Lecture Notes in Computer Science 1530

Edited by G. Goos, J. Hartmanis and J. van Leeuwen

Springer
Berlin
Heidelberg
New York
Barcelona
Hong Kong
London
Milan
Paris
Singapore
Tokyo

V. Arvind R. Ramanujam (Eds.)

Foundations of Software Technology and Theoretical Computer Science

18th Conference
Chennai, India, December 17-19, 1998
Proceedings

Springer

Volume Editors

V. Arvind
R. Ramanujam
The Institute of Mathematical Sciences, CIT Campus
Chennai 600 113, India
E-mail: {arvind,jam}@imsc.ernet.in

Cataloging-in-Publication data applied for

Die Deutsche Bibliothek - CIP-Einheitsaufnahme

Foundations of software technology and theoretical computer science : 18th conference, Chennai, India, December 17 - 19 1998 ; proceedings / V. Arvind ; R. Ramanujam (ed.). - Berlin ; Heidelberg ; New York ; Barcelona ; Hong Kong ; London ; Milan ; Paris ; Singapore ; Tokyo : Springer, 1998
(Lecture notes in computer science ; Vol. 1530)
ISBN 3-540-65384-8

CR Subject Classification (1998): F.1, F.3-4, G.2, F.2, D.2, D.1, D.3

ISSN 0302-9743
ISBN 3-540-65384-8 Springer-Verlag Berlin Heidelberg New York

Typesetting: Camera-ready by author
SPIN 10692914 06/3142 – 5 4 3 2 1 0 Printed on acid-free paper

Preface

This volume contains the proceedings of the 18th FST&TCS conference (Foundations of Software Technology and Theoretical Computer Science), organized under the auspices of the Indian Association for Research in Computing Science (*http://www.imsc.ernet.in/ iarcs*).

This year's conference attracted 93 submissions from as many as 22 countries. Each submission was reviewed by at least three independent referees. The Programme Committee met on August 1 and 2, 1998, at Chennai and selected 28 papers for inclusion in the conference programme. We thank the Programme Committee members and the reviewers for their sincere efforts.

We are fortunate to have six invited speakers this year, providing for a very attractive programme: Rajeev Alur, Ken McMillan, Neil Immerman, John Reif, Erik Meineche Schmidt, and Umesh Vazirani. The conference has two *theme sessions*: Model Checking (with invited talks by Alur and McMillan, and 4 contributed papers), and Quantum Computation (with invited talks by Schmidt and Vazirani). Moreover, the conference is preceded by a two-day workshop (December 14–15, 1998) on Molecular Computing (organized by Kamala Krithivasan), and a two-day school (December 15–16, 1998) on Finite Model Theory (organized by Anuj Dawar and Anil Seth). The Molecular Computation Workshop includes talks by Natasha Jonoska, Kamala Krithivasan, Georghe Paun, John Reif, Yasubumi Sakakibara, Rani Siromoney, and K. G. Subramanian. The speakers at the Finite Model Theory school include Anuj Dawar, Martin Grohe, Neil Immerman, Anil Seth, Wolfgang Thomas, Moshe Vardi, and Victor Vianu. Interestingly, Immerman's conference talk relates finite model theory and model checking, whereas Reif's conference talk is on comparing the molecular and quantum models of computation. We thank all the invited speakers for agreeing to talk at the conference, as well as for providing abstracts and articles for the proceedings.

The Institute of Mathematical Sciences and the Spic Mathematical Institute, both at Chennai, have co-hosted the conference. We thank these institutes, as well as the others who extended financial support, agencies of the Government of India, and private software companies in India.

We thank members of the organizing committee for making it happen. Special thanks go to the staff of our institute and Alfred Hofmann of Springer-Verlag for help with the proceedings.

IMSc, Chennai
September 1998

V. Arvind
R. Ramanujam

Program Committee

Manindra Agrawal *(IIT, Kanpur)*
V Arvind *(IMSc, Chennai)* ***(Co-Chair)***
Jin-Yi Cai *(SUNY, Buffalo)*
Ramesh Hariharan *(IISc, Bangalore)*
Kamala Krithivasan *(IIT, Chennai)*
Meena Mahajan *(IMSc, Chennai)*
Madhavan Mukund *(SMI, Chennai)*
Mogens Nielsen *(BRICS, Aarhus)*
Tobias Nipkow *(TU, Muenchen)*
C Pandurangan *(IIT, Chennai)*
Rohit Parikh *(CUNY, New York)*
Sanjiva Prasad *(IIT, Delhi)*
Jaikumar Radhakrishnan *(TIFR, Mumbai)*
R Ramanujam *(IMSc, Chennai)* ***(Co-chair)***
S Ramesh *(IIT, Mumbai)*
Abhiram Ranade *(IIT, Mumbai)*
Sandeep Sen *(IIT, Delhi)*
Natarajan Shankar *(SRI, California)*
G Sivakumar *(IIT, Mumbai)*
Aravind Srinivasan *(NUS, Singapore)*
K V Subrahmanyam *(SMI, Chennai)*
K G Subramanian *(MCC, Chennai)*
Moshe Vardi *(Rice Univ, Texas)*
Pascal Weil *(CNRS, Paris)*

Organizing Committee

Kamal Lodaya *(IMSc, Chennai)*
Meena Mahajan
(IMSc, Chennai) ***(Co-chair)***
Madhavan Mukund
(SMI, Chennai) ***(Co-chair)***
R Rama *(IIT, Chennai)*
Venkatesh Raman *(IMSc, Chennai)*
Anil Seth *(IMSc, Chennai)*

List of Reviewers

Luca Aceto
Pankaj K. Agarwal
Manindra Agrawal
E. Allender
Rajeev Alur
R. Amadio
Richard Anderson
Arne Andersson
Hiroki Arimura
S. Arun-Kumar
V. Arvind
Juergen Avenhaus
Sergey Berezin
Piotr Berman
Purandar Bhaduri
Binay K. Bhattacharya
M.R. Bhujade
Gerard Boudol
Franck van Breugel
Gerhard Brewka
Gerth Stølting Brodal
Darius Buntinas
Gerhard Buntrock
Marco Cadoli
J.-Y. Cai
Paul Caspi
Manuel Chakravarty
Vijay Chandru
Dmitri Chkliaev
Horatiu Cirstea
Manuel Clavel
Loic Correnson
Bruno Courcelle
David Cyrluk
Olivier Danvy
V. Rajkumar Dare
Nachum Dershowitz
Tamal K. Dey
D.M. Dhamdhere
A.A. Diwan
Shlomi Dolev
Dan Dougherty
Agostino Dovier
Devdatt Dubhashi
Steven Eker
E. A. Emerson
J. Esparza
Melvin Fitting
Marc Fuchs
Naveen Garg
Leszek Gasieniec
Konstantinos Georgatos
Jean Goubault-Larrecq
Thorsten Graf
Bernhard Gramlich
Radu Grosu
Rajiv Gupta
Peter Habermehl
David Harel
Ramesh Hariharan
Ryu Hasegawa
John Havlicek
Jean-Michel Helary
Mathew Hennessy
Jesper G. Henriksen
Kohei Honda
Jozef Hooman
Jieh Hsiang
Guan Shieng Huang
Dang Van Hung
Graham Hutton
Sanjay Jain
Mathai Joseph
Stasys Jukna
Prem Kalra
V. Kamakoti
M.V. Kameshwar
Gila Kamhi
Sampath Kannan
Deepak Kapur
Sanjeev Khanna
Samir Khuller
Claude Kirchner
Johannes Köbler
Ilkka Kokkarinen
Padmanabhan Krishnan
M.R.K. Krishna Rao
Kamala Krithivasan
Sandeep Kulkarni
M. Kwiatkowska
Yassine Lakhnech
Tak-wah Lam
Eric Laporte
Kim Larsen
Stefano Leonardi
Allen Leung
Francesca Levi
Francois Levy
Jean-Jacques Levy
Kamal Lodaya
Satyanarayana V. Lokam
Phil Long
Salvador Lucas
Bas Luttik
Meena Mahajan
Anil Maheshwari
S. N. Majumdar
D. Manivannan
Swami Manohar
Madhav Marathe
Claude Marché
Eric Martin
S.L. Mehndiratta
Daniele Micciancio
Aart Middeldorp
Peter Bro Miltersen
Swarup Kumar Mohalik
Madhavan Mukund
Ketan Mulmuley
Ian Munro
Praveen Murthy
S. Muthukrishnan
K. Narayan Kumar
P. Narendran
Gilbert Ndjatou
Ajay Nerurkar
R. De Nicola
Mogens Nielsen
Tobias Nipkow
Friedrich Otto
S. P. Pal
Alessandro Panconesi

C. Pandurangan
P. K. Pandya
Rohit Parikh
Joachim Parrow
Gh. Paun
Wojciech Penczek
Frank Pfenning
Teo Chung Piaw
Sanjiva Prasad
S. Qadeer
Paola Quaglia
J. Radhakrishnan
N. Raja
I. V. Ramakrishnan
Rajeev Raman
Venkatesh Raman
R. Ramanujam
S. Ramesh
Abhiram Ranade
K. Rangarajan
S. Ravi Kumar
Anders P. Ravn
Uday Reddy
Stefano Crespi Reghizzi
James Riely
Christine Roeckl
Michel de Rougemont
Albert Rubio
Alexander Russell
Oliver Rüthing
Marie-France Sagot
David Sands
Davide Sangiorgi
Sandeep Sen
N. Shankar
Priti Shankar
R. K. Shyamasundar
A. Prasad Sistla
D. Sivakumar
G. Sivakumar
Milind Sohoni
Harald Sondergaard
Aravind Srinivasan
Ian Stark
K. V. Subrahmanyam
K. G. Subramanian
P. R. Subramanya
Gerard Tel
Denis Therièn
P.S. Thiagarajan
T. Thierauf
Gnanaraj Thomas
Wolfgang Thomas
Ashish Tiwari
Mark Tullsen
Moshe Vardi
Margus Veanes
C. E. Veni Madhavan
K. Vidyasankar
V. Vinay
Sundar Vishwanathan
Uwe Waldmann
Igor Walukiewicz
Osamu Watanabe
Th. P. van der Weide
Pascal Weil
David Wolfram
Pierre Wolper
Nobuko Yoshida

Table of Contents

Invited Talk 1

Session 1(a)

Session 1(b)

Session 2(a)

Session 2(b)

Invited Talk 2

Session 3

Session 4

Invited Talk 3

Session 5(a)

Session 5(b)

Session 6(a)

Session 6(b)

Invited Talk 4

Invited Talk 5

Session 7

Session 8(a)

Session 8(b)

Session 9

Invited Talk 6

Descriptive Complexity and Model Checking

Neil Immerman*
Computer Science Dept.
University of Massachusetts
Amherst, MA 01003
`http://www.cs.umass.edu/~immerman`
`immerman@cs.umass.edu`

1 Introduction

Descriptive Complexity [I98] is an approach to complexity that measures the richness of a language or sentence needed to describe a given property. There is a profound relationship between the traditional computational complexity of a problem and the descriptive complexity of the problem. In this setting, the finite object being worked on is treated as a logical structure. Thus descriptive complexity is part of finite model theory [EF95].

An exciting application of Descriptive Complexity is to a part of computer-aided verification called Model Checking. For a long time, the area of formal methods had a reputation of claiming more than it could deliver.

The promise of proving large programs and systems correct was held out for decades as a technology that was right around the corner. Model checking is a modest approach to formal methods. This modesty is misleading; model checking is so modest that it is practical and useful. Many hardware design companies, including Intel, have adopted model checking as part of their basic design method [K97].

The idea is simple. When we design a program, distributed protocol, or circuit, we do so in a formal language. This might be a circuit design language such as VHDL, or a system specification language such as State Charts or Heitmeyer's SCR [BH].

*Research supported by NSF grant CCR-9505446.

Such a formal design determines a logical structure, $\mathcal{K} = \langle S, p_1, \ldots, p_k, R\rangle$, called a Kripke structure or transition system. S consists of the set of possible global states of the design, the set of all possible gate values for the circuit, or all possible assignments of values to the variables of a program, or all possible assignments of states to each processor in the distributed protocol. Binary relation R is the next move relation: $R(s, s')$ means that the move from s to s' is a possible atomic transition of the circuit or program. Unary relations $p_1, \ldots, p_k$ express properties of the global states, for example, being an initial state, being an accepting state, or that a particular variable has a special value. The size of S is often exponential in the size of the design. This phenomenon is typically referred to as the *state explosion problem.*

Once we have our formal design, a representation of the transition system can be automatically generated. We may now wish to write some simple correctness conditions in a formal language. For example, we might want to express the following:

1. If the Restart button is pressed, we eventually restart.
2. Doors are not opened between stations.
3. Division is performed correctly.
4. The motor is not turned on during maintenance.

These conditions express the fact that (1) if we press the Restart button on a personal computer it will eventually restart — without our having to unplug it and plug it in again; (2) the subway train controller meets some simple safety conditions; (3) Intel's new processor does its arithmetic correctly; and (4) the mixer in a nuclear waste storage container (which is designed to keep its contents mixed and thus less volatile) cannot turn on (and thus cause injury) during maintenance.

Now that we have formally expressed our design and our statement concerning its behavior, we can simply press a button and be told whether or not $\mathcal{K} \models \varphi$, that is, does the design satisfy the desired property?

This is the model checking problem: given $\mathcal{K}$ and φ, test whether $\mathcal{K}$ satisfies φ. Model checkers are being hailed as great debugging aides. We can write a simple property that our system should satisfy and press the button. If it does not satisfy the property then we will be told so. Typical model checking programs will present a counter-example run of the system, i.e., they produce the explicit bug. If the model does satisfy the property, then we will be told so. Note that this is better than just not finding a bug. Our model checker has automatically proved that our design has a certain desirable property.

Model Checking is a burgeoning field. It has already succeeded in finding many bugs in circuit designs that escaped less formal debugging and testing methods.

I believe the potential for model checking goes well beyond debugging circuit designs. As a user designs a circuit, program, web page, lecture, book, course, etc., the system on which it is designed can have a formal model of what is being constructed. The user can ask if the design will have a certain simple property. The system will answer, "no, and here is a bug", or "yes". If the answer is yes, then that can be something that this user or even other users can depend upon and build upon. Furthermore, the system could ask if the property should be checked for dynamically, i.e., the system could issue a warning if a later change in the design caused the desired property to be violated. In fact, there is an enormous potential here for rational, computer-aided design, verification, and maintenance. To accomplish this, it is necessary to maintain a formal model and to keep the query language simple.

Two popular query languages for model checking are the computational tree logics CTL and CTL* [E91]. These languages are usually translated to the modal mu calculus before being evaluated.

Moshe Vardi and I showed that the languages CTL and CTL* are naturally embedded in transitive closure logic, using only two domain variables [IV97]. This logic is more natural than the mu calculus for expressing the kind of reachability properties that we typically want to model check. Furthermore, transitive logic, a subset of NSPACE[$\log n$], is more feasible to check than the mu calculus. The latter is polynomial-time complete, where that means polynomial time in the size of the huge Kripke structures.

More recently, Natasha Alechina and I have extended the paper [IV97], showing the practical use of transitive closure logic in symbolic model checking [AI]. In particular, we have identified an expressive fragment of transitive closure logic that has linear-time data complexity and admits the above embedding of CTL*.

Descriptive complexity applies directly to model checking. In model checking we need to determine whether our huge logical structure satisfies a given formula. Since the structures are so large, the complexity of the query language is a crucial factor in whether it can be feasibly checked. This is the reason that our approach to reducing the complexity of the query languages in [IV97, AI] is so promising.

In this lecture, I will survey some recent work at the intersection of model checking and descriptive complexity. In particular I will emphasize the following three topics.

1. Efficient Query Languages: The transitive closure logics discussed in [IV97] and especially [AI] offer improvements in efficiency over current methods that use the mu calculus. We are currently studying the time-space tradeoffs in evaluating such queries.

2. Abstraction: We wish to test whether a huge Kripke structure $\mathcal{K}$ satisfies a simple query φ. The most promising way to do this is to project $\mathcal{K}$ down

to a homomorphic image $\mathcal{K}'$ that is smaller than $\mathcal{K}$ and yet satisfies a corresponding formula φ' iff the original structure $\mathcal{K}$ satisfies φ. It is easy to construct situations where the model checking problem is NSPACE[$\log n$]-complete in the size of the Kripke structure, and thus PSPACE-complete in the size of the design. However, many natural situations admit repeated abstractions whose composition drastically reduces the size of the structures, thus allowing feasible model checking. We are working to codify some of the situations where this occures.

3. Dynamic Model Checking: From both a practical and a theoretical point of view it is important to consider the dynamic complexity of model checking as the design and thus the structure $\mathcal{K}$ changes. We would like to be able to recheck a formula after slightly changing the design in less time than it took us to check the formula originally. Similarly, we would like to have the abstract structure $\mathcal{K}'$ automatically modified as we change the structure $\mathcal{K}$. These issues are closely tied to current work on the dynamic complexity of reachability [PI97].

References

[AI] N. Alechina and N. Immerman, "Efficient Fragments of Transitive Closure Logic," manuscript.

[AH] R. Alur and T. Henzinger, *Computer-Aided Verification*, to appear.

[BH] R. Bharadwaj and C. Heitmeyer, "Verifying SCR Requirements Specifications using State Exploration," Proceedings of First ACM SIGPLAN Workshop on Automatic Analysis of Software, Paris, France, January 14, 1997.

[CGP] E. Clarke, O. Grumberg and D. Peled, *Model Checking*, to appear.

[EF95] H.D. Ebbinghaus and J. Flum *Finite Model Theory,* 1995, Springer-Verlag.

[E91] E. A. Emerson, "Temporal and Modal Logic" in van Leeuwen, ed., *Handbook of Theoretical Computer Science,* M.I.T. Press, 1991.

[I98] N. Immerman, *Descriptive Complexity*, 1998, Springer-Verlag Graduate Texts in Computer Science, New York.

[Imm87] N. Immerman. Languages that capture complexity classes. *SIAM Journal of Computing*, 16(4):760–778, 1987.

[IV97] N. Immerman and M. Vardi. Model Checking and Transitive Closure Logic. *Proc. 9th Int'l Conf. on Computer-Aided Verification* (CAV'97), Lecture Notes in Computer Science, Springer-Verlag 291 - 302, 1997.

[Imm91] N. Immerman. DSPACE[n^k]=VAR[$k+1$]. *Sixth IEEE Structure in Complexity Theory Symposium*, 334-340, 1991.

[K97] R. Kurshan, "Formal Verification in a Commercial Setting," Design Automation Conference (1997).

[Kur94] R. Kurshan, *Computer-Aided Verification of Coordinating Processes,* 1994, Princeton University Press, Princeton, NJ.

[McM93] K. McMillan, *Symbolic Model Checking,* 1993, Kluwer.

[PI97] S. Patnaik and N. Immerman, "Dyn-FO: A Parallel, Dynamic Complexity Class," *J. Comput. Sys. Sci.* 55(2) (1997), 199-209.

Approximation Algorithms with Bounded Performance Guarantees for the Clustered Traveling Salesman Problem (Extended Abstract)

Nili Guttmann-Beck[1], Refael Hassin[1], Samir Khuller[2], and Balaji Raghavachari[3]

[1] Department of Statistics and Operations Research, Tel-Aviv University, Tel-Aviv 69978, Israel. {nili,hassin}@math.tau.ac.il

[2] Department of Computer Science and UMIACS, University of Maryland, College Park, MD 20742, USA. samir@cs.umd.edu

[3] Department of Computer Science, The University of Texas at Dallas, Richardson, TX 75083-0688, USA. rbk@utdallas.edu

Abstract. Let $G = (V, E)$ be a complete undirected graph with vertex set V, edge set E, and edge weights $l(e)$ satisfying triangle inequality. The vertex set V is partitioned into *clusters* $V_1, \ldots, V_k$. The *clustered traveling salesman problem* (CTSP) is to compute a shortest Hamiltonian cycle (tour) that visits all the vertices, and in which the vertices of each cluster are visited consecutively. Since this problem is a generalization of the traveling salesman problem, it is NP-hard. In this paper, we consider several variants of this basic problem and provide polynomial time approximation algorithms for them.

1 Introduction

Let $G = (V, E)$ be a complete undirected graph with vertex set V, edge set E, and edge weights $l(e)$ satisfying triangle inequality. The vertex set V is partitioned into *clusters* $V_1, \ldots, V_k$. The *clustered traveling salesman problem* (CTSP) is to compute a shortest Hamiltonian cycle (tour) that visits all the vertices, and in which the vertices of each cluster are visited consecutively. Applications and other related work may be found in [3, 9, 13] and an exact branch and bound algorithm is described in [15]. The traveling salesman problem (TSP) can be viewed as a special case of CTSP in which there is only one cluster $V_1 = V$ (alternatively, each V_i is a singleton). We deal with several variants of the problem depending on whether or not the starting and ending vertices of a cluster have been specified. Since all the variants are generalizations of TSP, they are all NP-hard.

In this paper we focus on the design of approximation algorithms with guaranteed performance ratios. These are algorithms that run in polynomial time, and produce suboptimal solutions. We measure the worst case ratio of the cost of the solution generated by the algorithm to the optimal cost. We present approximation algorithms with bounded performance ratios for several different variants of this problem. The previously known related results are a 3.5-approximation for the problem with given starting vertices [2] (and this result extends to the case where no starting or ending vertices are given, with the same approximation bound), a $\frac{3}{2}$-approximation for the problem in which there are only two clusters with unspecified end vertices and a prespecified starting vertex [10], and a $\frac{5}{3}$-approximation for the problem in which the order of visiting the clusters in the tour is specified as part of the problem [1].

In this paper we describe a 1.9091-approximation algorithm for the problem in which the starting and ending vertices of each cluster are specified. We give a 1.8-approximation algorithm if for each cluster the two end vertices are given, but we are free to choose any one as the starting vertex and the other one as the ending vertex. We give a 2.75-approximation algorithm for the case when we are only given clusters with no specific starting and ending vertices, and a 2.643-approximation algorithm if we are only given the starting vertex in each cluster.

Our solutions use known approximation algorithms to three closely related problems: the *traveling salesman path problem* (TSPP), the *stacker crane problem* (SCP) and the *rural postman problem* (RPP). These problems are discussed in Section 2. In fact one of the contributions of our paper is to design new algorithms for TSPP, and to show their use in improving the previously known approximation factors for CTSP; along with careful use of the algorithms for SCP and RPP.

Outline of the paper: In Section 2 we discuss some basic notation that is used in the paper. In addition, we review algorithms for approximating TSPP, SCP, and RPP. In Section 3 we address the case in which the starting and ending vertices in each cluster are specified. In Section 4 we address the case in which the end vertices are given, but either one could be chosen as the entry or exit vertex for the cluster. In Section 5 we address the case in which only the starting vertex in each cluster is specified. In Section 6 we address the case in which no entry or exit vertex is specified for any cluster. Finally, in Section 7 we study the problem when the number of clusters is a constant, and describe a $\frac{5}{3}$-approximation algorithm for all variants. We also show that obtaining an approximation ratio of α for k clusters ($k \geq 4$) with unspecified end vertices, implies an approximation ratio of α for TSPP with specified end vertices. Thus, improving the approximation ratio for a constant number of clusters is at least as hard as improving the approximation ratio for TSPP (for which the best approximation ratio is currently $\frac{5}{3}$ [8]).

2 Preliminaries

Some of our algorithms use a *directed cycle cover* routine in digraphs. The directed cycle cover problem is to find a set of directed cycles of minimum total weight that includes all the vertices in a given digraph. This problem is equivalent to weighted bipartite matching, which is also called the assignment problem [14]. We also use an *undirected cycle cover* algorithm that finds in an undirected graph a set of undirected cycles of minimum total weight that includes all its vertices. This problem can be solved by applying a weighted matching algorithm [16].

For a graph $G = (V, E)$ we denote by $l(e)$ the weight (also known as length) of an edge $e \in E$. For a subset $E' \subseteq E$ we denote $L(E') = \sum_{e \in E'} l(e)$, the total weight (length) of the edges. Let OPT denote both an optimal solution of the problem under consideration and its total length. Similarly, let $MST(G)$ denote both a minimum-weight spanning tree of G and its weight. We also assume that the edge weights obey the triangle inequality.

2.1 The traveling salesman path problem

Hoogeveen [8] considered three variations of TSPP, in which as part of the input instance the following constraints are placed on the end vertices of the resulting Hamiltonian path: (1) both end vertices are specified, (2) only one of the end vertices is specified, and (3) no end vertices are specified. For the latter two cases, it was shown that a straightforward adaptation of Christofides' algorithm yields an algorithm with a performance ratio of $\frac{3}{2}$. The case with two specified ends is more difficult as we now elaborate.

Let s and t be two specified vertices in G. We consider the problem of finding a path with s and t as its two ends, that visits all vertices of G. One can solve this problem in a manner similar to Christofides' algorithm for TSP [4], by starting with $MST(G)$, adding a suitable matching, and then finding an Eulerian walk of the resulting graph. We do not get a $\frac{3}{2}$ approximation ratio since in the TSPP the optimal solution is a path, and not a tour. The bound of $\frac{1}{2}OPT$ on the weight of a minimum-weight perfect matching of a subset of the vertices, which holds for TSP (tour), does not hold here.

We obtain a $\frac{5}{3}$ approximation ratio as follows.

Theorem 1. *There exists a polynomial-time algorithm for TSPP between given end vertices s and t, that finds solutions S_1 and S_2 which satisfy the following equations:*

$$\begin{aligned} l(S_1) &\leq 2\ MST(G) - l(s,t) \\ &\leq 2\ OPT - l(s,t), \\ l(S_2) &\leq MST(G) + \frac{1}{2}(OPT + l(s,t)) \\ &\leq \frac{3}{2}\ OPT + \frac{1}{2}\ l(s,t). \end{aligned}$$

Proof. We "double" the edges of $MST(G)$ except for those on the unique $s - t$ path on it. The result is a connected multigraph whose vertex degrees are all even except for those of s and t. We now find an Eulerian walk between s and t on this multigraph and turn it into a Hamiltonian path between s and t without increasing the weight by shortcutting and applying the triangle inequality. We call it S_1. The length of S_1 is at most $2MST(G) - l(s,t)$, which is at most $2OPT - l(s,t)$.

To obtain S_2, we adopt the following strategy. Consider adding the edge (s,t) to OPT, and making it a cycle. The length of this cycle is $OPT+l(s,t)$. The cycle can be decomposed into two matchings between any even-size subset of vertices, and the length of the smaller matching is at most $\frac{1}{2}(OPT + l(s,t))$. We use the strategy of Hoogeveen [8], and add to $MST(G)$ a minimum-weight matching of vertices selected based on their degree in $MST(G)$ (odd degree vertices of $V \setminus \{s,t\}$ and even degree vertices of $\{s,t\}$ in $MST(G)$), and output an Eulerian walk S_2 from s to t in the resulting graph. This Eulerian walk can be converted into a Hamiltonian path by shortcutting. Using the triangle inequality, we obtain that $l(S_2)$ is at most $MST(G) + \frac{1}{2}(OPT + l(s,t)) \leq \frac{3}{2}OPT + \frac{1}{2}l(s,t)$.

Corollary 1. *The shorter of the paths S_1 and S_2 is at most $\frac{5}{3}OPT$.*

Proof. Using Theorem 1, observe that if $l(s,t) > \frac{1}{3}OPT$, then $l(S_1) \leq \frac{5}{3}OPT$. Otherwise, $l(s,t) \leq \frac{1}{3}OPT$, in which case $l(S_2) \leq \frac{5}{3}OPT$.

Remark 1. Hoogeveen [8] proves the bound of $\frac{5}{3}OPT$ in a different way. Solution S_2 can be directly bounded as $MST(G) + w(M)$, where $w(M)$ is the weight of a min-weight perfect matching on the subset of odd degree vertices of $V \setminus \{s,t\}$ and even degree vertices of $\{s,t\}$ in $MST(G)$. He showed that $OPT \cup MST(G)$ can be decomposed into three matchings, and this shows that $w(M) \leq \frac{2}{3}OPT$. Our algorithm for TSPP with given end vertices is different, and this leads to improvements in the analysis of our algorithms for CTSP.

2.2 The stacker crane problem

Let $G = (V, E)$ be an arbitrary graph that satisfies the triangle inequality. Let $D = \{(s_i, t_i) : i = 1, \ldots, k\}$ be a given set of *special directed arcs*, each with length ℓ_i. The arc (s_i, t_i) denotes an object that is at vertex s_i and needs to be moved to vertex t_i using a vehicle (called the stacker crane). The *stacker crane problem* (SCP) is to compute a shortest walk that traverses each directed arc (s_i, t_i) at least once in the specified direction (from s_i to t_i). Let $D = \sum_i \ell_i$ and $A = OPT - D$.

The stacker crane problem is a generalization of TSP since TSP can be viewed as an instance of SCP in which each vertex is replaced by an arc of zero-length. It is possible to derive a 2-approximation algorithm for the problem using standard techniques such as "twice around the tree" heuristic. *Algorithm StackerCrane* by Frederickson, Hecht and Kim [7] is a 1.8-approximation algorithm for SCP. It applies two different algorithms and then selects the best of the two solutions generated by them. We briefly review the basic ideas behind the two algorithms (for details, see [7, 12]):

- *Algorithm ShortArcs*: Shrink the directed arcs and reduce the problem to an instance of TSP. Use an approximation algorithm for the TSP instance, and then recover a solution for the original problem (the algorithm itself is somewhat subtle and the reader is referred to the original paper). This algorithm works well when D is small compared to OPT.

- *Algorithm LongArcs*: Complete the set of directed arcs into a directed cycle cover. Then find a set of edges of minimum total weight to connect the cycles together; add two copies of each one of these edges, and orient the copies in opposite directions to each other. The resulting graph is Eulerian, and the algorithm outputs an Euler walk of this solution. The algorithm performs well when D is large.

The following theorem can be derived from [7].

Theorem 2. *Consider an instance of the stacker crane problem in which the sum of the lengths of the special directed arcs is D. Let OPT be an optimal solution, and let* $A = OPT - D$. *The walk returned by Algorithm ShortArcs has length at most* $\frac{3}{2}A + 2D$. *The walk returned by Algorithm LongArcs has length at most* $3A + D$.

2.3 The rural postman problem

Let $E' \subseteq E$ be a specified subset of *special edges*. The *rural postman problem* (RPP) is to compute a shortest walk that visits all the edges in E'. The Chinese postman problem is a special case of RPP in which $E' = E$, i.e., the walk must include *all* the edges. But the Chinese postman problem is solvable in polynomial time by reducing it to weighted matching, whereas RPP is NP-hard.

The two algorithms, defined above for SCP, can be modified to solve RPP. We define *Algorithm LongArcs2* that is similar to *LongArcs*, but in this case, D is a set of *undirected* edges, and we only change the algorithm so that it completes the set of edges into an undirected cycle cover. The second part of Theorem 2 holds for this case as well.

Algorithm *ShortArcs* greatly simplifies when applied to RPP and, turns to be a straightforward generalization of Christofides algorithm for TSP. As indicated by Frederickson [6], it produces a $\frac{3}{2}$-approximation algorithm for the problem (see the survey by Eiselt *et al.* [5] for more details and a paper by Jansen [11] for a generalization).

We denote by *Algorithm RuralPostman* the algorithm which executes these two algorithms and returns the shorter solution.

Remark 2. In some of our algorithms for CTSP, we generate instances of RPP (SCP) and run the above algorithms for them. In the RPP (SCP) instances that we generate the special edges (directed arcs) are vertex disjoint. This in fact guarantees that the walks are actually tours since each vertex is visited once. These instances are themselves CTSP instances with $|V_i| = 2$ $(i = 1, ..., k)$ *and given end vertices (starting and ending vertices, respectively). However, we note that if for some constant c,* $|V_i| \leq c (1 \leq i \leq k)$ *then we can obtain the same approximation ratios as for RPP (SCP) quite easily since within each cluster we can obtain an optimal solution.*

3 Given start and end vertices

In this section, we consider the CTSP in which the starting vertex s_i and ending vertex t_i is given for each cluster V_i. Our algorithm is based on the following idea. We decompose the problem into two parts. Inside each cluster V_i, we find $path_i$, a path from the start vertex s_i to the end vertex t_i that goes through all vertices of that cluster. This is TSPP with given end vertices. In addition, we need to connect the paths by adding edges into a single cycle. We replace each cluster by a special arc from s_i to t_i and get an instance of the stacker crane problem. Find a tour that includes all the special directed arcs. From this solution to SCP, we replace each arc (s_i, t_i) by the path $path_i$ computed within that cluster. Figure 1 describes the algorithm in detail.

Algorithm GivenST
Input
1. A graph $G = (V, E)$, $|V| = n$, with weights $l(e)$ $e \in E$.
2. A partition of V into clusters $V_1, ..., V_k$.
3. Start and end vertices s_i and t_i respectively, for each cluster V_i, $i = 1, \ldots, k$.
returns *A clustered tour.*
begin
1. For each V_i, compute $path_i$, a Hamiltonian path with end vertices s_i and t_i.
2. Apply Algorithm StackerCrane with special directed arcs $\{(s_i, t_i) \mid i = 1, ..., k\}$ to obtain tour T.
3. In T, replace the special directed arc (s_i, t_i) by $path_i$, $i = 1, ..., k$.
4. **return** *the resulting tour T_m.*
end *GivenST*

Fig. 1. Algorithm *GivenST*

Theorem 3. *Let T_m be the tour returned by Algorithm GivenST in Figure 1. Then,*

$$l(T_m) \leq \frac{21}{11}\ OPT < 1.9091 OPT.$$

Proof. The algorithm consists of solving two subproblems: TSPP with given end vertices, and SCP. Let L be the sum of the lengths of the paths of OPT through each cluster. Let A be the length of the other edges of OPT that are not in L (edges of OPT that connect the different clusters together). Let D be the total length of the directed arcs $(s_i, t_i), i = 1, \ldots, k$. By Theorem 1, the lengths of the two solutions to TSPP with given end vertices are at most $2L - D$ and $\frac{3}{2}L + \frac{1}{2}D$. Using the fact that the minimum of a set of quantities is at most any convex combination,

$$l(TSPP) \leq \min\left(2L - D, \frac{3}{2}L + \frac{1}{2}D\right)$$

$$
\begin{aligned}
&\leq \frac{9}{11}\Big(2L - D\Big) + \frac{2}{11}\Big(\frac{3}{2}L + \frac{1}{2}D\Big) \\
&= \frac{21}{11}L - \frac{8}{11}D.
\end{aligned}
$$

There exists a solution to SCP of length at most $A+D$. Hence by Theorem 2, the lengths of the two solutions to SCP are at most $\frac{3}{2}A+2D$ and $3A+D$. Therefore the solution returned by the SCP algorithm is at most

$$
\begin{aligned}
l(SCP) &\leq \min\Big(\frac{3}{2}A + 2D, 3A + D\Big) \\
&\leq \frac{8}{11}\Big(\frac{3}{2}A + 2D\Big) + \frac{3}{11}\Big(3A + D\Big) \\
&= \frac{21}{11}A + \frac{19}{11}D.
\end{aligned}
$$

In Step 3 of Algorithm GivenST, the two solutions are combined by replacing arcs of length D in the TSPP solution by the SCP solution. We obtain an upper bound on the length of the solution T_m thus obtained by combining the above equations.

$$
\begin{aligned}
l(T_m) &= l(TSPP) - D + l(SCP) \\
&\leq \Big(\frac{21}{11}L - \frac{8}{11}D\Big) - D + \Big(\frac{21}{11}A + \frac{19}{11}D\Big) \\
&= \frac{21}{11}\Big(L + A\Big) = \frac{21}{11}OPT.
\end{aligned}
$$

4 Given end vertices

In this section, we consider the CTSP in which for each i, $i = 1, \ldots, k$, we are given the two end vertices, $\{s_i^1, s_i^2\}$, of cluster V_i. The vertices of each cluster must be contiguous on the tour, and the end vertices of cluster V_i must be s_i^1 and s_i^2, but we are free to select any one of them as the start vertex and the other vertex as the end vertex. We modify *Algorithm GivenST* by executing *Algorithm RuralPostman* rather than *Algorithm StackerCrane*, since $path_i$ can be oriented in any direction. The solution obtained consists of the special edges $(s_i^1, s_i^2), i = 1, \ldots, k$ and other undirected edges between the end vertices. We replace the special edges by the corresponding paths between s_i^1 to s_i^2 computed in Step 1.

Theorem 4. *Let T_m be the tour returned by Algorithm GivenEnds. Then*

$$
l(T_m) \leq \frac{9}{5}\ OPT.
$$

5 Given starting vertices

In this section, we consider the version of CTSP in which, for each cluster i we are given only its starting vertex s_i and we are free to select its ending vertex. We give an algorithm with an approximation ratio of 2.643. We propose two different heuristics, and select the shorter of the tours generated. In the first heuristic, we combine a tour of the starting vertices with tours of the individual clusters to generate a clustered tour. In the second heuristic, for each cluster, we select the end vertex t_i to be the farthest vertex from s_i within the cluster. We then find a solution using *Algorithm GivenST* (Section 3) that finds a clustered tour when the start and end vertices of each cluster are given. Figure 2 describes the algorithm.

Algorithm GivenStart

Input

1. A graph $G = (V, E)$, $|V| = n$, with weights $l(e)$ $e \in E$.

2. A partition of V into clusters $V_1, ..., V_k$.

3. In each cluster i, starting vertex s_i.

returns *A clustered tour*

begin

1. Compute a tour T_i that visits all vertices of V_i, for each $i \in \{1, 2, \ldots, k\}$.
Compute a tour S of just the starting vertices $\{s_1, s_2, \ldots, s_k\}$.
Let T_s be a tour obtained by shortcutting $S \cup (\cup_{i=1}^{k} T_i)$.

2. For each cluster V_i, choose an end vertex t_i that is farthest from s_i. Let Algorithm GivenST return tour T_l with start vertices s_i and end vertices t_i.

3. **return** *the shorter of the tours T_s and T_l.*

end *GivenStart*

Fig. 2. Algorithm *GivenStart*

In Step 1, we compute $k + 1$ tours, one for each cluster V_i, and a tour that visits just the start vertices. All these tours can be computed using the TSP algorithm of Christofides [4]. The intuition behind this heuristic is that it does well when the sum of the distances between the start and end vertices of each cluster in the optimal solution is small relative to the total cost. In Step 2, we select an end vertex $t_i \in V_i$ that maximizes $l(s_i, t_i)$. With that selection of end vertices, we can now apply *Algorithm GivenST* to find a clustered tour.

We introduce some notation to analyze the algorithm. Let A be the total cost of those edges of OPT that connect vertices of two different clusters (there are exactly k such edges). Let L be the sum of the lengths of the paths of OPT through the clusters. By definition $OPT = A + L$. Let d be the sum of the distances between the start and end vertices of each cluster of OPT; note that we are summing the lengths of direct edges that connect start vertices to the end vertices chosen by OPT. Let D be the sum of distances between s_i and t_i, i.e.,

$D = \sum_{i=1}^{k} l(s_i, t_i)$. Since we chose t_i in V_i as the vertex that maximizes $l(s_i, t_i)$, $d \leq D$.

Lemma 1. *Let T_s be the tour computed in Step 1 of Algorithm GivenStart. Then,*

$$l(T_s) \leq \frac{3}{2} OPT + 2d.$$

Proof. The Hamiltonian paths through each cluster can be converted to cycles by adding an edge that connects s_i with the end vertex in that cluster of OPT. Hence there exists a collection of k tours, one through each cluster V_i, whose total cost is $L + d$. We now follow the analysis of Christofides [4]. The sum of costs of minimum spanning trees through each cluster is at most L. The cost of the matchings connecting odd-degree vertices of each cluster is at most $\frac{1}{2}(L + d)$. Therefore the sum of the k tours computed in Step 1 is at most $\frac{3}{2}L + \frac{1}{2}d$. There exists a tour of just the start vertices of length $A + d$, which is obtained from OPT by replacing the paths through each cluster of length L by a direct edge connecting the end vertices and deleting the intermediate vertices. Hence the cost of the tour S computed in Step 1 is at most $\frac{3}{2}(A + d)$. Tour T_s is obtained by combining all the above tours and its length is at most $\frac{3}{2}(L + A) + 2d = \frac{3}{2} OPT + 2d$.

Lemma 2. *Let T_l be the tour computed in Step 2 of Algorithm GivenStart. Then,*

$$l(T_l) \leq \frac{3}{2} OPT + 2L - \frac{3}{2} d.$$

Proof. The tour T_l is obtained by running *Algorithm GivenST* after choosing an end vertex t_i for each cluster. The algorithm computes a solution to SCP (Step 2), which is computed in turn by computing two solutions and taking the shorter of the two (see Section 2.2). We prove that if one just takes the SCP solution computed by *Algorithm ShortArcs*, we get the desired result. We observe that OPT can be shortcut to obtain a feasible solution to the corresponding stacker crane problem and therefore if *Algorithm ShortArcs* is applied to this problem, we get a tour whose length is at most $\frac{3}{2} OPT + \frac{1}{2} D$. In this tour, we replace each arc (s_i, t_i) by a path from s_i to t_i. By Theorem 1 the lengths of such paths is at most $2 \sum_{i=1}^{k} MST(G_i) - D \leq 2L - D$, where G_i is the subgraph induced by V_i. Hence the total length of the tour obtained is

$$\begin{aligned} l(T_l) &\leq \left(\frac{3}{2} OPT + \frac{1}{2} D\right) - D + (2L - D) \\ &= \frac{3}{2} OPT + 2L - \frac{3}{2} D \\ &\leq \frac{3}{2} OPT + 2L - \frac{3}{2} d, \end{aligned}$$

since $d \leq D$.

Theorem 5. *Let T_m be the clustered tour returned by Algorithm GivenStart in Figure 2. Then,*

$$l(T_m) \leq \frac{37}{14}\ OPT < 2.643\ OPT.$$

Proof. If $d \leq \frac{4}{7}L$, then by Lemma 1 and the obvious inequality $L \leq OPT$,

$$l(T_s) \leq \frac{3}{2}OPT + \frac{8}{7}L \leq \frac{37}{14}\ OPT.$$

If $d > \frac{4}{7}L$, then the same inequality holds for $l(T_l)$ by Lemma 2. Since the algorithm chooses the shorter of the tours, the theorem follows.

6 Unspecified end vertices

In this case we are only given the clusters and we are free to choose the start and end vertices in the clusters. We give a 2.75 approximation for an arbitrary number of clusters. We first apply a TSPP algorithm with unspecified ends within each cluster. We use the direct edges between the ends of these paths as special edges for an RPP instance. We compute an approximate tour of this instance and finally replace each special edge by the corresponding path to produce our first tour. To obtain our second tour, in each cluster, select two vertices s_i and t_i such that $l(s_i, t_i)$ is maximized, to be the end vertices in the cluster, and then apply *Algorithm GivenEnds* to obtain a tour. Finally, we select the shorter tour. Figure 3 describes the algorithm.

Algorithm UnspecifiedEnds

Input

1. A graph $G = (V, E)$, $|V| = n$, with weights $l(e)$ $e \in E$.

2. A partition of V into clusters $V_1, ..., V_k$.

returns *A clustered tour*

begin

1. Apply a TSPP algorithm with unspecified end vertices in each of $V_1, \ldots, V_k$. Let $path_i$ be the resulting path on V_i, and denote its end vertices by a_i and b_i. Apply Algorithm RuralPostman with special edges (a_i, b_i) $i = 1, ..., k$ and let T_s be the tour obtained by replacing special edge (a_i, b_i) by $path_i$ $i = 1, ..., k$.

2. In each cluster find vertices s_i and t_i that maximize $l(s_i, t_i)$. Apply Algorithm GivenEnds with end vertices $\{s_i, t_i\}$, and let T_l be the tour that it returns.

3. **return** *the shorter of the tours T_s and T_l.*

end *UnspecifiedEnds*

Fig. 3. Algorithm *UnspecifiedEnds*

Theorem 6. *Let T_m be the tour returned by Algorithm UnspecifiedEnds in Figure 3. Then,*

$$l(T_m) \leq \frac{11}{4} OPT.$$

7 Constant number of clusters

In this section, we consider the CTSP where the number of clusters, k, is a constant. The case $k = 1$ is the TSP. We show that the CTSP with given end vertices is equivalent to TSPP with given end vertices. Hence we can obtain the obvious $\frac{5}{3}$-approximation for this case by using the $\frac{5}{3}$ approximation for TSPP, but any further improvement in the approximation ratio is possible only if the approximation algorithm for TSPP with given end vertices is improved.

We also show that TSPP with given end vertices is equivalent to CTSP with unspecified end vertices for four or more clusters. This shows that an α-approximation algorithm for this problem, would imply an α-approximation algorithm for TSPP with given end vertices.

Theorem 7. *If there exists an α-approximation algorithm to the TSPP with given end vertices then there exists an α-approximation algorithm for CTSP for a constant number of clusters (for all the variants we consider in this paper).*

Corollary 2. *There exists a $\frac{5}{3}$-approximation algorithm to CTSP for constant number of clusters (in all the variants we consider for this paper).*

Remark 3. If there exists an α-approximation algorithm for TSPP with given end vertices there exists an α-approximation algorithm for CTSP when the order of the clusters and the start and end vertices are given. This follows by finding a path between each pair of end vertices inside each cluster using the approximation algorithm for the TSPP, and connecting the paths using the given order. If the order of the clusters is specified but the end vertices are not specified, Anily, Bramel and Hertz [1] give a $\frac{5}{3}$-approximation algorithm.

Theorem 8. *If there exists an α-approximation algorithm for CTSP with given end vertices and k clusters, for some $k \geq 2$, then there exists an α-approximation algorithm for the TSPP with given end vertices.*

Theorem 9. *If there exists an α-approximation algorithm for CTSP with unspecified end vertices and k clusters, for some $k \geq 4$, then there exists an α-approximation algorithm for the TSPP with given end vertices.*

Remark 4. The approximation given in [10] is for the CTSP with unspecified end vertices with three clusters, where one is a singleton. The main point of the last theorem is that we cannot obtain such a bound even when a single new cluster is added, unless the bound for TSPP of $\frac{5}{3}$ is improved.

Acknowledgment

The third author's research was supported in part by NSF CAREER Award CCR 9501355. The fourth author's research was supported in part by NSF Research Initiation Award CCR-9409625.

References

1. S. Anily, J. Bramel, and A. Hertz, "A $\frac{5}{3}$-approximation algorithm for the clustered traveling salesman tour and path problems," Manuscript, December 1997.
2. E. Arkin, R. Hassin, and L. Klein, "Restricted delivery problems on a network," *Networks* **29** (1997), pages 205-216.
3. J. A. Chisman, "The clustered traveling salesman problem," *Computers & Operations Research* **2** (1975), pages 115-119.
4. N. Christofides, "Worst-case analysis of a new heuristic for the traveling salesman problem," Technical Report 388, Graduate School of Industrial Administration, Carnegie-Mellon University (1976).
5. H. A. Eiselt, M. Gendreau, and G. Laporte, "Arc routing problems, part II: The rural postman problem," *Operations Research* **43** (1995), pages 399-414.
6. G. N. Frederickson, "Approximation algorithms for some postman problems," *J. Assoc. Comput. Mach.* **26** (1979), pages 538-554.
7. G. N. Frederickson, M. S. Hecht, and C. E. Kim, "Approximation algorithms for some routing problems," *SIAM J. Comput.* **7** (1978), pages 178-193.
8. J. A. Hoogeveen, "Analysis of Christofides' heuristic: Some paths are more difficult than cycles," *Operations Research Letters,* **10** (1991), pages 291-295.
9. M. Gendreau, A. Hertz, and G. Laporte, "The traveling salesman problem with backhauls," *Computers and Operations Research,* **23** (1996), pages 501-508.
10. M. Gendreau, G. Laporte and A. Hertz, "An approximation algorithm for the traveling salesman problem with backhauls," *Operations Research,* **45** (1997), pages 639-641.
11. K. Jansen, "An approximation algorithm for the general routing problem," *Information Processing Letters,* **41** (1992), pages 333-339.
12. D. S. Johnson and C. H. Papadimitriou, "Performance guarantees for heuristics," E. L. Lawler, J. K. Lenstra, A. H. G. Rinnooy Kan and D. B. Shmoys (eds). *The Traveling Salesman Problem: A Guided Tour of Combinatorial Optimization* Wiley (1985), pages 145-180.
13. K. Jongens and T. Volgenant, "The symmetric clustered traveling salesman problem" *European Journal of Operational Research* **19** (1985), pages 68-75.
14. E. L. Lawler, *Combinatorial Optimization: Networks and Matroids* Holt, Reinehart and Winston (1976).
15. F. C. J. Lokin, "Procedures for traveling salesman problems with additional constraints," *European Journal of Operational Research* **3** (1978), pages 135-141.
16. G. L. Nemhauser and L. A. Wolsey, *Integer and Combinatorial Optimization* Wiley & Sons (1988).

A Hamiltonian Approach to the Assignment of Non-reusable Frequencies*

DIMITRIS A. FOTAKIS[1,2] PAUL G. SPIRAKIS[1,2]

[1] Department of Computer Engineering and Informatics
University of Patras, 265 00 Rion, Patras, Greece
[2] Computer Technology Institute
Kolokotroni 3, 262 21 Patras, Greece
Email: fotakis@cti.gr, spirakis@cti.gr

Abstract. The problem of Radio Labelling is to assign distinct integer labels to all the vertices of a graph, such that adjacent vertices get labels at distance at least two. The objective is to minimize the label span. Radio labelling is a combinatorial model for frequency assignment in case that the transmitters are not allowed to operate at the same channel. We show that radio labelling is related to TSP(1,2). Hence, it is $\mathcal{NP}$-complete and MAX–SNP-hard. Then, we present a polynomial-time algorithm for computing an optimal radio labelling, given a coloring of the graph with constant number of colors. Thus, we prove that radio labelling is in $\mathcal{P}$ for planar graphs. We also obtain a $\frac{3}{2}$-approximation $\mathcal{NC}$ algorithm and we prove that approximating radio labelling in graphs of bounded maximum degree is essentially as hard as in general graphs. We obtain similar results for TSP(1,2). In particular, we present the first $\frac{3}{2}$-approximation $\mathcal{NC}$ algorithm for TSP(1,2), and we prove that dense instances of TSP(1,2) do not admit a PTAS, unless $\mathcal{P} = \mathcal{NP}$.

1 Introduction

The Frequency Assignment Problem (FAP) arises from the fact that radio transmitters operating at the same or closely related frequency channels have the potential to interfere with each other. FAP can be formulated as an optimization problem as follows: Given a collection of transmitters to be assigned operating channels and a set of interference constraints on transmitter pairs, find an assignment that fulfills all the interference constraints and minimizes the allocated bandwidth.

A common model for FAP is the *interference graph*. Each vertex of an interference graph represents a transmitter, while each edge represents an interference constraint between the adjacent transmitters. The frequency channels are usually assumed to be uniformly spaced in the spectrum and are labelled using positive integers. Frequency channels with adjacent integer labels are assumed adjacent in the spectrum [5, 6, 8]. Clearly, FAP is a generalization of graph coloring [6].

* This work was partially supported by ESPRIT LTR Project no. 20244—ALCOM–IT.

Instead of specifying the interference constraints for each pair of transmitters, FAP can be defined by specifying a minimum allowed spatial distance for each channel/spectral separation that is a potential source of interference [5, 6]. In [6] these are called *Frequency-Distance* (FD) constraints. FD-constraints can be given as a set of distances $\{D_0, D_1, \ldots, D_\kappa\}$, $D_0 \geq D_1 \geq \cdots \geq D_\kappa$, where the distance D_x, $x \in \{0, 1, \ldots, \kappa\}$, is the minimum distance between transmitters using channels at distance x.

The FD(κ)-coloring problem has been proposed as a model for FAP in unweighted interference graphs [8]. In FD(κ)-coloring we seek a function $\chi_\kappa : V \mapsto \{1, \ldots, \nu\}$ that fulfills the FD-constraints with respect to the graph distances $D_0 = \kappa + 1, D_1 = \kappa, \ldots, D_\kappa = 1$, and minimizes the largest color ν used (color span). Alternatively, $v, u \in V$ are only allowed to get colors at distance x, $|\chi_\kappa(v) - \chi_\kappa(u)| = x$, $x \in \{0, 1, \ldots, \kappa\}$, if v and u are at distance at least $\kappa - x + 1$ from each other in the interference graph. A polynomial-time exact algorithm for a variant of FD(κ)-coloring in lattices is presented in [8]. FD(2) -coloring ($\kappa = 2$) is a combinatorial model for the widely used "co-channel" and "adjacent-channel" interference constraints. FD(2)-coloring is also called *radio coloring* in [4]. A problem similar to FD(2)-coloring is studied [11] in the context of mobile networks, where each vertex may require more than one colors (multi-coloring). A polynomial-time approximation algorithm for triangular lattices is presented in [11].

In some practical applications the transmitters cover a local or metropolitan area. Hence, the transmitters are not allowed to operate at the same channel ($D_0 = \infty$, non-reusable frequency channels). In this paper we study *Radio Labelling*, which is the equivalent of FD(2)-coloring in the context of non-reusable frequency assignment. In particular, a valid radio labelling fulfills the FD-constraints with respect to $D_0 = \infty, D_1 = 2, D_2 = 1$. In radio labelling we seek an assignment of distinct integer labels to all the vertices of a graph, such that adjacent vertices get labels at distance at least two. The objective is to minimize the maximum label used (label span). The definition of radio labelling is communicated to us by [7].

Competitive algorithms and lower bounds for on-line radio labelling are presented in [4]. Moreover, radio labelling and similar combinatorial models for non-reusable frequency assignment are used for obtaining lower bounds on the optimal values of general FAP instances [1, 14]. These lower bounds are necessary for assessing the quality of the solutions found by heuristic algorithms.

1.1 Summary of Results

We start with proving that radio labelling is equivalent to Hamiltonian Path with distances one and two (HP(1,2)). Hence, radio labelling is MAX–SNP-hard and approximable in polynomial time within $\frac{7}{6}$ [13]. We also prove that both radio labelling and FD(2)-coloring remain $\mathcal{NP}$-complete for graphs of diameter two.

Next, we present a polynomial-time algorithm for computing an optimal radio labelling, given a coloring of the graph with constant number of colors. Therefore, we prove that radio labelling is in $\mathcal{P}$ for planar graphs and graphs colorable with constant number of colors in polynomial time.

We proceed to deal with radio labelling in general graphs and we obtain a $\frac{3}{2}$-approximation $\mathcal{NC}$ algorithm. In particular, if MC_G denotes the cardinality of the maximum clique and $\chi(G)$ denotes the chromatic number of the graph $G(V,E)$, the algorithm produces a radio labelling of value at most $|V|+\mathrm{MC}_G-1 \leq |V|+\chi(G)-1$, without assuming any knowledge on MC_G or $\chi(G)$. Therefore, it outperforms all known sequential approximation algorithms for graphs with clique number (chromatic number) less than $\frac{|V|}{6}$.

Additionally, we show that there exists a constant $\Delta^\star < 1$, such that, for all $\Delta \in [\Delta^\star, 1)$, radio labelling in graphs $G(V,E)$ of maximum degree $\Delta(G) \leq \Delta|V|$ is essentially as hard to approximate as in general graphs. This is in contrast with the fact that, if $\Delta(G) < \frac{n}{2}$, then an optimal radio labelling of value $|V|$ can be easily computed.

Since radio labelling is closely related to HP(1,2) and TSP(1,2), we also obtain similar results for these problems. In particular, given a partition of a graph G into constant number of cliques, we show how to decide in polynomial time if G is Hamiltonian. Moreover, we present the first $\frac{3}{2}$-approximation $\mathcal{NC}$ algorithm for TSP(1,2) and HP(1,2). The best previously known parallel algorithm for metric TSP and all the special cases is the algorithm of Christofides [2], which is in $\mathcal{RNC}$, but it is not known to be in $\mathcal{NC}$.

We also prove that dense instances of TSP(1,2) and HP(1,2) are essentially as hard to approximate as general instances, as opposed to the success in designing Polynomial Time Approximation Schemes (PTAS) for dense instances of many combinatorial optimization problems (cf. [10] for a survey). Recently a different proof of the same result appears independently in [3].

2 Preliminaries

Given a graph $G(V,E)$, $\chi(G)$ denotes the chromatic number, MIS_G is the cardinality of the Maximum Independent Set, MC_G is the cardinality of the Maximum Clique, and $d(v,u)$ denotes the length of the shortest path between $v,u \in V$. For all graphs G, $\mathrm{MC}_G \leq \chi(G)$. The complementary graph $\overline{G}$ is a graph on the same vertex set V that contains an edge $\{v,u\}$, iff $\{v,u\} \notin E$. Clearly, $\mathrm{MIS}_G = \mathrm{MC}_{\overline{G}}$. A graph $G(V,E)$ is called *Δ-bounded*, for some constant $1 > \Delta > 0$, if the maximum degree $\Delta(G)$ is no more than $\Delta|V|$. Also, a graph $G(V,E)$ is called *δ-dense*, for some constant $1 > \delta > 0$, if the minimum degree $\delta(G)$ is at least $\delta|V|$.

The Travelling Salesman Problem with distances one and two (TSP(1,2)) is the problem of finding a Hamiltonian cycle of minimum length in a complete graph, where all the edge lengths are either one or two. Clearly, given a graph $G(V,E)$, TSP(1,2) is a generalization of the Hamiltonian cycle problem in G, where each edge in E is considered of length one and each edge not in E (non-edge) of length two. TSP_G denotes the optimal value of the TSP(1,2) instance corresponding to the graph G. An interesting variant of TSP(1,2) is Hamiltonian Path with distances one and two (HP(1,2)), where the objective is to find a Hamiltonian path of minimum length. Since TSP(1,2) and HP(1,2) generalize the Hamiltonian cycle and path problems respectively, they are $\mathcal{NP}$-complete. Moreover, they are MAX–SNP-hard and there exists a polynomial-time $\frac{7}{6}$-approximation algorithm [13].

Definition 1. (FD(κ)-labelling)
INSTANCE: A graph $G(V, E)$.
SOLUTION: A valid FD(κ)-labelling, i.e. a function $\mathrm{L}_\kappa : V \mapsto \{1, \ldots, \nu\}$ such that, for all $v, u \in V$, $|\mathrm{L}_\kappa(v) - \mathrm{L}_\kappa(u)| = x$, $x \in \{1, \ldots, \kappa\}$, only if $d(v, u) \geq \kappa - x + 1$.
OBJECTIVE: Minimize the maximum label ν used (label span).

This paper is devoted to FD(2)-labelling, which is also called *Radio Labelling*. In the following, given a graph $G(V, E)$, RL(G) denotes the value of an optimal radio labelling for G and, for any $v \in V$, RL(v) denotes the label assigned to v by a valid radio labelling.

Since radio labelling assigns distinct integer labels to all the vertices of a graph, it is a vertex arrangement problem. In particular, given an arrangement $v_1, v_2, \ldots, v_n$, a valid radio labelling can be computed as follows: $\mathrm{RL}(v_1) = 1$, and for $i = 1, \ldots, n-1$, $\mathrm{RL}(v_{i+1}) = \mathrm{RL}(v_i) + 1$, if $\{v_i, v_{i+1}\} \notin E$, and $\mathrm{RL}(v_{i+1}) = \mathrm{RL}(v_i) + 2$, otherwise. Conversely, any radio labelling implies a vertex arrangement, in the sense that v precedes u, iff $\mathrm{RL}(v) < \mathrm{RL}(u)$. A radio labelling L is minimal, if there does not exist another radio labelling L' that corresponds to the same vertex arrangement and $\mathrm{RL}(L') < \mathrm{RL}(L)$. In the sequel, we only consider minimal radio labellings. It is not hard to verify the following.

Lemma 2. *Radio labelling is equivalent to HP(1,2) in the complementary graph.*

Hence, Dirac's Theorem implies that if $\Delta(G) < \frac{|V|}{2}$, a radio labelling of value $|V|$ exist and can be found in polynomial time. Given a coloring of G with χ colors, it is easy to find a radio labelling of value at most $|V| + \chi - 1$. Therefore, $|V| \leq \mathrm{RL}(G) \leq |V| + \chi(G) - 1$. Additionally, for graphs of diameter two, radio labelling is equivalent to FD(2)-coloring.

Lemma 3. *Radio labelling and* FD(2)*-coloring restricted to graphs of diameter two are $\mathcal{NP}$-complete.*

Proof sketch. Given a graph G of $\mathrm{diam}(G) = 2$, the problem of deciding if the complementary graph $\overline{G}$ contains a Hamiltonian path is $\mathcal{NP}$-complete. □

3 An Exact Algorithm for Constant Number of Colors

Since radio labelling is equivalent to HP(1,2) and a coloring corresponds to a partition into cliques of the complementary graph, we present the technical part of the proof in the context of Hamiltonian paths/cycles and partitions into cliques. In particular, we prove that, given a partition of a graph $G(V, E)$ into constant number of cliques, we can decide if G is Hamiltonian in polynomial time.

3.1 Hamiltonian Cycles and Partitions into Cliques

Theorem 4. *Given a graph $G(V,E)$, $|V| = n$, and a partition of V into $\kappa > 1$ cliques, there exists a deterministic algorithm that runs in time $\mathcal{O}(n^{\kappa(2\kappa-1)})$ and decides if G is Hamiltonian. If G is Hamiltonian, the algorithm outputs a Hamiltonian cycle.*

Proof. A set of inter-clique edges $M \subseteq E$ is an HC-set if M can be extended to a Hamiltonian cycle using only clique-edges, i.e. there exists a $M^{(c)} \subseteq E$ of clique edges such that $M \cup M^{(c)}$ is a Hamiltonian cycle.

We first show that, given a set of inter-clique edges M, we can decide if M is an HC-set and construct a Hamiltonian cycle from M in poly(n, κ) time (Proposition 5). Then, we prove that G is Hamiltonian iff there exists an HC-set of cardinality at most $\kappa(\kappa - 1)$ (Lemmas 6 and 7). The algorithm exhaustively searches all the sets of inter-clique edges of cardinality at most $\kappa(\kappa - 1)$ for an HC-set. Additionally, we conjecture that, if G is Hamiltonian, then there exists an HC-set of cardinality at most $2(\kappa - 1)$. We prove this conjecture for a special case (Lemma 8) and we use Lemma 6 to show the equivalence to Conjecture 9.

Let $\mathcal{C} = \{C_1, \ldots, C_\kappa\}$ be a partition of V into $\kappa > 1$ cliques. Given a set $M \subseteq E$ of inter-clique edges, the *clique graph* $T(\mathcal{C}, M)$ contains exactly κ vertices, that correspond to the cliques of $\mathcal{C}$, and represents how the edges of M connect the different cliques. If M is an HC-set, then the corresponding clique graph $T(C, M)$ is connected and eulerian. However, the converse is not always true.

Given a set of inter-clique edges M, we color an edge RED, if it shares a vertex of G with another edge of M. Otherwise, we color it BLUE. The corresponding edges of G are colored with the same colors, while the remaining edges $(E - M)$ are colored BLACK. Additionally, we color RED each vertex $v \in V$, which is the common end vertex of two or more RED edges. We color BLUE each vertex $v \in V$ to which exactly one edge of M (RED or BLUE) is incident. The remaining vertices of G are colored BLACK (Figure 1).

Let H be any Hamiltonian cycle of G and let M be the corresponding set of inter-clique edges. Obviously, RED vertices cannot be exploited for visiting any BLACK vertices belonging to the same clique. If H visits a clique C_i through a vertex v, and leaves C_i through a vertex u, then $v, u \in C_i$ consist a BLUE vertex pair. A BLUE pass through a clique C_i is a simple path of length at least one, that entirely consists of non-RED vertices of C_i. A clique C_i is covered by M, if all the vertices of C_i have degree at most two in M, and the existence of a non-RED vertex implies the existence of at least one BLUE vertex pair. The following proposition characterizes HC-sets.

Proposition 5. *A set of inter-clique edges M is an HC-set iff the corresponding clique graph $T(C, M)$ is connected, eulerian, and,*

(a) For all $i = 1, \ldots, \kappa$, C_i is covered by M; and
(b) There exists an eulerian trail R for T such that: For any RED *vertex $v \in V$, R passes through v exactly once using the corresponding* RED *edge pair.*

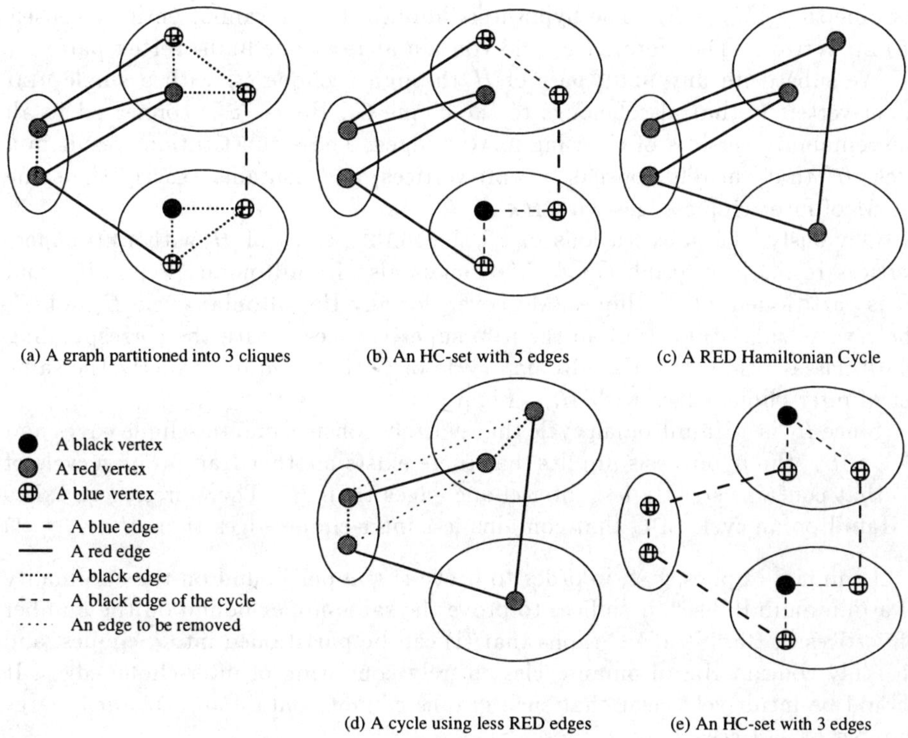

Fig. 1. An application of Lemmas 6 and 7.

Proof sketch: Any HC-set corresponds to a connected, eulerian clique graph $T(C, M)$ that fulfills both (a) and (b). Conversely, we can extend M into a Hamiltonian cycle H following the eulerian trail R. All the RED vertices can be included in H with degree two because of (b). Moreover, since R is an eulerian trail and (a) holds for M, all the BLUE and the BLACK vertices can be included in H with degree two. Therefore, H is a Hamiltonian cycle. □

The proof of Proposition 5 implies a deterministic procedure for deciding if a set of inter-clique edges is an HC-set in poly(n, κ) time. Moreover, in case that M is an HC-set, this procedure outputs a Hamiltonian cycle.

Lemma 6. *Let $B_\kappa \geq 2$ be some integer only depending on κ such that, for any graph $G(V, E)$ and any partition of V into κ cliques, if G is Hamiltonian and $|V| > B_\kappa$, then G contains at least one Hamiltonian cycle not entirely consisting of inter-clique edges* (RED *vertices*).
Then, for any graph $G(V, E)$ and any partition of V into κ cliques, G is Hamiltonian iff it contains a Hamiltonian cycle with at most B_κ inter-clique edges.

Proof. Let H be the Hamiltonian cycle of G containing the minimum number of inter-clique edges and let M be the corresponding set of inter-clique edges.

Assume that $|M| > B_\kappa$. The hypothesis implies that H cannot entirely consist of RED vertices. Therefore, H should contain at least one BLUE vertex pair.

We substitute any BLUE pass of H through a clique C_i with a single RED super-vertex $\hat{v}$, that also belongs to the clique C_i. Hence, $\hat{v}$ is connected to all the remaining vertices of C_i using BLACK edges. These substitutions result in a cycle H' that entirely consists of RED vertices, and contains exactly the same set M of inter-clique edges with H.

Obviously, the substitutions of all the BLUE passes of H with RED super-vertices result in a graph $G'(V', E')$ that is also Hamiltonian, $|V'| > B_\kappa$, and V' is partitioned into κ cliques. Moreover, for any Hamiltonian cycle $H_{G'}$ of G', the reverse substitutions of all the RED super-vertices $\hat{v}$ with the corresponding BLUE passes result in a Hamiltonian cycle of G that contains exactly the same set of inter-clique edges with $H_{G'}$ (Figure 1).

Since H' is a Hamiltonian cycle that entirely consists of inter-clique edges and $|V'| > B_\kappa$, the hypothesis implies that there exists another Hamiltonian cycle of G' that contains strictly less inter-clique edges than H'. Therefore, there exists a Hamiltonian cycle of G that contains less inter-clique edges than H. □

Lemma 6 implies that, in order to prove the upper bound on the cardinality of a minimum HC-set, it suffices to prove the same upper bound on the number of vertices of Hamiltonian graphs that (i) can be partitioned into κ cliques, and (ii) only contain Hamiltonian cycles entirely consisting of inter-clique edges. It should be intuitively clear that such graphs cannot contain an arbitrarily large number of vertices.

Lemma 7. *Given a graph $G(V, E)$ and a partition of V into κ cliques, G is Hamiltonian iff there exists an HC-set M such that $|M| \leq \kappa(\kappa - 1)$.*

Proof. By definition, the existence of an HC-set implies that G is Hamiltonian. Conversely, let H be the Hamiltonian cycle of G that contains the minimum number of inter-clique edges, and let M be the corresponding HC-set. If $|M| \leq \kappa(\kappa - 1)$, then we are done. Otherwise, Lemma 6 implies that it suffices to prove the same upper bound on $|V|$ for graphs $G(V, E)$ that only contain Hamiltonian cycles entirely consisting of inter-clique edges.

Assume that $|V| = |M|$ and the coloring of V under M entirely consists of RED vertices, and consider an arbitrary orientation of the Hamiltonian cycle H (e.g. a traversal of the edges of H in the clockwise direction). If there exist a pair of cliques C_i and C_j and four vertices $v_1, v_2 \in C_i$ and $u_1, u_2 \in C_j$, such that both v_x are followed by u_x ($x = 1, 2$) in a traversal of H, then the BLACK edges $\{v_1, v_2\}$ and $\{u_1, u_2\}$ can be used instead of $\{v_1, u_1\}$ and $\{v_2, u_2\}$ in order to obtain a Hamiltonian cycle containing less inter-clique edges than H. The previous situation can be avoided only if, for all $i = 1, \ldots, \kappa$, and $j = 1, \ldots, \kappa$, $j \neq i$, at most one vertex $v_j \in C_i$ is followed by a vertex $u \in C_j$ in any traversal of H. Hence, if $|V| > \kappa(\kappa - 1)$, then G contains at least one Hamiltonian cycle not entirely consisting of inter-clique edges. Alternatively, any HC-set M of minimum cardinality contains at most two edges between any pair of cliques C_i and C_j. Thus, M contains at most $\kappa(\kappa - 1)$ inter-clique edges. □

Therefore, we can decide if G is Hamiltonian in time $\mathcal{O}(n^{\kappa(2\kappa-1)})$, because the number of the different edge sets containing at most $\kappa(\kappa-1)$ inter-clique edges is at most $n^{2\kappa(\kappa-1)}$, and we can decide if a set of inter-clique edges is an HC-set in time $\text{poly}(n,\kappa)=\mathcal{O}(n^{\kappa})$. □

A BLUE Hamiltonian cycle is a Hamiltonian cycle that does not contain any RED vertices or edges. We can substantially improve the bound of $\kappa(\kappa-1)$ for graphs containing a BLUE Hamiltonian cycle.

Lemma 8. *Given a graph $G(V,E)$ and a partition of V into κ cliques, if G contains a* BLUE *Hamiltonian cycle, then there exists an HC-set M entirely consisting of* BLUE *edges, such that $|M| \leq 2(\kappa-1)$.*

Proof. Let H be the BLUE Hamiltonian cycle of G that contains the minimum number of inter-clique edges and let M be the corresponding HC-set. Assume that $|M| > 2(\kappa-1)$, otherwise we are done. Notice that, since RED vertices cannot be created by removing edges, any $M' \subseteq M$ that corresponds to an eulerian, connected, clique graph $T(C,M')$ is an HC-set that only contains BLUE edges.

Let $S_T(C,M_S)$ be any spanning tree of $T(C,M)$. Since $|M_S|=\kappa-1$, the graph $T^{(S)}(C,M-M_S)$, which is obtained by removing the edges of the spanning tree from T, contains at least κ edges. Therefore, $T^{(S)}$ contains a simple cycle L. The removal of the edges of L does not affect connectivity (the edges of L do not touch the spanning tree S_T), and subtracts two from the degrees of the involved vertices/cliques. Clearly, the clique graph $T'(C,M-L)$ is connected and eulerian, and $M-L$, $|M-L|<|M|$, is an HC-set. □

There exist HC-sets of cardinality exactly $2(\kappa-1)$ that correspond to a Hamiltonian cycle using the minimum number of inter-clique edges. Therefore, the bound of $2(\kappa-1)$ is tight. However, we are not able to construct HC-sets that contain more than $2(\kappa-1)$ edges and correspond to Hamiltonian cycles using the minimum number of inter-clique edges. Hence, we conjecture that the bound of $2(\kappa-1)$ holds for any graph and any partition into κ cliques. An inductive (on $|V|$) application of Lemma 6 suggests that this conjecture is equivalent to the following:

Conjecture 9. *For any Hamiltonian graph $G(V,E)$ of $2\kappa-1$ vertices and any partition of V into κ cliques, there exists at least one Hamiltonian cycle not entirely consisting of inter-clique edges.*

3.2 A Reduction from Radio Labelling to Hamiltonian Cycle

Lemma 10. *Given a graph $G(V,E)$, $|V|=n$, and a coloring of G with κ colors, an optimal radio labelling can be computed in $\mathcal{O}(n^{\kappa(2\kappa+1)})$ time.*

Proof sketch. Since $\text{RL}(G) \leq n+\kappa-1$, optimal HP(1,2)/TSP(1,2) solutions to the complementary graph $\overline{G}$ can be found by at most $\mathcal{O}(n^{2\kappa})$ calls to the algorithm of Theorem 4. □

Since any planar graph can be colored with constant number of colors in polynomial time, the following theorem is an immediate consequence of Lemma 10.

Theorem 11. *An optimal radio labelling of a planar graph can be computed in polynomial time.*

Remark. Conjecture 9 implies that, given a graph $G(V, E)$ and a coloring with κ colors, an optimal radio labelling can be computed in time $n^{\mathcal{O}(\kappa)}$.

4 An $\mathcal{NC}$ Approximation Algorithm for General Graphs

Then, we present a $\frac{3}{2}$-approximation $\mathcal{NC}$ algorithm for radio labelling in general graphs. For clarity of presentation, the algorithm is described and analyzed in the context of Hamiltonian paths and cycles. In particular, we obtain the first $\frac{3}{2}$-approximation $\mathcal{NC}$ algorithm for HP(1,2) and TSP(1,2).

Theorem 12. *The following inequalities hold for any graph $G(V, E)$, $|V| = n$:*

$$2\text{MIS}_G \leq \text{TSP}_G \leq n + \text{MIS}_G \tag{1}$$

Moreover, a tour and an independent set that fulfill (1) can be computed in $\mathcal{NC}$.

Proof. The algorithm TSP-MIS (Figure 2) proceeds in phases, such that the following holds for the ith phase:
For all the vertices v, $v \in V^i$ implies that $\deg_P(v) \leq 1$. Moreover, for each non-trivial path $p \in P$, exactly one of the end vertices of p is in V^i.

Therefore, at the end of the algorithm, the set P consists of simple paths (of 1-edges) and isolated vertices. If the isolated vertices are considered as trivial paths, the edge set P covers V with vertex disjoint simple paths. Additionally, the vertex sets S^i are independent sets, because M^i is a maximal matching in $G^i(V^i, E^i)$.
Performance: The performance of the algorithm is determined by the number of edges (of length 1) that are included in the set P at the end of the algorithm. Initially, the set P is empty. At each phase i, the edges of M^i are added to P in step (*). Let $|M^i|$ be the number of edges of a maximal matching M^i of the graph G^i. The algorithm runs for $K + 1$ phases, where K will be fixed later. Clearly, $|P| \geq \sum_{i=1}^{K} |M^i|$.

Since the vertices of V^i not covered by a maximal matching M^i form an independent set, we obtain that,

$$\frac{|V^i| - \text{MIS}_G}{2} \leq |M^i| \leq \frac{|V^i|}{2}$$

Furthermore, for any pair of vertices of V^i that are matched by M^i, exactly one vertex is added to V^{i+1}. Therefore,

$$\frac{|V^i|}{2} \leq |V^{i+1}| = |V^i| - |M^i| \leq \frac{|V^i| + \text{MIS}_G}{2}$$

The following inequality holds for all $i \geq 1$, and can be proved by induction.

$$|V^{i+1}| \leq \frac{|V^1| + (2^i - 1)\text{MIS}_G}{2^i} \tag{2}$$

```
Algorithm TSP-MIS
Input:  A graph G(V, E).
Output: A set P of edges that cover V with vertex disjoint simple paths.
        A set S* of independent vertices.
P := ∅;
i := 0;
repeat
    i := i + 1;      /* i^th phase */
    V^i := {v ∈ V : deg_P(v) = 0};
    For any non-trivial path p ∈ P,
        add exactly one of the end vertices of p to V^i;
    E^i := {{v, w} ∈ E : v ∈ V^i ∧ w ∈ V^i};
    Find a Maximal Matching M^i in G^i(V^i, E^i);
(*) P := P ∪ M^i;
    S^i := {v ∈ V^i : deg_{M^i}(v) = 0};
until M^i = ∅ or i > K;
S* := S^i of maximum cardinality;
return(P, S*);
```

Fig. 2. The Algorithm TSP-MIS.

If $K = \lceil \log n \rceil$, then inequality (2) implies that $|V^{K+1}| < \mathrm{MIS}_G + 1$. By summing the equalities $|V^{i+1}| = |V^i| - |M^i|$, for all $1 \leq i \leq K + 1$, we obtain that,

$$|V^{K+1}| = |V^1| - \sum_{i=1}^{K} |M^i| \geq |V| - |P|$$

Therefore, $|P| \geq n - \mathrm{MIS}_G$. Since the set P consists of simple paths of total length at least $n - \mathrm{MIS}_G$, we can construct a Hamiltonian cycle from P by adding no more than MIS_G edges of length two. Hence, $\mathrm{TSP}_G \leq n + \mathrm{MIS}_G$.

The proof of the inequality $2\mathrm{MIS}_G \leq \mathrm{TSP}_G$ is simple. Furthermore, if the cardinality of $S^\star$ was less than $\mathrm{TSP}_G - n$, then the previous analysis implies that the result of TSP-MIS would be a Hamiltonian cycle of length less than TSP_G.

There exist graphs G such that $\mathrm{TSP}_G = n + \mathrm{MIS}_G - 1$. For example, for any integer $x > 1$, consider the graph consisting of a clique on $n - x$ vertices and an independent set of x vertices, all of them connected to a single vertex of the clique. Clearly, $\mathrm{MIS}_G = x + 1$ and $\mathrm{TSP}_G = n + x$.

Complexity: The algorithm runs for at most $\lceil \log n \rceil + 1$ phases. Since the connected components of P are simple paths, the computation of G^i can be easily implemented in $\mathcal{NC}$. The complexity of the algorithm is dominated by the computation of the maximal matching. There exist a CRCW PRAM algorithm that produces a maximal matching in $\mathcal{O}(\log^3 n)$ time using $\mathcal{O}(n^2)$ processors [9]. Moreover, the sequential complexity of TSP-MIS is $\mathcal{O}(n^2 \log n)$. □

Obviously, the arguments above also apply to HP(1,2) and to radio labelling in the complementary graph $\overline{G}$. Therefore, the following is an immediate consequence of Theorem 12:

Corollary 13. *There exists an $\mathcal{NC}$ algorithm that runs in a CRCW PRAM in time $\mathcal{O}(\log^4 n)$ using $\mathcal{O}(n^2)$ processors and approximates,*

1. *Radio labelling, HP(1,2), and TSP(1,2) within $\frac{3}{2}$.*
2. *HP(1,2) and TSP(1,2) restricted to graphs G, such that $\mathrm{MIS}_G \leq \alpha n$, within $(1+\alpha)$.*
3. *Radio labelling restricted to graphs G, such that $\mathrm{MC}_G \leq \alpha n$ ($\chi(G) \leq \alpha n$), within $(1+\alpha)$.*
4. *Maximum Clique restricted to graphs G, such that $\mathrm{RL}(G) \geq (1+\beta)n$, within $\frac{2\beta}{1+\beta}$.*

5 Graphs of Bounded Maximum Degree

Even though radio labelling is in $\mathcal{P}$ for graphs $G(V,E)$ of $\Delta(G) < \frac{|V|}{2}$, we prove that there exists a constant $\frac{1}{2} < \Delta^\star < 1$, such that, for all $\Delta \in [\Delta^\star, 1)$, Δ-bounded instances of radio labelling (i.e. $\Delta(G) \leq \Delta|V|$) do not admit a PTAS.

Theorem 14. *There exists a constant $\frac{1}{2} < \Delta^\star < 1$, such that, for all $\Delta \in [\Delta^\star, 1)$, Δ-bounded instances of radio labelling do not admit a PTAS, unless $\mathcal{P} = \mathcal{NP}$.*

Proof sketch. Transform any graph $G(V,E)$ to a Δ-bounded graph by adding a clique on $\frac{1-\Delta}{\Delta}$ vertices. Since radio labelling is MAX–SNP-hard, there exists a constant $\epsilon^\star > 0$, such that radio labelling is not approximable within $(1+\epsilon^\star)$, unless $\mathcal{P} = \mathcal{NP}$. For any small constant α, $\epsilon^\star > \alpha > 0$, $\Delta^\star = \frac{1+\alpha}{1+\epsilon^\star} < 1$. □

For graphs with optimal values $\mathrm{RL}(G) \geq \frac{|V|}{\Delta}$, $\Delta \in [\Delta^\star, 1)$, the previous transformation is an L-reduction from such instances of radio labelling to Δ-bounded instances. A similar result also holds for dense instances of HP(1,2) and TSP(1,2).

Corollary 15. *There exists a constant $\delta^\star > 0$, such that, for all $0 < \delta \leq \delta^\star$, δ-dense instances of HP(1,2) and TSP(1,2) do not admit a PTAS, unless $\mathcal{P} = \mathcal{NP}$.*

6 Open Problems

An interesting direction for further research is to obtain a polynomial-time approximation algorithm for FD(2)-coloring in planar graphs using our exact algorithm for radio labelling. One approach may be to decompose the planar graph to subgraphs, such that almost all vertices of each subgraph get distinct colors by an optimal (or near optimal) assignment. Then, our exact algorithm can be used for computing an optimal radio labelling for each of the resulting subgraphs. Obviously, the decomposition of the planar graph and the combination of the partial assignments to a near optimal solution require an appropriate planar separator theorem.

Another research direction is the conjecture that, given a graph $G(V, E)$ and a partition of V into κ cliques, G is Hamiltonian iff there exists a Hamiltonian cycle containing at most $2(\kappa - 1)$ inter-clique edges. This would imply a $n^{\mathcal{O}(\kappa)}$ exact algorithm for radio labelling in the complementary graph $\overline{G}$, given a coloring of $\overline{G}$ with κ colors. In this paper, we prove the conjectured bound for graphs and partitions that contain at least one Hamiltonian cycle H, such that any vertex $v \in V$ has degree at most one in the set of inter-clique edges of H.

Additionally, it may be possible to improve the complexity of the algorithm of Theorem 4 to $\mathcal{O}(f(\kappa)p(n))$, where $f(\kappa)$ is a fixed function of κ, e.g. $f(\kappa) = 2^{\kappa^2}$, and $p(n)$ is a fixed polynomial in n of degree not depending on κ, e.g. $p(n) = n$. This is also suggested by Papadimitriou [12].

References

1. S.M. Allen, D.H. Smith, and S. Hurley. Lower Bounding Techniques for Frequency Assignment. Submitted to *Discrete Mathematics*, 1997.
2. N. Christofides. Worst-Case Analysis of a New Heuristic for the Travelling Salesman Problem. *Symposium on new directions and recent results in algorithms and complexity*, p. 441, 1976.
3. W. Fernandez de la Vega and M. Karpinski. On Approximation Hardness of Dense TSP and other Path Problems. Electronic Colloquium on Computational Complexity, TR98-024, 1998.
4. D. Fotakis, G. Pantziou, G. Pentaris, and P. Spirakis. Frequency Assignment in Mobile and Radio Networks. To appear in *Proc. of the Workshop on Networks in Distributed Computing*, DIMACS Series, AMS, 1998.
5. R.A.H. Gower and R.A. Leese. The Sensitivity of Channel Assignment to Constraint Specification. *Proc. of the 12th International Symposium on Electromagnetic Compatibility*, pp. 131-136, 1997.
6. W.K. Hale. Frequency Assignment: Theory and Applications. *Proceedings of the IEEE* **68**(12), pp. 1497–1514, 1980.
7. F. Harary. Personal Communication. 1997.
8. J. van den Heuvel, R.A. Leese, and M.A. Shepherd. Graph Labelling and Radio Channel Assignment. Manuscript available from `http://www.maths.ox.ac.uk/users/gowerr/preprints.html`, 1996.
9. A. Israeli and Y. Shiloach. An improved algorithm for maximal matching. *Information Processing Letters* **33**, pp. 57–60, 1986.
10. M. Karpinski. Polynomial Time Approximation Schemes for Some Dense Instances of $\mathcal{NP}$-hard Optimization Problems. *Proc. of the 1st Symposium on Randomization and Approximation Techniques in Computer Science*, pp. 1–14, 1997.
11. S. Khanna and K. Kumaran. On Wireless Spectrum Estimation and Generalized Graph Coloring. *Proc. of the 17th Joint Conference of IEEE Computer and Communications Societies - INFOCOM*, 1998.
12. C.H. Papadimitriou. Personal Communication. 1998.
13. C.H. Papadimitriou and M. Yannakakis. The Traveling Salesman Problem with Distances One and Two. *Mathematics of Operations Research* **18**(1), pp. 1–11, 1993.
14. A. Raychaudhuri. *Intersection assignments, T-colourings and powers of graphs.* PhD Thesis, Rutgers University, 1985.

Deadlock Sensitive Types for Lambda Calculus with Resources

Carolina Lavatelli

INRIA, Domaine de Voluceau-Rocquencourt, B.P. 105, 78153 Le Chesnay, France.
Carolina.Lavatelli@inria.fr

Abstract. We define a new type system for lambda calculi with resources which characterizes the flat operational semantics that distinguishes deadlock from divergence. The system follows the intersection style but with a special management of structural rules. The novel feature in comparison with previous works is the introduction of a controlled form of weakening that allows to deal with deadlock. To show the adequacy result we apply the realizability technique on a decorated calculus where the resources to be consumed are explicitly indicated.

1 Introduction

In this paper we address the problem of detecting possibly deadlocked terms of the lambda calculus with resources λ_r defined by Boudol [2], through a typing system. This lazy non-deterministic calculus was designed so as to narrow the gap between π-calculus and λ-calculus by introducing the possibility of raising a new form of irreducible term (that can be interpreted as deadlocked) during evaluation. As usual in lazy calculi, evaluations can diverge, that is infinite computations can arise, or converge to lambda abstractions; furthermore, evaluations can be blocked by lack of resources. Let us illustrate this with an example (we use integers and sum for simplicity though they do not belong to the formal definition of the calculus) : Define $M = \lambda fx.f(fx)$ and $S_i = \lambda y.y + i$. Then

$$\begin{aligned} M(S_1 \mid S_2)5 &\xrightarrow{\star}_r (f(fx))\langle S_1 \mid S_2/f\rangle\langle 5/x\rangle \rightarrow_r (S_1(fx))\langle S_2/f\rangle\langle 5/x\rangle \\ &\rightarrow_r (fx+1)\langle S_2/f\rangle\langle 5/x\rangle \quad\ \rightarrow_r (S_2x+1)\langle \mathbf{1}/f\rangle\langle 5/x\rangle \\ &\rightarrow_r (x+2+1)\langle \mathbf{1}/f\rangle\langle 5/x\rangle \quad \rightarrow_r (5+2+1)\langle \mathbf{1}/f\rangle\langle \mathbf{1}/x\rangle \\ &\xrightarrow{\star}_r 8\langle \mathbf{1}/f\rangle\langle \mathbf{1}/x\rangle \end{aligned}$$

Notice that arguments are multisets of terms e.g. $(S_1 \mid S_2)$, called resources, and that β-reduction transforms arguments into explicit substitution entries like $\langle S_1 \mid S_2/f\rangle$. Resources are then consumed non-deterministically by necessity and the symbol $\mathbf{1}$ denotes the absence of resources. In the case above, the resources were enough to reach a value and all possible evaluations gives the same result, but for instance, $M(S_1 \mid S_2 \mid S_3)5$ has three legal results (8, 9 and 10) depending on which resources S_i are used. Now consider the following situation :

$$M(S_1)5 \xrightarrow{\star}_r (fx+1)\langle \mathbf{1}/f\rangle\langle 5/x\rangle$$

In this case, the evaluation cannot proceed since there is no available resource for f. We say that the irreducible resulting term is deadlocked. Observe that such terms can arise in the presence of arguments composed of a finite number of resources only. In order to recover pure lazy lambda calculus, infinitely available resources are allowed. For instance, the resource S_1 is used twice during the evaluation $M(S_1^\infty)5 \xrightarrow{\star}_r 7\langle S_1^\infty/f\rangle\langle \mathbf{1}/x\rangle$.

Various operational semantics can be defined in this framework, depending on which irreducible terms are taken as valid results, studied in [2, 4–7, 9, 10]. Among them we have the standard semantics, which takes abstractions as values only -hence deadlocked and divergent terms are identified-, and the flat semantics where abstractions and deadlocked terms are different kinds of values. In this paper we propose a new intersection-like type system for λ_r, with a special management of hypotheses, that induces an adequate characterization of the flat semantics. The difficulties come from the fact that not only contraction of hypotheses is not sound (this corresponds to the finite availability of resources which means that resources cannot be duplicated, as for the standard semantics) but the usual structural rule for weakening is not applicable in general when deadlock is meaningful. Indeed, adding useless hypotheses can destroy deadlock. To overcome this problem, two kind of types (for assumptions) have been used, finite and infinite, the first one to keep track of deadlock (over which no weakening is possible), the second one to give account of ordinary derivations. The realizability proof-technique used to show the adequacy result has been also adapted to the new scenario : We introduce a decorated calculus which allows to memorize the relevant assumptions made during type-derivation, i.e. which β-reductions must be performed and which resources must be fetched to reach a value of the desired type. Using results by Boudol and Laneve about the embedding of lazy λ-calculus into π-calculus [6], we conclude that the semantics induced by the type system over pure λ-terms is at most as discriminating as the π-semantics.

2 The calculus

The set of terms of the lambda calculus with resources λ_r includes variables, abstractions, applications and terms with substitution entries like $M\langle B/x\rangle$; arguments are either the empty bag $\mathbf{1}$ or non empty multisets of resources, possibly with infinite multiplicity. The syntax is the following [1] :

$$\begin{array}{rrl} \text{(terms)}: & M ::= & x \mid \lambda x.M \mid (MB) \mid M\langle B/x\rangle \\ \text{(bags)}: & B ::= & \mathbf{1} \mid P \\ & P ::= & M \mid M^\infty \mid (P \mid P) \end{array}$$

Contexts are terms with some subterms replaced by a hole $[]$. The notation $C[M]$ stands for the term where the hole of C is replaced by M. We assume that application associates to the left. We use $M\tilde{R}$ as a short form for $MR_1 \ldots R_n$. For $\tilde{R}$ composed of substitution entries only, we often write $M\langle\tilde{P}/\tilde{x}\rangle$ or even $M\rho$ instead of $M\langle P_1/x_1\rangle \ldots \langle P_n/x_n\rangle$. Free and bound variables of terms are

[1] Remark that in our setting, bags cannot be composed of $\mathbf{1}$ and some other terms, while this is so in the definition of [2]. However, the two presentations are equivalent.

$$(P_0 \mid P_1) =_{ac} (P_1 \mid P_0) \qquad (P_0 \mid (P_1 \mid P_2)) =_{ac} ((P_0 \mid P_1) \mid P_2)$$

$$P =_{ac} Q \Rightarrow P \equiv Q \qquad M^\infty \equiv (M \mid M^\infty) \qquad P \equiv Q \Rightarrow \begin{cases} MP \equiv MQ \\ M\langle P/x\rangle \equiv M\langle Q/x\rangle \end{cases}$$

$$(\beta)\ (\lambda x.M)P \rightarrow_r M\langle P/x\rangle \qquad (v)\ (\lambda x.M)\langle P/z\rangle \rightarrow_r \lambda x.(M\langle P/z\rangle) \text{ if } x \notin fv(z,P)$$

$$(fetch)\ M\langle N/x\rangle \succ M' \text{ and } x \notin fv(N) \Rightarrow \begin{cases} M\langle N/x\rangle \rightarrow_r M'\langle \mathbf{1}/x\rangle \\ M\langle (N \mid Q)/x\rangle \rightarrow_r M'\langle Q/x\rangle \end{cases}$$

$$M \rightarrow_r M' \Rightarrow \begin{cases} MP \rightarrow_r M'P \\ M\langle P/x\rangle \rightarrow_r M'\langle P/x\rangle \\ N \rightarrow_r M' \qquad \text{if } M \equiv N \text{ or } M =_\alpha N \end{cases}$$

$$x\langle N/x\rangle \succ N \qquad M\langle N/x\rangle \succ M' \Rightarrow \begin{cases} MP\langle N/x\rangle \succ M'P \\ M\langle P/z\rangle\langle N/x\rangle \succ M'\langle P/z\rangle \text{ if } x \neq z, z \notin fv(N) \end{cases}$$

Fig. 1. Structural equivalence and Evaluation rules

defined as usual (both λ-abstractions and substitution entries are binders). We consider terms up to α-conversion ($M =_\alpha N$). The following terms will be used throughout the paper : $\mathbf{I} = \lambda x.x$, $\Omega = (\lambda x.xx^\infty)(\lambda x.xx^\infty)^\infty$ and $\mathbf{D} = y\langle \mathbf{1}/y\rangle$. Terms of the shape $\lambda x_1 \ldots x_n.\Omega$ are called *unsolvable*, and terms of the shape $\lambda x_1 \ldots x_n.\mathbf{D}$ are called *potentially deadlocked.* Their order is n, which can be zero. The structural equivalence [2] $\equiv$ and the lazy evaluation rules $\rightarrow_r$ are given in Fig. 2. Lazy λ-calculus is a sub-calculus of λ_r [3]. The encoding defined in [2] is the following (in the rest of the paper, E and F stand for pure λ-terms) : $[\![x]\!] = x$, $[\![\lambda x.E]\!] = \lambda x.[\![E]\!]$ and $[\![(EF)]\!] = [\![E]\!][\![F]\!]^\infty$.

We define the convergence/divergence predicates as follows :

$$\begin{array}{lll} M \Uparrow & \stackrel{def}{\Longleftrightarrow} & M \text{ may diverge} \\ & & \text{evaluation issued from } M). \\ M \Downarrow \delta(T) & \stackrel{def}{\Longleftrightarrow} & M \text{ may deadlock (i.e. } M \stackrel{\star}{\rightarrow}_r x\tilde{R}\langle \mathbf{1}/x\rangle\tilde{S} = \mathrm{T}). \\ M \Downarrow \gamma(T) & \stackrel{def}{\Longleftrightarrow} & M \text{ may converge (i.e. } M \stackrel{\star}{\rightarrow}_r \lambda x.M' = \mathrm{T}). \end{array}$$

---

[2] The standard definition of λ_r includes $P \equiv (\mathbf{1} \mid P)$.

[3] Two other calculi will be mentioned along the paper : lambda calculus with resources and convergence testing λ_r^c [9, 7], which incorporates a convergence testing operator in the style of [1], and lambda calculus with multiplicities λ_m, where only homogeneous bags $(M \mid \ldots \mid M)$ are allowed, with finite or infinite multiplicity. λ_r^c is non-deterministic, while λ_m is deterministic up to α-conversion.

The notations $M \Downarrow \delta$ and $M \Downarrow \gamma$ stand for $\exists T \; M \Downarrow \delta(T)$ and $\exists T \; M \Downarrow \gamma(T)$.

Definition 1. (operational semantics)

$$\begin{array}{rcll} \textit{standard} : M \sqsubseteq^{\natural} N & \stackrel{def}{\Longleftrightarrow} & \forall C & C[M] \Downarrow \gamma \;\Rightarrow\; C[N] \Downarrow \gamma . \\ \textit{flat} : M \sqsubseteq^{\flat}_{l} N & \stackrel{def}{\Longleftrightarrow} & \forall C & C[M] \Downarrow \gamma \;\Rightarrow\; C[N] \Downarrow \gamma \textit{ and} \\ & & & C[M] \Downarrow \delta \;\Rightarrow\; C[N] \Downarrow \delta . \\ \textit{over lambda-terms} : E \leq^{o}_{l} F & \stackrel{def}{\Longleftrightarrow} & & [\![E]\!] \sqsubseteq^{o}_{l} [\![F]\!] \end{array}$$

where $o = \natural, \flat$ and $l = m, r, rc$. The associated equivalences are $\simeq^{o}_{l}$, and $=^{o}_{l}$. Sometimes o and/or l will not appear, indicating that the kind of semantics and/or the language is irrelevant.

2.1 Standard and flat semantics compared

In the standard and flat scenarios, we have

$$\begin{array}{rcll} M\langle R/x\rangle & \simeq & M & x \notin fv(M) \\ (MP)\langle R/x\rangle & \simeq & (M\langle R/x\rangle)P & x \notin fv(P) \\ M\langle P/z\rangle\langle R/x\rangle & \simeq & M\langle R/x\rangle\langle P/z\rangle & z \neq x, x \notin fv(P), z \notin fv(R) \\ (MP)\langle L^{\infty}/x\rangle & \simeq & (M\langle L^{\infty}/x\rangle)P\langle L^{\infty}/x\rangle & \end{array}$$

Proposition 1. *All unsolvable resources except that of maximal order can be dropped from bags in the two semantics. Furthermore, Ω can be eliminated from bags in the standard semantics* [4].

Example 1. Let $P = (\lambda x_1 \ldots x_{n_1}.\Omega \mid \ldots \mid \lambda x_1 \ldots x_{n_j}.\Omega)$, $m = \max\{n_i\}$, and $Q = (\lambda x_1 \ldots x_m.\Omega)$. Then $NP \simeq NQ$: if $NP \Downarrow \gamma(V)$, at most one unsolvable was consumed from P, say $\lambda x_1 \ldots x_{n_i}.\Omega$; then $V = \lambda x_h \ldots x_{n_i}.\Omega\rho$, with $n_i \geq h$. Therefore $NQ \Downarrow \gamma(\lambda x_h \ldots x_m.\Omega\rho')$. If $NP \Downarrow \delta$, the unsolvables are not used; then $NQ \Downarrow \delta$.

Proposition 2. *In the standard semantics, potentially deadlocked terms can be discarded as unsolvable ones (recall that Ω and $\mathbf{D}$ are not distinguished). In the flat semantics, only repeated potentially deadlocked terms can be discarded.*

Example 2. Let $P = (\lambda x_1 \ldots x_n.\mathbf{D} \mid \lambda x_1 \ldots x_n.\mathbf{D} \mid \lambda x_1 \ldots x_k.\mathbf{D} \mid \lambda x_1 \ldots x_k.\mathbf{D})$, $Q_1 = (\lambda x_1 \ldots x_m.\mathbf{D})$, $Q_2 = (\lambda x_1 \ldots x_n.\mathbf{D} \mid \lambda x_1 \ldots x_k.\mathbf{D})$, with $m = \max\{n, k\}$. We have $NP \simeq^{\flat} NQ_2$, but $NP \not\sqsubseteq^{\flat} NQ_1$ in general : assume $N = \mathbf{I}$, $k < n$ and $C = [\,]P_1 \ldots P_k$; then $C[\mathbf{I}P] \stackrel{\star}{\rightarrow}_r \mathbf{D}\rho \Downarrow \delta$ but $C[\mathbf{I}Q_1] \stackrel{\star}{\rightarrow}_r \lambda x_{k+1} \ldots x_n.\mathbf{D}\rho' \Downarrow \gamma$ only.

Unlike $\sqsubseteq^{\natural}$, the flat preorder $\sqsubseteq^{\flat}$ does not verify η-expansion : for instance, $[\,]\langle \mathbf{1}/x\rangle$ separates the terms x and $\lambda y.xy$. Indeed, $x\langle \mathbf{1}/x\rangle \Downarrow \delta$ but $(\lambda y.xy)\langle \mathbf{1}/x\rangle \Downarrow \gamma$ only. Moreover, let $Q \equiv (P \mid Q')$, then $MP \sqsubseteq^{\natural} MQ$ and $M\langle P/x\rangle \sqsubseteq^{\natural} M\langle Q/x\rangle$ but this is not true in the flat scenario since $xx\langle \mathbf{I}/x\rangle \Downarrow \delta$ but $xx\langle \mathbf{I} \mid \Omega/x\rangle \Uparrow$. [5].

---

[4] This holds for λ_r and λ_m but not for λ_r^c, since the convergence testing combinator can be used to count the number of unsolvable or potentially deadlocked terms of order greater than zero (see [9] for detailed proofs about standard semantics).

[5] However, there are some cases for which these inequalities hold : when P is not used in the deadlocked evaluation, when P has an infinite resource, when Q contains a term which may deadlock. Something similar happens when one tries to group substitutions entries.

Example 3. We have $M\langle P_0/x\rangle Q\langle P_1/x\rangle \sqsubseteq^{\natural} (MQ)\langle P_0 \mid P_1/x\rangle$ for any P_0 and P_1. Let $P_0 = \mathbf{I}$ and $P_1 = \lambda zy.y$. We have $(xx)\langle P_0/x\rangle x\langle P_1/x\rangle \overset{\star}{\rightarrow}_r x\langle \mathbf{1}/x\rangle x\langle P_1/x\rangle \Downarrow \delta$, while $((xx)x)\langle P_0 \mid P_1/x\rangle \Downarrow \gamma(\mathbf{I})$ only.

2.2 On the expressiveness of resource calculi

In this section, we draw a comparison of expressiveness between calculi with resources, lazy lambda calculus and π-calculus. Besides the notions already introduced, we use Lévy [11] and Longo [12] intensional semantics for lambda calculus $\leq_{\mathcal{L}}$, based on a notion of approximation that distinguishes $\lambda x.\Omega$ from Ω, and its η-extension $\leq_{\mathcal{L}}^{\eta}$ defined by Ong [15] and used to characterize the local structure of Plotkin-Scott-Engeler model of λ-calculus. Moreover, $\sqsubseteq_\lambda$ stands for Morris preorder for lazy lambda calculus. As far as π-calculus is concerned, assume $[\![E]\!]u$ stands for the π-expression associated with the lambda term E, for a given channel u, and define $E \leq_\pi F \overset{def}{\Longleftrightarrow} [\![E]\!]u \sqsubseteq_\pi [\![F]\!]u$, where $\sqsubseteq_\pi$ is the contextual semantics of the π-calculus [14]. In the following, the single arrow $\longrightarrow$ stands for strict inclusion and the double arrow $\longleftrightarrow$ for equality :

$$\leq_{\mathcal{L}} \overset{[4]}{\longrightarrow} \leq_m^{\natural} \overset{[4]}{\longleftrightarrow} \leq_{\mathcal{L}}^{\eta} \overset{[15]}{\longrightarrow} \sqsubseteq_\lambda$$

$$\leq_{\mathcal{L}} \overset{[5]}{\longleftrightarrow} \leq_m^{\flat} \overset{[5]}{\longleftrightarrow} \leq_r^{\flat} \overset{[6]}{\longleftrightarrow} \leq_\pi$$

$$=_\pi \overset{[16]}{\longleftrightarrow} =_{\mathcal{L}} \overset{[4]}{\longleftrightarrow} =_m^{\natural} \overset{[9]}{\longleftrightarrow} =_{rc}^{\natural}$$

3 Type assignment system

The syntax for types is determined by the following grammar:

$$\text{(types for terms)} : \quad \phi ::= \omega \mid \delta \mid \pi \rightarrow \phi$$

$$\text{(types for bags)} : \quad \pi ::= \mathbf{1} \mid \psi \mid \psi \times \mathbf{1}$$

$$\psi ::= \phi \mid \psi \times \psi$$

The difference with respect to classical intersection type systems is that δ is the type for deadlock, and that the types for arguments involve $\mathbf{1}$, which is the type of the empty bag. The constructor $\times$ behaves much like the standard conjunction operator except that $\times$ is not idempotent. The classes of types $\mathcal{T}_\omega$ and $\mathcal{T}_\delta$ defined below are associated with the unsolvable and the possibly deadlocked terms respectively. Let $\mathcal{T}_\phi^0 = \{\phi\}$ and $\mathcal{T}_\phi^{i+1} = \{\omega \rightarrow \sigma \mid$ for any $\sigma \in \mathcal{T}_\phi^i\}$. Then : $\mathcal{T}_\omega = \bigcup \mathcal{T}_\omega^i$ and $\mathcal{T}_\delta = \bigcup \mathcal{T}_\delta^i$. Among the types for bags we distinguish the following subsets [6] :

(finite types) $\Theta = \{\phi_1 \times \ldots \times \phi_n \times \mathbf{1} \mid \phi_i \notin \mathcal{T}_\delta \cup \mathcal{T}_\omega\}$ ranged over by $\theta, \theta', \ldots$
(infinite types) $\Psi = \{\phi_1 \times \ldots \times \phi_n\}$ ranged over by $\psi, \psi', \ldots$

[6] Notice that $\Theta \cup \Psi$ does not cover the whole set of product types. For instance $\omega \times \mathbf{1}$ is neither finite nor infinite.

Definition 2. *The relation $\sim$ between types is the least equivalence verifying the usual laws for arrows in the weak theory of lambda-calculus (1. and 2.), together with additional laws for product (3. to 8.) :*

1. $\psi \to \omega \sim \omega \to \omega$
2. $\pi_1 \sim \pi_0$ *and* $\phi_0 \sim \phi_1 \;\Rightarrow\; (\pi_0 \to \phi_0) \sim (\pi_1 \to \phi_1)$

3. $\omega \times \pi \sim \pi$
4. $\pi_0 \times \pi_1 \sim \pi_1 \times \pi_0$
5. $\pi_0 \times (\pi_1 \times \pi_2) \sim (\pi_0 \times \pi_1) \times \pi_2$
6. $\pi_0 \sim \pi_0'$ *and* $\pi_1 \sim \pi_1' \;\Rightarrow\; \pi_0 \times \pi_1 \sim \pi_0' \times \pi_1'$

7. $\phi \in \mathcal{T}_\omega^p$ *and* $\sigma \in \mathcal{T}_\omega^q$ *and* $p \leq q \;\Rightarrow\; \sigma \sim \phi \times \sigma$
8. $\phi \in \mathcal{T}_\delta^p \;\Rightarrow\; \phi \sim \phi \times \phi$.

Rules 1. to 6. belong to the type theory of [2]. Remark that the operator $\times$ is not idempotent, that is, contraction of types is not allowed in general. Nevertheless, $\pi \sim \pi \times \pi$ holds for $\pi \in \mathcal{T}_\omega \cup \mathcal{T}_\delta$. Rules 7. and 8. are new and have no effect on finite types; their intended meaning is to collapse the typing of terms that differ either on the number of unsolvable terms or on the number of deadlocked terms as the operational semantics does (cf. examples 1 and 2).

The typing system associated with λ_r is a sequent calculus where the provable judgments are of the form $\Gamma \vdash M : \phi$, where Γ is a finite set of hypotheses $\{x_1 : \pi_1, \ldots, x_n : \pi_n\}$, with $x_i \neq x_j$ for $i \neq j$. We often write $x \in \Gamma$ for $\exists \pi \; x : \pi \in \Gamma$, and $\Gamma(x) = \pi$ if $x : \pi \in \Gamma$. We write $x : \pi, \Gamma$ instead of $\{x : \pi\} \cup \Gamma$ provided that $x \notin \Gamma$. The following notion of combination of contexts is needed to formalize the typing rules.

Definition 3. *The combination $\star$ of two product types is the commutative and associative operation satisfying :*

$$
\begin{aligned}
\theta \star \theta' &= \psi \times \theta' \quad \text{if } \theta = \psi \times \mathbf{1} \\
\psi \star \psi' &= \psi \times \psi' \\
\psi \star \theta &= \begin{cases} \psi \times \theta & \text{if } \psi \times \theta \text{ is a finite type} \\ \psi \times \psi' & \text{if } \theta = \psi' \times \mathbf{1} \text{ and } \psi \sim \delta \times \psi'' \\ \text{undefined} & \text{otherwise} \end{cases} \\
(\Gamma \star \Delta)(x) &= \begin{cases} \Gamma(x) & \text{if } x \notin \Delta \\ \Delta(x) & \text{if } x \notin \Gamma \\ \Gamma(x) \star \Delta(x) & \text{otherwise.} \end{cases}
\end{aligned}
$$

The type system is defined in Fig. 3. Unlike that of [2] for the standard semantics of λ_r, our system deals with two categories of types, finite (θ) and infinite (ψ) (if we forget the rules for finite types, these two systems are similar). Observe that rule (L0b) applies only to infinite types. In fact, we do not want $\omega \times \theta \sim \theta$ for otherwise, one could derive $\vdash x\langle \Omega/x \rangle : \delta$ by using rules (L1b), (L0a) and (L4b) (in this case $\theta = \mathbf{1}$). Roughly, finite types help in proving deadlock : the only way to introduce finite types in a derivation is by axiom (L1b) and the conditions imposed in definition 3 preserve deadlock.

all terms

$$(\text{L0a})\ \vdash M:\omega \qquad (\text{L0b})\ \frac{x:\psi,\Gamma\vdash M:\phi \quad \phi\sim\phi' \quad \psi\sim\psi'}{x:\psi',\Gamma\vdash M:\phi'}$$

variables

$$(\text{L1a})\ \frac{\phi\neq\omega}{x:\phi\vdash x:\phi} \qquad (\text{L1b})\ x:\mathbf{1}\vdash x:\delta$$

abstractions

$$(\text{L2a})\ \frac{x:\pi,\Gamma\vdash N:\phi}{\Gamma\vdash\lambda x.N:\pi\to\phi} \qquad (\text{L2b})\ \frac{\Gamma\vdash N:\phi \quad x\notin\Gamma}{\Gamma\vdash\lambda x.N:\omega\to\phi}$$

applications

$$(\text{L3a})\ \frac{\Gamma\vdash M:\psi\to\phi \quad \psi=\phi_1\times\ldots\times\phi_n \quad P\equiv(M_1\mid\ldots\mid M_n\mid Q) \quad \Delta_i\vdash M_i:\phi_i}{\Gamma\star(\Delta_1\star\ldots\star\Delta_n)\vdash(MP):\phi}\ (1)$$

$$(\text{L3b})\ \frac{\Gamma\vdash M:\theta\to\phi \quad \theta=\phi_1\times\ldots\times\phi_n\times\mathbf{1} \quad P{=_{ac}}(M_1\mid\ldots\mid M_n) \quad \Delta_i\vdash M_i:\phi_i}{\Gamma\star(\Delta_1\star\ldots\star\Delta_n)\vdash(MP):\phi}\ (2)$$

$$(\text{L3c})\ \frac{\Gamma\vdash M:\psi\to\phi}{\Gamma\vdash MB:\phi}\ (3) \qquad (\text{L3d})\ \frac{\Gamma\vdash M:\mathbf{1}\to\phi}{\Gamma\vdash M\mathbf{1}:\phi} \qquad (\text{L3e})\ \frac{\Gamma\vdash M:\delta}{\Gamma\vdash(MB):\delta}$$

closures

$$(\text{L4a})\ \frac{x:\psi,\Gamma\vdash M:\phi \quad \psi=\phi_1\times\ldots\times\phi_n \quad P\equiv(M_1\mid\ldots\mid M_n\mid Q) \quad \Delta_i\vdash M_i:\phi_i}{\Gamma\star(\Delta_1\star\ldots\star\Delta_n)\vdash M\langle P/x\rangle:\phi}\ (1)$$

$$(\text{L4b})\ \frac{x:\theta,\Gamma\vdash M:\phi \quad \theta=\phi_1\times\ldots\times\phi_n\times\mathbf{1} \quad P{=_{ac}}(M_1\mid\ldots\mid M_n) \quad \Delta_i\vdash M_i:\phi_i}{\Gamma\star(\Delta_1\star\ldots\star\Delta_n)\vdash M\langle P/x\rangle:\phi}\ (2)$$

$$(\text{L4c})\ \frac{x:\psi,\Gamma\vdash M:\phi}{\Gamma\vdash M\langle B/x\rangle:\phi}\ (3) \qquad (\text{L4d})\ \frac{x:\mathbf{1},\Gamma\vdash M:\phi}{\Gamma\vdash M\langle\mathbf{1}/x\rangle:\phi} \qquad (\text{L4e})\ \frac{\Gamma\vdash M:\phi \quad x\notin\Gamma}{\Gamma\vdash M\langle B/x\rangle:\phi}$$

with $\phi\neq\omega$ in (L3a) to (L3d) and (L4a) to (L4e)

and (1) $\psi\not\sim\omega$, (2) $n\geq 1$, (3) $\psi\sim\omega$.

Fig. 2. Type System

Example 4. Let $M = x(\lambda y.xy)\mathbf{I}$, $M_1 = M\langle\mathbf{I}/x\rangle$ and $M_2 = M\langle(\mathbf{I} \mid \mathbf{I})/x\rangle$. We have $M_1 \Downarrow \delta$ but $M_2 \Downarrow \gamma$ only. Let $\phi = \omega \to \delta$; then

$$\cfrac{x : \phi \to \phi \vdash x : \phi \to \phi \qquad \cfrac{\cfrac{x : \mathbf{1} \vdash x : \delta}{x : \mathbf{1} \vdash xy : \delta}\,(\text{L3e})}{x : \mathbf{1} \vdash \lambda y.xy : \omega \to \delta}\,(\text{L2b})}{x : (\phi \to \phi) \times \mathbf{1} \vdash M : \delta}\,(\text{L3a})$$

Using (L4b) and the fact that $\vdash \mathbf{I} : \phi \to \phi$ we conclude $\vdash M_1 : \delta$ as expected. Remark that asking for exactly one argument in rule (L4b) is essential. If this condition is relaxed, by allowing some kind of weakening, then we may have $\vdash M_2 : \delta$ too, which is not correct.

Let us examine the problem posed by weakening in the framework of a system that distinguishes between deadlock and divergence.

Example 5. Assume that we have a rule for weakening that allows to arbitrarily enlarge the types of the hypotheses as in [2]. Then we can build the following typing :

$$\cfrac{\cfrac{\cfrac{x : \delta \to \delta \vdash x : \delta \to \delta}{x : (\delta \to \delta) \times (\omega \to (\phi \to \phi)) \vdash x : \delta \to \delta}\,(\text{weak}) \qquad x : \mathbf{1} \vdash x : \delta}{x : (\delta \to \delta) \times (\omega \to (\phi \to \phi)) \times \mathbf{1} \vdash xx : \delta}\,(\text{L3a})}{x : (\delta \to \delta) \times (\omega \to (\phi \to \phi)) \times \mathbf{1} \vdash (xx)x : \delta}\,(\text{L3e})$$

Using rule (L4b) and the fact that $\vdash \mathbf{I} : \delta \to \delta$ and $\vdash \lambda y.\mathbf{I} : \omega \to (\phi \to \phi)$, one shows $\vdash M = (xx)x\langle(\mathbf{I} \mid \lambda y.\mathbf{I})/x\rangle : \delta$, but this is not correct, since the typing system is supposed to characterize convergence : Observe that $M \Downarrow \gamma(\mathbf{I})$ but $M \not\Downarrow \delta$.

The problem appears when the weakened hypothesis is combined with a finite type. This is why we do not allow useless hypotheses in axiom (L0a) and we ask for $\phi \neq \omega$ in axiom (L1a) (notice that to derive $\vdash \mathbf{I} : \omega \to \omega$ we must use (L0a) and then (L2b)) [7]. We finish our discussion about the typing system by showing why contraction is not sound.

Example 6. Let $M = (\lambda x.x(x\mathbf{I}))\mathbf{I}$ and $\tau = \phi \to \phi$. It is easy to see that $\vdash \mathbf{I} : \tau$, $\vdash \mathbf{I} : \tau \to \tau$ and $x : (\tau \to \tau) \times (\tau \to \tau) \vdash x(x\mathbf{I}) : \tau$. If contraction were allowed, then $x : \tau \to \tau \vdash x(x\mathbf{I}) : \tau$, which would imply $\vdash M : \tau$. That is M would have been given a functional type while it just evaluates to deadlock.

Definition 4. (type semantics)

$$\begin{array}{lll} \textit{For } \lambda_r\textit{-terms :} & M \sqsubseteq_\phi N & \overset{def}{\Longleftrightarrow} \ \forall \Gamma\, \forall \phi\ (\Gamma \vdash M : \phi \ \Rightarrow\ \Gamma \vdash N : \phi) \\ \textit{For } \lambda\textit{-terms :} & E \leq_\phi F & \overset{def}{\Longleftrightarrow} \ [\![E]\!] \sqsubseteq_\phi [\![F]\!] \end{array}$$

[7] Nothing similar happens when dealing with infinite types. In this case, the rules for applications and closures involve an implicit weakening since the bags in question can contain many terms (of any type) not used in the derivation.

$$\lceil M^\infty \rceil_o \equiv M^\infty \qquad\qquad \lceil M^\infty \rceil_{i+1} \equiv (\lceil M \rceil \mid \lceil M^\infty \rceil_i)$$

$$(\beta)\begin{cases}(\lambda x.M)\lceil B\rceil \rightarrow_{\lceil r\rceil} M\langle B/x\rangle \\ (\lambda x.M)\lceil \underline{B}\rceil \rightarrow_{\lceil r\rceil} M\langle B/\underline{x}\rangle\end{cases} \qquad (fetch)\begin{cases} x\langle\lceil N\rceil/x\rangle \succ N \\ x\langle\lceil N\rceil/\underline{x}\rangle \succ N\end{cases}$$

$M \Downarrow \lceil\delta\rceil(T) \overset{def}{\iff} M \overset{\star}{\rightarrow}_{\lceil r\rceil} x\tilde{R}\langle\mathbf{1}/x\rangle\tilde{S} = T$ and T has no brackets at all.
$M \Downarrow \lceil\gamma\rceil(T) \overset{def}{\iff} M \overset{\star}{\rightarrow}_{\lceil r\rceil} \lambda x.M' = T$

decorated-flat : $M \sqsubseteq^{\flat}_{\lceil r\rceil} N \overset{def}{\iff} \forall C\ C[M] \Downarrow \lceil\gamma\rceil \Rightarrow C[N] \Downarrow \lceil\gamma\rceil$ and $C[M] \Downarrow \lceil\delta\rceil \Rightarrow C[N] \Downarrow \lceil\delta\rceil$

Fig. 3. Decorated Semantics

4 Main results

The crucial point for establishing the adequacy of the type semantics, is to prove that the type system characterizes convergence, that is :

$$M \Downarrow \gamma \iff \vdash M : \omega \rightarrow \omega \quad \text{and} \quad M \Downarrow \delta \iff \vdash M : \delta\,.$$

The $\Rightarrow$ part follows essentially by subject expansion since abstractions have type $\omega \rightarrow \omega$ and deadlocked terms have type δ.

Lemma 1. (subject expansion) *$M \rightarrow_r M'$ and $\Gamma \vdash M' : \phi \Rightarrow \Gamma \vdash M : \phi$.*

As for the $\Leftarrow$ part, in order to apply the realizability technique, we work on the following decorated version of λ_r, with brackets and underscores :

$$\begin{array}{rl} \text{decorated-terms}: & M ::= x \mid \lambda x.M \mid (MB) \mid (M\lceil B\rceil) \mid (M\lceil \underline{B}\rceil) \mid M\langle B/x\rangle \mid M\langle B/\underline{x}\rangle \\ \text{decorated bags}: & B ::= \mathbf{1} \mid P \\ & P ::= M \mid M^\infty \mid (P \mid P) \mid \lceil M\rceil \mid \lceil M^\infty\rceil_n \end{array}$$

The notation $u(M)$ stands for the undecorated term obtained by erasing all brackets and underscores from M, and $d(M)$ stands for some decorated term such that $u(d(M)) = M$. Fig. 4 completes the definition of the decorated calculus. In this framework, the first line must be added to the definition of $\equiv$ and the new (β) and $(fetch)$ rules replace those for λ_r in Fig. 2. Brackets and underscores are introduced to control the possible evaluations of terms. Notice that the new evaluation rules say that only bracketed arguments can be β-reduced, and that only bracketed resources can be fetched. Moreover, underscored arguments become underscored variables by β-reduction. Observe that one has $M \Downarrow \lceil\delta\rceil(T)$ only if the head variable of T is bound by a substitution entry without underscore; nevertheless, some underscored variables may appear in T elsewhere.

Lemma 2. *Let M be a decorated λ_r-term and N be a λ_r-term. Assume α is either δ or γ. Then $(M \Downarrow \lceil\alpha\rceil \Rightarrow u(M) \Downarrow \alpha)$ and $(N \Downarrow \alpha \Rightarrow d(N) \Downarrow \lceil\alpha\rceil)$.*

To define the realizability predicate, we use a kind of type simplification with respect to rules 3., 7. and 8. of definition 2 defined as follows :

$$\begin{array}{ll} \text{if } \psi \sim \omega \text{ then} & \psi \mapsto \epsilon \text{ (the empty sequence)} \\ \text{if } \psi \not\sim \omega \text{ then} & \psi \mapsto \phi_1, \ldots, \phi_n \text{ with } n \geq 1 \text{ iff} \\ & \psi \sim \phi_1 \times \ldots \times \phi_n \text{ with } \phi_i \neq \omega \text{ and} \\ & \forall i \neq j \;\; \phi_i \in \mathcal{T}_\omega \Rightarrow \phi_j \notin \mathcal{T}_\omega \text{ and} \\ & \forall i \neq j \;\; (\phi_i \in \mathcal{T}_\delta^p \text{ and } \phi_j \in \mathcal{T}_\delta^q) \Rightarrow p \neq q . \end{array}$$

Definition 5. (realizability predicate over decorated terms)

1. $\models M : \omega \quad \stackrel{def}{\Longleftrightarrow} \quad true$
2. $\models M : \delta \quad \stackrel{def}{\Longleftrightarrow} \quad M \Downarrow \lceil \delta \rceil$
3. $\models M : \pi \rightarrow \phi \stackrel{def}{\Longleftrightarrow} M \Downarrow \lceil \gamma \rceil \; and \; \forall B \models B : \pi \Rightarrow \begin{cases} \models M \lceil B \rceil : \phi & if\; \pi \in \Theta \\ \models M \lceil \underline{B} \rceil : \phi & if\; \pi \in \Psi \end{cases}$
4. $\models \mathbf{1} : \mathbf{1} \quad \stackrel{def}{\Longleftrightarrow} \quad true$
5. $\models P : \theta = \phi_1 \times \ldots \times \phi_n \times \mathbf{1} \stackrel{def}{\Longleftrightarrow} P =_{ac} (\lceil M_1 \rceil \mid \ldots \mid \lceil M_n \rceil) \; and \; \forall i \; \models M_i : \phi_i$
6. $\models B : \psi \mapsto \epsilon \quad \stackrel{def}{\Longleftrightarrow} \quad true$
7. $\models B : \psi \mapsto \phi_1, \ldots, \phi_n \quad \stackrel{def}{\Longleftrightarrow} \quad B \equiv (\lceil M_1 \rceil \mid \ldots \mid \lceil M_n \rceil \mid P) \; and \; \forall i \; \models M_i : \phi_i$

For open terms, assume $\Gamma = x_1 : \theta_1, \ldots, x_m : \theta_m, z_1 : \psi_1, \ldots, z_n : \psi_n$ *and* $fv(M) = \{x_1, \ldots, x_m\} \cup \{z_1, \ldots, z_n\} \cup \{y_1, \ldots, y_k\}$ *with* $m, n, k \geq 0$. *Then*

$$\Gamma \models M : \phi \stackrel{def}{\Longleftrightarrow} \forall \tilde{P}\tilde{Q} \; (\forall ij \; \models P_i : \theta_i \; and \models Q_j : \psi_j) \Rightarrow \models M \langle \tilde{P}/\tilde{x} \rangle \langle \tilde{Q}/\tilde{z} \rangle \langle \tilde{\Omega}/\tilde{y} \rangle : \phi$$

In comparison with classical realizability predicates, the interesting case is 3. Assume $\phi = \delta$. The use of brackets in the inductive part of the definition guarantees that M can consume B (that is, M evaluates to an abstraction). Moreover, if π is infinite, the fact that B is underscored ensures that deadlock (remember that $\phi = \delta$) does not come from B even if all its resources have been used during evaluation. Finally, recall that the typing system makes useful hypothesis only, that is, some free variables of M may not be captured by Γ in a derivation $\Gamma \vdash M : \phi$. In the definition of $\Gamma \models M : \phi$, this aspect is taken into account by imposing substitution entries $\langle \Omega/y \rangle$ (certainly useless for convergence) for these free variables.

Theorem 1. (soundness) $\Gamma \vdash M : \phi \; \Rightarrow \; \Gamma \models d(M) : \phi$.

Proof. We indicate the main steps of the proof, which is by induction on the derivation $\Gamma \vdash M : \phi$. For rules (L0) to (L2), the inductive hypothesis together with the following easy properties are enough :

(1) If $M \sqsubseteq^{b}_{\lceil r \rceil} N$ and $\Gamma \models M : \phi$, then $\Gamma \models N : \phi$.
(2) If $x : \pi, \Gamma \models M : \phi$ and $\pi \sim \pi', \phi \sim \phi'$ then $x : \pi', \Gamma \models M : \phi'$.

In the case of applications and closures, properties (3) and (4) are needed to combine the multiple inductive hypotheses (see example below). Assume $\models P : \pi_0 \star \ldots \star \pi_n$ and

$P \equiv (P_0 \mid \ldots \mid P_n)$ with $\models P_i : \pi_i$. Define $Q = (\lceil H_1\langle P_1/x\rangle\rceil \mid \ldots \mid \lceil H_n\langle P_n/x\rangle\rceil \mid Q')$, with $x \notin fv(Q')$:

$$(3) N\langle P_0/x\rangle Q\rho \sqsubseteq^{\flat}_{\lceil r\rceil} N(\lceil H_1\rceil \mid \ldots \lceil H_n\rceil \mid Q')\langle P/x\rangle\rho.$$
$$(4) N\langle P_0/x\rangle\langle Q/y\rangle\rho \sqsubseteq^{\flat}_{\lceil r\rceil} N\langle(\lceil H_1\rceil \mid \ldots \mid \lceil H_n\rceil \mid Q')/y\rangle\langle P/x\rangle\rho.$$

Consider the following example : $M_1 = (yy^{\infty})$, $M_2 = (yy)\mathbf{D}$, $M = M_1M_2$, $N = \lambda x.xxx$ and $\sigma : \omega \to (\delta \to \delta)$. It is easy to see that

$$\frac{y : \sigma \vdash M_1 : \delta \to \delta \quad y : \sigma \vdash M_2 : \delta}{\Gamma = y : \sigma \times \sigma \vdash M : \delta}\,(\mathrm{L3a})$$

To prove $\Gamma \models d(M) : \delta$, we show $\models d(M)\langle P/y\rangle : \delta$ for an arbitrary bag P such that $\models P : \sigma \times \sigma$: we decompose P into P_0, P_1 both verifying $\models P_i : \sigma$, we use the inductive hypotheses $\models d(M_1)\langle P_0/y\rangle : \delta \to \delta$ and $\models d(M_2)\langle P_1/y\rangle : \delta$, and then we apply (3).

In order to prove (3) and (4), one uses property (5), which allows to conclude that, under some assumptions, it is possible to group substitution entries on the same variable (cf. discussion in section 2.1, in particular example 3).

(5) If $\models P : \pi_0{\star}\pi_1$, $P \equiv (P_0 \mid P_1)$, $\models P_i : \pi_i$ then $M\langle P_0/x\rangle\tilde{R}\langle P_1/x\rangle\tilde{S} \sqsubseteq^{\flat}_{\lceil r\rceil} M\tilde{R}\langle P/x\rangle\tilde{S}$.

Let us illustrate why (5) does not hold if we replace $\sqsubseteq^{\flat}_{\lceil r\rceil}$ by $\sqsubseteq^{\flat}_{r}$. Indeed, to prove (5) we reproduce in the right side term the evaluation steps issued from the left side term. This is not possible if we consider all evaluations and not only decorated ones. Define $P = (\lceil\lambda z.\mathbf{I}\rceil \mid \lceil\lambda z.\mathbf{I}\rceil \mid N)$, $P_0 = (\lceil\lambda z.\mathbf{I}\rceil \mid N)$ and $P_1 = (\lceil\lambda z.\mathbf{I}\rceil)$. Then $\models P : \sigma \times \sigma$ and $\models P_i : \sigma$ for $i = 0, 1$. We have $d(M_1)\langle P_0/y\rangle d(M_2)\langle P_1/y\rangle \Downarrow \lceil\delta\rceil$, and also $d(M_1M_2)\langle P/y\rangle \Downarrow \lceil\delta\rceil$. But if we ignore decorations, then $M_1\langle P_0/y\rangle M_2\langle P_1/y\rangle \xrightarrow{\star}_r (y\langle y^{\infty}/x\rangle\langle\mathbf{1}/y\rangle)(M_2\langle P_1/y\rangle)) \Downarrow \delta$ by fetching N first (although it is not decorated inside brackets), but this move gives the following when performed in the term at the right : $(M_1M_2)\langle P/x\rangle \xrightarrow{\star}_r yM_2\langle y^{\infty}/x\rangle\langle\lambda z.\mathbf{I}/y\rangle\mathbf{I}\langle M_2/z\rangle\langle y^{\infty}/x\rangle\langle\mathbf{1}/y\rangle \Downarrow \gamma$.

Theorem 2. (adequacy for λ_r-terms) $M \sqsubseteq_{\phi} N \;\Rightarrow\; M \sqsubseteq^{\flat}_{r} N$.

An immediate corollary of this theorem and results stated in section 2.2 is:

Theorem 3. (adequacy for π-encoded λ-terms) $E \leq_{\phi} F \;\Rightarrow\; E \leq_{\pi} F$.

5 Conclusion

We have proposed an intersection-like type system for the lambda calculus with resources which provides an adequate abstract counterpart to the flat operational semantics that distinguishes divergence from deadlock. The question about completeness (that is, $M \sqsubseteq_{\phi} N \;\Leftarrow\; M \sqsubseteq^{\flat}_{r} N$) seems delicate since its proof would involve the definition of a convenient notion of approximant (cf. [10] for a proposal in the framework of the standard semantics) and a non-trivial separation technique. Indeed, a proof by definability is not feasible since convergence testing lacks to the calculus. The problem is maybe easier over pure lambda terms, for which we have already $E \leq_{\mathcal{L}} F \iff E \leq^{\flat}_{r} F$. Concerning the type system itself, it would be interesting to study to what extent it relates to other systems for concurrent languages dealing with deadlock, such us those presented in [3, 8], at least in the restricted universe of pure functions (indeed, the support languages of both references -an extension of π and λ for the first one, and a π-like process calculus for the second one- contain lambda calculus through appropriate encodings). We leave these topics for further work.

Acknowledgments. I would like to thank Jean-Jacques Lévy for his helpful suggestions.

References

1. S. Abramsky, L. Ong. *Full Abstraction in the lazy lambda calculus.* Information and Computation, 105(2). 1993.
2. G. Boudol. *The lambda calculus with multiplicities.* Rapport de Recherche 2025, INRIA Sophia-Antipolis. 1993.
3. G. Boudol. *Typing the use of resources in a Concurrent Calculus.* Proceedings of ASIAN'97. 1997.
4. G. Boudol, C. Laneve. *The discriminating power of multiplicities in the λ-calculus.* Information and Computation, 126 (1). 1996.
5. G. Boudol, C. Laneve. *Termination, deadlock and divergence in the λ-calculus with multiplicities.* Proc. 11th Mathematical Foundations of Programming Semantics Conference. Electronic Notes in Computer Science. 1995.
6. G. Boudol, C. Laneve. *λ-Calculus, Multiplicities and the π-Calculus.* Rapport de Recherche 2581, INRIA Sophia-Antipolis. 1995.
7. G. Boudol, C. Lavatelli. *Full Abstraction for lambda-calculus with resources and convergence testing.* CAAP'96. LNCS 1059. 1996.
8. N. Kobayashi. *A partially deadlock-free types process calculus.* Proceedings of LICS'97. 1997.
9. C. Lavatelli. *Sémantique du Lambda Calcul avec Ressources.* Thèse de Doctorat. Université Paris VII. France. 1996.
10. C. Lavatelli. *Algebraic Interpretation of the Lambda Calculus with Resources.* CONCUR'96. LNCS 1119. 1996.
11. J.-J.Lévy. *An algebraic interpretation of the $\lambda\beta K$-calculus; and an application of a labeled λ-calculus.* Theoretical Computer Science, 2(1). 1976.
12. G. Longo. *Set Theoretical Models of Lambda Calculus : Theories, expansions and isomorphisms.* Annals of Pure and Applied Logic, 24. 1983.
13. R. Milner, J. Parrow, D. Walker. *A Calculus of Mobile Processes, Parts I and II.* Information and Computation, 100(1). 1992.
14. R. Milner. *Functions as Processes.* Mathematical Structures in Computer Science, 2. 1992.
15. C.-H. Luke Ong. *Fully Abstract Models of the Lazy Lambda Calculus.* In Proceedings of the 29th Conference on Foundations of Computer Science. The Computer Science Press. 1988.
16. D. Sangiorgi. *The Lazy Lambda Calculus in a Concurrency Scenario.* Information and Computation, 120(1). 1994.

On Encoding $p\pi$ in $m\pi$

Paola Quaglia*[1] David Walker[2]

[1] BRICS**, Aarhus University, Denmark
[2] Oxford University Computing Laboratory, U.K.

Abstract. This paper is about the encoding of $p\pi$, the polyadic π-calculus, in $m\pi$, the monadic π-calculus. A type system for $m\pi$ processes is introduced which captures the interaction regime underlying the encoding of $p\pi$ processes respecting a sorting. A full-abstraction result is shown: two $p\pi$ processes are typed barbed congruent iff their $m\pi$ encodings are monadic-typed barbed congruent.

1 Introduction

The π-calculus is a model of computation in which one can naturally express systems where the inter-connection structure among the parts changes during evolution. Its basic entities are names. They may be thought of as names of communication links. Processes, terms expressing systems, use names to interact, and pass names to one another by mentioning them in interactions. Names received by a process may be used and mentioned by it in further interactions.

In $m\pi$, the monadic π-calculus [MPW92], an interaction between processes involves the transmission of a single name. In $p\pi$, the polyadic π-calculus [Mil92], a tuple of names is passed in an interaction. As shown in [MPW92] atomic communication of tuples of names is expressible in the monadic calculus. Using standard notation (a reader unfamiliar with π-calculus may care to refer to Section 2) the key clauses in an inductively-defined translation $[\![\cdot]\!]$ from polyadic processes to monadic processes are

$$[\![x(z_1 \ldots z_n).\,P]\!] = x(w).\,w(z_1).\,\ldots.\,w(z_n).\,[\![P]\!]$$

and

$$[\![\overline{x}\langle a_1 \ldots a_n\rangle.\,Q]\!] = \nu w\,\overline{x}w.\,\overline{w}a_1.\,\ldots.\,\overline{w}a_n.\,[\![Q]\!]$$

where in each case w is a fresh name, i.e. is not free in the translated process. The transmission of a tuple $\vec{a} = a_1 \ldots a_n$ is expressed by

$$\begin{array}{ll} & [\![x(z_1 \ldots z_n).\,P \mid \overline{x}\langle a_1 \ldots a_n\rangle.\,Q]\!] \\ = & [\![x(z_1 \ldots z_n).\,P]\!] \mid [\![\overline{x}\langle a_1 \ldots a_n\rangle.\,Q]\!] \\ \longrightarrow & \nu w\,(w(z_1).\,\ldots.\,w(z_n).\,[\![P]\!] \mid \overline{w}a_1.\,\ldots.\,\overline{w}a_n.\,[\![Q]\!]) \\ \longrightarrow^n & [\![P]\!]\{\vec{a}/\vec{z}\} \mid [\![Q]\!] \\ = & [\![P\{\vec{a}/\vec{z}\} \mid Q]\!] \end{array}$$

where $\vec{z} = z_1 \ldots z_n$. Although communication of an n-tuple is represented using $n+1$ interactions, it can be considered atomic since

$$\nu w\,(w(z_1).\,\ldots.\,w(z_n).\,[\![P]\!] \mid \overline{w}a_1.\,\ldots.\,\overline{w}a_n.\,[\![Q]\!]) \approx [\![P]\!]\{\vec{a}/\vec{z}\} \mid [\![Q]\!]$$

* Funded by the EU, under the Marie Curie TMR Programme.
** Basic Research in Computer Science, Centre of the Danish National Research Foundation.

where $\approx$ is (weak) barbed congruence. The first interaction creates a private link, and the subsequent semantically-inert communications transfer the names $a_1 \ldots a_n$ from sender to receiver via that link.

In the polyadic calculus there is a pressing need for some kind of typing discipline, as among the processes are terms – $w(v).\, v(yz).\, \mathbf{0} \mid \overline{w}\langle x\rangle.\, \overline{x}\langle abc\rangle.\, \mathbf{0}$ is an example – where the components disagree on the length of the tuple to be passed – in the second communication in the example. Even on well-typed processes, however, the translation $[\![\cdot]\!]$ is not fully abstract when barbed congruence is adopted as process equivalence. If P and Q are well-typed polyadic processes then the equivalence of $[\![P]\!]$ and $[\![Q]\!]$ implies that of P and Q, but the converse does not hold, the reason being, briefly, that there are monadic contexts that do not conform to the interaction regime that underlies the translation. A simple example is $P = \overline{x}y.\, \overline{x}y.\, \mathbf{0}$ and $Q = \overline{x}y.\, \mathbf{0} \mid \overline{x}y.\, \mathbf{0}$: the monadic processes $\mathcal{K}[[\![P]\!]]$ and $\mathcal{K}[[\![Q]\!]]$ are not barbed bisimilar where $\mathcal{K}$ is the monadic context $[\cdot] \mid x(z).\, x(w).\, a(v).\, \mathbf{0}$.

In this paper we introduce a typing system for monadic processes that captures the interaction regime underlying the translation, and use it to obtain a full-abstraction result. The following informal and incomplete account is filled out in the paper. Fix a set $\mathcal{S}$ of sorts and a polyadic sorting λ, a partial function from $\mathcal{S}$ to $\mathcal{S}^*$, of the kind introduced in [Mil92]. Write $\Psi \vdash_\lambda P$ if P is well-typed under λ assuming its free names have the sorts recorded in Ψ, a finite partial function from names to $\mathcal{S}$-sorts. Write $P \approx_\lambda Q$ if P and Q are mutually well-typed and $\mathcal{C}[P] \approx \mathcal{C}[Q]$ for every suitably well-typed context $\mathcal{C}$, where $\dot{\approx}$ is barbed bisimilarity. We construct a set $\mathcal{S}^m$ of monadic sorts and a monadic sorting λ^m expressed using a graph. We give a typing system for inferring judgments of the form $\Psi; \Delta; \Gamma \vdash^m_\lambda M$ where M is a monadic process and Δ, Γ are finite partial functions from names to $\mathcal{S}^m$-sorts. One property of the system is that $\Psi \vdash_\lambda P$ iff $\Psi; \emptyset; \emptyset \vdash^m_\lambda [\![P]\!]$. As a guide, in a judgment $\Psi'; \Delta; \Gamma \vdash^m_\lambda M$ appearing in an inference of a judgment $\Psi; \emptyset; \emptyset \vdash^m_\lambda [\![P]\!]$, the functions Δ and Γ will record the monadic sorts of the monadic names introduced in translating P that are free in M and that M may use immediately for receiving and for sending, respectively. The sort of name that M may receive or send via a monadic name w is determined by λ^m; in general, that sort changes from one use of w to the next. Using the typing system we define $\approx^m_\lambda$ on monadic processes by setting $M \approx^m_\lambda N$ if M and N are mutually well-typed in the monadic system and $\mathcal{K}[M] \approx \mathcal{K}[N]$ for every suitably well-typed monadic context $\mathcal{K}$. The main theorem is that if P and Q are well-typed polyadic processes then

$$P \approx_\lambda Q \quad \text{iff} \quad [\![P]\!] \approx^m_\lambda [\![Q]\!].$$

Thus the monadic typing system captures the interaction regime that underlies the polyadic-monadic translation. The main theorem is not easy to prove. The proof, however, sheds light on an important class of monadic processes, and several of the techniques used in it may be useful in other situations.

There has been much work on typing for π-calculus processes; a sample of papers is [Hon93,Kob97,KPT96,LW95,Mil92,NS97,PS93,PS97,San97,Tur96,VH93]. The work to which that presented here is most closely related is [Yos96]. We will explain the relationship at the end of the paper. In Section 2 we recall necessary background material, in Section 3 we introduce the typing system for monadic processes, and in Section 4 we outline the proof of the main theorem. The full proof is too long to present in detail here, so we concentrate on describing the main ideas.

2 Background

In this section we recall necessary definitions and notations. We refer to the papers cited in the Introduction for further explanation.

We presuppose a countably-infinite set of names, ranged over by lower-case letters. We write $\vec{x}$ for a tuple $x_1 \ldots x_n$ of names.

The *prefixes* are given by

$$\pi \ ::= \ \overline{x}\vec{y} \ \mid \ x(\vec{z})$$

where $\vec{z}$ is a tuple of distinct names.

The *processes* are given by

$$P \ ::= \ \mathbf{0} \ \mid \ \pi.P \ \mid \ P \mid P' \ \mid \ \nu z\, P \ \mid \ !P.$$

We write $\mathcal{P}$ for the set of processes; P, Q, R range over $\mathcal{P}$.

A *context* is an expression obtained from a process by replacing an occurrence of '0' by the *hole* $[\cdot]$. C ranges over contexts. We write $C[P]$ for the process obtained by replacing the occurrence of the hole in C by P.

We sometimes refer to processes and contexts collectively as *terms* and use T to range over terms. A term is *monadic* if for each subterm $\overline{x}\vec{y}.T$ or $x(\vec{y}).T$ of it, $|\vec{y}| = 1$. We write $\mathcal{M}$ for the set of monadic processes; M, N, K range over $\mathcal{M}$. Also, $\mathcal{K}, \mathcal{H}$ range over monadic contexts.

In $x(\vec{z}).P$ and in $\nu z\, P$ the displayed occurrences of $\vec{z}$ and z are *binding* with *scope* P. An occurrence of a name in a term is *free* if it is not within the scope of a binding occurrence of the name. We write $\mathrm{fn}(P)$ for the set of names that have a free occurrence in P, and $\mathrm{fn}(P, Q, \ldots)$ for $\mathrm{fn}(P) \cup \mathrm{fn}(Q) \cup \ldots$. We write also $\mathrm{bn}(P)$ for the set of names that have a binding occurrence in P.

A *substitution* is a function on names which is the identity except on a finite set. We use θ to range over substitutions, and write $x\theta$ for θ applied to x. The *support* of θ, $\mathsf{supp}(\theta)$, is $\{x \mid x\theta \neq x\}$, and the *cosupport* is $\mathsf{cosupp}(\theta) = \{x\theta \mid x \in \mathsf{supp}(\theta)\}$. If $\mathsf{supp}(\theta) = \{x_1, \ldots, x_n\}$ and $x_i\theta = y_i$ for each i, we write $\{y_1 \cdots y_n / x_1 \ldots x_n\}$ for θ. If X is a set of names we write $X\theta$ for $\{x\theta \mid x \in X\}$. We write $P\theta$ for the process obtained by replacing each free occurrence of each name x in P by $x\theta$, with change of bound names to avoid captures.

We adopt the following conventions. We identify processes that differ only by change of bound names. Further, when considering a collection of processes and substitutions we tacitly assume that the free names of the processes are different from their bound names, that no name has more than one binding occurrence, and that no bound name is in the support or cosupport of any of the substitutions.

Structural congruence is the smallest congruence, $\equiv$, on processes such that

1. $P_1 \mid (P_2 \mid P_3) \equiv (P_1 \mid P_2) \mid P_3$, $P_1 \mid P_2 \equiv P_2 \mid P_1$, $P \mid \mathbf{0} \equiv P$
2. $\nu z\, \nu w\, P \equiv \nu w\, \nu z\, P$, $\nu z\, \mathbf{0} \equiv \mathbf{0}$
3. $\nu z\, (P_1 \mid P_2) \equiv P_1 \mid \nu z\, P_2$ provided $z \notin \mathrm{fn}(P_1)$
4. $!P \equiv P \mid !P$.

An occurrence of one term in another is *unguarded* if it is not underneath a prefix.

Lemma 1. If $P \equiv Q$ then $P\theta \equiv Q\theta$ and $\mathrm{fn}(P) = \mathrm{fn}(Q)$ and for each unguarded $\pi.P'$ in P there is an unguarded $\pi.Q'$ in Q with $P' \equiv Q'$.

Intraaction is the smallest relation, $\longrightarrow$, on processes such that

1. $\overline{x}\vec{y}.P \mid x(\vec{z}).Q \longrightarrow P \mid Q\{\vec{y}/\vec{z}\}$ provided $|\vec{y}|=|\vec{z}|$
2. $P \longrightarrow P'$ implies $P \mid Q \longrightarrow P' \mid Q$
3. $P \longrightarrow P'$ implies $\nu z\, P \longrightarrow \nu z\, P'$
4. $P \equiv Q \longrightarrow Q' \equiv P'$ implies $P \longrightarrow P'$.

We write $\Longrightarrow$ for the reflexive and transitive closure of $\longrightarrow$.

Lemma 2. If $P \longrightarrow Q$ then $\mathrm{fn}(Q) \subseteq \mathrm{fn}(P)$.

In writing terms we assume composition associates to the left. Any intraaction arises from two complementary unguarded prefixes not underneath replications:

Lemma 3. If $P \longrightarrow Q$ then $P \equiv P' = \nu\vec{w}\,(\overline{x}\vec{y}.P_1 \mid x(\vec{z}).P_2 \mid P_3)$ where $|\vec{y}|=|\vec{z}|$ and $Q \equiv Q' = \nu\vec{w}\,(P_1 \mid P_2\{\vec{y}/\vec{z}\} \mid P_3)$ and $P' \mapsto Q'$, i.e. $P' \longrightarrow Q'$ may be inferred without use of the structural rule (rule 4).

If x is a name then $\overline{x}$ is a *co-name*. We use μ to range over names and co-names.

The ***observability predicates***, $\downarrow_\mu$, are defined by: $P\downarrow_x$ if P has an unguarded subterm $x(\vec{z}).Q$ and $x \in \mathrm{fn}(P)$; and $P\downarrow_{\overline{x}}$ if P has an unguarded subterm $\overline{x}\vec{y}.Q$ and $x \in \mathrm{fn}(P)$. Further, $\Downarrow_\mu$ is $\Longrightarrow\downarrow_\mu$.

Lemma 4. The relations $\downarrow_\mu$ are closed under $\equiv$, and $P\downarrow_x$ iff $P \equiv \nu\vec{w}\,(x(\vec{z}).Q \mid Q')$ where $x \notin \vec{w}$, and $P\downarrow_{\overline{x}}$ iff $P \equiv \nu\vec{w}\,(\overline{x}\vec{y}.Q \mid Q')$ where $x \notin \vec{w}$.

Barbed bisimilarity is the largest symmetric relation, $\dot{\approx}$, such that if $P \dot{\approx} Q$ then $P\downarrow_\mu$ implies $Q\Downarrow_\mu$, and $P \longrightarrow P'$ implies $Q \Longrightarrow\, \dot{\approx}\, P'$.

Monadic processes M and N are ***monadic barbed congruent***, $M \approx^m N$, if $\mathcal{K}[M] \dot{\approx} \mathcal{K}[N]$ for every monadic context $\mathcal{K}$.

A simple but important observation is

Lemma 5. If $w \notin \mathrm{fn}(M, N, \vec{y})$ and $\vec{y} = y_1 \ldots y_n$ and $\vec{z} = z_1 \ldots z_n$, then

$$\nu w\,(\overline{w}y_1.\ \ldots .\overline{w}y_n.M \mid w(z_1).\ \ldots .w(z_n).N) \approx^m M \mid N\{\vec{y}/\vec{z}\}.$$

Definition 1. The translation $[\![\cdot]\!]$ from terms to monadic terms is defined as follows:

$$[\![\overline{x}\langle y_1 \ldots y_n\rangle.T]\!] = \nu w\,\overline{x}w.\overline{w}y_1.\ \ldots .\overline{w}y_n.[\![T]\!]$$
$$[\![x(z_1 \ldots z_n).T]\!] = x(w).w(z_1).\ \ldots .w(z_n).[\![T]\!]$$

and $[\![[\cdot]]\!] = [\cdot]$, $[\![0]\!] = 0$, $[\![T \mid T']\!] = [\![T]\!] \mid [\![T']\!]$, $[\![\nu z\,T]\!] = \nu z\,[\![T]\!]$, and $[\![!T]\!] = ![\![T]\!]$.

The translation enjoys the following properties.

Lemma 6. $\mathrm{fn}([\![P]\!]) = \mathrm{fn}(P)$ and $[\![P\theta]\!] = [\![P]\!]\theta$.

Lemma 7. If $P \equiv Q$ then $[\![P]\!] \equiv [\![Q]\!]$.

Lemma 8. $P\downarrow_\mu$ iff $[\![P]\!]\downarrow_\mu$.

Lemma 9. If $P \longrightarrow Q$ then $[\![P]\!] \longrightarrow M \Longrightarrow [\![Q]\!]$ with $M \approx^m [\![Q]\!]$.

We now consider typing of polyadic processes. Fix a set $\mathcal{S}$ of *sorts*, ranged over by s, t, and a *sorting* $\lambda : \mathcal{S} \rightharpoonup \mathcal{S}^*$.

We use Ψ to range over finite partial functions from names to sorts. We write $\mathrm{n}(\Psi)$ for the domain of Ψ. If $\mathrm{n}(\Psi) = \{x_1, \ldots, x_n\}$ and $\Psi(x_i) = s_i$ for each i, we write $\{x_1 : s_1, \ldots, x_n : s_n\}$ for Ψ. We write $\Psi(x) \simeq s$ to mean 'if $x \in \mathrm{n}(\Psi)$ then $\Psi(x) = s$'. Ψ and Ψ' are *compatible* if $x \in \mathrm{n}(\Psi) \cap \mathrm{n}(\Psi')$ implies $\Psi(x) = \Psi'(x)$. If Ψ and Ψ' are compatible we write Ψ, Ψ' for $\Psi \cup \Psi'$, and we abbreviate $\Psi, \{x : s\}$ to $\Psi, x : s$. We write $\Psi\theta$ for $\{x\theta : s \mid x : s \in \Psi\}$.

Definition 2. P is a λ-*process* if $\Psi \vdash P$ may be inferred for some Ψ using the rules in Table 1, where the side conditions are

1. $z \notin \mathrm{n}(\Psi)$,
2. $\lambda(s) = (t_1 \ldots t_n)$ where $n \geq 1$, $\Psi(x) \simeq s$, $\Psi(y_i) \simeq t_i$, $x = y_i$ implies $s = t_i$, and $y_i = y_j$ implies $t_i = t_j$,
3. $\lambda(s) = (t_1 \ldots t_n)$ where $n \geq 1$, $\Psi(x) \simeq s$, and $z_i \notin \mathrm{n}(\Psi)$.

$$\frac{}{\Psi \vdash 0} \qquad \frac{\Psi \vdash P}{\Psi \vdash !P} \qquad \frac{\Psi \vdash P_1 \quad \Psi \vdash P_2}{\Psi \vdash P_1 \mid P_2} \qquad \frac{\Psi, z : s \vdash P}{\Psi \vdash \nu z\, P} \quad (1)$$

$$\frac{\Psi \vdash P}{\Psi, x : s, y_1 : t_1, \ldots, y_n : t_n \vdash \overline{x}\langle y_1 \ldots y_n \rangle . P} \quad (2)$$

$$\frac{\Psi, z_1 : t_1, \ldots, z_n : t_n \vdash P}{\Psi, x : s \vdash x(z_1 \ldots z_n). P} \quad (3)$$

Table 1. The polyadic typing rules

The type system enjoys the following properties.

Lemma 10. If $\Psi \vdash P$ then $\mathrm{fn}(P) \subseteq \mathrm{n}(\Psi)$ and $\mathrm{bn}(P) \cap \mathrm{n}(\Psi) = \emptyset$.

In view of the last assertion, when we write a judgment $\Psi \vdash P$ we tacitly assume that the bound names of P are chosen not to be in $\mathrm{n}(\Psi)$.

Lemma 11. If $\Psi \vdash P$ and $\Psi' \subseteq \Psi$ and $\mathrm{fn}(P) \subseteq \mathrm{n}(\Psi')$, then $\Psi' \vdash P$.

Lemma 12. If $\Psi \vdash P$ and $\mathrm{n}(\Psi') \cap \mathrm{n}(\Psi) = \emptyset$, then $\Psi, \Psi' \vdash P$.

Lemma 13. If $\Psi \vdash P$ and $Q \equiv P$, then $\Psi \vdash Q$.

Lemma 14. If $\Psi \vdash P$ and $P \longrightarrow P'$, then $\Psi \vdash P'$.

Lemma 15. If P is a λ-process and $P \Longrightarrow Q \equiv \nu\vec{w}\,(\overline{x}\vec{y}.\,Q_1 \mid x(\vec{z}).\,Q_2 \mid Q_3)$, then $|\vec{y}|=|\vec{z}|$.

We write $\Psi \vdash P, Q$ if $\Psi \vdash P$ and $\Psi \vdash Q$. The rules for typing contexts are like the rules for typing processes, with the addition of the rule: $\Psi \vdash [\cdot]$ for any Ψ. A context C is a $\lambda(\Psi)$-*context* if using the rule-instance $\Psi \vdash [\cdot]$ we can infer $\Psi' \vdash C$ for some Ψ'. If $\Psi \vdash P$ and C is a $\lambda(\Psi)$-context, then $C[P]$ is a λ-process.

Definition 3. P and Q are *barbed λ-congruent*, $P \approx_\lambda Q$, if there is Ψ such that $\Psi \vdash P, Q$ and $C[P] \stackrel{\cdot}{\approx} C[Q]$ for every $\lambda(\Psi)$-context C.

3 The monadic type system

We now introduce the monadic type system and establish some of its properties. Fix a set $\mathcal{S}$ of sorts and a sorting λ.

Definition 4. The set of *m-sorts*, ranged over by σ, τ, is

$$\mathcal{S}^m = \{\circ, \bullet\} \cup \{s^i \mid 1 \leq i \leq |\lambda(s)|, s \in \mathcal{S}\}.$$

For example, if $\mathcal{S} = \{s, t, r\}$ and $\lambda(s) = (t\,r)$, $\lambda(t) = (s)$ and $\lambda(r) = ()$, then $\mathcal{S}^m = \{\circ, \bullet, s^1, s^2, t^1\}$.

Definition 5. The labelled directed graph $\mathcal{G}_\lambda$ has nodes $\mathcal{S}^m$, labels $\mathcal{S}$, and arrows

$$\circ \xrightarrow{s} s^1 \xrightarrow{t_1} s^2 \xrightarrow{t_2} \ldots \xrightarrow{t_{n-1}} s^n \xrightarrow{t_n} \bullet$$

if $\lambda(s) = (t_1 \ldots t_n)$. In particular, if $\lambda(s) = ()$ it has an arrow $\circ \xrightarrow{s} \bullet$.

For the example sorting above the arrows are

$$\circ \xrightarrow{s} s^1 \xrightarrow{t} s^2 \xrightarrow{r} \bullet \text{ and } \circ \xrightarrow{t} t^1 \xrightarrow{s} \bullet \text{ and } \circ \xrightarrow{r} \bullet.$$

We use Δ, Γ to range over finite partial functions from names to $\mathcal{S}^m - \{\bullet\}$, and use analogous notations to those mentioned earlier in connection with functions Ψ.

The following notion will be important in typing compositions.

Definition 6. Suppose Δ_1 and Γ_1 are compatible, and Δ_2 and Γ_2 are compatible. Then Δ_1, Γ_1 and Δ_2, Γ_2 are *complementary* if $\mathrm{n}(\Delta_1) \cap \mathrm{n}(\Delta_2) = \emptyset$, $\mathrm{n}(\Gamma_1) \cap \mathrm{n}(\Gamma_2) = \emptyset$, and Δ_1, Δ_2 and Γ_1, Γ_2 are compatible.

Definition 7. A monadic process M is a λ^m-*process* if $\Psi; \Delta; \Gamma \vdash M$ may be inferred for some Ψ, Δ, Γ using the rules in Table 2.

In the rules for prefixes, $\{w : \bullet\}$ is read as $\emptyset$; this saves writing. Note that in the rules for input prefix, $z \neq x$ by the convention on free and bound names.

The rules are best understood via an example. Assuming the example sorting above, let $P = !\nu a\,(Q \mid R)$ where $Q = \overline{a}\langle bc\rangle.\,\mathbf{0}$ and $R = a(uv).\,\mathbf{0}$. Then

$$[\![P]\!] = !\nu a\,((\nu w\;\overline{a}w.\,\overline{w}b.\,\overline{w}c.\,\mathbf{0}) \mid a(z).\,z(u).\,z(v).\,\mathbf{0})$$

and we have, in full,

$$\frac{}{\Psi;\emptyset;\emptyset \vdash \mathbf{0}}$$

$$\frac{\Psi;\emptyset;\{y:\sigma\}\vdash M}{\Psi, x:s;\emptyset;\{y:\circ\}\vdash \overline{x}y.\,M} \quad \circ \xrightarrow{s} \sigma \text{ and } \Psi(x)\simeq s \text{ and } y \notin \mathrm{n}(\Psi,x)$$

$$\frac{\Psi;\emptyset;\{x:\tau\}\vdash M}{\Psi, y:s;\emptyset;\{x:\sigma\}\vdash \overline{x}y.\,M} \quad \circ \neq \sigma \xrightarrow{s} \tau \text{ and } \Psi(y)\simeq s \text{ and } x \notin \mathrm{n}(\Psi,y)$$

$$\frac{\Psi;\{z:\sigma\};\emptyset\vdash M}{\Psi, x:s;\emptyset;\emptyset\vdash x(z).\,M} \quad \circ \xrightarrow{s} \sigma \text{ and } \Psi(x)\simeq s \text{ and } z \notin \mathrm{n}(\Psi)$$

$$\frac{\Psi, z:s;\{x:\tau\};\emptyset\vdash M}{\Psi;\{x:\sigma\};\emptyset\vdash x(z).\,M} \quad \circ \neq \sigma \xrightarrow{s} \tau \text{ and } x,z \notin \mathrm{n}(\Psi)$$

$$\frac{\Psi;\Delta_1;\Gamma_1\vdash M_1 \qquad \Psi;\Delta_2;\Gamma_2\vdash M_2}{\Psi;\Delta_1,\Delta_2;\Gamma_1,\Gamma_2\vdash M_1 \mid M_2} \quad \Delta_1,\Gamma_1 \text{ and } \Delta_2,\Gamma_2 \text{ are complementary}$$

$$\frac{\Psi, z:s;\Delta;\Gamma\vdash M}{\Psi;\Delta;\Gamma\vdash \nu z\, M} \quad z\notin \mathrm{n}(\Psi,\Delta,\Gamma) \qquad\qquad \frac{\Psi;\Delta;\Gamma, z:\circ\vdash M}{\Psi;\Delta;\Gamma\vdash \nu z\, M} \quad z\notin \mathrm{n}(\Psi,\Delta,\Gamma)$$

$$\frac{\Psi;\Delta, z:\sigma;\Gamma, z:\sigma\vdash M}{\Psi;\Delta;\Gamma\vdash \nu z\, M} \quad z\notin \mathrm{n}(\Psi,\Delta,\Gamma) \text{ and } \sigma\neq\circ \qquad\qquad \frac{\Psi;\emptyset;\emptyset\vdash M}{\Psi;\emptyset;\emptyset\vdash !M}$$

Table 2. The monadic typing rules

$$\dfrac{\dfrac{\dfrac{\dfrac{\dfrac{\dfrac{}{\emptyset;\emptyset;\emptyset\vdash \mathbf{0}}}{\{c:r\};\emptyset;\{w:s^2\}\vdash \overline{w}c.\,\mathbf{0}}}{\{b:t,c:r\};\emptyset;\{w:s^1\}\vdash \overline{w}b.\,\overline{w}c.\,\mathbf{0}}}{\{a:s,b:t,c:r\};\emptyset;\{w:\circ\}\vdash \overline{a}w.\,\overline{w}b.\,\overline{w}c.\,\mathbf{0}}}{\{a:s,b:t,c:r\};\emptyset;\emptyset\vdash [\![Q]\!]} \qquad \dfrac{\dfrac{\dfrac{\dfrac{}{\{u:t,v:r,b:t,c:r\};\emptyset;\emptyset\vdash \mathbf{0}}}{\{u:t,b:t,c:r\};\{z:s^2\};\emptyset\vdash z(v).\,\mathbf{0}}}{\{b:t,c:r\};\{z:s^1\};\emptyset\vdash z(u).\,z(v).\,\mathbf{0}}}{\{a:s,b:t,c:r\};\emptyset;\emptyset\vdash [\![R]\!]}}{\dfrac{\dfrac{\{a:s,b:t,c:r\};\emptyset;\emptyset\vdash [\![Q]\!] \mid [\![R]\!]}{\{b:t,c:r\};\emptyset;\emptyset\vdash \nu a\,([\![Q]\!] \mid [\![R]\!])}}{\{b:t,c:r\};\emptyset;\emptyset\vdash [\![P]\!]}}$$

Note that in the judgment

$$\{a:s,b:t,c:r\};\emptyset;\{w:\circ\}\vdash \overline{a}w.\,\overline{w}b.\,\overline{w}c.\,\mathbf{0}$$

the name w is recorded in the Γ-component with m-sort $\circ$, and that the second of the restriction rules is applied to infer

$$\{a:s, b:t, c:r\}; \emptyset; \emptyset \vdash [Q].$$

In the judgment

$$\{b:t, c:r\}; \emptyset; \{w:s^1\} \vdash \overline{w}b.\overline{w}c.\mathbf{0}$$

w is ascribed m-sort s^1, indicating that the process can immediately send on w. The graph $\mathcal{G}_\lambda$ stipulates that the name which can be sent via w must be of sort t. In the judgment

$$\{c:r\}; \emptyset; \{w:s^2\} \vdash \overline{w}c.\mathbf{0}$$

w has m-sort s^2 and c sort r as given by $\mathcal{G}_\lambda$. After being used for sending for the second and last time, w disappears from the Γ-component.

In a complementary way, m-sorts are ascribed to z in the Δ-components of the judgments involving subterms of R to indicate how they use the name for receiving.

We now state some properties of the type system (several auxiliary results are omitted).

Lemma 16. Suppose $\Psi; \Delta; \Gamma \vdash M$. Then: (1) Δ and Γ are compatible. (2) $\mathsf{n}(\Psi) \cap \mathsf{n}(\Delta, \Gamma) = \emptyset$. (3) $\mathsf{fn}(M) \subseteq \mathsf{n}(\Psi, \Delta, \Gamma)$. (4) $\mathsf{n}(\Delta, \Gamma) \subseteq \mathsf{fn}(M)$. (5) $\circ \notin \mathsf{cosupp}(\Delta)$. (6) $\Gamma(x) = \circ$ implies $x \notin \mathsf{n}(\Delta)$. (7) $\mathsf{bn}(M) \cap \mathsf{n}(\Psi, \Delta, \Gamma) = \emptyset$.

In view of the last part, when we write a judgment $\Psi; \Delta; \Gamma \vdash M$ we tacitly assume that the bound names of M are chosen not to be in $\mathsf{n}(\Psi, \Delta, \Gamma)$.

We write $|T|$ for the number of operators in the term T.

Lemma 17. If $\Psi; \Delta; \Gamma \vdash M$ then there is $M' \equiv M$ such that $|M'| \leq |M|$ and:

1. If $w : \circ \in \Gamma$ then $M' = \nu\vec{w}\, \overline{x}w.N$ or $M' = \nu\vec{w}\, (\overline{x}w.N \mid K)$ where $w \notin \vec{w}$.
2. If $w : \sigma \in \Gamma$ and $\sigma \neq \circ$, then $M' = \nu\vec{w}\, \overline{w}x.N$ or $M' = \nu\vec{w}\, (\overline{w}x.N \mid K)$ where $w \notin \vec{w}$.
3. If $w : \sigma \in \Delta$ then $M' = \nu\vec{w}\, w(z).N$ or $M' = \nu\vec{w}\, (w(z).N \mid K)$ where $w \notin \vec{w}$.
4. If $w : \sigma \in \Delta \cap \Gamma$ then $M' = \nu\vec{w}\, (\overline{w}x.N \mid w(z).N')$ or $M' = \nu\vec{w}\, (\overline{w}x.N \mid w(z).N' \mid K)$ where $w \notin \vec{w}$.

The reason this lemma takes the form it does is that to carry out later arguments by induction on type inference, a handle on the size of terms is needed.

Typing is, as would be expected, invariant under structural congruence:

Lemma 18. If $\Psi; \Delta; \Gamma \vdash M$ and $N \equiv M$, then $\Psi; \Delta; \Gamma \vdash N$.

The final result in this section shows how typing changes under intraaction. To prove the lemma it is necessary to examine the effects of substitution on typing.

Lemma 19. If $\Psi; \Delta; \Gamma \vdash M$ and $M \longrightarrow M'$, then $\Psi; \Delta'; \Gamma' \vdash M'$ where

1. $\Delta' = \Delta$ and $\Gamma' = \Gamma$, or
2. $\Delta' = \Delta, y : \sigma$ and $\Gamma' = \Gamma - \{y : \circ\} \cup \{y : \sigma\}$ where $y : \circ \in \Gamma$ and $\circ \overset{s}{\rightarrow} \sigma$, or
3. $\Delta' = \Delta - \{y : \sigma\} \cup \{y : \tau\}$ and $\Gamma' = \Gamma - \{y : \sigma\} \cup \{y : \tau\}$ where $y : \sigma \in \Delta \cap \Gamma$ and $\circ \neq \sigma \overset{s}{\rightarrow} \tau$.

The rules for typing monadic contexts are like the rules in Tab. 2, with the addition of the rule: $\Psi; \Delta; \Gamma \vdash [\cdot]$ for any Ψ, Δ, Γ. A monadic context $\mathcal{K}$ is a $\lambda^m(\Psi, \Delta, \Delta')$*-context* if assuming $\Psi; \Delta; \Delta \vdash [\cdot]$ we can infer $\Psi'; \Delta'; \Delta' \vdash \mathcal{K}$ for some Ψ'.

Definition 8. M and N are *barbed* λ^m*-congruent*, $M \approx^m_\lambda N$, if there are Ψ, Δ such that $\Psi; \Delta; \Delta \vdash M, N$ and $\mathcal{K}[M] \dot{\approx} \mathcal{K}[N]$ for every $\lambda^m(\Psi, \Delta, \emptyset)$-context $\mathcal{K}$.

Recalling the counterexample $P = \overline{x}y.\overline{x}y.\mathbf{0}$ and $Q = \overline{x}y.\mathbf{0} \mid \overline{x}y.\mathbf{0}$ to full abstraction of the translation, and the monadic context $\mathcal{K} = [\cdot] \mid x(z).x(w).a(v).\mathbf{0}$ such that $\mathcal{K}[[P]] \not\dot{\approx} \mathcal{K}[[Q]]$, note that $\mathcal{K}$ is not a $\lambda^m(\Psi, \Delta, \emptyset)$-context for any Ψ and Δ.

4 Main results

In this section we outline the main results. First we relate typing of P under λ and typing of $[P]$ under λ^m.

Lemma 20. If $\Psi \vdash P$ then $\Psi; \emptyset; \emptyset \vdash [P]$.

Lemma 21. If $\Psi; \Delta; \Gamma \vdash [P]$ then $\Delta = \Gamma = \emptyset$ and $\Psi \vdash P$.

This lemma does not hold if we remove the very minor restriction '$n \geq 1$' from the side conditions of the typing rules for polyadic prefixes. For example if $\lambda(s) = (s)$, then $\emptyset; \emptyset; x : s^1 \vdash [\overline{x}\langle\rangle.\mathbf{0}], [x().\mathbf{0}]$.

We now outline the proof that the translation is sound.

Theorem 1. If $[P] \approx^m_\lambda [Q]$ then $P \approx_\lambda Q$.

Proof. Consider first $\mathcal{B} = \{(R, [R]) \mid R \text{ a } \lambda\text{-process}\}$. We noted in Section 2 that

1. $R \downarrow_\mu$ iff $[R] \downarrow_\mu$, and
2. if $R \longrightarrow R'$ then $[R] \longrightarrow N \Longrightarrow [R']$ with $N \approx^m [R']$.

We show that

$$\text{if } [R] \longrightarrow N \text{ then } N \approx^m [R'] \text{ where } R \longrightarrow R'. \tag{1}$$

Assertion (1) does not hold without the assumption that R is a λ-process: consider for instance $R = \overline{a}\langle bc\rangle.\mathbf{0} \mid a(z).\mathbf{0}$. Assertion (1) is harder to prove than it may at first sight appear. The reason is that the structural rule may be applied arbitrarily in inferring $[R] \longrightarrow N$, and it takes some work to see that a suitable R' can always be found. The monadic type system plays a key role in carrying out that work.

Note that $P \equiv Q$ iff $P \equiv_1^* Q$, where $P' \equiv_1 Q'$ if there are a context C and processes P'', Q'' comprising an instance of one of the axioms of structural congruence such that $P' = C[P'']$ and $Q' = C[Q'']$.

We write $\langle \Psi; \Delta; \Gamma \vdash M \rangle$ for an inference of the judgment $\Psi; \Delta; \Gamma \vdash M$. We say w is *monadic in* $\langle \Psi; \Delta; \Gamma \vdash M \rangle$ if for some judgment $\Psi'; \Delta'; \Gamma' \vdash M'$ in $\langle \Psi; \Delta; \Gamma \vdash M \rangle$ we have $w \in \mathrm{n}(\Delta', \Gamma')$. We write $M \rightsquigarrow M'$ if there are $\langle \Psi; \Delta; \Gamma \vdash M \rangle$ and w monadic in it such that M' is obtained from M by replacing a subterm N by N' where

1. $N = \nu w\, \nu z\, K$ and $N' = \nu z\, \nu w\, K$ where z is not monadic in $\langle \Psi; \Delta; \Gamma \vdash M \rangle$, or
2. $N = \nu w\, (K \mid K')$ and $N' = K \mid \nu w\, K'$ where $w \notin \mathrm{fn}(K)$, or
3. $N = \nu w\, (K \mid K')$ and $N' = \nu w\, K \mid K'$ where $w \notin \mathrm{fn}(K')$.

Note that $M \rightsquigarrow M'$ implies $M' \equiv_1 M$. In a structural manipulation of $[\![R]\!]$, a $\rightsquigarrow$-transformation involving νw changes the term structure in such a way as to move the restriction towards the prefix of the form $\overline{x}w$ introduced in translating R. The $\rightsquigarrow$-transformations and their inverses have no direct counterparts in a manipulation of R. We have, however,

Lemma 22. If $[\![R]\!] \equiv M$ then $M \rightsquigarrow^* [\![R'']\!]$ where $R'' \equiv R$.

Now returning to the proof of (1), suppose $[\![R]\!] \equiv M = \nu\vec{w}\,(\overline{x}w.\,M_1 \mid x(z).\,M_2 \mid M_3)$ and $M \mapsto M' = \nu\vec{w}\,(M_1 \mid M_2\{{}^{w}\!/\!{}_{z}\} \mid M_3) \equiv N$. Then $R \equiv R''$ where $M \rightsquigarrow^* [\![R'']\!]$. By the form of M, $R'' = \nu\vec{v}\,(\overline{x}\vec{y}.\,P_1 \mid x(\vec{z}).\,P_2 \mid P_3)$ and $R'' \mapsto R' = \nu\vec{v}\,(P_1 \mid P_2\{\vec{y}/\vec{z}\} \mid P_3)$ where $\nu w\,\overline{x}w.\,M_1 \rightsquigarrow^* [\![\overline{x}\vec{y}.\,P_1]\!]$, $x(z).\,M_2 \rightsquigarrow^* [\![x(\vec{z}).\,P_2]\!]$, and $\nu\vec{u}\,M_3 \rightsquigarrow^* [\![P_3]\!]$ where $\vec{w}$ is a permutation of $\vec{v}w\vec{u}$. Further $N \Longrightarrow [\![R']\!]$ and $[\![R']\!] \approx^m N$ as required. By 1, 2 and (1) we have

Corollary 1. If R is a λ-process then $[\![R]\!] \approx R$.

To complete the proof of the theorem, suppose $[\![P]\!] \approx^m_\lambda [\![Q]\!]$ and Ψ is such that $\Psi;\emptyset;\emptyset \vdash [\![P]\!],[\![Q]\!]$ and $\mathcal{K}[[\![P]\!]] \approx \mathcal{K}[[\![Q]\!]]$ for every $\lambda^m(\Psi,\emptyset,\emptyset)$-context $\mathcal{K}$. Then $\Psi \vdash P,Q$ and if $\mathcal{C}$ is a $\lambda(\Psi)$-context then $[\![\mathcal{C}]\!]$ is a $\lambda^m(\Psi,\emptyset,\emptyset)$-context and so

$$\mathcal{C}[P] \approx [\![\mathcal{C}[P]]\!] = [\![\mathcal{C}]\!][[\![P]\!]] \approx [\![\mathcal{C}]\!][[\![Q]\!]] = [\![\mathcal{C}[Q]]\!] \approx \mathcal{C}[Q].$$

Hence $P \approx_\lambda Q$. □

We now outline the proof that the translation is complete.

Theorem 2. If $P \approx_\lambda Q$ then $[\![P]\!] \approx^m_\lambda [\![Q]\!]$.

Proof. Suppose $P \approx_\lambda Q$ and Ψ_0 is such that $\Psi_0 \vdash P,Q$ and $\mathcal{C}[P] \stackrel{.}{\approx} \mathcal{C}[Q]$ for every $\lambda(\Psi_0)$-context $\mathcal{C}$. Then $\Psi_0;\emptyset;\emptyset \vdash [\![P]\!],[\![Q]\!]$. Suppose $\mathcal{K}$ is a $\lambda^m(\Psi_0,\emptyset,\emptyset)$-context. The crucial fact is:

There is a $\lambda(\Psi_0)$-context $\mathcal{C}$ such that $\mathcal{K}[[\![P]\!]] \stackrel{.}{\approx} [\![\mathcal{C}]\!][[\![P]\!]]$ and $\mathcal{K}[[\![Q]\!]] \stackrel{.}{\approx} [\![\mathcal{C}]\!][[\![Q]\!]]$. (2)

From this, using Corollary 1 we have

$$\mathcal{K}[[\![P]\!]] \stackrel{.}{\approx} [\![\mathcal{C}]\!][[\![P]\!]] = [\![\mathcal{C}[P]]\!] \stackrel{.}{\approx} \mathcal{C}[P] \stackrel{.}{\approx} \mathcal{C}[Q] \stackrel{.}{\approx} [\![\mathcal{C}[Q]]\!] = [\![\mathcal{C}]\!][[\![Q]\!]] \stackrel{.}{\approx} \mathcal{K}[[\![Q]\!]].$$

To establish (2) we show

Lemma 23. Suppose $\Psi;\Delta;\Delta,\vec{w} : \circ \vdash \mathcal{K}$ assuming $\Psi_0;\Delta_0;\Delta_0,\vec{w}_0 : \circ \vdash [\cdot]$. Then there exists $\mathcal{C}$ such that

1. $\Psi \vdash \mathcal{C}$ assuming $\Psi_0 \vdash [\cdot]$, and
2. if $\Psi_0;\Delta_0;\Delta_0,\vec{w}_0 : \circ \vdash M$ then $\nu\vec{v}\vec{w}\,\mathcal{K}[M] \approx^m_\lambda [\![\mathcal{C}]\!][\nu\vec{v}_0\vec{w}_0\,M]$ where $\vec{v} = \mathrm{n}(\Delta)$ and $\vec{v}_0 = \mathrm{n}(\Delta_0)$.

The proof is by induction on the derivation of $\Psi;\Delta;\Delta,\vec{w} : \circ \vdash \mathcal{K}$. Note that the assertion concerns $\approx^m_\lambda$ and not $\stackrel{.}{\approx}$; this is important in the induction.

The most difficult cases are the prefixes. We outline the argument for the input prefix; the argument for output prefix is dual to it.

Suppose $\mathcal{K} = x(z).\,\mathcal{K}_0$. Then by the typing rules $\Psi = \Psi' \cup \{x : s\}$ and $\Delta,\vec{w} = \emptyset$ and $\Psi';\{z : s^1\};\emptyset \vdash \mathcal{K}_0$ (where $\circ \stackrel{s}{\rightarrow} s^1$). For clarity we assume that $\lambda(s) = (t_1t_2)$ – this retains the essence of the problem. By Lemma 17 we have (in the most complicated of the four possible combinations),

$$\mathcal{K} \equiv \mathcal{K}' = x(z).\, \nu\vec{u}_1\, (z(z_1).\, \nu\vec{u}_2\, (z(z_2).\, \mathcal{K}_3 \mid \mathcal{K}_2) \mid \mathcal{K}_1)$$

with $|\,\mathcal{K}'\,| \leq |\,\mathcal{K}\,|$. (We abuse notation here: each $\mathcal{K}_i$ is a term, i.e. a process or a context.) From the typing rules, setting $\vec{u}_3 = \emptyset$, in $\langle \Psi; \emptyset; \emptyset \vdash \mathcal{K}' \rangle$ the judgment for $\mathcal{K}_i$ is of the form

$$\Psi_i, \vec{x}_1, \vec{x}_2; \Delta_i; \Delta_i, \vec{v}_i : \circ \vdash \mathcal{K}_i \text{ where } \vec{x}_i\vec{r}_i\vec{v}_i = \vec{u}_i \text{ where } \mathrm{n}(\Delta_i) = \vec{r}_i.$$

By the inductive hypothesis there are C_1, C_2, C_3 such that $\Psi_i, \vec{x}_1, \vec{x}_2 \vdash C_i$ assuming $\Psi_0 \vdash [\cdot]$, and if $\Psi_0; \Delta_0; \Delta_0, \vec{w}_0 : \circ \vdash M$ then $\nu\vec{r}_i\vec{v}_i\ \mathcal{K}_i[M] \approx^m_\lambda [\![C_i]\!][\nu\vec{r}_0\vec{w}_0\ M]$ where $\vec{r}_0 = \mathrm{n}(\Delta_0)$. Then set

$$C = x(z_1 z_2).\, \nu\vec{x}_1\vec{x}_2\, (C_3 \mid C_2 \mid C_1).$$

We then show that for every M such that $\Psi_0; \Delta_0; \Delta_0, \vec{w}_0 : \circ \vdash M$,

$$\mathcal{K}'[M] \approx^m_\lambda [\![C]\!][\nu\vec{r}_0\vec{w}_0\ M]. \tag{3}$$

As an aside, note here the fundamental role of typing in the inductive argument. It is not in general the case that $\mathcal{K}'[M] \approx^m [\![C]\!][\nu\vec{r}_0\vec{w}_0\ M]$. For example if $\nu\vec{u}_1\ \mathcal{K}_1 \downarrow_\mu$ for some μ then $\mathcal{H}'[\mathcal{K}'[M]] \not\approx \mathcal{H}'[[\![C]\!][\nu\vec{r}_0\vec{w}_0\ M]]$ where $\mathcal{H}'$ is $[\cdot] \mid \nu w\ \overline{x}w.\mathbf{0}$.

Returning to the main proof, if $\Psi_0; \Delta_0; \Delta_0, \vec{w}_0 : \circ \vdash M$ then $\mathcal{K}''[M] \approx^m_\lambda [\![C]\!][\nu\vec{r}_0\vec{w}_0\ M]$ where

$$\mathcal{K}'' = x(z).\, z(z_1).\, z(z_2).\, \nu\vec{u}_1\vec{u}_2\, (\mathcal{K}_3 \mid \mathcal{K}_2 \mid \mathcal{K}_1).$$

So assertion (3) follows from

$$\mathcal{K}'[M] \approx^m_\lambda \mathcal{K}''[M].$$

This in turn follows from

Lemma 24. Suppose $\Psi; \emptyset; \emptyset \vdash K', K''$ where

$$K' = x(z).\, \nu\vec{u}_1\, (z(z_1).\, \nu\vec{u}_2\, (z(z_2).\, K_3 \mid K_2) \mid K_1)$$
$$K'' = x(z).\, z(z_1).\, z(z_2).\, \nu\vec{u}_1\vec{u}_2\, (K_3 \mid K_2 \mid K_1).$$

Then $K' \approx^m_\lambda K''$.

Let $\Theta = \{\{\vec{y}/\vec{x}\} \mid$ for each i, $x_i : s \in \Psi$ and $y_i : t \in \Psi$ implies $s = t\}$. The strategy for the proof of this lemma is to show that

$$\mathcal{R} = \{(\mathcal{H}[K'\theta], \mathcal{H}[K''\theta]) \mid \theta \in \Theta \text{ and } \mathcal{H} \text{ is a } \lambda^m(\Psi\theta, \emptyset, \emptyset)\text{-context}\} \cup \dot{\approx}$$

is a barbed bisimulation up to $\approx^m$. Then for any $\lambda^m(\Psi, \emptyset, \emptyset)$-context $\mathcal{H}$ we have $\mathcal{H}[K'] \dot{\approx} \mathcal{H}[K'']$, and hence $K' \approx^m_\lambda K''$. □

A final remark: in the translation the clause for output prefix could alternatively be

$$[\![\overline{x}\langle a_1 \ldots a_n\rangle.\, Q]\!] = \nu w\ \overline{x}w.\, (\overline{w}a_1.\, \ldots.\, \overline{w}a_n.\mathbf{0} \mid [\![Q]\!]).$$

The same results hold in this case, the type system and Lemma 5 showing clearly why the two translations are in essence the same.

As mentioned in the Introduction, the work to which that presented here is most closely related is [Yos96]. There a notion of graph type for monadic processes is introduced and studied. Nodes of a graph type represent atomic actions, and edges an activation ordering between them. Among other results, a full abstraction theorem for the translation of polyadic processes to monadic processes is shown. The present paper is not, therefore, the first to prove such a result. We believe, however, that the approach introduced in this paper is considerably simpler and clearer. The type system is of a kind which is well understood, and its rules are very natural, given the idea of the graph $\mathcal{G}_\lambda$ arising from a polyadic sorting λ. We found the ability to argue by induction on type inference invaluable to the proof of full abstraction. We believe the techniques introduced here may be useful in other circumstances.

References

[Hon93] K. Honda. Types for Dyadic Interaction. In E. Best, editor, *Proc. 4th Conf. CONCUR*, volume 715 of *LNCS*, pages 509–523. Springer-Verlag, 1993.

[Kob97] N. Kobayashi. A partially deadlock-free typed process calculus. In *Proc. 12th IEEE Symp. LICS*, pages 128–139, 1997.

[KPT96] N. Kobayashi, B.C. Pierce, and D.N. Turner. Linearity and the Pi-Calculus. In *Proc. 23rd ACM Symp. POPL*, pages 358–371, 1996.

[LW95] X. Liu and D. Walker. A Polymorphic Type System for the Polyadic π-calculus. In I. Lee and S.A. Smolka, editors, *Proc. 6th Conf. CONCUR*, volume 962 of *LNCS*, pages 103–116. Springer-Verlag, 1995.

[Mil92] R. Milner. The Polyadic π-Calculus: a Tutorial. In F.L. Bauer, W. Brauer, and H. Schwichtenberg, editors, *Logic and Algebra of Specification*, pages 203–246. Springer-Verlag, 1992.

[MPW92] R. Milner, J. Parrow, and D. Walker. A Calculus of Mobile Processes, Part I and II. *Information and Computation*, 100(1):1–77, 1992.

[NS97] U. Nestmann and M. Steffen. Typing Confluence. In S. Gnesi and D. Latella, editors, *Proc. 2nd Int. ERCIM Workshop on Formal Methods in Industrial Critical Systems*, pages 77–101, 1997.

[PS93] B.C. Pierce and D. Sangiorgi. Typing and Subtyping for Mobile Processes. In *Proc. 8th IEEE Symp. LICS*, pages 376–385, 1993.

[PS97] B.C. Pierce and D. Sangiorgi. Behavioral Equivalence in the Polymorphic Pi-Calculus. In *Proc. 24th ACM Symp. POPL*, pages 242–255, 1997.

[San97] D. Sangiorgi. The name discipline of uniform receptiveness. In P. Degano, R. Gorrieri, and A. Marchetti-Spaccamela, editors, *Proc. 24th ICALP*, volume 1256 of *LNCS*, pages 303–313. Springer, 1997.

[Tur96] D.N. Turner. *The Polymorphic Pi-Calculus: Theory and Implementation*. PhD thesis, Comp. Sc. Dep., Edinburgh University, 1996. Report ECS-LFCS-96-345.

[VH93] V.T. Vasconcelos and K. Honda. Principal typing schemes in a polyadic π-calculus. In E. Best, editor, *Proc. 4th Conf. CONCUR*, volume 715 of *LNCS*. Springer-Verlag, 1993.

[Yos96] N. Yoshida. Graph Types for Monadic Mobile Processes. In *Proc. 16th Conf. FST&TCS*, volume 1180 of *LNCS*, pages 371–386. Springer, 1996.

Improved Methods for Approximating Node Weighted Steiner Trees and Connected Dominating Sets (Extended Abstract)

Sudipto Guha[1] and Samir Khuller[2]

[1] Dept. of Computer Science, Stanford University, Stanford, CA 94305.
sudipto@cs.stanford.edu

[2] Computer Science Department, University of Maryland, College Park, MD 20742.
samir@cs.umd.edu

Abstract. In this paper we study the Steiner tree problem in graphs for the case when vertices as well as edges have weights associated with them. A greedy approximation algorithm based on "spider decompositions" was developed by Klein and Ravi for this problem. This algorithm provides a worst case approximation ratio of $2\ln k$, where k is the number of terminals. However, the best known lower bound on the approximation ratio is $(1-o(1))\ln k$, assuming that $NP \not\subseteq DTIME[n^{O(\log\log n)}]$, by a reduction from set cover.

We show that for the unweighted case we can obtain an approximation factor of $\ln k$. For the weighted case we develop a new decomposition theorem, and generalize the notion of "spiders" to "branch-spiders", that are used to design a new algorithm with a worst case approximation factor of $1.5\ln k$. We then generalize the method to yield an approximation factor of $(1.35+\epsilon)\ln k$, for any constant $\epsilon > 0$. These algorithms, although polynomial, are not very practical due to their high running time; since we need to repeatedly find many minimum weight matchings in each iteration. We also develop a simple greedy algorithm that is practical and has a worst case approximation factor of $1.6103\ln k$. The techniques developed for this algorithm imply a method of approximating node weighted network design problems defined by 0-1 proper functions as well.

These new ideas also lead to improved approximation guarantees for the problem of finding a minimum node weighted connected dominating set. The previous best approximation guarantee for this problem was $3\ln n$ due to Guha and Khuller. By a direct application of the methods developed in this paper we are able to develop an algorithm with an approximation factor of $(1.35+\epsilon)\ln n$ for any fixed $\epsilon > 0$.

1 Introduction

The Steiner tree problem is a classical problem in networks, and is of wide interest. The problem is known to be NP-hard for graphs, as well as in most metrics

[5]. Much effort has been devoted to the study of polynomial time approximation algorithms for this problem [1,9–11,14]. For other results on the Steiner tree problem see the book by Hwang, Richards and Winter [8].

The Steiner tree problem is defined as follows: given a graph $G = (V, E)$ and a subset of vertices $S \subseteq V$ we wish to compute a minimum weight tree that includes the vertices in S. The tree may include other vertices not in S as well. The vertices in S are also called *terminals* (sometimes these are referred to as "required" vertices). For results on edge weighted problems see [1, 2, 9, 11, 14, 15]. In this paper, we concentrate on the study of the node weighted version, where the nodes, rather than the edges have weights. This is a more general problem, since one can reduce the edge weighted problem to the node weighted problem by subdividing edges and giving the new vertices the weight corresponding to the subdivided edge.

The first non-trivial polynomial time approximation factor for this problem was achieved by Klein and Ravi [10]. Their algorithm achieves a worst case approximation factor of $2 \ln k$ where k is the number of terminals. They showed that the problem is at least as hard to approximate as the set-cover problem, for which a polynomial time approximation algorithm with a factor of $(1 - \epsilon) \ln k$, for any constant $\epsilon > 0$ would imply that $NP \subseteq DTIME[n^{O(\log \log n)}]$ [4].

The Klein-Ravi algorithm [10] is based on an earlier heuristic by Rayward-Smith [13] and may be viewed as a generalization of the set-cover greedy approach [3]. In this scheme, at each step a "spider" is chosen so as to minimize the **ratio** of the weight of spider to the number of terminals that it connects. They prove that the process of greedily picking spiders yields a good solution.

Our first algorithm is based on a new decomposition theorem, using which we can establish a bound of $1.5 \ln k$ for the approximation factor. We show that we can decompose the solution into more complex objects called branch-spiders. We also show how to compute the min-ratio branch spider in polynomial time. This algorithm is described in Section 3. We then show how to use generalizations of branch-spiders to develop a new algorithm with an approximation factor of $(1.35 + \epsilon) \ln k$, for any $\epsilon > 0$. Unfortunately, finding branch-spiders of minimum ratio is computationally intensive as it uses weighted matchings repeatedly, so this algorithm is not practical for large graphs.

Our second approach yields a much faster algorithm and also addresses generalizations to the case when the optimal solution is a collection of connected components. It has a worst case approximation factor of $1.6103 \ln k$. It is not difficult to observe that this algorithm can be extended easily to problems defined by 0-1 proper functions (see [6, 10]). This algorithm is described in Section 4.

Due to lack of space we omit a description of the $\ln k$ approximation algorithm for the case when all node weights are 1.

In Section 6 we show how to use the methods developed in this paper to solve the Connected dominating set (CDS) problem. This improves the $3 \ln n$ factor shown for the weighted CDS problem in [7].

2 Preliminaries

We assume that the input graph is connected and that only the vertices have weights. In the case where both edges and vertices have weights, we can subdivide the edges to introduce a vertex of degree two which has the same weight as the edge. In this way we can reduce the version where both the nodes and edges have weights, to the version where only the nodes have weights. Without loss of generality the subset of required vertices, also called terminals have zero weight since they are included in every solution. We assume that these have degree one, since for each terminal s, we can create a new vertex s' and add the edge (s, s') and consider s' as the terminal.

Definition 1. *A spider is defined as a tree having at most one node of degree more than two. Such a node (if one exists) is called the center of the spider.*

Definition 2. *An m spider ($m > 2$) is defined as a spider with a center of degree m.*
A 2 spider is one with no node of degree more than two.

An m spider has m leaves, and each path to a leaf from its center is called a *leg*. A 2 spider is a path. (By our assumption on the terminals, all terminals are leaves.)

Definition 3. *An m+ spider ($m > 2$) is defined as a spider with a center of degree at least m.*

The *weight* of a subgraph is the sum of the weights of the nodes in the subgraph. The *ratio* of a subgraph is the ratio of its cost to the number of terminals included in it. The terminals are always degree one by construction.

Contracting a subgraph is the operation of contracting all nodes of the subgraph to form one vertex. If we contract a subgraph S in graph G, making the contracted vertex into a terminal, then it is easy to argue that the weight of the optimal solution is at most the weight of the subgraph together with the weight of the optimal solution for the new graph. In the algorithms discussed below, we will contract small trees. The shrunken node has zero weight, and we make it a degree one node once again.

Klein and Ravi [10] give an algorithm that repeatedly contracts the min-ratio spider. The reason one obtains a $2 \ln k$ factor as opposed to a $\ln k$ factor (as in set cover), is that one may repeatedly contract 2 spiders, and each time a spider is contracted, we create a new terminal to denote the contracted spider, so the number of terminals decreases by one and not two (see [10] for the proof). If we could restrict our attention to larger spiders, then we get a better algorithm. However, we cannot show that a decomposition into large spiders exists – to achieve this, we modify spiders into more general structures.

The next two lemmas are due to Klein and Ravi [10], and used in their proof for the approximation factor of $2 \ln k$.

Lemma 1. *Any solution to the node weighted Steiner tree problem can be decomposed into spiders having terminals as leaves.*

Lemma 2. *If there are n_i terminals that need to be connected then the minimum ratio spider has min ratio $\gamma_m \leq \frac{w(OPT)}{n_i}$.*

Note that minimum ratio spiders can be computed in polynomial time as was shown in [10].

3 Algorithm for Node Weighted Steiner Trees

Before describing the new decomposition theorem, we introduce the notion of branch-spiders.

Definition 4. *A branch is defined as a tree with at most three leaves. We refer to one of the leaves as the root.*

Definition 5. *A branch-spider is constructed by identifying the roots of a collection of disjoint branches into a single vertex, called the center.*

Definition 6. *A* 3+ branch-spider *is one with at least three terminals.*

We now show a decomposition of a solution to the node weighted Steiner tree problem into 3+ branch-spiders. This proof is similar to the proof by Wolsey given in [10].

Lemma 3. *Any solution to the node weighted Steiner tree problem, with at least three terminals, can be decomposed into* 3+ *branch-spiders having terminals as leaves.*

Proof. Consider a solution to the node weighted Steiner tree problem. This is a tree that includes all the terminals as leaf nodes. The depth of a node is the distance of a node from an arbitrarily chosen root. The theorem can be proven by induction on the number of terminals. Choose a node v of maximum depth, such that the subtree rooted at v contains at least three terminals. We immediately obtain a branch-spider (with at least three terminals) rooted at v. Note that no proper descendant of v has three terminals in its subtree, hence this satisfies the requirement of being a branch-spider. Delete the subtree rooted at v. If the tree still contains at least three terminals, by the induction hypothesis we can find a decomposition of the remaining tree into 3+ branch-spiders, and we are done. If there are at most two terminals remaining, we can attach them to v while maintaining a branch-spider rooted at v. This concludes the proof.

We now address the issue of computing minimum ratio 3+ branch-spiders. (The ratio of a branch-spider is defined in the same way as for spiders, the total weight divided by the number of terminals that it connects.)

We show how to find a minimum weight branch-spider centered at vertex v that has exactly ℓ terminals in it. Actually what we find is a connected subgraph that has the same ratio as this branch-spider. Using this procedure it is easy to compute the minimum ratio branch-spider with at least three terminals by simply enumerating over all possible centers and sizes of branch-spiders ($\ell \geq 3$).

Algorithm for finding a minimum weight 3+ branch-spider (G^*, v, ℓ)

Step 1. Build a weighted graph $G'_v = (V'_v, E'_v)$ with $V'_v = \{$all terminals in $G^*\}$ and $w(x, y)$ = weight of a min weight Steiner tree in G^* connecting terminals $\{x, y, v\}$ (in this calculation we do not include the weight of the center v).

Step 2.

Case (a) If ℓ is odd, for each terminal x, we find a minimum weight matching M_x of cardinality $\lfloor \frac{\ell}{2} \rfloor$ in $G'_v - \{x\}$. The total weight of the spider is $w(v) + w(M_x) + w(x)$ where $w(x)$ is the distance[1] from v to x in the graph G^*. We take the minimum weight spider over all choices of x.

Case (b) If ℓ is even, we find a a minimum weight matching M of cardinality $\frac{\ell}{2}$ in G'_v. The total weight of the spider is $w(v) + w(M)$.

(The problem of finding a min weight matching of cardinality $\lfloor \frac{\ell}{2} \rfloor$ in $H = (V_H, E_H)$ may be reduced to minimum weight perfect matching by creating $|V_H| - 2\lfloor \frac{\ell}{2} \rfloor$ dummy vertices, and by adding zero weight edges from each vertex in H to each dummy vertex. A minimum weight perfect matching in the new graph permits all vertices, except for $2\lfloor \frac{\ell}{2} \rfloor$ vertices, to be matched at zero cost to the dummy vertices. The remaining vertices are forced to match each other at minimum cost, yielding a matching M of cardinality $\lfloor \frac{\ell}{2} \rfloor$.)

Lemma 4. *The algorithm described above computes a connected subgraph with ratio at most the ratio of the 3+ branch-spider of minimum ratio.*

Proof. Let the minimum ratio 3+ branch-spider have its center at vertex v' and have ℓ terminals. A pair of branches, each having a single terminal, can be viewed as a single branch with two terminals. In this way we can pair up branches with only one terminal, leaving at most one unpaired branch. This naturally induces a matching in G'_v of cardinality $\lfloor \frac{\ell}{2} \rfloor$. This shows that there is a matching of size (cardinality) $\lfloor \frac{\ell}{2} \rfloor$, the center vertex and possibly a single branch of total weight at most the cost of the branch-spider. When the algorithm tries v' as its center, with the correct choice of ℓ and tries x as the unpaired branch, we should compute a connected subgraph, which is really a union of Steiner trees, having v as a leaf node, of weight at most the weight of the 3+ branch-spider.

The algorithm works iteratively. In each iteration, let n_i denote the number of terminals remaining at the start of iteration i. Initially, $n_1 = k$ the number of terminals in S.

Node Steiner Tree Algorithm:I

Repeat the following steps until we have at most two terminals left, and then connect the terminals optimally.

Step 1. Find a 3+ branch-spider in G with minimum ratio.

[1] To compute the distance from v to x we do not include the weight of the vertex v, since this has already been included in the weight of the spider. The distance is simply the weight of the minimum weight path from v to x.

Step 2. Contract the chosen branch-spider, and update G.

The following lemma follows from Lemma 3.

Lemma 5. *In iteration i having n_i terminals to connect, the minimum ratio branch-spider has ratio at most $\frac{w(OPT)}{n_i}$.*

Theorem 1. *The algorithm described above yields a node weighted Steiner tree of cost at most $1.5 \ln k$ times the optimal, where k is the initial number of terminals.*

Proof. Denote the cost of the spider chosen at iteration i to be C_i. We will prove that

$$C_i \leq 1.5w(OPT) \ln \frac{n_i}{n_{i+1}}. \tag{1}$$

Summing up all the C_i values (over all z iterations) gives the required bound.

$$\sum_{i=1}^{z} C_i \leq \sum_{i=1}^{z} 1.5w(OPT) \ln \frac{n_i}{n_{i+1}}$$

$$\sum_{i=1}^{z} C_i \leq 1.5w(OPT) \ln k$$

Notice that if the algorithm stopped when there were two terminals left, $C_i \leq w(OPT)$, and the above equation follows.

We will now prove Equation (1). Assume the minimum ratio 3+ branch-spider has t terminals. Since $t \geq 3$, we have $t - 1 \geq \frac{2}{3}t$. From Lemma 5,

$$\frac{C_i}{t} \leq \frac{w(OPT)}{n_i}$$

This gives us that $\frac{t}{n_i} \geq \frac{C_i}{w(OPT)}$. Since $n_{i+1} = n_i - (t-1)$, we get

$$n_{i+1} \leq n_i - \frac{2}{3}t \leq n_i(1 - \frac{2C_i}{3w(OPT)}).$$

$$\ln \frac{n_i}{n_{i+1}} \geq -\ln(1 - \frac{2C_i}{3w(OPT)}) \geq \frac{C_i}{1.5w(OPT)}.$$

The last step uses the fact that $-\ln(1-x) \geq x$. We conclude that

$$C_i \leq 1.5w(OPT) \ln \frac{n_i}{n_{i+1}}.$$

Further Improvements:

We can improve the approximation ratio by restricting ourselves to minimum ratio objects that have size at least four. However, to decompose the optimal solution into structures of size at least four, we need to prove a decomposition property like Lemma 3.

Definition 7. *A bramble is defined as a tree with at most four leaves. We refer to one of the leaves as the root. A full bramble is one with exactly four leaves.*

Definition 8. *A bramble-spider is constructed by identifying the roots of a collection of disjoint brambles into a single vertex, called the center.*

Definition 9. *A* 4+ bramble-spider *is one with at least four terminals.*

Along the lines of Lemma 3 we can prove the following.

Lemma 6. *Any solution to the node weighted Steiner tree problem with at least four terminals can be decomposed into* 4+ *bramble spiders having the terminals as leaves.*

The difficulty is that we do not know how to find the min ratio 4+ *bramble-spider* in polynomial time. We will use a greedy algorithm to approximate this structure. However this approximation helps only if the size of the bramble spiders is sufficiently large. To ensure this we need to find optimal bramble-spiders that have a small number of full brambles.

Node Steiner Tree Algorithm:II

The input to this algorithm is a node weighted graph G, a constant $\epsilon > 0$ and a set S of terminals.

Let $w = w(OPT)/n_i$ and $\delta = 1.35$, and $C = \frac{1}{\epsilon}$.

Repeat the following steps until we have at most $3C$ terminals left, and then connect the remaining terminals optimally.

Step 1. Compute the best ratio spider, let the ratio be γ_m.

Step 2. Compute the best ratio 3+ spider, let the ratio be γ_{3+}.

Step 3. For each $j = 0 \ldots C$ compute the min ratio 4+ branch-spider with at least 4 terminals, and exactly j full brambles attached to it. Let the ratio be γ.

(This can be done in a manner similar to the computation of branch-spiders, except that we have to try all choices of terminals that will be included as part of the full brambles. Since there are at most C such sets, this can be done in polynomial time for a fixed value of C.)

Step 4. Compute γ^{apx}, an approximate min ratio bramble spider that has at least C terminals. We will try each vertex as the root and pick full brambles of minimum weight greedily. For a fixed root, pick the full bramble with least weight and mark the three terminals used. Repeatedly, pick the lightest bramble with no marked terminals, and mark the three terminals, until all terminals have been marked. While doing this (for each possible root) we will construct a series of bramble-spiders. We will then select the lowest ratio bramble-spider having at least C terminals, from all the bramble-spiders considered. Precise details of this step are provided in Lemma 8.

Step 5. If $2\gamma_m \leq \delta w$ then shrink spider from step 1. If $1.5\gamma_{3+} \leq \delta w$ then shrink spider from step 2. Else shrink the spider found in Step 3 or 4, whichever achieves the minimum in $\min(\delta\gamma, \gamma^{apx})$.

For this algorithm to work, we have to know the weight $w(OPT)$ of the optimal solution. Since we only know an upper bound on the weight $w(OPT)$

(sum of the weight of all vertices), we have to "guess" the weight approximately, and run the algorithm for each possible guessed value. Suppose the cost of each iteration is C_i. In each iteration, let n_i denote the number of terminals remaining at the start of iteration i. Initially, $n_1 = k$ the number of terminals in S.

We first prove the following theorem.

Theorem 2. *If C_i is the cost of the spider contracted in iteration i, then $C_i \leq \delta(\frac{1+\epsilon}{1-\epsilon})w(OPT)\ln\frac{n_i}{n_{i+1}}$, for any $\epsilon > 0$.*

We will prove Theorem 2 in two steps.

Lemma 7. *In step 5 if we contract the spider chosen in Step 1 or Step 2, then $C_i \leq \delta w(OPT)\ln\frac{n_i}{n_{i+1}}$.*

Proof. Assume we contracted the spider chosen in Step 1. Suppose the minimum ratio spider has t terminals. Since $t \geq 2$, we have $t - 1 \geq \frac{t}{2}$. By the condition in Step 5, we have

$$2\gamma_m \leq \delta w, \quad \text{which reduces to} \quad 2\frac{C_i}{t} \leq \delta\frac{w(OPT)}{n_i}.$$

Thus $\frac{t}{2} \geq \frac{n_i C_i}{\delta w(OPT)}$. Since $n_{i+1} = n_i - (t-1)$, we get

$$n_{i+1} \leq n_i - \frac{t}{2} \leq n_i(1 - \frac{C_i}{\delta w(OPT)}).$$

Simplifying, we conclude that

$$C_i \leq \delta w(OPT)\ln\frac{n_i}{n_{i+1}}.$$

Now suppose we contracted the spider chosen in Step 2. Suppose the minimum ratio 3+ spider has t terminals. Since $t \geq 3$, we have $t - 1 \geq \frac{2t}{3}$. By the condition in Step 5, we have

$$\frac{3}{2}\gamma_{3+} \leq \delta\frac{w(OPT)}{n_i} \quad \text{which implies} \quad \frac{3}{2}\frac{C_i}{t} \leq \delta\frac{w(OPT)}{n_i}.$$

This gives us that $\frac{2t}{3} \geq \frac{n_i C_i}{\delta w(OPT)}$. As before, we get $n_{i+1} \leq n_i - \frac{2t}{3} \leq n_i(1 - \frac{C_i}{\delta w(OPT)})$. Simplifying, we get that

$$C_i \leq \delta w(OPT)\ln\frac{n_i}{n_{i+1}}.$$

Lemma 8. *If the first two conditions in Step 5 are not met, and the min ratio bramble-spider has $> C$ full brambles then $\gamma^{apx} \leq \delta(1+\epsilon)w$ where w is $w(OPT)/n_i$.*

Proof. (Of Theorem 2). If we contract the spider chosen in Step 1, or Step 2, we can use Lemma 7 to prove the claim. If we contract the spider chosen in Step 3 or Step 4, we have to consider the following cases.

Case 1: **suppose the best ratio bramble-spider has $\leq C$ full brambles**

(a) $\delta\gamma \leq \gamma^{apx}$. In this case $\gamma \leq w$. Since $\frac{C_i}{t} \leq \frac{w(OPT)}{n_i}$ and $t-1 \geq \frac{3}{4}t$ (we contract at least 4 terminals), we get $C_i \leq \frac{4}{3}w(OPT)\ln\frac{n_i}{n_{i+1}}$.

(b) $\gamma^{apx} \leq \delta\gamma(\leq \delta w)$. Since in step 4 we find a spider with at least C terminals, we get a bound of $C_i \leq \frac{\delta}{1-\epsilon}w(OPT)\ln\frac{n_i}{n_{i+1}}$.

Case 2: **suppose the best ratio bramble-spider has> C full brambles**

(a) $\delta\gamma \leq \gamma^{apx}$ In this case, by Lemma 8, $\delta\gamma \leq \gamma^{apx} \leq \delta(1+\epsilon)w$ and we get $C_i \leq \frac{4}{3}(1+\epsilon)w(OPT)\ln\frac{n_i}{n_{i+1}}$.

(b) By Lemma 8 $\gamma^{apx} \leq \delta(1+\epsilon)w$. Since it has at least C terminals, we obtain $C_i \leq \delta\frac{1+\epsilon}{1-\epsilon}w(OPT)\ln\frac{n_i}{n_{i+1}}$.

Theorem 3. *The node weighted Steiner tree problem can be approximated to a factor of* $1.35(1+\epsilon')\ln k$ *for any* $\epsilon' > 0$.

Proof. Summing up all the C_i values gives a total weight of $\delta(\frac{1+\epsilon}{1-\epsilon})w(OPT)\ln k$. Recall that $\delta = 1.35$. For any given $\epsilon' > 0$, we set $\epsilon = \frac{\epsilon'}{2+\epsilon'}$ so that $\frac{1+\epsilon}{1-\epsilon} = 1+\epsilon'$ to obtain the required approximation factor.

4 Faster Approximation Algorithm

We present a greedy algorithm for node weighted Steiner trees, which is practical and extends to the class of 0-1 proper functions as well (see Section 5). This algorithm has the same complexity as the original algorithm of Klein and Ravi [10].

Algorithm

Repeat the following steps until we have at most two terminals left, and then connect the terminals optimally. Let n_i be the number of terminals in iteration i (initially, $n_1 = k$).

Step 1. Find a spider with the minimum ratio. (this can be done by using the method by Klein and Ravi [10]). Let the ratio be γ_m. If it is a 3+ spider contract it.

Step 2. Else if the minimum ratio spider is a 2 spider, find the 3+ spider with the minimum ratio. Let this ratio be γ_{3+}.

For each terminal j find its closest terminal, with the distance being the sum of the weights of the nodes on the path. Call this path P_j. Order these P_j's in increasing order of weight. (For convenience, we use P_j to denote both the path and its weight.)

Define $S = \{j | P_j \leq 2 \cdot \min\left[\frac{4\gamma_m}{3}, \gamma_{3+}\right]\}$. Let the number of distinct paths P_j such that $j \in S$ be ℓ_i. Denote the forest induced by these ℓ_i paths be T. Let $Cost(T)$ denote the weight of this forest.

Consider $\min\left[\frac{Cost(T)}{-\ln(1-\frac{\ell_i}{n_i})}, 2n_i\gamma_m, \frac{3}{2}n_i\gamma_{3+}\right]$.

Subcase (a). If the first term is the smallest, contract the forest induced by the paths.

Subcase (b). If the second term is the smallest, contract the minimum ratio spider.

Subcase (c). If the third term is the smallest, contract the minimum ratio 3+ spider.

4.1 Proof of Approximation Factor

In this section we prove the following theorem.

Theorem 4. *The algorithm described above yields a node weighted Steiner tree of weight at most* $1.6103 \ln k$ *times the optimal, where* k *is the initial number of terminals.*

Denote the weight paid at iteration i to be C_i.

Lemma 9. *In iteration* i, *if only step 1 is executed, then* $C_i \leq 1.5w(OPT) \ln \frac{n_i}{n_{i+1}}$.

This proof is the same as the proof of Theorem 1.

Lemma 10. *In iteration* i, *if step 2 is taken, then* $\min \left[\frac{Cost(T)}{-\ln(1-\frac{\ell_i}{n_i})}, 2n_i\gamma_m, \frac{3}{2}n_i\gamma_{3+}\right] <$ $1.6103\ w(OPT)$.

Lemma 11. *In iteration* i, *if step 2 is taken, then* $C_i < 1.6103w(OPT) \ln \frac{n_i}{n_{i+1}}$.

Proof. If subcase (a) is chosen, then $C_i = Cost(T)$ and $n_{i+1} = n_i - \ell_i$. Since $1 - \frac{\ell_i}{n_i} = \frac{n_{i+1}}{n_i}$, and $\frac{Cost(T)}{w(OPT)} < 1.6103(-\ln(1 - \frac{\ell_i}{n_i}))$,

$$\frac{C_i}{w(OPT)} < 1.6103 \ln \frac{n_i}{n_{i+1}}$$

If subcase (b) is chosen then $C_i = 2\gamma_m$, and $n_{i+1} = n_i - 1$. From Lemma 10, $2\gamma_m n_i < 1.6103\ w(OPT)$, we get $\frac{1.6103w(OPT)}{n_i} > C_i$.

$$\ln \frac{n_i}{n_{i+1}} = -\ln(1 - \frac{1}{n_i}) > \frac{1}{n_i}.$$

Thus,

$$1.6103\ w(OPT) \ln \frac{n_i}{n_{i+1}} > C_i.$$

If subcase (c) is chosen, let the minimum ratio 3+ spider have t legs. Then $C_i = t\gamma_{3+}$, and $n_{i+1} = n_i - (t - 1)$. By Lemma 10,

$$\frac{3C_i n_i}{2t} < 1.6103\ w(OPT).$$

Now,

$$\ln \frac{n_i}{n_{i+1}} = \ln \frac{n_i}{n_i - t + 1} = -\ln(1 - \frac{t-1}{n_i}) \geq \frac{t-1}{n_i}.$$

Since $t \geq 3$, thus $(t - 1) \geq \frac{2t}{3}$,

$$\ln \frac{n_i}{n_{i+1}} \geq \frac{t-1}{n_i} \geq \frac{2t}{3n_i} > \frac{C_i}{1.6103\ w(OPT)}.$$

The proof of Theorem 4 now follows easily.

Proof. (Of Theorem 4) Let there be $z-1$ iterations. Then $n_z = 1$. Also if initially there were k terminals to connect, $n_1 = k$. For all iterations i, we have $1.6103w(OPT)\ln\frac{n_i}{n_{i+1}} > C_i$. Summing over the iterations, the theorem follows.

5 0-1 Proper functions

A considerable effort has been spent on solving a generalized network design problem where the connectivity requirements are specified as a function of a subset of vertices. These problems assume edge and node weights, and the objective function is to minimize the sum of the weights. For any subset S of vertices, define $\Gamma(S)$ to be the set of edges in the set $(S, V-S)$ (these are the edges with exactly one end point in S). There is a 0-1 function f defined on subsets of vertices. The cut $\Gamma(S)$ belongs to a family of cuts if $f(S) = 1$. Goemans and Williamson [6] proposed a class of cut families and showed that they are useful in modeling network design problems. These are defined via proper functions f, which are required to obey the following properties: $f(S) = f(V-S)$ for all $S \subseteq V$; and if A and B are disjoint, then $f(A) = f(B) = 0$ implies that $f(A \cup B) = 0$.

Klein and Ravi show that the node weighted Steiner tree algorithm can be modified to find a solution for the more general class of problems defined via proper functions [10]. A subset of vertices S which has $f(S) = 1$ is called an active component. They show that active components behave as terminals in a node weighted Steiner tree formulation. However the final solution need not have a single connected component; hence the decomposition lemma developed for branch-spiders does not hold. It may be the case that the optimal solution has connected components having only two terminals in each. In any case, the faster algorithm proposed in Section 4 can be modified to obtain an approximation guarantee of $1.6103\ln k$. Typical problems include generalizations of Steiner trees.

6 Application to Connected Dominating Sets

The *connected dominating set* (CDS) problem is defined as follows: given a node weighted graph G, find a subset S of vertices of minimum weight, such that S induces a connected subgraph and the vertices in S form a dominating set in G. See [7] for applications and other results for the CDS problem on unweighted graphs.

We can develop a similar approximation scheme for connected dominating sets. As the algorithm proceeds, certain vertices are added to the current CDS. Initially, the CDS is empty, and finally it forms a valid CDS when the algorithm terminates. We use the following color notation – each vertex in the CDS is colored black. All vertices which are adjacent to a black vertex are colored gray. The remaining vertices are colored white.

Define a *piece* as a black connected component or a white vertex. Treat each piece as a terminal. Define spiders as in Section 3, but include only the weight of non-leaf gray and white nodes when computing the weight of a spider. In this algorithm, we only shrink black connected components, and not complete spiders.

It is easy to observe that a spider connecting ℓ pieces, reduces the number of pieces by $\ell - 1$. And ultimately when we have found a solution only one piece should be remaining. Notice that all the decomposition claims in Section 3 follow. We can proceed analyzing in a similar way to achieve an approximation ratio of $(1.35 + \epsilon) \ln k$.

Acknowledgments: Part of this work was done while Sudipto Guha was at the University of Maryland and his research was supported by NSF Research Initiation Award CCR-9307462. Samir Khuller's research was supported by NSF Research Initiation Award CCR-9307462, and NSF CAREER Award CCR-9501355. We thank Yoram Sussmann and the reviewers for useful comments on an earlier draft of the paper.

References

1. P. Berman and V. Ramaiyer, "Improved approximation algorithms for the Steiner tree problem", *J. Algorithms*, 17:381–408, (1994).
2. M. Bern and P. Plassmann, "The Steiner problem with edge lengths 1 and 2", *Information Processing Letters*, 32: 171–176, (1989).
3. T. Cormen, C. Leiserson, and R. Rivest, *Introduction to Algorithms*, The MIT Press, 1989.
4. U. Feige, "A threshold of ln n for approximating set-cover", *28th ACM Symposium on Theory of Computing*, pages 314–318, (1996).
5. M. R. Garey and D. S. Johnson, "Computers and Intractability: A guide to the theory of NP-completeness", *Freeman, San Francisco* (1978).
6. M. X. Goemans and D. P. Williamson, "A general approximation technique for constrained forest problems", *SIAM Journal on Computing*, 24:296–317, (1995).
7. S. Guha and S. Khuller, "Approximation algorithms for connected dominating sets", *Algorithmica*, 20:374–387, (1998).
8. F. K. Hwang, D. S. Richards and P. Winter, *The Steiner tree problem*, Annals of Discrete Mathematics: 53, North-Holland, (1992).
9. L. Kou, G. Markowsky and L. Berman, "A fast algorithm for Steiner trees", *Acta Informatica*, 15, pp. 141–145, (1981).
10. P. N. Klein and R. Ravi, "A nearly best-possible approximation algorithm for node-weighted Steiner trees", *J. Algorithms*, 19(1):104–114, (1995).
11. M. Karpinsky and A. Zelikovsky, "New approximation algorithms for the Steiner tree problem", *Journal of Combinatorial Optimization*, 1(1):47–66, (1997).
12. C. Lund and M. Yannakakis, "On the hardness of approximating minimization problems", *Journal of the ACM*, 41(5): 960–981, (1994).
13. V. J. Rayward-Smith, "The computation of nearly minimal Steiner trees in graphs", *Internat. J. Math. Educ. Sci. Tech.*, 14: 15–23, (1983).
14. H. Takahashi and A. Matsuyama, "An approximate solution for the Steiner problem in graphs", *Math. Japonica*, Vol. 24, pp. 573–577, (1980).
15. A. Zelikovsky, "An 11/6 approx algo for the network Steiner problem", *Algorithmica*, 9: 463–470, (1993).

Red-Black Prefetching: An Approximation Algorithm for Parallel Disk Scheduling*

Mahesh Kallahalla and Peter J. Varman

Dept. of ECE, Rice University, Houston, TX 77005, USA.
{kalla, pjv}@rice.edu

Abstract. We address the problem of I/O scheduling of read-once reference strings in a multiple-disk parallel I/O system. We present a novel online algorithm, Red-Black Prefetching (RBP), for parallel I/O scheduling. In order to perform accurate prefetching RBP uses L-block lookahead. The performance of RBP is analyzed in the standard parallel disk model with D independent disks and a shared I/O buffer of size M. We show that the number of parallel I/Os performed by RBP is within a factot $\Theta(\max\{\sqrt{MD/L}, D^{1/3}\})$ of the number of I/Os done by the optimal offline algorithm. This ratio is within a canstant factor of the best possible when L is $L = O(MD^{1/3})$.

1 Introduction

Continuing advances in processor architecture and technology have resulted in the I/O subsystem becoming the bottleneck in many applications. The problem is exacerbated by the advent of multiprocessing systems that can harness the power of hundreds of processors in speeding up computation. Improvements in I/O technology are unlikely to keep pace with processor-memory speeds, causing many applications to choke on I/O. The increasing availability of cost-effective multiple-disk storage systems [6] provides an opportunity to improve the I/O performance through the use of parallelism.

By prefetching data from idle disks the increased disk bandwidth can be used to eliminate the disk latency seen by later I/O requests. The prefetched data needs to be cached in an I/O buffer till it is actually requested by the computation. As the size of the I/O buffer is limited, care must be taken to prefetch the most useful data from the disks. This is the central problem addressed in this paper: determine which blocks to prefetch in each parallel I/O operation so that the overall I/O time is minimized.

We use the intuitive Parallel Disk Model introduced by Vitter and Shriver [13]: the I/O system consists of D independently-accessible disks with an associated shared I/O buffer of capacity M blocks. The data for the computation is stored on the disks in blocks; a block is the unit of access from a disk. In each I/O up to D blocks, at most one from each disk, can be read into

* Supported in part by the National Science Foundation under grant CCR-9704562 and a grant from the Schlumberger Foundation.

the buffer. From the viewpoint of the I/O, the computation is characterized by a *reference string* consisting of the ordered sequence of blocks that the computation accesses. A block should be present in the I/O buffer before it can be accessed by the computation. Serving the reference string requires performing I/O operations to provide the computation with blocks in the order specified by the reference string. The measure of performance is the number of I/Os required to service a given reference string.

In several applications, a particular data block is accessed either once or very infrequently. Examples of such applications include database operations such as external merging [2, 10] (including carrying out several of these concurrently), and streamed applications like real-time retrieval and playback of multiple streams of multimedia data. To model such access patterns, we assume that the reference string consists of read I/Os to distinct blocks; such a string is called a read-once reference string. Surprisingly, in the multiple-disk case even with this simplification intuitive I/O schedules are sub-optimal.

To prefetch accurately a scheduling algorithm needs some information regarding future accesses. In several circumstances it may not have the entire reference string available at the start of the computation; instead at any time it has a lookahead of a fixed number of future requests, called the *lookahead window*. In this paper we consider L-block lookahead [3], through which at any instant the scheduler knows the sequence of next L blocks to be requested by the computation.

We motivate the underlying scheduling problem in the parallel disk model with an example. Consider a system with $D = 3$ and $M = 6$. Assume that blocks labeled A_i (respectively B_i, C_i) are placed on disk 1 (respectively 2, 3), and that the reference string $\Sigma = A_1A_2A_3A_4B_1C_1A_5B_2C_2A_6B_3C_3A_7B_4C_4C_5C_6C_7$. For purposes of this example we assume that an I/O is initiated only when the referenced block is not present in the buffer. Figure 1 (a) shows an I/O schedule constructed by a simple greedy algorithm which always fetches blocks in the order of the reference string, and maximizes the disk parallelism at each step. At step 1, blocks A_1 B_1 and C_1 are fetched concurrently in one I/O. Similarly in step 2, blocks A_2, B_2 and C_2 are fetched in parallel. In step 3, there is buffer space for just 1 additional block besides A_3, and the choice is between fetching B_3, C_3 or neither. Fetching greedily in the order of Σ means that we fetch B_3; continuing in this manner we obtain a schedule of length 9.

In Figure 1 (b), at step 2 disk 2 is idle (even though there is buffer space) and C_2 which occurs later than B_2 in Σ is prefetched; similarly, at step 3, C_3 which occurs even later than B_2 is prefetched. However, the overall length of the schedule is 7, better than the schedule that fetched greedily in the order of Σ. The problem is to find a schedule that services the reference string in the least number of I/Os with the given I/O buffer.

The main contribution of this paper is an algorithm, Red-Black Prefetching (RBP), for parallel disk scheduling with superior I/O performance. The algorithm is easy to implement and requires time linear in the length of the reference string. We analyze the performance of RBP using the *competitive ratio*; this is

Disk 1	A_1	A_2	A_3	A_4	A_5	A_6	A_7		
Disk 2	B_1	B_2	B_3		B_4				
Disk 3	C_1	C_2			C_3	C_4	C_5	C_6	C_7

(a)

Disk 1	A_1	A_2	A_3	A_4	A_5	A_6	A_7
Disk 2	B_1				B_2	B_3	B_4
Disk 3	C_1	C_2	C_3	C_4	C_5	C_6	C_7

(b)

Fig. 1. Schedules for reference string Σ.

the worst-case ratio between the number of I/Os done by RBP and the number of I/Os done by the optimal off-line algorithm to service the same reference string. We show that the competitive ratio of RBP with L-block lookahead is $\Theta(C)$, where $C = \max\{\sqrt{DM/L}, D^{1/3}\}$. It can also be shown that the competitive ratio of any algorithm with L-block lookahead is $\Theta(\sqrt{DM/L})$. The details are omitted from this paper. Hence RBP is comparable to the best on-line algorithm when $L \leq MD^{1/3}$. The previous best algorithm [3] is optimal only for $L = M$.

Studies on parallel disk I/O scheduling have usually concentrated on particular applications such as external merging and sorting [2, 10, 13]. The general question of designing on-line prefetching algorithms using bounded lookahead for read-once reference strings in the parallel disk model was first addressed in [3]. One of their results showed that any algorithm having M-block lookahead can require $\Omega(\sqrt{D})$ times as many I/Os as the optimal off-line algorithm. They also presented an algorithm, NOM, that achieves this bound. Though NOM has the best competitive ratio achievable with M-block lookahead, the fact that it uses only the next M requests in making its scheduling decisions is intrinsic to the algorithm and there does not seem to be any way to generalize it to make use of additional lookahead.

Classical buffer management [4, 11] has focussed on the problem of caching to optimize eviction decisions. Lately, an alternate model to study integrated prefetching and caching was proposed in [5]. In this model the time required to consume a block is an explicit parameter, and the total elapsed time is the performance metric. Off-line approximation algorithms for a single-disk and multiple-disk systems in this model were addressed in [5] and [9] respectively. Recently a polynomial time optimal algorithm for the single disk case was discovered in [1]. In the parallel disk model of this paper, a randomized caching and scheduling algorithm with bounded expected performance was presented in [8]. Using a distributed buffer configuration, in which each disk has its own private buffer, [12] presented an optimal deterministic off-line I/O scheduling algorithm to minimize the number of I/Os.

2 Algorithm RBP

In this section we present the I/O scheduling algorithm, Red-Black Prefetching. We partition the reference string into *phases*, each phase corresponding to a buffer-load of I/O requests. As mentioned before, the competitive ratio will be used as the performance index of algorithm RBP that uses L-block lookahead. We use OPT to denote the optimal off-line algorithm, and $T_A(\Sigma)$ to denote the number of I/Os done by algorithm A to service the reference string Σ.

Algorithm RBP uses L-block lookahead to schedule I/Os.

- Partition the I/O buffer into two parts, *red* and *black*, each of size $M/2$. Each half of the buffer will be used to hold only blocks of that color.
- All blocks in the lookahead are colored either red or black. A block of *phase*(j) at depth i is colored red if the width of *phase*(j) at depth i is less than the threshold width W, $w_i < W$; else it is colored black.
- On a request for block b, one of the following actions are taken:
- If b is present in either the red or the black buffer, service the request and evict block b from the corresponding buffer.
- If b is not present in either buffer then
  - Begin a batched-I/O operation as follows: If b is red (black), fetch the next $M/2$ red (respectively black) blocks beginning with b in order of reference, into the red (respectively black) buffer. Fetch these $M/2$ blocks with maximal parallelism.
  - Service the request and evict block b from the buffer.

Fig. 2. Algorithm RBP

Definition 1. *Let the reference string be* $\Sigma = \langle r_0, r_1, \cdots, r_{N-1} \rangle$.

- *The ith phase,* $i \geq 0$*, phase*(i)*, is the substring* $\langle r_{iM}, \cdots, r_{(i+1)M-1} \rangle$.
- *If the last block referenced is* r_i*, then an on-line scheduling algorithm has L-block lookahead if it knows the substring* $\langle r_{i+1}, \cdots, r_{i+L} \rangle$.
- *An on-line scheduling algorithm* $\mathcal{A}$ *has a competitive ratio of* C_A *if there is a constant* b *such that for any reference string* Σ, $T_{\text{A}}(\Sigma) \leq C_A T_{\text{OPT}}(\Sigma) + b$.

Fetching blocks one phase at a time can yield sub-optimal schedules. In fact the optimal algorithm will obtain additional parallelism by prefetching blocks belonging to several phases at the same time. However, since blocks prefetched from future phases occupy buffer space till they are consumed they need to be carefully chosen. In order to decide which blocks ought to be fetched in a phase-by-phase fashion and which ought to be prefetched across phases, RBP colors each block either *red* or *black*. This coloring is based on a parameter W called *threshold width*. Intuitively, the red blocks of a phase span a small (less than W) number of disks and form a narrow portion of a phase, while the black blocks constitute a wide portion. The intent is to fetch black blocks together to obtain parallelism within a phase, while fetching red blocks together to obtain parallelism across phases. The coloring scheme is given in the following definition; the details of the algorithm are presented in Figure 2.

Definition 2. *Within a phase, a block on some disk has a depth* k *if there are* $k-1$ *blocks from that disk referenced before it in that phase. The width of a phase at height* i*, denoted by* w_i*, is the number of blocks in that phase with depth* i*. A block at depth* i *is colored red if* $w_i < W$*; else it is colored black.*

Figure 3 illustrates these definitions with an example. The system consists of $D = 5$ disks and an I/O buffer of size $M = 16$. The illustrated phase is

$phase(p) = \langle a_1a_2b_1c_1d_1b_2b_3c_2e_1e_2c_3a_3e_3a_4a_5c_4 \rangle$. Figure 3(a) shows the location of blocks on the disks. Figure 3(b) shows the depth of each block and the width of the phase at different heights. Finally Figure 3(c) shows the red (shown in grey) and black blocks assuming $W = 3$.

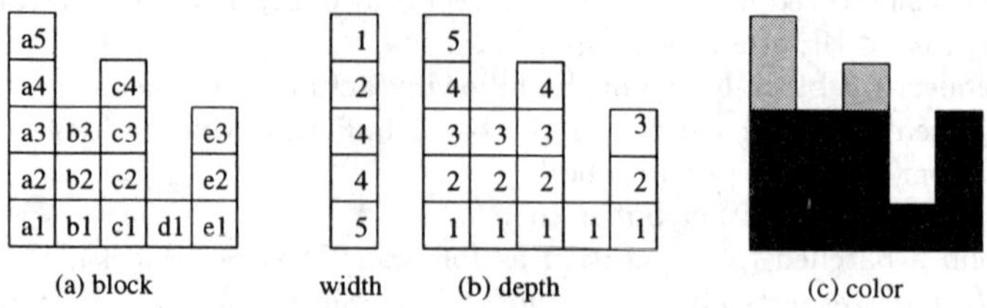

Fig. 3. Illustration of definitions.

3 Analysis of RBP

In order to bound the competitive ratio of RBP, we need to compare the number of I/Os done by RBP with L-block lookahead to the number of I/Os done by the optimal off-line algorithm. We do this by lower bounding the number of I/Os done by OPT, parameterized by the difference in the number of I/Os done by RBP and OPT. To simplify our analysis we implicitly assume that in the schedules considered no block is evicted before it has been referenced. It can be noted that any I/O schedule can be transformed into another schedule of the same length, or smaller, for which this property holds.

Theorem 1. *The competitive ratio of RBP with L-block lookahead is*

$$\begin{array}{lll} \Theta(\sqrt{DM/L}) & \text{if } M \leq L < MD^{1/3} & \text{choosing } DM^2/L^2 \geq W \geq L/M \\ \Theta(D^{1/3}) & \text{if } L \geq MD^{1/3} & \text{choosing } W = D^{1/3} \end{array}$$

Proof. To simplify the presentation, we assume that L is an integral multiple of M. The I/Os for RBP can be divided into I/Os done to fetch black blocks and the I/Os to fetch red blocks. Correspondingly, we break our analysis into two parts. We shown in Lemma 4 that the ratio between the number of I/Os done by RBP to fetch black blocks, and the total number of I/Os done by OPT is $O(\sqrt{D/W})$. Lemma 8 shows that the ratio between the number of I/Os done by RBP to fetch red blocks and the total number of I/Os done by OPT is $O(\max\{\sqrt[4]{DW}, \sqrt{DM/L}\})$. When $M \leq L < MD^{1/3}$ it can be seen that for all values of W, $DM^2/L^2 \geq W \geq L/M$, $\sqrt{DM/L}$ is the dominating term. Similarly, when $L \geq MD^{1/3}$ it can be seen that by choosing $W = D^{1/3}$ the number of I/Os done by RBP to fetch red and black blocks are of the same order and $D^{1/3}$ is the dominating term.

These bounds can be shown to be tight by constructing reference strings such that the above bounds are matched in both the ranges of L. The details of these constructions are omitted from this paper.

3.1 I/Os for Black Blocks

In this section we present a bound on the ratio between the number of I/Os done by RBP to fetch black blocks and the total number of I/Os done by OPT. To measure the advantage OPT gains over RBP due to its off-line knowledge, we define some of the blocks fetched by OPT to be *useful blocks*. A count of such blocks is a measure of the reduction in the number of I/Os done by OPT to service the black blocks of a phase relative to RBP.

Definition 3. *Let the set of black blocks of phase(i) be B_i. At some instant let the blocks in OPT's buffer be $\mathcal{M}$.*

- *The residual height of phase(i) at that time is the maximum number of blocks from a single disk in the set $B_i - \mathcal{M}$.*
- *The number of useful blocks prefetched in phase(j) for a phase(i), $i > j$, is the difference between the residual height of phase(i) at the start of phase(j) and the residual height of phase(i) at the end of phase(j).*
- *The number of useful blocks prefetched for phase(i) is the number of useful blocks prefetched for phase(i) in prior phases.*

From the above definition, if OPT prefetches B useful blocks for a single phase, then at least B blocks must be fetched from a single disk, and hence at least B I/Os must be done to fetch them. Of course, if the B useful blocks belong to different phases then less than B I/Os may be sufficient to fetch them.

Lemma 1. *If B useful blocks are prefetched by OPT for phase(i) in phase(j), then OPT must have done at least B I/Os in phase(j).*

For ease of notation we use $\sum_P$ to denote the sum over all i such that *phase*(i) belongs to the reference string.

Lemma 2. *If the number of I/Os done by OPT is T_{OPT}, and T^b_{RBP} is the number of I/Os done by RBP to fetch black blocks, then*

$$T^b_{\text{RBP}}/2 \leq T_{\text{OPT}} + B$$

where B is the number of useful blocks prefetched by OPT.

Proof. The total number of black blocks in a phase is at most M. In each batched-I/O operation RBP fetches $M/2$ black blocks; hence at most 2 batched-I/O operations are required to fetch the black blocks of *phase*(i). If the maximum number of black blocks from any single disk in *phase*(i) is $H_b(i)$, in each batched-I/O operation for black blocks RBP does no more than $H_b(i)$ I/Os. Hence, $T^b_{\text{RBP}} \leq 2\sum_P H_b(i)$.

By definition, OPT needs to do at least $H_b(i) - b_i$ I/Os in *phase*(i), where b_i is the number of useful blocks prefetched for *phase*(i). Since the number of useful blocks fetched is B, $T_{\text{OPT}} \geq \sum_P H_b(i) - \sum_P b_i \geq T^b_{\text{RBP}}/2 - B$.

Lemma 3 gives a measure of the cost of useful blocks in terms of the buffer space that they occupy.

Lemma 3. *If at some instant, the buffer contains B useful blocks, then the buffer should contain at least WB black blocks, where W is the threshold width.*

Proof. By definition, the number of useful block prefetched for $phase(i)$ is the reduction in the maximum number of black blocks that need to be fetched from any single disk in $phase(i)$. However, by Definition 2 at least W black blocks must be fetched to reduce the maximum number of black blocks on any single disk by one. Hence there must be at least WU black blocks in the buffer if there are U useful prefetched blocks in the buffer.

Lemma 4. *The ratio between the number of I/Os done by RBP to fetch black blocks and the total number of I/Os done by OPT is $O(\sqrt{D/W})$.*

Proof. Let the reference string be Σ. We shall show that $T_{\text{OPT}} = \Omega(B\sqrt{W/D})$, whence the lemma follows by Lemma 2. Let the number of useful blocks prefetched by OPT in $phase(i)$ be b_i. Let α_l, $\alpha_l \geq 0$, denote the number of these blocks prefetched for $phase(i+l)$, $l \geq 1$. Note that $\sum_P \alpha_l = b_i$ and $\sum_P b_i = B$. Let $I_{\text{OPT}}(i)$ denote the number of I/Os done by OPT in $phase(i)$.

$$T_{\text{OPT}} = \sum_P I_{\text{OPT}}(i) \tag{1}$$

Since α_l useful blocks are prefetched for $phase(i+l)$ in $phase(i)$, by Lemma 1 the number of I/Os done by OPT in $phase(i)$, $I_{\text{OPT}}(i) \geq \alpha_l$, for all $l \geq 1$. In all $l-1$ phases between $phase(i)$ and $phase(i+l)$ there are at least α_l useful blocks intended for $phase(i+l)$ in the buffer. Then, from Lemma 3 the number of blocks occupying space in the buffer during $phase(i+s)$, $s < l$, is at least $W\alpha_l$. Hence at least $W\alpha_l$ blocks, that are referenced in $phase(i+s)$, are not present in the buffer at the start of $phase(i+s)$. Due to this at least $\alpha_l W/D$ I/Os need to be done by OPT in $phase(i+s)$. That is, the number of I/Os chargeable to the blocks prefetched by $phase(i)$ intended for $phase(i+l)$, is at least $(l-1)\alpha_l W/D$. Let $phase(i+n)$ be the last phase to which a useful block is fetched in $phase(i)$. The number of I/Os chargeable to useful blocks prefetched in $phase(i)$ is therefore

$$\sum_{l=1}^{n}(l-1)\alpha_l W/D = \sum_{l=1}^{n} l\alpha_l W/D - b_i W/D$$

We know that $\alpha_l \leq I_{\text{OPT}}(i)$. In order to minimize $\sum_{l=1}^{n} l\alpha_l$ set $\alpha_r \geq \alpha_s$ whenever $r < s$. Therefore to lower bound the first term of the summation, set each of the first $\lfloor b_i/I_{\text{OPT}}(i)\rfloor$ α_ls to their maximum value, $I_{\text{OPT}}(i)$.

$$\sum_{l=1}^{n} l\alpha_l \;\geq\; \sum_{l=1}^{b_i/I_{\text{OPT}}(i)-1} l I_{\text{OPT}}(i) \;\geq\; \frac{b_i^2}{2I_{\text{OPT}}(i)} - \frac{b_i}{2}$$

Hence,

$$T_{\text{OPT}} \geq \sum_P \left(\frac{b_i^2}{2I_{\text{OPT}}(i)} - \frac{3b_i}{2}\right)\frac{W}{D} \tag{2}$$

Since b_i useful blocks are fetched in *phase*(i), by Lemma 3 the number of blocks fetched is at least $W \sum_P b_i$. As at best these could have been fetched with full parallelism $T_{\text{OPT}} \geq W \sum_P b_i/D$. Hence, Equation 2 can be rewritten as

$$T_{\text{OPT}} \geq \sum_P (b_i^2 W)/(5DI_{\text{OPT}}(i)) \tag{3}$$

Combining Equations 1 and 3

$$T_{\text{OPT}} \geq \frac{1}{2}\sum_P \left(I_{\text{OPT}}(i) + \frac{Wb_i^2}{5DI_{\text{OPT}}(i)} \right) \geq \frac{1}{2}\sum_P b_i\sqrt{W/5D} = \Omega(B\sqrt{W/D})$$

3.2 I/Os for Red Blocks

In this section we shall bound the ratio between the number of I/Os done by RBP to fetch red blocks and the total number of I/Os done by OPT. Let us first group red blocks from contiguous phases into sets of M blocks.

Definition 4. *Let the reference string be Σ.*

- *Σ is partitioned into contiguous sequences of L references called windows; the i th window is denoted by window(i).*
- *A swath is a minimal sequence of contiguous phases of a window such that there are at least M red blocks in these phases. The end portion of a window which may not have M red blocks is appended to the previous swath of the window if any; else the whole window constitutes a swath. The j th swath, $j \geq 0$, is denoted by swath(j); every phase is in exactly one swath and phase(0) is in swath(0).*

Note that the definition of a swath depends only upon the reference string and the threshold parameter W; it is independent of the I/O scheduling algorithm. By definition, RBP fetches the red blocks of a swath $M/2$ blocks at a time. On the other hand OPT may prefetch blocks for future swaths while servicing the current swath. To bound the advantage that OPT gets over RBP by doing so, we redefine *useful blocks* in the current context. These definitions parallel those in Section 3.1, but deal with swaths rather than phases.

Definition 5. *Let the set of red blocks of swath(i) be R_i. At some instant let the blocks in OPT's buffer be $\mathcal{M}$.*

- *The residual height of swath(i) at that time is the maximum number of red blocks from a single disk in the set $R_i - \mathcal{M}$.*
- *The number of useful blocks prefetched in swath(j) for swath(i), $i > j$, is the difference between the residual height of swath(i) at the start of swath(j) and the residual height of swath(i) at the end of swath(j). Further if swath(i) and swath(j) are in the same window then these useful blocks are called short, else they are called long.*
- *The number of useful blocks prefetched for swath(i) is the number of useful blocks prefetched for swath(i) in prior swaths.*

The following lemma follows directly from the above definition.

Lemma 5. *If R useful blocks are prefetched by OPT for swath(i), then OPT must have done at least R I/Os.*

From the above definitions, if u long useful blocks are prefetched in $window(i)$ for $window(j)$, at least u blocks are present in the buffer while servicing any $window(t)$, $i < t < j$. Hence at least $u/D \times L/M$ I/Os are chargeable to these blocks in $window(t)$. By using this observation and an analysis similar to Lemma 4, the following bound on T_{OPT} can be shown.

Lemma 6. *If the number of long useful blocks fetched by OPT is U, then*

$$T_{\text{OPT}} = \Omega(U\sqrt{L/DM})$$

We next bound the number of I/Os done by OPT by considering short useful blocks. Though OPT may prefetch blocks from several swaths at the same time, the bounded buffer presents a constraint: the number of blocks in the buffer cannot be more than M. To capture this constraint we define *super-swaths*, which is a collection of swaths in which the number of blocks prefetched by OPT is bounded.

Definition 6. *Each window is partitioned into minimal length sequences of contiguous swaths, called super-swaths, such that in each super-swath the number of useful blocks prefetched by OPT for swaths in the same super-swath is at least M. The end portion of the window is appended to the previous super-swath if any, else the entire window constitutes a super-swath. The k th super-swath, $k \geq 0$, is denoted by $superswath(k)$.*

The following lemma gives a lower bound on the number of I/Os done by OPT relative to that done by RBP to fetch the red blocks in a super-swath. For ease of notation we use $\sum_{SS_k}$ to denote the sum over all j such that $swath(j)$ is in $superswath(k)$.

Lemma 7. *If $\mathcal{W}^r_{\text{RBP}}(k)$ is the number of I/Os done by RBP to fetch red blocks of $superswath(k)$, and $T_{\text{OPT}}(k)$ is the total number of I/Os done by OPT in $superswath(k)$, then*

$$\mathcal{W}^r_{\text{RBP}}(k) = O(T_{\text{OPT}}(k) + U_k + R_k)$$

where U_k and R_k are the number of long and short useful blocks, respectively, prefetched for $superswath(k)$.

Proof. By the definition of a swath and the fact that there can be at most M red blocks in any phase, the total number of red blocks in a swath is at most $3M - 2$. In each batched-I/O operation RBP fetches $M/2$ red blocks; hence at most 6 batched-I/O operations are required to fetch the red blocks of $swath(j)$. If the number of red blocks from any single disk in $swath(j)$ is $H_r(j)$, in each batched-I/O operation for red blocks RBP performs no more than $H_r(j)$ I/Os. Hence

$$\mathcal{W}^r_{\text{RBP}}(k) \leq 6 \sum_{SS_k} H_r(j)$$

Consider the I/Os done by OPT to fetch red blocks of a super-swath. The total number of useful blocks prefetched for *superswath*(k) is $U_k + R_k$.

$$T_{\text{OPT}}(k) \geq \sum_{SS_k} H_r(j) - (U_k + R_k) \geq \mathcal{W}^r_{\text{RBP}}(k)/6 - (U_k + R_k)$$

Note that in the above lemma $U_k \leq M$ due to the bound on the buffer size . Let U' be the total number of long useful blocks fetched to super-swaths in which $U_k \geq R_k$ and R' be the total number of short useful blocks fetched to super-swaths in which $U_k < R_k$.

Corollary 1. *If T^r_{RBP} is the number of I/Os done by RBP to fetch red blocks then $T^r_{\text{RBP}} \leq T_{\text{OPT}} + 2U' + 2R'$.*

Lemma 8. *The ratio between the number of I/Os done by RBP to fetch red blocks and the total number of I/Os done by OPT is $O(\max\{\sqrt[4]{DW}, \sqrt{DM/L}\})$.*

Proof. If $U' \geq R'$ then the lemma follows by Lemma 6 and Corollary 1, as $U' \leq U$.

In the other case when $U' < R'$, consider any *superswath*(k) in which $R_k > U_k$. We shall show that the number of I/Os done by OPT in *superswath*(k) is lower bounded by $\Omega(R_k/\sqrt[4]{DW})$. This will then imply that $T_{\text{OPT}} \geq R'/\sqrt[4]{DW}$, whence the lemma follows by Corollary 1. Two cases are possible depending on whether *superswath*(k) is the entire window or not.

Case 1. *superswath*(k) is not an entire window.

In this case *superswath*(k) has $\Theta(M)$ short useful blocks prefetched for it within the same super-swath and at most M from without, $R_k = \Theta(M)$. Let the number of swaths in *superswath*(k) be n. By the definition of a super-swath $n \geq 2$. Consider a set of two swaths, *swath*(j) and *swath*$(j+1)$, in *superswath*(k). Let the number of phases in these swaths combined be β_j, and the number of I/Os done by OPT in them be y_j. The maximum number of red blocks from any phase in these swaths, not present in the buffer at the start of *swath*(j) is Wy_j. Hence the number of red blocks fetched in these swaths is no more than $\beta_j W y_j$. At most M red blocks could have been prefetched for these two swaths in previous swaths. Hence at least M red blocks need to be fetched during these swaths. Hence,

$$\beta_j \geq M/Wy_j$$

The number of phases in the super-swath is therefore

$$\sum_{SS_k} \beta_j/2 \geq \sum_{SS_k} M/2Wy_j$$

From the fact that the arithmetic mean is greater than the harmonic mean, $\sum_{SS_k} 1/y_j \geq n^2/\sum_{SS_k} y_j$.

$$\sum_{SS_k} \beta_j \geq n^2 M/W \sum_{SS_k} y_j = \Omega\left(n^2 M/W \sum_{SS_k} y_j\right)$$

OPT has to do at least M/D I/Os in every two phases. Hence the number of I/Os done by OPT in *superswath*(k) is at least

$$T_{\text{OPT}}(k) \geq \frac{M}{D} \times \frac{1}{2} \sum_{SS_k} \beta_j/2 = \Omega\left(n^2 M^2/(DW \sum_{SS_k} y_j)\right)$$

This together with the fact that $T_{\text{OPT}}(k) \geq \sum_{SS_k} y_j/2$ yields $T_{\text{OPT}}(k) = \Omega(nM/\sqrt{DW})$. Two cases are possible depending on the number of swaths in *superswath*(k), n.

Case 1a. n $\geq \sqrt[4]{DW}$: Then clearly $T_{\text{OPT}}(k) = \Omega(M/\sqrt[4]{DW})$.

Case 1b. n $< \sqrt[4]{DW}$: By assumption, at least M blocks are fetched and consumed in the same super-swath. Hence, there is at least one swath in *superswath*(k) for which at least M/n useful blocks were fetched. Therefore, by Lemma 5 OPT should have done at least M/n I/Os in *superswath*(k).

Case 2: *superswath*(k) is an entire window.

As the entire window is a super-swath no short useful block could have been prefetched for this super-swath in previous super-swaths. Hence all R_k short useful blocks are fetched in the same super-swath. By an analysis similar to Case 1 it can be shown that in *superswath*(k),

$$T_{\text{OPT}}(k) = \Omega\left(R_k/\sqrt[4]{DW}\right)$$

Finally as $U_k < R_k$, by Corollary 1 $\mathcal{W}^r_{\text{RBP}}(k) = O(T_{\text{OPT}}(k) + R_k)$.

Hence in either case if $R_k > U_k$, $T_{\text{OPT}}(k) = \Omega\left(R_k/\sqrt[4]{DW}\right)$.

4 Conclusions

In this paper we considered the problem of prefetching and I/O scheduling of read-once reference strings in a parallel I/O system. We presented a novel on-line algorithm, Red-Black Prefetching (RBP), for this problem and bounded its competitive ratio. We analyzed the performance of RBP in the standard parallel disk model with D disks and a buffer of size M. We showed that the number of I/Os performed by RBP is within $\Theta(C)$, where $C = \max\{\sqrt{MD/L}, D^{1/3}\}$, of the optimal schedule. It can be shown that the competitive ratio of any on-line algorithm with L-block lookahead is $\Theta(\sqrt{DM/L})$; hence RBP is asymptotically optimal when $L \leq MD^{1/3}$. RBP is easy to implement and computationally requires time linear in the length of the reference string.

An interesting alternate measure of performance is the on-line ratio [7]. This is the ratio between the number of I/Os done by an on-line algorithm to the number of I/Os done by the optimal *on-line* algorithm with the same amount of lookahead. This measure attempts to measure the efficiency with which the on-line algorithm uses the lookahead available to it. The analysis of this paper can be extended to show that the on-line ratio of RBP is $\Theta(C)$, where $C = \min\{L/M, (DL/M)^{1/5}, D^{1/3}\}$, with the corresponding choice of the threshold width W being L^2, $(D^3M^2/L^2)^{1/5}$ and $D^{1/3}$, respectively.

References

1. S. Albers, N. Garg, and S. Leonardi.: Minimizing Stall Time in Single and Parallel Disk Systems. Proc. of Symp. on Theory of Computing. (1998)
2. R. D. Barve, E. F. Grove, and J. S. Vitter.: Simple Randomized Mergesort on Parallel Disks. Parallel Computing. Vol. 23 **4** (1996): 601–631
3. R. D. Barve, M. Kallahalla, P. J. Varman, and J. S. Vitter.: Competitive Parallel Disk Prefetching and Buffer Management. Proc. of ACM Wkshp. on IOPADS (1997). 47–56
4. L. A. Belady.: A Study of Replacement Algorithms for a Virtual Storage Computer. IBM Systems Journal, Vol. 5 **2**. (1966) 78–101
5. P. Cao, E. W. Felten, A. R. Karlin, and K. Li.: A Study of Integrated Prefetching and Caching Strategies. Proc. of the Joint Int. Conf. on Measurement and Modeling of Comp. Sys. ACM (1995) 188–197
6. P. M. Chen, E. K. Lee, G. A. Gibson, R. H. Katz, and D. A. Patterson.: RAID: High Performance Reliable Secondary Storage. ACM Computing Surveys, Vol. 26 **2**. (1994) 145–185
7. M. Kallahalla and P. J. Varman.: ASP: Adaptive Online Parallel Disk Scheduling. Proc. of DIMACS Wkshp. on Ext. Memory Algorithms and Visualization, DIMACS. (1998) (To appear)
8. M. Kallahalla and P. J. Varman.: Improving Parallel-Disk Buffer Management using Randomized Writeback. Proc. of Int. Conf. on Parallel Procesing. (1998) 270–277
9. T. Kimbrel and A. R. Karlin.: Near-Optimal Parallel Prefetching and Caching. Proc. of Foundations of Computer Science. IEEE (1996) 540–549
10. V. S. Pai, A. A. Schäffer, and P. J. Varman.: Markov Analysis of Multiple-Disk Prefetching Strategies for External Merging. Theoretical Computer Science, Vol. 128 **1–2**. (1994) 211–239
11. D. D. Sleator and R. E. Tarjan.: Amortized Efficiency of List Update and Paging Rules. Communications of the ACM, Vol. 28 **2**. (1985) 202–208
12. P. J. Varman and R. M. Verma.: Tight Bounds for Prefetching and Buffer Management Algorithms for Parallel I/O Systems. Proc. of FST&TCS. LNCS Vol. 16. (1996)
13. J. S. Vitter and E. A. M. Shriver.: Optimal Algorithms for Parallel Memory, I: Two-Level Memories. Algorithmica, Vol. 12 **2–3**. (1994) 110–147

A Synchronous Semantics of Higher-Order Processes for Modeling Reconfigurable Reactive Systems

Jean-Pierre Talpin and David Nowak

INRIA-Rennes and IRISA, Campus de Beaulieu, F-35042 Rennes

Abstract. Synchronous languages are well suited for the design of dependable real-time systems: they enable a very high-level specification and an extremely modular implementation of complex systems by structurally decomposing them into elementary synchronous processes. To maximize the support for the generic implementation and the dynamic reconfigurability of reactive systems, we introduce a semantics of higher-order processes in a seamless extension of the synchronous language SIGNAL. To enable the correct specification and the modular implementation of systems, we introduce an expressive type inference system for characterizing their temporal and causal invariants.

1 Introduction

Synchronous languages, such as SIGNAL [2], LUSTRE [9], ESTEREL [3] have been specifically designed to ease the development of reactive systems. The synchronous hypothesis provides a deterministic notion of concurrency where operations and communications are instantaneous. In a synchronous language, concurrency is meant as a logical way to decompose the description of a system into a set of elementary communicating processes. Interaction between concurrent components is conceptually performed by broadcasting events. Synchronous languages enable a very high-level specification and an extremely modular design of complex reactive systems by structurally decomposing them into elementary processes. The compilation of such specifications consists of the proof of global safety requirements and of the assembly of processes to form automata or circuits of fixed interaction topology. In practice, however, fixing the topology of a system makes it difficult to model practical situations requiring an optimal reaction to a major environmental change, e.g., the tele-maintainance of processing algorithms on a satellite; the adaptation of an event handler to a context-sensitive, menu-driven, user-interface; loading an applet in a browser; the dynamic configuration of a flight-assistance system with respect to the flight phase. Reconfigurations should be taken into account early in the design of the system in order to prevent accidental alteration of services or interferences during execution. The reactivity and safety invariants of the system should be preserved. A simple and intuitive way to express the dynamic configurability and the generic assembly of reactive system components in a synchronous language is to introduce a semantics of higher-order processes. Higher-order processes have been extensively studied in the context of process calculi [8, 14] and allow reasoning on state and mobility in distributed system. Contemporary work has demonstrated the practicality of higher-order programming languages for hardware-design (e.g. LAVA [4], HAWK [13]) and the introduction of LUCID-synchrone [6] has been a first step towards the generalization of the principles of synchronous programming to higher-order languages. To model reconfigurable reactive systems, we give a seamless extension of the synchronous language SIGNAL with first-class processes (section 2). We introduce an inference system (section 3 and 4) for determining the temporal and causal invariants of processes. We state the formal properties of our inference systems (section 5).

2 Semantics

We adopt the synchronous programming model of SIGNAL [2] and regard a reactive system as the composition of co-iterative simultaneous equations on discrete signals. A signal represents an infinite sequence of values defined over a discrete and totally ordered set of instants. Each equation in the system specifies an elementary and instantaneous operation on input signals which produces outputs. An instant is the time elapsed between two successive occurrences of messages at the signal. This simple and intuitive notion of time allows concurrency to meets determinism: *synchronous composition* concerns signals present at the same time. The systematization of this hypothesis has several immediate consequences: communication becomes broadcast and is immediate (inputs and outputs are present at the same time). But it also imposes a programming style which slightly differ from conventions, in that consideration on the logical notion of time imposed by the model are essential. This can be illustrated by considering the definition of a counter from m to n: let x = (pre x m) + 1 in when (x $\leq$ n) x. At each instant, it is either silent or reacts to input events and provide values to its environment. The value of x is initially $x_0 = m$. At each instant $i > 0$, it is the previous value x_{i-1} of x added to 1 and is returned until the bound n is reached. In other words, $x_0 = m$ and $x_i = x_{i-1} + 1, \forall i \in [1..n - m]$.

Syntax A signal is named x, y or z. A value v is either a boolean b or a closure c. A closure c consists of a closed (i.e. s.t. $\mathrm{fv}(e) = \{x\}$) and finite expression e parameterized by a signal x. Expressions e consist of values v, pervasives p, references to signals x, abstractions $\mathsf{proc}\, x\, e$, applications $e(e')$, synchronous compositions $e \mid e'$ and scoped definitions let $x = e$ in e'

x	signal	$e ::= v$	value	$p ::=$ sync	synchro
		$\mid x \mid p$	reference	$\mid$ pre	delay
$b ::=$ true $\mid$ false	boolean	$\mid e(e')$	application	$\mid$ when	sample
$c ::= \mathsf{proc}\, x\, e$	closure	$\mid e \mid e'$	composition	$\mid$ default	merge
$v ::= b \mid c$	value	$\mid$ let $x = e$ in e'	definition	$\mid$ reset	reset

Fig. 1. Syntax of expressions e

By extension, $x_1^{1..m_1} = e_1 \mid \ldots x_n^{m_n} = e_n$ simultaneously defines $(x_i^j)_{i=1..n}^{j=1..m_i}$ by the expressions $e_{1..n}$ of $(m_i)_{i=1..n}$ outputs. The pervasive sync $e\ e'$ synchronizes e and e'; pre $e\ e'$ references the previous value of e (initially e'); when $e\ e'$ outputs e' when e is present and true; default $e\ e'$ outputs the value of e when it is present or else that of e'. We write $x_{1..n}$ or $\tilde{x}$ for a sequence. We write $\mathrm{fv}(e)$ for the signals lexically free in e. For a relation R, $\mathrm{dom}(R)$ is the domain of R and $R \uplus (x, P)$ the addition of (x, P) s.t. $x \notin \mathrm{dom}(R)$ to R.

Operational Semantics We define a small step operational semantics which describes how a system e evolves over time. A step defines an instant. The evolution of the system over time is modeled by co-iteration. The relation consists of an environment E, an initial state represented by an expression e, a (composition of) result(s) $\tilde{r}$ and a final state e'. It means that e reacts to E by producing $\tilde{r}$ and becoming e'. Environments E associate signals x to results r (either absent, i.e. abs, or present, i.e. v). The axioms (val) defines the transition for values v (either v or absent to preserve stuttering), the axiom (sig) that for signals x (the result r associated to x in the environment is emitted). The rule (let) defines the meaning of let $x = e$ in e'. Since inputs and outputs are simultaneous, the hypothesis (x, r) is required to conclude that e_1 has result r (e.g., example 1). The rule (par) synchronizes the events E used to produce the result $(\tilde{r}_1, \tilde{r}_2)$ of a composition $e_1 \mid e_2$. The rules (pre_1) and (pre_2) define the meaning of a delay statement pre $e_1\ e_2$. When the result v_1 of e_1 is present, it is stored in place of e_2 of which the result v_2 is emitted. The rules (abs_1) and (abs_2) mean that the emission of a closure c from an abstraction $\mathsf{proc}\,x\,e$ require all signals y free in e to be present in E.

$E \vdash e \xrightarrow{\tilde{r}} e'$	instant	$r ::= \mathsf{abs} \mid v$	result
$(E_i \vdash e_i \xrightarrow{\tilde{r}_i} e_{i+1})_{i \geq 0}$	execution	$E \ni (x, r)$	environment

Fig. 2. Semantics domains

$$E \vdash v \xrightarrow{v} v \quad E \vdash v \xrightarrow{\mathsf{abs}} v \quad \text{(val)}$$

$$E \uplus (x, r) \vdash x \xrightarrow{r} x \quad \text{(sig)}$$

$$\frac{E \uplus (x, r_1) \vdash e_1 \xrightarrow{r_1} e_1' \quad E \uplus (x, r_1) \vdash e_2 \xrightarrow{\tilde{r}} e_2'}{E \vdash \mathsf{let}\ x = e_1\ \mathsf{in}\ e_2 \xrightarrow{\tilde{r}} \mathsf{let}\ x = e_1'\ \mathsf{in}\ e_2'} \ \text{(let)}$$

$$\frac{E \vdash e_1 \xrightarrow{\tilde{r}_1} e_1' \quad E \vdash e_2 \xrightarrow{\tilde{r}_2} e_2'}{E \vdash e_1 \mid e_2 \xrightarrow{(\tilde{r}_1, \tilde{r}_2)} e_1' \mid e_2'} \ \text{(par)} \qquad \frac{E \vdash e_1 \xrightarrow{r_1} e_1' \quad E \vdash r_1(e_2) \xrightarrow{\tilde{r}} r_1'(e_2')}{E \vdash e_1(e_2) \xrightarrow{\tilde{r}} e_1'(e_2')} \ \text{(app)}$$

$$\frac{E \vdash e_1 \xrightarrow{v_1} e_1' \quad E \vdash e_2 \xrightarrow{v_2} e_2'}{E \vdash \mathsf{pre}\ e_1\ e_2 \xrightarrow{v_2} \mathsf{pre}\ e_1'\ v_1} \ (\mathrm{pre}_1) \qquad \frac{E \vdash e_2 \xrightarrow{r} e_2' \quad (x, r) \vdash e_1 \xrightarrow{\tilde{r}} e_1'}{E \vdash (\mathsf{proc}\,x\,e_1)(e_2) \xrightarrow{\tilde{r}} (\mathsf{proc}\,x\,e_1')(e_2')} \ (\mathrm{cls}_1)$$

$$\frac{E \vdash e_1 \xrightarrow{\mathsf{abs}} e_1' \quad E \vdash e_2 \xrightarrow{\mathsf{abs}} e_2'}{E \vdash \mathsf{pre}\ e_1\ e_2 \xrightarrow{\mathsf{abs}} \mathsf{pre}\ e_1'\ e_2'} \ (\mathrm{pre}_2) \qquad \frac{E \vdash e_2 \xrightarrow{r} e_2'}{E \vdash \mathsf{abs}(e_2) \xrightarrow{\mathsf{abs}} \mathsf{abs}(e_2')} \ (\mathrm{cls}_2)$$

$$\frac{c = (\mathsf{proc}\,x\,e)[v/y]_{(y,v) \in E}^{y \in \mathrm{fv}(e) \setminus \{x\}}}{E \vdash \mathsf{proc}\,x\,e \xrightarrow{c} \mathsf{proc}\,x\,e} \ (\mathrm{abs}_1) \qquad \frac{E \vdash e_1 \xrightarrow{\mathsf{abs}} e_1' \quad E \vdash e_2 \xrightarrow{r} e_2' \quad E \vdash r(e_3) \xrightarrow{\tilde{r}} r'(e_3')}{E \vdash (\mathsf{reset}\ e_1\ e_2)(e_3) \xrightarrow{\tilde{r}} (\mathsf{reset}\ e_1'\ r')(e_3')} \ (\mathrm{rst}_1)$$

$$\frac{y \in \mathrm{fv}(e) \setminus \{x\} \quad (y, \mathsf{abs}) \in E}{E \vdash \mathsf{proc}\,x\,e \xrightarrow{\mathsf{abs}} \mathsf{proc}\,x\,e} \ (\mathrm{abs}_2) \qquad \frac{E \vdash e_1 \xrightarrow{c} e_1' \quad E \vdash c(e_3) \xrightarrow{\tilde{r}} c'(e_3')}{E \vdash (\mathsf{reset}\ e_1\ e_2)(e_3) \xrightarrow{\tilde{r}} (\mathsf{reset}\ e_1'\ c')(e_3')} \ (\mathrm{rst}_2)$$

Fig. 3. Operational semantics $E \vdash e \xrightarrow{\tilde{r}} e'$

The inductive definition of values v further excludes co-inductive closures, e.g. $c = \mathsf{proc}\,x\,c(x)$ from let $f = \mathsf{proc}\,x\,f(x)$ (the causal analysis, section 4, detects and rejects "instantaneously recursive" closures). The rule (app) evaluates e_1 to a state e_1' and result r_1. If it is absent, rule (cls_2), so is the result. If it is a closure $\mathsf{proc}\,x\,e_1$, rule (cls_1), x is bound to r_2 and e_1 evaluated to e_1' and to $\tilde{r}$. The keyword reset allows to store the internal state of a process when necessary (e.g., the watch, below). If the reset e_1 is absent, rule (rst_1), no reconfiguration takes place. The initial process e_2 is evaluated to r and applied to e_3. The application produces a result $\tilde{r}$ and a new state, consisting of r' and e_3'. It is stored in place of e_2 and e_3. If e_1 emits a new process c, rule (rst_2), the previous state is discarded and the new state c' results from applying c to e_3. Pervasives sync, when and default incur no state transition. The operator default e e' outputs the value of e when e is present. If e returns abs, the result is that of e'. The operator when e e' outputs the value of e' when e is present with the value true. All operators on booleans (e.g. and, or, not) and on integers (e.g. +, -, *) are synchronous: inputs and outputs are present simultaneously or absent.

x	abs	v
y	abs	v'
sync x y	abs	unit

x	abs	v	v	abs
y	abs	v'	abs	v
default x y	abs	v	v	v

x	abs	v	abs	false	true
y	abs	abs	v	v	v
when x y	abs	abs	abs	abs	v

Fig. 4. Pervasives sync, when and default

Example 1. Let us consider a variant of the example 1 which reacts to an input tick by counting from an initial value start down to 0 to emit a timeout. At each instant, all expressions are simultaneously executed. The signal count is reset to start when the timeout occurs. Otherwise it takes a decrement of its previous value last. Using the timer, we define a watch that emits seconds and minutes by constructing the higher-order processes count_seconds and count_minutes). We resource to reconfiguration to store the internal state of each process (i.e. instances of count and start). Given a predefined tick signal that represents milliseconds, we assemble the watch.

```
let timer = proc (start)
    proc (tick) let count = (start when (last ≤ 1)) default (last - 1)
                | last = pre count start | sync (count, tick)
                in when (last ≤ 1) true
let watch = proc (start)
    proc (tick) let count_seconds = timer(1000) | count_minutes = timer(60)
                | seconds = (reset (when start count_seconds) count_seconds)(tick)
                | minutes = (reset (when start count_minutes) count_minutes)(seconds)
                in seconds | minutes
```

Fig. 5. The timer and the watch

3 Temporal Invariants

As outlined in the operational semantics, the execution of processes requires the resolution of temporal relations between signals in order to ensure the respect of synchronization constraints. Determining clock relations is usually specified in terms of a *clock calculus* [2]. A clock calculus abstracts a process by a system of boolean equations which denotes the temporal relations between signals. This system must be satisfiable in order to accept the process as an executable specification. In the spirit of an effect system [18], we express both temporal and causal invariants of synchronous processes within an expressive type system.

Type System A type τ is either a data-type bool, a type variable α, a composition $\tau \times \tau'$, a process type $\tau \rightarrow \tau'$ (of input τ and output τ'). The type of a signal x is represented by a data-type τ annotated with a clock κ. The data-type τ denotes the structure of values transported by the signal and the clock κ denotes the discrete set of instants at which data are present. A clock κ is represented by a boolean polynomial which denotes a discrete set of instants. A clock is either 0 (which denotes absence), 1 (which denotes over-sampling), a clock variable δ (which denotes a set of instants), the additive $\kappa + \kappa'$ (equivalent to the proposition $(\kappa \wedge \neg\kappa') \vee (\kappa' \wedge \neg\kappa)$), which denotes the disjoint union of the instants denoted by κ and κ', or the multiplicative $\kappa \times \kappa'$ (equivalent to $\kappa \wedge \kappa'$), which denotes the intersection of the instants denoted by κ and κ'.

$\tau ::= \mathsf{bool} \mid \alpha \mid \tau \rightarrow \tau' \mid \tau \times \tau' \mid \tau_\kappa$	type
$\kappa ::= 0 \mid 1 \mid \delta \mid \kappa + \kappa' \mid \kappa \times \kappa'$	clock
$\sigma ::= \tau \mid \forall\alpha.\sigma \mid \forall\delta.\sigma \mid \exists!\delta.\sigma$	type scheme
$\Gamma \ni (x : \sigma_\kappa),\ \Delta \ni \delta$	hypothesis

$$\overline{\Gamma}(\Delta, \tau_\kappa) = \exists\Delta\backslash\Delta'.[\forall(\mathrm{ftv}(\tau)\backslash\mathrm{ftv}(\Gamma)).\forall(\Delta'\backslash\Delta).\exists!(\Delta\cap\Delta').\tau_\kappa] s.t. \Delta' = \mathrm{fcv}(\tau)\backslash\mathrm{fcv}(\Gamma)\backslash\mathrm{fcv}(\kappa)$$

Fig. 6. Type system

We refer to the type hypothesis Γ as a relation between signals names and polymorphic types. We refer to the control hypothesis Δ as a set of abstract clocks introduced for sampling signals (e.g., example 3). A polymorphic type σ denotes the family of all types of a signal. It is universally quantified over free type variables (written $\forall\alpha.\sigma$) and clock variables (written $\forall\delta.\sigma$) and existentially quantified over its free abstract clock variables (written $\exists!\delta.\sigma$). The generalization $\overline{\Gamma}(\Delta, \tau_\kappa)$ of the type τ_κ of a signal with respect to the type hypothesis Γ and the control hypothesis Δ is a pair $\exists\Delta''.\sigma_\kappa$ consisting of the polymorphic type of the signal and of the context-sensitive control hypothesis (i.e. which refer to signals defined in Γ). A polymorphic type σ_κ is constructed by universally quantifying τ_κ with the set of its *context-free* type variable $\alpha_{1..m}$ (i.e. free in τ but not in Γ) and clock variables $\Delta'\backslash\Delta$ (i.e. free in τ, but neither in Γ nor in κ), and by existentially quantifying it with its set of context-free control hypothesis $\Delta \cap \Delta'$ (i.e. free both in τ and Δ, but neither in Γ or κ). *Context-sensitive* control-hypothesis $\Delta'' = \Delta \backslash \Delta'$ remains. The relation of instantiation, written $\exists\Delta.\tau_\kappa \preceq \sigma_\kappa$ means that τ belongs to the family σ given the control hypothesis Δ. A pair $\exists\Delta''.\tau_\kappa$ is an instance of the polymorphic type $\forall\alpha_{1..m}\forall\Delta\exists!\Delta'.\tau'_\kappa$ iff τ equals τ' modulo a substitution from $\alpha_{1..m}$ to $\tau_{1..m}$, a substitution from Δ to $\kappa_{1..n}$ and a bijection from Δ' to Δ''.

Inference system The sequent $\Delta, \Gamma \vdash e:\tau$ inductively defines the type and clock of expressions e given hypothesis Γ and Δ. The rule (let) typechecks the definition e of a signal x with the type hypothesis Γ by giving it a type τ_κ and control hypothesis Δ. Then, the type of x is generalized as $\exists\Delta'.\sigma_\kappa$ with respect to Γ. The expression e' is then typechecked with $\Gamma \uplus (x, \sigma_\kappa)$ to built the type τ' and the control hypothesis Δ'' of e'. The conclusion accepts let e in e' as well-typed with $\Delta' \uplus \Delta''$. In the rule (var), the control hypothesis Δ introduced by instantiating the polymorphic type $\Gamma(x)$ of a signal x to τ are added to the sequent. The rule (par) for the composition $e \mid e'$ accepts two well-typed expressions e and e' and merge the disjoint control hypothesis Δ and Δ' introduced by e and e'. The rule (abs) introduces a type hypothesis τ' for x in order to accepts e as well-typed with Δ and τ. Since a process is a value, it can be assigned any clock κ provided that all signals y free in e are present (i.e. at clock κ'). The rule (app) checks the application of a process e to a signal e'. The type τ' of e' must match that expected as formal parameter by the result of e. However, no output can be present if the process itself is absent. Therefore, the clock of the output τ must be combined with κ: the presence of an output requires the presence of e (at the clock κ). This requirement is written $\tau \times \kappa$ and defined by $(\tau_\kappa) \times \kappa' = \tau_{\kappa\times\kappa'}$ and $(\tau_{1..n}) \times \kappa = (\tau_1 \times \kappa) \times \ldots (\tau_n \times \kappa)$. The types of sync and pre mean that input and output are synchronous at clock κ. The types of reset and default mean that the output is present at the clock $\kappa \vee \kappa'$ of both inputs. The clock of when defines an existentially quantified clock δ which abstracts the instants at which its first argument is present with the value true. The result is present when that clock intersects with that of the second argument: $\delta \times \kappa'$.

$$\frac{\Delta, \Gamma \vdash e:(\tau' \to \tau)_\kappa \quad \Delta', \Gamma \vdash e':\tau'}{\Delta \uplus \Delta', \Gamma \vdash e(e'):\tau \times \kappa}\ (\text{app}) \qquad \frac{\Delta, \Gamma \vdash e:\tau \quad \Delta', \Gamma \vdash e':\tau'}{\Delta \uplus \Delta', \Gamma \vdash e \mid e':\tau \times \tau'}\ (\text{par})$$

$$\frac{\exists\Delta.\tau \preceq \Gamma(x)}{\Delta, \Gamma \vdash x:\tau}\ (\text{var}) \qquad \frac{\Delta, \Gamma \vdash e:\tau \quad \Delta, \Gamma \vdash e':\tau' \quad \Delta'', \Gamma \vdash p:\tau \to \tau' \to \tau''}{\Delta \uplus \Delta' \uplus \Delta'', \Gamma \vdash p\ e\ e':\tau''}\ (\text{pvs})$$

$$\frac{\Delta, \Gamma \uplus (x, \tau') \vdash e:\tau}{\Delta, \Gamma \vdash \mathsf{proc}\, x\, e:(\tau' \to \tau)_{\kappa\times\kappa'}}\ (\text{abs}) \quad s.t.\ \kappa' = \Pi^{y \in fv(e)\setminus\{x\}}_{(y,\sigma_{\kappa''})\in\Gamma}\ \kappa''$$

$$\frac{\Delta, \Gamma \uplus (x, \tau_\kappa) \vdash e:\tau_\kappa \quad \Delta'', \Gamma \uplus (x, \sigma_\kappa) \vdash e':\tau'}{\Delta' \uplus \Delta'', \Gamma \vdash \mathsf{let}\ x = e\ \mathsf{in}\ e':\tau'}\ (\text{let}) \quad s.t.\ \overline{\Gamma}(\Delta, \tau_\kappa) = \exists\Delta'.\sigma_\kappa$$

$$\begin{array}{ll} \Gamma \vdash b:\mathsf{bool}_\kappa & \Gamma \vdash \mathsf{default}:\tau_\kappa \to \tau_{\kappa'} \to \tau_{\kappa\vee\kappa'} \\ \Gamma \vdash \mathsf{pre}:\tau_\kappa \to \tau_\kappa \to \tau_\kappa & \Gamma \vdash \mathsf{reset}:\tau_\kappa \to \tau_{\kappa'} \to \tau_{\kappa\vee\kappa'\vee\kappa''} \\ \Gamma \vdash \mathsf{sync}:\tau_\kappa \to \tau'_\kappa \to \mathsf{unit}_\kappa & \exists!\delta, \Gamma \vdash \mathsf{when}:\mathsf{bool}_{\delta+\kappa} \to \tau_{\kappa'} \to \tau_{\delta\times\kappa'} \end{array}$$

Fig. 7. Inference system $\Delta, \Gamma \vdash e:\tau$

Example 2. How do these considerations translate in the example of the timer? Since count, tick are synchronous, they share the same clock κ'. This clock is down-sampled in order to produce timeout signals. Hence, it it composed of an abstract clock δ and of a disjoint sub-clock κ, i.e., $\kappa' = \delta + \kappa$.

```
let count = (start when (last ≤ 1)) default (last − 1)   int_{δ+κ}
|   last = pre count start | sync(count, tick)           int_{δ+κ}
in  when (last ≤ 1) true                                 bool_δ
```

What is the polymorphic type of the timer process? It has parameters start and tick which we said are of clock $\delta + \kappa$. The result is of clock δ. Since both δ and κ are context-free, we can generalize them (i.e. by considering $\kappa = \delta'$). In each place the timer is used (e.g. for sampling seconds and minutes in the watch), its existentially quantified clock receives a fresh instance, in order to distinguish it from other clocks. In the case of the watch, we actually have $\kappa_1 = \kappa_2 + \delta_2$.

$$\begin{array}{rl} \mathsf{timer}: & \exists!\delta, \forall\delta'.(\mathsf{int}_{\delta+\delta'} \rightarrow (\mathsf{bool}_{\delta+\delta'} \rightarrow \mathsf{bool}_{\delta})_{\delta+\delta'})_{\kappa''} \\ \delta_1 \vdash \mathsf{timer(60)}: & (\mathsf{bool}_{\delta_1+\kappa_1} \rightarrow \mathsf{bool}_{\delta_1})_{\delta_1+\kappa_1} \\ \delta_1, \delta_2 \vdash \mathsf{timer(100)}: & (\mathsf{bool}_{\delta_2+\kappa_2} \rightarrow \mathsf{bool}_{\delta_2})_{\delta_2+\kappa_2} \end{array}$$

4 Causal Invariants

The clock calculus allows the compilation of parallelism within a process by defining a hierarchy of tasks according to clock relations [1] (see section 5). To generate executable code, additional information on the causal dependencies between signals is needed in order to serialize the emission of outputs in each task. In SIGNAL, this information is obtained by a flow analysis [2]. This analysis detects cyclic causal dependencies, which may incur dead-locks at runtime. Similarly, higher-order processes may define "instantaneously" recursive processes. Just as cyclic causal dependencies between first-order signals may denote dead-locks, cyclic higher-order processes may denote non-terminating processes. We address the issue of determining causal relation between signals by generalizing the flow analysis of SIGNAL in terms of an effect system (e.g., [18]) which relates each signal to the set of signals ϕ required for its computation (e.g. in $x = y + z$, x requires y and z).

Causality Inference A causality flow ϕ is either a variable φ (which identifies a signal) or an assembly φ, ϕ (which identifies signals ϕ that φ depends on). Flows are right-idempotent (i.e. $\varphi, \phi, \phi = \varphi, \phi$) and right-commutative (i.e. $\varphi, \phi, \phi' = \varphi, \phi', \phi$). A substitution $[\phi/\varphi]$ is defined by $(\varphi', \phi')[\phi/\varphi] = (\varphi'[\phi/\varphi]), (\phi'[\phi/\varphi])$. We reuse the symbols τ, σ and Γ to name flow-annotated types and environments. We write $\overline{\Gamma}(\tau^{\phi})$ for the generalization of a type τ^{ϕ} over its set of free type and flow variables.

$$\phi ::= \varphi \mid \varphi, \phi \quad \text{flow} \qquad \tau ::= \ldots \mid \tau^{\phi} \quad \text{type} \qquad \sigma ::= \ldots \mid \forall\varphi.\sigma \quad \text{scheme}$$

Fig. 8. Types and causalities τ^{ϕ}

$$\overline{\Gamma}(\tau^{\phi}) = \forall\alpha_{1..m}.\forall\varphi_{1..n}.\tau^{\phi} \;\textit{where}\; \alpha_{1..m} = \mathrm{ftv}(\tau)\backslash\mathrm{ftv}(\Gamma) \;\textit{and}\; \varphi_{1..n} = \mathrm{ffv}(\tau)\backslash\mathrm{ffv}(\Gamma)\backslash\mathrm{ffv}(\phi)$$

Fig. 9. Generalization $\overline{\Gamma}(\tau^{\phi})$

The sequent $\Gamma \Vdash e : \tau$ checks that the flow hypothesis Γ is consistent with the assertion that e has flow and type τ. The rule (var) allows the instantiation of the polymorphic flow type $\Gamma(x)$ of a signal x by a monomorphic flow type τ. In the rule (par), the expressions e and e' may have different flows. The rules (let), (abs) and (app) are structurally equivalent to those of the clock calculus.

We write $(\tau^{\phi}) \times \phi' = \tau^{\phi,\phi'}$ and $(\tau_{1..n}) \times \phi = (\tau_1 \times \phi) \times \ldots (\tau_n \times \phi)$. The type of pre denotes no causality from the inputs (flows ϕ and ϕ') to the output ϕ''. The type of when denotes a causal dependency from the second input (flow ϕ) to the output (flow ϕ'', ϕ). The type of default denotes a causality from the inputs (ϕ and ϕ') to the output (ϕ'', ϕ, ϕ').

$$\frac{\Gamma \uplus (x, \tau^{\phi}) \Vdash e : \tau^{\phi} \quad \Gamma \uplus (x, \overline{\Gamma}(\tau^{\phi})) \Vdash e' : \tau'}{\Gamma \Vdash \mathsf{let}\ x = e\ \mathsf{in}\ e' : \tau'}\ (\text{let}) \qquad \frac{\Gamma \Vdash e : (\tau' \to \tau)^{\phi} \quad \Gamma \Vdash e' : \tau'}{\Gamma \Vdash e(e') : \tau \times \phi}\ (\text{app}) \qquad \frac{\Gamma \Vdash e : \tau \quad \Gamma \Vdash e' : \tau'}{\Gamma \Vdash e \mid e' : \tau \times \tau'}\ (\text{par})$$

$$\frac{\tau \preceq \Gamma(x)}{\Gamma \Vdash x : \tau}\ (\text{var}) \qquad \frac{\Gamma \Vdash e : \tau \quad \Gamma \Vdash e' : \tau' \quad \Gamma \Vdash p : \tau \to \tau' \to \tau''}{\Gamma \Vdash p\ e\ e' : \tau''}\ (\text{pvs})$$

$$\frac{\Gamma \uplus (x, \tau') \Vdash e : \tau}{\Gamma \Vdash \mathsf{proc}\, x\, e : (\tau' \to \tau)^{\phi,\phi'}}\ (\text{abs}) \quad s.t.\ \phi' = \bigcup_{(y, \sigma^{\phi''}) \in \Gamma}^{y \in fv(e) \setminus \{x\}} \phi''$$

$$\Gamma \Vdash \mathsf{bool}^{\phi} \qquad \Gamma \Vdash \mathsf{sync} : \tau^{\phi} \to \tau'^{\phi'} \to \mathsf{unit}^{\phi''} \qquad \Gamma \Vdash \mathsf{default} : \tau^{\phi} \to \tau^{\phi'} \to \tau^{\phi'',\phi,\phi'}$$

$$\Gamma \Vdash \mathsf{pre} : \tau^{\phi} \to \tau^{\phi'} \to \tau^{\phi''} \qquad \Gamma \Vdash \mathsf{reset} : \tau^{\phi} \to \tau^{\phi'} \to \tau^{\phi'',\phi,\phi'} \qquad \Gamma \Vdash \mathsf{when} : \mathsf{bool}^{\phi'} \to \tau^{\phi} \to \tau^{\phi'',\phi}$$

Fig. 10. Inference system $\Gamma \Vdash e : \tau$

Example 3. The information inferred by the causality calculus is depicted below for the process timer. Each signal is assigned a record that contains the flow variable that identifies it (form φ_1 to φ_5) and the flow of signals required for its computation. A linear checking of the equations in the process allows to infer the needed information. For instance count (flow φ_3) requires start (flow φ_1) or last (flow φ_4). Hence, its flow is $\varphi_3, \varphi_1, \varphi_4$. The signature of timer in the flow calculus is $\mathsf{int}^{\varphi_1} \to \mathsf{bool}^{\varphi_2} \to \mathsf{bool}^{\varphi_5}$.

$$\begin{bmatrix} \mathsf{start} : \mathsf{int}^{\varphi_1} \\ \mathsf{tick} : \mathsf{bool}^{\varphi_2} \end{bmatrix} \Vdash \begin{array}{ll} \mathsf{let\ count} = (\mathsf{start\ when\ (last} \leq 1)) \mathsf{\ default\ (last} - 1) & \mathsf{int}^{\varphi_3,\varphi_1,\varphi_4} \\ \mid\ \mathsf{last} = \mathsf{pre\ count\ start} \mid \mathsf{sync(count, tick)} & \mathsf{int}^{\varphi_4} \\ \mathsf{in\ when\ (last} \leq 1)\ \mathsf{true} & \mathsf{bool}^{\varphi_5} \end{array}$$

5 Formal Properties

Typing rules are now required for reasoning on evaluated expressions r: axioms to mean that the absence has any type, clock and flow and rules for sequences.

$$\Delta, \Gamma \vdash \mathsf{abs} : \tau_{\kappa} \qquad \Gamma \Vdash \mathsf{abs} : \tau^{\phi} \qquad \frac{\Delta, \Gamma \vdash r : \tau \quad \Delta', \Gamma \vdash r' : \tau'}{\Delta \uplus \Delta', \Gamma \vdash (r, r') : \tau \times \tau'} \qquad \frac{\Gamma \Vdash r : \tau \quad \Gamma \Vdash r' : \tau'}{\Gamma \Vdash (r, r') : \tau \times \tau'}$$

Fig. 11. Typing rules $\Delta, \Gamma \vdash r : \tau$ and $\Gamma \Vdash r : \tau$ for results

Consistency We establish a consistency relation between environments E and hypothesis Δ, Γ to express the fact that clock relations model synchronizations and causality relations model data dependencies.

Definition 1 (Consistency). We write $\Delta, \Gamma \vdash E$ iff $\mathrm{dom}(E) = \mathrm{dom}(\Gamma)$ and for all $(x, r) \in E$ there exists $\exists \Delta'.\tau_{\kappa} \preceq \Gamma(x)$ such that $\Delta \supseteq \Delta'$, $\Delta \vdash v : \tau_{\kappa}$ and, for all $(x', r') \in E$ and $(x' : \sigma'_{\kappa'}) \in \Gamma$, $\kappa \geq \kappa'$ implies ($r = \mathsf{abs}$ iff $r' = \mathsf{abs}$). We write $\Gamma \Vdash E$ iff $\mathrm{dom}(E) = \mathrm{dom}(\Gamma)$ and for all $(x, r) \in E$ there exists $\tau^{\phi} \preceq \Gamma(x)$ such that $\Vdash v : \tau^{\phi}$ and, there exists $(x', r') \in E$ and $(x' : \sigma'^{\phi'}) \in \Gamma$ such that $\phi \supseteq \phi'$ implies ($r = \mathsf{abs}$ iff $r' = \mathsf{abs}$).

Invariance The theorem 1 states the invariance of temporal and causal properties determined by the inference systems with respect to a step in the operational semantics. It says that, if a system e is well-typed, given well-typed inputs E and executed, then the outputs $\tilde{r}$ and final state e' have same type.

Theorem 1. *If $\Delta, \Gamma \vdash e : \tau$, $\Delta, \Gamma \vdash E$ and $E \vdash e \xrightarrow{\tilde{r}} e'$ then $\Delta, \Gamma \vdash \tilde{r} : \tau$ and $\Delta, \Gamma \vdash e' : \tau$. If $\Gamma \Vdash e : \tau$, $\Gamma \Vdash E$ and $E \vdash e \xrightarrow{\tilde{r}} e'$ then $\Gamma \Vdash \tilde{r} : \tau$ and $\Gamma \Vdash e' : \tau$.*

The proof of theorem 1 requires a substitution lemma in which θ stands for a substitution of type variables α by types τ, of clock variables δ by clocks κ and of flow variables φ by flows ϕ.

Lemma 1. *If $\Delta, \Gamma \vdash e : \tau$ then $\Delta, \theta\Gamma \vdash e : \theta\tau$ for all θ s.t. $\Delta = \theta\Delta$. If $\Gamma \Vdash e : \tau$ then $\theta\Gamma \Vdash e : \theta\tau$ for all θ.*

Endochrony Endochrony refers to the Ancient Greek: "$\varepsilon\nu\delta o$", and literally means "time defined from the inside". An endochronous expression e defines a reactive system where "time defined from the inside" translates into the property that the production of its outputs only depends on the presence of its inputs. An endochronous system reacts to inputs (by having clocks computable from that of its inputs) and terminates within a predictable amount of time (by avoiding deadlocks and recursions). Hierarchization is the implementation of endochrony. It is the medium used in SIGNAL for compiling parallelism [1]. It consists of organizing the environment Γ as a tree Θ that defines a correct scheduling of computations into tasks. Each node of the tree consists of synchronous signals. It denotes the task of computing them when the clock is active. Each relation of a node with a sub-tree represents a sub-task of smaller clock. A tree of tasks being computed, expressions in each task can be serialized by following the causal relations determined by the flow analysis.

Example 4. A good example of exochronous specification is the expression count = (start when (last $\leq$ 1)) default (last $-$ 1) of the timer. Out of its context, it may be possible to give the signal count clock $\kappa_{\mathsf{c}} = (\kappa_{\mathsf{s}}) \vee (\kappa + \delta)$ given $\kappa_{\mathsf{l}} = \kappa + \delta$ the clock of last. Endochrony is achieved by synchronizing count with start and last (with the pre statement) and count with the input tick (the sync statement). This hierarchizes the output of the timer w.r.t. the input tick and all local signals.

We express the property of hierarchization as a relation $\mathcal{H}_\Delta(\Gamma, \kappa)$ between the clock κ of an expression e and its environment Δ, Γ.

Definition 2 (Hierarchization). The clock κ is hierarchizable in Δ, Γ, written $\mathcal{H}_\Delta(\Gamma, \kappa)$ iff $\kappa \neq 0$, $\kappa \neq 1$ and there exists $(x, \sigma_{\kappa'}) \in \Gamma$ such that $\kappa \leq \kappa'$ and $\kappa' \not\leq \Sigma_{\delta \in \Delta}\delta$. We write $\mathcal{H}_\Delta(\Gamma, \tau)$ iff all clocks κ occurring free in τ satisfy $\mathcal{H}_\Delta(\Gamma, \kappa)$.

The property of deadlock-freedom $\mathcal{A}$ resources to flow annotations. It means that a signal $(x, \sigma^{\varphi, \phi}) \in \Gamma$ s.t. $\varphi \in \phi$ may be defined by a fixed-point equation. This means that its computation may dead-lock (e.g. let $x = x + 1$) or may not terminate (e.g. let $f = \mathsf{proc}\, x\, f(x)$).

Definition 3 (Cycle-Freedom). The flow φ, ϕ is acyclic, written $\mathcal{A}(\varphi, \phi)$, iff $\varphi \notin \phi$. We write $\mathcal{A}(\tau)$ iff all flows ϕ occurring in τ satisfy $\mathcal{A}(\phi)$.

Given $\mathcal{H}$ and $\mathcal{A}$, we define endochrony as an inductive and decidable property.

Definition 4 (Endochrony). A judgments satisfy $\mathcal{E}[\![\Gamma \Vdash e:\tau]\!]$ iff $\mathcal{A}(\tau)$. A proof tree $P/\Gamma \Vdash e:\tau$ (resp. $P'/\Delta, \Gamma \vdash e:\tau$) is endochronous iff P (resp. P') is endochronous and $\mathcal{E}[\![\Gamma \Vdash e:\tau]\!]$ (resp. $\mathcal{E}[\![\Delta, \Gamma \vdash e:\tau]\!]$). A system e is endochronous iff it has endochronous proofs $P/\Gamma \Vdash e:\tau$ and $P'/\Delta, \Gamma \vdash e:\tau$.

$$\mathcal{E}[\![\Delta, \Gamma \vdash x:\tau]\!] \text{ iff } \mathcal{H}_\Delta(\Gamma, \tau) \quad \mathcal{E}[\![\Delta \uplus \Delta', \Gamma \vdash e(e'):\tau]\!] \text{ iff } \mathcal{H}_\Delta(\Gamma, \tau)$$

$$\mathcal{E}[\![\Delta, \Gamma \vdash e \mid e':\tau]\!] \text{ iff } \mathcal{H}_\Delta(\Gamma, \tau) \quad \mathcal{E}[\![\Delta, \Gamma \vdash \mathsf{let}\ x = e\ \mathsf{in}\ e':\tau']\!] \text{ iff } \Delta, \Gamma \uplus (x:\tau) \vdash e:\tau$$

$$\mathcal{E}[\![\Delta, \Gamma \vdash \mathsf{proc}\, x\, e:\tau]\!] \text{ iff } \mathcal{H}_\Delta(\Gamma^{\{x\} \cup fv(e)}, \tau) \qquad \textit{and } \mathcal{H}_\Delta(\Gamma, \tau),\ \mathcal{H}_\Delta(\Gamma, \tau')$$

Fig. 12. Endochrony $\mathcal{E}[\![\Delta, \Gamma \Vdash e:\tau]\!]$

Example 5. An example of non-endochronous specification is $\mathsf{x} + (\mathsf{x}\ \mathsf{when}\ \mathsf{x} > 0)$. It requires $x : \exists\delta.\mathsf{int}_\delta$ to reflect that x is present iff $x > 0$ (i.e. at the abstract clock δ). If $x \leq 0$, the expression deadlocks. As in SIGNAL, our definition of endochrony allows to detect and rejects such a constrained specification.

Safety The theorem 1 and the property of endochrony characterize the expressions e which "cannot go wrong".

Theorem 2. *If E and e are endochronous (with $\Delta, \Gamma \vdash E$, $\Gamma \Vdash E$, $\Gamma \Vdash e:\tau$ and $\Delta, \Gamma \vdash e:\tau$) then $E \vdash e \xrightarrow{\tilde{r}} e'$ and $\tilde{r}$ and e' are endochronous.*

6 Implementation

We can easily derive an algorithm $\mathrm{inf}(\Delta', \Gamma)[\![e]\!] = (\Delta, \tau, \theta)$ from the inference system. It constructs a set of constants Δ, a type τ and a substitution θ on types and clock variables from an initial Δ', a set of type hypothesis Γ and an expression e. Whereas the clock calculus introduces clocks κ and types τ, the inference system introduces fresh variables δ and α. Whereas the clock calculus specifies type matches, the inference system determines equations $\tau' =^? \tau''$ to be unified. The equational problem $\tau' =^? \tau''$ is decomposed in the resolution of equations on data-types and on clocks. Unification of boolean clock equations is decidable and unitary (i.e. boolean equations have a unique most general unifier [12]). In inf, we refer to $\mathrm{mgu}_\Delta(\kappa =^? \kappa')$ as the boolean unification algorithm of [12] determining the most general unifier of the equation $\kappa =^? \kappa'$ with constants Δ. Similarly, causality information φ, ϕ is represented by a simple form of extensible record [16] of prefix φ and members ϕ, for which we know the resolution of equations $\phi =^? \phi'$ to be a decidable and unitary equational problem. A clever implementation of our type system would account for the simplification of clock and flow annotations by resourcing to eliminations rules for clocks: $\Delta, \Gamma \vdash e:\tau$ iff $\Delta \uplus \delta, \Gamma \vdash e:\tau$ and $\delta \notin \mathrm{fcv}(\Gamma, \tau)$; and for flows: $\Gamma \Vdash e:\tau^\phi$ iff $\Gamma \Vdash e:\tau^{\phi,\varphi}$ and $\varphi \notin \mathrm{left}(\Gamma, \tau, \phi)$ (s.t.$\mathrm{left}(\varphi, \phi) = \{\varphi\}$). Showing that the inference of types, clocks and flows reduces to solving a system of boolean and record equations demonstrates its decidability.

7 Related Work

Contemporary work demonstrated the practicality of higher-order programming languages for the design of circuits (e.g. LAVA [4], HAWK [13]). Our type-theoretical modeling of synchronous interaction would find an interesting application in serving as a medium for specifying behavioral abstractions of circuit components in such systems. The introduction of LUCID-synchrone [6] was a first step towards the generalization of the principles of synchronous programming to higher-order languages. The proposal of [6] is a model of synchronous recursive functions over lazy streams. Our programming model is co-iterative and implements exochronous operators (i.e. when and default, as in SIGNAL). The clock calculus of [6] uses symbolic types c annotated with expressions ($c \textsf{ on } e$, $c \xrightarrow{x} c'$). The use dependent types limits the expression of decidable clock relations (i.e. $c \geq c \textsf{ on } e$), of polymorphism (e.g. for eliminating let-bound identifiers x), imposes restrictions for typing functions $\lambda x.e$ (i.e. the x must be universally quantifiable). As types contain expressions and expressions model state transitions, specifying invariants under subject reduction becomes sophisticated ([6, Theorem 1] states the preservation of typability under reduction). Our type system proposes a both simpler and more expressive representation of both the temporal and causal invariants of synchronous processes. Other approaches for characterizing reactivity are proposed in [10], where an intuitive and expressive numerical model of time is presented for determining length-preserving recursive list functions in a purely functional language. Other interpretations of reactivity, mainly consisting of a programming model, are the object-oriented approach of [5], the functional approach of [15], or the transposition of synchronous programming paradigms under the concept of concurrent constraints in [17], or the notion of continuous time employed in [7]. None of the frameworks considered in [6, 10, 7, 15, 17] characterize the property of *endochrony* for reactive systems.

8 Conclusions

Our main contribution is to transpose the notion of *endochrony*, as modelled in SIGNAL, in the context of a higher-order and typed synchronous programming model. We introduce an expressive type system for specifying the temporal and causal relations between events. This system generalizes previous studies on clock calculi [2] in terms of effect systems [18]. It implements an abstraction of the temporal invariants of signals using boolean expressions, called *clocks*. A subject reduction property (section 5, theorem 1) states the correctness of clock invariants. A property of *hierarchization* and of *deadlock-freedom* allows to decide a safety property (theorem 2) and to characterize the compilation of parallelism in a process as the organization of its expressions as a tree of serialized actions. Our approach generalizes the semantics of equational synchronous programming languages (such as LUSTRE or SIGNAL) for the support higher-order processes. It allows to express the dynamic configuration and the generic specification of reactive system components while preserving the hypotheses on the synchrony of communications and on the instantaneousness of computations.

References

1. T. P. Amagbegnon, L. Besnard, P. Le Guernic. Implementation of the data-flow synchronous language SIGNAL. In *Conference on Programming Language Design and Implementation.* ACM, 1995.
2. A. Benveniste, P. Le Guernic, C. Jacquemot. Synchronous programming with events and relations: the SIGNAL language and its semantics. In *Science of Computer Programming,* v. 16, 1991.
3. G. Berry, G. Gonthier. The ESTEREL synchronous programming language: design, semantics, implementation. In *Science of Computer Programming,* v. 19, 1992.
4. P. Bjesse, K. Claessen, M. Sheeran. LAVA: hardware design in HASKELL. In *International Conference on Functional Programming.* ACM, 1998.
5. F. Boussinot. ICOBJ programming. *Technical report* n. 3028. INRIA, 1996.
6. P. Caspi, M. Pouzet. Synchronous Kahn networks. In *International Conference on Functional Programming.* ACM, 1996.
7. C. Elliott, P. Hudak. Functional reactive animation. In *proceedings of the International Conference on Functional Programming.* ACM, 1997.
8. C. Fournet, G. Gonthier. The reflexive CHAM and the join calculus. In *Symposium on Principles of Programming Languages.* ACM Press, 1996.
9. N. Halbwachs, P. Caspi, P. Raymond, D. Pilaud. The synchronous data-flow programming language LUSTRE. In *Proceedings of the* IEEE, v. 79(9). IEEE, 1991.
10. J. Hughes, L. Pareto, A. Sabry. Proving the correctness of reactive systems using sized types. In *Symposium on Principles of Programming Languages.* ACM, 1996.
11. T. Jensen. Clock analysis of synchronous dataflow programs. In *Symposium on Partial Evaluation and Semantics-Based Program Manipulation.* ACM, 1995.
12. U. Martin, T. Nipkow. Unification in boolean rings. In *Journal of Automated Reasoning,* v. 4. Kluwer Academic Press, 1988.
13. J. Matthews, B. Cook, J. Launchburry. Microprocessor specification in HAWK. In *International Conference on Computer Languages.* IEEE, 1998.
14. R. Milner, J. Parrow, D. Walker. A calculus of mobile processes. In *Information and Computation.* Academic Press, 1992.
15. R. Pucella. Reactive programming in STANDARD ML. In *International Conference on Computer Languages.* IEEE, 1998.
16. D. Remi. Type inference for records in a natural extension of ML. *Research report n. 1431.* INRIA, 1991.
17. V. Saraswat, R. Jagadeesan, V. Gupta. Foundation of timed concurrent constraint programming. In *Symposium on Logic in Computer Science.* IEEE, 1994.
18. J.-P. Talpin, P. Jouvelot. The type and effect discipline. In *Information and Computation,* v. 111(2). Academic Press, 1994.

Testing Theories for Asynchronous Languages *

Ilaria Castellani[1] and Matthew Hennessy[2]

[1] INRIA, BP 93, 06902 Sophia-Antipolis Cedex, France
[2] COGS, University of Sussex, Brighton BN1 9QH, UK

Abstract. We study testing preorders for an asynchronous version of *CCS* called *TACCS*, where message emission is non blocking. We first give a labelled transition system semantics for this language, which includes both external and internal choice operators. By applying the standard definitions of may and must testing to this semantics we obtain two behavioural preorders based on asynchronous observations, $\sqsubseteq_{may}$ and $\sqsubseteq_{must}$. We present alternative behavioural characterisations of these preorders, which are subsequently used to obtain equational theories for the finite fragment of the language.

1 Introduction

The asynchronous π-calculus [5, 9] is a very simple but powerful formalism for describing distributed and mobile processes, based on the asynchronous exchange of names. Its descriptive power as a programming calculus has been demonstrated theoretically in papers such as [5, 9, 10, 13] and practically in [14], where a minor variant takes the role of the target implementation language for the sophisticated distributed and higher-order programming language *Pict*.

However a calculus should not only be computationally expressive. The most successful process calculi, such as *CCS* [12], on which the asynchronous π-calculus is based, *CSP* [8] and *ACP* [2], also come equipped with a powerful equational theory with which one may reason about the behaviour of processes. For the asynchronous π-calculus, much work still remains to be done in developing suitable equational theories; to our knowledge the only proposed axiomatisations concern a variation of strong bisimulation equivalence called *strong asynchronous bisimulation*[1] and an asynchronous version of *may testing* [4].

A major attraction of the asynchronous π-calculus is its simplicity. In spite of its expressive power, it consists of very few process combinators: blocking input and non blocking output on a named channel, parallelism, recursion, and the powerful scoping mechanism for channels from the standard π-calculus. But operators which may be of limited attraction from a computational point of view can play a significant role in an equational theory. The choice operator + of *CCS* is a typical example. In this paper we demonstrate that such operators can also help in providing interesting behavioural theories for asynchronous languages.

---

* Research partially funded by the EU Working Group CONFER II and the EU HCM Network EXPRESS. The second author was also supported by the EPSRC project GR/K60701.

We examine a simplification of the asynchronous π-calculus, an asynchronous variant of *CCS* equipped with internal and external choice operators, which we call *TACCS* ; essentially an asynchronous version of the language studied in [7]. In Section 2 we define an operational semantics for *TACCS* . In the following section we apply the standard definitions of *testing* to this operational semantics to obtain two preorders on asynchronous processes [6, 7], the *may* testing preorder $\sqsubseteq_{may}$ and the *must* testing preorder $\sqsubseteq_{must}$. The main result of this section is an alternative characterisation of these contextual preorders, defined in terms of properties of the operational semantics of processes. These characterisations are similar in style to those for the corresponding preorders on the synchronous version of the language, studied in [7], but at least for the *must* case, are considerably more subtle. In Section 4 we present our main result, namely an equational characterisation of the preorder $\sqsubseteq_{must}$ for the finitary part of *TACCS*; the extension to recursion can be handled using standard techniques. In the full paper we also give an axiomatisation of $\sqsubseteq_{may}$, along the lines of that proposed in [4] for a variant of our language. Here we outline the equational characterisation of the must preorder: this requires the standard theory of internal and external choice [7], the axioms for asynchrony used in [1], a law accounting for the interplay between output and choice, and three new conditional equations.

The paper ends with a brief conclusion and comparison with related work. In this extended abstract all proofs are omitted. They may be found in the full version of the paper.

2 The language and operational semantics

Given the set Names ranged over by a, b, c, we use $\mathsf{Act} = \{\, a, \bar{a} \mid a \in \mathsf{Names} \,\}$ to denote the set of visible actions, and $\mathsf{Act}_\tau = \mathsf{Act} \cup \{\tau\}$ for the set of all actions, ranged over by α, β, γ. The syntax of the language *TACCS* is given by

$$t ::= 0 \mid a.t \mid \widehat{a}.t \mid \bar{a} \mid t \parallel t \mid t \oplus t \mid t + t$$
$$x \in \mathsf{Var} \mid \mathsf{rec}\, x.\, t$$

We have the empty process 0, two choice operators, external choice + and internal choice $\oplus$, parallelism $\parallel$ and recursive definitions $\mathsf{rec}\, x.\, t$ from [7]. We also have input prefixing $a.\, t$ and the new construct of *asynchronous output prefixing* $\widehat{a}.\, t$, where the emission on channel a is non blocking for the process t. The atom $\bar{a}$ is introduced to facilitate the semantics of asynchronous output.

We have not included the hiding and renaming constructs from *CCS*; they can be handled in a straighforward manner in our theory and would simply add uninteresting detail to the various definitions. Note however that unlike the version of asynchronous *CCS* considered in [15] or the presentation of the asynchronous π-calculus in [1] we do not require a separate syntactic class of guarded terms; the external choice operator may be applied to arbitrary terms.

As usual the recursion operator binds variables and we shall use p, q, r to denote *closed* terms of *TACCS*, which we often refer to as processes. The usual abbreviations from *CCS* will also be employed, for example omitting trailing occurrences of 0; so e.g. we abbreviate $a.0$ to a.

The operational semantics of processes in *TACCS* is given in Figure 1 (where some obvious symmetric rules are omitted) in terms of three transition relations:

- $p \xrightarrow{a} q$, meaning that p can receive a signal on channel a to become q
- $p \xrightarrow{\bar{a}} q$, meaning that p can asynchronously transmit a signal on channel a to become q
- $p \xrightarrow{\tau} q$, meaning that p can reduce to q after an internal step, possibly a communication

This semantics differs from the standard operational semantics for synchronous *CCS*, given in [7], only for the asynchronous behaviour of outputs. More precisely:

- An asynchronous output prefix $\widehat{a}.p$ can only perform an internal action, whose effect is to spawn off an atom $\overline{a}$ which will then run in parallel with p

$$\widehat{a}.p \xrightarrow{\tau} \overline{a} \parallel p$$

- Only a spawned off atom $\overline{a}$ can emit a signal on channel a

$$\overline{a} \xrightarrow{\bar{a}} 0$$

- Atoms $\overline{a}$ behave asynchronously with respect to external choice $+$: in particular they are not consumed when the choice is resolved. We have for instance

$$\overline{a} + b \xrightarrow{\tau} \overline{a} \parallel 0 \xrightarrow{\bar{a}} 0 \parallel 0$$

We feel that the first two properties correspond to a natural behavioural interpretation of the intuitive idea of non blocking output. The third ensures the asynchrony of output, even in the presence of external choice. Intuitively, asynchronous actions should not affect the behaviour of the rest of the system, e.g. by preventing other actions as would be the case with the usual rule for $+$.

3 Testing asynchronous processes

In this section we apply the standard testing scenario to *TACCS* to obtain asynchronous versions of the *may* and *must* testing preorders. After discussing the difference between synchronous and asynchronous testing we give alternative behavioural characterisations of the preorders.

We first recall the standard definition of testing from [7]. Let ω be a new action representing "success". Then a *test* or *observer* e is simply a process which may contain occurrences of ω. The definitions of the *may* and *must* testing preorders are just the standard ones.

$$\text{Input}\quad \frac{}{a.\,p \xrightarrow{a} p}$$

$$\text{Output}\quad \frac{}{\widehat{a}.\,p \xrightarrow{\tau} \overline{a} \parallel p} \qquad \text{Atom}\quad \frac{}{\overline{a} \xrightarrow{\overline{a}} 0}$$

$$\text{Par}\quad \frac{p \xrightarrow{\alpha} p'}{p \parallel q \xrightarrow{\alpha} p' \parallel q}$$

$$\text{Com}\quad \frac{p \xrightarrow{a} p', \qquad q \xrightarrow{\overline{a}} q'}{p \parallel q \xrightarrow{\tau} p' \parallel q'}$$

$$\text{Int}\quad \frac{}{p \oplus q \xrightarrow{\tau} p} \qquad \frac{}{p \oplus q \xrightarrow{\tau} q}$$

$$\text{Ext}\quad \frac{p \xrightarrow{a} p'}{p + q \xrightarrow{a} p'} \qquad \frac{p \xrightarrow{\tau} p'}{p + q \xrightarrow{\tau} p' + q} \qquad \frac{p \xrightarrow{\overline{a}} p'}{p + q \xrightarrow{\tau} \overline{a} \parallel p'}$$

$$\text{Rec}\quad \frac{}{\mathsf{rec}\, x.\, t \xrightarrow{\tau} t[\mathsf{rec}\, x.\, t/x]}$$

Fig. 1. Operational Semantics

For any process p and test e let

- p may e if there exists a maximal computation
$$e \parallel p = e_0 \parallel p_0 \xrightarrow{\tau} \cdots e_k \parallel p_k \xrightarrow{\tau} \cdots$$
such that $e_n \xrightarrow{\omega}$ for some $n \geq 0$.
- p must e if for every such maximal computation, $e_n \xrightarrow{\omega}$ for some $n \geq 0$.

Then the testing preorders and the induced equivalences are defined as usual:

- $p \sqsubseteq_{may} q$ if p may e implies q may e for every test e
- $p \sqsubseteq_{must} q$ if p must e implies q must e for every test e
- $p \sqsubseteq q$ if $p \sqsubseteq_{may} q$ and $p \sqsubseteq_{must} q$

- $p \simeq_{may} q$ if $p \sqsubseteq_{may} q$ and $q \sqsubseteq_{may} p$
- $p \simeq_{must} q$ if $p \sqsubseteq_{must} q$ and $q \sqsubseteq_{must} p$
- $p \simeq q$ if $p \sqsubseteq q$ and $q \sqsubseteq p$

Note that the definitions of the preorders are formally the same as in the synchronous case [7], but because they are applied to an asynchronous semantics we expect these relations to be weaker. It has been argued in previous work on asynchronous calculi [10, 1], that an *asynchronous observer* should not be capable of observing the inputs of a process, since this would amount to detecting when its own outputs are consumed; indeed this restriction on what can be observed seems to be the essence of asynchrony. In our testing scenario this restriction is automatically enforced; the observer loses control over the inputs of the process being tested because its own output actions are non blocking, and thus in particular they cannot block a success action ω.

Let us look at some examples. In these examples p will always denote the left-hand process and q the right-hand one.

Example 1. $a \sqsubseteq 0$

To see that $p \sqsubseteq_{must} q$, note that in any test that p must pass, an output on a can never block a success action ω. Typically the test $e = \widehat{a}.\,\omega$ cannot serve as a failing test for q as in the synchronous case. So if $p\,\mathsf{must}\,e$ this is because all the internal sequences of e itself lead to success, hence also $q\,\mathsf{must}\,e$. In a similar way one argues that $p \sqsubseteq_{may} q$.

Example 2. $0 \not\sqsubseteq_{must} a$ $\quad$ $0 \sqsubseteq_{may} a$

The distinguishing test in the must case is $(a.\,\omega \,\|\, \overline{a})$.

As this example shows, the tests $(a.\,\omega \,\|\, \overline{a})$ allow inputs to be observed to some extent. In the synchronous case the test normally used to observe the input a is $e = (\omega \oplus \omega) + \overline{a}$. However with our "asynchronous" rule for $+$ the test e could silently move to $\overline{a}$, and thus fail for every process. Note that the asynchronous test $(a.\,\omega \,\|\, \overline{a})$ is weaker than the corresponding test e in the synchronous case: it cannot distinguish the inability to perform an action a from the possibility of performing an a immediately followed by an $\overline{a}$. This is illustrated by the next example.

Example 3. $0 \simeq a.\overline{a}$

We leave the reader to verify the various inequalities. Let us just remark, as regards $0 \sqsubseteq_{must} a.\overline{a}$, that the test $(a.\,\omega \,\|\overline{a})$ cannot be used here as a discriminating test as in Example 2, since $a.\overline{a}\,\mathsf{must}\,(a.\,\omega\,\|\overline{a})$. Note that with the standard rule for $+$ we would have $0\,\mathsf{must}\,(\omega \oplus \omega) + \overline{a}$ and therefore it would *not* be true that $0 \sqsubseteq_{must} a.\overline{a}$. On the other hand this seems to be a basic law for asynchrony.

The testing preorders $\sqsubseteq_{may}$ and $\sqsubseteq_{must}$ are *contextual*, in the sense that they are defined using a quantification over the behaviour of processes in all contexts of a certain form. We now give alternative characterisations for them, which are independent of these contexts. To motivate these characterisations it will be convenient to refer to similar results in the synchronous case. So we let $\sqsubseteq^{s}_{may}$ and $\sqsubseteq^{s}_{must}$ denote the synchronous may and must testing preorders; that is the preorders based on the standard operational semantics of *CCS*, as defined in [7].

3.1 Characterising may testing

Let us start with some terminology. We define *weak transitions* as usual:

$$p \stackrel{\varepsilon}{\Longrightarrow} p' \Leftrightarrow p \stackrel{\tau}{\longrightarrow}^* p'$$
$$p \stackrel{\alpha}{\Longrightarrow} p' \Leftrightarrow p \stackrel{\varepsilon}{\Longrightarrow} \cdot \stackrel{\alpha}{\longrightarrow} \cdot \stackrel{\varepsilon}{\Longrightarrow} p'$$

Note the difference between $p \stackrel{\varepsilon}{\Longrightarrow} p'$ and $p \stackrel{\tau}{\Longrightarrow} p'$ (the latter involving at least one τ step). The weak transitions are extended to sequences of observable actions in the standard way:

$$p \stackrel{s}{\Longrightarrow} p' \Leftrightarrow p \stackrel{\alpha_1}{\Longrightarrow} \cdots \stackrel{\alpha_n}{\Longrightarrow} p' \qquad\qquad s = \alpha_1 \cdots \alpha_n, \quad \alpha_i \neq \tau$$

Thus $p \stackrel{s}{\Longrightarrow} p'$ means that p can carry out the observable sequence of actions s to arrive at p'. In a synchronous world this is exactly the same as saying that p can react to the sequence of messages $\bar{s}$ (or to the obvious sequential process constructed from $\bar{s}$) to arrive at p'. Let $\equiv$ denote the structural congruence over terms generated by the monoidal laws for $\|$. Formally we have, using the notation $p \stackrel{\alpha}{\longrightarrow} \equiv p'$ to mean $\exists\, p''.\, p \stackrel{\alpha}{\longrightarrow} p'' \equiv p'$

$$p \stackrel{s}{\Longrightarrow} p' \text{ if and only if } p \,\|\, \bar{s} \stackrel{\varepsilon}{\Longrightarrow} \equiv p'$$

However in an asynchronous world these two statements no longer coincide. First of all, the notion of "sequence of messages" is not as clear, since output messages are non blocking for the rest of the sequence. The asynchronous operational semantics allows for a larger number of computations from $p \| \bar{s}$ (where $\bar{s}$ represents here the process obtained by replacing output actions with asynchronous prefix in the corresponding sequence). For example if $\bar{s}$ is the sequence $\bar{b}b$ then we can have $p \,\|\, \bar{s} \stackrel{\varepsilon}{\Longrightarrow} p$, which means that in the asynchronous world we should allow p to move to itself via the sequence s. To formalise this idea we introduce new transition relations $\stackrel{\alpha}{\Longrightarrow}_a$ and $\stackrel{s}{\Longrightarrow}_a$.

Definition 1. *Let the strong* asynchronous transition relation $\stackrel{\alpha}{\longrightarrow}_a$ *be the least relation over processes such that*

- $\stackrel{\alpha}{\longrightarrow} \subseteq \stackrel{\alpha}{\longrightarrow}_a$
- *for any* $b \in \mathsf{Names}$, $p \stackrel{b}{\longrightarrow}_a p \,\|\, \bar{b}$

The weak transition relations $\stackrel{\alpha}{\Longrightarrow}_a$ *and* $\stackrel{s}{\Longrightarrow}_a$ *are then defined as above.*

Note that the $\stackrel{\alpha}{\longrightarrow}_a$ determine a kind of *input-enabled* transition system, similar to that introduced in [10] by Honda and Tokoro for the asynchronous π-calculus.

Lemma 1. $p \stackrel{s}{\Longrightarrow}_a p'$ *and* $q \stackrel{\bar{s}}{\Longrightarrow} q'$ *imply* $p \,\|\, q \stackrel{\varepsilon}{\Longrightarrow} \equiv p' \,\|\, q'$

For any process p, let $\mathcal{L}(p)$ denote the language of observable sequences of p:

$$\mathcal{L}(p) = \{\, s \mid \exists p'.\, p \stackrel{s}{\Longrightarrow} p' \,\}$$

We define similarly the language of observable *asynchronous sequences* of p:

$$\mathcal{L}^a(p) = \{\, s \mid \exists p'.\, p \stackrel{s}{\Longrightarrow}_a p' \,\}$$

We call $\mathcal{L}^a(p)$ the *asynchronous language* of p. It is well-known that in the synchronous case may testing is characterised by language inclusion; that is, for synchronous processes

$$p \sqsubseteq^s_{may} q \text{ if and only if } \mathcal{L}(p) \subseteq \mathcal{L}(q)$$

As it turns out, this result can be naturally adapted to the asynchronous case:

Theorem 1. (Characterisation of may testing). *In TACCS :*

$$p \sqsubseteq_{may} q \textit{ if and only if } \mathcal{L}(p) \subseteq \mathcal{L}^a(q)$$

3.2 Characterising must testing

Unlike that of $\sqsubseteq_{may}$, the characterisation of $\sqsubseteq_{must}$ is rather involved. In order to motivate it, it will be helpful to recall the corresponding characterisation for the synchronous case. To do so we need the following notation:

Input and Output sets $I(p) = \{ a \mid p \xrightarrow{a} \}$, $O(p) = \{ \bar{a} \mid p \xrightarrow{\bar{a}} \}$
Ready sets $R(p) = I(p) \cup O(p)$
Acceptance sets $\mathcal{A}(p, s) = \{ R(p') \mid p \overset{s}{\Longrightarrow} p' \overset{\tau}{\not\longrightarrow} \}$
Convergence predicate Let $\Downarrow$ be the least predicate over processes which satisfies

- $p \Downarrow \varepsilon$ if there is no infinite reduction of the form $p \xrightarrow{\tau} \cdots$
- $p \Downarrow \alpha s$ if $p \Downarrow \varepsilon$ and $p \overset{\alpha}{\Longrightarrow} q$ implies $q \Downarrow s$.

Definition 2. *Let $p \ll^s q$ if for every $s \in \mathsf{Act}^*$, $p \Downarrow s$ implies*

- $q \Downarrow s$
- *for every $A \in \mathcal{A}(q, s)$ there exists some $A' \in \mathcal{A}(p, s)$ such that $A' \subseteq A$.*

The classical result for synchronous processes [7] is

$$p \sqsubseteq^s_{must} q \text{ if and only if } p \ll^s q$$

We wish to adapt this result to the asynchronous case. Consider first the convergence predicate. An asynchronous version can be defined in the obvious way:

- $p \Downarrow^a \varepsilon$ if there is no infinite reduction of the form $p \xrightarrow{\tau} \cdots$
- $p \Downarrow^a \alpha s$ if $p \Downarrow^a \varepsilon$ and $p \overset{\alpha}{\Longrightarrow}_a q$ implies $q \Downarrow^a s$.

Acceptance sets will also require considerable modification. An immediate remark is that they should not include input actions. This is illustrated by a simple example, already encountered in Section 3.

Example 4. Let $p = a$ and $q = 0$. We have seen that $p \sqsubseteq_{must} q$. On the other hand $\mathcal{A}(q, \varepsilon) = \{\emptyset\}$ and $\mathcal{A}(p, \varepsilon) = \{\{a\}\}$, so the condition on acceptance sets of Definition 2 is not satisfied.

This example suggests that the $\mathcal{A}(p,s)$ should be restricted to output actions, i.e. replaced by *output acceptance sets* $\mathcal{O}(p,s) = \{\, O(p') \mid p \stackrel{s}{\Longrightarrow} p' \stackrel{\tau}{\not\longrightarrow} \}$, in keeping with the intuition that only outputs should be directly observable.

A consequence of the synchronous characterisation is that $p \sqsubseteq^{s}_{must} q$ implies $\mathcal{L}(q) \subseteq \mathcal{L}(p)$, since $s \in \mathcal{L}(p) \Leftrightarrow \mathcal{A}(p,s) \neq \emptyset$. This is not true in the asynchronous case; $p \sqsubseteq_{must} q$ does not imply $\mathcal{L}(q) \subseteq \mathcal{L}(p)$, as shown by the next example.

Example 5. Let $p = 0$ and $q = a.\overline{a}$. We have $p \sqsubseteq_{must} q$ (as seen earlier in this section) and $a \in \mathcal{L}(q)$, but $a \notin \mathcal{L}(p)$.

This indicates that p should be allowed to match the execution sequences of q in a more liberal way than in the synchronous case: if q executes a sequence s then p should be allowed to execute s "asynchronously". This is where the new transition relation $\stackrel{s}{\Longrightarrow}_a$ comes into play for must testing. Intuitively we expect $p \sqsubseteq_{must} q \Rightarrow \mathcal{L}(q) \subseteq \mathcal{L}^a(p)$.

These two remarks lead to our first attempt at a definition. We will use two kinds of acceptance sets: $\mathcal{O}(p,s) = \{\, O(p') \mid p \stackrel{s}{\Longrightarrow} p' \stackrel{\tau}{\not\longrightarrow} \}$ and $\mathcal{O}^a(p,s) = \{\, O(p') \mid p \stackrel{s}{\Longrightarrow}_a p' \stackrel{\tau}{\not\longrightarrow} \}$.

Definition 3. *Let $p \ll' q$ if for every $s \in \mathsf{Act}^*$, $p \Downarrow^a s$ implies*

- $q \Downarrow^a s$
- *for every $O \in \mathcal{O}(q,s)$ there exists some $O' \in \mathcal{O}^a(p,s)$ such that $O' \subseteq O$.*

It may be shown that $p \sqsubseteq_{must} q$ implies $p \ll' q$. On the other hand $\ll'$ is still too generous and it is not true that $p \ll' q$ implies $p \sqsubseteq_{must} q$.

Example 6. Let $p = a.\overline{b}$ and $q = 0$. Then

- $p \ll' q$, because $\mathcal{O}(q,\varepsilon) = \{\emptyset\}$ and $\mathcal{O}^a(p,\varepsilon) = \{\emptyset\}$.
- $p \not\sqsubseteq_{must} q$, because p must e while q $\not{\mathsf{must}}$ e, where e is the test $\overline{a} \parallel b.\omega$.

This example suggests that to compute the acceptance set of p after s we should not only consider its s-derivatives but also look further at their input-derivatives (derivatives via a sequence of inputs). Intuitively this is because an observer with output capabilities interacting with a process may or may not discharge some of these outputs by communication with the process. In the above example the observer provokes the derivation $p \stackrel{\varepsilon}{\Longrightarrow} p' \stackrel{a}{\longrightarrow} p''$ where $p' = p$ and $p'' = \overline{b}$ and this should be reflected in some manner in the acceptance set of p after ε.

We thus want to generalise the sets $\mathcal{O}^a(p,s)$ by looking at the input-derivatives of p after s. For a reason that will soon become clear we need to consider multisets of inputs rather than sets. In the following $\uplus$ denotes multiset union. We use the notation $\{\!|\ \ |\!\}$ for multisets, writing for instance $\{\!|\, a, a \,|\!\}$.

Definition 4. *For any finite multiset of* input *actions I let $\stackrel{}{\rightsquigarrow}_I$ be the binary predicate defined by*

- *$(p \stackrel{\tau}{\not\longrightarrow}$ and $I(p) \cap I = \emptyset)$ implies $p \rightsquigarrow_I p$*
- *$(p \stackrel{a}{\Longrightarrow} p'$, and $p' \rightsquigarrow_I p''\,)$ implies $p \rightsquigarrow_{I \uplus \{\!|\, a \,|\!\}} p''$*

Intuitively $p \not\rightsquigarrow_I p'$ means that by performing a subset of the input actions in I, p can arrive at the stable state p' which cannot perform any of the remaining actions in I. Note that if p is stable then $p \not\rightsquigarrow_\emptyset p$.

Based on this predicate, we can define the generalised acceptance sets:

$$\mathcal{O}^a_I(p,s) = \{\, O(p'') \mid p \overset{s}{\Longrightarrow}_a p', p' \not\rightsquigarrow_I p'' \,\}$$

Let $IM(p,s)$, the set of *input multisets* of p after s, be given by

$$IM(p,s) = \{\, \{\!|\, a_1, \ldots, a_n \,|\!\} \mid a_i \in \mathsf{Names},\ p \overset{s}{\Longrightarrow}_a \overset{a_1}{\Longrightarrow} \cdots \overset{a_n}{\Longrightarrow} p_n \,\}$$

We can now finally define our alternative preorder:

Definition 5. *Let $p \ll q$ if for every $s \in \mathsf{Act}^*$, $p \Downarrow^a s$ implies*

- $q \Downarrow^a s$
- *for every $A \in \mathcal{A}(q,s)$ and every $I \in IM(p,s)$ such that $I \cap A = \emptyset$ there exists some $O \in \mathcal{O}^a_I(p,s)$ such that $O \backslash \overline{I} \subseteq A$.*

Two comments about this definition will be helpful.

- The requirement $I \cap A = \emptyset$ can be justified as follows. The multiset I represents the inputs that p could be doing (after s) in reaction to some test, that is the complement of the outputs that the test is offering. Since the process q has reached a *stable state* with ready set A, where it is confronted with the same test, the test should be unable to make q react. Thus in particular the complement I of its outputs $\overline{I}$ should be disjoint from the inputs in A. Note that without this requirement we would have e.g. $a.\bar{b} \not\ll a.\bar{b}$!
- The condition $O \backslash \overline{I} \subseteq A$ can also be explained intuitively. In an asynchronous setting, an observer providing some outputs $\overline{I}$ to the environment, will have subsequently no way of telling, when observing these outputs, whether they come from himself or from the observed process p. So all he can require is that when p reaches a stable state p'', with outputs, say, O, the *remaining* outputs of p'', $O \backslash \overline{I}$, be included in the actions A of the corresponding state of q. In fact the condition $O \backslash \overline{I} \subseteq A$ could be reformulated as $O \subseteq A \uplus \overline{I}$, which is reminiscent of the definition of *asynchronous bisimulation* in [1].

Theorem 2. (Characterisation of must testing) *In TACCS :*

$$p \sqsubseteq_{must} q \text{ if and only if } p \ll q$$

4 Equational Characterisation

In this section we restrict attention to finite terms, without recursion. Standard techniques may be used to extend equational theories to recursive terms.

In what follows $\mu, \nu \in \mathsf{Act}$ will denote visible actions. We will use the notation $\mu.t$ to represent $a.t$ when μ is the input action a and $\widehat{a}.t$ when μ is the output action $\bar{a}$. With this convention the basic testing axioms for $\sqsubseteq$ (concerning the

Asynchrony:

$$X = X + a.(\overline{a} \parallel X)$$
$$\widehat{a}.X = \overline{a} \parallel X$$

Fig. 2. Extra laws for asynchronous testing

choice operators and their interplay with prefixing and parallelism) are exactly the same as in [7] and are not reported here.

In addition we need two axioms for asynchrony, given in Figure 2. The first is a law holding also for weak asynchronous bisimulation, taken from [1]. The second is the natural law for asynchronous output prefixing. Indeed it shows that in the presence of the atoms $\overline{a}$ this form of prefix is redundant in our language. However its presence facilitates the comparison between the operational semantics of synchronous and asynchronous outputs.

We shall not present the characterisation of $\sqsubseteq_{may}$ here, since it is a simple adaptation of that given in [4] for a variant of our language. Let us just recall some interesting laws holding for asynchronous may testing. Let $a \in \mathsf{Names}$, $\mu \in \mathsf{Act}$. Then $\sqsubseteq_{may}$ satisfies:

$$a.\mu.X \leq \mu.a.X$$
$$a.(\overline{a} \parallel X) \leq X$$

In fact, for $\sqsubseteq_{may}$ the first law in Figure 2 can be derived from these two laws.

We give now the equational characterisation for must testing. To obtain the theory for $\sqsubseteq_{must}$ we add to the standard laws and those of Figure 2 the usual axiom for must testing:

$$X \oplus Y \leq X$$

However this is not sufficient to yield a complete theory for $\sqsubseteq_{must}$. For instance we have the inequality $\overline{a}+b.\overline{a} \sqsubseteq_{must} \overline{a}$, which the reader may want to check using the alternative characterisation of Theorem 2. This inequality is not derivable from the axioms considered so far. More generally we have the law

$$p + b.p \sqsubseteq_{must} p$$

In our theory this will be an instance of the conditional rule **R1** in Figure 3.

Two more conditional rules are required, **R2** and **R3**, which we briefly motivate. As regards **R2**, note that the may testing law $a.(\overline{a} \parallel X) \leq X$ is not valid

$$X \oplus Y \leq X \qquad\qquad \mathbf{R1}\ \frac{X + Y \leq X}{X + a.\,Y \leq X}$$

$$\mathbf{R2}\ \frac{X + Y \leq X}{X + a.\,(\overline{a} \,\|\, Y) \leq X}$$

$$X + \widehat{a}.\,Y = (X + \widehat{a}.\,Y) \oplus \widehat{a}.\,Y \qquad\qquad \mathbf{R3}\ \frac{X + Y \leq X}{(X + \widehat{a}.\,Z) \oplus Y \leq X}$$

Fig. 3. Extra laws for must testing

for must testing. For instance $p = a.(\overline{a} \,\|\, \overline{b}) \not\sqsubseteq_{must} \overline{b} = q$, since $\mathcal{A}(q, \overline{b}) \neq \emptyset$ while $\mathcal{O}^a_I(p, \overline{b}) = \emptyset$ for any I. For must testing we have the more restricted law

$$X \ + \ a.(\overline{a} \,\|\, X) \ \leq \ X$$

which is one half of the asynchrony law in Figure 2. However, this is not enough since it does not allow one to derive for instance: $\overline{a} \ + \ c.(\overline{c} \,\|\, b.\,\overline{a}) \ \leq \ \overline{a}$. Whence the need for the more general conditional rule **R2**.

Similarly, the use of **R3** can be exemplified by the simple inequality

$$(\overline{a} \ + \ \overline{b}) \oplus 0 \ \leq \ \overline{a}$$

which again appears not to be derivable from the other laws.

Finally, we have a law expressing the asynchronous behaviour of outputs with respect to external choice

$$X + \widehat{a}.\,Y \ = \ (X + \widehat{a}.\,Y) \ \oplus \ \widehat{a}.\,Y$$

This shows that a process of the form $X + \widehat{a}.\,Y$ can spontaneously resolve its choice by releasing its output to the environment.

Let $\vdash_{must} p \leq q$ mean that $p \leq q$ is provable in the theory obtained by adding the equations in Figure 3 to the standard laws and those of Figure 2.

Theorem 3. *For finite asynchronous processes* $p \sqsubseteq_{must} q$ *iff* $\vdash_{must} p \leq q$.

5 Conclusions

We have given an asynchonous operational semantics to a version of *CCS* with internal and external choice operators, called *TACCS*. Based on this asynchonous semantics we developed semantic theories of may and must testing. In particular we gave alternative behavioural characterisations of the resulting preorders, and equational characterisations for the finite fragment of the language.

Some interesting questions remain. For example, is it possible to eliminate the use of conditional equations in the characterisation of $\sqsubseteq_{must}$? Or would there be a simpler algebraic characterisation for the sublanguage in which the external choice operator is only applied to input prefixes, essentially the language studied in [3, 1]? But perhaps the most important question is the extent to which our approach can be generalised to yield an equational characterisation of must testing over the π-calculus.

The may testing preorder has been equationally characterised for an asynchronous version of *CCS* and for the asynchronous π-calculus in [4]. But both these languages have syntactic restrictions that we do not impose; specifically external choice may only be applied to input prefixes. Strong bisimulation has also been characterised for the asynchronous π-calculus in [1], again with the same restriction on external choice. As regards weak asynchronous bisimulation, the recent work [11] shows how restrictions on the behaviour of asynchronous π-processes can bring up interesting new algebraic laws.

References

1. R. Amadio, I. Castellani, and D. Sangiorgi. On bisimulations for the asynchronous π-calculus. *Theoretical Computer Science*, 195:291–324, 1998.
2. J. C. M. Baeten and W. P. Weijland. *Process Algebra*, volume 18 of *Cambridge Tracts in Computer Science*. Cambridge University Press, 1990.
3. M. Boreale, R. DeNicola, and R. Pugliese. Asynchronous observations of processes. In *Proc. FOSSACS'98*, LNCS 1378, 1998.
4. M. Boreale, R. DeNicola, and R. Pugliese. Laws for asynchrony, 1998. Draft.
5. G. Boudol. Asynchrony and the π-calculus. Research Report 1702, INRIA, Sophia-Antipolis, 1992.
6. R. DeNicola and M. Hennessy. Testing equivalences for provesses. *Theoretical Computer Science*, 43:83–133, 1984.
7. M. Hennessy. *Algebraic Theory of Processes.* MIT Press, Cambridge, Massachusetts, 1988.
8. C.A.R. Hoare. *Communicating Sequential Processes.* Prentice-Hall, 1985.
9. K. Honda and M. Tokoro. An object calculus for asynchronous communication. In *Proc. ECOOP'91*, LNCS 512, 1991.
10. K. Honda and M. Tokoro. On asynchronous communication semantics. In *Proc. Object-Based Concurrent Computing,* LNCS 612, 1992.
11. M. Merro and D. Sangiorgi. On asynchrony in name-passing calculi. In *Proc. ICALP'98,* LNCS 1443, 1998.
12. R. Milner. *Communication and Concurrency.* Prentice Hall, 1989.
13. U. Nestmann and B. Pierce. Decoding choice encodings. In *Proc. CONCUR'96,* LNCS 1119, 1996.
14. Benjamin C. Pierce and David N. Turner. Pict: A programming language based on the pi-calculus. Technical Report CSCI 476, Computer Science Department, Indiana University, 1997. To appear in *Proof, Language and Interaction: Essays in Honour of Robin Milner*, Gordon Plotkin, Colin Stirling, and Mads Tofte, editors, MIT Press.
15. P. Selinger. First-order axioms for asynchrony. In *Proc. CONCUR'97,* LNCS 1243, 1997.

Alternative Computational Models: A Comparison of Biomolecular and Quantum Computation

Extended Abstract

John H. Reif

Department of Computer Science
Duke University

Abstract. *Molecular Computation (MC)* is massively parallel computation where data is stored and processed within objects of molecular size. *Biomolecular Computation (BMC)* is MC using biotechnology techniques, e.g. recombinant DNA operations. In contrast, *Quantum Computation (QC)* is a type of computation where unitary and measurement operations are executed on linear superpositions of classical states. Both BMC and QC may be executed at the micromolecular scale by a variety of methodologies and technologies. This paper surveys various methods for doing BMC and QC and discusses the considerable theoretical and practical advances in BMC and QC made in the last few years. We compare bounds on key resource such as time, volume (number of molecules times molecular density), energy and error rates achievable, taking particular note of the scalability of these methods with the size of the problem solved. In addition to NP search problems and database search problems, we enumerate a wide variety of further potential practical applications of BMC and QC. We observe that certain problems if solved with polynomial time bounds appear to require exponentially large volume for BMC (e.g., NP search problems) and QC (e.g., the observation operation). We discuss techniques for decreasing errors in BMC (e.g., annealing errors) and QC (e.g., decoherence errors), and volume where possible, to insure the scalability of BMC and QC to problems of large input size. In addition, we consider how BMC might be used to assist QC (e.g., to do observation operations for Bulk QC) and also how quantum techniques might be used to assist BMC (e.g., to do exquisite detection of very small quantities of a molecule in solution within a large volume).

1 Introduction

Conventional silicon based methods for computation have made great strides in the later 20th century, both in miniaturization as well as the use of innovative architectures, e.g., parallel architectures. However, there may well be limitations to the size of components using silicon technology, due to manufacturing limitations (e.g., the wavelength used in lithography) or device limitations in the function of very small components.

1.0 Molecular Computation (MC). A molecule will be (somewhat arbitrary) termed a *micromolecule* if it has at most 10^4 atoms, and otherwise a macromolecule. We may envision in the perhaps near future doing computation at an *ultra-scale*: that is submicroscopic and even micromolecular scale. In particular, we will define *MC* to be parallel computation, where data is stored and processed within micromolecule size objects. Some key resource bounds for MC are:

(i) time of computation (which if the computation is synchronous, this is the time duration of each operations times the number of steps of the computation),

(ii) volume (if the computing media is homogeneous, this is the the number of molecules (size) times molecular density), and
(iii) energy.

Furthermore, we need to bound the errors of MC, to insure the computations are correct. A key issue is the *scalability* of MC methods: that is by how much do these resource metrics increase with the size of the problem solved? There is not just one way to do MC, and in fact there are a number of quite distinct alternative technologies which will be discussed in this paper.

1.1 Biomolecular Computation (BMC). A large number of biotechnology laboratory techniques, known collectively as *recombinant DNA operations*, have be developed for manipulating DNA and related techniques have been developed to manipulate RNA and certain other bio-molecules in sophisticated ways. One basic approach to MC, which will be termed *Biomolecular Computation (BMC)* is to apply such biotechnology operations to do computation. In this approach, data may be encoded within individual molecules, for example via DNA or RNA base coding. This data may be stored as vast numbers of DNA or RNA molecules in solution in a test tube or in solid support on a surface.

• **Distributed Molecular Parallelism.** In the *distributed molecular parallelism (DP-BMC)* paradigm for BMC, the operations of a computation are executed in parallel on a large number of distinct molecules in a distributed manner, using the massive parallelism inherent in BMC. Feynman [F61] first proposed doing computation via distributed molecular parallelism, but his idea was not tested for a number of decades.

• **Initial Work in BMC.** Adleman was the first to actually do an experiment demonstrating BMC, solving a small NP search problem. NP search problems are considered intractable via conventional methods for macroscopic sequential and parallel computation. The *Hamiltonian path* problem is to find a path in a graph that visits each node exactly once. Adleman [A94] (also ee [G94,KTL97] and Fu et al [FBZ98] for improvements) employed molecular parallelism in the solution of the Hamiltonian path problem, by forming a set of DNA strings encoding sequences of nodes of the graph and restricting the set of sequences to only Hamiltonian paths. The number of recombinant DNA operations grew linearly with the size of the input graph. In a lab experiment, he tested his techniques on DNA for a 7 node Hamiltonian path problem. This was the first major experimental milestone achieved in the field of BMC.

1.2 Quantum Computation (QC). Another basic approach to MC is to apply quantum mechanics to do computation. A single molecule or collection of molecules may have a number n of degrees of freedom known as *qubits*. A *classical state* is associated with each fixed setting (to classical Boolean values) of the qubits. Quantum mechanics allows for a linear superposition (also termed an *entangled quantum state*) of these classical states to exist simultaneously. Each classical state of the superposition is assigned a given complex amplitude and the sum of the squares of the magnitudes of the amplitudes of all classical states is 1. QC is a method of computation where various operations can be executed on these superpositions:

– **unitary operations** (which are reversible operations on the superpositions, and can be represented by unitary matrices)

– **observation operations**, which allow for the (strong) measurement of each qubit, providing a mapping from the current superposition to a superposition where the measured qubit is assigned a classical Boolean value with probability given by the square of the amplitude of the qubit in its original superposition.

• **Initial Work in QC.** Benioff [Ben82] and Feynman [Fey86] were the first to suggest the use of quantum mechanical principles for doing computation. Deutsch and Jozsa [DJ92] give the first example of a quantum algorithm that gave a rapid solution of an example problem, and they proved that the problem (for a given a black box function) is not quickly solvable by any conventional computing machine. Costantini, Smeraldi [CS97] gave a generalization of Deutsch's example and Collins et al [CKH98] simplified the Deutsch-Jozsa algorithm (also see Jozsa [Joz96,Joz97,Joz98] further elaborated on quantum computation and complexity).

• **Surveys of QC.** The following are reviews and surveys have been made of QC: Bennett et al [BD95a, BD95b], Barenco [Bar96], Benio [Ben96], Brassard [Bra96], Haroche, Raimond [HR96], Brassard [Bra97], Preskill [Pre97a], Scarani [Sca98], Steane [Ste98], Vedral, Plenio [VP98]. Also, Williams and Clearwater [WC97] is the first text book in QC. (Also, Taubes [Tau96] and Gershenfeld, Chuang [GC98] give popular press descriptions of QC.)

1.3 Organization of this Paper. In this Section 1 we have introduced BMC and QC. In Section 3 we discuss resource bounds for BMC and QC, including time, volume, and energy. In Section 2 we describe mathematical models and complexity bounds for BMC and QC. In Section 4 we discuss enabling technologies and experimental paradigms for doing BMC and QC. In Section 5 we discuss the type of errors encountered in BMC and QCC, and methods for decreasing errors. In Section 6 we discuss applications of BMC and QC. In Section 7 we discuss hybrids of BMC and QC, including as an example of an applications of QC to BMC as well as an example of an application of BMC to QC. In Section 8 we give conclusion and acknowledgements.

2 Models and Complexity Bounds for BMC.

2.1 Models for BMC.

• **Splicing Models.** *Splicing* is a paradigm for BMC which provides a theoretical model of enzymatic systems operating on DNA. Splicing models a solution with enzymatic actions (restrictions and the ligations) operating on DNA in parallel in a common test tube. The DNA strands are modeled as strings over a finite alphabet. Splicing allows for the generation of new strings from an initially chosen set of strings, using a specified set of splicing operations. The splicing operations on the DNA are string editing operations such as cutting, appending, etc. These operations can be applied in any order, and thus the splicing system can be considered to be autonomously controlled. Also, the operations may be nondeterministic: a large number of possible results may be obtained from a small number of operations. Splicing predates all other BMC paradigms and it has its roots in formal language theory [H87] and Lindenmayer systems [H92]. Pioneering work on splicing was done by Head [H92]. There is now a rather extensive literature (including thirty or so papers) in splicing and related string rewrite systems, written by a dozen researchers, including Paun [P96a,P96b,P97] and Paun et al [CFKP96,HPP96,PRS96], Culik and Harju [CH89] Pixton[Pi95,Pi96,Pi97], [StM97], Yokomori and Kobayashi [YK97a,YK97b], Kim and Kyungpook [KK97]. All of these investigations were theoretical in nature, and established the computational power of splicing systems of various sorts. Surveys of DNA computing in the context of the splicing model are given by Kari [Kar98,Kar97B,Kar96] and Kari, Sakakibara [KS97]. In summary, splicing provided the first theoretical studies of BMC and and has contributed to our understanding of the potential power of BMC. It has evolved to be a very active subfield of formal language theory. At this time, splicing is primarily a theoretical rather than an experimental area of BMC.

• **Models for Distributed Molecular Parallelism.**

– **Test Tube and Memory Models.** Lipton [L94] defined the first abstract model of BMC that takes into account distributed molecular parallelism. The elements of his *test tubes* are strings as in the case of DNA. His model allowed a number of operations on test tubes to be executed in one lab step. The subsequent *Memory* model of Adleman [A95] refined the model of Lipton by restricting the set of operations to the following: (i) *Merge:* Given tubes T_1, T_2, produce the union $T_1 \cup T_2$. (ii) *Copy:* Given a tube T_1, produce a tube T_2 with the same contents. (iii) *Detect:* Given a tube T, say 'yes' if T contains at least one element and say 'no' if it contains none. (iv) *Separation:* Given a tube T_1 and a word w, produce a tube T_2 with all elements of T_1 that contain w.

– **A Surface-Based Model for BMC.** An abstract model of surface-based BMC computation has been developed by [LGCCL+96] (comparable with Lipton and Adelman's models), and it is shown that the surface-based model is also capable of general circuit simulation.

– **A Parallel Associative Memory Model for BMC.** This is a very high level model proposed by Reif [R95] which (i) allows any of the operations for the Memory model of Adleman to be executed in one step, and also (ii) has a Parallel Associative Matching (PA-Match) operation, which provides for the combination of all pairs of DNA strings with subsequences that have a complementary match at a specified location. This PA-Match operation is very similar to the data base join operation.

– **A Recombinant DNA Model for BMC.** Is a low level model for BMC proposed by Reif [R95] which allows operations that are abstractions of very well understood recombinant DNA operations and provides a graph representation, known as a *complex*, for the relevant structural properties of DNA. To insure realism, the RDNA model allows complementary pairing of only very short sequences of DNA in constant time. Reif [R95] showed that the PA-Match operation of the PAM model can be simulated in the RDNA model with a slow down which is linear in the pattern match length.

– **Other Models of BMC.** Yokomori and Kobayashi [YK97b] developed a model of BMC based on equality checking, which may be related to the PAM model. Kurtz, Mahaney, Royer, and Simon [KMRS96] formulated a model of BMC which takes into account solution concentrations.

– **Speed-Ups using Molecular Parallelism.** Beaver [BeA95] and Reif [R95] (also Papadimitriou [P95]) independently proved that any linear space bounded sequential computation can be exponentially speeded up by PMC; in particular, they showed that sequential Turing Machine computations with space s and time $2^{O(s)}$ can be simulated by BMC in polynomial time. All their proofs made use of a pointer jumping technique (this pointer jumping technique dates to the 1978 work of Fortune and Wyllie [FW78], who gave a parallel simulation of a space bounded TM by a PRAM) which required a large volume to implement in BMC. The paper of [R95] proved this speed-up result for the (very high level) PAM model, and then [R95] described in detail its implementation by recombinant DNA operations in the RDNA model. The proof of [B95] used a DNA string-editing operation known as site-directed local mutagenesis (see [WGWZ92], page 192-193, [OP94], page 191-206, and Chapter 5 of [SFM89]) to implement pointer jumping. Khodor and Gifford [KG98] have recently implementated BMC methods using programmed mutagenesis.

– **Molecular PRAMs.** A Parallel Random Access Machine (PRAM) is a parallel machine with a large shared memory. It is CREW if its memory allows concurrent reads and exclusive writes. This same technique of pointer jumping is essential also for Reif's [R95] BMC simulation of a CREW PRAM. Given a CREW PRAM with time bound D, with M memory cells, and processor bound P, [R95] showed that the PRAM can be simulated in the PAM model using t PA-Match operations as well as $O(s \log s)$ PAM operations where $s = O(\log(PM))$ and $t = O(D + s)$. This result immediately implied that in $t = O(D + s)$ PAM steps, one can evaluate and find the satisfying inputs to a Boolean circuit constructable in s space with n inputs, unbounded fan-out, and depth

D. Subsequently, Ogihara and Ray [OR97b] obtained a similar result as [R95] for parallel circuit evaluation, implicitly assuming a model similar to the PAM model. (Also see [HA97] for BMC methods for parallel evaluation of a Boolean μ-formulas.) To allow the PRAM to use shared global memory, we need to do massively parallel message (DNA strand) routing. As a consequence, the volume bounds for this simulation of a PRAM required volume growing at least quadratically with size of the storage of the PRAM. Gehani and Reif [GR98a] propose a MEMS micro-flow device technology that requires a substantial decreased volume to do the massively parallel message routing required for the shared memory operations of the PRAM.

2.2 Models and Complexity Bounds for QC.

• **Quantum TMs and other Automata.** Deutsch [Deu85b] gave the first formal description of a quantum computer, known as a *quantum TM*. The tape contents of the TM are qubits. *Quantum configurations* of the QTM are superpositions of classical TM configurations. A transition of the QTM is a unitary mapping on quantum configurations of the QTM. Thus, a computation of the QTM is a unitary mapping from the initial quantum configuration to the final quantum configuration. Various papers generalize classical language and automata to the quantum case. Moore, Crutchfield [MC97] propose quantum finite-state and push-down automata, and regular and context-free grammars, and they generalize several classical theorems, e.g. pumping lemmas, closure properties, rational and algebraic generating functions, and Greibach normal form. Kondacs and Watrous [KW97] partially characterize the power of quantum finite state automata. Dunlavey [Dun98] gives a space-efficient simulation of a deterministic finite state machine (FSM) on a quantum computer (using Grover's search algorithm discussed below). Watrous [Wat95] investigates quantum cellular automata and Drr et al [DTS96,DS96] give decision procedures for unitary linear (one dimensional) quantum cellular automata.

• **Quantum Complexity Classes and Structural Complexity.** Berthiaume, Brassard [BB92a] survey open QC structural complexity problems (also see Berthiaume [Ber95]). QC can clearly execute deterministic and randomized computations with no slow down. P (NP, QP, respectively) are the class of problems solved by deterministic (nondeterministic, quantum, respectively) polynomial time computations. Thus QP is the quantum analog of the time efficient class P. It is not known if QP contains NP, that is if QC can solve NP search problems in polynomial time. It is also not known whether QP is a superset of P, nor if there are any problems QC can solve in polynomial time that are not in P (but this is true given quantum oracles; see Berthiaume, Brassard [BB92b, BB94], Machta [MAC98], van Dam [Dam98a, Dam98b] for complexity bounds for computing with quantum oracles).

• **Bounded Precision QC.** Practical implementations of QC most likely will need to be done within some bounded amplitude precision, and with this motivation Bernstein, Vazirani [BV93, BV97] investigated the power of QTMs that have bounded amplitude precision. Let *BQP* be the class of polynomial time QTM computations that are computed within amplitude precision bounded by an inverse polynomial in the input size. Most of the algorithms we will mention (such as Shor's) are in the class BQP. [BV93, BV97] showed that BQP computations can be done using unitary operations with a fixed irrational rotation. Adleman et al [ADH97] improved this to show that BQP can be computed using only unitary operations with rational rotations, and that BQP is in the class PSPACE of polynomial space computations of classical TMs.

• **Quantum Gates.** A set of Boolean gates are *universal* if any Boolean operation on arbitrarily many bits can be expressed as compositions of these gates. Toffoli [Tof80] defined an extended XOR 3-bit gate (which is an XOR gate condition on one of the inputs and is known as the *Toffoli gate*) and showed that this gate, in combination with certain 1-bit gates, is universal. A set of quantum qubit gates are *universal* for Boolean computations for QC if any unitary operation on arbitrarily many qubits can be expressed as compositions of these gates. Deutsch defined the extended quantum XOR 3-qubit gate (known as the Deutsch-Toffoli gate) and proved this gate, in combination with certain one qubit gates, is universal. Barenco [Bar95], Sleator et al [DMS+95], Barenco et al [BBC+95], and DiVincenzo [DiV95] proved the 2-qubit XOR gates with certain 1-qubit gates can implement the Deutsch-Toffoli gate, so are universal for QC (also see Smolin and DiVincenzo [SD95], DiVincenzo et al [DiV96, DS98], Poyatos et al [PCZ96], Mozyrsky et al [MPH96a,MPH97, MPH98], Poyatos et al [PCZ96]). Lloyd [Llo97c] then proved that almost any 2-qubit quantum logic gate (with certain 1-qubit gates) is universal for QC. Monroe et al [MMK95], DiVincenz et al [DVL98] gave experimental demonstrations of quantum gates. [Deu89] defined a quantum computing model known as a *quantum gate array* which allows execution of a (possibly cyclic) sequence of quantum gates, where each input is a qubit, and each gate computes a unitary transformation.

• **Quantum Circuits.** Yao [Yao93] restricted the concept to (acyclic) *quantum circuits* which are a generalization of Boolean logic circuits for quantum gates. It suffices that a quantum circuit use only these universal gates. Yao [Yao93] proved that QTM computations are equivalent to uniform quantum circuit families. Aharonov et al [AKN97] discusses a generalization of quantum circuits to allow mixed states, where measurements can be done in the middle of the computation, and showed that such quantum circuits are equivalent in computational power to standard quantum circuits. This generalized an earlier result of Bernstein and Vazirani [BV93] that showed that all observation operations can be pushed to the end of the computation, by repeated use of a quantum XOR gate construction.

• **Quantum Parallel Complexity Classes.** Let NC (QNC, respectively) be the class of (quantum, respectively) circuits with polynomial size and polylog depth. Thus QNC is the quantum analog of the processor efficient parallel class NC. Moore, Nilsson [MN98a] define QNC and show various problems are in QNC, for example they show that the quantum Fourier transform can be parallelized to linear depth and polynomial size.

• **Lower Bounds on Quantum Communication.** Cleve et al [CDN+98] prove linear lower bounds for the quantum communication complexity of the inner product function, and give a reduction from the quantum information theory problem to the problem of quantum computation of the inner product. Knill, Laflamme [KL98] characterize the communication complexity of one qubit.

• **Quantum Programming Languages and Their Compilers.** Malhas [May96] defines a quantum version of the lambda calculus (the lambda calculus is a formal programming system similar to lisp) and Malhas [May97] shows that it can efficiently simulate quantum computations. Tucci [Tuc 98] describes a procedure for compiling unitary quantum transformations into elementary 2-qubit gates.

3 Resource Bounds

The energy consumption, processing rate, and volume, are all important resources to consider in miniaturized and mobile computing devices, and in particular molecular scale computations. Conventional electronic computers computers of the size of a work station operate in the range of 10^{-9} Joules per operation, at up to about 50 giga-ops per second, with memory of about 10 to 100 giga-bytes, and in a volume of about 10 cm^2.

3.1 Resource Bounds for BMC

• **Energy Bounds for BMC.**

– **Energy Consumption and Reversible Computation.** *Reversible computations* are computations where each state transformation is a reversible function, so that any computation can be reversed without loss of information. Landauer [Lan61] showed that irreversible computations must generate heat in the computing process, and that reversible computations have the property that if executed slowly enough, they (in the limit) can consume no energy in an adiabatic computation. Bennett [Ben73] (also see Bennett, Landauer [BL85], Landauer [Lan96]) showed that any computing machine (e.g., an abstract machine such as a Turing Machine) can be transformed to do reversible computations. Bennett's reversibility construction required extra space to store information to insure reversibility; Li, Vitanyi [LV96] give trade-offs between time and space in the resulting reversible machine.

Many recombinant DNA operations such as denaturing and annealing, are reversible, so they require arbitrarily small energy (they require heating or cooling, but this can be done using heat baths). Other recombinant DNA operations such as separation, do not seem to be reversible, and use approximately 10^{-19} Joules per operation.

• **Volume Bounds for BMC.** A small amount of water can contain a vast number of DNA molecules. A reasonable solution concentration to do recombinant DNA operations is 5 grams of DNA per one liter of water. Then a liter of water contains in solution about 10^{21} DNA bases. For an associative memory (see Baum [B95]) of this scale, we can provide a few bytes of memory per DNA strand, by use of at most 100 base pairs per DNA strand. Thus a liter of solution provides an associative memory with 10^{19} to 10^{20} bytes, which is 10^7 to 10^8 tera-bytes. It is important to note that the scale of the BMC approach is limited by the volume. Known BMC techniques can solve any NP search problem in time polynomial in the input size, but require volume which grows linearly with the combinatorial search space, and thus exponentially with the input size (However, some recent approaches (Hagiya and Arita [HA97] and Cukras et al [CFL+98]) to solving NP search problems via BMC have decreased the volume by iterative refinement of the search space).

• **Processing Rate Bounds for BMC.** The time duration of the recombinant DNA operations such as annealing, which depends on hybridization, is strongly dependent on the length of sequences to be matched and may also depend on temperature, pH, solution concentration, and possibly other parameters. These recombinant DNA and other biotechnology operations can take from a few seconds up to 100 minutes. A DNA strand may need $1,000$ base pairs to encode a processor state and so a liter of solution encodes the state of approximately 10^{18} distinct processors. Since a liter of water contains in solution about 10^{21} DNA bases, the overall potential for BMC using DNA is 10^{15} to 10^{16} operations per second in the liter of solution, which is $1,000$ tera-ops. While this number is very large, it is finite, so there is a finite constant upper limit to the enhanced power of MC using BMC within moderate volume. Nevertheless, the size of this constant is so large that it way well be advantageous in certain key applications, as compared to conventional (macroscopic) computation methods.

3.2 Resource Bounds for QC

• **Energy Bounds for QC.** The conventional linear model of QC allows only unitary state transformations and so by definition is reversible, with the possible exception of the observation operation which does quantum state reduction. Benioff [Ben82] noted that as a consequence of the reversibility of the unitary state transformations, QC these transformations dissipate no energy. The energy bounds for the observation operation are not well understood, and depend on the technology used.

• **Processing Rate of QC.** The rate of execution unitary operations in QC depend largely on the implementation technology; techniques can execute unitary operations in microseconds (e.g., Bulk MNR) and some might execute at microsecond or even picosecond rates (e.g., photonic techniques for MNR) The time duration to do observation can also be very short, but may be highly dependant on the size of the measuring apparatus and on the required precision (see the below discussion on the observation operation and its volume).

• **Volume Bounds for QC.** In this paper we consider (perhaps more closely than usual in the quantum literature due to our interest in MC) the volume bounds of QC. Potentially, the modest volume bounds of QC may be the one significant advantage over other methods for MC. (In contrast, BMC methods for solving an NP search problems such as integer factoring requires volume growing linearly with the combinatorial search space, and thus exponentially with the input size.) Due to the *quantum parallelism* (i.e., the superposition of the classical states allow each classical state to exist in parallel), the volume would at *appear* to be no more that the number of qubits. This may be true, but there are a number of substantial issues that need to be carefully considered.

– **QC Observation.** Recall the observation operation both provides a measurement of a qubit with a resulting state reduction. However, the QC literature has not yet carefully considered the volume bounds for the observation operation and it is not at all clear what the volume is required. In conventional descriptions of quantum mechanics, the observation is considered to be done in by a macroscopic measuring device; the precise size or molecular volume of such a measuring device (say as a function of the number of qubits) is unclear. The experimental evidence of the volume bounds for observation is unclear as well, since the QC experiments have not yet been scaled to large or even moderate numbers (say dozens) of qubits. (see Shnirman, Schoen [SS98], D'Helon, Milburn [HM97] Ozawa [Oza98]) Also, not much else about observation is clearly understood, since the precise nature of quantum state reduction via a strong quantum measurement remains somewhat of a mystery. We first consider a related question:

– **Approximate Observation Operations.** An approach to this difficulty is to only do the observation operation approximately within accuracy ϵ; this may suffice for many QC applications. However, even if the observation operation is done ϵ-approximately by unitary operations, it appears to require a number of additional qubits n' growing exponentially with the n, the original number of qubits of the QC. In fact, we know of no upper bound on n' better than $2^n \log(1/\epsilon)$.

– **Volume Bounds for Observation.** where ϵ is the inverse of a polynomial. Since the size of the classical state space grows as 2^n in the general case, it is reasonable to assume (e.g., where the physics of the strong measurement is defined by a diffusion process [Got66,DL94] that is rapidly mixing) that the likelihood of reversibility of the observation, within polynomial time bounds, drops exponentially with n. In the full paper [R98], we give an informal argument that even an ϵ-approximate observation can not be done in polynomial time using polynomial volume. In spite of informal nature of this argument, it does provide evidence that (with the above assumption), QC with the observation operation does not scale to a large number of qubits within small volumes, and in particular that a polynomial time ϵ-approximate observation operation requires very large volume and can not be done at the micromolecular scale for moderate large n.

– **Avoiding Observation Operations.** An alternative approach is to completely avoid observation operations on the basis that the observation operation is not actually essential to many quantum computations. Let some particular qubit (of a linear superposition of classical states) be *ϵ-near classical* if had the qubit been observed, the measured value would be a fixed value (either be 0 or 1) with ϵ probability. In the full paper [R98], we note (using known techniques) that quantum computations with observation operations and classic output can be modified to entirely eliminate any observation operations, and have output qubits that are ϵ-near classical, for arbitrarily small ϵ. This alternative approach can entirely eliminate the observation operation from many quantum computations, and so provides small volume, but has the drawback of providing a non-classical output.

4 Enabling Technologies and Experiments

4.1 Enabling Technologies and Experimental Paradigms for BMC. An *enabling technology* is a technology that allows a task to be done. Here we discuss various alternative enabling technologies for BMC and QC, and discuss their experiment in BMC and QC using these technologies.

• **Recombinant DNA Technology.** In the last two decades, there have been revolutionary advances in the field of biotechnology. Biotechnology has developed a large set of procedures for modifying DNA, known collectively known as *recombinant DNA*. DNA is a molecule consisting of a linear sequence of nucleotides. There are 4 types of nucleotides, which are complementary in pairs. A key property of DNA is *Watson-Crick complementation*, which allows the binding of complementary nucleotides. DNA may be single stranded (ssDNA) or double stranded. An ssDNA has an orientation $3' - 8'$ or $5' - 3'$. If two ssDNA are Watson-Crick complementary and $3' - 8'$ and $5' - 3'$ oriented in opposite directions, they are said to be *sticky*. At the appropriate conditions (determined by temperature and salinity, etc.), they may hybridize into double-stranded DNA. This resulting double-stranded DNA has complementary strands in opposite orientation. This allows the *annealing* of large strands of single DNA into double DNA, and the formation of complex 3D structures (this is known as *secondary structure*). The reverse process (usually induced by heating) is the *denature* of complex structures into single stranded linear structures. See [MH87,PP97,W97,RDGS97,HG97] for mathematical models of DNA hybridization and their simulation via thermodynamics. Short strands of ssDNA of length n are sometimes called *n-mers*. Many recombinant DNA operations use hybridization and are specific to a DNA segment with a prescribed n-mer subsequence. Such recombinant DNA operations include *cleavage* of DNA strands, *separation* of DNA strands, *detection* of DNA strands, and *fluorescent tagging* of specific DNA words. In addition, there are operations that are not specific, including *ligation* of DNA segments to form covalent bonds that join the DNA strands together, *merging* of test tube contents, the denature operation discussed above, and separation by molecular weight. Basic principles of recombinant DNA technology are described in [WGWZ92] [WHR87,OP94]. Detailed theoretical discussions of dynamics, thermodynamics, and structure of DNA, RNA and certain proteins are given by [BKP90,S94,EC]. Also see [ER82,MH87] for the dynamics and chemistry of nucleic acids and enzymes.

Due to the industrialization of the biotechnology field, laboratory techniques for recombinant DNA and RNA manipulation are becoming highly standardized, with well written lab manuals (e.g. [SFM89]) detailing the elementary lab steps required for recombinant DNA operations. Many of those recombinant DNA operations which where once considered highly sophisticated are now routine, and many have been automated by robotic systems. As a further byproduct of the industrialization of the biotechnology field, many of the constraints (such as timing, pH, and solution concentration, contamination etc.) critical to the successful execution of recombinant DNA techniques for conventional biological and medical applications (but not necessarily for all BMC applications), are now quite well understood, both theoretically and in practice.

• **Alternative Recombinant DNA Methodologies.** The most pervasive enabling biotechnology for BMC is solution-based recombinant DNA, that is the recombinant DNA operations are done on test tubes with DNA in solution. However, their are a number of alternative enabling biotechnologies, that allow similar and sometimes enhanced capabilities.

– **Solid Support BMC.** An example of an alternative recombinant DNA methodology is the *solid support* of individual DNA, for example by *surface attachments.* In solid support, the DNA strands are affixed to supports of some sort. In surface-based chemistry, surface attachments are used to affix DNA strands to organic compounds on the surface of a container. This can allow for more control of recombinant DNA operations, since this insures (i) that distinct DNA strands so immobilized can not interact, and also (ii) allows reagents and complementary DNA to have easy access to the DNA, and (iii) allows for easy removal of reagents and secondary by-products. Also, handling of samples is simpler and more readily automated. Surface-based chemistry has been used in protein sequencing, DNA synthesis, and peptide synthesis [S88]. Surface attachment methods can also be used for optical read-out (e.g., via fluorescent tagging of specific DNA words) on 2D arrays. A possible drawback of surface attachment technology, in comparison to solution-based recombinant DNA techniques, is a reduction on the total number of DNA strands that can be used.

– **Automation and Miniaturization of BMC.** MEMS is the technology of miniature actuators, valves, pumps, sensors and other such mechanisms, and when controlling fluids it is known as *MEMS micro-flow device technology.* [EE92,VSJMWR92,MEBH92]. Some of the current limits of BMC stem from the labor intensive nature of the laboratory work, the error rates, and the large volumes needed for certain bio-molecular reactions to occur (e.g., for searching and associative matching in wet data bases). [GR98a] (also see Ikuta [Iku96], Suyama [Suy98] for biological applications) propose the use of MEMS micro-flow device technology for BMC for automation of the laboratory work, parallel execution of the steps of a BMC algorithm (for improved speed and reliability), and for transport of fluids and DNA among multiple micro-test tubes. [GR98a] provide a model for micro-flow based bio-molecular computation (MF-BMC) which uses abstractions of both the recombinant DNA (RDNA) technology as well as of the micro-flow technology, and takes into account both of their limitations (e.g., concentration limitations for reactants in RDNA, and the geometric limitations of the MEMS device fabrication technology). [GR98a] also give a time and volume efficient MF-BMC architecture for routing DNA strands among multiple micro-test tubes (this gives a substantial decrease in the volume required for the PRAM simulation of [R95]).

• **Experimental Paradigms for BMC.** Even within BMC, there are a number of distinct methods to do computation: *(A) Splicing,* which provides a (theoretical) model of enzymatic systems operating on DNA, *(B) Distributed Molecular Parallelism*, where a operations are done on a large number of molecules in parallel, and the operations execute within a molecule in a sequential fashion (either synchronously or asynchronous with other molecules), *(C) Local Molecular Parallelism*, where operations are done within each molecule in a parallel fashion, and does computation by assembly of DNA tiles, and *(D) Cellular Processing*, where BMC is done using a microorganism such as bacteria to do computation, by re-engineering the regulatory feedback systems used in cellular metabolism. We now consider the experimental demonstration of each of these paradigms for BMC.

(A) Splicing. At this time, splicing is primarily a theoretical rather than an experimental area of BMC. There are a number of practical issues (e.g., the number of distinct enzymes with distinct recognition sequences for DNA splicing operations are limited to at most a few hundred) that may limit the scale of experimental implementations of splicing, but it is quite possible that evolutionary techniques (using RNA enzymes) may be used to solve such difficulties. Recently an experimental test of splicing was done by Laun and Reddy [LR97], which provided a laboratory demonstration of splicing, testing

a system with enzymatic actions (restrictions and the ligations) operating on DNA in parallel in a test tube.
(B) The Distributed Molecular Parallelism Paradigm. In this paradigm for BMC, the operations are executed in parallel on a large number of distinct molecules in a distributed manner, using the massive parallelism inherent in BMC.
• **NP Search using DP-BMC.** As mentioned in the introduction, Adleman [A94] did the first experiment demonstrating BMC, solving the Hamiltonian path problem on 7 nodes. This and many other BMC experiments have used distributed molecular parallelism to solve small NP search problems (see a discussion of NP search experiments in Section 6).
• **General-purpose Molecular Computers using DP-BMC.** BMC machines using molecular parallelism and providing large memories, are being constructed at Wisconsin [LGCCL+96], [CCCFF+97,LTCSC97] and USC [A95,RWBCG+96,ARRW96]. In both projects, a large number of DNA strands are used, where each DNA strand stores multiple memory words. Both these machines will be capable of performing, in parallel, certain classes of simple operations on words within the DNA molecules used as memory. Both projects developed error-resistant word designs. The Wisconsin project is employing a surface to immobilize the DNA strands which correspond to the solution space of a NP search problem. In contrast, the USC project uses a combination of solution-based and solid support methods, which are used to improve the efficiency of the separation operations.
• **Parallel Arithmetic.** To compete with silicon, it is important to develop the capability of BMC to quickly execute basic operations, such as arithmetic and Boolean operations, that are executed in single steps by conventional machines. Furthermore, these basic operations should be executable in massively parallel fashion (that is, executed on multiple inputs in parallel).

Guarnieri and Bancroft [GB96] developed a DNA-based addition algorithm employing successive primer extension reactions to implement the carries and the Boolean logic required in binary addition (similar methods can be used for subtraction). Guarnieri, Fliss, and Bancroft prototyped [GFB96] the first BMC addition operations (on single bits) in recombinant DNA. Subsequent proposed methods [RKL98], [OGB97,LKSR97,GPZ97], and [RKL98] for basic operations such as arithmetic (addition and subtraction) permit chaining of the output of these operations into the inputs to further operations, and to allow operations to be executed to be executed in massive parallel fashion.
(C) The Local Assembly Paradigm. The *local parallelism (LP-BMC)* paradigm for BMC allows operations to be executed in parallel on a given molecule (in contrast to the parallelism where operations are executed in parallel on a large number of distinct molecules but execute sequentially within any given molecule).
• **DNA Nano-Fabrication Techniques.** Feynman [F61] proposed nano-fabrication of structures of molecular size. Nanotechnology, without use of DNA, is discussed in the texts [CL92,M93]. Nano-fabrication of structures in DNA was pioneered by Seeman (e.g., see [SZC94]) in the 1990s. His work may well be of central importance to the progress of the emerging field of BMC. Seeman and his students such as Chen and Wang nano-fabricated in DNA (see [ZS92,ZS94,SWLQ+96,SQLYL+96,SZDC95] and [SZC94,SC91,SZDWM+94,SQLYL+96]): *2D polygons,* including interlinked squares, and *3D polyhedra,* including a cube and a truncated octahedron. Seeman's ingenious constructions used for basic constructive components: *DNA junctions:* i.e., immobile and partially mobile DNA n-armed branched junctions [SCK89], *DNA knots:* i.e., ssDNA knots [MDS91,DS92] and Borromean rings[MS97], *DNA crossover molecules:* i.e., DX molecules of Fu and Seeman[FS93]. Many of Seeman's constructions used DX molecules

for rigidity or dsDNA for partial rigidity. Most of the constructions utilized hybridization in solution, usually followed by ligation. The octahedron used solid-support [S88], to avoid interaction between constructed molecules [ZS92]. See [CRFCC+96,MLMS96] for other work in DNA nano-structures. Recently, Seeman et al [SMY+98] constructed from DNA a nanomechanical device capable of controlled movement.

• **Tiling.** A class of *(domino) tiling problems* were defined by Wang [W61] as follows: we are given a finite set of tiles of unit size square tiles each with top and bottom sides labeled with symbols over a finite alphabet. These labels will be called *pads*. We also specify the initial placement of a specified subset of these tiles, and the borders of the region where tiles must be placed defining the *extent of tiling*. The problem is to place the tiles, chosen with replacement, in all these square regions within the specified borders, so that each pair of vertical abutting tiles have identical symbols on their contacting sides. Let the *size* of the tiling assembly be the number of tiles placed. Berger [B66] (also see Buchi [B62]) proved that given a finite set of tile types, the tiling problem is undecidable if the extent of tiling is infinite. Direct simulations TMs are given in [R71,LP81,GJP77] and [LP81] proved that the domino tiling problem is NP-complete if the extent of tiling is a rectangle of polynomial size. (see the servey of Grunbaum, Branko, and Shepard [GBS87])

• **Computation via Local Assembly.** Winfree [W96] proposed a very intriguing idea: to do these tiling constructions by application of the DNA nano-fabrication techniques of Seeman et al [SZC94], which may be used for the construction of small DNA molecules that can function as square tiles with pads on the sides. The pads are ssDNA. Recall that if two ssDNA are sticky (i.e., Watson-Crick complementary and $3'-8'$ and $5'-3'$ oriented in opposite directions), they may hybridize together at the appropriate conditions into doubly stranded DNA. The assembly of the tiles is due to this hybridization of pairs of matching sticky pads on the sides of the tiles. We will call this innovative paradigm for BMC *unmediated self-assembly* since the computations advance with no intervention by any controllers. The computations advance with no intervention by any controllers, and require no thermal cycling. It is a considerable paradigm shift from dDP-BMC, which requires the recombinant DNA steps (which implement the molecular parallelism) to be done in sequence.

To simulate a $1D$ parallel automata or a one tape TM, Winfree et al [W96,WYS96] proposed self-assembly of $2D$ arrays of DNA molecules, applying the recombinant DNA nano-fabrication techniques of Seeman et al [SZC94], in combination with the tiling techniques of Berger [B66]. Winfree et al [WYS96] used this idea to solve a variety of computational problems using unmediated DNA self-assembly, e.g., directed Hamiltonian path problem, using a tiling of polynomial size extent. Winfree et al [WYS96] also provided a valuable experimental test validating the preferential pairing of matching DNA tiles over partially non-matching DNA tiles. Winfree [Win98a] made computer simulations of computing by self-assembly of DNA tiles, with a detailed simulation model of the kenetics of annealing during the self assembly of DNA tiles.

• **Assemblies of Small Size and Depth.** To increase the likelihood of success of assembly, Reif [R97] proposed a *step-wise assembly* which provides control of the assembly in distinct steps. The total number of steps is bound by the depth of the assembly. Also, [R97] proposed the use of *frames*, which are rigid DNA nano-structures used to constrain the geometry of the assembly and to allow for the placement of input DNA strands on the boundaries of the tiling assembly. Using these assembly techniques, [R97] proposed LP-BMC methods to solve a number of fundamental problems that form the basis for the design of many parallel algorithms, for these decreased the size of the assembly to linear in the input size and and significantly decreased the number of time steps.

For example, the *prefix computation problem* is the problem of applying an associative operation to all prefixes of a sequence of n inputs, and can be used to solve arithmetic problems such as integer addition, subtraction, multiplication by a constant number, finite state automata simulation, and to fingerprint (hash) a string. [R97] gave step-wise assembly algorithms, with linear assembly size and logarithmic time, for the prefix computation problem. As another example, *normal parallel algorithms* [S71,U84,L92] are a large class of parallel algorithms that can be executed in logarithmic time on shuffle-exchange networks (for example DFT, bitonic merge, and an arbitrary fixed permutation of n data elements in logarithmic time). [R97] gave LP-BMC methods for perfect shuffle and pair-wise exchange using a linear size assembly and constant assembly depth, and thus constant time. This allows one to execute normal parallel algorithms using LP-BMC in logarithmic time. Also, this implies a method for parallel evaluation of a bounded degree Boolean circuit in time bounded by the circuit depth times a logarithmic factor. Previously, such operations had been implemented using DP-BMC techniques [R95] in similar time bounds but required a large amount of volume; in contrast the LP-BMC methods of [R97] require very modest volume. All of these LP-BMC algorithms of [R97] can also use DP-BMC to simultaneously solve multiple problems with distinct inputs (e.g. do parallel arithmetic on multiple inputs, or determine satisfying inputs of a circuit), so they are an enhancement of the power of DP-BMC. Jonoska et al [JKS98] describes techniques for solving the Hamiltonian path problem by self assembly of single strand DNA into three dimensional DNA structures representing a Hamiltonian path.

(D) The Cellular Processor Paradigm. BMC may make use of microorganisms such as bacteria to do computation. A *cellular processor* is a microorganism such as a bacteria, which does computation via a re-engineered regulatory feedback system for cellular metabolism. The re-engineering involves the insertion of modified regulatory genes. whose DNA has been modified and engineered so that the cell can compute using regulatory feedback systems used in cellular metabolism. This paradigm for BMC was first discussed in a science fiction article of Bear [Bea83]. The recent papers Ji [Ji98] and Kazic [Kaz98] discuss models for doing BMC using cellular processors. A group at the Lab for CS, MIT is designing an experimental demonstration of a cellular processor.

Alternative Paradigms for BMC. There may well be further alternative paradigms for BMC. For example, Landweber [La96] proposes the use of RNA rather than DNA as the basis of the biotechnology.

4.2 Enabling Technologies and Experimental Paradigms for QC. As noted above, any QC can be realized by a *universal* set of gates consisting of the 2-qubit XOR operation along with some 1-qubit operations. There are two basic approaches known to do QC:

(A) Micromolecular QC. Here QC on n qubits is executed using n individual atoms, ions or photons, and each qubit is generally encoded using the quantized states of each individual atom, ion or photon. The readout (observation operation) is by measurement of the (eigen) state of each individual atom, ion or photon. In the following we enumerate a number of proposed micromolecular QC methods (see the full paper [R98] for a more detailed description):

• **Quantum Dots.** (Burkard [BLD98], Loss et al [LD97], Meekhof et al [MMK+96] describe the use of coupled quantum dots to do QC),

Ion Trap QC (Cirac, Zoller [CZ95], James [Jam97]) proposed using a linear array of ions trapped by electromagnetic fields, whose energy states are used to store the qubits; see Cirac, Zoller [CZ95], James [Jam97], Meekhof et al [Mee96], Wineland et al [WMM+96, WMI+98], King et al [KWM98], Turchette et al [TWK+98], Hughes[Hug97], Hughes et al [HJG+98], James [JGH+98]),

• **Cavity QED.** (A group at Cal Tech (Turchette [THL+95]) have experimentally demonstrated the use of trapped photons in a cavity QED system to execute 2-qubit XOR gates and thus in principle can do universal QC),

• **Photonics.** (see Chuang et al [CY95, CVZ+98] , Torma, Stenholm [TS96], who experimentally demonstrated QC using optical systems where qubits are encoded by photon phases and universal quantum gates are implemented by optical components consisting of beamsplitters, phase shifters and nonlinear media.),

• **Heteropolymer.** (This is a polymer consisting of a linear array of atoms, each of which can be either in a ground or excited energy state; see Teich et al [TOM88], Lloyd [Llo93]),

• **Nuclear Spin.** (see DiVincenzo [DiV97b] Wei et al [WXM98a, WXM98b]),

• **Propogation Delays.** (see Castagnoli [Cas97]).

Of these, Ion Trap QC, Cavity QED QC, and Photonics have been experimentally demonstrated up to a very small number of qubits (about 3 bits). The apparent intention of such micromolecular methods for QC is to have an apparatus for storing qubits and executing unitary operations (but not necessarily executing observation operations) which requires only volume linear in the number of qubits. One difficulty (addressed by Kak [Kak98], Murao et al [MPP+97]) is *purification of the initial state*: if the state of a QC is initially in an entangled state, and each of the quantum gate transformations introduces phase uncertainty during the QC, then effect of these perturbations may accumulate to make the output to the QC incorrect. A more basic difficulty for these micromolecular methods is that they all use experimental technology that is not well established as might be; in particular their approaches each involve containment of atomic size objects (such as individual atoms, ions or photons) and manipulations of their states. A further difficulty of the micromolecular methods for QC is that apperatus for the observation operation, for even if observation is approximated, seems to require volume growing exponential with the number of qubits, as described ealier in this paper.

(B) Bulk (or NMR) QC. Nuclear magnetic resonance (NMR) spectroscopy is an imaging technology using the spin of the nuclei of a large collection of atoms. Bulk QC is executed on a macroscopic volume containing, in solution a large number of identical molecules, each of which encodes all the qubits. The molecule can be chosen so that it has n distinct quantized spins modes (e.g., each of the n nuclei may have a distinct quantized spins). Each of the n qubits is encoded by one of these spin modes of the molecule. The coupling of qubits is via spin-spin coupling between pairs of distinct nuclei. Unitary operations such as XOR can be executed by radio frequency (RF) pulses at resonance frequencies determined in part by this spin-spin coupling between pairs of nuclei (and also by the chemical structure of the molecule). Bulk QC was independently proposed by Cory, Fahmy, Havel [CFH96] and Gershenfeld, Chuang [GC97, GC98] (Also see Berman et al [BDL+98] and the proposal of Wei et al [WXM98b] for doing MNR QC on doped crystals rather than in solutions.)

• **Bulk QC was experimentally tested** for the following: the quantum baker's map on 3 qubits (Brun, Schack [BS98]), quantum search (Jones et al [JMH98] and Jones [Jon98]), approximate quantum counting (Jones, Mosca [JM98a]) Deutsch's problem (Jones, Mosca [JM98b]), Deutsch-Jozsa algorithm on a 3 qubits (Linden, Barjat, Freeman[LBR98]).

• **Advantages of Bulk QC:** (i) it can use well established NMR technology and in particular macroscopic devices, The main advantages are (ii) the long time duration until decoherence (due to a low coupling with the environment) and (iii) it currently scales to more qubits than other proposed technologies for QC.

• **Disadvantages of Bulk QC:** A disadvantage of Bulk QC is that it appears to allow only a *weak* measurement of the ensemble average which does not provide a quantum state reduction; that is the weak measurement does not alter (at least by much) the superposition of states. (Later we suggest an interesting BMC technique for doing observations (with quantum state reduction) for Bulk QC.) Another disadvantage of Bulk QC is that it appears to require, for a variety of reasons, macroscopic volumes, and in particular volumes which grow exponential with the number of qubits. Macroscopic volumes appear to be required for measurement via conventional means. Also, Bulk QC requires the initialization to close to a pure state. If Bulk QC is done at room temperature, the initialization methods of Cory, Fahmy, Havel [CFH96] (using logical labeling) and Gershenfeld, Chuang [GC97, GC98] (using spatial averaging) yield a pseudo-pure state, where the number of molecules actually in the pure state drops exponentially as $1/c^n$ with the number n of qubits, for some constant c (as noted by Warren [War95]). In the full paper [R98], we observe that to overcome this measurement error, we need the volume N to grow exponentially with n. Recently, there have been various other proposed methods for initialization to a pure state: (see Barnes[Bar98], Gershenfeld, Chuang [GC98], Knill et al [KCL97], Schulman, Vezeroni [SV98]) the latter provides polynomial volume for initialization, with the assumption of an exponential decrease in spin-spin correlations with the distance between the nuclei located within a molecule. Although their methods may provide a solution in practice, most inter-atomic interactions such as the spin-spin correlations seem to decrease by inverse polynomial power laws rather than by an exponential decrease. It has not yet been experimentally established which of these pure state initialization methods scale to a large number of qubits without large volume.

(Note: Some physicists feel that it has not been clearly established whether: (a) MNR is actually a quantum phenomenon with quantum superposition of classical states, or (b) if MNR just mimics a quantum phenomenon and is actually just classical parallelism, where the quantum superposition of classical states is encoded using multiple molecules where each molecule is in a distinct classical state. If the latter is true with each molecule is in a distinct classical state, then (see Williams and Clearwater [WC96]) the volume may grow grow exponentially with the number n of qubits, since each classical state may need to be stored by at least one molecule, and the number of classical states can be 2^n. Also, even if each molecule is in some partially mixed quantum state (see Zyczkowski et al [ZHS98]), the volume may still need to grow very large.)

In summary, some potential disadvantages of Bulk QC that may make it difficulty to scale are (i) the inability to do observation (strong measurement with quantum state reduction), (ii) the difficulty to do even a weak measurement without the use of exponential volume, (iii) difficulty (possibly now resolved) to obtain pure initial states without the use of exponential volume, (iv) the possibility that Bulk QC is not a quantum phenomena at all (an unresolved controversy within physics), and so may require use of exponential volume.

It is interesting to consider whether NNR can be scaled down from the macroscopic to molecular level. DiVincenzo [DiV97b] Wei et al [WXM98a, WXM98b] propose doing QC using the nuclear spins of atoms or electrons in a single trapped molecule. The main advantages are (i) small volume and (ii) the long time duration until decoherence (an advantage shared with NMR). The key difficulty of this approach is the measurement of the state of each spin, which does not appear to be feasible by the mechanical techniques for detection of magnetic resonance usual used in MNR, which can only do detection of the spin for large ensembles of atoms.

5 Correcting Errors

5.1 Correcting Errors in BMC. BMC has certain requirements not met by conventional recombinant DNA technology. Various methods have been developed which improve conventional recombinant DNA to obtain high yields and to allow for repeatability of operations. Also, analytic and simulation models of key recombinant DNA operations are being developed. In the full paper [R98], we discuss methods for efficient error-resistant separations, minimizing ligation errors, and DNA word design for BMC.

5.2 Correcting Errors in QC.

• **Decoherence Errors in QC.** *Quantum decoherence* is the gradual introduction of errors of amplitude in the quantum superposition of classical states. All known experimental implementations of QC suffer from the gradual decoherence of entangled states. The rate of decoherence per step of QC depends on the specific technology implementing QC. Although the addition of decoherence errors in the amplitudes may at first not have a major effect on the QC, the affect of the errors may accumulate over time and completely destroy the computation. Researchers have dealt with decoherence errors by extending classical error correction techniques to quantum analogs. Generally, there is assumed a decoherence error model where the errors introduced are assumed to be uniform random with bounded magnitude, independently for each qubit. In the full paper [R98], we discuss quantum codes, quantum coding theory, and quantum compression.

6 Applications

6.1 Applications of BMC. There are a wide variety of problems (up to moderate sizes) that may benefit from the massive parallelism and nano-scale miniaturization available to BMC. In the full paper [R98], we discuss these applications in more detail.

• **NP search problems.** NP search problems may be solved by BMC by (a) assembling a large number of potential solutions to the search problem, where each potential solution is encoded on a distinct strand of DNA, and (b) then performing recombinant DNA operations which separate out the correct solutions of the problem. DP-BMC has been proposed for the following NP search problems: (*i*) *Hamiltonian path* (Adleman[A94], [G94,KTL97], Fu et al [FBZ98],[MoS97]), (*ii*) *Boolean Formula Satisfiability (SAT)* (Lipton [L94], [BDLS95], Eng [Eng98], and the Whiplash PCR of Hagiya and Arita [HA97],Winfree [Win98b]), (*iii*) *graph coloring* (Jonoska and Karl [JK96]) (*iv*) *shortest common superstring problem* (Gloor et al [GKG+98]), (*v*) *integer factorization* (Beaver [Be94]), (*vi*) *breaking the DES cryptosystem* ([BDL95] and [ARRW96]), (*vii*) *protein conformation* (Conrad and Zauner [CZ97]).

– **Decreasing the Volume Used in NP search.** In all these methods, the number of steps grows as a polynomial function of the size of the input, but the volume grows exponentially with the input. For exact solutions of NP complete problems, we may benefit from a more general type of computation than simply brute force search. The molecular computation needs to be general enough to implement sophisticated heuristics, which may result in a smaller search space and volume. For example, Ogihara and Ray [OR97a] proposed a DP-BMC method for decreasing the volume (providing a smaller constant base of the exponential growth rate) required to solve the SAT problem. The difficulty with many of these approaches for NP search is that they initially generate a very large volume containing all possible solutions. An alternative heuristic approach of iteratively refining the solution space. to solve NP search problems has been suggested by Hagiya and Arita [HA97] and Cukras et al [CFL+98], and may in practice give a significant decrease in the volume.

• **Huge Associative Memories.** BMC has the potential to provide huge memories. Each individual strand of DNA can encode binary information. A small volume can contain a vast number of molecules. As we have discussed in Section 3, DNA in weak solution in one liter of water can encode 10^7 to 10^8 tera-bytes, and we can perform massively parallel associative searches on these memories. Baum [B95] (also see Lipton [L96]) proposed a parallel memory where DNA strands are used to store memory words, and provided a method for doing associative memory searches using complementary matching. Lipton [Lip98] describes the use of web data bases and associative search within them to do cryptoanalysis.

• **Massively Parallel Machines.** BMC also has the potential to supply massive computational power. BMC can be used as a parallel machine where each processor's state is encoded by a DNA strand. BMC can perform massively parallel computations by executing recombinant DNA operations that act on all the DNA molecules at the same time. These recombinant DNA operations may be performed to execute massively parallel local memory read/write, logical operations and also further basic operations on words such as parallel arithmetic. As we have discussed in Section 3, DNA in weak solution in one liter of water can encode the state of about 10^{18} processors, and since certain recombinant DNA operations can take many minutes, the overall potential for a massively parallel BMC machines is about $1,000$ tera-ops.

• **Combinatorial Chemistry as NP Searches.** *Combinatorial chemistry* techniques (also known as *diversity* techniques) have been used by biochemists to do combinatorial searches for biological objects with special properties. The disciplines of combinatorial chemistry and BMC may benefit by combining some of their techniques. For example, the search space of combinatorial chemistry might be decreased by sophisticated heuristics used in NP search methods.

• **Other Algorithmic Applications of DP-BMC.** DP-BMC may also be used to speed up computations that would require polynomial time on conventional machines: Beigel and Fu [BF97] discuss approximation algorithm for NP search problems, Baum and Boneh discuss DP-BMC methods for executing dynamic programming algorithms, and Oliver [O96] discusses DP-BMC methods for matrix multiplication.

• **Neural Network Learning and Image Recognition.** Mills, Yurke, and Platzman [MYP98] propose a rather innovative BMC system for error-tolerant learning in a neural network, which is intended to be used for associative matching of images. They make innovative use of DNA chips for I/O.

• **DNA Nano-fabrication and Self-assembly.** BMC techniques combined with Seeman's DNA nano-fabrication techniques allow for the self-assembly of DNA tiles into lattices in 2 and 3 dimensions and the construction of complex nano-structures that encode computations.

• **Biological Applications: Processing of Natural DNA.** BMC may also be used in problems that are not implicitly digital in nature, for example the processing of natural (biologically derived) DNA. These techniques may be used to provide improved methods for the sequencing and fingerprinting of natural DNA, and the solution of other biomedical problems. The results of processing natural DNA can be used to form *wet data bases* with re-coded DNA in solution, and BMC can be used to do fast searches and data base operations on these wet databases. BMC techniques might be ideally suited to solve problems in molecular biology which inherently involve *natural DNA*, that is DNA that is biologically derived (as opposed to artificially synthesized DNA which is coded over a given word alphabet). Lipton, Boneh, and Landweber [LBL96] considered such a class of problems, including sequencing, fingerprinting and mutation detection. These may well be the *killer applications* of BMC. An experimental demonstration, at moderate scale, of a BMC method for solving a significant problem in molecular biology with natural DNA inputs, will be a major milestone in BMC.

• **Approximate Counting of DNA.** Faulhammer, Lipton, and Landweber [FLL98] give a BMC method for estimating the number of DNA strands within a test tube.
6. 2 Applications of QC. The early literature in QC provided some examples of QC algorithms for problems constructed for the reasonable purpose of showing that QC can solve some problems more efficiently than conventional sequential computing models. Later, quantum algorithms were developed for variety of useful applications. Again further details are given in In the full paper [R98].
• **Quantum Fourier Transforms.** Drutsch, Jazsa [DJ92] gave an $O(n)$ time quantum algorithm for creating a uniform superposition of all possible values of n bits, which is a *quantum Fourier transform* over the finite field of size 2. Extensions of the quantum Fourier transform are given by Coppersmith [Cop94], Griffiths, Niu [GN96], Hoyer [Hoy97], Beals [Bea98], Pueschel, Roetteler, Bet [PRB98], and to applications to arithmetic and polynomial problems are described in Vedral, Barenco, Ekert [VBE96] and Grigoriev [Gri97].
• **Quantum Factoring.** The most notable algorithmic result in QC to date is the quantum algorithm of Shor [Sho94, Sho97] (also see the review by Ekert and Jozsa [EJ96]) for discrete logarithm and integer factorization in polynomial time (with modest amplitude precision). Shor's algorithm uses efficient reduction from integer factoring to the problem of approximately computing the period (length of a orbit) within an integer ring. The period is approximated by repeated the use of a quantum Fourier transform over the integer ring and greatest common divisor computations. Further work is done by Zalka [Zal98], Beckman et al [BCD+96], Obenland, Despain [OD96a], Plenio, Knight [PK96], Kitaev [Kit95].
• **Quantum Search.** Another significant efficient QC algorithmic result is the algorithm of Grover [Gro96], which searches within a data base of size N in time $\sqrt{N}$ Grover refined his result in [Gro97,Gro98], Bounds on quantum search are given by Zalka [Zal97], Pati [PAT98],[FGG+98] Biron et al [BBB+98], and applications to data bases are given by Cockshott [Coc97], and Benjamin, Johnson [BJ98] Brassard et al [BNT96] combine the techniques of Grover and Shor to give a fast quantum algorithm for approximately counting.

While Grover's algorithm is clearly an improvement over linear sequential search in a data base, it appears less impressive in the case of an explicitly defined data base which needs to be stored in volume N. Methods for BMC (and in fact ma number of methods for massively parallel computation) can do search in a data base of size N in time at most polylogarithmic with N, by relatively straightforward use of parallel search Moreover, Grover's algorithm may not have a clear advantage even in the case of an implicitly defined data base, which does not need to be stored, but instead can be constructed on the fly (e.g., that arising from NP search methods). In this case, Grover's search algorithm can be used to speed up combinatorial search within a domain of size N to a time bound of $O(\sqrt{N})$ (see Hogg [Hog96], Hogg, Yanik [HY98]), and in this case Grover's algorithm appears to require only volume logarithmic in the (combinatorial) search space size N. In contrast, BMC takes volume linear in the search space, but takes just time polylogorithmic in the search space.
• **Quantum Simulations in Physics.** The first application proposed for QC (Feynman [Fey82]) was for simulating quantum physics. In principle, quantum computers provide universal quantum simulation of any quantum mechanical physical system (Lloyd [Llo96], Zalka[Zal96a], Boghosian [Bog98])).Proposed QC simulations of quantum mechanical systems include: many-body systems (Wiesner[Wie96]), many-body Fermi systems (Abrams, Lloyd [AL97]), multiparticle (ballistic) evolution (Benioff [Ben96]), quantum lattice-gas models (Boghosian, Taylor [BT96]), Meyer [Mey96a, Mey96b]), Ising spin

glasses (Lidar, Biham [LB97]), the thermal rate constant (Lidar, Wang [LW98], quantum chaos (Schack [Sch97]).

• **Quantum Cryptography.** Bennett et al [BBB+82] gave the first methods for quantum cryptography using qubits as keys, which are secure against all possible types of attacks. Surveys of quantum cryptography are given in Bennett, Brassard, Ekert [BBE92], Brassard [Bra93], Bennett, Brassard [BB84b], Brassard [Bra94].

• **Distributed Quantum Networks.** Future hardware will have to be fast, scalable, and highly parallelizable. A *quantum network* is a network of QCs executing over a spatially distributed network, where quantum entanglement is distributed among distant nodes in the quantum network. Thus, using *distributed entanglement*, a quantum network distributes the parts of an entangled state to various processors, which can to act on the parts independently. Various basic difficulties were overcome: *How can one do state transfer distribution?* (see Bennett et al [BBC93, BBP+96], Brassard [Bra96]), and *how can one cope with communication errors and attenuation in a quantum network?* (see the *quantum repeaters* that do quantum error correction in Ekert et al [CZ97], Knill, Laflamme, Zurek [KLZ96]).

• **Quantum Learning.** (see Bshouty, Jackson [BJ95], Ventura, Martinez [VM98c], Yu, Vlasov [YV96], Tucci [Tuc98], Ventura, Martinez [VM98b])

• **Quantum Robotics.** Benioff [Ben97] considers a distributed QC system with mobile *quantum robots* that can carry out carrying out measurements and physical experiments on the environment.

• **Winding Up quantum Clocks.** The precision of atomic clocks are limited by the spontaneous decay lifetimes of excited atomic states, but Huelga [HMP+97]) and Bollinger et al [Bol96] extend these lifetimes by using quantum error correcting codes.

7 Hybrids of BMC and QC

7.1 Applications of QC to BMC. It is interesting to envision a BMC that uses quantum affects to aid in its I/O. We can apply the quantum Zeno affect (similar to that used by Kwiat et al [KWHZK95,KWZ96]) to do exquisite detection (of say, of a single molecule) within a large container of fluid, by taking quantum samples of the volume, and doing repeated rounds of sensing. If the molecule to be detected is in fact in the fluid, then the amount of sensing is very small quantity quickly decreasing with the number of rounds. However, if a molecule is not in the fluid, then the amount of sensing by this method can be quite large. (A result of Reif [Rei98] shows that quantum techniques can not reduce the amount of sensing for both cases.)

7.2 Applications of BMC to QC. One interesting application of BMC is to do the observation operation for Bulk QC. Here we assume that the Bulk QC is being executed on a macroscopic volume of solution, containing a large number of micromolecules which are the quantum components for the Bulk QC unitary operations. Recall that Bulk QC can only do a weak measurement of the state of the spins; the weak measurement does not much affect the state superposition. We would like instead to do an observation operation which reduces the current state superposition. A possible technique is to place each of these micromolecule onto or within a host (e.g., a natural or artificial cell, or a macromolecule such as a protein, DNA, or RNA). The host should be much larger than the micromolecule, but still microscopic. There are a number of techniques where by the host might be used to a do an observation of the state of the qubit spins of the micromolecule (perhaps via a nearly irreversible chemical reaction), which results in a reduction of the micromolecule's state superposition. A key reservation to this technique is the apparent growth of the size of the measurement apparatus with the number of qubits.

8 Conclusion and Acknowledgements

Comparison of Current BMC with early VLSI. BMC is a new field, with largely unexplored methodologies. In the full paper, we compare BMC and QC in the later 1990's with the state of VLSI in 1970s, and note that they suffer from similar difficulties. For example, currently the design and execution of a BMC or QC experiment in the laboratory is supported with only a few software tools for design and simulation prior to doing the experiment:

• **Computer Simulations of BMC.** A preliminary version of a Java software tool for simulating BMC has been developed by Gehani, Reif [GR98b].

• **Computer Simulations of QC.** Obenland, Despain [OD97, D98a, D98b] have given efficient computer simulations of QC, including errors and decoherence, and Cerf, S. E. Koonin [CK98] have given Monte Carlo simulations of QC.

In spite of advanced technologies for Recombinant DNA and for quantum apparatus, experiments in BMC and QC are highly prone to errors. We have discussed techniques that alleviate some of these errors, but this clearly motivates the need to further develope software tools for design and simulation of BMC and QC experiments.

Also, there is at this time no consensus on which methods for doing BMC are the best; as we have seen there are multiple approaches that may have success. While some of the current experiments in BMC are using conventional solution-based recombinant DNA technology, others are employing alternative biotechnology (such as surface attachments). It is also not yet clear which of the paradigms for BMC will be preeminent. There is a similar lack of consensus within QC of the best and most scalable technologies. To a degree, this diversity of approaches may in itself be an advantage, since it will increase the likelihood of prototyping and establishing successful methodologies.

Acknowledgements. We would like to thank G. Brassard for his clear explanation of numerous results in the field of QC. Supported by Grants NSF CCR-9725021, NSF IRI-9619647, NSF/DARPA CCR-92725021, and ARO contract DAAH-04-96-1-0448.

References

[R98] Reif, J.H., *Alternative Computational Models: A Comparison of Biomolecular and Quantum Computation*, (Sept., 1998), Full version of the extended abstract appearing in these proceedings.
(a postscript preprint is online at
http://www.cs.duke.edu/~ reif/paper/paper.html/altcomp.ps).

Note: Due to page length constraints, the references in have been removed from the extended abstract appearing in these proceedings. The full paper [Rei98] has 646 references (including 265 references to BMC and 381 references to QC), and many additional discussions of experimental techniques, applications and error correction.

Optimal Regular Tree Pattern Matching Using Pushdown Automata

Maya Madhavan
Priti Shankar

Department of Computer Science and Automation
Indian Institute of Science
Bangalore 560012
India

Abstract. We propose a construction that augments the precomputation step of a regular tree pattern matching algorithm to include cost analysis. The matching device generated is a pushdown automaton in contrast with the conventionally generated tree pattern matching automaton. Our technique can handle a larger class of cost augmented regular tree grammars than can be preprocessed by conventional methods, and has been tested on some input problem instances representing instruction sets for processors.

1 Introduction

The use of regular tree grammars and rewriting systems for the description of machine instructions for use in code generation tools is well known [4] [2] [7] [14] [8] [15] [13]. The problem addressed in this paper can be stated as follows: *Given a regular tree grammar whose productions are augmented with costs, and an input subject tree, compute a minimum cost derivation tree for the input tree.* In a typical application, the subject tree is an intermediate code representation for a source program undergoing compilation; the minimum cost derivation tree yields a cheapest assembly level code sequence for the tree. Most algorithms for regular tree pattern matching draw heavily from the seminal work of [9] and [3] for the problem of tree pattern matching with a single wildcard. The algorithms employ a *preprocessing* phase, which constructs tables encoding the finite state tree pattern matching automaton, and a *matching* phase which traverses the input subject tree and reports matches at the appropriate nodes. For *optimal* regular tree pattern matching there is the additional requirement of choosing a *minimal cost* pattern that matches at the root. Algorithms such as [4] [15] [2] and [14] perform cost computations at preprocessing time, whereas [7] [1] [13] [5] perform them at matching time. Graham and Glanville [6] used $LR(0)$ parsing techniques for retargettable code generation. However, their technique cannot be applied to regular tree pattern matching in general, as it does not carry forward all choices until an optimal decision can be made. Our technique may be viewed as an extension of the $LR(0)$ technique in order to simultaneously track all derivations and precompute costs. We have incorporated a variation of a technique proposed in [2] into an algorithm introduced in [17] for this purpose. A sufficient condition for termination of the algorithm is given. We have also presented the results from preprocessing regular tree grammars representing instruction sets of two machines, and compared the table sizes so obtained with those output by a preprocessor which generates a finite state tree pattern matching automaton [16].

2 Background

Let A be a finite alphabet consisting of a set of operators OP and a set of terminals T. Each operator *op* in OP is associated with an *arity*, *arity*(*op*). Elements of T have arity 0. The set $TREES(A)$ consists of all trees with internal nodes labeled with elements of OP, and leaves with labels from T. The number of children of a node labeled *op* is *arity*(*op*). Special symbols called *wildcards* are assumed to have arity 0. If N is a set of wildcards, the set $TREES(A \cup N)$ is the set of all trees with wildcards also allowed as labels of leaves.
We begin with a few definitions drawn from [2].
Definition 2.1 A *regular tree grammar* G is a four tuple (N, A, P, S) where
1. N is a finite set of *nonterminal* symbols
2. $A = T \cup OP$ is a *ranked alphabet*, with the ranking function denoted by arity. T is the set of *terminal* symbols and OP is the set of *operators*.
3. P is a finite set of *production rules* of the form $X \to t$, where $X \in N$ and t is an encoding of a tree in $TREES(A \cup N)$.
4. S is the *start symbol* of the grammar.
A *tree pattern* is thus represented by the righthand side of a production of P in the grammar above. A production of P is called a *chain rule*, if it is of the form $A \to B$, where both A and B are nonterminals. For purposes of the discussion here we will be dealing with grammars in *normal form* defined below:
Definition 2.2 A production is said to be in normal form if it is in one of the three forms below.
1. $A \to opB_1B_2 \dots B_k$ where $A, B_i, i = 1, 2, \dots k$ are all non terminals, and *op* has arity k.
2. $A \to B$, where A and B are non terminals.
3. $B \to b$, where b is a terminal.
A grammar is in normal form if all its productions are in normal form. Any regular tree grammar can be put into normal form by the introduction of extra nonterminals.
Below is an example of a regular tree grammar in normal form. For the time being, we ignore the costs associated with the productions.
Example 2.1
$G = (\{V, B, G\}, A, P, V)$ where, $A = \{a, b\}$ and the arities are 2 and 0 respectively. The productions P, augmented with cost are as follows:

$V \to aVB[0]$	$V \to aGV[1]$	$V \to G[1]$
$G \to B[1]$	$V \to b[7]$	$B \to b[4]$

Derivation sequences are defined in the usual way. However, we note that the objects being derived are trees. Two derivation trees for the subject tree

$a(a(b,b),b)$ in the language generated by the regular tree grammar of example 2.1 above, are displayed in Figure 2.1.

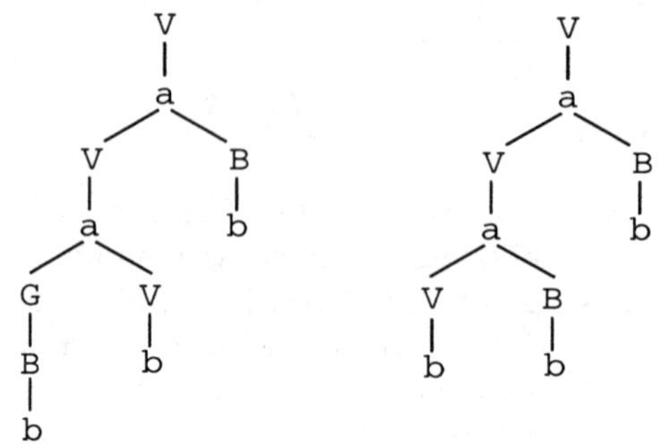

Figure 2.1 Two derivation trees for the subject tree $a(a(b,b),b))$ in the grammar of example 2.1.

A tree pattern is said to *match* at a node in the subject tree, if a production with righthand side corresponding to the tree pattern is used at that node in the derivation tree. Each derivation tree thus defines a set of matches, (a *set* because there may be chain rules that match) at each node in the subject tree. The regular tree pattern matching problem may thus be phrased as :*Given a regular tree grammar G and a subject tree t, find a representation of all derivation trees for t in G.*

The regular tree pattern matching problem for a grammar G can be converted into a string parsing problem for a context free grammar by constructing a new grammar G' from G, by converting righthand sides of all productions of G into postorder listings of the corresponding tree patterns. Any listing will work; however, a postorder listing is appropriate for a bottom up algorithm. Since each operator has a fixed arity, the postorder listing uniquely defines the tree. Let $post(t)$ denote the postorder listing of a tree t. We note that the grammar G' is in general ambiguous. It is shown in [17] that finding all derivation trees in G corresponds to finding all derivations in G'.

We assume that the reader is familiar with the notions of right sentential forms, handles, viable prefixes, and $LR(0)$ items being valid for viable prefixes. Definitions may be found in [10].

The three key ideas used in the algorithm in [17] are the following:

1. Refinement of the notion of a pattern matching at a particular node to that of a *pattern matching in a left context* at that node.
2. Equivalence of the problems of detecting pattern matches in left contexts in regular tree grammars, and obtaining rightmost derivation sequences in reverse in the corresponding context free grammars.
3. The observation that all viable prefixes induced by any input string are of the

same length.(By a viable prefix *induced* by an input string we mean the string representing the stack contents after consuming the input string using a shift reduce parsing strategy. The normal form of the grammar is essential for the last property).

Definitions and theorems formalizing these ideas from [17] are presented below. By an X-derivation tree we mean a subtree of a derivation tree with root labeled X.

Definition 2.3 Let $G = (N, T, P, S)$ be a regular tree grammar in normal form, and t be a subject tree. Then pattern β represented by production $X \to \beta$ matches at node j in left context $\alpha, \alpha \in N^*$ if

1. β matches at node j or equivalently, $X \Longrightarrow \beta \Longrightarrow^* t'$ where t' is the subtree rooted at j.

2. If α is not ϵ, then the sequence of maximal complete subtrees of t to the left of j, listed from left to right is $t_1, t_2, \ldots t_k$, with t_i having an X_i-derivation tree,$1 \leq i \leq k$, where $\alpha = X_1 X_2 \ldots X_k$.

3. The string $X_1 X_2 \ldots X_k X$ is a prefix of the postorder listing of some tree in $TREES(A \cup N)$ with an $S-$derivation.

Example 2.2 In the derivation tree on the left in figure 2.1, pattern represented by production $B \longrightarrow b$ matches in left contexts ϵ and V. In the derivation tree on the right both instances match in left context V.

Theorem 2.1 Let $G = (N, T, P, S)$ be a regular tree grammar, and G' the context free grammar constructed as before. Let t be a subject tree with postorder listing $a_1 \ldots a_j w, a_i \in A, w \in A^*$. Then pattern β represented by production $X \to post(\beta)$ of G' matches at node j in left context α if and only if there is a rightmost derivation in the grammar G' of the form

$$S \Longrightarrow^* \alpha X z \Longrightarrow \alpha post(\beta) z \Longrightarrow^* \alpha a_h \ldots a_j z \Longrightarrow^* a_1 \ldots a_j z, z \in A^*$$

where $a_h \ldots a_j$ is the subtree rooted at node j.

Theorem 2.2 Let G' be a context free grammar constructed from a regular tree grammar in normal form. Then for any input string w which is a prefix of a string in $L(G')$, all viable prefixes induced by w are of the same length.

The property stated in the last theorem suggests an augmentation of the LR parsing technique for preprocessing the context free grammar. The construction of the deterministic finite automaton(dfa) that recognizes viable prefixes of an LR grammar can be modified to produce one that recognizes *sets* of viable prefixes of a context free grammar derived from a regular tree grammar. The dfa has two kinds of transitions, those on terminals, and those on *sets* of nonterminals. Any path from the start state of the dfa to a reduce state will spell out a string of the form $S_1 S_2 \ldots S_n a$, where the S_i are sets of nonterminals. The associated viable prefixes are of the form $X_1 X_2 \ldots X_n a$ where $X_i \in S_i$. (Note, however, that not all concatenations of elements of the sets S_i are viable prefixes).

With regular tree pattern matching reduced to parsing, all we need to store during matching, is the equivalent of the LR parsing table for the input grammar. In the next section we show that we can modify the preprocessing algorithm so as to produce an extended $LR(0)$ automaton which is augmented with costs.

3 Precomputation of Costs

3.1 Definitions

Our starting point here is a context free grammar derived from a regular tree grammar augmented with costs. Thus each production is associated with a non negative integer which is the cost of the instruction represented by the tree pattern. We denote this by $rulecost(p)$ for production p. Our aim is to create a LR like parsing table as in the previous section, where each state of the dfa also has relative cost information encoded into it. The technique used in this section is adaptated from [2]. We begin by defining certain entities. Let $G = (N, T, P, S)$ be a cost augmented regular tree grammar in normal form.

Definition 3.1 The absolute cost of a nonterminal X matching an input symbol a in left context ϵ, is represented by $abscost(\epsilon, X, a)$. For a derivation sequence d represented by $X \Longrightarrow X_1 \Longrightarrow X_2 \ldots \Longrightarrow X_n \Longrightarrow a$, let $C_d = rulecost(X_n \longrightarrow a) + \sum_{i=1}^{n-1} rulecost(X_i \longrightarrow X_{i+1}) + rulecost(X \longrightarrow X_1)$, then, $abscost(\epsilon, X, a) = min_d(C_d)$

Definition 3.2 The *absolute cost* of a nonterminal X matching a symbol a in left context α is defined as follows:
$abscost(\alpha, X, a) = abscost(\epsilon, X, a)$ if X matches in left context α
$abscost(\alpha, X, a) = \infty$ otherwise

Definition 3.3 The *relative cost* of a nonterminal X matching a symbol a in left context α is: $cost(\alpha, X, a) = abscost(\alpha, X, a) - min_{y \in N}\{abscost(\alpha, Y, a)\}$.
Having defined costs for trees of height one we next look at trees of height greater than one. Let t be a tree of height greater than one.

Definition 3.4 $abscost(\alpha, X, t) = \infty$ if X does not match t in left context α;
If X matches t in left context α, let $t = a(t_1, t_2, \ldots t_q)$ and $X \longrightarrow aY_1Y_2 \ldots Y_q$ where Y_i matches $t_i, 1 \leq i \leq q$;
Define $abscost(\alpha, X \longrightarrow Y_1Y_2 \ldots Y_q a, t) = rulecost(X \longrightarrow Y_1 \ldots Y_q a) + cost(\alpha, Y_1, t_1) + cost(\alpha Y_1, Y_2, t_2) + \ldots + cost(\alpha Y_1 Y_2 \ldots Y_{q-1}, Y_q, t_q)$
Then $abscost(\alpha, X, t) = min_{X \Longrightarrow \beta \Longrightarrow^* t}\{abscost(\alpha, X \longrightarrow \beta, t)\}$

Definition 3.5 The relative cost of a nonterminal X matching a tree t in left context α is:
$cost(\alpha, X, t) = abscost(\alpha, X, t) - min_{Y \Longrightarrow^* t}\{abscost(\alpha, Y, t)\}$
Having defined the cost of a nonterminal matching in a left context, we next introduce the notion of an augmented rightmost derivation of a context free grammar derived from the regular tree grammar as in the previous section. To avoid complicating notation, we assume from now on, that $G = (N, T, P, S)$ is the context free grammar

Definition 3.6
A single *augmented derivation step* is of the form $\alpha < A, c > w \Longrightarrow \alpha < X_1, d_1 > \ldots < X_k, d_k >< a, 0 > w$ where
1. α is a sequence of $< nonterminal, cost >$ pairs, such that if α' is the concatenation of first members of pairs of α then $S \Longrightarrow^* \alpha' A w \Longrightarrow \alpha' X_1 X_2 \ldots X_k a w$
2. $\exists t s.t. A \Longrightarrow X_1 X_2 \ldots X_k a \Longrightarrow^* t$ with $X_i \Longrightarrow^* t_i, i \leq i \leq k$ and $t = t_1 t_2 \ldots t_k a$
3. $cost(\alpha', X_1, t_1) = d_1, cost(\alpha' X_1, X_2, t_2) = d_2, \ldots cost(\alpha' X_1 X_2 \ldots X_{k-1}, X_k, t_k) =$

d_k and $c = rulecost(A \longrightarrow X_1 \ldots X_k) + \sum_{i=1}^{k} d_i - min_B\{abscost(\alpha\prime, B, t)\}$.

Definition 3.7 An *augmented viable prefix* is any prefix of an augmented right sentential form such that the concatenation of the first elements yields a viable prefix.

Definition 3.8 An augmented item $[A \rightarrow \alpha\,.\,\beta,\, c]$ is valid for an augmented viable prefix $\gamma =< X_1, c_1 >< X_2, c_2 > \cdots < X_n, c_n >$ if,

1. $[A \rightarrow \alpha\,.\,\beta]$ is valid for viable prefix $X_1 X_2 \cdots X_n$.
2. If $\alpha = X_i \cdots X_n$ then, if $\beta \neq \epsilon$ then $c = c_i + c_{i+1} \ldots + c_n$ else $c = c_i + c_{i+1} \ldots + c_n + rulecost(A \longrightarrow \alpha)$

We are actually interested in a similar definition of validity for sets of augmented viable prefixes (which we term *set viable prefixes*), where the costs associated with the items are relative costs. Thus we are naturally led to the following definition.

Definition 3.9 An augmented item $[A \rightarrow \alpha.\beta, c]$ is valid for set viable prefix $S_1 S_2 \ldots S_n$ if

1. There exists a viable prefix $\gamma =< X_1, c_1 >, < X_2, c_2 > \ldots, < X_n, c_n >$ in $S_1 S_2 \ldots S_n$ with $[A \rightarrow \alpha.\beta, c']$ valid for γ
2. If $\beta \neq \epsilon$ then $c = c'$ else $c = c' - min_{\gamma' \in S_1 S_2 \ldots S_n}\{c\prime\prime : [\beta \rightarrow \delta., c\prime\prime]$ is valid for γ'.

3.2 The Preprocessing Algorithm

If the grammar is $LR(0)$, each prefix of a string in the language, induces exactly one viable prefix before any reduction, and there is at most one reduction possible at any step. In this case there may be several augmented viable prefixes induced by the same string. However, as these are all of the same length [17], shifts and reductions may be carried out using a single stack. This permits the use of a simple extension of the $LR(0)$ parsing technique. We first augment the grammar with the production $Z \longrightarrow S\$, [0]$ where \$ is a symbol not in the alphabet, in order to make the language prefix free. We next precompute sets of augmented items that are valid for augmented viable prefixes induced by the same input string. All these are included in a single state. We can then construct a finite state automaton M which we will call the Auxiliary Automaton(AA) as follows:

$M = (Q, \Sigma, \delta, q_0, F)$

where $Q = \{I | I$ is a distinct set of augmented items$\}$

$\Sigma = A \cup 2^{<N,c>}$, where $< N, c >$ is a $(non\ terminal, cost)$ pair

q_0 is the state associated with the initial set of augmented items.

F is the state containing the augmented item $[Z \longrightarrow S\$., 0]$.

δ is the transition function made up of δ_A, the set of transitions on elements of A, and δ_{LC}, those on sets of (*nonterminal*, *cost*) pairs. The function δ can be extended to strings of symbols in the usual way.

This is the controlling automaton for a parser for the language generated by the grammar G', the parser performing the additional role of minimum cost tree selection. The auxiliary automaton plays a role analogous to the dfa for canonical sets of $LR(0)$ items in an $LR(0)$ parser.

Although we can use a technique similar to the technique for construction of the automaton for recognizing viable prefixes of an LR grammar, there is one striking difference. The transitions out of a state of the automaton that recognizes viable prefixes of the LR grammar are determined by just the items associated with the state. Here, the transitions on sets of $(nonterminal, cost)$ pairs can be deduced only *after computing sets of such pairs that match in the same left context*. There are three functions required. The first, called the *goto* function, which is similar to the corresponding function of an $LR(0)$ automaton, restricted to only terminal symbols, computes the new set of augmented items obtained by making a transition from the old set on a terminal or operator symbol, and computes relative costs. Because our grammar is in normal form, all such transitions will always lead to complete items. Such a set of items in our terminology, is called a *matchset*.

The function *reduction* has two parameters. The first is a set of complete items all of which call for reductions. The second is a set of augmented items $\mathcal{I}$ associated with a state which will be uncovered on stack when the righthand sides of all these productions are simultaneously popped off the stack. (For the time being let us not concern ourselves with how exactly such a set of items is identified). We call such a set of items an *LCset*, and we say that a state associated with such a set is a *valid left context state* for the matchset. *reduction* first collects the left hand side $(nonterminal, cost)$ pairs associated with a *matchset* into a set $\mathcal{R}$. It then augments $\mathcal{R}$ with $(nonterminal, cost)$ pairs that can be added using chain rules that are applicable, updating costs as it proceeds. Finally, it creates a new set of augmented items by making transitions on elements of $\mathcal{R}$ from $\mathcal{I}$. For a given matchset m we use S_m to denote the set of lefthand side non terminals of complete items. The *closure* function is is similar to the conventional function used in the construction of itemsets in the dfa for viable prefixes. These functions are described in detail in [12]. The function $ClosureReduction(itemset_1, itemset_2)$ is defined as $closure(reduction(itemset_1, itemset_2))$.

To identify states that can be valid left context states for a given matchset, we follow a simple technique that tests a condition that is necessary but not sufficient. As a consequence some spurious states may be generated (which are unreachable at run time). The choice of this over the exact technique [17] was dictated by considerations of efficiency, and the fact that for all the examples tested out by us, the approximate test gave the same results as the exact test, except in one case where it produced one extra state. Informally speaking, we check if each item of the form $[A \longrightarrow \alpha., c]$ in a matchset has a corresponding item of the form $[A \longrightarrow .\alpha, 0]$ in the state under test for the valid left context property, and that the state under test does not contain any other item of the form $[C \longrightarrow .\alpha, 0]$ if an item of the form $[C \longrightarrow \alpha., d]$ is not in the matchset. The condition is not sufficient because there may be another production of the form $B \longrightarrow \beta$ that always matches in this left context along with the other productions, but whose corresponding complete item is not in the matchset. We omit a formal definition of this test here, and refer to it as a boolean function *validlc*(p, m) (where p is an LCset and m is a matchset) which returns true if p satisfies the condition to be eligible as a valid LCset for m.

Algorithm *Preprocess*
Input A cost augmented context free grammar $G' = (N, T, P, S)$ representing a regular tree grammar G in normal form.
Output The auxiliary automaton represented by tables δ_A, δ_{LC}, which represent transitions on elements of A and 2^N respectively

```
begin
lcsets := φ;
matchsets := φ;
list := closure({[S → .α] | S → α ∈ P});
    while list is not empty do

    delete next element q from list and add it to lcsets;
    for each a ∈ A such that goto(q, a) is not empty do
        m := goto(q, a);
        δ_A(q, a) := (match(m), S_m);
        if m is not in matchsets then
            matchsets := matchsets ∪ {m};
            for each state r in lcsets do
                if validlc(r, m) then
                p := ClosureReduction(r, m);
                δ_LC(r, S_m) := (match(p), p);
                if p is not in list or lcsets then append p to list endif
                endif
            endfor
        endif
    endfor
    for each state t in matchsets do
        if validlc(q, t) then
            s := ClosureReduction(q, t);
            δ_LC(q, S_t) := (match(s), s);
            if s is not in list or lcsets then append s to list endif;
        endif
    endfor

    endwhile
end
```

We next prove that the automaton constructed by the algorithm satisfies the property below:

Property
Augmented $LR(0)$ Item $[A \rightarrow \alpha.\beta, c]$ is valid for augmented viable prefix $\gamma = Y_1Y_2 \ldots Y_k$ in $S_1S_2 \ldots S_k$ if and only if $\delta(q_0, S_1S_2 \ldots S_k)$ contains $[A \rightarrow \alpha.\beta, c]$.
Proof We give an informal proof that the property is satisfied, ignoring costs. The argument is based on the fact that a similar property (differing from the

one above only in that the function δ is applied on a single viable prefix instead of a set of viable prefixes) holds for a dfa for canonical set of $LR(0)$ items [10]. The construction using algorithm *Preprocess* may be viewed as a subset construction beginning with the $LR(0)$ dfa. We begin with the start state. Suppose m is a matchstate reached during some point in the algorithm, with $S_m = \{X_1, X_2, \dots X_l\}$. In the $LR(0)$ dfa we would have individual transitions from valid left context states on each of $X_1, X_2, \dots X_l$ to different states. Here, we collect the items in all those states into a single state, and then augment the items with those obtained with the application of chain rules and got by the closure operation.(This is exactly what *ClosureReduction* does given a matchstate and an LCstate). Thus the state we reach in the auxiliary automaton on a label sequence $S_1 S_2 \dots S_k$ is got by merging individual states we would have reached by following individual viable prefixes of the form $Y_1 Y_2 \dots Y_k$ in the dfa for $LR(0)$ item sets induced by the same input string. The property follows from the fact that it holds for each of the viable prefixes in the $LR(0)$ automaton. That the property holds when costs are included in the itemsets follows directly from the definition of an augmented item being valid for a set viable prefix.

3.3 A Sufficient Condition for Termination

In some cases, the input augmented grammar may be such that the algorithm *Preprocess* does not terminate. Thus, there is no finite automaton that can store the precomputed cost information. In such cases, the only alternative is to perform dynamic cost computations. Recall that the states of the auxiliary automaton consist of sets of $(LR(0)item, cost)$ pairs. Thus the number of states is unbounded if and only if the cost component is unbounded. This will happen whenever there is a pair of nonterminals, such that both elements of the pair match in the same left context, and derive the same sequence of infinite trees with increasing cost differences. This is illustrated in the example below.

Example 3.1

Consider the grammar, $G = (\{S, A, B, C\}, \{d, b, a, e\}, P, S)$, where the arities of the terminals (in the order that they appear in the set) are 2,0,0 and 0, and the augmented productions are,

$S \to A\,S\,d[0]$	$S \to B\,S\,d[0]$	$A \to C\,A\,d[0]$
$B \to C\,B\,d[5]$	$A \to b[1]$	$B \to b[1]$
$C \to a[1]$	$S \to c[1]$	

The nonterminals A and B match an infinite sequence of input trees in the same left context, with increasing relative costs(which increase in multiples of 5). As a result, Algorithm *Preprocess* will not terminate on this input instance.

The use of left-contextual information, results in the generation of finite parsing tables for problem instances on which conventional techniques that produce finite state tree pattern matching automata do not terminate. One such example is given below.

Example 3.2

$S \to X\,S\,d[0]$	$S \to Y\,S\,d[0]$	$X \to L1\,A\,e[0]$
$Y \to L2\,B\,e[0]$	$A \to C\,A\,d[0]$	$B \to C\,B\,d[5]$
$A \to b[1]$	$B \to b[1]$	$C \to a[1]$
$S \to c[1]$	$L1 \to l1[0]$	$L2 \to l2[0]$

Since the non-terminals A and B do not match in the same left context, it does not matter that these non-terminals match the same infinite sequence of trees with unbounded cost difference. The table construction for this example using our algorithm terminates with 25 states (13 LCsets and 12 matchsets). However, the computation using any bottom algorithm that constructs a bottom up finite state tree pattern matching automaton will not terminate.

We now give a sufficient condition for termination of the algorithm. The condition is *sufficient* but not *necessary*, as it disqualifies a grammar if there is a pair of nonterminals that match in the same left context, and generate the same sequence of infinite trees, without checking the condition on costs. We first motivate the development of the sufficiency condition.

Let m be a matchset. For each valid left context state p for m, one can associate an enhancement of m by associating with each complete item $[A \longrightarrow \alpha.]$in m a set of nonterminals representing the completion of A using all chain rules applicable in p. Thus, we can associate with each matchset, a collection of enhanced matchsets. Each element of an enhanced matchset is a set of complete items, each item associated with a set of nonterminals, obtained as described above. Let us use the symbol $\mathcal{C}_m$ to describe the collection of nonterminal sets associated with enhanced matchset m. Let $\mathcal{M}$ be the collection of enhanced matchsets associated with the auxiliary automaton without costs.

We also define an *aligned nonterminal set* below:

Definition 3.10 Let m be a matchset with complete items $[A_1 \to X_{11}X_{12}\cdots X_{1n}.]$, $[A_2 \to X_{21}X_{22}\cdots X_{2n}.]$, ..., $[A_k \to X_{k1}X_{k2}\cdots X_{kn}.]$.

The sets $\{X_{11}, X_{21}, \ldots, X_{k1}\}$, $\{X_{12}, X_{22}, \ldots, X_{k2}\}$, ...,$\{X_{1n}, X_{2n}, \ldots, X_{kn}\}$ are all termed aligned non-terminal sets for matchset m. Aligned nonterminal sets are sets of non terminals that match in the same left context.

We next construct a directed graph $\mathcal{G} = (\mathcal{M}, \mathcal{E})$ from the automaton (without costs) [17]. $\mathcal{M}$, the vertex set consists of all enhanced matchsets. There is an edge from node m_1 to node m_2 if and only if it is possible to form a set by selecting at least one element from the nonterminal set associated with each complete item in m_1 so that the set thus formed is an aligned non-terminal set for node m_2.

The graph constructed above, encapsulates certain properties of *fused* derivation trees defined below. Consider a subject tree t, and a derivation tree for it. The derivation tree induces a labeling of the nodes of the tree as follows. Each node is labeled with the set of nonterminals that match at that node. (In general, there will be a *set* because of the existence of chain rules). Suppose now, that we superimpose all derivation trees for this subject tree. Instead of a set of nonterminals, there will be a *collection* of sets labeling each node. Let us call this tree with a collection of sets labeling each node a *fused* tree for t.

The following relationship exists between the graph $\mathcal{G}$ and the set of fused derivation trees for the grammar:

1.Each node of a fused derivation tree corresponds to an enhanced matchset.
2.There is a node with label set $\mathcal{C}_1$ with parent with label set $\mathcal{C}_2$ in some fused derivation tree for the grammar if and only if there is a edge from an enhanced matchset with associated collection $\mathcal{C}_1$ to another with associated collection $\mathcal{C}_2$ in the graph $\mathcal{G}$.
A moments reflection will convince the reader that both these statements are true. Using the second property inductively, we can conclude that it holds with the word *parent* replaced by *proper ancestor* and *egde* replaced by *path.* Finally if the sets $\mathcal{C}_1$ and $\mathcal{C}_2$ are the same, then the path is a cycle. The last statement implies that a cycle exists in $\mathcal{G}$ if and only if there is an ancestor-descendant path in some fused derivation tree with both the nodes having the same collection as label. This in turn implies that the tree can nest itself, which is the same thing as saying that there is an infinite sequence of trees matching a set of nonterminals in the same left context. We have given an informal argument in support of the following theorem:
Theorem 3.3 Algorithm *Preprocess* will terminate if the graph $\mathcal{G}$ constructed above has no cycles.
That the condition is only sufficient and not necessary can be verified by modifying the grammar of example 3.1 so that the costs of the recursive productions for the nonterminals A and B are the same. The corresponding graph $\mathcal{G}$ has a cycle but algorithm *Preprocess* terminates.

4 Conclusion

We have given an algorithm that solves the problem of optimal linear regular tree pattern matching by constructing a pushdown automaton that performs matching in linear time, and precomputes costs. We have run the algorithm on some input instances that represent instruction sets for two machines. The first set of patterns(Intel Pentium) had 351 productions, 26 non-terminals and 212 terminals and operators; the second set(IBM R6000) had 60 productions, 13 non-terminals, and 30 terminals and operators. Total table sizes(including index maps) and execution times (on a Sun UltraSPARC 60)with and without cost precomputation (the latter within parentheses) are given below:
Intel Pentium: 4423(2367), 27.3(6.3)seconds
IBM R6000: 1264(1020), 1.0(0.7)seconds
Corresponding figures for the conventional algorithm using Chase compression techniques[3][16] are:
Intel Pentium: 46566(32505), 2.29(1.5)seconds
IBM R6000 : 2747(2747), 0.22(0.22)seconds
Thus though the new algorithm offers savings in auxiliary space for these examples, preprocessing requires more time. More experimentation is necessary to study space/time tradeoffs using this algorithm. The fact that our optimal matcher(or instruction selector), operates like an LR parser(quite different from the Graham Glanville technique, as it carries forward all choices, finally selecting

an optimal one), allows the use of attributes, which may prove useful for carrying out other tasks in code generation.

References

1. Aho, A.V., and Ganapathi, M., Efficient tree pattern matching: an aid to code generation, in: *Proc. 12th ACM Symp. on Priciples of Programming Languages* (1985) 334-340.
2. Balachandran, A., Dhamdhere, D.M., and Biswas, S., Efficient retargetable code generation using bottom up tree pattern matching, *Comput. Lang.* **3**(15)(1990) 127-140.
3. Chase, D., An improvement to bottom up tree pattern matching, in: *Proc. 14th Ann. ACM Symp. on Principles of Programming Languages* (1987) 168-177.
4. Ferdinand, C., Seidl, H., and Wilhelm, R., Tree Automata for Code Selection, *Acta Informatica*, **31**,(1994) 741-760.
5. Gantait, A., Design of a bottom up tree pattern matching algorithm and its application to code generation, ME Project Report, Department Of Computer Science and Automation, Indian Institute of Science, Bangalore, 1996.
6. Glanville, R.S., and Graham, S.L., A new approach to compiler code generation, in: *Proc. 5th ACM Symposium on Principles of Programming Languages*, (1978) 231-240.
7. Hatcher, P., and Christopher, T., High-quality code generation via bottom-up tree pattern matching, in:*Proc. 13th ACM Symp. on Principles of Programming Languages* (1986) 119-130.
8. Henry, R.R., Encoding optimal pattern selection in a table-driven bottom-up tree pattern matcher, Technical Report 89-02-04, Computer Science Department, University of Washington,(1989).
9. Hoffmann, C., and O'Donnell, M.J., Pattern matching in trees, *J. ACM* **29**(1)(1982) 68-95.
10. Hopcroft, J.E., and Ullman, J.D., An Introduction to Automata Theory, Languages and Computation, Addison Wesley(1979).
11. Madhavan, M., Optimal linear regular tree pattern matching using pushdown automata, MSc (Engineering) Thesis(submitted), Department of Computer Science and Automation, Indian Institute of Science, Bangalore, 1998.
12. Madhavan, M., Shankar, P., Finding minimal cost derivation trees for regular tree grammars, Technical report IISC-CSA-98-07, Department of Computer Science and Automation, Indian Institute of Science, Bangalore, India, August 1998.
13. Nymeyer, A., and Katoen, J.P., Code generation based on formal BURS theory and heuristic search, *Acta Informatica*, **34**(8),(1997) 597-636.
14. Pelegri-Llopart, E., and Graham, S.L., Optimal code generation for expression trees: An application of BURS theory, in:*Proc. 15th ACM Symposium on Principles of Programming Languages*, (1988) 119-129.
15. Proebsting, T.A., BURS automata generation, *ACM Trans. on Prog. Lang. and Sys.* **3**(17),(1995) 461-486.
16. Ravi Kumar, S., Retargettable code generation using bottom up tree pattern matching, M.E Project Report, Department of Computer Science and Automation, Indian Institute of Science, Bangalore, 1992.
17. Shankar, P., Gantait, A., Yuvaraj, A.R., and Madhavan, M., A New algorithm for linear regular tree pattern matching, (To appear in *Theoretical Computer Science*).

Locating Matches of Tree Patterns in Forests

Andreas Neumann and Helmut Seidl

Department of Computer Science, University of Trier, Germany
neumann,seidl@psi.uni-trier.de

Abstract. We deal with matching and locating of patterns in forests of variable arity. A pattern consists of a structural and a contextual condition for subtrees of a forest, both of which are given as tree or forest regular languages. We use the notation of constraint systems to uniformly specify both kinds of conditions. In order to implement pattern matching we introduce the class of pushdown forest automata. We identify a special class of contexts such that not only pattern matching but also locating all of a forest's subtrees matching in context can be performed in a single traversal. We also give a method for computing the reachable states of an automaton in order to minimize the size of transition tables.

1 Introduction

In Standard Generalized Markup Language (SGML) [Gol90] documents are represented as trees. A node in a document tree may have arbitrarily many children, independent of the symbol at that node. A sequence of documents or subdocuments is called a forest. A main task in document transformation and information retrieval is locating one or all of a forest's subtrees matching a pattern. A pattern is made up of a structural condition on the subtrees themselves and a contextual condition on their location in the forest, relative to its siblings and ancestors. Due to the potentially enormous size of documents, it is highly desirable to perform pattern localization "on the fly" during one pass through the document. Here, we present a solution for an interesting subclass of contextual conditions. To the best of our knowledge, no single-pass localization algorithm has been suggested so far.

A structural condition is given by a regular language over trees or forests. Tree regular languages have first been characterized (under the name of recognizable sets of pseudoterms) as projections of the derivation trees of context free grammars by [Tha67]. The author also defines a class of so-called pseudo-automata which accept the class of tree regular languages. Restricting himself to ranked trees, [Bra69] gives a slightly different definition of finite tree automata. Under the name bilanguages, [PQ68] define tree regular languages to be homomorphic images of tree-local sets. [Tak75] shows that a string representation of forest regular languages using pairs of parentheses indexed by a node's symbol is a nest language, i.e., a special case of context-free languages. [Mur96] uses pointed tree representations, as introduced by [Pod92], for specifying contextual conditions in patterns. The author then gives a method for locating matching subtrees in two passes, namely a bottom-up and a top-down traversal of the tree. The idea is similar to [BKR96]: here the bottom-up traversal is preceded by a top-down traversal, the so-called guide, labeling each node with information about its upper context. In contrast to our automaton, however, the guide may not take into account information about left siblings.

In this paper we use constraint systems as a uniform method for specifying both structural and contextual conditions in patterns. We introduce the class of pushdown forest automata, and show how they can be used for efficiently recognizing forest regular languages: during a depth-first, left-to-right traversal of the forest, each node is visited twice: once before and once immediately after processing its children. This is closely related to SGML parsing, where each node a is represented by a pair of markers <a> and </a> enclosing the representation of its children. We identify an interesting subclass of contextual conditions, namely those referring only to nodes that are visited earlier in a left-to-right depth-first traversal. This class allows, e.g., searching for list items that are nested deeper than a certain level n, or locating all captions in figures. We show that the decision whether a subtree satisfies both the structural and this special class of contextual condition can already be taken when its root is visited for the second time. We also give a method for computing the reachable states of the constructed automaton.

[Tak75] already proposed so called P-tracers as a special class of pushdown automata for accepting the string representation of tree regular languages. Her construction, however, is non-deterministic, and she does not provide a method for making it deterministic. [SGYM98] use the string representation of ranked trees for the purposes of code generation. They use LR-parsing, and exploit the property that even in the non-deterministic case moves on the stack are directed by the tree structure. Thus alternative runs can be tracked simultaneously. LR-parsing is mainly a bottom-up strategy: the pushdown is used for determining possible points for reductions, i.e. whether the right hand side of a production is satisfied. In our case these points are determined by the tree structure without having to look at the pushdown. Instead, our algorithm uses the pushdown for gathering information about the part of forest visited so far. It uses this information for selecting sensible expansions when descending to a node's children, and is therefore more closely related to recursive descent parsing. A different class of pushdown tree automata was given in [Mor94]: a two-way automaton can arbitrarily change its direction from bottom-up to top-down and vice versa and thus visit each node several times. As opposed to our approach, a transition proceeds from a node to all of its children simultaneously. It is not clear how this can be efficiently implemented by a left-to-right traversal.

The remainder of this paper is organized as follows: the next section introduces our notion of trees and forests and defines constraint systems and patterns. In Section 3 we present the class of pushdown forest automata which are shown to be well suited for implementing constraint systems in the following section. Section 5 demonstrates how matches of a pattern can be located. Section 6 explains how to compute the reachable states of an automaton, and the last section discusses extensions to the pattern language.

2 Trees, Forests and Patterns

Various notations have been proposed for specifying tree regular languages, e.g. by F-local sets or F-grammars. In this paper we use constraint systems for convenient specification of forest regular languages. Let us first formalize the notion of trees and forests.

Definition 1: Let Σ be an alphabet. The sets $\mathcal{T}_\Sigma$ of *trees* t and $\mathcal{F}_\Sigma$ of *forests* f over Σ are given by the following grammar (in contrast to graph theory, a forest is a sequence rather than an unordered set of trees):

$$t ::= a\langle f\rangle, a \in \Sigma \qquad\qquad f ::= \varepsilon \mid tf$$

For brevity, we often omit the ε in a forest $t_1 \ldots t_n\varepsilon$. For the remainder we refer to a fixed alphabet Σ unless explicitly stated otherwise. Thus we can omit the subscript Σ and simply write $\mathcal{T}$ and $\mathcal{F}$.

A forest language over Σ is a subset of $\mathcal{F}_\Sigma$. Constraint systems provide a convenient way of denoting forest languages:

Definition 2: A *constraint system* over Σ is a quadruple $C = (X, Y, y_\sharp, S)$, where X and Y are sets of *tree variables* and *forest variables* such that $X \cap Y = \emptyset$. $y_\sharp \in Y$ is the *start variable* of C, and S is a set of constraints[1] of the form

$$\begin{array}{ll} y \sqsupseteq \varepsilon & \text{with } y \in Y, \\ y \sqsupseteq xy_1 & \text{with } y, y_1 \in Y \text{ and } x \in X, \text{ or} \\ x \sqsupseteq a\langle y\rangle & \text{with } x \in X, y \in Y \text{ and } a \in \Sigma. \end{array}$$

We use the following naming convention: $x, x_1, \ldots$ are always tree variables in X, whereas $y, y_1, \ldots$ denote forest variables in Y. Variables from either X or Y are named z. When the context is clear, we abbreviate $z \sqsupseteq r \in S$ to $z \sqsupseteq r$.

In order to define the meaning of constraint systems, we need the concept of substitutions:

Definition 3: A *substitution* $\sigma : X \cup Y \to 2^\mathcal{T} \cup 2^\mathcal{F}$ assigns sets of trees to tree variables and sets of forests to forest variables. We can now define the meaning function $[\![.]\!]$ for right hand sides of constraints w.r.t. an input substitution σ:

$$[\![\varepsilon]\!]\,\sigma = \{\varepsilon\} \qquad\qquad [\![a\langle y\rangle]\!]\,\sigma = \{a\langle f\rangle \mid f \in \sigma y\}$$

$$[\![xy]\!]\,\sigma = \{tf \mid t \in \sigma x, f \in \sigma y\}$$

The least solution $[\![C]\!]$ of a constraint system C is obtained by fixpoint iteration, i.e., in terms of a sequence of substitutions $\sigma_0, \sigma_1, \ldots$ The value of σ_{i+1} for variable z is obtained by evaluating all right hand sides for z w.r.t. σ_i:

[1] Note that what we consider as a constraint corresponds closely to a rule of a grammar. The constraint notation, however, has the advantage of allowing more easily for generalizations (c.f. Section 7).

$$\sigma_0\, z = \emptyset \qquad \sigma_{i+1}\, z = \bigcup_{z \sqsupseteq r} [\![r]\!]\, \sigma_i \qquad [\![C]\!]\, z = \bigcup_{i>0} \sigma_i\, z$$

The *language* of C is $\mathcal{L}_C = [\![C]\!]\, y_\sharp$. It turns out that the languages described by constraint systems coincide with the *forest regular languages* in [Tak75].

Example 1: Suppose that $\Sigma = \{a, b\}$ and consider constraint system $C = (\{x_1, x_\top\}, \{y_\sharp, y_\top\}, y_\sharp, S)$ with constraints:

$$\begin{array}{llll} x_\top \sqsupseteq a\langle y_\top\rangle & y_\top \sqsupseteq x_\top y_\top & y_\sharp \sqsupseteq x_1 y_\top & x_1 \sqsupseteq a\langle y_\top\rangle \\ x_\top \sqsupseteq b\langle y_\top\rangle & y_\top \sqsupseteq \varepsilon & y_\sharp \sqsupseteq x_\top y_\sharp & \end{array}$$

First note that $[\![C]\!]\, x_\top = \mathcal{T}$ and $[\![C]\!]\, y_\top = \mathcal{F}$, and thus x_1 represents all trees with root a. Therefore $\mathcal{L}_C$ is the language of all forests one of whose trees has a at its root. For the remainder of this paper we assume that each constraint system implicitly contains variables $x_\top$ and $y_\top$ with appropriate constraints to make them represent $\mathcal{T}$ and $\mathcal{F}$. □

In document processing we are often not interested in whether a whole forest f satisfies a constraint system C. We rather want to locate *subtrees* of f satisfying a structural condition and being in a specified context. A context can be viewed as a forest that contains a hole $\bullet$ indicating the position of the desired subtree: e.g., the forest $a\langle\varepsilon\rangle\bullet b\langle\varepsilon\rangle$ is a context at the second position of a forest with three trees, the first and third one having symbols a and b and no children. A contextual condition is a set of contexts. Here we are interested in contextual conditions which can be tested just by inspecting ancestors and left siblings of $\bullet$. These are the nodes visited before $\bullet$ during a depth-first, left-to-right traversal of a forest.

Definition 4: The sets $\mathcal{T}^\circ_\Sigma$ of *pointed trees* t° and $\mathcal{F}^\circ_\Sigma$ of *pointed forests* f° over Σ are defined as follows:

$$t^\circ ::= \bullet \mid a\langle f^\circ\rangle, a \in \Sigma \qquad\qquad f^\circ ::= t^\circ f \mid t f^\circ$$

Note that similar to the definition of [Pod92], a pointed tree or forest contains exactly one hole. Again we often omit subscript Σ and simply use $\mathcal{T}^\circ$ and $\mathcal{F}^\circ$. The hole serves as a fill-in for a tree: for a pointed forest f° and a tree t, we denote by f°/t the tree obtained by replacing the $\bullet$ in f° with t.

Contextual conditions are described by an extended form of constraint systems:

Definition 5: A context system is a tuple $C^\circ = (X, X^\circ, Y, Y^\circ, y^\circ_\sharp, S^\circ)$, such that X, X°, Y, Y° are mutually disjoint, $y^\circ_\sharp \in Y^\circ$ and S is a set of constraints such that:

1) For $y^\circ \in Y^\circ$ and $y^\circ \sqsupseteq r$, either $r = x^\circ y_\top$ with $x^\circ \in X^\circ \cup \{\bullet\}$, or $r = x y^\circ_1$ with $x \in X$ and $y^\circ_1 \in Y^\circ$;
2) for $x^\circ \in X^\circ$ and $x^\circ \sqsupseteq r$, r is of the form $a\langle y^\circ\rangle$, with $y^\circ \in Y^\circ$;
3) for $z \in X \cup Y$ and $z \sqsupseteq r$, r is as in Def. 2 (and thus contains no variables from X° or Y°).

X° and Y° are called *context* variables. Naming conventions are as for the non-pointed case, except that context variables have a superscript $^\circ$. The meaning $[\![C^\circ]\!]$ of a context system is defined as for constraint systems with the addition:

$[\![\bullet y_\top]\!]\,\sigma = \{\bullet f \mid f \in \mathcal{F}\}$

The language of C° is $\mathcal{L}_{C^\circ} = [\![C^\circ]\!]\,y^\circ_\sharp$. Note that 1)-3) ensure that each $f \in \mathcal{L}_{C^\circ}$ contains exactly one hole. Furthermore, only $y_\top$ can occur right to a context variable. We can thus only specify *upper left contexts*.

Example 2: Let $\Sigma=\{a,b,c\}$ and $C^\circ = (\{x_\top, x\}, \{x^\circ_1\}, \{y_\top\}, \{y^\circ_\sharp, y^\circ_1, y^\circ_2\}, y^\circ_\sharp, S^\circ)$ where S° consists of the constraints:

$$\begin{array}{llll} y^\circ_\sharp \sqsupseteq x_\top y^\circ_\sharp & x^\circ_1 \sqsupseteq b\langle y^\circ_1\rangle & y^\circ_1 \sqsupseteq x^\circ_1 y_\top & x \sqsupseteq c\langle y_\top\rangle \\ y^\circ_\sharp \sqsupseteq x^\circ_1 y_\top & y^\circ_1 \sqsupseteq x_\top y^\circ_\sharp & y^\circ_1 \sqsupseteq x y^\circ_2 & y^\circ_2 \sqsupseteq \bullet y_\top \end{array}$$

C° requires $\bullet$ to be the immediate right sibling of a node labeled c which is the first child of node labeled b all of whose ancestors are b. □

We are now ready to define our notion of a pattern:

Definition 6: A *pattern system* is a pair $\Pi = (C^\circ, x_\sharp)$ such that $C^\circ = (X, X^\circ, Y, Y^\circ, y^\circ_\sharp, S^\circ)$ is a context system and $x_\sharp \in X$ is a distinguished *target variable*. The language $\mathcal{L}_\Pi$ is the set of all forests $f = f^\circ/t$ with $f^\circ \in \mathcal{L}_{C^\circ}$ and $t \in [\![C^\circ]\!]\,x_\sharp$. Then we also say that t *matches* $x_\sharp$ *in* f *with context* $y^\circ_\sharp$. Note that substituting $x_\sharp$ for $\bullet$ in each right hand side in S° yields a constraint system C_Π with $\mathcal{L}_\Pi = \mathcal{L}_{C_\Pi}$. The language of a pattern system is therefore a forest regular language.

Example 3: Consider again context system C° from Example 2. Adding a target variable $x_\sharp$ and a constraint $x_\sharp \sqsupseteq a\langle y_\top\rangle$ yields a pattern Π. $\mathcal{L}_\Pi$ consists of all forests containing a tree labeled a as the immediate right sibling of a tree labeled c which has no left siblings and all of whose ancestors are labeled b. □

3 Pushdown Forest Automata

How can we implement constraint systems with automata? A common approach (e.g., [Tha67], [Bra69], [Mur96]) are finite state bottom-up forest automata with a transition relation $\alpha : \Sigma \times 2^{Q^*} \times Q$ such that R is regular for all $(a, R, q) \in \alpha$. In other words, a node is assigned a state by checking the word of states assigned to its children for membership in a string regular language R over Q. Representation of R is usually by the set of all transitions (a, w, q) with $w \in R$. This has the major disadvantage that the automaton may have infinitely many transitions.

Our approach is to represent R by a finite string automaton with a separate state space $Q_\mathcal{F}$ integrated into the forest automaton. This has the effect that each subtree of the forest becomes marked with a state in $Q_\mathcal{F}$ during a run of the automaton. These marks can be used to determine whether a subtree is at a position that might satisfy a contextual condition.

As a further enhancement we adopt the depth-first, left-to-right visiting order of SGML parsers as the traversing strategy of the automaton: each node is visited twice, once before and once after its children. Thus we can, in a single traversal, first pass some finite information down to a node's children, modify it during the children's traversal and then hand it back to the parent node. We even go one step further equipping the automaton with a pushdown: only an interesting part of the information is handed to the children while the current state is stacked onto the pushdown. This stacked information is later combined with the new information returned from the children. Note that our traversing strategy is the same as used for evaluation of L-attributed grammars (e.g. [MW95]).

Definition 7: A *(non-deterministic) pushdown forest automaton* (PFA) is a tuple $P = (Q_\mathcal{T}, Q_\mathcal{F}, I, F, \mathit{Entry}, \mathit{Exit}, \mathit{Comb})$, where $Q_\mathcal{T}$ and $Q_\mathcal{F}$ are sets of *tree states* and *forest states*, $I \subseteq Q_\mathcal{F}$ and $F \subseteq Q_\mathcal{F}$ are sets of *start states* and *final states*, $\mathit{Entry} : \Sigma \to Q_\mathcal{F} \times Q_\mathcal{F}$ is the *entry function*, $\mathit{Exit} : \Sigma \to Q_\mathcal{F} \times Q_\mathcal{T}$ is the *exit function*, and $\mathit{Comb} \subseteq Q_\mathcal{F} \times Q_\mathcal{T} \times Q_\mathcal{F}$ is the *transition relation*. As a shorthand for $\mathit{Entry}\ a$ and $\mathit{Exit}\ a$ we use Entry_a and Exit_a.
Now we define two transition relations $\delta^P_\mathcal{T} \subseteq Q_\mathcal{F} \times \mathcal{T} \times Q_\mathcal{T}$ and $\delta^P_\mathcal{F} \subseteq Q_\mathcal{F} \times \mathcal{F} \times Q_\mathcal{F}$ (when the context is clear we omit superscript P):

$$
\begin{array}{rl}
(q, \varepsilon, q) \in \delta_\mathcal{F} & \text{for all } q; \\
(q_1, tf, q_2) \in \delta_\mathcal{F} & \text{iff there are } p \in Q_\mathcal{T}, q \in Q_\mathcal{F} \text{ such that} \\
& \qquad (q_1, t, p) \in \delta_\mathcal{T}, (q_1, p, q) \in \mathit{Comb} \text{ and } (q, f, q_2) \in \delta_\mathcal{F}. \\
(q, a\langle f\rangle, p) \in \delta_\mathcal{T} & \text{iff there are } q_0, q_1 \in Q_\mathcal{F} \text{ with } (q, q_0) \in \mathit{Entry}_a, \\
& \qquad (q_0, f, q_1) \in \delta_\mathcal{F}, \text{ and } (q_1, p) \in \mathit{Exit}_a.
\end{array}
$$

The *language* of P is $\mathcal{L}_P = \{f \mid (q, f, q_1) \in \delta_\mathcal{F} \text{ for some } q \in I, q_1 \in F\}$. P is called deterministic (DPFA) if I is a singleton, $\mathit{Entry}_a : Q_\mathcal{F} \to Q_\mathcal{F}$ and $\mathit{Exit}_a : Q_\mathcal{F} \to Q_\mathcal{T}$ are functions for all a and Comb is also a function: $Q_\mathcal{F} \times Q_\mathcal{T} \to Q_\mathcal{F}$. In this case $\delta_\mathcal{T} : Q_\mathcal{F} \times \mathcal{T} \to Q_\mathcal{T}$ and $\delta_\mathcal{F} : Q_\mathcal{F} \times \mathcal{F} \to Q_\mathcal{F}$ are functions as well.

Note that *Comb* and $Q_\mathcal{F}$ form a finite string automaton over $Q_\mathcal{T}$, with the difference that initial and accepting states are determined by *Entry* and *Exit*. When the automaton reaches a node of the input forest, the current forest state is stacked and then passed to the children through Entry_a. The forest state obtained by traversing the children is then transformed into a tree state via the *Exit* function, which is combined with the stacked forest state via *Comb*. The result is passed to the right sibling or if there is no such sibling, to the parent node via *Exit*.
It is worth mentioning that this is close to an idea of [Tak75]: there forests are uniquely mapped to a string representation using pairs of parentheses marked with symbols from Σ. The image of a forest regular language is then a *nest language*, i.e. a special class of context free languages which can therefore be parsed by non-deterministic pushdown string automata.
As opposed to string automata theory, we succeed in constructing for our non-deterministic pushdown forest automata equivalent deterministic ones.

Theorem 1: For each PFA P there is a DPFA D such that $\mathcal{L}_P = \mathcal{L}_D$.

The proof is by subset construction. The conventional approach is to use as states the subsets of $Q_\mathcal{T}$ and $Q_\mathcal{F}$. But this does not suffice: after the Exit_a step, a forest state q may only be combined with a tree state p if p was obtained starting from an initial state in $\mathit{Entry}_a\ q$ (for the same q!). This relationship is not determinable with sets of tree or forest states. Instead we need sets of pairs

(q, p) as tree states and sets of pairs (q, q_1) as forest states, indicating that state p or q_1 was obtained as a consequence of $\mathit{Entry}_a\, q$. The details of the construction are omitted for brevity. □

A special case of PFAs are those where $\mathit{Entry}_a\, q = I$ for all a and q. These automata correspond closely to the finite state bottom-up automata mentioned at the beginning of this section and are therefore called ***bottom-up forest automata*** (BFAs). Although BFAs do not use the pushdown, they accept the same languages as PFAs:

Lemma 1: For each PFA P there is a BFA B with $\mathcal{L}_P = \mathcal{L}_B$.

We only give the idea of the proof: B simulates P's $\mathit{Entry}_a\, q$ step by guessing a and q non-deterministically. As forest states, B has triples (q, a, q_1) indicating that q_1 was reached due to guessing q and a. *Exit* can then check whether a was guessed correctly, yielding a tree state (q, p) meaning that p was obtained as a consequence of guessing q. The *Comb* function can then check whether q was the correct guess. □

We conclude that the pushdown does add nothing to expressiveness as compared to bottom-up automata. It may, however, add to succinctness of representation: it can drastically reduce the size of the automaton in the deterministic case:

Lemma 2: There is a sequence of languages $\mathcal{L}^1, \mathcal{L}^2, \ldots$ such that for all $n > 0$, there is a DPFA P accepting $\mathcal{L}^n$ with $O(n)$ states whereas each DBFA B accepting $\mathcal{L}^n$ has at least $O(2^n)$ states.

Proof: let $\mathcal{L}^n$ be the language of all unary trees having symbol a at the node of depth n. For $n > 0$, $\mathcal{L}^n$ is accepted by $P = (\{-1, 0\}, \{-1, 0, \ldots, n, \infty\}, \{1\}, \{0\}, \mathit{Entry}, \mathit{Exit}, \mathit{Comb})$ with

$$\begin{array}{rcll} \mathit{Entry}_b\, i &=& i{+}1, & 1 \le i < n, b \in \Sigma \\ \mathit{Entry}_a\, n &=& \infty & \\ \mathit{Entry}_b\, n &=& -1, & b \neq a, b \in \Sigma \\ \mathit{Entry}_b\, \infty &=& \infty, & b \in \Sigma \\ \mathit{Entry}_b\, q &=& -1, & q \in \{0, -1\}, b \in \Sigma \end{array} \qquad \begin{array}{rcll} \mathit{Exit}_b\, q &=& 0, & b \in \Sigma, q \in \{0, \infty\} \\ \mathit{Exit}_b\, q &=& -1, & b \in \Sigma, q \notin \{0, \infty\} \\ \mathit{Comb}(q, 0) &=& 0, & q \in \{1, \ldots, n, \infty\} \\ \mathit{Comb}(p, q) &=& -1, & p \in \{0, -1\} \\ && & \text{or } q = -1 \end{array}$$

Here, -1 is an error state, whereas 0 indicates that the first tree of a forest has been successfully traversed. For $1 \le i \le n$, state i means that level i has just been entered, and ∞ represents a depth greater than n. Now it is easy to see that P accepts $\mathcal{L}^n$, and it has $n{+}5 = O(n)$ states. Now suppose that there is a DBFA B with initial state q_I accepting $\mathcal{L}^n$. Then, for deciding whether a tree t is in $\mathcal{L}^n$, $\delta_{\mathcal{T}}(q_I, t)$ must denote whether t has symbol a at depth n. But for deciding whether $b\langle t\rangle \in \mathcal{L}^n$, it must contain that information also for depth $n{-}1$, and analogously for $n{-}2, \ldots, 1$. The smallest domain capable of expressing this information consists of all subsets of $\{1, \ldots, n\}$, and there are 2^n such sets. Thus, B must have at least 2^n tree states. □

We conclude that for some languages, our pushdown automata are exponentially more succinct than, e.g., the bottom-up automata of [Tha67] or the LR-automata of [SGYM98]. Observe that the decisive point in the last example is the PFA's awareness of the left upper context. Another approach to enhancing BFAs is to provide knowledge only about the parent node's symbol. This leads to a subclass of PFAs where $Entry_a\ q$ is equal for all q and thus depends only on a. They are related to the approach of [BMW91] for trees of fixed arity. Here an n-ary transition function: $Q^n \times \Sigma \to Q$ is simulated by a finite automaton with states Q_a for each element a of Σ, requiring a unary transition function: $Q_a \times Q \to Q_a$ only. The initial state for a is a weak version of our $Entry_a$. Though this class of automata is more succinct than BFAs, it still requires $\Omega(2^n)$ states for the above example in the deterministic case.

4 The Construction

In [NS98] a one-to-one correspondence between constraint systems and BFAs is established. Especially it is shown that for each constraint system an equivalent DBFA can be constructed, that has $2^{Y\times Y}$ as forest states. A BFA, however, is not aware of the upper context and therefore unsuited for checking contextual conditions. Therefore we will now give an algorithm for constructing, for a given constraint system C, an equivalent DPFA D_C with the same set of forest states $2^{Y\times Y}$. We then give a modification of the base method that computes just the reachable states of the automaton. Later on we shall see that our method is also suited for verifying contextual conditions.

Definition 8: Let $C = (X, Y, y_\sharp, S)$ be a constraint system. The DPFA D_C is defined as $(2^X, 2^{Y\times Y}, \{q_\sharp\}, F, \mathit{Entry}, \mathit{Exit}, \mathit{Comb})$, where

$$\begin{aligned} q_\sharp &= \{(y_\sharp, y_\sharp)\} \\ F &= \{q \mid (y_\sharp, y_0) \in q \text{ for some } y_0 \text{ with } y_0 \sqsupseteq \varepsilon\} \\ \mathit{Entry}_a\ q &= \{(y,y) \mid (y_1, y_2) \in q, y_2 \sqsupseteq x y_3, \text{ and } x \sqsupseteq a\langle y\rangle\} \\ \mathit{Exit}_a\ q &= \{x \mid x \sqsupseteq a\langle y\rangle \text{ and there is a } (y, y_0) \in q \text{ with } y_0 \sqsupseteq \varepsilon\} \\ \mathit{Comb}(q,p) &= \{(y, y_2) \mid (y, y_1) \in q, y_1 \sqsupseteq x y_2 \text{ and } x \in p\} \end{aligned}$$

Assume the automaton wants to verify that $a\langle f\rangle$ belongs to the language of variable x (i.e., $[\![C]\!]\ x$). Then it needs to verify that f is in the language of some y with $x \sqsupseteq a\langle y\rangle$. In order to show this, it maintains, during traversal of f, pairs (y, y_1). The first component simply records y, whereas the second component is a variable to be verified for the remaining part of f. Thus, the entry function produces pairs of the form (y, y). Accordingly, if after complete traversal of f a pair (y, y_0) with $y_0 \sqsupseteq \varepsilon$ is obtained, then $a\langle f\rangle$ belongs to the languages of all x with $x \sqsupseteq a\langle y\rangle$. This is reflected by the *Exit*-function.

Theorem 2: For each constraint system C, $\mathcal{L}_{D_C} = \mathcal{L}_C$.

We omit the proof and instead illustrate the construction by an example:

Example 4: Consider constraint system C from Ex. 1. Then D_C has tree states $Q_\mathcal{T} = 2^{\{x_1, x_\top\}}$ and forest states $Q_\mathcal{F} = 2^{\{y_\sharp, y_\top\}^2}$. The start state is $\{\{(y_\sharp, y_\sharp)\}\}$, and the final states are all that contain $(y_\sharp, y_\top)$.
A run of D_C for $f = b\langle\varepsilon\rangle a\langle b\langle\varepsilon\rangle\rangle b\langle\varepsilon\rangle$ is illustrated in Fig. 1. Let us explain some steps of this run: node a is entered with forest state $1 = \{(y_\sharp, y_\sharp)\}$. In order to proceed to its child, the *Entry* function is applied:

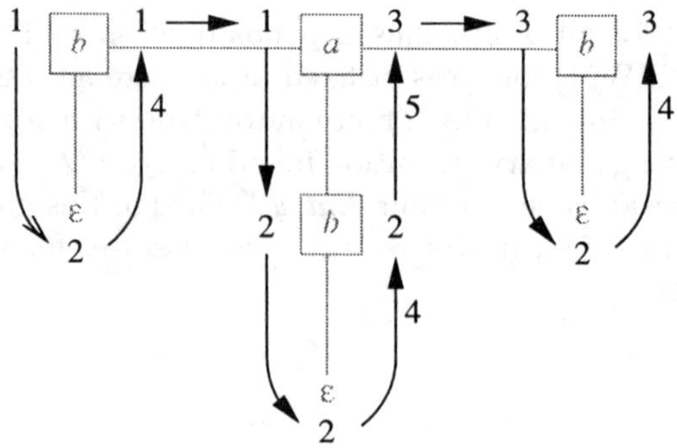

where:

$1 = \{(y_\sharp, y_\sharp)\}$
$2 = \{(y_\top, y_\top)\}$
$3 = \{(y_\sharp, y_\sharp), (y_\sharp, y_\top)\}$
$4 = \{x_\top\}$
$5 = \{x_1, x_\top\}$

Fig. 1. A run of D_C from Ex. 4 for $f = b\langle\varepsilon\rangle a\langle b\langle\varepsilon\rangle\rangle b\langle\varepsilon\rangle$.

$$Entry_a\, 1 = \{(y, y) \mid (y_1, y_2) \in 1, y_2 \sqsupseteq xy_3, x \sqsupseteq a\langle y\rangle\} = \{(y_\top, y_\top)\} = 2$$

Node b is thus entered with state 2. This state is reproduced through inspecting its (zero) children, then fed into the *Exit*-function when returning to node a:

$$Exit_a\, 2 = \{x \mid x \sqsupseteq a\langle y\rangle, (y, y_0) \in 2, y_0 \sqsupseteq \varepsilon\} = \{x \mid x \sqsupseteq a\langle y_\top\rangle\} = \{x_1, x_\top\} = 5$$

The so obtained tree state 5 is now combined with the previously stacked forest state $1 = \{(y_\sharp, y_\sharp)\}$:

$$\begin{aligned} Comb(1,5) &= \{(y, y_2) \mid (y, y_1) \in 1, y_1 \sqsupseteq xy_2, x \in 5\} \\ &= \{(y_\sharp, y_2) \mid y_\sharp \sqsupseteq xy_2, x \in 5\} = \{(y_\sharp, y_\sharp), (y_\sharp, y_\top)\} = 3 \end{aligned}$$

This forest state 3 is preserved by traversing the last subtree $b\langle\varepsilon\rangle$. Since 3 is a final state, D_C accepts f. □

5 Locating Matches

The previous section showed how we can use DPFAs for accepting the language of a constraint system and thus also of a pattern. But how can we, for a pattern system $(C^\circ, x_\sharp)$, *locate* subtrees t that match target variable $x_\sharp$ in a forest f? We will show that we recognize t by looking at the input and output state of the $\delta_\mathcal{T}$-call for t. We can further observe that if these states indicate a match, then the whole run of the automaton is always successful.

Let us first define the notion of a labeling produced by a run of a DPFA:

Definition 9: Let $D = (Q_\mathcal{T}, Q_\mathcal{F}, \{q_\sharp\}, F, Entry, Exit, Comb)$ be a DPFA and f_0 be a forest. Then the *labeling* λ of f_0 by D is a mapping from subtrees and subforests of f_0 to forest states of D, assigning each subtree or subforest[2] the input state of the corresponding call of $\delta_\mathcal{T}$ or $\delta_\mathcal{F}$ during the run of D on f_0. Formally speaking,

- $\lambda f_0 = q_\sharp$;
- if $\lambda t = q$ and $t = a\langle f\rangle$, then $\lambda f = Entry_a\, q$;

[2] More precisely, we should rather speak of *occurrences* of subtrees and subforests.

- if $\lambda f = q$ and $f = tf_1$, then $\lambda t = q$ and $\lambda f_1 = \mathit{Comb}(q, \delta_{\mathcal{T}}(q,t))$.

We can now formulate the main result of this paper:

Theorem 3: Let $\Pi = (C^\circ, x_\sharp)$ be a pattern system. We obtain a constraint system C by substituting $x_\sharp$ for all occurrences of $\bullet$ in C°. Now let D_C be defined as in the previous section and, for a fixed forest f_0, let λ be the labeling of f_0 produced by D_C. Then for all subtrees t of f_0 the following two statements are equivalent:

(1) t matches $x_\sharp$ in f_0;

(2) there are $y, y_1 \in Y$ such that $(y, y_1) \in \lambda t$, $y_1 \sqsupseteq x_\sharp y_\top$, and $x_\sharp \in \delta_{\mathcal{T}}(\lambda t, t)$.

The proof is omitted. □

We conclude that during a run of D_C, we can identify candidates t fulfilling the context of a pattern by looking at λt. Then it only remains to verify that t satisfies target variable $x_\sharp$, i.e. $x_\sharp \in \delta_{\mathcal{T}}(\lambda t, t)$. In that case we have detected a match of the pattern. Therefore, in a single run, we not only determine whether a forest contains a match, but we can also locate all matching subtrees. Thus we can find all matches of a pattern in an SGML document during the parse process, without the need for constructing a copy of the document in memory.

6 Computing Reachable States

We have presented a method for constructing an equivalent DPFA for a given constraint system. The set of forest states of D_C is $2^{Y \times Y}$ which is still large. In most cases, however, a considerable subset of states is not reachable from the automaton's start state. An implementation of D_C will therefore compress the transition tables by storing transitions for the reachable states only. In order to describe reachable states we make up a system of inclusion constraints for each $q \in Q_{\mathcal{F}}$:

$$r_{\mathcal{T}}[q] \supseteq \{\mathit{Exit}_a\, q_1 \mid q_1 \in r_{\mathcal{F}}[\mathit{Entry}_a\, q], a \in \Sigma\}$$
$$r_{\mathcal{F}}[q] \supseteq \{q\}$$
$$r_{\mathcal{F}}[q] \supseteq \{\mathit{Comb}(q_1, p) \mid q_1 \in r_{\mathcal{F}}[q] \text{ and } p \in r_{\mathcal{T}}[q_1]\}$$

Variable $r_{\mathcal{F}}[q]$ describes the set of all forest states reachable from q at the same level, i.e., $q_1 \in r_{\mathcal{F}}[q]$ iff there is an f such that $q_1 = \delta_{\mathcal{F}}(q, f)$. Similarly, $r_{\mathcal{T}}[q]$ describes the set of all tree states reachable from q by consuming exactly one tree, i.e., $p \in r_{\mathcal{T}}[q]$ iff $p = \delta_{\mathcal{T}}(q, t)$ for some t.

In order to compute $r_{\mathcal{F}}[q]$ for some state q, $r_{\mathcal{F}}[q_1]$ and $r_{\mathcal{T}}[q_1]$ must be computed for all q_1 reachable from $\mathit{Entry}_a\, q$. In order to compute these, all states reachable from $\mathit{Entry}_a\, q_1$ have to be considered, and so on. Therefore, computing a partial least solution for all $r_{\mathcal{F}}[q]$ and $r_{\mathcal{T}}[q]$ necessary to compute $r_{\mathcal{F}}[q_\sharp]$ for the start state $q_\sharp$ involves exactly the reachable states of D_C. [LH92] propose *local solvers* for computing such a solution. Because the only operation required for solving the system is set union, *differential local solvers* as in [FS98] can also be applied. The interested reader may consult that paper for efficient algorithms.

Example 5: Consider automaton D_C from Ex. 4. Running a local solver yields:

$r_{\mathcal{F}}[1] = \{1,3\}$, $r_{\mathcal{F}}[3] = \{3\}$, $r_{\mathcal{F}}[2] = \{2\}$, and $r_{\mathcal{T}}[1] = r_{\mathcal{T}}[2] = r_{\mathcal{T}}[3] = \{5,4\}$. I.e., states $1,\ldots,5$ from Fig. 1 are the only reachable ones among the twenty states of D_C. □

7 Extensions

We have suggested a mechanism for specifying forest regular languages, namely constraint systems. This formalism has the advantage of allowing for convenient extensions. For instance, we can add conjunctions:

$$x \sqsupseteq a\langle \sqcap M\rangle \qquad \text{with } M \subseteq Y \text{ and} \qquad [\![a\langle \sqcap M\rangle]\!]\,\sigma = \bigcap_{y\in M} [\![a\langle y\rangle]\!]\,\sigma$$

On the automaton side this introduces the concept of *alternation*: $Exit_a$ is extended to be a subset of $2^{Q_{\mathcal{F}}} \times Q_{\mathcal{T}}$ (instead of $Q_{\mathcal{F}} \times Q_{\mathcal{T}}$), and $\delta_{\mathcal{T}}$ is redefined:

$$(q, a\langle f\rangle, p) \in \delta_{\mathcal{T}} \text{ iff there is an } M \subseteq Q_{\mathcal{F}} \text{ with } (M,p) \in Exit_a \text{ and for all } q_1 \in M \text{ there is a } q_0 \in Entry_a\, q \text{ with } (q_0, f, q_1) \in \delta_{\mathcal{F}}.$$

Since alternation can be removed by a subset construction similar to the one removing non-determinism, the construction of D_C can also handle conjunctions, provided we change the definition of *Entry* and *Exit*:

$$Entry_a\, q = \{(y,y) \mid (y_1,y_2) \in q, y_2 \sqsupseteq xy_3, x \sqsupseteq a\langle \sqcap M\rangle \text{ and } y \in M\}$$
$$Exit_a\, q = \{x \mid x \sqsupseteq a\langle \sqcap M\rangle \text{ and for } y \in M, (y,y_0) \in q \text{ with } y_0 \sqsupseteq \varepsilon\}$$

But we have to be careful: conjunctions may only occur in constraints for non-context variables. Otherwise locating matches becomes complicated.
Interestingly enough, it is also complicated to allow conjunctions in constraints for forest variables, like $y \sqsupseteq \sqcap_{i=1}^{n} x_i y_i$. Carried over to automata, this would imply alternation in traversing a forest from left to right. Removing this kind of alternation results in a state space that is doubly exponential – provided we preserve the direction of traversal [CKS81]. In order to do with single exponential blowup (needed anyway for removing non-determinism) we would have to change direction of traversal. Clearly, this is contrary to our intention of running the automaton during one left-to-right parse of a document tree.

8 Conclusion

We presented constraint systems for denoting regular languages of trees and forests of variable arity and used them for uniformly specifying both structural and contextual conditions in patterns. Then we introduced the class of forest pushdown automata which we showed to be well-suited for recognizing forest regular languages. We identified an interesting subset of contextual conditions and showed how PFAs can be used for locating all subtrees of a forest that match a pattern. For this purpose a single traversal through the forest is sufficient, and the decision whether a subtree matches can be made in-place, i.e. at the time of visiting that subtree. We gave an algorithm for computing the reachable states of pushdown forest automata and observed that this can considerably reduce the size of the transition tables.

It remains to be investigated whether we can extend our method to deal with arbitrary contexts. Future work includes integrating these methods into a document processing system.

Acknowledgements: We thank Priti Shankar for kindly providing us with a preliminary version of his paper [SGYM98].

References

[BKR96] M. Biehl, N. Klarlund, and T. Rauhe. Algorithms for guided tree automata. In *First International Workshop on Implementing Automata (WIA'96)*, LNCS 1260. Springer, 1996.

[BMW91] J. Börstler, U. Möncke, and R. Wilhelm. Table Compression for Tree Automata. *ACM TOPLAS*, 13(3):295–314, 1991.

[Bra69] W.S. Brainerd. Tree Generating Regular Systems. *Information and Control*, 14:217–231, 1969.

[CKS81] A.K. Chandra, D.C. Kozen, and L.J. Stockmeyer. Alternation. *J. ACM*, 28(1):114–133, 1981.

[FS98] C. Fecht and H. Seidl. Propagating Differences: An Efficient New Fixpoint Algorithm for Distributive Constraint Systems. In *ESOP '98*, LNCS 1381, pages 90–104. Springer, 1998.

[Gol90] C.F. Goldfarb. *The SGML Handbook*. Clarendon Press, Oxford, 1990.

[LH92] B. LeCharlier and P. Van Hentenryck. A Universal Top-Down Fixpoint Algorithm. Technical Report CS-92-25, Brown University, Providence, 1992.

[Mor94] E. Moriya. On two-way tree automata. *IPL*, 50:117–121, 1994.

[Mur96] M. Murata. Transformations of Trees and Schemas by Patterns and Contextual Conditions. In C. Nicolas and D. Wood, editors, *Principles of Document Processing (PODP'96)*, LNCS 1293, pages 153–169. Springer, 1996.

[MW95] D. Maurer and R. Wilhelm. *Compiler Design*. Addison-Wesley, 1995.

[NS98] A. Neumann and H. Seidl. Locating Matches of Tree Patterns in Forests. Technical Report 98-08, Mathematik/Informatik, Universität Trier, 1998.

[Pod92] A. Podelski. A Monoid Approach to Tree Automata. In M. Nivat and A. Podelski, editors, *Tree Automata and Languages*, pages 41–56. North Holland, 1992.

[PQ68] C. Pair and A. Quere. Définition et Etude des Bilangages Réguliers. *Information and Control*, 13:565–593, 1968.

[SGYM98] P. Shankar, A. Gantait, A.R. Yuvaraj, and M. Madhavan. A New Algorithm for Linear Regular Tree Pattern Matching. Submitted to TCS, 1998.

[Tak75] M. Takahashi. Generalizations of Regular Sets and their Application to a Study of Context-Free Languages. *Information and Control*, 27:1–36, 1975.

[Tha67] J.W. Thatcher. Characterizing Derivation Trees of Context-Free Grammars through a Generalization of Finite Automata Theory. *JCSS*, 1:317–322, 1967.

Benefits of Tree Transducers for Optimizing Functional Programs

Armin Kühnemann

Grundlagen der Programmierung, Institut für Softwaretechnik I,
Fakultät Informatik, Technische Universität Dresden, D–01062 Dresden, Germany,
e–mail: kuehne@orchid.inf.tu-dresden.de

Abstract. We present a technique to prevent the construction of intermediate data structures in functional programs, which is based on results from the theory of tree transducers. We first decompose function definitions, which correspond to macro tree transducers, into smaller pieces. Under certain restrictions these pieces can be composed to an attributed tree transducer using a composition result for attribute grammars. The same construction can be used to compose the attributed tree transducers, which represent the initial function definitions.

1 Introduction

In functional programs compositions of functions are frequently used in order to support a modular style of programming. Thus, one function can produce an intermediate result, which is consumed by another function. If these intermediate results are structured objects, like lists or trees, then this programming style can cause inefficiencies. For instance, Wadler has tackled this problem by inventing the deforestation technique for transforming programs using intermediate data structures into programs that do not (cf. [18]). The original transformation terminates for treeless first-order programs, where essentially every occurrence of a function in the right-hand side of an equation is only applied to variables.

Attribute grammars have been introduced by Knuth in [12] to assign meaning to programs which are produced by context-free grammars. Johnsson even considers them as functional programming paradigms (cf. [11]). At least they suffer from the same problems, if they are used in a compositional programming style. Ganzinger has shown in [8] that restricted attribute grammars, which are called language morphisms, are closed under composition. Ganzinger and Giegerich have presented this composition in the framework of attribute coupled grammars (cf. [9, 10]). The imposed restriction is called *syntactic single use requirement*, which essentially means that every attribute value in a tree may be used at most once to calculate other attribute values.

Attributed tree transducers (for short *atts*) have been defined by Fülöp in [7] as formal models to study properties of attribute grammars. They abstract from attribute grammars in the sense that they translate trees into trees, which are constructed over ranked alphabets. Fülöp has shown that the class of atts is not closed under composition, but closed under right-composition with the class of *top-down tree transducers* (for short *tdtts*; cf. [15, 17]). Tdtts can be seen as atts without inherited attributes and thus as models for S-attribute grammars.

In this paper we present a technique to prevent intermediate data structures of primitive-recursive tree functions, which is based on the composition result for attribute grammars. For this purpose we consider *macro tree transducers* (for short *mtts*), which have been introduced by Engelfriet in [4] (also cf. [2, 6]). Mtts extend the scheme of primitive recursion, additionally allowing simultaneous definitions of functions and nesting of trees in parameter positions. In order to generalize our results, we actually present them for *macro attributed tree transducers* (for short *matts*), which we have invented in [14] as integration of atts and mtts. Since the classes of mtts and of matts generally are not closed under composition (cf. [6, 14]), we have to impose restrictions.

We project the syntactic single use requirement on matts. Since matts can copy context parameters, this projection still allows that an attribute value is used more than once to calculate other attribute values. Thus, we call our restriction *weakly single-use*. In this paper we additionally take advantage of the *noncopying* restriction for matts. This restriction means that context variables of functions may be used at most once in the right-hand sides of function definitions. Since atts have no context variables, the weakly single-use restriction for atts is called *single-use* restriction.

In [14] we have decomposed matts into atts and yield functions, which perform substitutions of parameter values. According to Engelfriet (cf. [5]), also yield functions can also be realized by atts. In [13] we have shown that the decomposition carries over the weakly single-use restriction from an matt to the first att. If the matt is noncopying, then the second att is single-use. Thus, under both restrictions, the single-use atts can be composed to one single-use att.

In consequence, also restricted matts, and in particular restricted primitive-recursive functions, can be composed to one single-use att. Thus, intermediate data structures are no more constructed!

With this method also compositions of functions can be handled, which deforestation does not optimize. An example which demonstrates this is the twofold reversal of monadic trees, where the accumulating parameter (cf. e.g. [16]) causes the trouble in deforestation. In [13] we have presented another example, in which three restricted mtts for the translation of binary numbers (cf. also [12]) into programs for an abstract machine were composed to one att.

Correnson et al. apply in [1] the same strategy as we did in [13]. They perform the transformation of functions into attribute grammars directly without decomposition and composition steps. But in contrast to our work, they do not specify the class of functions, which their strategy can treat. Further they state, that the strategy of composition via attribute grammars is more powerful than deforestation. We cannot agree with this statement, because there are also examples, which deforestation can handle, but not attribute grammar composition. An example is the composition of a tdtt, which produces for a monadic tree a full binary tree of the same height, with an mtt, which produces again a monadic tree with a height that is equal to the number of leaves of the binary tree.

2 Preliminaries

We denote the set of natural numbers including 0 by $\mathbb{N}$. For every $m \in \mathbb{N}$, the set $\{1, \ldots, m\}$ is denoted by $[m]$. We will use the set $Y = \{y_1, y_2, y_3, \ldots\}$ of *variables* and for every $k \in \mathbb{N}$ the abbreviation $Y_k = \{y_1, \ldots, y_k\}$. If Σ is an alphabet, then Σ^* denotes the set of *strings* over Σ. The empty string is denoted by ε. For a string v and two lists $u_1, \ldots, u_n$ and $v_1, \ldots, v_n$ of strings such that no pair u_j and u_l overlaps in v, we abbreviate by $v[u_1/v_1, \ldots, u_n/v_n]$ (or by $v[u_j/v_j\ ;\ j \in [n]]$) the string which is obtained from v by replacing every occurrence of u_j in v by v_j. Let $\Rightarrow$ be a binary relation on a set K. Then, $\Rightarrow^*$ denotes the transitive, reflexive closure of $\Rightarrow$. If $k \Rightarrow^* k'$ for $k, k' \in K$ and if there is no $k'' \in K$ such that $k' \Rightarrow k''$, then k' is called a *normal form of k with respect to* $\Rightarrow$, which is denoted by $nf(\Rightarrow, k)$, if it exists and if it is unique.

A *ranked alphabet* is a pair $(\Sigma, rank_\Sigma)$ where Σ is a finite set and $rank_\Sigma : \Sigma \longrightarrow \mathbb{N}$ is a mapping. For every $\sigma \in \Sigma$, $rank_\Sigma(\sigma)$ is called the *rank of* σ. If Σ is known and $rank_\Sigma(\sigma) = n$, then we write $\sigma^{(n)}$. $\Sigma^{(n)}$ denotes the set of elements with rank n. The set of *trees over* Σ, denoted by $T\langle\Sigma\rangle$, is the smallest set T such that for every $n \geq 0$, $\sigma \in \Sigma^{(n)}$, and $t_1, \ldots, t_n \in T$: $\sigma(t_1, \ldots, t_n) \in T$. Let $t \in T\langle\Sigma\rangle$. Then, $paths(t) \subseteq \mathbb{N}^*$ is the *set of paths of* t. If $t \in \Sigma^{(0)}$, then $paths(t) = \{\varepsilon\}$. If $t = \sigma(t_1, \ldots, t_n)$ with $\sigma \in \Sigma^{(n)}$, $n \geq 1$, and $t_1, \ldots, t_n \in T\langle\Sigma\rangle$, then $paths(t) = \{\varepsilon\} \cup \{jp \mid j \in [n], p \in paths(t_j)\}$. Every path $p \in paths(t)$ determines exactly one node of t. The *label* $\sigma \in \Sigma$ of the node of t which is reached by a path $p \in paths(t)$ is denoted by $label(t, p)$.

Let Σ, Δ, and Ω be ranked alphabets. A total function $\tau : T\langle\Sigma\rangle \longrightarrow T\langle\Delta\rangle$ is called *tree transformation*. If $\tau_1 : T\langle\Sigma\rangle \longrightarrow T\langle\Delta\rangle$ and $\tau_2 : T\langle\Delta\rangle \longrightarrow T\langle\Omega\rangle$ are tree transformations, then we denote the *composition* of τ_1 and τ_2 by $\tau_1 \circ \tau_2$. Thus, for every $t \in T\langle\Sigma\rangle$, $\tau_1 \circ \tau_2 : T\langle\Sigma\rangle \longrightarrow T\langle\Omega\rangle$ is defined by $(\tau_1 \circ \tau_2)(t) = \tau_2(\tau_1(t))$. If $\mathcal{T}_1$ and $\mathcal{T}_2$ are two classes of tree transformations, then $\{\tau_1 \circ \tau_2 \mid \tau_1 \in \mathcal{T}_1, \tau_2 \in \mathcal{T}_2\}$ is denoted by $\mathcal{T}_1 \circ \mathcal{T}_2$.

A function $h : \Omega^{(0)} \longrightarrow T\langle\Delta\rangle(Y)$ such that $h(\omega)$ contains for every $\omega \in \Omega^{(0)}$ and $y_j \in Y$ at most one occurrence of y_j is called *yield base function*. The following *yield function* $yield_h : T\langle\Omega\rangle \longrightarrow T\langle\Delta\rangle(Y)$ interprets every occurrence of a symbol $\omega \in \Omega^{(n+1)}$ as substitution, which replaces every occurrence of a variable y_j with $j \in [n]$ in the interpretation of the first subtree of ω by the interpretation of the $(j+1)$-st subtree of ω: For every $\omega \in \Omega^{(0)}$, $yield_h(\omega) = h(\omega)$ and for every $n \geq 0$, $\omega \in \Omega^{(n+1)}$, and $t_0, t_1, \ldots, t_n \in T\langle\Omega\rangle$, $yield_h(\omega(t_0, t_1, \ldots, t_n)) = yield_h(t_0)[y_j/yield_h(t_j)\ ;\ j \in [n]]$. The class of yield functions is denoted by *YIELD*.

3 Macro Attributed Tree Transducers

We recall the definition of a macro attributed tree transducer from [14]. Note that the first argument of every function is a path of a tree t. If the *path variable* z in the rules is instantiated by a path p to a node of t, then the path zj is instantiated by the path pj to the j-th successor of this node.

Definition 3.1 A *macro attributed tree transducer* (for short *matt*) is a tuple $M = (S, I, \Sigma, \Delta, s_{in}, root, R)$ where

- S is a ranked alphabet of *synthesized functions*; for every $s \in S$, $rank_S(s) \geq 1$.
- I is a ranked alphabet of *inherited functions*; for every $i \in I$, $rank_I(i) \geq 1$.
- Σ is a ranked alphabet of *input symbols.*
- Δ is a ranked alphabet of *output symbols.*
- s_{in} is a unary symbol, called the *initial synthesized function.*
- *root* is a unary symbol, called the *root symbol.*

We assume that S, I, Σ, Δ, $\{s_{in}\}$, and $\{root\}$ are disjoint in pairs.
For every $k \geq 0$, $I' \in \{I, \emptyset\}$, and $n \geq 0$ the set of *right-hand sides over* S, $[k]$, I', Δ, *and* Y_n, denoted by $RHS(S, [k], I', \Delta, Y_n)$, is the smallest set RHS with:

1. For every $m \geq 0$, $s \in S^{(m+1)}$, $j \in [k]$, and $\varrho_1, \ldots, \varrho_m \in RHS$: $s(zj, \varrho_1, \ldots, \varrho_m) \in RHS$.
2. For every $m \geq 0$, $i \in I'^{(m+1)}$, and $\varrho_1, \ldots, \varrho_m \in RHS$: $i(z, \varrho_1, \ldots, \varrho_m) \in RHS$.
3. For every $r \geq 0$, $\delta \in \Delta^{(r)}$, and $\varrho_1, \ldots, \varrho_r \in RHS$: $\delta(\varrho_1, \ldots, \varrho_r) \in RHS$.
4. $Y_n \subseteq RHS$.

- $R = \bigcup_{\sigma \in \Sigma \cup \{root\}} R_\sigma$ is the set of *rules* with:
  - R_{root} contains
    - exactly one rule $s_{in}(z) \to \rho$ with $\rho \in RHS(S, [1], \emptyset, \Delta, Y_0)$ and
    - for every $n \geq 0$ and $i \in I^{(n+1)}$ exactly one rule $i(z1, y_1, \ldots, y_n) \to \varrho$ with $\varrho \in RHS(S, [1], \emptyset, \Delta, Y_n)$.
  - For every $k \geq 0$ and $\sigma \in \Sigma^{(k)}$, R_σ contains
    - for every $n \geq 0$ and $s \in S^{(n+1)}$ exactly one rule $s(z, y_1, \ldots, y_n) \to \varrho$ with $\varrho \in RHS(S, [k], I, \Delta, Y_n)$ and
    - for every $n \geq 0$, $i \in I^{(n+1)}$, and $j \in [k]$ exactly one rule $i(zj, y_1, \ldots, y_n) \to \varrho$ with $\varrho \in RHS(S, [k], I, \Delta, Y_n)$. □

Example 3.2 Let $\Sigma_{rv} = \{A^{(1)}, B^{(1)}, E^{(0)}\}$. We define the matts M_{rv} and M^*_{rv}:
$M_{rv} = (S_{rv}, \emptyset, \Sigma_{rv}, \Sigma_{rv}, s_{in}, root, R_{rv})$ with $S_{rv} = \{rv^{(2)}\}$ and

$(R_{rv})_{root} = \{s_{in}(z) \to rv(z1, E)\}$ $\quad(R_{rv})_A = \{rv(z, y_1) \to rv(z1, A(y_1))\}$
$(R_{rv})_E = \{rv(z, y_1) \to y_1\}$ $\quad(R_{rv})_B = \{rv(z, y_1) \to rv(z1, B(y_1))\}$

M_{rv} reverses the occurrences of As and Bs in a tree $t \in T\langle\Sigma_{rv}\rangle$ by accumulating them in the second parameter of rv. M_{rv} represents the four equations $s_{in}\ (root\ x) = rv\ x\ E$, $rv\ E\ y_1 = y_1$, $rv\ (A\ x)\ y_1 = rv\ x\ (A\ y_1)$, and $rv\ (B\ x)\ y_1 = rv\ x\ (B\ y_1)$ of a functional program in Haskell-like notation, where $root$, A, B, and E are data constructors, and x and y_1 are variables.
$M^*_{rv} = (S^*_{rv}, I^*_{rv}, \Sigma_{rv}, \Sigma_{rv}, s_{in}, root, R^*_{rv})$ with $S^*_{rv} = \{s^{(1)}\}$, $I^*_{rv} = \{i^{(1)}\}$, and

$(R^*_{rv})_{root} = \{s_{in}(z) \to s(z1),\ \ i(z1) \to E\}$
$(R^*_{rv})_A = \{s(z) \to s(z1),\ \ i(z1) \to A(i(z))\}$
$(R^*_{rv})_B = \{s(z) \to s(z1),\ \ i(z1) \to B(i(z))\}$
$(R^*_{rv})_E = \{s(z) \to i(z)\}$

M^*_{rv} reverses a tree $t \in T\langle\Sigma_{rv}\rangle$, collecting the labels of the nodes of t in reverse order by i and passing the resulting tree by s unchanged to the root of t. □

An matt translates *input trees* (of $T\langle\Sigma\rangle$) into *output trees* (of $T\langle\Delta\rangle$). For every $e \in T\langle\Sigma\rangle$, the tree $root(e)$, abbreviated by $\tilde{e}$, is called *control tree* and we choose the value of s_{in} at the root of $\tilde{e}$ as output tree (cf. Definition 3.8). We use the abbreviations $F = S \cup I$, $F_+ = F \cup \{s_{in}\}$, $S_+ = S \cup \{s_{in}\}$ and $\Sigma_+ = \Sigma \cup \{root\}$. A function $f \in F_+^{(1)}$ is called *attribute*. For every $k \geq 0$ and $\sigma \in \Sigma^{(k)}$ we define the set of *inside* and *outside function occurrences of* σ as $in_M(\sigma) = \{s(z) \mid s \in S\} \cup \{i(zj) \mid i \in I, j \in [k]\}$ and $out_M(\sigma) = \{i(z) \mid i \in I\} \cup \{s(zj) \mid s \in S, j \in [k]\}$, respectively. $in_M(root) = \{s_{in}(z)\} \cup \{i(z1) \mid i \in I\}$ and $out_M(root) = \{s(z1) \mid s \in S\}$ are the sets of *inside* and *outside function occurrences of root*. An *attribute occurrence* is a function occurrence with function component of rank 1.

Definition 3.3 Let $M = (S, I, \Sigma, \Delta, s_{in}, root, R)$ be an matt.

- M is a *macro tree transducer* (for short *mtt*), if $I = \emptyset$.
- M is an *attributed tree transducer* (for short *att*), if $S = S^{(1)}$ and $I = I^{(1)}$.
- M is a *top-down tree transducer* (for short *tdtt*), if $S = S^{(1)}$ and $I = \emptyset$. □

Example 3.4 M_{rv} is an mtt and M_{rv}^* is an att. □

The set of sentential forms of an matt M is the set of trees over Δ and functions which are applied to paths of a control tree $\tilde{e}$ in their first arguments. $\tilde{e}$ itself will parameterize the derivation relation. With regard to the derivation relation we define the set of sentential forms for an arbitrary superset $\Delta' \supseteq \Delta$.

Definition 3.5 Let $M = (S, I, \Sigma, \Delta, s_{in}, root, R)$ be an matt. Let $e \in T\langle\Sigma\rangle$ and let Δ' be a ranked alphabet with $\Delta \subseteq \Delta'$. The set $SF(F, s_{in}, paths(\tilde{e}), \Delta')$ of *sentential forms over* F, s_{in}, $paths(\tilde{e})$ *and* Δ' is the smallest set SF such that:

1. $s_{in}(\varepsilon) \in SF$.
2. For every $n \geq 0$, $f \in F^{(n+1)}$, $p \in (paths(\tilde{e}) - \{\varepsilon\})$, and $t_1, \ldots, t_n \in SF$: $f(p, t_1, \ldots, t_n) \in SF$.
3. For every $r \geq 0$, $\delta \in \Delta'^{(r)}$, and $t_1, \ldots, t_r \in SF$: $\delta(t_1, \ldots, t_r) \in SF$. □

For an matt M and for a control tree $\tilde{e}$, the set of *function instances of* $\tilde{e}$ is the set $\{s_{in}(\varepsilon)\} \cup \{f(p) \mid f \in F, p \in (paths(\tilde{e}) - \{\varepsilon\})\}$.

Definition 3.6 Let $M = (S, I, \Sigma, \Delta, s_{in}, root, R)$ be an matt. Let $e \in T\langle\Sigma\rangle$. The *derivation relation of* M *with respect to* $\tilde{e}$, denoted by $\Rightarrow_{M,\tilde{e}}$, is a binary relation on $SF(F, s_{in}, paths(\tilde{e}), \Delta)$ defined as follows:
For every $t_1, t_2 \in SF(F, s_{in}, paths(\tilde{e}), \Delta)$, $\quad t_1 \Rightarrow_{M,\tilde{e}} t_2, \quad$ iff

- there is $t' \in SF(F, s_{in}, paths(\tilde{e}), \Delta \cup \{u\})$ with exactly one occurrence of the 0-ary symbol $u \notin (F_+ \cup \Delta \cup \mathbb{N}^*)$,
- there is $n \in \mathbb{N}$, a function $f \in F_+^{(n+1)}$, and a path $p \in paths(\tilde{e})$,
- there are $t'_1, \ldots, t'_n \in SF(F, s_{in}, paths(\tilde{e}), \Delta)$ with
- $t_1 = t'[u/f(p, t'_1, \ldots, t'_n)]$, and

1.
   - either $f \in S_+$,
   - there is $k \geq 0$ and $\sigma \in \Sigma_+^{(k)}$ with $label(\tilde{e}, p) = \sigma$, and
   - there is a rule $(f(z, y_1, \ldots, y_n) \to \varrho) \in R_\sigma$, such that
   - $t_2 = t'[u/\varrho[z/p][y_l/t'_l\,;\, l \in [n]]]$,

2. – or $f \in I$,
   – there is $p' \in paths(\tilde{e})$, $k \geq 1$, $\sigma \in \Sigma_+^{(k)}$, and $j \in [k]$ with $label(\tilde{e}, p') = \sigma$ and $p = p'j$, and
   – there is a rule $(f(zj, y_1, \ldots, y_n) \to \varrho) \in R_\sigma$, such that
   – $t_2 = t'[u/\varrho[z/p'][y_l/t'_l\,;\, l \in [n]]]$. □

If M or $\tilde{e}$ are known, then we drop the corresponding indices from $\Rightarrow$.

Example 3.7 Let $\tilde{e} = root(A(A(B(E))))$. Then we can derive as follows:

- $s_{in}(\varepsilon) \Rightarrow_{M_{rv}} rv(1, E) \Rightarrow_{M_{rv}} rv(11, A(E)) \Rightarrow_{M_{rv}} rv(111, A(A(E))) \Rightarrow_{M_{rv}} rv(1111, B(A(A(E)))) \Rightarrow_{M_{rv}} B(A(A(E)))$
- $s_{in}(\varepsilon) \Rightarrow_{M^*_{rv}} s(1) \Rightarrow_{M^*_{rv}} s(11) \Rightarrow_{M^*_{rv}} s(111) \Rightarrow_{M^*_{rv}} s(1111) \Rightarrow_{M^*_{rv}} i(1111) \Rightarrow_{M^*_{rv}} B(i(111)) \Rightarrow_{M^*_{rv}} B(A(i(11))) \Rightarrow_{M^*_{rv}} B(A(A(i(1)))) \Rightarrow_{M^*_{rv}} B(A(A(E)))$ □

Matts can be *circular* as attribute grammars, i.e. a function instance may depend on itself. Only *noncircular* matts induce noetherian and confluent derivation relations and thus every sentential form has a unique normal form (cf. [14]).

Definition 3.8 Let $M = (S, I, \Sigma, \Delta, s_{in}, root, R)$ be a noncircular matt. The *tree transformation* $\tau(M) : T\langle\Sigma\rangle \longrightarrow T\langle\Delta\rangle$ *computed by* M, is defined as follows. For every $e \in T\langle\Sigma\rangle$, $\tau(M)(e) = nf(\Rightarrow_{M,\tilde{e}}, s_{in}(\varepsilon))$. □

In the following we always mean noncircular matts when we talk about matts.

Definition 3.9 An matt $M = (S, I, \Sigma, \Delta, s_{in}, root, R)$ is called

- *noncopying*, if for every $(f(\eta, y_1, \ldots, y_n) \to \varrho) \in R$ and for every $j \in [n]$, the variable y_j occurs at most once in ϱ,
- *weakly single-use*, if for every $k \geq 0$, $\sigma \in \Sigma_+^{(k)}$, and $f(\eta) \in out_M(\sigma)$, $f(\eta)$ occurs in a right-hand side of at most one rule in R_σ and there exactly once,
- and *single-use*, if M is a weakly single-use att. □

Example 3.10 The mtt M_{rv} is noncopying and weakly single-use. The att M^*_{rv} is (trivially) noncopying and weakly single-use. Thus M^*_{rv} is also single-use. □

The *classes of tree transformations*, which are computed by tdtts, atts, mtts, and matts are denoted by T, AT, MT, and MAT, respectively. We add an index *wsu* and an index *nc* to these classes, if we deal with weakly single-use tts and noncopying tts, respectively, where tt is an abbreviation for tree transducer. Instead of AT_{wsu} and T_{wsu} we use AT_{su} and T_{su}, respectively.

4 Decomposition

Engelfriet and Vogler have shown that an mtt can be simulated by the composition of a tdtt with a yield function (cf. [4, 6]). We have generalized this result in [14] to matts, proving that an matt can be simulated by the composition of an att with a yield function. Here we informally recall the construction for the decomposition of an matt M into an att M' and a function $yield_h$.

The key idea is to simulate the task of an $(n+1)$-ary function f of M by a unary function f' of M'. Since f' is unary, it does not know the current values for the Y-parameters to which f is applied. Instead of it, f' introduces a new 0-ary symbol Π_j, wherever f uses its j-th parameter in a calculation. For this purpose, every variable y_j in the right-hand sides of the rules of M are substituted by Π_j.

The function $yield_h$ has to substitute every occurrence of Π_j in a sentential form by the j-th current Y-parameter, thus we define $h(\Pi_j) = y_j$. The current Y-parameters themselves are integrated into the calculation of M' by the substitution of a right-hand side of the form $f(\eta, t_1, \ldots, t_n)$ in M by $SUB_n(f'(\eta), t'_1, \ldots, t'_n)$, where SUB_n is a new $(n+1)$-ary output symbol and $t'_1, \ldots, t'_n$ result from $t_1, \ldots, t_n$ by recursive substitutions. Roughly speaking, $yield_h$ interprets an occurrence of SUB_n as substitution, which replaces every occurrence of Π_j in the subtree, which is generated by $f'(\eta)$, by t'_j.

To avoid the distinction of SUB-symbols from output symbols with a rank greater than 0 in the yield function, also for every r-ary output symbol δ of M a 0-ary output symbol δ' in M' is used. Thus, right-hand sides of the form $\delta(t_1, \ldots, t_r)$ in M are substituted by $SUB_r(\delta', t'_1, \ldots, t'_r)$ and $h(\delta') = \delta(y_1, \ldots, y_r)$ is defined to undo this substitution later. This should be improved in implementations.

This decomposition result and the corresponding composition result (cf. [6, 14]), which is not relevant for our aim, have the following consequences.

Theorem 4.1 $MAT = AT \circ YIELD$ ([14]) and $MT = T \circ YIELD$ ([4, 6]) □

Example 4.2 For M_{rv} we construct a tdtt M'_{rv} and a yield base function h_{rv} such that $\tau(M'_{rv}) \circ yield_{h_{rv}} = \tau(M_{rv})$. $M'_{rv} = (S'_{rv}, \emptyset, \Sigma_{rv}, \Omega_{rv}, s'_{in}, root, R'_{rv})$ with $S'_{rv} = \{rv'^{(1)}\}$, $\Omega_{rv} = \{A'^{(0)}, B'^{(0)}, E'^{(0)}, \Pi_1^{(0)}, SUB_0^{(1)}, SUB_1^{(2)}\}$, and

$$(R'_{rv})_{root} = \{s'_{in}(z) \to SUB_1(rv'(z1), SUB_0(E'))\}$$
$$(R'_{rv})_A \;\;= \{rv'(z) \to SUB_1(rv'(z1), SUB_1(A', \Pi_1))\}$$
$$(R'_{rv})_B \;\;= \{rv'(z) \to SUB_1(rv'(z1), SUB_1(B', \Pi_1))\}$$
$$(R'_{rv})_E \;\;= \{rv'(z) \to \Pi_1\}$$

Note that M'_{rv} is single-use. The function $h_{rv} : \Omega_{rv}^{(0)} \longrightarrow T\langle\Sigma_{rv}\rangle(Y_1)$ is defined by $h_{rv}(A') = A(y_1)$, $h_{rv}(B') = B(y_1)$, $h_{rv}(E') = E$, and $h_{rv}(\Pi_1) = y_1$. □

The decomposition and the composition, respectively, carries over the weakly single-use restriction from the matt to the att and vice versa, respectively:

Theorem 4.3 $MAT_{wsu} = AT_{su} \circ YIELD$ and $MT_{wsu} = T_{su} \circ YIELD$ ([13])
Proof. Let M be a weakly single-use matt (a weakly single-use mtt, respectively). The construction for the decomposition result delivers an att (a tdtt, respectively) which is single-use, because every outside function occurrence in a right-hand side of a rule of M is translated into exactly one outside attribute occurrence in a right-hand side of a rule of M'. The proof for the composition result is not relevant for the aim of this paper (cf. [13]). □

5 Realization of Yield Functions

Engelfriet has demonstrated, how a yield function can be calculated by an attribute grammar with only one synthesized attribute (cf. [5]). In our framework we can construct an att as follows.

Let $yield_h : T\langle\Omega\rangle \longrightarrow T\langle\Delta\rangle(Y_{mx})$ be a yield function with $mx \in \mathbb{N}$ and $h : \Omega^{(0)} \longrightarrow T\langle\Delta\rangle(Y_{mx})$. The instances of the unique synthesized attribute s represent the results of applying $yield_h$ to the subtrees of a tree in $T\langle\Omega\rangle$. The parameters $y_1, \ldots, y_{mx}$ are represented by inherited attributes $i_1, \ldots, i_{mx}$.

Since for every $\omega \in \Omega^{(0)}$ (thus for Π_j- and δ'-symbols from Section 4), $yield_h(\omega) = h(\omega)$, the value of s at an occurrence of ω is obtained from $h(\omega) \in T\langle\Delta\rangle(Y_{mx})$, where for every occurrence of y_j in $h(\omega)$ the value of i_j at ω is used.

For every occurrence of $\omega \in \Omega^{(n+1)}$ (thus for SUB_n-symbols from Section 4) the substitution principle is imitated as follows. The value of s at the first successor of ω is passed to s at ω itself. For every $j \in [mx]$, the value of i_j at ω is passed to i_j at every successor of ω, but the first. If $n \leq mx$, then i_j at the first successor of ω gets for every $j \in [n]$ the value from s at the $(j+1)$-st successor, and for every $j \in [mx] - [n]$ the value from i_j at ω. If $n > mx$ (which cannot appear in yield functions constructed in our decompositions), then for every $j \in [mx]$, i_j at the first successor gets the value from s at the $(j+1)$-st successor. In Figure 1 the situation for $mx = 3$ and for a symbol SUB_2 is shown.

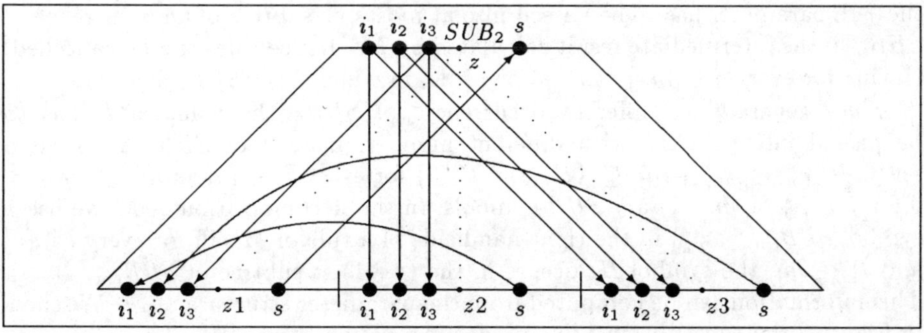

Fig. 1. Substitution principle for $mx = 3$ and SUB_2.

Lemma 5.1 *YIELD* $\subseteq AT$ ([5]) □

Example 5.2 We give for h_{rv} the att M''_{rv} such that $\tau(M''_{rv}) = yield_{h_{rv}}$. $M''_{rv} = (S''_{rv}, I''_{rv}, \Omega_{rv}, \Sigma_{rv} \cup \{y_1\}, s_{in}, root, R''_{rv})$ with $S''_{rv} = \{s^{(1)}\}$, $I''_{rv} = \{i_1^{(1)}\}$ and

$$(R''_{rv})_{root} = \{s_{in}(z) \rightarrow s(z1),\ i_1(z1) \rightarrow y_1\}$$
$$(R''_{rv})_{\Pi_1} = \{s(z) \rightarrow i_1(z)\}$$
$$(R''_{rv})_{E'} = \{s(z) \rightarrow E\}$$
$$(R''_{rv})_{A'} = \{s(z) \rightarrow A(i_1(z))\}$$
$$(R''_{rv})_{B'} = \{s(z) \rightarrow B(i_1(z))\}$$
$$(R''_{rv})_{SUB_0} = \{s(z) \rightarrow s(z1),\ i_1(z1) \rightarrow i_1(z)\}$$
$$(R''_{rv})_{SUB_1} = \{s(z) \rightarrow s(z1),\ i_1(z1) \rightarrow s(z2),\ i_1(z2) \rightarrow i_1(z)\}$$

Note that M''_{rv} is single-use. Further note that y_1 in the second rule of $(R''_{rv})_{root}$ is an output symbol of M''_{rv}, which does not occur in any output tree. □

In [13] we have shown $YIELD \not\subseteq AT_{su}$. Thus, the observation from our example cannot be generalized. The reason is, that the value of an attribute i_j at $\omega \in \Omega^{(n+1)}$ may be used for the value of i_j at more than one successor (cf. Figure 1). In the following we show, under which conditions a yield function resulting from a decomposition of an matt can be realized by a single-use att.

If the yield base function is constructed according to Section 4, then in the case $n \leq mx$ we can cancel[1] unconditionally for every $\omega \in \Omega^{(n+1)}$ and $j \in [mx] - [n]$ the rule for i_j at the first successor of ω (in Figure 1 for i_3 at $z1$). This holds, because in the decomposition an occurrence of SUB_n in the right-hand side of a rule of the att M' is used, iff an $(n+1)$-ary function or an n-ary output symbol occurs in a right-hand side of a rule of the matt M. Thus the calculation inside the first subtree t_0 of a subtree $SUB_n(t_0, t_1, \ldots, t_n)$ generated by M' only depends on $t_1, \ldots, t_n$, which are passed into t_0 via $i_1, \ldots, i_n$.

A rule for i_j with $j \in [mx]$ at another successor of ω may only be cancelled, if the j-th parameter is not used there. Unfortunately this property cannot be deduced from a yield function alone. One has to consider the structure of possible input trees for the yield function. The structure of these trees is known, if they are output trees of an att M' resulting from a decomposition of an matt M.

In particular, if M is noncopying, then every subtree of every right-hand side of M' has at most one occurrence of a symbol Π_j with $j \in [mx]$. This holds in particular for subtrees, which are labeled by a symbol SUB_n at their roots. Thus, the j-th parameter has to be passed into at most one subtree of an occurrence of SUB_n in the intermediate result calculated by M'. Hence rules can be cancelled, leaving for every $j \in [mx]$ at most one rule, in which i_j at SUB_n is used.

Since generally at different occurrences of SUB_n the value of i_j has to be passed into subtrees with different number, instead of SUB_n we need a set $\{SUB_{(m_1,\ldots,m_n)} \mid m_j \subseteq \{\Pi_1, \ldots, \Pi_{mx}\}$ for every $j \in [n]$ and $m_j \cap m_{j'} = \emptyset$ for $j \neq j'\}$ of $(n+1)$-ary SUB-symbols. In the decomposition of M we use a symbol $SUB_{(m_1,\ldots,m_n)}$ in the right-hand side of a rule of M', iff for every $l \in [n]$ and $\Pi_j \in m_l$, the symbol Π_j occurs in the $(l+1)$-st subtree of $SUB_{(m_1,\ldots,m_n)}$. This information can be computed from the parameter structure of M. We show in Figure 2 the substitution principle for $mx = 3$ and for $SUB_{(\{\Pi_2\},\{\Pi_1,\Pi_3\})}$.

Lemma 5.3 $MAT_{nc} \subseteq AT \circ AT_{su}$ and $MAT_{wsu,nc} \subseteq AT_{su} \circ AT_{su}$ □

There is a possibility to simulate general yield functions by weakly single-use tts. In [6] it was shown, how an "(input-) linear mtt" can calculate a yield function. In our framework this means, that for every input symbol $\sigma^{(k)}$ with $k \geq 0$, for every $j \in [k]$ and for every synthesized function s, the path zj occurs at most once in the right-hand side ϱ of the rule $s(z, \ldots) \to \varrho$ in R_σ. Since this mtt has only one function, this restriction induces the weakly single-use property.

Lemma 5.4 $YIELD \subseteq MT_{wsu}$ ([6, 13]) □

[1] Actually, to cancel a rule means to define its right-hand side as arbitrary 0-ary symbol, in order to fulfill the completeness condition for rules of an matt.

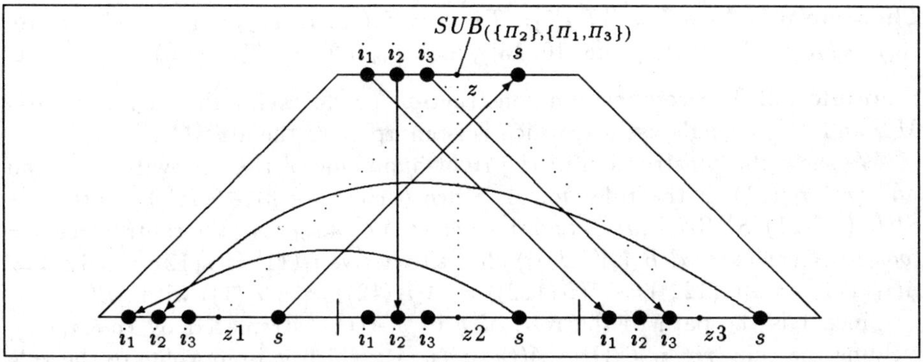

Fig. 2. Substitution principle for $mx = 3$ and $SUB_{(\{\Pi_2\},\{\Pi_1,\Pi_3\})}$.

6 Composition

Fülöp has shown that generally two atts cannot be composed to one att (cf. [7]). Two restrictions are known, under which two atts M_1 and M_2 can be composed to an att M: The construction in [7] requires that M_2 is a tdtt. It takes the cartesian product of the attribute sets of M_1 and M_2 as attribute set of M and computes the right-hand sides of rules of M by "translating" the right-hand sides of rules of M_1 with the help of M_2. The other construction is based on composition results for language morphisms (cf. [8]) and for attribute coupled grammars (cf. [9, 10]) and restricts M_1 to be single-use. In the framework of tts it was presented in [13] by generalizing the translation technique of [7]:

Let $M_1 = (S_1, I_1, \Sigma, \Omega, s_{in,1}, root, R_1)$ and $M_2 = (S_2, I_2, \Omega, \Delta, s_{in,2}, root, R_2)$ be atts. For the att $M = (S, I, \Sigma, \Delta, s_{in}, root, R)$ we define $S = (S_1 \times S_2) \cup (I_1 \times I_2)$ and $I = (S_1 \times I_2) \cup (I_1 \times S_2)$. For every $\sigma \in \Sigma_+^{(k)}$ the rules in R_σ are constructed as follows. For every $s_1(z) \to \varrho$ (and $i_1(zj) \to \varrho$, respectively) in $(R_1)_\sigma$ with $s_1 \in S_1$ ($i_1 \in I_1$ and $j \in [k]$, respectively), ϱ serves as input tree for M_2:

- If a derivation of M_2 is started with $s_2 \in S_2$ at the root of ϱ, then its result is the right-hand side of the rule in R_σ with left-hand side $(s_1, s_2)(z)$ (and $(i_1, s_2)(zj)$, respectively).
- If a derivation of M_2 is started with $i_2 \in I_2$ at a leaf of ϱ, which is labeled by an $a_1(zj') \in out_{M_1}(\sigma)$ with $a_1 \in S_1 \cup I_1$ and $j' \in [k] \cup \{\varepsilon\}$, then its result is the right-hand side of the rule in R_σ with left-hand side $(a_1, i_2)(zj')$.

If during a derivation of M_2 an $i_2' \in I_2$ hits the root of ϱ, then it is replaced by $(s_1, i_2')(z)$ (by $(i_1, i_2')(zj)$, respectively). If an $s_2' \in S_2$ hits an $\hat{a}_1(z\hat{j}) \in out_{M_1}(\sigma)$ with $\hat{a}_1 \in S_1 \cup I_1$ and $\hat{j} \in [k] \cup \{\varepsilon\}$, then it is replaced by $(\hat{a}_1, s_2')(z\hat{j})$.

In general, for every $i_2 \in I_2$ and $a_1(zj') \in out_{M_1}(\sigma)$, the rule with left-hand side $(a_1, i_2)(zj')$ is not unique, because more than one leaf of the right-hand sides of rules in $(R_1)_\sigma$ may be labeled by $a_1(zj')$. This can be avoided, if one of our two restrictions holds, i.e. if M_1 is single-use or M_2 has no inherited attributes.

Since the construction carries over the single-use restriction from M_2 to M (cf. [13]) and since also the corresponding decomposition results hold, we get:

Theorem 6.1 $AT \circ T = AT$ ([7]), $T \circ T = T$ ([15]), $AT_{su} \circ AT = AT$ ([8, 10, 13]), $AT_{su} \circ AT_{su} = AT_{su}$ ([8, 10, 13]), and $T_{su} \circ T_{su} = T_{su}$ ([13]) □

Example 6.2 The composition construction produces for the single-use atts M'_{rv} and M''_{rv} a single-use att, which is isomorphic to the att M^*_{rv}.

We show the construction of the right-hand side of the rule with left-hand side $(rv', i_1)(z1)$ in the rules for A: Since $(rv'(z) \to \varrho) \in (R'_{rv})_A$ with $\varrho = SUB_1(rv'(z1), SUB_1(A', \Pi_1))$ and since $rv'(z1) \in out_{M_1}(A)$, the control tree $\tilde{\varrho} = root(SUB_1(rv'(z1), SUB_1(A', \Pi_1)))$ allows to derive $i_1(11) \Rightarrow s(12) \Rightarrow s(121) \Rightarrow A(i_1(121)) \Rightarrow A(s(122)) \Rightarrow A(i_1(122)) \Rightarrow A(i_1(12)) \Rightarrow A(i_1(1))$ with M''_{rv}.

Since 1 is the path to the root of ϱ in $\tilde{\varrho}$, $i_1(1)$ is replaced by $(rv', i_1)(z)$, yielding the rule $(rv', i_1)(z1) \to A((rv', i_1)(z))$, which is isomorphic to the rule $i(z1) \to A(i(z))$ in $(R^*_{rv})_A$. □

It is interesting that M_{rv}, which corresponds to the most natural way to describe the reversal by a functional program, is transformed into M^*_{rv}, which corresponds to the most natural way to describe the reversal by an attribute grammar. Since M^*_{rv} is single-use, it can also be composed with itself (cf. [10]). Note that the construction for the result $AT \subseteq MT$ (cf. [2]) can transform the composition result again into a functional program, which does not use an intermediate result!

7 Theoretical Consequences

The first result shows the limited power of weakly single-use matts. Note that we have proved $MAT = AT \circ AT$ in [14] for the unrestricted class of matts.

Theorem 7.1 $MAT_{wsu} \subseteq AT$
Proof. $MAT_{wsu} = AT_{su} \circ YIELD \subseteq AT_{su} \circ AT = AT$ by Theorem 4.3, Lemma 5.1, and Theorem 6.1. □

We do not know yet, whether MAT_{wsu} is strictly included in AT or whether these classes are equal. Adding the noncopying restriction, we get a characterization, which reflects the theoretical background of our running example:

Theorem 7.2 $MAT_{wsu,nc} = AT_{su}$
Proof. $MAT_{wsu,nc} \subseteq AT_{su} \circ AT_{su} = AT_{su}$ by Lemma 5.3 and Theorem 6.1 and $AT_{su} \subseteq MAT_{wsu,nc}$, since atts have no parameters from Y. □

If we use Lemma 5.4 to calculate yield functions, then we get a nice characterization for the class MAT_{wsu} and the result, that MT_{wsu} is closed under left-composition with T_{su}, in analogy to the result $MT = T \circ MT$ from [6].

Theorem 7.3 $MAT_{wsu} = AT_{su} \circ MT_{wsu}$ and $MT_{wsu} = T_{su} \circ MT_{wsu}$
Proof.

MAT_{wsu}	MT_{wsu}	
$= AT_{su} \circ YIELD$	$= T_{su} \circ YIELD$	(Theorem 4.3)
$\subseteq AT_{su} \circ MT_{wsu}$	$\subseteq T_{su} \circ MT_{wsu}$	(Lemma 5.4)
$= AT_{su} \circ T_{su} \circ YIELD$	$= T_{su} \circ T_{su} \circ YIELD$	(Theorem 4.3)
$\subseteq AT_{su} \circ YIELD$	$= T_{su} \circ YIELD$	(Theorem 6.1)
$= MAT_{wsu}$	$= MT_{wsu}$	(Theorem 4.3) □

8 Further Research Topics

The strategies deforestation and composition are incomparable, since both can solve problems, which the other cannot solve. Is it possible, to integrate both strategies? At least a formal characterization of problems would be useful, for which deforestation has advantages compared with composition, and vice versa.

We think that matts are not only suitable to present composition and decomposition results for tts in a uniform way. Since overlapping research in functional programming and attribute grammars is often hampered by their different formalisms as stated e.g. in [3], we also consider matts to be an interesting possibility to compare or even to integrate the composition results for both concepts.

References

1. L. Correnson, E. Duris, D. Parigot, and G. Roussel. Symbolic composition. Technical Report 3348, INRIA, France, 1998.
2. B. Courcelle and P. Franchi-Zannettacci. Attribute grammars and recursive program schemes. *Theoret. Comput. Sci.*, 17:163–191, 235–257, 1982.
3. E. Duris, D. Parigot, G. Roussel, and M. Jourdan. Attribute grammars and folds: generic control operators. Technical Report 2957, INRIA, France, 1996.
4. J. Engelfriet. Some open questions and recent results on tree transducers and tree languages. In R.V. Book, editor, *Formal language theory; perspectives and open problems*, pages 241–286. New York, Academic Press, 1980.
5. J. Engelfriet. Tree transducers and syntax directed semantics. Technical Report Memorandum 363, Technische Hogeschool Twente, 1981.
6. J. Engelfriet and H. Vogler. Macro tree transducers. *J. Comp. Syst. Sci.*, 31:71–145, 1985.
7. Z. Fülöp. On attributed tree transducers. *Acta Cybernetica*, 5:261–279, 1981.
8. H. Ganzinger. Increasing modularity and language-independency in automatically generated compilers. *Science of Computer Programming*, 3:223–278, 1983.
9. H. Ganzinger and R. Giegerich. Attribute coupled grammars. In *Symposium on Compiler Construction, SIGPLAN Notices Vol.19, No.6*, pages 157–170, 1984.
10. R. Giegerich. Composition and evaluation of attribute coupled grammars. *Acta Informatica*, 25:355–423, 1988.
11. T. Johnsson. Attribute grammars as a functional programming paradigm. In *FPCA'87, Portland*, volume 274 of *LNCS*, pages 154–173. Springer-Verlag, 1987.
12. D.E. Knuth. Semantics of context-free languages. *Math. Syst. Th.*, 2:127–145, 1968. Corrections in *Math. Syst. Th.*, 5:95-96, 1971.
13. A. Kühnemann. *Berechnungsstärken von Teilklassen primitiv-rekursiver Programmschemata.* PhD thesis, Technical Univ. of Dresden, 1997. Shaker Verlag.
14. A. Kühnemann and H. Vogler. Synthesized and inherited functions - a new computational model for syntax-directed semantics. *Acta Informatica*, 31:431-477, 1994.
15. W.C. Rounds. Mappings and grammars on trees. *Math. Syst.Th.*, 4:257–287, 1970.
16. H. Seidl and M.H. Sørensen. Constraints to stop higher-order deforestation. In *POPL'97, Paris*, pages 400–413. ACM Press, 1997.
17. J.W. Thatcher. Generalized^2 sequential machine maps. *J.Comp.Syst.Sci.*, 4:339–367, 1970.
18. P. Wadler. Deforestation: Transforming programs to eliminate trees. *Theor. Comp. Sci.*, 73:231–248, 1990.

Implementable Failure Detectors in Asynchronous Systems

Vijay K. Garg* and J. Roger Mitchell**

Electrical and Computer Engineering Department
The University of Texas, Austin, TX 78712
email: garg@ece.utexas.edu, http://maple.ece.utexas.edu

Abstract. The failure detectors discussed in the literature are either impossible to implement in an asynchronous system, or their exact guarantees have not been discussed. We introduce an *infinitely often accurate* failure detector which can be implemented in an asynchronous system. We provide one such implementation and show its application to the fault-tolerant server maintenance problem. We also show that some natural timeout based failure detectors implemented on Unix are not sufficient to guarantee infinitely often accuracy.

1 Introduction

Failure detection is one of the most fundamental modules of any fault-tolerant distributed system. Typically, a fault-tolerant distributed system uses one of the two techniques - maintain replicas of a process, or use primary-backup approach. Both of these approaches rely on detection of failures. While most commercial fault-tolerant systems use some sort of failure detection facility typically based on timeouts, we show that many of them are inadequate in providing accuracy guarantees in failure detection.

The first systematic study of failure detection in asynchronous systems was done by [CHT92,CT96]. The weakest failure detector they studied, called $\Diamond\mathcal{W}$, can be used to solve the consensus problem in asynchronous systems. It follows from [FLP85] that failure detectors in [CT96] are not implementable in asynchronous systems. The failure detector introduced in this paper, called Infinitely Often Accurate detector (IO detector for short), can be implemented efficiently in asynchronous systems.

An IO detector is required to satisfy even weaker accuracy than eventually weak accuracy proposed by Chandra and Toueg [CT96]. Intuitively, eventually weak accuracy requires that for all runs the detector eventually never suspects at least one correct process. It is precisely this requirement which makes it possible to solve the consensus problem by using, for example, the rotating coordinator

* supported in part by the NSF Grants ECS-9414780, CCR-9520540, a Texas Education Board Grant ARP-320, a General Motors Fellowship, and an IBM grant
** supported in part by a Virginia & Ernest Cockrell fellowship

technique[CT96]. On the other hand, this is also the requirement which is impossible to implement in an asynchronous system. An IO detector only requires that a correct process is not permanently suspected. By assuming that a channel delivers the messages infinitely often, this requirement can be easily met. In fact, the algorithm is based on an earlier work by Dwork et al. [DLS88]. Our contribution lies in formalizing the exact properties guaranteed by that algorithm and showing its usefulness in asynchronous systems. We also show that some other natural "timeout" implementation of failure detectors for Unix [HK95] and other systems do not satisfy the properties of an IO detector.

Although no algorithm can solve the consensus problem in an asynchronous system for all runs, it is desirable that the processes reach agreement in finite time for runs which satisfy *partial synchrony* condition. Following [DLS88], a run is defined as partially synchronous if there exists a non-failed process such that eventually all messages it sends reach their destinations in bounded delay. We show that for these runs our failure detector will provide eventual weak accuracy and hence processes using the approach in [CT96] will reach agreement in finite time. Thus, our failure detector provides *conditional* eventual weak accuracy guarantee. In other words, whereas $\diamond\mathcal{W}$ insists on eventual weak accuracy for all runs, we require eventual weak accuracy only in partially synchronous runs and infinitely often accuracy for all runs.

While the IO detector cannot be used to solve the consensus problem, we show that it is useful for other applications. In particular, we give its application to a fault-tolerant server maintenance problem. This problem requires presence of at least one server during the computation. Our solution works in spite of up to $N-1$ failures in a system of N processes.

2 IO Failure Detectors

We assume the usual model of an asynchronous system [FLP85]. The message delays are unbounded but finite. A *run* of any algorithm in an asynchronous system results in a set of *local* states denoted by S. We use s, t and u to denote the local states of processes, i, j and k to denote process indices, and the notation $s.v$ to denote the value of the variable v in the local state s. The relation $s < t$ means that s and t are states at the same process and s occurred before t. The relation $s \leq t$ means that $s < t$ or s is equal to t. The relation, $\rightarrow$, is used to order states in the same manner as Lamport's happened before relation on events [Lam78]. Therefore, $s \rightarrow t$ is the smallest transitive relation on S satisfying 1) $s < t$ implies $s \rightarrow t$, and 2) if s is the state immediately preceding the send of a message and t is the state immediately following the receive of that message then $s \rightarrow t$.

A global state G is a set of local states, one from each process, such that no two of them are related by the happened-before relation. We use symbols G and H to denote global states and $G[i]$ to denote the state of the process i in the global state G. We say that $G \preceq H$ (or $H \succeq G$) iff $\forall i : G[i] \leq H[i]$.

A processor crashes by ceasing all its activities. We assume that once a process has failed (or crashed) it stays failed throughout the run. The predicate $failed(i)$ holds if the process i has failed in the given run. A process that has not failed is called a *correct* process. We denote the set of all processes and the set of correct processes by Π and Π_c respectively. The set $C \subseteq S$ denotes the set of states on the correct processes and the set C_j denotes the states for any correct process j.

The predicate $s.suspects[i]$ holds if the process i is suspected in the state s (by the process which contains s). A failure detector is responsible for maintaining the value of the predicate $suspects[i]$ at all processes. The value of $suspects[i]$ is true at P_k, if P_k suspects that P_i has failed. We would like our failure detectors to satisfy certain completeness and accuracy properties of these suspicions.

Definition 1. *An IO failure detector is a failure detector that satisfies strong completeness, infinitely often accuracy, and conditional eventual weak accuracy.*

These properties are described next.

2.1 Strong Completeness Property

Let the predicate $permsusp(s, i)$ be defined as

$$permsusp(s, i) \equiv \forall t \geq s : t.suspects[i]$$

The *strong completeness* property requires the failed process to be eventually suspected by *all* correct processes. Formally, for all runs,

$$\forall i, j : \langle failed(i) \wedge \neg failed(j) \Rightarrow \exists s \in C_j : permsusp(s, i)\rangle$$

The *weak completeness* property requires that every failed process is eventually permanently suspected by some correct process. Formally, for all runs,

$$\forall i : \langle failed(i) \Rightarrow \exists s \in C : permsusp(s, i)\rangle$$

Since strong completeness is quite useful in the design of distributed algorithms, and is easily achieved by simple timeout mechanisms, we require that IO detectors satisfy strong completeness.

2.2 Infinite Often Accuracy

In [CT96], four accuracy properties have been presented. The weakest of these properties is *eventual weak accuracy.* A detector satisfies eventual weak accuracy if for all runs eventually some correct process is never suspected by any correct process. Formally, for all runs

$$\exists i \in \Pi_c, \forall j \in \Pi_c, \exists s \in C_j, \forall t \geq s : \neg t.suspects[i]$$

However, as shown by [CT96] a failure detector which satisfies weak completeness and eventual weak accuracy, called eventually weak detector ($\diamond\mathcal{W}$)

can be used to solve the consensus problem in an asynchronous system. This implies that $\Diamond\mathcal{W}$ is impossible to implement in an asynchronous system. We now introduce a weaker accuracy property which we call infinitely often accuracy. A detector is infinitely often accurate if no correct process permanently suspects an unfailed process. Formally,

Definition 2. *A detector is infinitely often accurate if for all runs*

$$\forall i : \langle \neg failed(i) \Rightarrow \forall s \in C : \neg permsusp(s, i) \rangle$$

Note that infinitely often accuracy is simply the converse of the weak completeness requirement. By combining the two properties, we get the following pleasant property of an IO detector.

$$\forall i : failed(i) \equiv \exists s \in C : permsusp(s, i)$$

Intuitively, this says that a failure of a process is equivalent to permanent suspicion by some correct process.

2.3 Conditional Eventual Weak accuracy

We now introduce another useful property of failure detectors, *conditional eventual weak accuracy*, which is also implementable in an asynchronous environment. The property says that if we happen to be lucky in *some* asynchronous run in the sense that eventually all messages sent by at least one process reach their destination under some bound then the failure detector will eventually be accurate with respect to that process *in that run*.

We first introduce the notion of a *partially synchronous* run similar to that used in [DLP+86].

Definition 3. *A run is partially synchronous if there exists a state s in a correct process P_i and a bound δ such that all messages sent by P_i after s take at most δ units of time.*

In the above definition we do not require the knowledge of P_i, s, or δ. This lets us define:

Definition 4. *A failure detector satisfies conditional eventual weak accuracy if for all partially synchronous runs it satisfies eventual weak accuracy.*

Observe that the conditional eventual weak accuracy is weaker than the eventual weak accuracy. The former requires that the failure detector satisfy eventual weak accuracy only when the run is partially synchronous, while the latter requires it for all runs.

Remark: We also require that a correct process never suspect itself. This property is trivial to satisfy by ensuring that a process never sets its own suspicion to true. We will always assume this property.

3 Comparison of IO detector with $\Diamond\mathcal{W}$

How does an IO detector compare to $\Diamond\mathcal{W}$? First note that if a failure detector satisfies weak accuracy, then it does not necessarily satisfy infinitely often accuracy. The detector may be accurate with respect to one process but permanently suspect some other correct process. However, another way to compare failure detectors is by using the notion of reduction between detectors as introduced by [CT96]. We show that an IO detector can be implemented using a $\Diamond\mathcal{W}$ detector.

Our implementation of an IO detector uses a $\Diamond\mathcal{S}$ detector. A $\Diamond\mathcal{S}$ detector [CT96] is a failure detector that satisfies strong completeness and eventual weak accuracy. It can be built using $\Diamond\mathcal{W}$ detector as shown in [CT96]. Let *IO.suspects* and *ES.suspects* be the set of processes suspected by the IO detector and $\Diamond\mathcal{S}$ detector respectively. The algorithm (given in Figure 1) is based on two activities. Each process sends a message "alive" to all other processes infinitely often. On receiving such a message from P_i, P_j queries the $\Diamond\mathcal{S}$ suspector and removes the suspicion of P_i and P_j.

```
var
        IO.suspects: set of processes initially ES.suspects − {j};

(I1) send "alive" to all processes infinitely often;

(I2) On receiving "alive" from P_i;
        IO.suspects := ES.suspects − {i, j};
```

Fig. 1. Implementation of an IO detector at P_j using a $\Diamond\mathcal{S}$ detector

We now have the following Lemma.

Lemma 1. *The algorithm in Fig. 1 implements an IO detector.*

Proof. We first show the strong completeness property. Consider any process P_i that has failed. This implies that eventually P_i will be in *ES.suspects* for P_j, by the property of $\Diamond\mathcal{S}$ detector. Further, eventually P_j will stop receiving "alive" message from P_i. This implies that P_i will be permanently in *IO.suspects* of P_j.

To see infinitely often accuracy property, consider any process P_i that has not failed. Any correct process will receive "alive" message from P_i infinitely often. Therefore, P_i will be not be in *IO.suspects* infinitely often.

We show that the algorithm satisfies *eventual weak accuracy* and therefore *conditional eventual weak accuracy*. The detector only removes suspicion from the set *ES.suspects*. Since $\Diamond\mathcal{S}$ satisfies eventual weak accuracy it follows that the IO detector built from $\Diamond\mathcal{S}$ also satisfies this property. ∎

We now consider the converse question. Is there an asynchronous algorithm that implements $\Diamond\mathcal{W}$ using IO-detector? We answer this question in negative by giving an implementation of an IO-detector in Fig. 2. This implementation is similar to that proposed by [DLS88]. The algorithm maintains a timeout period for each process. The variable *watch*[i] is the timer for the process P_i. When the timer expires, the process is suspected. On the other hand when a message is received while a process is suspected, the timeout period for that process is increased.

```
var
        IO.suspects : set of processes initially ∅;
        timeout: array[1..N] of integer initially t;
        watch: array[1..N] of timer initially set to timeout;

(A1) send "alive" to all processes after every t units;

(A2) On receiving "alive" from Pi;
        if i ∈ IO.suspects then
                IO.suspects := IO.suspects − {i};
                timeout[i]++;
        Set watch[i] timer for timeout[i];

(A3) on expiry of watch[i]
        IO.suspects := IO.suspects ∪ {i};
```

Fig. 2. Implementation of an IO detector at P_j

Theorem 1. *The algorithm in Fig.2 implements an IO detector.*

Proof. First we show the strong completeness property. If a process P_i has failed then it will stop sending messages and due to rule (A3) it will permanently be in the set *IO.suspects* of all processes.

The property of infinitely often accuracy follows from the proof of Lemma 1.

The algorithm also satisfies conditional eventual weak accuracy. Consider any partially synchronous run. Let P_i be the correct process in that run for which messages obey the partial synchrony condition after some state s. Since messages sent after that state are received in less than δ units of time, there can only be a bounded number of false suspicions of P_i by any process (because the timeout period is increased by 1 after every false suspicion). Thus, eventually there is a time after which P_i is not suspected by any process. ■

Observe that one needs to be careful with designing algorithms for failure detectors. Some natural approaches do not satisfy the IO-property. Consider the algorithm in Fig. 3 which is similar to the *watchd* process implemented on Unix and reported in [HK95]. It is tempting to implement failure detectors using the algorithm in Fig. 3 since it only requires the failure detector to listen for incoming messages during the timeout interval. This algorithm, however, does not satisfy IO accuracy. It may suspect some process P_i at all times even when P_i is alive and just slow.

```
var
        watchd.suspects: set of processes initially ∅;

(B1) infinitely often broadcast a query message to all processes

(B2) After broadcast wait for timeout[i] time units (timeout period)
        watchd.suspects := { Pi|Pi did not respond to the query in the timeout period }

(B3) On receiving a query from Pi
        send "I am alive" to Pi
```

Fig. 3. A Detector at P_j that does not satisfy IO accuracy

4 Detectors with Stronger Properties

4.1 Failure detectors with small suspicion list

So far we had assumed that up to $N-1$ out of N processes may fail. If we assume that at most f processes may fail, then we can build a failure detector which will never suspect more than f processes and yet provide strong completeness, infinitely often accuracy, and conditional eventual weak accuracy. An implementation of this detector, called f-IO detector, is shown in Fig. 4. Note that when f equals $N-1$, it is equivalent to IO detector (because a process never suspects itself).

The algorithm maintains a queue of slow processes in addition to the list of suspected processes. When a process is suspected it is added to the list only if the size of the list is less than f; otherwise, it is inserted in the queue of slow processes. When a process is unsuspected if the slow queue was non-empty, the process at the head is removed from the queue and inserted in the suspicion list.

Theorem 2. *The algorithm provides all properties of IO detector assuming there are at most f failures. Further, it suspects at most f processes at any time.*

Proof. Strong completeness: If a process has failed it will eventually be permanently suspected by IO.suspects. If it is put in the suspicion list, it will never be removed. If it is kept in the slow queue, then we show that the number of processes ahead in the slow queue will decrease by 1. By our assumption that at most f processes fail, and there are f suspected processes, there is at least one

```
var
        fIO.suspects : set of processes initially ∅;
        slow : FIFO queue of processes initially empty;

(A1) On change of IO.suspects[k] from false to true and not inqueue(slow,k)
        if |fIO.suspects| < f then fIO.suspects[k]:= true;
        else insert(slow,k);

(A2) On change of IO.suspects[k] from true to false
        if fIO.suspects[k] then
                fIO.suspects[k] := false;
                if not empty(slow)
                        i := deletehead(slow);
                        fIO.suspects[i] := true;
        else delete(slow,k); // delete it from the queue
```

Fig. 4. An IO Detector at P_j with small suspicion list

process which is suspected incorrectly. This is because one of the failed process is in the slow queue. By IO accuracy the process that is incorrectly suspected will eventually be unsuspected. At that point the head of the slow queue will be removed.
The *IO-accuracy* and *Conditional eventual weak accuracy* follow from the accuracy properties of IO detector. ■

4.2 Infinitely Often Global Accuracy

So far our detectors only guaranteed that an unfailed process is not permanently suspected. This implies that every process will be accurate about any other process infinitely often. However, it may not have accurate suspicions of all processes at the same time. Thus, it is quite possible that when P_1 is accurate about P_2 it is not so for P_3 and when it is accurate for P_3, it is not accurate for P_2. Surprisingly, it is possible in an asynchronous system to build a detector which guarantees that each process is correct about all other processes infinitely often. We call it an IOG detector.

The main idea behind an IOG detector is as follows. Each process keeps an ordered list of suspected processes. This order is based on the timestamp of the last message received from a process. Thus, in this list P_i appears before P_j if the last message received from P_i was earlier than that of P_j. A process P_k is unsuspected whenever a message is received from a suspected process, say P_i, with the property that timestamp(P_i) is less than or equal to timestamp(P_k). The formal description is given in Fig. 5.

Theorem 3. *The algorithm in Fig.5 implements an IOG detector.*

```
var
        IOG.suspects : set of processes initially ∅;
        timeout: array[1..N] of integer initially t;
        watch: array[1..N] of timer initially set to timeout;
        timestamp: array[1..N] of integer initially 0;

(A1) send "alive" to all processes after every t units;

(A2) On receiving "alive" from P_i;
        timestamp[i] := time; // any increasing counter will do
        if i ∈ IOG.suspects then
                timeout[i]++;
                for k ∈ {1,..,n} do
                        if k ∈ IOG.suspects ∧ timestamp[i] ≤ timestamp[k] then
                                IOG.suspects := IOG.suspects − {k};
                                Set watch[k] timer for timeout[k];

(A3) on expiry of watch[i]
        IOG.suspects := IOG.suspects ∪ {i};
```

Fig. 5. Implementation of an IOG detector (at P_j)

Proof. First we show the strong completeness property. If a process P_i has failed then it will stop sending messages. Eventually its timestamp will be older than that of any correct process. It will then be permanently suspected.

Now consider the property of infinitely often global accuracy. Since failed processes do not send messages and other do, eventually the timestamp of all failed processes are older than that of correct processes. Consider the correct process with the oldest timestamp. Eventually a message will be received from this process. At that point all correct processes will be unsuspected. After any incorrect suspicion, this cycle will repeat and therefore, the detector is accurate globally infinitely often.

The proof for conditional eventual accuracy is identical to that for an IO detector. ■

5 Applications of IO failure detectors

Since IO detectors are implementable, it is clear that they cannot be used for solving the consensus problem in an asynchronous system. What good are they then? We now discuss a practical problem that can be solved using IO detectors. Another example can be found in [GM98]. Consider a service that is required in a distributed system consisting of N processes. We require that at least one process always act as the provider of that service. As a simple example, assume that the servers are stateless and any request from the client is broadcast to all servers.

The problem requires that at least one (preferably exactly one) server respond to the request. We abstract this requirement using the concept of a token. Any process that has a token considers itself as the provider of the service. Since the process holding a token may fail, we clearly need a mechanism to regenerate a token to avoid interruption of the service. To avoid triviality, we only consider those runs in which at most $N-1$ out of N processes fail. The following predicates are used for specifying the requirements.

- $G[i].token$ is true iff process P_i has a token in the global state G.
- $hastoken(G)$ is true iff the global state G has a token. It may have multiple tokens.
$$hastoken(G) \equiv \exists i : G[i].token$$
- $noduplicate(G)$ is true iff the global state G has at most one token. It may have none.
$$noduplicate(G) \equiv \forall i, j : i \neq j : \neg G[i].token \vee \neg G[j].token$$
- $boundedafter(G, i)$ is true iff there exists a bound δ such that all messages sent by P_i after G take at most δ units of time.

Ideally, we would like all global states to have exactly one token. However, even the weaker requirement that eventually there exists exactly one token is impossible to implement in an asynchronous system. Therefore, we consider a weaker set of requirements given below.

1. *Availability:* There exists a global state such that all later global states have at least one token. Formally,
$$\exists G, \forall H \succeq G : hastoken(H)$$
2. *Efficiency:* For every global state G in which two different processes have tokens, there exists a later global state in which the token from at least one of the processes is removed. Formally, for all G, i, j such that $i \neq j$,
$$G[i].token \wedge G[j].token \Rightarrow \exists H \succeq G : \neg H[i].token \vee \neg H[j].token$$
3. *Eventually exactly one token under partial synchrony:* If after any global state G all messages sent by some correct process P_i arrive in less than a pre-determined bounded delay, then there exists a later global state H such that all global states after H have exactly one token. Formally,
$$\forall G : boundedafter(G, i) \Rightarrow \exists H, \forall H' \succeq H : hastoken(H') \wedge noduplicate(H')$$

In practice, for most cases the partial synchrony condition would be true and therefore eventually we will have exactly one token. However, when the partial synchrony is not met we would still have properties of availability and efficiency. This illustrates the methodology that we propose for asynchronous algorithms. They provide useful guarantees even when the run is not well behaved and provide more desirable guarantees when the run is well behaved (i.e. partially synchronous).

We now present a solution which meets all requirements. In addition to the suspicion list maintained by the failure detector, each process maintains a timestamp for each process called *ticket time*. The ticket time of a process P_k is the logical time[Lam78] when it was suspected by some process P_i such that according to P_i, P_k had a token before the suspicion and P_i gets it after the suspicion. P_i will then send out a message to all processes informing them of the suspicion along with this ticket time.

Process P_i has a token if all processes that are currently not suspected by P_i have ticket times that are greater than that of P_i. If a process with a token is suspected its ticket time will become greater than all other ticket times. In this way the token is moved from a slow process to the next process which is alive. The formal description of the algorithm is given in Fig. 6. The algorithm assumes that all channels are FIFO.

```
var
        ticket:array[1..N] of (integer,integer) initially ∀i : ticket[i] = (0, i)
        suspected: array[1..N] of boolean; /* set by the failure detector */

        token(k) ≡ (∀i ≠ k : suspected[i] ∨ (ticket[i] > ticket[k])) ∧ ¬suspected[k]

        (R1) Upon change from unsuspicion to suspicion of P_k with token(k)
                if token(j) then
                        ticket[k] := Lamport's_logical_clock;
                        send "slow", k, ticket[k] to all processes

        (R2) Upon receiving "slow",k,t
                ticket[k] := max(ticket[k], t);
```

Fig. 6. Algorithm for Alive Token Problem at P_j

Theorem 4. *The algorithm in Fig. 6 satisfies all three required properties.*

Proof. Availability: First consider the global state G after which no failures occur. We show that if there is a process with a token in G, then some process will always have a token. A process with a token can lose it only if its own ticket time increases. This can happen only when a process with a token (after the suspicion) sends it a "slow" message. Thus, in this case some other process has a token.

Now, consider the scenario when failures occur. If a process that does not have a token fails then no harm is done. We show that if a process with a token fails and there are no more tokens in the system then a token is regenerated. Of all the processes that are correct consider the process with the smallest ticket. By strong completeness, this process will eventually suspect all the failed processes. At that point, it will have a token.

Efficiency: Consider the global state G in which two processes P_i and P_j have tokens. Since there is a total order on all tickets, this can only happen when the process with the smaller ticket number, say P_i, is suspected by the other process, P_j. For any continuation of run after G, in which P_i or P_j fails we have a global state state H in which $\neg H[i].token \vee \neg H[j].token$. Otherwise, by the IO accuracy property of IO detector, P_j will eventually remove the suspicion of P_i. In that global state H, $\neg H[j].token$ holds.

Eventually exactly one token under partial synchrony: Consider any global state G such that $boundedafter(G, i)$ holds. This implies that IO detector for any process P_j will eventually never suspect P_i. If there are multiple values of i such that $boundedafter(G, i)$ holds, then we choose the process with the smallest ticket number in G. This process is never suspected by anybody else after G and therefore no other process will ever have a token. Further, this process will never lose the token since no process which is unsuspected can have a smaller ticket number. ∎

Remark: If suspicions are perfect, that is, a process is suspected only when it is failed, the algorithm ensures that there is at most one token. Thus, the algorithm can also be seen as a fault-tolerant mutual exclusion algorithm with perfect failure detectors.

References

[CHT92] Tushar Deepak Chandra, Vassos Hadzilacos, and Sam Toueg. The weakest failure detector for solving consensus. In *Proc. of the 11th ACM Symposium on Principles of Distributed Computing*, pages 147–158, August 1992.

[CT96] Tushar Deepak Chandra and Sam Toueg. Unreliable failure detectors for reliable distributed systems. *JACM*, 43(2):225–267, March 1996.

[DLP+86] Danny Dolev, Nancy A. Lynch, Shlomit S. Pinter, Eugene W. Stark, and William E. Weihl. Reaching approximate agreement in the presence of faults. *JACM*, 33(3):499–516, July 1986.

[DLS88] Cynthia Dwork, Nancy Lynch, and Larry Stockmeyer. Consensus in the presence of partial synchrony. *Journal of the ACM*, 35(2):288–323, April 1988.

[FLP85] M. J. Fischer, N. Lynch, and M. Paterson. Impossibility of distributed consensus with one faulty process. *Journal of the ACM*, 32(2), April 1985.

[GM98] V. K. Garg and J. R. Mitchell. Detection of global predicates in a faulty environment. In *Proc. of the IEEE International Conference on Distributed Computing Systems*, pages 416–423, Amsterdam, May 1998.

[HK95] Y. Huang and C. Kintala. Software fault tolerance in the application layer. In Michael Lyu, editor, *Software Fault Tolerance*, pages 249–278. Wiley, Trends in Software, 1995.

[Lam78] L. Lamport. Time, clocks, and the ordering of events in a distributed system. *Communications of the ACM*, 21(7):558–565, July 1978.

BRICS and Quantum Information Processing

Erik Meineche Schmidt

BRICS
Department of Computer Science
University of Aarhus
Building 540, Ny Munkegade, DK-8000 Aarhus C, Denmark
E-mail: ems@brics.dk

Abstract. BRICS is a research centre and international PhD school in theoretical computer science, based at the University of Aarhus, Denmark. The centre has recently become engaged in quantum information processing in cooperation with the Department of Physics, also University of Aarhus.
This extended abstract surveys activities at BRICS with special emphasis on the activities in quantum information processing.

1 Introduction

BRICS (Basic Research In Computer Science) started in 1994 as one out of a total of 23 centres funded by the newly established Danish National Research Foundation [1]. The centre is based at the Universities of Aalborg and Aarhus and it's goal is to conduct basic research in the central areas of theoretical computer science, *logic*, *semantics*, and *algorithmics* (the latter covering both algorithms and complexity theory). A specific goal for the first five year period has been to strengthen activities in logic and algorithmics, taking advantage of the already existing strong expertise in semantics. The first grant, covering the period 1994-1998, has recently been extended until the end of 2003.

BRICS experienced a significant expansion in 1997, when the International PhD School was established in Aarhus. The goal of the school is to establish a strong, internationally competitive, doctoral program in (theoretical) computer science in Denmark. The school offers a significant number of PhD-fellowships to foreign PhD students, and is expected to have a total of 40-50 PhD students when fully operational (approximately half of which will be foreign).

The most recent development around BRICS is the establishment of the Thomas B. Thrige Center for Quantum Informatics in the beginning of 1998. Here BRICS researchers cooperate with colleagues from the Department of Physics, University of Aarhus, on quantum computing in general and on building a (protoype of) a quantum encryption device in particular.

It is perhaps interesting to notice that the centre has inherited its name from its principal sponsor, the Thomas B. Thrige Foundation, a private industrial foundation devoted to promoting the interests of Danish industry.

2 Scientific activities

BRICS has managed to establish an active scientific environment with a strong research profile in core areas of theoretical computer science.

The rest of this section outlines some of the work, the reader is refered to the BRICS homepage (http://www.brics.dk) for references and further information.

2.1 Highlights

The following represents a brief description of some of the scientific highlights.

- **Semantics.** *Foundations* (domain theory, operational semantics), *Concurrency* (theoretical work unifying different approaches, tools), *Programming Language Theory* (semantics and implementation of programming-language features such as type systems, constraint systems etc.).
- **Algorithmics.** *Lower Bounds* (lower bounds in various models of computation, with emphasis on lower bounds for dynamic algorithms and data structures)., *Algorithms* (dynamic algorithms and (analysis) of randomised algorithms, internal and external memory data structures),
  Data Security and Cryptography
  (design and analysis of interactive protocols, construction of digital signatures and practical methods for construction of encryption systems).
- **Logic.** *Constructive and categorical logic* (application of categorical methods, contributions to recent advances in verification techniques, semantics and domain theory),
  Logic and Automata
  (the interplay between automata theory and logic has been exploited to yield advances in logics for verification and their automation),
  Logic and Complexity
  (logics of bounded strength and their relation to complexity theory).
- **Tools for Verification.** General proof systems like HOL, and variants, development and use of MONA (based on monadic second-order logic), more specialised systems like UPPAAL concentrating on real-time verification.

We aim to further consolidate our expertise in these areas, but also to engage in carefully chosen (more experimentally oriented) areas on the fringe of the kernel activities.

2.2 Other activities

A total of approximately 90 persons are associated with BRICS, and the centre is visited by more than 100 foreign scientists per year. A number of visitors offer *mini courses*, where a topic within their area of expertise is presented in the form of a compact course aimed at PhD-students and colleagues.

Another central aspect of the BRICS activities are the *themes* that have been taking place each year since the start in 1994. The topics of the first five themes have been *Complexity Theory, Logic, Verification, Algorithms in Quantum Information Processing (AQIP'98)*, and *Logic and Complexity*.

AQIP'98 is possibly of special interest since it was the fist meeting that was (almost) entirely devoted to the *algorithmic* aspects of quantum information processing.

3 Quantum Information Processing

The activities in quantum information processing represent an interesting example of interdisciplinary activities, involving expertise from both physics and computer science, and being of both experimental and theoretical nature.

3.1 Experimental Activities

On the experimental side, the main activity is building a prototype of a quantum cryptography device doing *quantum key distribution*, i.e. allowing two parties to establish a secret shared keyword, which can then be used for securing conventional communication.

The apparatus will use phase encoding and interferometry to transport information, like many known experiments. A crucial property, necessary for the security of any quantum key distribution protocol is that each classical bit of information is sent encoded in the state of only one photon. Sources of photons that can be built in practice are never perfect in this respect, i.e. the states actually produced are not pure states containing only one photon. Recent research has shown that this problem can be quite serious when using so called faint pulses, the source of photons commonly used in such experiments [2].

Several possible photon sources are expected to be included in the experiment, including a promising technique based on so called parametric down-conversion which produces pairs of photons in an entangled state [2]. This in turn allows for better approximations to pure single photon states.

Future plans include experimental research in quantum information storage.

In particular, the storage of a quantum state of light seems more and more feasible due to the development of the atomic systems extremely well isolated from the environment.

Those systems include cold atoms and ions in traps as well as atoms frozen in a solid host at He temperatures.

3.2 Theoretical activities

When two communicating parties have exchanged information using a quantum channel, the information sent will contain errors, and parts of it may have become known to an attacker.

The analysis of the security of the system being built is therefore a main theoretical activity. This is a joint computer science and physics endavour, since secure quantum cryptography can only be obtained by supplementing the quantum transmission with postprocessing using error correction and privacy amplification techniques.

Other theoretical activities include the study of implementing more advanced cryptographic tools than key distribution, e.g. *bit commitment*. Although this is known to be impossible without assumptions, some recent work has shown that under reasonable physical assumptions (but no computational assumptions) bit commitment is indeed possible [3].

Other work goes towards establishing transmission of quantum states while correcting errors in the transmission [4]. Note that this is not possible using traditional error correcting codes since this would require measuring the states sent, thereby necessarily loosing some of the quantum information.

In the future it is planned to increase the effort on theoretical research in quantum computing in general.

Acknowledgements

Thanks to Ivan Damgård for his assistance in preparing this abstract.

References

1. *How To Be Better Than Good*, The Danish National Research Foundation, 1996.
2. Gilles Brassard, Tal Mor, and Barry C.Sanders: *Quantum Cryptography via Parametric Downconversion*, Manuscript 1998. To be presented at the Algorithms in Quantum Information Processing Workshop (AQIP'99).
3. Louis Salvail: *Quantum Bit Commitment from a Physical Assumption*, Proc. of Crypto 98, LNCS 1462, Springer Verlag.
4. Anders Sørensen and Klaus Mølmer: *Error-free quantum communication through noisy channels*, Manuscript 1998. To appear in Phys. Rev. A, September 1998.

Martingales and Locality in Distributed Computing

Devdatt P. Dubhashi *

Department of Computer Science and Engg.
Indian Institute of Technology, Delhi
Hauz Khas, New Delhi 110016
INDIA
dubhashi@cse.iitd.ernet.in,
WWW home page:http://bhim.cse.iitd.ernet.in/dubhashi

Abstract. We use Martingale inequalities to give a simple and uniform analysis of two families of distributed randomised algorithms for edge colouring graphs.

1 Introduction

The aim of this paper is to advocate the use of certain Martingale inequalities known as "The Method of Bounded Differences" (henceforth abbreviated to MOBD) [9] as a tool for the analysis of distributed randomized algorithms that work in the *locality* paradigm. The form of the inequality we employ and its application here is significantly different from previous successful uses of the method in Computer Science applications in that it exerts much finer control on the effects of the underlying variables to get significantly strobger bounds , and it succeeds in spite of the lack of complete independence. This last feature particularly, makes it a valuable tool in Computer Science contexts where lack of independence is omnipresent. This aspect of the MOBD has, to the best of our knowledge, never been adequately brought out before. Our contribution is to highlight its special relevance for Computer Science applications by demonstrating its use in the context of a class of distributed computations in the locality paradigm.

We give a high probability analysis of a two classes of distributed edge colouring algorithms, [2, 4, 11]. Apart from its intrinsic interest as a classical combinatorial problem, and as a paradigm example for locality in distributed computing, edge colouring is also useful from a practical standpoint because of its connection to scheduling. In distributed networks or architectures an edge colouring corresponds to a set of data transfers that can be executed in parallel. So, a partition of the edges into a small number of colour classes – i.e. a "good" edge colouring– gives an efficient schedule to perform data transfers (for more details,

* Work partly done while at BRICS, Department of Computer Science, University of Aarhus, Denmark. Partially supported by the ESPRIT Long Term Research program of the EU under contract No. 20244 (ALCOM–IT)

see [11, 2]). The analysis of edge colouring algorithms published in the literature is extremely long and difficult and that in [11] is moreover, based an a certain *ad hoc* extension of the Chernoff-Hoeffding bounds. In contrast, our analysis is a very simple, short and streamlined application of the MOBD, only two pages long, and besides, also yields slightly stronger bounds. These two examples are intended moreover, as a dramatic illustration of the versatility and power of the method for the analysis of locality in distributed computing in general, a framework for which is sketched at the end..

In a **message-passing** distributed network, one is faced with the twin problems of *locality* and *symmetry breaking*. Each processor can gather data only locally so as to minimise communication which is at a premium rather than computation. Moreover all processors are identical form the point of view of the network which makes it hard, if not impossible, to schedule the operations of the various processors at different times in order to avoid congestion and converge toward the common computing goal. An often successful way to circumvent these difficulties– the locality bottleneck and symmetry-breaking– is to resort to randomization. When randomization is used, one is required to prove performance guarantees on the results delivered by a randomised algorithm. Notice that in truly distributed environments the usual solution available in sequential or other centralized settings such as a PRAM, namely to restart the randomized algorithm in case of bad outcome, is simply not available. This is because of the cost of collecting and distributing such information to every node in the network. In this context then, it becomes especially important to be able to certify that the randomized algorithm will almost surely work correctly i.e. provide a high probability guarantee.

Even for simple algorithms, this is a challenging task, and the analysis of edge colouring algorithms in the literature are very long and complicated, often requiring *ad hoc* stratagems, as noted above. We show how these analyses can be dramatically simplified and streamlined. The main technical tool used in this paper is a version of the "Method of Bounded Differences" that is more powerful and versatile than the generally known and used version. This version typically yields much stronger bounds. Perhaps even more significantly, the restriction on independence on the underlying random variables which is necessary for the usual version is removed and this greatly extends the scope of applicability of the method. Although these facts are implicit in some of the existing literature, they have never been explicitly noted and highlighted, to the best of our knowledge. For instance, in the (otherwise excellent) survey of McDiarmid [9], the simpler version is stated right at the outset (Lemma 1.2) and illustrated with a number of examples from combinatorics. But the more powerful version is buried away in an obscure corollary towards the end (Corollary 6.10) rather than highlighted as we feel it it deserves to be, and finds no applications. It is our intention here to highlight the more powerful version, especially those aspects that are crucial to make it particularly suitable for analysis of the edge colouring algorithms and more generally, for locality in distributed computing.

2 Distributed Edge Colouring

Vizing's Theorem shows that every graph G can be edge coloured sequentially in polynomial time with Δ or $\Delta + 1$ colours, where Δ is the maximum degree of the input graph (see, for instance, [1]).

It is a challenging open problem whether colourings as good as these can be computed fast in a distributed model. In the absence of such a result one might aim at the more modest goal of computing reasonably good colourings, instead of optimal ones. By a trivial modification of a well-known *vertex* colouring algorithm of Luby it is possible to edge colour a graph using $2\Delta - 2$ colours in $O(\log n)$ rounds (where n is the number of processors) [6].

We shall present and analyze two classes of simple localised distributed algorithms that compute near optimal edge colourings. Both algorithms proceed in a sequence of rounds. In each round, a simple randomised heuristic is invoked to colour a significant fraction of the edges successfully. The remaining edges are passed over to succeeding rounds. This continues until the number of edges is small enough to employ a brute–force method at the final step. For example, the algorithm of Luby mentioned above can be invoked when the degree of the graph becomes small i.e. when the condition $\Delta \gg \log n$ is no longer satisfied.

One of the classes of algorithms involves a standard reduction to bipartite graphs described in [11]: the graph is split into two parts T ("top") and B (bottom). The bipartite graph $G[T, B]$ induced by the edges connecting top and bottom vertices is coloured by invoking the Algorithm P described below. The algorithm is then invoked recursively in parallel on $G[T]$ and $G[B]$, the graphs respectively induced by the top and bottom vertices. Both graphs are coloured using the same set of colours. Thus it suffices to describe the algorithm used for colouring bipartite graphs.

We describe the action carried out by both algorithms in a single round. For the second class of algorithms, we describe the action only for bipartite graphs; additionally, each vertex knows whether it is top or bottom. At the beginning of each round, there is a palette of fresh new available colours, $[\Delta]$, where Δ is the maximum degree of the graph at the current stage. For simplicity we will assume that the graph is Δ–regular.

Algorithm I(Independent): Each edge *independently* picks a colour. This *tentative* colour becomes permanent if there are no conflicting edges picking the same tentative colour at either endpoint.

Algorithm P(Permutation): There is a two step protocol:

- Each bottom vertex, in parallel, makes a *proposal* independently of other bottom vertices by assigning a random *permutation* of the colours to their incident edges.
- Each top vertex, in parallel, then picks a *winner* out of every set of incident edges that have the same colour. Tentative colours of winner edges become final.
- The *losers*– edges who are not winners– are decoloured and passed to the next round.

For the purposes of the high probability analysis below, the exact rule used for selecting the winner edge is unimportant – it can be chosen arbitrarily from any of the edges of the relevant colour; we merely require that it should not depend on edges of different colours. This is another illustration of the power of the martingale method.

It is apparent that both algorithms are truly distributed. That is to say, each vertex need only exchange information with the neighbours to execute the algorithm. This and its simplicity make the algorithms amenable for implementations in a distributed environment. Algorithm I is used with some more modifications in a number of edge colouring algorithms [2, 4]. Algorithm P is exactly the algorithm used in [11].

We focus all our attention in the analysis of one round of both algorithms. Let Δ denote the maximum degree of the graph at the beginning of the round and Δ' denote the maximum degree of the leftover graph. One can easily show that both algorithms, $\mathrm{E}[\Delta' \mid \Delta] \leq \beta\Delta$, for some constant $\beta < 1$. For algorithm I, $\beta = 1 - e^{-2}$ while for algorithm P, $\beta = 1/e$. The goal is to show that this holds with high probability. This is done in § 4 after the relevant tools – the Martingale inequalities – are introduced in the next section.

For completeness, we sketch a calculation of the total number of colours $\mathrm{BC}(\Delta)$ used by Algorithm P for the bipartite colouring of a graph with maximum degree Δ: with high probability, it is,

$$\begin{aligned}\mathrm{BC}(\Delta) &= \Delta + \frac{(1+\epsilon)\Delta}{e} + \frac{(1+\epsilon)^2\Delta^2}{e} + \ldots \\ &\leq \frac{1}{1-(1+\epsilon)e}\Delta \approx 1.59\Delta \text{ for small enough } \epsilon.\end{aligned}$$

To this, one should add $O(\log n)$ colours at the end of the process. As can be seen by analyzing the simple recursion describing the number of colours used by the outer level of the recursion, the overall numbers of colours is the same $1.59\Delta + O(\log n)$, [11].

3 Martingale Inequalities

We shall use martingale inequalities in the *avataras* of the "Method of Bounded Differences" [9]. We shall use the following notations and conventions: $X_1, \ldots, X_n$ will denote random variables with X_i taking values in some set A_i for each $i \in [n]$. For each $i \in [n]$, a_i, a_i' will denote arbitrary elements from A_i. For a function f of several arguments, $f(*, a_i, *)$ will denote that all arguments except the indicated one are held fixed. We shall use boldface notation to abbreviate the sequences: so $\mathbf{X}$ denotes $X_1, \ldots, X_n$, and $\mathbf{a}$ denotes $a_1, \ldots, a_n$. Finally, for each $i \in [n]$, we abbreviate $X_1 = a_1, \ldots, X_i = a_i$ by $\mathbf{X}_i = \mathbf{a}_i$.

3.1 Method(s) of Bounded Differences

The most widely known and used form of the "Method of Bounded Differences" is as follows:

Theorem 1 (Method of Bounded Differences). *Let f be a function that is* **Lipschitz** *with constants $c_i, i \in [n]$ i.e.*

$$|f(*, a_i, *) - f(*, a_i', *)| \leq c_i, \quad \text{for } i \in [n]. \tag{1}$$

Then, if $X_1, \ldots, X_n$ are **independent** *random variables, for any $t > 0$,*

$$\Pr[|f - \mathrm{E}[f]| > t] \leq 2\exp\left(\frac{-2t^2}{\sum_i c_i^2}\right).$$

While extremely convenient to use, this version has two drawbacks. First the bound obtained can be quite weak (because $\sum_i c_i^2$ is large) and second, the assumption of independence limits its range of applicability. A stronger form of the inequality that removes both these limitations is the following

Theorem 2 (Method of Bounded Average Differences). *Let f be a function and $X_1, \ldots, X_n$ a set of random variables (not necessarily independent) such that there are constants $c_i, i \in [n]$, for which*

$$|\mathrm{E}[f \mid \mathbf{X}_{i-1} = \mathbf{a}_{i-1}, X_i = a_i] - \mathrm{E}[f \mid \mathbf{X}_{i-1} = \mathbf{a}_{i-1}, X_i = a_i']| \leq c_i, \tag{2}$$

for each $i \in [n]$ and for every two assignments $\mathbf{X}_{i-1} = \mathbf{a}_{i-1}, X_i = a_i, a_i'$ that are separately consistent (hence of non-zero probability). Then, for any $t > 0$,

$$\Pr[|f - \mathrm{E}[f]| > t] \leq 2\exp\left(\frac{-2t^2}{\sum_i c_i^2}\right).$$

For a discussion of the relative strengths of these methods, see [3].

3.2 Coupling

In order to make effective use of the Method of Average Bounded Differences, we need to get a good handle on the bound (2), for the difference in the expected values of a function under two different conditioned distributions. A very useful technique for this is the method of *coupling*. Suppose that we can find a joint distribution $\pi(\mathbf{Y}, \mathbf{Y}')$ such that the marginal distribution for Y is the same as the distribution of $\mathbf{X}$ conditioned on $\mathbf{X}_{i-1} = \mathbf{a}_{i-1}, X_i = a_i$ and the marginal distribution for $\mathbf{Y}'$ is the same as the distribution $\mathbf{X}$ conditioned on $\mathbf{X}_{i-1} = \mathbf{a}_{i-1}, X_i = a_i'$. Such a joint distribution is called a coupling of the two original distributions. Then,

$$\begin{aligned} |\mathrm{E}[f \mid \mathbf{X}_{i-1} = \mathbf{a}_{i-1}, X_i = a_i] - \mathrm{E}[f \mid \mathbf{X}_{i-1} = \mathbf{a}_{i-1}, X_i = a_i']| &= \\ |\mathrm{E}_\pi[f(\mathbf{Y})] - \mathrm{E}_\pi[f(\mathbf{Y}')]| = |\mathrm{E}_\pi[f(\mathbf{Y}) - f(\mathbf{Y}')]| & \end{aligned} \tag{3}$$

If the coupling π is well–chosen so that $|f(\mathbf{Y}) - f(\mathbf{Y}')|$ is usually very small, we can get a good bound on the difference (2). For example, suppose that

- For any sample point $(\mathbf{y}, \mathbf{y}')$ we have $|f(\mathbf{y}) - f(\mathbf{y}')| \leq d$ for some constant $d > 0$; and

– For most sample points $(\mathbf{y}, \mathbf{y}'$, $f(\mathbf{y}) = f(\mathbf{y}')$. That is, $\pi[f(\mathbf{Y}) - f(\mathbf{Y}')] \leq p$, for some $p << 1$.

Then, we can conclude using (3) that

$$|\mathrm{E}[f \mid \mathbf{X}_{i-1} = \mathbf{a}_{i-1}, X_i = a_i] - \mathrm{E}[f \mid \mathbf{X}_{i-1} = \mathbf{a}_{i-1}, X_i = a_i']| \leq pd.$$

We shall construct suitable couplings to bound the difference in (2).

4 High Probability Analyses

4.1 Top Vertices

The analysis is particularly easy when v is a top vertex in Algorithm P. For, in this case, the incident edges all receive colours independently of each other. This is exactly the situation of the classical balls and bins experiment: the incident edges are the "balls" that are falling at random independently into the colours that represent the "bins". One can apply the method of bounded differences in the simplest form. Let $T_e, e \in E$, be the random variables taking values in $[\Delta]$ that represent the tentative colours of the edges. Then the number of edges successfully coloured around v is a function $f(T_e, e \in N^1(v))$, where $N^1(v)$ denotes the set of edges incident on v.

It is easily seen that this function has the *Lipschitz* property with constant 1: changing only one argument while leaving the others fixed only changes the value of f by at most 2. Note that this is true *regardless of the rule for choosing winners*, as long as this rule does not depend on edges of different colours. This will also be true of the remaining analyses below and illustrates once again, the power of the martingale methods.

Moreover, the variables $T_e, e \in N^1(v)$ are independent when v is a "top" vertex. Hence, by the method of bounded differences in the simplest form, we get the following sharp concentration result by plugging into Theorem 1:

Theorem 3. *Let v be a top vertex in algorithm P and let f be the number of edges around v that are successfully coloured in one round of the algorithm. Then,*

$$\Pr[|f - \mathrm{E}[f]| > t] \leq \exp\left(\frac{-t^2}{2\Delta}\right),$$

For $t := \epsilon\Delta$ $(0 < \epsilon < 1)$, this gives an exponentially decreasing probability for deviations around the mean. If $\Delta \gg \log n$ then the probability that the new degree of any vertex deviates far from its expected value is inverse polynomial, i.e. the new max degree is sharply concentrated around its mean.

4.2 Other Vertices: The Difficulty

The analysis for the "bottom" vertices in Algorithm P is more complicated in several respects. It is useful to see why so that one can appreciate the need for using a more sophisticated tool such as the Method of Bounded Average Differences. To start with, one could introduce an indicator random variable X_e for each edge e incident upon a bottom vertex v. These random variable are not independent however. Consider a four cycle with vertices v, a, w, b, where v and w are bottom vertices and a and b are top vertices. Let's refer to the process of selecting the winner (step 2 of the algorithm P) as "the lottery". Suppose that we are given the information that edge va got tentative colour red and lost the lottery— i.e. $X_{va} = 0$— and that edge vb got tentative colour green. We'll argue intuitively that given this, it is more likely that $X_{vb} = 0$. Since edge va lost the lottery, the probability that edge wa gets tentative colour red increases. In turn, this increases the probability that edge wb gets tentative colour green, which implies that edge vb is more likely to lose the lottery. So, not only are the X_e's not independent, but the dependency among them is particularly malicious.

One could hope to bound this effect by using the MOBD in it simplest form. This is also ruled out however, for two reasons. The first is that the tentative colour choices of the edges around a vertex are not independent. This is because the edges incident on vertex are assigned a permutation of the colours. The second reason applies also to algorithm I where all edges act independently. The new degree of v, a bottom vertex in algorithm P or an arbitrary vertex in algorithm I, is a function $f = f(T_e, e \in N(v))$, where $N(v)$ is the set of edges at distance at most 2 from v. Thus f depends on as many as $\Delta(\Delta - 1) = \Theta(\Delta^2)$ edges. Even if f is Lipshitz with constants $d_i = 2$, this is not enough to get a strong enough bound because $d = \sum_i d_i^2 = \Theta(\Delta^2)$. Applying the method of bounded differences in the simple form, Theorem 1, would give the bound

$$\mathtt{Pr}[|f - \mathtt{E}[f]| > t] \leq 2\exp\left(-\frac{t^2}{\Theta(\Delta^2)}\right).$$

This bound however is useless for $t = \epsilon\mathtt{E}[f]$ since $\mathtt{E}[f] \approx \Delta/e$.

We will use the Method of Bounded Average Differences, Theorem 2, to get a much better bound. We shall invoke the two crucial features of this more general method. Namely that it does not presume that the underlying variables are independent [1] , and that, as we shall see, it allows us to bound the effect of individual random choices with constants much smaller than those given by the MOBD in simple form.

Let's now move on to the analysis. A similar analysis applies to both cases: when v is a bottom vertex in algorithm P or an arbitrary vertex in algorithm I. Let $N^1(v)$ denote the set of "direct" edges– i.e. the edges incident on v– and let $N^2(v)$ denote the set of "indirect edges" that is, the edges incident on a neighbour of v. Let $N(v) := N^1(v) \bigcup N^2(v)$. The number of edges successfully coloured at vertex v is a function $f(T_e, e \in N(v))$. Note that in Algorithm P, even though f seems to depend on edges at distance 3 from v via their effect on

[1] A referee pointed out that one can redefine variables in the analysis of Algorithm P to make them independent; however, this is unnecessary since Theorem to be applied does not need independence. Moreover, in general, it may not always be possible to make such a redefinition of variables. But the general method will still apply.

edges at distance 2, f can still be regarded as a function of the edges in $N(v)$ only (i.e. f is fixed by giving colours to all edges in $N(v)$ regardless of what happens to other edges) and hence only these edges need be considered in the analysis.

Let us number the variables so that the direct edges are numbered *after* the indirect edges (this will be important for the calculations to follow). We need to compute

$$\lambda_k := |\mathrm{E}[f \mid \mathbf{T}_{k-1}, T_k = c_k] - \mathrm{E}[f \mid \mathbf{T}_{k-1}, T_k = c'_k]|. \tag{4}$$

We decompose f as a sum to ease the computations later. Introduce the indicator functions $f_e, e \in E$:

$$f_e(\mathbf{c}) := \begin{cases} 1; & \text{if edge } e \text{ is successfully coloured in colouring } \mathbf{c}, \\ 0; & \text{otherwise.} \end{cases}$$

Then $f = \sum_{v \in e} f_e$.

Hence we are reduced, by linearity of expectation, to computing for each $e \in N^1(v)$,

$$|\mathrm{Pr}[f_e = 1 \mid \mathbf{T}_{k-1}, T_k = c_k] - \mathrm{Pr}[f_e = 1 \mid \mathbf{T}_{k-1}, T_k = c'_k]|.$$

For the computations that follows we should keep in mind that in algorithm P bottom vertices assign colours independently of each other. This implies that in either algorithm, the colour choices of the edges incident upon a neighbour of v are independent of each other. In Algorithm I, *all* edges have their colours assigned independently.

4.3 General Vertex in Algorithm I

To compute a good bound for λ_k in (4), we shall construct a suitable coupling of the two different conditioned distributions. The coupling $(\mathbf{Y}, \mathbf{Y}')$ is almost trivial: $\mathbf{Y}$ is distributed as $\mathbf{T}$ conditioned on $\mathbf{T}_{k-1}, T_k = c_k$ and $\mathbf{Y}'$ is identically equal to $\mathbf{Y}$ except that $\mathbf{Y}'_k = c'_k$. It is easily seen that by the independence of all tentative colours, the marginal distributions of $\mathbf{Y}$ and $\mathbf{Y}'$ are exactly the two conditioned distributions $[\mathbf{T} \mid \mathbf{T}_{k-1}, T_k = c_k]$ and $[\mathbf{T} \mid \mathbf{T}_{k-1}, T_k = c'_k]$ respectively.

Now let us compute $|\mathrm{E}[f(\mathbf{Y}) - f(\mathbf{Y}')]|$.

- First, let us consider the case when $e_1, \ldots, e_k \in N^2(v)$, i.e. only the choices of indirect edges are exposed. Let $e_k = (w, z)$, where w is a neighbour of v. Then for a direct edge $e \neq vw$, $f_e(\mathbf{y}) = f_e(\mathbf{y}')$ because in the joint distribution space, $\mathbf{y}$ and $\mathbf{y}'$ agree on all edges incident on e. So we only need to compute $|\mathrm{E}[f_{vw}(\mathbf{Y}) - f_{vw}(\mathbf{Y}')]|$. To bound this simply, we observe first that $f_{vw}(\mathbf{y}) - f_{vw}(\mathbf{y}') \in [-1, 1]$ and second that $f_{vw}(\mathbf{y}) = f_{vw}(\mathbf{y}')$ unless $y_{vw} = c_k or c'_k$. Thus we can conclude that

$$\mathrm{E}[f_{vw}(\mathbf{Y}) - f_{vw}(\mathbf{Y}')]| \leq \mathrm{Pr}[Y_e = c_k \vee Y_e = c'_k] \leq \frac{2}{\Delta}.$$

In fact one can do a tighter analysis using the same observations. Let us denote $f_e(\mathbf{y}, y_{w,z} = c_1, y_e = c_2)$ by $f_e(c_1, c_2)$. Note that $f_{vw}(c_k, c_k) = 0$ and similarly $f_{vw}(c'_k, c'_k) = 0$. Hence

$$\begin{aligned}&\mathrm{E}[f_e(\mathbf{Y}) - f_e(\mathbf{Y}') \mid z] = \\ &\quad (f_{vw}(c_k, c_k) - f_{vw}(c'_k, c_k))\Pr[Y_e = c_k] + (f_{vw}(c_k, c'_k) - f_{vw}(c'_k, c'_k))\Pr[Y_e = c'_k] \\ &\quad = (f_{vw}(c_k, c'_k) - f_{vw}(c'_k, c_k))\frac{1}{\Delta}\end{aligned}$$

(Here we used the fact that the distribution of colour around v is unaffected by the conditioning around z and that each colour is equally likely.) Hence $|\mathrm{E}[f_e(\mathbf{Y}) - f_e(\mathbf{Y}')]| \leq \frac{1}{\Delta}$.

- Now let us consider the case when $e_k \in N^1(v)$, i.e. choices of all indirect edges and of some direct edges have been exposed. In this case, we merely observe that f is Lipshitz with constant 2: $|f(\mathbf{y}) - f(\mathbf{y}')| \leq 2$ whenever $\mathbf{y}$ and $\mathbf{y}'$ differ in only one co-ordinate. Hence we can easily conclude that $|\mathrm{E}[f(\mathbf{Y}) - f(\mathbf{Y}')]| \leq 2$.

Overall,

$$\lambda_k \leq \begin{cases} 1/\Delta; & \text{for an edge } e_k \in N^2(v), \\ 2; & \text{for an edge } e_k \in N^1(v) \end{cases},$$

and we get

$$\sum_k \lambda_k^2 = \sum_{e \in N^2(v)} \frac{1}{\Delta^2} + \sum_{e \in N^1(v)} 4 \leq 4\Delta + 1.$$

We thus arrive at the following sharp concentration result by plugging into Theorem 2:

Theorem 4. *Let v be an arbitrary vertex in algorithm I and let Let f be the number of edges successfully coloured around v in one stage of either algorithm. Then,*

$$\Pr[|f - \mathrm{E}[f]| > t] \leq 2\exp\left(-\frac{t^2}{2\Delta + \frac{1}{2}}\right).$$

A referee observed that a similar result can be obtained very simply for Algorithm I by applying Theorem 1: regard f as a function of 2Δ variables: $T_e, v \in e$ and $\mathbf{T}(w), (v, w) \in E$, where $\mathbf{T}(w)$ records the colours of all edges incident on w except vw. Since f is Lipshitz with constant 2 with respect to each of these variables, we get the bound:

$$\Pr[|f - \mathrm{E}[f]| > t] \leq 2\exp\left(-\frac{t^2}{4\Delta}\right).$$

4.4 Bottom Vertices in Algorithm P

Once again, to compute a good bound for λ_k in (4), we shall construct a suitable coupling of the two different conditioned distributions $\mathbf{T}_{k-1}, T_k = c_k$ and

$\mathbf{T}_{k-1}, T_k = c'_k$. Suppose e_k is an edge zy where z is a bottom vertex. The coupling $(\mathbf{Y}, \mathbf{Y}')$ in this case is the following: $\mathbf{Y}$ is distributed as $\mathbf{T}$ conditioned on $\mathbf{T}_{k-1}, T_k = c_k$ and $\mathbf{Y}'$ is identically equal to $\mathbf{Y}$ except on the edges incident on z, where the colours c_k and c'_k are switched. We can think of the distribution as divided into two classes: on the edges incident on a vertex other than z, the two variables $\mathbf{Y}$ and $\mathbf{Y}'$ are identically equal. In particular, when z is not v, they have the same uniform distribution on all permutations of colours on the edges around v. However, on the edges incident on z, the two variables differ on exactly two edges where the colours c_k and c'_k are switched. It is easily seen that by the independence of different vertices, the marginal distributions of $\mathbf{Y}$ and $\mathbf{Y}'$ are exactly the two conditioned distributions $[\mathbf{T} \mid \mathbf{T}_{k-1}, T_k = c_k]$ and $[\mathbf{T} \mid \mathbf{T}_{k-1}, T_k = c'_k]$ respectively.

Now let us compute $|\mathrm{E}[f(\mathbf{Y}) - f(\mathbf{Y}')]|$. Recall that f was decomposed as a sum $\sum_{v \in e} f_e$. Hence by linearity of expectation, we need only bound each $|\mathrm{E}[f_e(\mathbf{Y}) - f_e(\mathbf{Y}')]|$ separately.

- First, let us consider the case when $e_1, \dots, e_k \in N^2(v)$, i.e. only the choices of indirect edges are exposed. Let $e_k = (w, z)$ for a neighbour w of v. Note that since

  $$\mathrm{E}[f(\mathbf{Y}) - f(\mathbf{Y}')] = \mathrm{E}[\mathrm{E}[f(\mathbf{Y}) - f(\mathbf{Y}') \mid \mathbf{Y}_e, \mathbf{Y}'_e, z \in e]],$$

  it suffices to bound $|\mathrm{E}[f(\mathbf{Y}) - f(\mathbf{Y}') \mid \mathbf{Y}_e, \mathbf{Y}'_e, z \in e]|$. Hence, fix some distribution of the colours around z. Recall that $\mathbf{Y}_{w,z} = c_k$ and $\mathbf{Y}'_{w,z} = c'_k$. Suppose $\mathbf{Y}_{z,w'} = c'_k$ for some other neighbour w' of z. Then by our coupling construction, $\mathbf{Y}'_{z,w'} = c_k$ and on the remaining edges $\mathbf{Y}$ and $\mathbf{Y}'$ agree identically. Moreover, by the independence of the other vertices, the distributions of $\mathbf{Y}$ and $\mathbf{Y}'$ on the remaining edges conditioned on the distribution around z is unaffected. let us denote the conditioned joint distribution by $[(\mathbf{Y}, \mathbf{Y}') \mid z]$. We thus need to bound $|\mathrm{E}[f(\mathbf{Y}) - f(\mathbf{Y}') \mid z]|$.
  Then for a direct edge $e \notin vw, vw'$, $f_e(\mathbf{y}) = f_e(\mathbf{y}')$ because in the joint distribution space, $\mathbf{y}$ and $\mathbf{y}'$ agree on all edges incident on e. So we only need to compute $|\mathrm{E}[f_e(\mathbf{Y}) - f_e(\mathbf{Y}')]|$ for $e \in vw, vw'$. To bound this simply, we observe that for either $e = vw$ or $e = vw'$, first, $f_e(\mathbf{y}) - f_e(\mathbf{y}') \in [-1, 1]$ and second that $f_e(\mathbf{y}) = f_e(\mathbf{y}')$ unless $y_e = c_k or c'_k$. Thus we can conclude that

  $$\mathrm{E}[f_e(\mathbf{Y}) - f_e(\mathbf{Y}')]| \leq \Pr[Y_e = c_k \vee Y_e = c'_k] \leq \frac{2}{\Delta}.$$

  Thus taking the two contributions for vw and vw' together, $|\mathrm{E}[f(\mathbf{Y}) - f(\mathbf{Y}') \mid z]| \leq \frac{4}{\Delta}$.
  In fact one can do a tighter analysis using the same observations. Let us denote $f_e(\mathbf{y}, y_{w,z} = c_1, y_e = c_2)$ by $f_e(c_1, c_2)$. Note that $f_{vw}(c_k, c_k) = 0 = f_{vw}(c'_k, c'_k)$ and similarly $f_{vw'}(c_k, c_k) = 0 = f_{vw'}(c'_k, c'_k)$. Thus, for $e = vw$ or $e = vw'$,

  $$\mathrm{E}[f_e(\mathbf{Y}) - f_e(\mathbf{Y}') \mid z] =$$
  $$(f_e(c_k, c_k) - f_e(c'_k, c_k))\Pr[Y_e = c_k] + (f_e(c_k, c'_k) - f_e(c'_k, y'_e = c'_k))\Pr[Y_e = c'_k]$$

$$= (f_e(c_k, c'_k) - f_e(c'_k, c_k))\frac{1}{\Delta}$$

Hence $|\mathbf{E}[f_e(\mathbf{Y}) - f_e(\mathbf{Y}') \mid z]| \leq \frac{1}{\Delta}$. Taking the two contributions for edges vw and vw' together, $|\mathbf{E}[f(\mathbf{Y}) - f(\mathbf{Y}') \mid x]| \leq \frac{2}{\Delta}$.

- Now let us consider the case when $e_k \in N^1(v)$, i.e. choices of all indirect edges and of some direct edges have been exposed. In this case, we observe again that $|f(\mathbf{y}) - f(\mathbf{y}')| \leq 2$ since $\mathbf{y}$ and $\mathbf{y}'$ differ on exactly two edges. Hence we can easily conclude that $|\mathbf{E}[f(\mathbf{Y}) - f(\mathbf{Y}')]| \leq 2$.

Overall,

$$\lambda_k \leq \begin{cases} 2/\Delta; & \text{for an edge } e_k \in N^2(v), \\ 2; & \text{for an edge } e_k \in N^1(v) \end{cases},$$

and we get

$$\sum_k \lambda_k^2 = \sum_{e \in N^2(v)} \frac{4}{\Delta^2} + \sum_{e \in N^1(v)} 4 \leq 4(\Delta + 1).$$

We thus arrive at the following sharp concentration result by plugging into Theorem 2:

Theorem 5. *Let v be an arbitrary vertex in algorithm I and let f be the number of edges successfully coloured around v in one stage of algorithm P. Then,*

$$\Pr[|f - \mathbf{E}[f]| > t] \leq 2\exp\left(-\frac{t^2}{2\Delta + 2}\right).$$

Comparing this with the corresponding bound for Algorithm I, we see that the failure probabilities for both algorithms are almost identical. For $t = \epsilon\Delta$, both a probability that decreases exponentially in Δ. As remarked earlier, if $\Delta \gg \log n$, this implies that the new max degree is sharply concentrated around the mean (with failure probability inverse polynomial in n). The constant in the exponent here is better than the one in the analysis in [11].

4.5 Extensions

It is fairly clear that the method extends more generally to cover similar scenarios in distributed computing. We sketch such a general setting: One has a distributed randomised algorithm that requires vertices to assign labels to themselves and incident edges. Each vertex acts independently of the others, and furthermore is symmetric with respect to the labels (colours). The function of interest, f depends only on a small local neighbourhood around some vertex v, is Lipschitz and satisfies some version of the following *locality* property: the labels on vertices and edges far away from v only effect f if certain events are triggered on nearer vertices and edges; these triggering events correspond to the setting of the nearer vertices and edges to specific values. For example, in edge colouring, the colour of an idirect edge only affects f if the incident direct edge has the same colour. One can extend the same arguments as above virtually intact for this general setting. This encompasses all the edge colouring algorithms mentioned above as well as the vertex colouring algorithms in [10] and [5].

5 Acknowledgement

Edgar Ramos pointed out an error in the original analysis during a talk at the Max–Planck–Institut für Informatik soon after I had submitted the paper. I showed him the coupling proof the next day. An anonymous referee also spotted the error and independently developed the same coupling argument. I am grateful for his detailed write–up containing several other comments and suggestions (some of which are acknowledged above) which helped immensely in preparing the revision. I also acknowledge the helpful comments of two other anonymous referees. I would like to thank Alessandro Panconesi for his help in drafting this paper, for invaluable discussions and for resolutely prodding me to pursue the "demise of the permanent" from [11]. Now, finally, R.I.P.

References

1. Bollabas, B. : Graph Theory: An Introductory Course. Springer–Verlag 1980.
2. Dubhashi, D., Grable, D.A., and Panconesi, A.: Near optimal distributed edge colouring via the nibble method. Theoretical Computer Science 203 (1998), 225–251, a special issue for ESA 95, the 3rd European Symposium on Algorithms.
3. Dubhashi, D. and Panconesi, A: Concentration of measure for computer scientists. Draft of a monograph in preparation.
4. Grable, D., and Panconesi, A: Near optimal distributed edge colouring in $O(\log\log n)$ rounds. Random Structures and Algorithms **10**, Nr. 3 (1997) 385–405
5. Grable, D., and Panconesi, A: Brooks and Vizing Colurings, SODA 98.
6. Luby, M.: Removing randomness in parallel without a processor penalty. J. Computer and Systems Sciences **47**:2 (1993) 250–286.
7. Marton, K.: Bounding $\bar{d}$ distance by informational divergence: A method to prove measure concentration. Annals of Probability **24** (1996) 857–866.
8. Marton, K.: On the measure concentration inequality of Talagrand for dependent random variables. submitted for publication. (1998).
9. McDiarmid, C.J.H.: On the method of bounded differences. in J. Siemons (ed): Surveys in Combinatorics, London Mathematical Society Lecture Notes Series 141, Cambridge University Press, (1989).
10. Molloy, M. and Reed, B.: A bound on the strong chromatic index of a graph. J. Comb. Theory (B) **69** (1997) 103–109.
11. Panconesi, A. and Srinivasan, A.: Randomized distributed edge coloring via an extension of the Chernoff–Hoeffding bounds. SIAM J. Computing **26**:2 (1997) 350–368.
12. Spencer, J.: Probabilistic methods in combinatorics. In proceedings of the International Congress of Mathematicians, Zurich, Birkhauser (1995).
13. Talagrand, M.: Concentration of measure and isoperimetric inequalities in product spaces. Publ. math. IHES, **81**:2 (1995) 73–205..

Space Efficient Suffix Trees

Ian Munro[1], Venkatesh Raman[2], S. Srinivasa Rao[2]

[1] Department of Computer Science, University of Waterloo, Canada N2L 3G1
[2] The Institute of Mathematical Sciences, Chennai, India 600 113.

Abstract. We first give a representation of a suffix tree that uses $n \lg n + O(n)$ bits of space and supports searching for a pattern in the given text (from a fixed size alphabet) in $O(m)$ time, where n is the size of the text and m is the size of the pattern. The structure is quite simple and answers a question raised by Muthukrishnan in [17]. Previous compact representations of suffix trees had a higher lower order term in space and had some expectation assumption [3], or required more time for searching [5]. Then, surprisingly, we show that we can even do better, by developing a structure that uses a suffix array (and so $n\lceil \lg n \rceil$ bits) and an additional $o(n)$ bits. String searching can be done in this structure also in $O(m)$ time. Besides supporting string searching, we can also report the number of occurrences of the pattern in the same time using no additional space. In this case the space occupied by the structures is much less compared to many of the previously known structures to do this. When the size of the alphabet k is not a constant, our structures can be easily extended, using standard tricks, to those that use the same space but take $O(m \lg k)$ time for string searching or to those that use an additional $O(m \lg k)$ bits but take the same $O(m)$ time for searching.

1 Introduction and Motivation

Given a text string, indexing is the problem of preprocessing the text so that search for a pattern can be answered efficiently. Two popular data structures for indexing are suffix trees and suffix arrays. A suffix tree [12] is a trie representing all the suffixes of the given text. Standard representations of suffix trees for texts of length n take about $4n$ words or pointers (each word taking $\log n$ bits of storage) and a search for a pattern of size m can be performed in $O(m)$ time (see Section 3 for details). A suffix array [11] keeps an array of pointers to the suffixes of the given text in lexicographic order, and another array of longest common prefixes of some of those suffixes to aid the search. Standard representation of suffix array takes about $2n$ words [5] and a search in a suffix array can be performed in $O(m + \log n)$ time [11]. So in [17], Muthukrishnan asked whether there exists a data structure that uses only $n + o(n)$ words and answers indexing questions in $O(m)$ time. In this paper, we propose two such structures. The first one uses $n + O(n/\lg n)$ words, or equivalently $n \lg n + O(n)$ bits and supports string searching in optimal $O(m)$ time. The second structure takes $n\lceil \lg n \rceil + o(n)$ bits of space and supports searching in $O(m)$ time. It is interesting to note that $o(n)$ additional bits are enough besides the n pointers for indexing.

Previously, Colussi and De Col [5] reported a data structure that uses $n \lg n + O(n)$ bits, but a search in the structure takes $O(m + \lg\lg n)$ time. In [3], Clark and Munro gave a version of suffix tree that uses n plus an expected $O(n \lg\lg n / \lg n)$ words under the assumption that the given binary (encoded) text is generated by a uniform symmetric random process and that the bit strings in the suffixes are independent. So our structure is not only more space efficient (in the lower order term), it doesn't need any assumption about the distribution of characters in the input string.

The main idea in our first representation is the recent $2n + o(n)$ bits encoding of a static binary tree on n nodes [16]. First we observe that a few more operations, than those given in [16] are needed to support our suffix tree algorithms. The next section reviews the binary tree representation and describes algorithms to support the additional operations. Section 3 reviews the suffix tree data structure and explains how our binary tree representation can be used to obtain a space efficient suffix tree. In Section 4 we give a structure that uses a suffix array and a couple of sparse suffix trees taking $n\lceil \lg n \rceil + o(n)$ bits of space which also supports searching in optimal time bounds. Section 5 gives concluding remarks and lists open problems.

Our model of computation is the standard unit cost RAM model where we assume that standard arithmetic and boolean operations on $\lg n$ bit words and reading and writing $\lg n$ bit strings can be performed in constant time. Also lg denotes the logarithm to the base 2 throughout the paper. And by a suffix array, we mean an array of pointers to the suffixes of the given text in lexicographic order (without any extra information).

2 Succinct Representation of Trees

A general rooted ordered tree on n vertices can be represented by a nested balanced string of $2n$ parenthesis as follows. Perform a preorder traversal of the tree starting from the root, and write an open parenthesis when a node is first encountered, going down the tree, and then a closing parenthesis while going up after traversing the subtree. However, if we represent a binary tree by such a sequence, it is not possible to distinguish a node with a left child but no right child and one with a right child and no left child.

So Munro and Raman[16] first use the well known isomorphism between the class of binary trees and the class of rooted ordered trees to convert the given binary tree into a general rooted ordered tree and then represent the rooted ordered tree using the above parenthesis representation. In the ordered tree there is a root which does not correspond to any node in the binary tree. Beyond this, the left child of a node in the binary tree corresponds to the leftmost child of the corresponding node in the ordered tree, and the right child in the binary tree corresponds to the next sibling to the right in ordered tree. (See the figure for an example). A node is represented, by convention, by its corresponding left parenthesis. It is not obvious still, how the navigational operations can be performed in constant time. Munro and Raman[16] show that using $o(n)$ additional

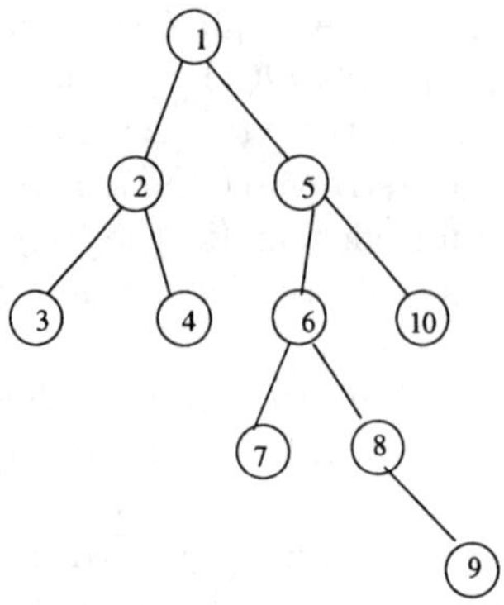

Fig 1.1: The Given Binary Tree on 10 Nodes

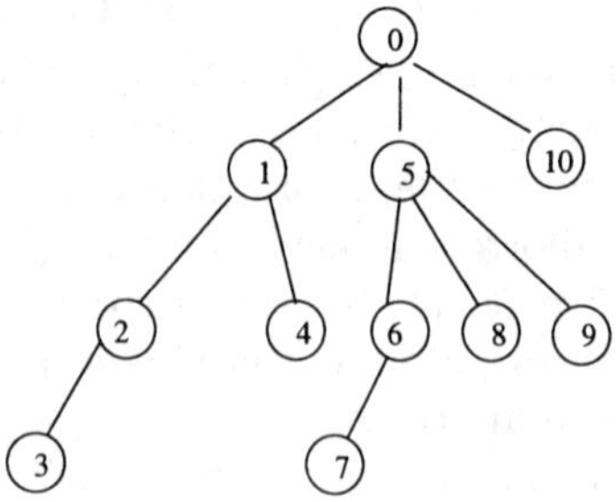

Fig 1.2: Equivalent Rooted Ordered Tree

0 1 2 3 3 2 4 4 1 5 6 7 7 6 8 8 9 9 5 10 10 0
(((( )) ( ))((( )) ( )( )) ( ))

Fig 1.3: The Parenthesis Representation

bits, the standard operations like the *left child*, *right child* and *parent* of a given node can be found in constant time. They also show that given a node, the size of the subtree rooted at that node can be found in constant time.

To use this tree representation to represent a suffix tree, we need the following additional operations and we first observe that these operations can be supported in constant time. We represent a node in the binary tree by its preorder number. Let i be any node in the given binary tree.

- $leafrank(i)$: find the number of leaves to the left (in the preorder numbering) of node i
- $leafsize(i)$: find the number of leaves in the subtree rooted at node i
- $leftmost(i)$: find the leftmost leaf in the subtree rooted at node i and
- $rightmost(i)$: find the rightmost leaf in the subtree rooted at node i.

To support these operations, we first need the two popular operations described below - *rank* and *select* in a binary string, which can be supported in constant time using $o(n)$ bits[8, 15].

- $rank(i)$: the number of 1's up to and including the position i and
- $select(i)$: the position of the ith 1.

The following generalization is easy to prove.

Theorem 1. *Given a binary string of length n, and a pattern p which is a binary string of fixed length m, let $rank_p(i)$ be the number of (possibly overlapping) occurrences of pattern p up to and including the position i and $select_p(i)$ be the position of the ith occurrence of p in the given binary string. Then both $rank_p(i)$ and $select_p(i)$ can be supported in constant time using $o(n)$ bits in addition to the space required for the given binary string.*

Proof. The algorithms to support (original) *rank* and *select* [8, 15] follow the following basic idea: Divide the given bit string into blocks of size $\lg^2 n$, and keep the rank information for the first element of every block. Within a block of size $\lg^2 n$ keep a recursive structure. After a couple of levels, the block sizes are small enough that the number of distinct blocks is small enough to keep a precomputed table of answers in $o(n)$ bits. The precomputed table stores the number of occurrences of the pattern up to the position for each small block (of length roughly $(\lg n)/2$) and for each position in the block.

This structure can easily be adapted to keep the $rank_p$ information for every block (assuming m is less than the block sizes). The precomputed table, in this case, stores the number of occurrences for every possible triple consisting of a block b of size $(\lg n)/2$, a bit string x of size $m-1$, and a position i in the block. The table entry stores the number of occurrences of the pattern p in the string x concatenated with the bit string in the first i positions of b. These extra information is to take care of an occurrence of the pattern in a span of two consecutive blocks. Since the size of m is fixed, the space requirement for the table is bounded above by 2^m times the original space requirement (which is $o(n)$). □

Remarks:

- Though, for our later application, the above theorem (assuming m is a fixed constant) is sufficient, we note that the above proof works also for m up to $(1/2-c)(\lg n)$ for some constant c. This is because the space used for the earlier table is $O(n^{1/2} \log^d n)$ for some constant d.
- When m is $\omega(\lg n)$, we can find the maximum number of non-overlapping occurrences of p up to any position (using $o(n)$ extra space) as follows: First divide the given bit string into blocks of size m. Then store in each block head (the first bit of the block), the answer for that position. Also if a pattern that does not overlap with the previous occurrences of the pattern ends in that block, then the position where the the pattern ends is also kept with the block head. There can be at most one such position in each block since the pattern length is more than the block size. Here we use the fact that the non-overlapping occurrences of the pattern obtained by starting with the leftmost occurrence of the pattern and picking the next available occurrence (in a greedy way) will give us the maximum number of occurrences.

Now, we prove the main theorem of this section.

Theorem 2. *Given a static binary tree on n nodes, we can represent it using* $2n+o(n)$ *bits in such a way that given a node* x*, in addition to finding its parent, left child, right child and the size of the subtree rooted at that node, we can also support the operations* $leafrank(x)$*,* $leafsize(x)$*,* $leftmost(x)$ *and* $rightmost(x)$ *in constant time.*

Proof. As before, we first convert the binary tree into an equivalent rooted ordered tree. The fact that *parent, left child, right child and the subtree size* are supported in constant time is already known [16].

Any leaf in the binary tree is a leaf in the general tree, but not vice versa. In fact, any leaf in the general tree is a leaf in the binary tree only if it is the last child of its parent. In other words, leaves in the binary tree correspond to the rightmost leaves in the general tree. In the parenthesis notation, a rightmost leaf corresponds to an open-close pair followed by a closing parenthesis (see Figure). Thus to compute $leafrank(x)$ we need to find the $rank_p(x)$, where p is the pattern ())), in the parenthesis sequence corresponding to the tree. Also $leafsize(x)$ is the difference between $rank_p(x)$ and $rank_p(f(x))$ where $f(x)$ denotes the closing parenthesis corresponding to x's parent.

The leftmost leaf of the subtree rooted at a node in the binary tree is the leaf whose $leafrank$ is one more than the $leafrank$ of the given node. Thus it can be found using the expression: $leftmost(x) = select_p(rank_p(x) + 1)$, where p is the pattern ())). The rightmost leaf of the subtree rooted at the node in the binary tree is the rightmost leaf of its parent in the general tree. Now the rightmost leaf of a node in the general tree is the node corresponding to the closing parenthesis immediately before the closing parenthesis of the given node. Thus $rightmost(x) = open(close(parent(x)) - 1)$, where $open$ ($close$) gives the position of the corresponding opening (closing) parenthesis of a given closing (opening) parenthesis. □

3 Applications to Suffix Tree Representation

Suffix trees[1] are data structures that admit efficient online string searches. They have also been applied to fundamental string problems such as finding the longest repeated substring [20], finding all squares or repetitions in a string [1], approximate string matching [10], and string comparison. They have also been used to address other types of problems such as text compression [18], compressing assembly code [6], inverted indices [2], and analyzing genetic sequences [4].

A suffix tree for a text string x of length n is an ordered trie whose entries are all the suffixes of x. In order to ensure that each suffix corresponds to a unique position in the text, a special character '\$', not in Σ, is appended to x. Each suffix has a minimal prefix that distinguishes it from the other suffixes. At a leaf node we keep the starting position, in the text, of the suffix ending at that node. Since the sum of the lengths of all the suffixes is of order $O(n^2)$, the tree size would be of the same order. Various tricks have been employed to reduce the number of nodes in the tree to $O(n)$ [12, 13, 20]. One trick is to compress the nodes with single child, and store the starting position in the text and the length of the compressed string at each node. Another trick is to store only the length (called the "skip value") of the compressed string at the nodes. For the rest of the paper, we will stick to the latter trick of keeping only the "skip value" at the compressed nodes. Since we have $n + 1$ leaf nodes (including the end-marker) and at most n internal nodes (as each internal node is of degree more than one), the tree has at most $2n + 1$ nodes.

Given a pattern p of length m and the suffix tree for a string x of length n, to search for p in x, we start at the root of the tree following the search string. At any node, we take the branch that matches the current character of the given pattern. At compressed nodes, we skip those many characters as specified by the "skip" value at that node, before comparing with the pattern. The search is continued until the pattern is exhausted or the current character of the pattern has no match at the current node. In the latter case, there is no copy of the pattern in the text. In the former case, if the search ends at a node, the position of any leaf in the subtree rooted at the node where the pattern is exhausted gives a possible starting point of the pattern in the text. Since we skipped bits in the middle, we start at a position given by any of the leaves of the subtree rooted at the node where search has ended, and confirm if the pattern exists in the text starting from that position. Clearly the above procedure takes $O(m)$ time to check the existence of the pattern in the text.

The storage requirement of suffix trees comprise of three quantities[3]:

- The storage for the tree (trie),
- the storage for the skip values at the compressed nodes, and
- the position indices at the leaves.

The position indices at the leaves take $n\lceil \lg n \rceil$ bits. Our goal is to show that the rest of the information can be represented using $O(n)$ bits using our succinct tree representation given in the last section. First note that even if the given text is on a binary alphabet, the suffix tree is a ternary tree (due to the extra \$ character). So first we will consider a binary alphabet by converting each symbol of the alphabet and the symbol \$ into binary. Thus, given a string x, we encode all the suffixes of $x\$$ in binary and construct a trie for them, which will be a binary tree. (This is same as the PAT tree of Gonnet et al.[7].) Since there are $n+1$ suffixes, there will be n internal nodes and $n+1$ external nodes in the trie. We can represent this $2n+1$ node binary tree with $4n+o(n)$ bits using the representation given in the previous section. This will take care of the storage for the first item above. We don't keep the skip values at all in our structure, and find them online, whenever needed (the algorithmic details are given in the next subsection). And finally we will have an array of pointers to the starting positions of the suffixes in the (lexicographically) sorted order, i.e. a suffix array, which requires $n\lceil \lg n \rceil$ bits. Thus it is easy to see that our structure takes $n\lceil \lg n \rceil + 4n + o(n)$ bits of storage. (Note that if the goal is to simply get a lower order term of $O(n)$ (not necessarily $4n$), then we can simplify our succinct tree represention using the additional bits available).

3.1 Algorithm for Searching

To search for a pattern, we start at the root as before. Navigating in the suffix tree is possible in our tree representation. At each internal node, to find the skip value at a node we first go to the leftmost and rightmost leaves in the subtree rooted at that node. Then we start comparing the text starting at these positions until there is a disagreement. (We don't have to compare the suffixes from the starting position. We already know that they agree up to the portion of the string represented by the node. So we can start matching from that position onwards.) Once we find the characters of disagreement, we find their binary encodings which may give raise to further agreement. The number of bits matched is the skip value at that node. Finding the leftmost or rightmost leaf of the subtree rooted at a node, in our tree representation takes constant time using the leftmost(x) and rightmost(x) operations of Theorem 2 in Section 2.

Now we continue the search as before. If the search terminates at a leaf node, then the pattern is compared with suffix pointed to by the leaf to see if it matches. To find the suffix pointed to by the leaf, we first find the *leafrank* of the leaf, and then find the value of that index in the array of pointers (suffix array). If the end of the pattern is encountered before we reach a leaf, then the suffix pointed to by a representative leaf from the subtree rooted at the node, at which the search has stopped, is compared with the pattern. This leaf can be found by the *leftmost*(x) or *rightmost*(x) operations of Theorem 2. The pattern matches the suffix if and only if any (or equivalently all) of suffixes in the subtree match the pattern.

The time to find a skip value is $O(\lg k + \textit{the skip value})$ where k is the size of the alphabet. This is because once we find the characters where the disagreement happens, we find their binary representations and find further agreements. Now the sum of the skip values in the search is at most m. So the total time spent in figuring out skip values is only $O(m \lg k)$. It turns out that we have atmost doubled the search cost by getting rid of the storage required for the skip values.

Once we confirm that the pattern exists in the text, the number of leaves in the subtree rooted at the node where the search ended, gives the number of occurrences of the pattern in the text. This can be found in constant time using the *leafsize* operation of Theorem 2. Thus we have

Theorem 3. *A suffix tree for a text of length n can be represented using $n \lg n + O(n)$ bits such that given a pattern of size m, the number of occurrences of the pattern in the string can be found in $O(m \lg k)$ time where k is the alphabet size.*

The trie representing all the suffixes, in binary, of the given string, is a special case of a binary tree, namely that each node has either zero or two children. So, we can even represent it directly using a preorder numbering sequence of balanced parentheses (without going through the general tree representation). This further simplifies the tree representation.

Recently Munro and Benoit[14] have extended the succinct representation for binary trees to represent an ordered k-ary tree (where each node has exactly k, possibly empty, children) using $2n + O(n \lg k)$ bits where navigational operations can be performed in constant time. Instead of converting the text and the suffixes to binary, we can represent the k-ary suffix tree using this k-ary tree representation directly. Then we have

Theorem 4. *A suffix tree for a text of length n can be represented using $n \lg n + O(n \lg k)$ bits such that given a pattern of size m, the number of occurrences of the pattern in the string can be found in $O(m)$ time where k is the alphabet size.*

Note that the time bounds match the bounds for the standard suffix tree operations while the higher order term in the space bound remains $n \lg n$.

We also remark that the above representation can be built in $O(n)$ time as once we build the suffix tree which takes $O(n)$ time [20], the succinct tree representation can be built in $O(n)$ time.

4 A Structure using a Suffix Array and $o(n)$ bits

In [5], Colussi and Col have given a structure that takes $n \lg n + O(n)$ bits and takes $O(m + \lg \lg n)$ time to search for a pattern of length m. This structure has a sparse suffix tree for every $(\lg n)$th suffix and suffix arrays (with extra information about longest common prefixes to aid efficient searching) for each block of size $\lg n$ in the sorted array of suffixes of the given text. We first observe that with an additional $o(n)$ bits, this structure can be modified into a structure that takes $O(m)$ time for searching. Note that the search time is $\omega(m)$ only when the pattern size m is small, i.e. when it is $o(\lg \lg n)$. To take care of small patterns, we store a precomputed table of answers. This table stores, for every string of length at most $\lg \lg n$, the positions in the suffix array of the first and the last suffix for which the string is a prefix. The difference between these two indices gives the number of occurrences of the string in the text. The table takes $O(2^{\lg \lg n} \lg n)$ or $O(\lg^2 n)$ bits. Given a pattern of length m, if $m \leq \lg \lg n$ then we look into the table and answer the query (in constant time). Otherwise we revert back to algorithm given in [5] to answer the query, which takes $O(m)$ time (since $m > \lg \lg n$). Though this gives another simple structure for indexing that takes $n \lg n + O(n)$ bits of space and supports searching in optimal time, the constant factor in the lower order term in space is more compared to our previous structure.

In what follows we show that $o(n)$ bits are sufficient in addition to a suffix array to support searching in $O(m)$ time, in the case of a fixed size alphabet. For an arbitrary alphabet of size k, the space required will remain the same but the search time will be $O(m \lg k)$. We will give the structure for the case of a fixed size alphabet. The general alphabet case is a straightforward extension of this structure, as explained in the previous section.

The structure mainly consists of three levels built on top of a suffix array. First, we divide the suffix array into blocks of size $\lg^2 n$ and build a suffix tree for every suffix starting at the first position in each block. This step is quite similar to the structures in [5, 9]. Then we subdivide each block into sub-blocks of size $(\lg \lg n)^2$. For each block, we construct a suffix tree for every suffix starting at the first position in each sub-block. Thus, first level consists of a suffix tree for every $(\lg^2 n)$th suffix in the suffix array. The second level will have suffix trees, one for each block, for every $((\lg \lg n)^2)$th suffix of each block of size $\lg^2 n$. The third level consists of a table structure which gives the following information: given an array of $(\lg \lg n)^2$ bit strings in sorted order, each of length at most $(\lg \lg n)^2$ and a pattern string of length at most $(\lg \lg n)^2$, it gives the first and last positions of the occurrences of the pattern, in the array, if the pattern matches with a string in the array. There is a table entry for *every* bit string array of size $(\lg\lg n)^2$ where each bit string is of size at most $(\lg\lg n)^2$ and for every pattern string of length at most $(\lg\lg n)^2$. The table is stored in the lexicographic order of its entries.

The first level suffix tree is stored using any standard suffix tree representation, with skip values and pointers (tree pointers, leaf pointers as well as pointers at the compressed nodes, to the suffix array for the positions where the compressed string starts in the text). The space occupied by this tree is $O(n/\lg n)$ bits. In the second level suffix tree, for the pointers to the suffix array including the leaf pointers, we store them with respect to the beginning of the block, i.e. we store only the offset values from the starting position of that block in the suffix array. Thus each of these pointers take $2\lg\lg n$ bits. Since the number of nodes in each of these trees is $O(\lg^2 n/(\lg\lg n)^2)$, we can also store the tree pointers using $\lg\lg n$ bits (i.e. we don't need to store the tree using the bracket representation). We don't keep the skip values (since they can be as large as n) at the compressed nodes. The skip values can be found online (as described in the last section). If we don't store the tree using the bracket representatin, then we have to store the pointers to the leftmost and rightmost leaves with each internal node, which again will take $2\lg\lg n$ bits for each node. Thus the space occupied by all these trees is $O(\frac{n}{\lg^2 n} \frac{\lg^2 n}{(\lg\lg n)^2} \lg\lg n) = O(n/\lg\lg n)$ bits. The space occupied by the table structure is atmost $O(2^{(\lg\lg n)^4} 2^{(\lg\lg n)^2} \lg\lg n)$ which is $o(n)$. Thus the overall space requirement for the structure (including $n\lceil\lg n\rceil$ bits for the suffix array) is $n\lceil\lg n\rceil + o(n)$ bits.

To search for a pattern string of length m, we first match the pattern in the first level suffix tree. If we have successfully matched the pattern in this tree (without any mismatch), then all the nodes in the subtree rooted at the node where the search has ended, will have the pattern as a common prefix. To find the number of occurrences of the pattern, we have to find the first and last occurrences of the pattern which can be found respectively from the blocks before the leftmost leaf and after the rightmost leaf. If the pattern does not match completely, we will find the only block in which the patern might occur. Thus, in either case, we are left with the problem of finding the first and last occurrences of the pattern in a block of length $\lg^2 n$ in the suffix array.

To search for the pattern in this smaller block, we again match it in the suffix tree corresponding to that block. Applying the same method as above, we are now left with finding the first and last occurrences of the pattern in a smaller sub-block of length $(\lg\lg n)^2$ in the suffix array.

Note that, if we recursively continue this process, by storing the sparse suffix trees in each level, the search time will be $O(m\lg^* n)$. Also this structure will take $n\lceil\lg n\rceil + O(n/\lg^* n)$ bits of space. However, we observe that after the two levels, the simple table structure of $o(n)$ bits we described earlier can aid to complete the search in $O(m)$ time.

Given an array of $(\lg\lg n)^2$ strings, each of length (atmost) $(\lg\lg n)^2$, in sorted order, and a pattern string of length (atmost) $(\lg\lg n)^2$, the table has the beginning and ending positions of the occurrences of the pattern in the array.

Now we read the first $(\lg\lg n)^2$ bits of each of the suffixes in the sub-block, and the first $(\lg\lg n)^2$ bits of the pattern and index into the table to find the first and last occurrences of the part of the pattern in the sub-block. If this gives a non-empty range, we will read the next $(\lg\lg n)^2$ bits of each of the suffixes in this range and the next $(\lg\lg n)^2$ bits of the pattern and find the sub-range of suffixes that match the first $2(\lg\lg n)^2$ bits of the pattern. We will do this repeatedly until either the pattern is exausted or the range has become empty (or a single suffix). The number of table look-up's is atmost $m/(\lg\lg n)^2$ and each table look-up takes $O((\lg\lg n)^2)$ time. So the overall time to search for a pattern is $O(m)$. Thus we have

Theorem 5. *Given a text of length n from a fixed alphabet, there exists a data structure that uses $n\lceil\lg n\rceil + o(n)$ bits such that given a pattern of size m, the number of occurrences of the pattern in the string can be found in $O(m)$ time.*

5 Conclusions

We have given two indexing structures - one a suffix tree using $n\lceil\lg n\rceil+4n+o(n)$ bits of storage, and another using $n\lceil\lg n\rceil + o(n)$ bits where indexing queries can be answered in optimum time. Not only can these structures support standard operations using less space, but they can also find the number of occurrences of the pattern using no additional space. We find it quite interesting that $o(n)$ bits in addition to a suffix array is sufficient for an index structure.

Some open problems that arise (remain) are:

- Is there an efficient indexing structure when the given text resides in the secondary memory? Our structures are well suited if the entire text resides in the main memory. However, the number of external memory accesses made in our structures is quite high (close to m), if the given text resides in the external memory. In fact, this problem remains in all the standard representations of suffix trees where, along with the skip value, the starting position of the compressed string is also kept. In such a representation, the text is looked at at every compressed node. So constructing an $n\lg n+O(n)$ bit suffix tree for a text in external memory (i.e. one that uses as few external accesses as possible) is an interesting open problem.
- Is there a structure that uses only $n + o(n)$ words of memory and supports searching in $m + o(m)$ time (or character comparisons) for a fixed size alphabet?
- Can we construct our suffix tree representations without using extra space, i.e. using only $n\lg n + O(n)$ bits of space while construction? (One obvious way to construct our suffix tree representation is to construct the usual suffix tree first and then construct the parenthesis representation of the tree from it, but this uses more space than required, while construction.)
- What is the optimal space for indexing? For example, can we construct an efficient indexing structure using $O(n\lg k)$ space where k is the size of the alphabet?

References

1. A. Apostolico and F. P. Preparata, "Structural properties of the string statistics problem", *Journal of Computer and System Sciences* **31** (1985) 394-41.
2. A. F. Cardenas, "Analysis and performance of inverted data base structures", *Communications of the ACM* **18,5** (1975) 253-263.
3. D. R. Clark and J. I. Munro, "Efficient Suffix Trees on Secondary Storage", *Proceedings of the 7th ACM-SIAM Symposium on Discrete Algorithms* (1996) 383-391.
4. B. Clift, D. Haussler, R. McConnel, T. D. Schneider, and G. D. Stormo, "Sequence landscapes", *Nucleic Acids Research* **4,1** (1986) 141-158.
5. L. Colussi and Alessia De Col, "A time and space efficient data structure for string searching on large texts", *Information Processing Letters* **58** (1996) 217-222.
6. C. Fraser, A. Wendt, and E. W. Myers, "Analysing and compressing assembly code", *Proceedings of the SIGPLAN Symposium on Compiler Construction* (1984).
7. G. H. Gonnet, R. A. Baeza-Yates, and T. Snider, "New indices for text: PAT trees and PAT arrays", *Information Retrieval: Data Structures and Algorithms*, Frakes and Baeza-Yates Eds., Prentice-Hall, (1992) 66-82.
8. G. Jacobson, "Space-efficient Static Trees and Graphs", *Proceedings of the IEEE Symposium on Foundations of Computer Science* (1989) 549-554.
9. J. Kärkkäinen and E. Ukkonen, "Sparse suffix trees", *Proceedings of the Second Annual International Computing and Combinatorics Conference (COCOON 96)*, LNCS 1090 (1996), 219-230.
10. G. M. Landau and U. Vishkin, "Introducing efficient parallelism into approximate string matching", *Proc. 18th ACM Symposium on Theory of Computing* (1986), 220-230.
11. U. Manber and G. Myers, "Suffix Arrays: A New Method for On-line String Searches", *SIAM Journal on Computing* **22(5)** (1993) 935-948.
12. M. E. McCreight, "A space-economical suffix tree construction algorithm", *Journal of the ACM* **23** (1976) 262-272.
13. D. R. Morrison, "PATRICIA: Practical Algorithm To Retrieve Information Coded In Alphanumeric", *Journal of the ACM* **15** (1968) 514-534.
14. J. I. Munro and D. Benoit, "Succinct Representation of k-ary trees", manuscript.
15. J. I. Munro, "Tables", *Proceedings of the 16th FST & TCS*, LNCS 1180 (1996) 37-42.
16. J. I. Munro and V. Raman, "Succinct representation of balanced parentheses, static trees and planar graphs", *Proceedings of the IEEE Symposium on Foundations of Computer Science* (1997) 118-126.
17. S. Muthukrishnan, "Randomization in Stringology", *Proceedings of the Preconference Workshop on Randomization*, December 1997, Kharagpur, India.
18. M. Rodeh, V. R. Pratt, and S. Even, "Linear algorithm for data compression via string matching", *Journal of the ACM* **28,1** (1991) 16-24.
19. H. Shang, Trie methods for text and spatial data structures on secondary storage, PhD Thesis, McGill University, (1995).
20. P. Weiner, "Linear pattern matching algorithm", *Proc. 14th IEEE Symposium on Switching and Automata Theory* (1973) 1-11.

Formal Verification of an O.S. Submodule

N.S.Pendharkar and K.Gopinath*
Computer Science & Automation
Indian Institute of Science, Bangalore

Abstract: The verification of concurrent systems with a large number of interacting components poses a significant challenge to the existing verification methodologies. We consider in this paper the formal verification of buffer cache algorithms of SVR3-type Unix systems using PVS.

1 Introduction

In the concurrent environment, it is often difficult to say with full confidence that a given algorithm works correctly. Testing and simulation usually cannot test all the possible behaviors. Hence verification is one viable approach, though not practiced to the extent desirable due to lack of appropriate tools. Though correctness of systems software (OSes, compilers, for example) is of paramount importance, they have presented a difficult target for verification. This is primarily due to two reasons: the size of these software and the difficulty of abstracting systems software to yield tractable models that are sufficiently interesting for taking the trouble to prove them correct. In addition, model checking is of little use in these domains directly unless used in conjunction with theorem provers. Systems software subcomponents are typically infinite state or almost close to it compared to hardware subsystems. Buffer cache algorithms, among many other critical components, are typically part of a kernel or runtime system and hence the importance of verifying them.

We consider in this paper the formal verification of buffer cache algorithms of SVR3-type Unix systems. SVR3-type buffer caches are present in SVR3-derived/inspired systems such as SCO Unix 3.2 or Linux 2.x. SVR4-type systems (such as Solaris 2.x, Unixware 2.x) are typically multithreaded and hence more complex. SVR3-type Unixes support concurrency to let multiple processes in the kernel but only one can be executing at any time with the rest suspended due to either interrupt processing or sleeping. The concurrency is of the interleaving variety on the processor with I/O devices only providing scope for true concurrency. The multithreaded kernels support true concurrent execution of kernel code through the use of appropriate locking.

1.1 Approach to Verification

One approach for verifying modules in systems software is to prove a smaller version of a specification and use state enumeration approaches. However, while proving a downscaled version of specification is effective at finding bugs, it is not

* Author for correspondence: gopi@csa.iisc.ernet.in

enough as it is possible that some bugs do not show up in the simplified case but do so in the full version. Theorem proving can handle the general case but the proofs are often very long and time consuming. One method of combining automated model checking and interactive theorem proving is to establish a property preserving abstraction for the general case. Theorem proving is used to justify the validity of the abstraction whereas model checking is used to prove the abstracted version of the general case[7, 2]. We follow this approach in this paper. Such an approach is likely to be fruitful for systems software as there are many modules, each with its own submodules and each submodule in turn using many unbounded data structures like lists, etc. Theorem proving is useful to handle the unbounded aspects of the problem. Though the initial investment in such a mixed approach could be high, it gives us the tools needed to investigate verification in the large.

Consider a concurrent system with N processes. Each process P consists of a initialization predicate I, internal action G and external (allowed) action R: $< I, G, R >$. The final program is the composition of the programs corresponding to all the processes. Processes are composed by taking the interleaving conjunction[3]. For example, the composition of two programs P_1 and P_2 ($P_1 || P_2$) can be written as: $< (I_1 \bigwedge I_2), ((G_1 \bigwedge R_2) \bigvee (G_2 \bigwedge R_1)), (R_1 \bigwedge R_2) >$. Any run of P_i ($i = 1, 2$) is a run of $P_1 || P_2$, so any property of P_i is a property of $P_1 || P_2$.

The strategy for proving some desired property of the concurrent system is to induct on the number of processes. The base case can be discharged by interactive theorem proving. Using the induction hypothesis that the property is true for k processes, we need to prove that it is true for $k+1$ processes. If our problem domain admits of a tournament style elimination, with only one "winner" from the k processes, we can abstract these k processes as a single process, and the $k+1^{th}$ process as the second process. These two processes can now be modelled as a two process concurrent system and model checking now can be attempted on this simpler system. Hence our approach requires a valid abstraction from k processes to a single process but this is quite often seen in many situations (caches, failover in clustered distributed systems, etc.). The *validity* of the abstraction is proved by checking the following properties:
1: Initialization (I) of concrete program should imply that of abstract program.
2: The internal action (G) and the external allowed actions (R) of the concrete program should imply that of the abstract program.
3: The validity of the final lemma in the abstract state should imply that of the concrete state.

Formally[2], given: a concrete program $< I_C, C >$, an abstract program $< I_A, A >$, a concrete invariant f, a concrete property c, an abstract property a and a good abstraction h that maps concrete to abstract states, then if

$$I_C(u) \supset I_A(h(u))$$

$$[C/f](u, v) \supset A(h(u), h(v)), \text{ and}$$

$$f(u) \bigwedge a(h(u)) \supset c(u),$$

then $I_C \supset AGc$ follows from $I_A \supset AGa$

If the four properties necessary for proving the validity of the abstraction are proved and also the validity of the safety property in the abstract state space is proved, then safety in the concrete space follows.

Currently, much work is being done in the formal verification of the communication protocols, such as the formal verification of the bounded retransmission protocol[4] and cache coherence protocols[1, 2]. One example of a complex hardware system that has been formally verified is the AAMP5 microprocessor[5].

2 Overview of Buffer Cache in SVR3 Unix

An operating system allows processes to concurrently store or retrieve the data from the mass storage devices such as disk. When a process needs data from the disk, it makes the requests through a system call. The system call results in the process entering the kernel and assuming kernel privileges. The reading or writing of data is effected by the kernel in the requesting process's context by accessing the disk. However, if every request results in a disk access, the response time as seen by processes will be very high and throughput will be low. Hence, the kernel maintains an in-core structure of buffers (the buffer cache) which contains the recently accessed disk blocks. It also tries to prefetch some of the data in the cache in order to exploit spatial locality. The replacement policy used in the cache is the least recently used (LRU). In addition, the kernel can attempt additional optimizations in deciding when to flush a "dirty" buffer onto the disk. Since the process is expected to frequently access the buffer, a kernel can "delay" the write of the buffer to some extent so that multiple writes on the disk block could be clubbed into a single disk write. In case the file is deleted soon after creation (like the temporary files generated during compilation), the buffer may never need to be flushed onto the disk. During system initialization, the number of buffers in the cache is configured and remains fixed thereafter.

2.1 Structure of Buffer Header

A kernel maintains a header for each buffer with following important fields[6]:
a: Device number and block number fields that uniquely identify the buffer.
b: A pointer to the in-core data which corresponds to this buffer.
c: Pointers which keep the buffer on a hash queue and on a free list, both of which are circular, doubly linked lists.
d: Status of the buffer (locked?, valid?, delayed write?[2], in use?, waited on by a process?)

A kernel organizes buffers in hash queues hashed as a function of [device number, block number] combination. Each buffer always exists on a hash queue though there is no significance to the position of the buffer in that queue. If a buffer is free, the kernel also keeps the buffer on a free list. Every buffer is on

[2] dirty buffer, hence must write the contents of the buffer to disk before reusing it

the free list when the system is booted. When the kernel wants any free buffer, it removes the buffer which is at the head of the list. When it wants a particular buffer, it may remove the buffer from anywhere in the free list. When I/O on a buffer is done and the kernel wants to place the buffer on the free list, it appends the buffer to the end of the list (unless there is some I/O error in which case it attaches the buffer in front of the list, for fairness reasons), but in no case does it place the buffer inside the list. This always ensures that the buffers at the head of the list are least frequently used as compared to those buffers which are farther from the head of the list[6].

Whenever a kernel wants to access a disk block, it searches for a buffer. Rather than searching the entire cache (which would be inefficient), it searches the buffer in the hash queues hashed as a function of [device number, block number]. If it finds the buffer containing the block, it checks if it is free. If so, it marks the buffer busy so that other processes cannot access it. But if the buffer is busy (some other process has already marked it busy), then this process must sleep. If the disk block is not hashed at all, then it is not present anywhere in the cache. In this case, the kernel must get a free buffer from the free list, change its device and block numbers and put it on the corresponding hash queue, and mark it busy. If kernel does not get any free buffer, then the process must sleep on the event that some buffer becomes free.

2.2 Correctness Conditions

The algorithm for buffer allocation should guarantee that:

1: At all times, a particular disk block can be cached in at most one buffer (consistency property). If there exist two buffers that cache the same disk block, then the kernel will not know which of them contains the most recent copy of data and hence the content of the disk block is determined by the order in which the two buffers are written to the disk.

2: If multiple processes try to access the same disk block, only one of them will get a locked buffer which contains the block (mutual exclusion property). All other processes must wait till the buffer is released by the process which has locked the buffer. Otherwise, if two processes write to the disk block, the final contents of the disk block would be the contents of the last writing process while the other process thinks that it has sole access to the block. Also, if one process that has got the buffer issues an I/O and the I/O fails making the contents of the buffer invalid, the other processes (if at all it has also got the buffer) may read invalid contents.

3: All the processes waiting for buffers will eventually wake up. Since a kernel allocates buffers during the execution of system calls and frees them before returning, processes cannot purposely hog buffers. This will ensure that a process cannot sleep indefinitely for a buffer. This fairness property will not be considered further in this paper as it requires modelling of all system calls (essentially, the whole of the OS kernel).

Ensuring these properties is necessary for the proper working of the file subsystem. Note that the underlying problem and the consistency conditions are quite different from the ones for processor caches.

2.3 The Buffer Cache Algorithms

The algorithms *getblk()* and *brelse()* are given in the appendix; they are exactly as given in [6] where high level pseudo-code is given, with all the important complications that the SVR3 Unix kernel code takes care of.

When a process enters *getblk()* algorithm, it first checks if the block is hashed in the cache (line 2). If hashed, it checks if the corresponding buffer is busy. If so, it sleeps on an event that the buffer becomes free (line 4); otherwise, the process locks the buffer.

If the block is not at all hashed in the cache, then the process must look for a free buffer from the free list. If a free buffer exists, it changes the device number, block number in the buffer header so that the buffer now refers to the disk block the process wants, puts the buffer in the respective hash queue and finally locks it. If there are no free buffers, the process must sleep for the event that any buffer becomes free (line 12).

One condition which may arise when a block is not hashed is delayed writes (line 16). If the buffer in the free list that is being replaced is valid (it contains *valid* contents of some other disk block) and it has not yet been written to the disk (the write was delayed to take advantage of temporal locality), the process must write the contents of the buffer to the disk before using it. The process initiates I/O on this buffer and continues *getblk* again from the beginning. In the current verification effort, we have abstracted this aspect out to reduce complexity but it can be incorporated with some additional effort.

The algorithm *brelse()* is invoked to free the buffer locked by a process. The algorithm is usually invoked in the interrupt context when the I/O corresponding to a buffer (to be released) is completed. The algorithm first wakes up all the processes waiting on the relevant events. Then it raises the processor execution level and attaches the buffer in the free list (in the front if the buffer was marked delayed write and at the end if it was not marked delayed write).

In the algorithm as given, following problems may arise:

1: Assume that a process finds that a buffer is hashed in the cache but busy (another process has locked the buffer and is possibly doing I/O on it). After this point (just after line 3), the process which had locked that buffer completes its I/O and, on account of a corresponding interrupt, the first process gets preempted. The second process frees the buffer (*brelse()*). Now assume that the first process gets scheduled again. It has already found out that the buffer is busy and hence goes to sleep on the event that the buffer becomes free *even though the buffer is not busy as it has already been released.* The process may never wake up.

2: Next, consider that a process has checked that the buffer is not hashed in the cache and there are no buffers in the free list (line 16). Assume that the I/O corresponding to one of the locked buffers gets completed and the first process gets preempted. The second process frees the buffer (*brelse()*). Now the first process gets scheduled and goes to sleep on the event that any buffer becomes free (line 18). But this results in an incorrect operation since it sleeps on the condition which is no longer true (one buffer is free now!).

3: Also, while manipulating the free list of buffers, there is a possibility of an interrupt being occurring and *brelse()* algorithm being executed. Since *brelse()* also manipulates the free list, this may result in corrupting the free list (p 31-32[6]).

All of the three problems occur due to non-atomicity in testing a condition and acting on it. Hence even though the algorithm looks plausible, there may be subtle errors in the presence of concurrency. There are other problems still (see exercises in [6] (page 58))! Raising the interrupt processor level is one solution. Some of these problems are handled in our model by redefining the unit of interleaving, especially with respect to interrupts.

3 Verification of Consistency

In general, when writing specifications, we should model only those aspects which are relevant to the properties of interest[2]. In this case, the property of interest is that a disk block should not be cached in more than one buffer. Since each disk block is independent of the other, we can consider the changes in the state of the buffer cache only with respect to one particular disk block and then prove that there can be only one buffer at the most hashed in the cache corresponding to this block. Also we are concerned only about the state of the buffer cache, no matter which process alters it. We only wish to prove that if the buffer cache can be modified in the ways which are permitted by *getblk()*, the above property is *always* valid. For the model checking part, we model a simple case of only two buffers and verify the property.

3.1 General and Abstract Specifications

The General Case The buffer cache is defined as an array of buffers. If the *valid* field in the buffer is true, the particular disk block (around which the specification is written and referred to as *blk*) is present in the buffer. If false, the disk block is not present in the buffer. However, it does not state which disk block the buffer contains. There may be any other disk block in the buffer (with which we are not concerned with) or even actually be invalid (may not represent any disk block). The *locked* field states whether the buffer is free (i.e. on the free list) or busy. The system's state is that of the buffer cache. In the specification, *b_init(s)* specifies the initial state of the buffer cache with the block *blk* being not present. *b_next(s, s1)* specifies the allowed next state transitions of the buffer cache, from *s* to *s*1. *b_safe(s)* is the safety property: if there exist two buffers that are valid (recall that valid means that it contains disk block *blk*), then they must be the same. In other words, there cannot exist two different buffers which have the same disk block *blk*.

The various cases in *getblk()* and the possible state changes are as follows:
1: the idle transition that leaves the state of buffer cache unchanged.

2: if *blk* is already hashed but the buffer in which it is hashed is locked then the state does not change, as a process that needs it sleeps until it becomes free.
3: if *blk* is hashed and the buffer in which it is hashed is not locked, then the buffer may get locked. This happens when a process trying for *blk* finds the block in the cache with the buffer free, and locks the buffer.
4: when *blk* is not hashed and also there is no free buffer in the cache (i.e. all the buffers are locked and the free list is empty), a process needing *blk* sleeps on the event that any buffer becomes free. There is no change in the state of the buffer cache.
5: when *blk* is not hashed and there are some free buffers, a process picks up the buffer at the head of the free list, changes the device and block number of the buffer so that the buffer now represents *blk* and locks it.
6: the transition corresponding to the release of buffer.

The property to be proved is that if we start in state $s0$ satisfying initialization predicate *b_init* then for all the states that are generated from *b_next*, the property *b_safe* is satisfied.

Downscaled Version This version has only 2 buffers but as the model checker provided with PVS cannot handle numeric subranges[2], changes were required to check this simplified specification: convert subranges to explicit enumerations, and use AND and OR instead of FORALL and EXISTS. The consistency property is proved by just typing "model-check" as the first proof command to PVS.

Property Preserving Abstraction Define a type ***astate*** (abstract state) and a function ***abstr*** which maps a state in concrete space (which corresponds to general case specification) to the abstract space, such that four properties hold:

initialstate_lemma: $\boldsymbol{b\_init(s) \Rightarrow ab\_init(abstr(s))}$
nextstep_lemma: $\boldsymbol{b\_next(s0, s1) \Rightarrow ab\_next(abstr(s0), abstr(s1))}$
safety_preserved: $\boldsymbol{ab\_safe(abstr(s)) \Rightarrow b\_safe(s)}$
safety: $\boldsymbol{ab\_init(as0) \Rightarrow AG(ab\_next, ab\_safe)(as0)}$

$AG(N, f)$ is a CTL formula that says that f is valid in all futures reached with N as the transition function. It is defined in a PVS library using the mu operator and other CTL operators as follows:

```
AG(N,f):pred[state] = NOT EF(N, NOT f)
EF(N,f):pred[state] = EU(N,(LAMBDA u: TRUE),f)
EU(N,f,g):pred[state] = mu (LAMBDA Q: (g OR (f AND EX(N,Q))))
EX(N,f)(u):bool =  (EXISTS v: (f(v) AND N(u, v)))
```

Of the above four lemmas, the fourth can be proved by model checking and the first three can be verified using theorem proving. The abstracted state consists of two fields of type *block_state* and *buffercache_state*. The *block_state* is enumeration of following: *not_present* (*blk* is not hashed in the buffer cache), *locked_once* (*blk* is present only once and the buffer containing *blk* is locked), *notlocked_once* (*blk* is present only once but the buffer containing *blk* is not locked), *notlocked_shared* (*blk* is present in more than one buffer in the buffer cache but all the buffers containing *blk* are free), *locked_shared* (*blk* is present in many buffers but at least one buffer is locked). The *buffercache_state* is just one of *all_locked* or *some_free.*

The Abstract Specification Of the five states of block *blk*, only the first three should be valid states. But we cannot assume it without proof. The specification written for the abstract state has an almost 1-1 correspondence with the general case specification. The initialization predicate states that *blk* is not present in the cache. The next state predicate corresponds to the six cases specified in the general case:

1: First, an idle transition that corresponds to that of the general case.

2: If *blk* is hashed (i.e. present) and its state is *locked_once*, then the system's state does not change as a process sleeps without changing the state of the buffer cache. But if *blk*'s state is *locked_shared*, we have a problem as the algorithm does not say anything about it. Though this state should never occur, we can not just assume it. Hence we allow a transition corresponding to this state, not worrying about what the final state will be.

3: If *blk* is hashed and the buffer containing *blk* is not locked, then there are two cases: block may be in *notlocked_once* state or *notlocked_shared* state. In the first case, *blk*'s state changes into *locked_once* and the state of the buffer cache may change to *all_locked* (if all buffers are now locked) or *some_free* (some buffers are free even after locking). But in the case of *notlocked_shared* state, the final block state will be *locked_shared* and the state of the buffer cache will be *some_free* (as its earlier state being *notlocked_shared* means that there were at least two buffers free. Locking one will still leave some buffer free).

4: If *blk* is not hashed and all the buffers are locked, then the state of the system does not change as the process trying for *blk* should sleep on the event any buffer becomes free.

5: When *blk* is not hashed and there exist some free buffers, then the state of the system can be changed in two possible ways. The state of the block in this case will be *locked_once* but the state of the buffer cache can be either *all_locked* or *some_free* depending on how many buffers remain free after locking one buffer which is free.

6: If a buffer is released by a process, *blk* can be locked_once or locked_shared. Correspondingly, the final state will be either *notlocked_once*, or (*locked shared* or *notlocked_shared*). In either case the state of the buffer cache will be *some_free.*

The safe predicate states that at state ***as*** the block state can be only in one of the three states: *not_present, notlocked_once, locked_once.* The safety property specifies that if the abstract program is initialized with the initialization predicate then for all the states generated from the next state predicate starting from the initial state, the safe predicate is always true.

3.2 Proof of Consistency

Safety for the abstract algorithm can be easily verified using the command "model-check" (see the discussion earlier on downscaled version). To prove the validity of abstraction, three lemmas have to be proved:

1: **initialstate_lemma** This is required to show that initializing the concrete (the general case) program is equivalent to initializing the abstract program. The proof is interactive but is relatively simple. First, it uses "skosimp*" strategy to introduce skolem constants. Then it uses a PVS strategy called "grind : if-match nil" which tells the PVS prover to make repeated skolemizations, if-lifting and not to make any instantiations on its own. Proper instantiation completes the proof.

2: **nextstate_lemma** This requires to be proved to establish that the next state transitions of the concrete specification imply the next state transitions of abstract specification. The proof of this is relatively lengthy and requires more than 550 proof commands to achieve the desired proof. Most of the difficulty lies in the need to expand the CTL operators (which are defined in terms of mu calculus) and then reasoning using lemmas on least fix points. We give some idea of the effort involved below by giving the definitions of mu operator in the PVS library along with one lemma useful in one of the proofs:

```
mu(pp): pred[T] = lfp(pp)
lfp (pp):pred[T] = glb({p | pp(p) <= p})
glb (setofpred):pred[T] =
    LAMBDA s: (FORALL p: member(p,setofpred) IMPLIES  p(s))
lfp_lem3: LEMMA ismono(ff) IMPLIES FORALL f: ff(f) <= f IMPLIES lfp(ff) <= f
```

For this reason, just to prove the simple base case takes 60 steps! We have included in an appendix an edited fragment of the proof of the base case of a simpler system as an illustration. The full proof script of this case as seen in PVS runs to 488 lines (the formulae become very large after substitutions and get repeated in the subsequent steps, hence the size) with 22 steps.

3: **safety_preserved** This lemma states that the proof of safety property in abstracted specification implies the proof of safety property in the concrete version. The proof of this lemma is relatively easy. The strategy "grind : if-match nil" first tries repeated skolemizations and if-liftings. This yields three subgoals to be proved. All the three subgoals can be proved using proper instantiations.

The proof of consistency property now directly follows from [2]. This completes the verification of the cache consistency property that a block can not reside in more than one buffer at a time. The proof takes around 650 manual proof commands and is mostly interactive except for the proof of downscaled specification and the abstract specification which are automated due to the model checker provided with PVS.

4 Verification of Mutual Exclusion

Whenever multiple processes try to acquire the same disk block, only one of the processes should succeed in getting a locked buffer corresponding to the disk block. i.e. there should not exist two distinct processes that have acquired the same buffer simultaneously. By an appropriate reformulation of this problem, we can convert this verification problem to that of verifying Peterson n-process mutual exclusion. This latter problem has been done earlier by N.Shankar at SRI (on an older version of PVS). Our PVS specification has a few minor modifications (for example, some additional lemmas were required) with the complete proof having been done from scratch. Due to lack of space, we give our argument for the reformulation and only a very brief proof outline as its novelty is not high due to the earlier work of Shankar.

4.1 Reformulation of the Problem

Consider an unknown number of processes that try to access the same disk block (say *blk*). Since the consistency of buffer cache has already been proved, we now know that there can be at most one buffer allocated to this disk block in the buffer cache. This simplifies the verification.

Each process can be in one of three states: *init* (process has not yet started accessing the block, equivalent to *try*=0 in Peterson's algorithm), *trying* (process has just started access, *try*=1) or *got_buf* (process has successfully got the buffer and locked it, equivalent to entry into the critical section in Peterson's algorithm *cs*=1). There can be one more state: the process is sleeping, i.e. the process does not busy wait but is awakened by an event. After waking up, it goes into the *trying* state.

If we can map the sleeping state also to that of *trying*, we can map the buffer cache mutual exclusion problem to that of n-process Peterson. Such a mapping is actually incorrect (results in a deadlock!) on a uniprocessor but not so in the abstract model of interleaving assumed in the PVS model (Section 1.1). (Also, the sleeping state *will have to be taken into account* when we are concerned with fairness issues, such as a process not sleeping infinitely on some condition.) Hence the verification of the mutual exclusion property follows from that of n-Peterson. We will still outline the proof in the context of buffer cache below, as its mapping to n-Peterson is clear enough.

4.2 Outline of Proof

Formally, if there exist processes j and k such that both of them have their state *got_buf*, then $j = k$. The strategy for the proof is induction on the number of processes trying for the same block. The base case of mutual exclusion is true if there is only one process. The induction hypothesis assumes validity for k processes and we need to show validity for $k + 1$. Assuming the hypothesis, we abstract the k processes as a single process (say A) and the $k+1^{th}$ process as the other process (say B). The state of A now is a function of states of k processes. We define a function ***abstr*** that maps a concrete state into the abstract state of A as follows: *got_buf* (if there exists a process out of the k processes which has state *got_buf*; there can be only one such process as mutual exclusion is valid for k processes), *trying* (if there exists at least one process with the state *trying*) or *init* (when the states of all them is *init*). The state of process B is same as the state of $k + 1^{th}$ process. Also, the state of buffer in the abstract state will be the same as that in the concrete state. We now should not only prove that mutual exclusion is true in the abstract state, but also that the abstraction itself is valid.

Fourteen lemmas were proved separately and applied in the proof. These lemmas include those for the proof of validity of abstraction: proofs of transition of k processes implying that of A, empty action of k processes implying that of A, transition of $k + 1^{th}$ process implying that of B, empty action of $(k + 1)^{th}$ process implying that of B and initialization of k processes implying that of A.

5 Conclusion and future work

The consistency and mutual exclusion properties of buffer caches have been successfully verified. Our experience underscores the importance of more mechanization in the use of formal methods. We plan to develop suitable languages to describe a domain closely (the OS area, more specifically, filesystems) and develop a translator to PVS along with some automatically derived proof strategies. This could reduce the amount of manual intervention in the proof.

References

1. K. L McMillan. Symbolic Model Checking: *An approach to the state explosion problem.* PhD thesis, School of Computer Science, CMU, 1992
2. John Rushby. Specification, proof checking, and model checking for protocols and distributed systems with PVS. Tutorial presented at FORTE X/PSTV XVII '97.
3. N. Shankar. A lazy approach to compositional verification. Technical Report SRI-CSL-93-8, SRI Intl, Menlo Park, CA, Dec 1993.
4. Klaus Havelund and N. Shankar. Experiments in theorem proving and model checking for protocol verification. In FME'96, LNCS 1051, Mar 1996.
5. Steven P. Miller and M. Srivas. Formal Verification of the AAMP5 Microprocessor. WIFT'95, Boca Raton, Florida, Apr 1995.
6. Maurice J. Bach. The Design of the UNIX Operating System. Prentice Hall New Delhi, India, 1994.
7. E.M. Clarke, O. Grumberg and D.E. Long. Model Checking and Abstraction. *ACM Transaction on Programming Languages & Systems*, Sep 1994

A Buffer Cache Algorithms Pseudocode

algorithm *getblk*
input: file system number, block number
output : locked buffer that can now be used for block

```
while (buffer not found) {
    if (block in hash queue) {
        if (buffer busy) {
            sleep (event buffer becomes free)
            continue
        }
        mark buffer busy
```

```
            remove buffer from free list
            return buffer
      } else {
            if (there are no buffers on free list) {
                  sleep (event any buffer becomes free)
                  continue
            }
            remove buffer from free list
            if (buffer marked for delayed write) {
                  asynch write of buffer to disk
                  continue
            }
            remove buffer from old hash queue
            put buffer onto new hash queue
            return buffer
      }
}
```

algorithm *brelse*
input: locked buffer
output: none

```
wake up all procs: event, waiting for any buf to become free
wake up all procs: event, waiting for this buf to become free
raise processor execution level to block interrupts
if (buffer contents are valid and buffer not old) {
      enqueue buffer at end of free list
} else enqueue buffer at the beginning of the free list
lower processor execution level to allow interrupts
unlock(buffer)
```

Appendix B: Edited fragment of proof of safety.1 (mutual exclusion)

```
[1]     (NOT mu(LAMBDA (Q: pred[state]):
                (NOT (LAMBDA (s: state[N]): TRUE) OR
                   ((LAMBDA u: TRUE) AND
                      EX((LAMBDA (s0: state[N]), (s1: state[N]):
                            (G_N(0)(s0, s1) OR R_N(0)(s0, s1))), Q)))))(s!1)
Rerunning steps: (EXPAND "NOT"), (EXPAND "mu"), (LEMMA "lfp_lem3"), we get:
{-1}    (FORALL (ff: [pred[state] -> pred[state]]):
         ismono(ff) IMPLIES FORALL (f: pred[state]): ff(f) <= f IMPLIES lfp(ff) <= f)

[-2]     lfp(LAMBDA (Q: pred[state]):
             ((LAMBDA (u): FALSE) OR
                ((LAMBDA u: TRUE) AND
                   EX((LAMBDA (s0: state[N]), (s1: state[N]):
                         (G_N(0)(s0, s1) OR R_N(0)(s0, s1))), Q))))(s!1)
Running step (INST?) yields 5 subgoals, each of which can be proved through
(PROP), (INST - "LAMBDA (u : state[N]): FALSE"), (EXPAND "<="), (INST?),
(BETA), (SKOSIMP), (EXPAND "OR"), (EXPAND "AND"), (GRIND), (ASSERT),...
```

Infinite Probabilistic and Nonprobabilistic Testing

K Narayan Kumar[1*] Rance Cleaveland[1] Scott A. Smolka[1]

Dept. Comput. Sci., SUNY at Stony Brook, Stony Brook, NY 11794
{kumar,rance,sas}@cs.sunysb.edu
(Research supported in part by NSF Grant CCR-9505562 and AFOSR Grants F49620-93-1-0250 and F49620-95-1-0508.)

Abstract. We introduce three new notions of infinite testing for probabilistic processes, namely, simple, Büchi and fair infinite testing. We carefully examine their distinguishing power and show that all three have the same power as finite tests. We also consider Büchi tests in the non-probabilistic setting and show that they have the same distinguishing power as finite tests. Finally, we show that finite probabilistic tests are stronger than nondeterministic fair tests.

1 Introduction

Testing preorders [DNH83, Hen88] have proved to be a very versatile paradigm for relating specifications and their implementations. The basic idea is first to define when a process *may pass* a test (there exists a successful interaction between the process and test) and *must pass* a test (all process-test interactions are successful). The *may* preorder is then defined as follows: a process P is *may* less than a process Q if whenever P *may* pass a test T, then Q *may* passes T as well. The *must* preorder is defined similarly. The *testing* preorder is then the conjunction of the *may* and *must* preorders.

These preorders extend in a natural and useful way to *probabilistic processes*; see, for example, [CDS+98, WSS97, YL92, Seg96, JY95]. A probabilistic process can be viewed as a *labeled Markov chain*, where the label attached to a Markovian transition indicates the communication action that takes place in conjunction with the transition. Testing preorders for probabilistic processes can be thought of as relating processes in terms of their relative reliability in different operating environments. Such environments can be modeled by *tests*, i.e. probabilistic processes equipped with a set of *success* states.

The majority of previous research on testing preorders has focused on finite testing. In the case of nondeterministic processes (which we also sometimes refer to as "nonprobabilistic processes") there are, however, two notable exceptions.

* On leave from SPIC Mathematical Institute, Chennai, India.

Hennessey [Hen88] has shown that a certain simple extension of finite testing to infinite testing offers no additional distinguishing power in terms of the induced preorders. Natarajan and Cleaveland [NC95] and Brinksma et al. [BRV95] have shown that *fair testing* induces a finer testing preorder than finite testing, and has practical ramifications in applications such as protocol verification.

In this paper, we introduce several new notions of infinite testing, for both probabilistic and nonprobabilistic processes, and carefully examine their distinguishing power. In particular, we consider the testing preorders induced by the following success criteria for infinite tests: *simple infinite tests*: a finite execution ending in a success state is deemed successful while all infinite executions are treated as unsuccessful; *Büchi tests*: tests are equipped with a set of special states called Büchi states, and an infinite execution is considered successful if it visits the set of Büchi state infinitely often; and *fair testing*: a state of a test from which a success state can be reached is said to be "potentially successful," and an infinite execution is successful if it remains among the set of potentially successful states.

Simple tests and fair tests have been studied in the literature and a motivation for their consideration may be found there. The motivation for Büchi tests is the following. A Büchi test corresponds to an environment that acts as a monitor, continously interacting with the system and periodically indicating whether the interaction up to that point is admissible. The entire computation is successful if the monitor reports success infinitely often.

As alluded to above, it is already known that, for nondeterministic processes, simple infinite tests offer no additional distinguishing power than finite tests [Hen88] (i.e. the induced preorders coincide), and that the fair testing preorder is finer than the one induced by finite tests [NC95, BRV95]. We complete this picture by showing that Büchi testing also coincides with finite testing.

In the probabilistic setting, only finite testing has been considered previously [CDS$^+$98]. We show that infinite tests offer no more distinguishing power than finite tests; i.e., the simple, Büchi, and fair testing preorders all coincide with the testing preorder induced by finite tests. Thus, fairness adds to the expressive power of nondeterministic testing but fails to do so in probabilistic testing.

Finally, we show that the probabilistic testing preorder refines the fair testing preorder for nondeterministic processes in the following sense: if two probabilistic processes are related by the probabilistic testing preorder, then their images under the forgetful homomorphism that erases probabilities are related by the fair testing preorder for nondeterministic processes.

2 Infinite Testing for Nondeterministic Processes

We begin by recalling the definitions of the testing preorders of [DNH83, Hen88]. Let Act denote a finite set of *actions* and let $\tau \notin \mathsf{Act}$. τ represents the distinguished unobservable internal action.

A *process* P over an alphabet Act is a labeled transition system $\langle K_P, \longrightarrow, p^I \rangle$ where K_P is a (countable) set of states, $p^I \in K_P$ is the initial state and $\longrightarrow \subseteq K_P \times \mathsf{Act} \cup \{\tau\} \times K_P$ is an image-finite *transition relation*. We write $p \xrightarrow{a} p'$ for $(p, a, p') \in \longrightarrow$ and $p \longrightarrow$ when there is an a and a p' such that $p \xrightarrow{a} p'$. A state p is *terminal* if $p \not\longrightarrow$.

A *finite execution fragment* of a process P is a sequence $p_0 \xrightarrow{a_1} p_1 \xrightarrow{a_2} \dots \xrightarrow{a_n} p_n$ where $p_i \xrightarrow{a_i} p_{i+1}$. An *infinite execution fragment* is a sequence $p_0 \xrightarrow{a_1} p_1 \xrightarrow{a_2} \dots \xrightarrow{a_n} p_n \xrightarrow{a_{n+1}} \dots$ where $p_i \xrightarrow{a_i} p_{i+1}$. An *execution* is a finite or an infinite execution fragment with $p_0 = p^I$. The set of all executions of a process P is denoted by $Exec_P$. An execution is said to be *complete* if it is infinite or if it is finite and ends in a terminal state. A state p is said to be *divergent* if there is an infinite execution fragment of the form $p \xrightarrow{\tau} p_1 \xrightarrow{\tau} p_2 \dots$ emanating from p. A process without divergent states is said to be divergence-free.

Given processes P and Q, the *composition* of P and Q is the process $P \| Q = \langle K_P \times K_Q, \longrightarrow_{P\|Q}, (p^I, q^I) \rangle$ where $\longrightarrow_{P\|Q}$ is given by

$$p \xrightarrow{\tau} p' \Rightarrow (p, q) \xrightarrow{\tau}_{P\|Q} (p', q)$$
$$q \xrightarrow{\tau} q' \Rightarrow (p, q) \xrightarrow{\tau}_{P\|Q} (p, q')$$
$$a \neq \tau \;\&\; p \xrightarrow{a} p' \;\&\; q \xrightarrow{a} q' \Rightarrow (p, q) \xrightarrow{a}_{P\|Q} (p', q')$$

A process P is said to be *finite* if it is finite-state and the relation $\longrightarrow$ is acyclic. Every execution of a finite process is finite. The composition of a finite process with any divergence-free process yields a finite process.

A *test* $T = \langle K_T, \longrightarrow_T, t^I, Suc_T \rangle$ is a process $\langle K_T, \longrightarrow_T, t^I \rangle$ with a distinguished set of *success* states $Suc_T \subseteq K_T$. (We often use T to refer its underlying process $\langle K_T, \longrightarrow_T, t^I \rangle$.) An execution of a test T is said to be *successful* if it ends in a state in Suc_T.

In this paper we require that processes be divergence-free and that every success state be a terminal state. The results in [CDS+98] that we build on assume that processes are divergence-free. The assumption on success states is for consistency with [NC95] and [CDS+98]. Traditional testing does not require that success states be terminal but any run that passes through a success state is considered successful. Thus, w.l.o.g., we may restrict success states to terminal states.

Given a process P and a test T, $P \| T$ is a test with $Suc_{P\|T} = \{(p, t) \mid t \in Suc_T \wedge (p, t) \not\longrightarrow\}$. We say that a process P may pass the test T, written

$P\ may\ T$, if the test $P \,||\, T$ has a successful execution. We say that a process P must pass the test T, written $P\ must\ T$, if every complete execution of the test $P \,||\, T$ is successful. (Usually success is indicated by a distinguished action w (see [Hen88, NC95]). It is easy to verify that our formulation using terminal success states is equivalent to the one presented in [NC95] for divergence-free processes).

A test T is said to be finite if its underlying process is finite. The *may-testing* preorder $\sqsubseteq_{may}$ is given by $P \sqsubseteq_{may} Q$ if for every finite test T, $P\ may\ T \Rightarrow Q\ may\ T$ and the *must-testing* preorder $\sqsubseteq_{must}$ is given by $P \sqsubseteq_{must} Q$ if for every finite test T, $P\ must\ T \Rightarrow Q\ must\ T$. Further, we say $P \sqsubseteq_{test} Q$ if $P \sqsubseteq_{may} Q$ and $P \sqsubseteq_{must} Q$.

If we remove the restriction that the tests be finite we get preorders $\sqsubseteq_{smay}$, $\sqsubseteq_{smust}$ and $\sqsubseteq_{s}$, respectively. We call such tests *simple infinite tests.* In [DNH83, Hen88], alternative characterizations of these preorders are derived and as a consequence it turns out that $\sqsubseteq_{may} = \sqsubseteq_{smay}$, $\sqsubseteq_{must} = \sqsubseteq_{smust}$ and $\sqsubseteq_{test} = \sqsubseteq_{s}$.

Natarajan and Cleaveland [NC95] and Brinksma et al. [BRV95] present a different criterion for deciding which infinite executions are successful. A state t of a test is said to be *potentially successful* if there is an execution fragment starting at t that leads to a success state. Under fair testing, a complete finite execution is successful if it ends in a success state and an infinite execution is successful if every state it visits is potentially successful. When a process P may/must satisfy a test T is defined analogous to the finite case and let the resulting preorders be $\sqsubseteq_{fmay}$, $\sqsubseteq_{fmust}$ and $\sqsubseteq_{f}$. It turns out that $\sqsubseteq_{fmay}$ is the same as $\sqsubseteq_{may}$ while $\sqsubseteq_{fmust}$ is finer than $\sqsubseteq_{must}$.

We now propose a third kind of infinite test. *Büchi* tests, as the name suggests, are inspired by the theory of automata over infinite sequences. A Büchi test T is a tuple $\langle K_T, \longrightarrow_T, t^I, Suc_T, \mathrm{B}\rangle$ where $\langle K_T, \longrightarrow_T, t^I, Suc_T\rangle$ is a test and $\mathrm{B} \subseteq K_T$. A finite execution of a Büchi test is successful if it ends in a state in Suc_T. An infinite execution of a Büchi test is successful if it visits the set B infinitely often.

Given a process P and a Büchi test T we treat $P \,||\, T$ as a Büchi test with $\mathrm{B}_{P||T} = \{(p,t) \mid t \in \mathrm{B}\}$. We say $P\ may_b\ T$ if $P \,||\, T$ has a successful execution and $P\ must_b\ T$ if every complete execution of $P \,||\, T$ is successful. As in the case of finite tests, these relations induce three preorders $\sqsubseteq_{bmay}$, $\sqsubseteq_{bmust}$ and $\sqsubseteq_{b}$.

Let T be the test $\langle \{t,t'\}, \{(t,a,t),(t,b,t),(t,b,t'),(t',b,t')\}, t, \emptyset, \{t'\}\rangle$. Then, $P\ may_b\ T$ if and only if P has an infinite execution with finite number of a-transitions, a property seemingly beyond the reach of finite tests. Nevertheless, the following theorem shows that the preorders induced by Büchi test are no different from those induced by finite tests.

Theorem 1. $\sqsubseteq_{bmay} = \sqsubseteq_{may}$ *,* $\sqsubseteq_{bmust} = \sqsubseteq_{must}$ *and* $\sqsubseteq_{b} = \sqsubseteq_{test}$.

Theorem 1 critically depends on the image-finiteness assumption. Büchi tests do not coicide with simple tests for processes with infinite branching. Divergence can be used to simulate infinite branching and consequently Theorem 1 also does not hold for processes with divergence. It is possible to modify the definition of Büchi tests to generalize this theorem to arbitrary processes, but such modifications are technical and an operational justification seems hard.

3 Probabilistic Processes and Testing

In this section, we recall the basic ingredients of the probabilistic testing framework of [CDS+98], namely, probabilistic processes and tests, the notion of a process passing a test with a certain probability, the probabilistic testing preorder, and the alternative characterization of the preorder. To simplify the presentation, we restrict ourselves to processes and tests without τ-moves. However, all our results extend to divergence-free processes and tests with τ-moves.

Let Act be a finite set of *atomic actions* and let a, b, ... range over Act. A *probabilistic process* P over Act is a tuple $\langle K_P, \longrightarrow, p^{\mathrm{I}}, \mu_P\rangle$ where $\langle K_P, \longrightarrow, p^{\mathrm{I}}\rangle$ is a process and $\mu_P : (K_P \times \mathsf{Act} \times K_P) \to [0,1]$ is the *transition distribution function* such that for each $p \in K_P$,

$$\sum_{\substack{a\in\mathsf{Act},\\ p'\in K_P}} \mu_P(p,a,p') \in \{0,1\}$$

Further, $p \xrightarrow{a} p'$ if and only if $\mu_P(p,a,p') > 0$. Intuitively, $\mu_P(p,a,p')$ is the probability that atomic action a is executed from state p to become state p'. We write $\mu_P(p,a)$, for $\sum_{p'\in P} \mu_P(p,a,p')$.

Notice that we are working in the generative model of probabilistic processes [GSS95]. Let $P = \langle K_P, \longrightarrow_P, p^{\mathrm{I}}, \mu_P\rangle$ and $Q = \langle K_Q, \longrightarrow_Q, q^{\mathrm{I}}, \mu_Q\rangle$ be probabilistic processes. Then their *composition*, denoted $P \,||\, Q$, is the tuple $\langle K_P \times K_Q, \longrightarrow_{P\,||\,Q}, (p^{\mathrm{I}}, q^{\mathrm{I}}), \mu_{P\,||\,Q}\rangle$ such that

$$\mu_{P\,||\,Q}((p,q),a,(p',q')) = \begin{matrix} \frac{\mu_P(p,a,p')\cdot\mu_Q(q,a,q')}{\nu(p,q)} & \text{if } \nu(p,q) > 0 \\ 0 & \text{otherwise} \end{matrix}$$

where $\nu(p,q) = \sum_{b\in\mathsf{Act}} \mu_P(p,b) \cdot \mu_Q(q,b)$.

Although P is a generative process it cannot autonomously decide which transitions to offer while interacting with an environment. The set of enabled transitions is determined by the environment and the probability assigned to an enabled transition is the conditional probability that this transition is taken from the set of all enabled transitions. In this sense, our processes are reactive and different from (labeled) Markov processes. As we shall see later, however, the interaction system consisting of a process and a test may be analyzed as a Markov chain.

A probabilistic *test* is a probabilistic process with some of its states designated as success states. That is, a probabilistic test is a tuple of the form $\langle K_T, \longrightarrow_T, t^{\mathrm{I}}, \mu_T, Suc_T\rangle$ where $\langle K_T, \longrightarrow_T, t^{\mathrm{I}}, \mu_T\rangle$ is a probabilistic process and $Suc_T \subseteq K_T$ is the set of *success states*. Further we will assume that if $t \in Suc_T$ then $\sum_{a\in\mathsf{Act}} \mu_T(t,a) = 0$. That is, as in the nondeterministic case, there are no transitions out of success states. Once the test has reached a success state the run is deemed successful (and thus the rest of the run is of no interest). In this section we assume that tests are finite, i.e., they are finite-state and the transition relation $\longrightarrow$ of a test is acyclic.

For an execution $\sigma = p_1 \xrightarrow{a_1} p_2 \xrightarrow{a_2} \ldots \xrightarrow{a_{n-1}} p_n$, let

$$Prod(\sigma) = \prod_{1\leq i\leq n-1} \mu_P(p_i, a_i, p_{i+1})$$

For any finite process P, the *execution probability distribution function* $\Pr : Exec_P \to [0,1]$ is defined inductively as follows:

$$\begin{aligned}\Pr(p_1 \xrightarrow{a_1} p_2 \ldots \xrightarrow{a_{n-1}} p_n) &= Prod(p_1 \xrightarrow{a_1} p_2 \ldots \xrightarrow{a_{n-1}} p_n) && \text{if } p_n \text{ is terminal}\\ &= 0 && \text{otherwise}\end{aligned}$$

and is lifted to sets $\mathcal{E} \subseteq Exec_P$ of executions as, $\Pr(\mathcal{E}) = \sum_{\sigma\in\mathcal{E}} \Pr(\sigma)$

Intuitively, $\Pr(\sigma)$ is the probability that the process P engages in execution σ. We assume that an execution always proceeds to completion and thus the probability of incomplete executions is taken to be 0.

Since tests are finite processes the execution probability function is defined. The *success probability* of a test T is given by $Pr(\mathrm{SE}_T)$, where SE_T is the set of all executions of T that end in success states. Every test can be treated as a process by disregarding its set of success states. Thus, given a probabilistic process $P = \langle K_P, \longrightarrow_P, p^I, \mu_P\rangle$ and a test $T = \langle K_T, \longrightarrow_T, t^I, \mu_T, Suc_T\rangle$, we can define the composition $P \,||\, T$. $P \,||\, T$ can also be treated as a test with $Suc_{P\,||\,T} = \{(p,t) \mid p \in K_P,\ t \in Suc_T\}$. By the definition of composition, there are no transitions out of states in $Suc_{P\,||\,T}$. Further, if T is a finite process then so is $P \,||\, T$. The *probability that P passes T* is simply the success probability of $P \,||\, T$. We write $P\ pass_\pi\ T$ if $Prob(\mathrm{SE}_{P\,||\,T}) \geq \pi$.

The testing preorder for probabilistic processes [CDS+98] can now be defined as follows. Let P and Q be processes. Then $P \sqsubseteq^{pr}_{test} Q$ if for all tests T, $\pi \in [0,1]$, $P\ pass_\pi\ T$ implies $Q\ pass_\pi\ T$ (or equivalently $\Pr(\mathrm{SE}_{P\,||\,T}) \leq \Pr(\mathrm{SE}_{Q\,||\,T})$).

A distribution over Act is a map $D : \mathsf{Act} \to [0,1]$ such that $\sum_{a\in\mathsf{Act}} D(a) \in \{0,1\}$. Let Dist denote the set of all distributions. A *probabilistic trace* $(a_1, D_1)\cdots(a_n, D_n)$ over Act is an element of $(\mathsf{Dist} \times \mathsf{Act})^*$. Tr_{Act} denotes the set of all probabilistic traces over Act, and $\varepsilon \in Tr_{\mathsf{Act}}$ denotes the empty probabilistic trace.

Intuitively, a probabilistic trace represents a possible "interaction session" with a probabilistic process; each distribution defines the probabilities with which different actions are enabled by the environment, while the action component specifies the action that the environment and process agree to execute. The function M_P defined next computes the probability that a process P, from a given state, engages in such an interaction session.

Let $P = \langle K_P, \longrightarrow_P, p^{\mathrm{I}}, \mu_P \rangle$ be a probabilistic process. Function $M_P : K_P \times Tr_{\mathsf{Act}} \rightarrow [0,1]$ is defined as follows:

$$M_P(p, \varepsilon) = 1$$

$$M_P(p, (a, D)\, s') = \begin{cases} \sum_{p' \in K_P} \frac{\mu_P(p,a,p') \cdot D(a) \cdot M_P(p',s')}{\nu(p,D)} & \text{if } \nu(p,D) > 0 \\ 0 & \text{otherwise} \end{cases}$$

where $\nu(p, D) = \sum_{b \in \mathsf{Act}} \mu_P(p, b) \cdot D(b)$.

The preorder induced by probabilistic traces, $\ll$, is defined by $P \ll Q$ if for all $s \in Tr_{\mathsf{Act}}, M_P(p^{\mathrm{I}}, s) \leq M_Q(q^{\mathrm{I}}, s)$.

Theorem 2 [CDS⁺98]. $P \sqsubseteq^{pr}_{test} Q$ if and only if $P \ll Q$

A Probability Measure on Sets of Executions: For any finite execution σ, let $[\sigma]$ denote the set of finite and infinite executions of P that extend σ. A set of executions is said to be *simple basic measurable* if it is either of the form $[\sigma]$ or $\{\sigma\}$ where $\{\sigma\} \neq [\sigma]$. We assign probabilities to simple basic measurable sets as follows: *Prob*$([\sigma])$ = *Prod*(σ) and *Prob*$(\{\sigma\}) = 0$ when $\{\sigma\} \neq [\sigma]$. A standard result tells us that this function extends to a probability measure over the σ-algebra generated by these sets. The reader is referred to [WSS97] for the details.

4 Simple Infinite Tests

As mentioned earlier, an execution of a simple infinite test is considered successful if it is finite and ends in a success state. Since there are no outgoing transitions from success states, $[\sigma] = \{\sigma\}$ for any successful execution σ. The probability of success is given by *Prob*$(\mathrm{SE}_T) = \sum_{\sigma \in \mathrm{SE}_T}$ *Prob*$([\sigma])$.

Given a probabilistic process P and a simple infinite test T the probability with which P passes T is just the success probability of $P \,||\, T$. The class of simple infinite tests induce a preorder $\sqsubseteq^{pr}_{s}$ given by $P \sqsubseteq^{pr}_{s} Q$ if and only if for all probabilistic tests T, *Prob*$(\mathrm{SE}_{P\,||\,T}) \leq$ *Prob*$(\mathrm{SE}_{Q\,||\,T})$.

Theorem 3. $\sqsubseteq^{pr}_{test} \; = \; \ll \; = \; \sqsubseteq^{pr}_{s}$

Proof. It is easy to see that $\sqsubseteq^{pr}_{s} \subseteq \ll$. We now prove the converse. Let P and Q be probabilistic processes such that $P \ll Q$. Let us examine the set of successful executions of $R \,||\, T$ for any process R. Let σ be any execution of T. Let $\mathrm{E}_{R\,||\,T}(\sigma)$

denote the set of executions of $R\,||\,T$ whose projection onto the T component extends σ. In [CDS+98] it is shown that there is a probabilistic trace $tr(\sigma)$ and a constant v (that depends on T and σ) such that $Prob(\mathrm{E}_{R\,||\,T}(\sigma)) = \frac{M_R(r^I, tr(\sigma))}{v}$.

Let P and Q be probabilistic processes with $P{\ll}Q$. Then,

$$Prob(\mathrm{E}_{P\,||\,T}(\sigma)) \;=\; \frac{M_P(p^I, tr(\sigma))}{v} \;\leq\; \frac{M_Q(q^I, tr(\sigma))}{v} \;=\; Prob(\mathrm{E}_{Q\,||\,T}(\sigma))$$

But $\mathrm{SE}_{P\,||\,T} = \bigcup_{\sigma\in \mathrm{SE}_T} \mathrm{E}_{P\,||\,T}(\sigma)$. Moreover, $\mathrm{E}_{P\,||\,T}(\sigma) \cap \mathrm{E}_{P\,||\,T}(\sigma') = \emptyset$ whenever $\sigma \neq \sigma'$. Thus,

$$Prob(\mathrm{SE}_{P\,||\,T}) \;\leq\; Prob(\mathrm{SE}_{Q\,||\,T})$$

5 Büchi Tests

We next consider infinite probabilistic tests with a Büchi acceptance condition. Formally, a *Büchi test* is a tuple $\langle K_T, \longrightarrow_T, t^I, \mu^T, Suc_T, \mathrm{B}\rangle$ where $\langle K_T, \longrightarrow_T, t^I, \mu_T, Suc_T\rangle$ is a probabilistic test and B is a subset of K_T. T is said to be a *pure* Büchi test when Suc_T is empty. An execution of a Büchi test is said to be successful if either it is finite and ends in a state in Suc_T or it is infinite and visits B infinitely often. We use SE_T to denote the set of successful executions of a Büchi test T. This set is measurable.

If P is a probabilistic process and T is a Büchi test then $P\,||\,T$ is a Büchi test with $\mathrm{B}_{P\,||\,T} = \{(r,t) \mid t \in \mathrm{B}\}$. The probability with which P passes T is given by $Prob(\mathrm{SE}_{P\,||\,T})$. The class of Büchi tests induces a preorder $\sqsubseteq_b^{pr}$ on the set of probabilistic processes such that $P \sqsubseteq_b^{pr} Q$ if and only if, for all Büchi tests T, $Prob(\mathrm{SE}_{P\,||\,T}) \leq Prob(\mathrm{SE}_{Q\,||\,T})$.

Proposition 4. *For every Büchi test T there is a pure Büchi test T^b and a simple infinite test T^u such that, for any probabilistic process P, $Prob(\mathrm{SE}_{P\,||\,T}) = Prob_{P\,||\,T^b}(\mathrm{SE}_{P\,||\,T^b}) + Prob_{P\,||\,T^u}(\mathrm{SE}_{P\,||\,T^u})$.*

Theorem 5. $\sqsubseteq_{test}^{pr} \;=\; \ll \;=\; \sqsubseteq_b^{pr}$

Proof. (sketch) As every finite test may be treated as a Büchi test the preorder induced by Büchi tests is finer than $\ll$.

Let P and Q be probabilistic processes with $P{\ll}Q$. Let T be any pure Büchi test and R be any probabilistic process. It is easy to show that $Prob(\mathrm{SE}_{R\,||\,T}) = Prob(\bigcap_{i\in\omega} S_i^R)$, where S_i^R is the set of executions of $R\,||\,T$ that contain at least i states whose T component is from B.

Let T_i be the set of executions of T that end in a state from B and contain precisely i occurrences of states from B. Then, $S_i^R = \bigcup_{\sigma\in T_i} \mathrm{E}_{R\,||\,T}(\sigma)$. Using this characterization of S_i^R, an argument identical to that in the proof of Theorem 3 shows that $Prob(S_i^P) \leq Prob(S_i^Q)$.

Thus, $Prob(P \,||\, T) = \lim_i \{Prob(S_i^P)\}_{i \in \omega} \leq \lim_i \{Prob(S_i^Q)\}_{i \in \omega} = Prob(Q \,||\, T)$.

If T is a general Büchi test, by Proposition 4, we can decompose T into a pure Büchi test and a simple infinite test. We then use the property of pure Büchi tests established above and Theorem 3 to derive the desired result.

6 Fair Tests

In this section we will restrict ourselves to finite-state processes and tests. A state t of a fair test T is said to be *potentially successful* if there is a finite execution fragment $t = t_1 \xrightarrow{a_1} \dots \xrightarrow{a_{n-1}} t_n$ with $t_n \in Suc_T$. It is said to be *dead* otherwise. A potentially successful state that is not a success state is called a *live* state.

A finite execution of a test is said to be *successful* if it ends in a success state. An infinite execution is said to be successful if every state in the execution is potentially successful. It is not difficult to show that this set is measurable. Thus we can define the probability of a process passing a fair test and the associated preorder $\sqsubseteq_f^{pr}$.

A finite execution is said to be *potentially successful* if it ends in a potentially successful state and is said to be dead otherwise. An execution is said to be *unsuccessful* if it is not successful. An execution that ends in a live state is a *live execution.* We use SE_T, FSE_T, PSE_T, LE_T and DE_T to denote the sets of successful, finite successful, potentially successful, live and dead executions of T, respectively.

6.1 Turning Probabilistic Processes into Markov Chains

Given a probabilistic test T the process

$$Mv(T) = \langle K_T^M, \longrightarrow_T^M, t^I, \mu_T^M, Suc_{Mv(T)} \rangle$$

is defined as follows: :

$$\begin{aligned} K_T^M &= \{t^I\} \cup \{(t,a) \mid t \in K_T \;\&\; a \in Act\} \\ \mu_T^M((t,a),b,(t',b)) &= \mu_T(t,b,t') \\ \mu_T^M(t^I,a,(t',a)) &= \mu_T(t^I,a,t') \\ \mu_T^M((t,a),b,(t',c)) &= 0 \qquad\qquad \{b \neq c\} \\ \mu_T^M(t^I,a,(t,b)) &= 0 \qquad\qquad \{a \neq b\} \end{aligned}$$

The initial state of $Mv(T)$ is t^I. The set of success states of $Mv(T)$ is $Suc_{Mv(T)} = \{(t,a) \mid t \in Suc_T\}$.

We have made multiple copies of each state so that in the resulting process there is at most one transition from a given state to another. Furthermore, the transitions used in an execution can be determined merely from the sequence of states involved in the execution.

There is an obvious bijective correspondence between the set of executions of T beginning at t^I and that of *Mv*(T) beginning at t^I: The finite execution $\sigma = t^I \xrightarrow{a_1} t_2 \xrightarrow{a_2} \ldots t_N$ corresponds to the execution $Mv(\sigma) = t^I \xrightarrow{a_1} (t_2, a_1) \xrightarrow{a_2} (t_3, a_2) \ldots (t_n, a_{n-1})$ and similarly for infinite executions. We use ρ to denote this bijection.

The process *Mv*(T) is almost a Markov chain (see [Fel50]). In a Markov chain the sum of the probabilities of the transitions out of every state must be 1 while in *Mv*(T) this sum is zero for some states (at least at every success state). We make one final modification to *Mv*(T), without sacrificing the correspondence mentioned above, to turn it into a Markov chain. For each state x that has no outgoing transitions, add a self-loop labeled δ with $\mu_T^M(x, \delta, x) = 1$, where δ does not appear in Act. We continue to refer to this process as *Mv*(T).

Clearly ρ is still a bijective correspondence between executions of T beginning at t^I and those of *Mv*(T) that begins at t^I which do not make use of transitions on δ. An execution of the Markov chain *Mv*(T) is said to be *successful* if it is infinite and all the states that it visits are potentially successful or if it is finite and it visits a success state. An execution of *Mv*(T) is said to be minimally good if it ends in a success state and none of its prefixes end in success states. We write $\text{MGE}_{Mv(T)}$ for the set of minimally good executions of *Mv*(T).

Lemma 6. *The map ρ relates minimally dead executions of T with minimally dead executions of Mv(T) in a bijective manner. The map ρ (bijectively) relates the finite successful executions of T with the minimally good executions of Mv(T). Further ρ preserves probability, that is Prod(σ) = Prod($\rho(\sigma)$). The probability of success of T equals the probability of success of Mv(T).*

Lemma 7. *The success probability of Mv(T) is $\sum_{\gamma \in \text{MGE}_{Mv(T)}} Prod(\gamma)$.*

Proof. Recall, that an execution of *Mv*(T) is successful iff it is infinite and if every state it visits is potentially successful or it is finite and visits a success state. This set can be partitioned in two: the set of successful executions that visit a success state and those that don't.

Clearly, any successful execution that enters some success state necessarily belong to $[\gamma]$ for some $\gamma \in \text{MGE}_{Mv(T)}$. On the other hand, the only transition out of a success state is a self-loop and so, every execution that is in $[\gamma]$, with $\gamma \in \text{MGE}_{Mv(T)}$, is successful. Let $\text{L}_{Mv(T)}$ be the set of infinite executions of *Mv*(T) that are successful but never visit a success state.

$$\text{SE}_{Mv(T)} = \Big(\bigcup_{\gamma \in \text{MGE}_{Mv(T)}} [\gamma] \Big) \cup \text{L}_{Mv(T)}$$

Thus

$$Prob(\mathrm{SE}_{Mv(T)}) = \sum_{\gamma \in \mathrm{MGE}_{Mv(T)}} Prob([\gamma]) + Prob(\mathrm{L}_{Mv(T)})$$

We now show that $Prob(\mathrm{L}_{Mv(T)}) = 0$. (Note that since $\mathrm{L}_{Mv(T)}$ is the difference between two measurable sets it must indeed be measurable). Let

$$L_n = \bigcup_{\gamma \in \mathrm{LE}_{Mv(T)}, |\gamma|=n} [\gamma]$$

Then, $L_{n+1} \subseteq L_n$ and $\mathrm{L}_{Mv(T)} = \bigcap_{n \geq 0} L_n$. Thus,

$$Prob(\mathrm{L}_{Mv(T)}) = \lim_n \{Prob(L_n)\}_{n \in \omega}$$

Consider the underlying graph of the Markov chain $Mv(T)$ whose vertices are the states and whose edges are defined by transitions of nonzero probability. In the decomposition of this graph into its maximal strongly connected components, components containing live states will consist entirely of live states; each success state lies in a singleton maximal strongly connected component and live states are not reachable from dead states. Further the components that contain live states will necessarily have outgoing edges. In the terminology of Markov chains (see [Fel50, Shi80]) every live state is transient (or nonrecurrent). A basic result in the theory of Markov chains states that for any finite Markov chain and state q, the probability that an m length execution beginning at q ends in a transient state approaches 0 as m goes to ∞. But $Prob(L_n)$ is at most the probability that a n length run from q^I ends in a transient state. Thus the sequence $\{Prob(L_n)\}_{n \in \omega}$ must converge to 0 and thus, $Prob(Mv(S)) = \sum_{\gamma \in \mathrm{MGE}_{Mv(T)}} Prod(\gamma)$.

Now, using Lemmas 6 and 7 it is easy to establish the following theorem. In contrast, nondeterministic fair tests induce a finer preorder than finite tests even when restricted to finite-state τ-free processes and tests.

Theorem 8. $\sqsubseteq_{test}^{pr} = \ll = \sqsubseteq_f^{pr}$

6.2 Finite Probabilistic Testing Refines Fair Testing

We now show that finite probabilistic testing induces a preorder that is finer than that induced by nondeterministic fair testing. Let Erase be the mapping defined by $\mathrm{Erase}(\langle K_P, \longrightarrow_P, p^{\mathrm{I}}, \mu_P \rangle) = \langle K_P, \longrightarrow_P, p^{\mathrm{I}} \rangle$.

Theorem 9. *For finite-state probabilistic processes P and Q, $P \sqsubseteq_{test}^{pr} Q \Rightarrow$* $\mathrm{Erase}(P) \sqsubseteq_f \mathrm{Erase}(Q)$.

7 Conclusions

We have carefully examined the distinguishing power of infinite testing. For nonprobabilistic testing, we showed that Büchi testing offers no additional distinguishing power over finite testing. In the probabilistic setting, we showed that nothing new is gained by considering infinite tests, as their induced preorders coincide with finite testing. Thus, fairness fails to add to the distinguishing power of probabilistic tests. Finally, we showed that the probabilistic testing preorder refines the fair testing preorder for nondeterministic processes.

All our results assume divergence-free processes and only finite-state processes are considered in the case of probabilistic fair testing. However, the results of [CDS+98] can be extended to probabilistic processes with divergence and consequently our results for simple tests and fair tests extend to processes with divergence. As future work, we would like to investigate the probabilistic preorder induced by infinite-state fair tests.

References

[BRV95] E. Brinksma, A. Rensink, and W. Vogler. Fair testing. In *Proceedings of CONCUR '95, LNCS 962.* Springer-Verlag, 1995.

[CDS+98] R. Cleaveland, Z. Dayar, S. A. Smolka, S. Yuen, and A. Zwarico. Testing preorders for probabilistic processes. *Information and Computation*, 1998. To Appear.

[DNH83] R. De Nicola and M. C. B. Hennessy. Testing equivalences for processes. *Theoretical Computer Science*, 34:83–133, 1983.

[Fel50] William Feller. *Probability Theory and its Applications.* John Wiley and Sons, 1950.

[GSS95] R. J. van Glabbeek, S. A. Smolka, and B. Steffen. Reactive, generative, and stratified models of probabilistic processes. *Information and Computation*, 121(1):59–80, August 1995.

[Hen88] M. C. B. Hennessy. *Algebraic Theory of Processes.* MIT Press, Boston, Mass., 1988.

[JY95] B. Jonsson and W. Yi. Compositional testing preorders for probabilistic processes. In *Proceedings of LICS '95*, pages 431–441, 1995.

[NC95] V. Natarajan and R. Cleaveland. Divergence and fair testing. In *Proceedings of ICALP '95, LNCS 944*, Springer-Verlag, 1995.

[Seg96] R. Segala. Testing probabilistic automata. In *Proccedings of CONCUR '96, LNCS 1119.* Springer-Verlag, 1996.

[Shi80] A. N. Shiryayev. *Probability.* Graduate Texts in Mathematics, Springer-Verlag, 1980.

[WSS97] S.-H. Wu, S. A. Smolka, and E. W. Stark. Composition and behaviors of probabilistic I/O automata. *Theoretical Computer Science*, 176, 1997.

[YL92] W. Yi and K. G. Larsen. Testing probabilistic and nondeterministic processes. In *Protocol Specification, Testing and Verification XII*, pages 47–61. North-Holland, 1992.

On Generating Strong Elimination Orderings of Strongly Chordal Graphs

N.Kalyana Rama Prasad P.Sreenivasa Kumar

Department of Computer Science & Engineering,
Indian Institute of Technology, Madras 600 036, India

Abstract. We present a conceptually simple algorithm to generate an ordering of the vertices of an undirected graph. The ordering generated turns out to be a strong elimination ordering if and only if the given graph is a strongly chordal graph. This algorithm makes use of maximum cardinality search and lexicographic breadth first search algorithms which are used to generate perfect elimination orderings of a chordal graph. Our algorithm takes $O(k^2n)$ time where k is the size of the largest minimal vertex separator and n denotes the number vertices in the graph. The algorithm provides a new insight into the structure of strongly chordal graphs and also gives rise to a new algorithm of the same time complexity for recognition of strongly chordal graphs.

1 Introduction

The class of chordal graphs is an important and well-studied subclass of perfect graphs. Chordal graphs find applications in modeling sparse matrix computations [10], acyclic database theory[1, 2] and the theory of totally balanced matrices [7]. Strongly chordal graphs are an interesting subclass of chordal graphs. They were introduced by Farber [3], who also provided a forbidden subgraph characterization for the class. Farber and Anstee [4] showed that strongly chordal graphs are closely related to totally balanced matrices and proposed an $O(n^4)$ algorithm to recognize these graphs. Lubiw [8] proposed an $O(m^2 \log n)$ algorithm to generate a double lexical ordering of a matrix with n rows and m nonzero entries. This ordering can be used to recognize totally balanced matrices and also to recognize strongly chordal graphs. Tarjan and Paige [14] improved the complexity of the above algorithm to $O(m \log n)$ and hence recognition of strongly chordal graphs has $O(m \log n)$ time complexity. Spinrad [12] further improved this complexity to $O(n^2)$ in case the given graph is a dense graph.

Algorithms for several problems on strongly chordal graphs assume that a strong elimination ordering is given. These problems include determining independent dominating set, minimum weighted dominating set, domatic partition and minimum dominating clique [5, 9]. Thus the problem of efficiently generating a strong elimination ordering assumes a lot of importance. The algorithm of Tarjan and Paige generates a strong elimination ordering of a strongly chordal graph. For the class of chordal graphs, the LexBFS (Lexicographic Breadth First

Search) and the MCS (Maximum Cardinality Search) are two linear-time graph-traversal based algorithms that generate a perfect elimination ordering. The fact that there is no such graph-traversal based algorithm for generating strong elimination orderings is intriguing and motivated us to look for it.

Our contribution in this paper is an algorithm that generates an ordering of the vertices of a given undirected graph such that the ordering is a strong elimination ordering if and only if the given graph is strongly chordal. We find that a particular way of breaking ties when using a LexBFS algorithm leads us to the generation of a strong elimination ordering. The properties of minimal vertex separators of strongly chordal graphs and the forbidden subgraph characterization are used to prove the correctness of the new algorithm. The minimal vertex separators in turn are obtained with the help of MCS peos of chordal graphs. The complexity of the algorithm is linear except for constructing the weighted separator graph $S(G)$ (defined below) of the given graph G which takes $O(k^2n)$ time and dominates the overall time complexity. Here k denotes the maximum size of a minimal vertex separator. Lubiw shows that a matrix can be checked for Γ-freeness property in linear time which can in turn be used to check if a given ordering of the vertices is indeed a strong elimination ordering. Thus our algorithm can be used in conjunction with the above to recognize if a given graph is strongly chordal in $O(k^2n)$ time. Though the new algorithm performs better than the existing algorithm only when the separator sizes are small, it gives a new insight into the structure of strongly chordal graphs.

The paper is organized as follows. In Section 2 we give the preliminaries required. In Section 3, we present the theorems that are used in designing the algorithm. Section 4 gives the algorithm. In Section 5 we present the correctness of the algorithm. The time complexity of the algorithm is analyzed in Section 6. Section 7 contains concluding remarks and open problems.

2 Preliminaries

Through out this paper we assume that the graph $G = (V, E)$ is undirected, connected and simple. Let $N(v)$ denote the set of all vertices adjacent to v in G and $N[v]$ denote the set $N(v) \cup \{v\}$. If $S \subseteq V$ then $G[S]$ denotes the graph induced by the vertices of S in G. An undirected graph $G = (V, E)$, with $|V| = n$ and $|E| = m$ is *chordal* if every cycle of length at least four contains a chord, i.e., an edge between two vertices that are not consecutive in the cycle. A vertex v is *simplicial* if its neighbors induce a complete subgraph. An elimination ordering σ of a graph G is a bijection σ: $\{1, 2, .., n\} \rightarrow V$. Accordingly, $\sigma(i)$ is the ith vertex in the elimination ordering and $\sigma^{-1}(v)$, $v \in V$ gives the position of v in σ. We represent the graph induced by the vertex set $\{v_i, v_{i+1}, .., v_n\}$ by G_i. Neighborhood of a vertex u in G_i denoted by $N_i[u]$. A *perfect elimination ordering* (*peo*) is an elimination ordering $\sigma = (v_1, v_2, .., v_n)$ where v_i, $(1 \leq i \leq n)$ is simplicial in the graph G_i. A well known characterization of chordal graphs is that a graph is chordal if and only if it has a perfect elimination ordering [6].

A subset S of vertices $V(G)$ of a chordal graph G is a minimal *u-v separator* of G if $G[V - S]$ has at least two connected components with vertices u and v in different components, and no proper subset of S has this property with respect to u and v. A *minimal vertex separator* is a minimal *u-v separator* for some u and v of G. Through out this paper we use the word separator for minimal vertex separator.

A *strongly chordal graph* is a chordal graph in which every even cycle of length at least six has an odd chord. An odd chord is a chord joining two vertices that are at an odd distance in the cycle. A vertex v is called *simple* if the set $\{N[u] : u \in N[v]\}$ is linearly ordered by set inclusion. Note that a simple vertex is also a simplicial vertex but the converse may not be true. Farber has shown that every induced subgraph of a strongly chordal graph has a simple vertex. Successive removal of simple vertices results in a special elimination ordering. An ordering of vertices $(v_1, v_2, .., v_n)$ is called a *strong elimination ordering,* if it is a perfect elimination ordering and for each $i < j < k$ if $v_j, v_k \in N_i[v_i]$ implies $N_i[v_j] \subseteq N_i[v_k]$.

Theorem 1. *[3] A chordal graph is strongly chordal if and only if its vertices admit a strong elimination ordering.*

A *trampoline* is a chordal graph G on $2n$ vertices, for some $n \geq 3$, whose vertex set can be partitioned into two sets, $W = \{w_1, w_2, .., w_n\}$ and $U = \{u_1, u_2, .., u_n\}$, so that W is independent and for each i and j, w_i is adjacent to u_j if and only if $i = j$ or $i = j + 1(mod\ n)$ and $G[U]$ is a complete graph. A trampoline on $2n$ vertices is also called an *n- sun.* The following forbidden subgraph characterization of strongly chordal graphs is given by Farber [3].

Theorem 2. *[3] A chordal graph is strongly chordal if and only if it contains no induced* n-sun.

3 Algorithm Development

For a chordal graph $G = (V, E)$, let $S(G)$ be a weighted graph defined as follows: The vertex set of $S(G)$ consists of those vertices of G that are present in one or more separators of G and there is an edge between a pair of vertices if they both belong to same separator. The weight of an edge is the number of separators in which both of its end-points are present. We use $S(G)$ to guide the LexBFS process on G. Current-separator-weight (cur-sep-wt) of a vertex in $S(G)$ is sum of the weights of the edges incident on it and whose other end vertices have already been numbered. The cur-sep-wt of all vertices is zero before numbering of the vertices of G.

We start numbering the vertices of the given graph using LexBFS [11] from n to 1. As in LexBFS algorithm, a label, which is a string of integers, is associated with each of the vertices of the graph. A vertex is chosen arbitrarily and numbered n. All the neighbors of this vertex are given a label n. If it has neighbors in $S(G)$ then the cur-sep-wt of each of its neighbors in the graph is incremented by making use of the edge weights in $S(G)$. At any stage, the next vertex to be numbered is the one that has the lexicographically highest label. If there is a tie one of the vertices with maximum cur-sep-wt is chosen. The above process is continued until there are no more vertices to be numbered. Clearly, we are developing a perfect elimination ordering since we are using lexBFS on a chordal graph. We show that this kind of numbering in fact yields a strong elimination ordering of the vertices if the given graph is a strongly chordal graph.

We make use of Maximum Cardinality Search algorithm which was proposed by Tarjan et al [15] to test the chordality of a graph to get all the *minimal vertex separators* of a given chordal graph. This algorithm runs in $O(n+m)$ time and gives an ordering of vertices(known as MCS-peo) in case the given graph is a chordal graph. An MCS ordering σ of a chordal graph with n vertices is obtained as follows: Number the vertices from n to 1 in decreasing order. $\sigma(i)$ is the vertex that receives the number i. $\sigma(n)$ is chosen arbitrarily. As the next vertex to number, select the vertex that is adjacent to the largest number of currently numbered vertices, breaking the ties arbitrarily.

Given a peo σ of a chordal graph G, $N(v,\sigma)$ denotes the set of vertices adjacent to v that appear later than v in σ. That is

$$N(v,\sigma) = \{x \in N(v), \sigma^{-1}(x) > \sigma^{-1}(v)\}$$

The set $N(v,\sigma)$ is called the *monotone adjacency set* of v, with respect to σ. Note that graph G can be constructed by starting with an empty graph and by adding vertices in the order $\sigma(n), \sigma(n-1)...\sigma(1)$ making each added vertex v adjacent to all the vertices of $N(v,\sigma)$. For a chordal graph G and peo σ, $G_i(\sigma)$ is the subgraph of G induced by the set $V_i(\sigma) = \{\sigma(j) : j \geq i\}$.

An algorithmic characterization of minimal vertex separators of a chordal graph in terms of the monotone adjacency sets of an MCS-peo was given in [13] which we mention here for ease of reference. The following Lemma 3 and Lemma 4 show that during maximum cardinality search of a chordal graph G, whenever the size of the monotone adjacency set doesn't increase from one stage to the next, a minimal vertex separator of G is detected and all the minimal vertex separators can be detected this way.

Algorithm MinimalVertexSeparators;
Input: A chordal graph and a MCS peo σ
Output: All the Minimal Vertex Separators
begin
    for all $v \in V(G)$ determine $N(v,\sigma)$;
    for $i = n-1$ down to 1 do
        begin
            if $|N(\sigma(i),\sigma)| \leq |N(\sigma(i+1),\sigma)|$ then
            $N(\sigma(i),\sigma)$ is a minimal vertex separator.
        end
end.

Lemma 3. *[13] Let σ be an MCS peo of a chordal graph G and $\sigma(t) = v, \sigma(t+1) = u$. If $|N(v,\sigma)| > |N(u,\sigma)|$ then $N(v,\sigma) = N(u,\sigma) + 1$ and $N(v,\sigma) = N(u,\sigma) \cup \{u\}$.Further $N(v,\sigma)$ is not a minimal vertex separator of $G_t(\sigma)$.*

Lemma 4. *[13] Let σ be an MCS peo of a chordal graph G and $\sigma(t) = v$, $\sigma(t+1) = u$. If $|N(v,\sigma)| \leq |N(u,\sigma)|$ then $N(v,\sigma)$ is a minimal vertex separator of G.*

Thus, given a chordal graph G and an MCS peo σ for G all of its minimal vertex separators can be determined using the algorithm **MinimalVertexSeparators**.

4 Algorithm

Algorithm SEO-Ordering
Input : A chordal graph
Output: An elimination ordering
begin

1. Find all the separators of the given chordal graph making use of MCS and form the weighted graph $S(G)$. Give a weight to each edge of the graph $S(G)$ which is equal to the number of separators in which the edge is present. Set the *cur-sep-wt* of all the vertices of G to zero.
2. Start numbering the vertices of the graph G from n to 1 using Lex-BFS. Number any vertex with n. If it has neighbors in $S(G)$ then increment the cur-sep-wt of each of its neighbors by the corresponding edge weight. Update the labels of the neighbors (in G) of the numbered vertex just as in LexBFS (i.e., by appending the number n to their labels).
3. Pick a vertex, say u, that has the lexicographically highest label. Number this vertex with the next available highest number, say x. If it has neighbors in $S(G)$ then update their cur-sep-wt. Also update the labels of the neighbors of u in G by appending x to the labels.
4. If there is a tie in the above step choose any vertex that has the maximum cur-sep-wt.
5. Repeat the steps 3 and 4 until there is no vertex that is to be numbered.

end

5 Correctness

We establish the correctness of the algorithm presented in the previous section with the help of a crucial observation that captures the two basic conditions that arise when a violation of the strong elimination property of the peo being generated by the algorithm occurs for the first time. We state the observation in the following lemma. For convenience, we refer to the vertices of G by the numbers assigned to them by the numbering scheme. Note that if $x > y$ then vertex x is numbered before y.

Lemma 5. *Let a numbering scheme be generated by the algorithm SEO-ordering. Let the vertices r, p, q, and j be such that $r > p > q > j$. Let r, p, q form a clique, $jq \in E$, $jr \in E$, and $jp \notin E$. Then either*
(i) there exists a vertex $w > q$ such that $wp \in E$, $wr \in E$ and $wq \notin E$, or
(ii) there exists $w > p, w' > j$, such that r, p, q and w form a 4-clique with $w'p \in E$, $w'w \in E$, $w'q \notin E$, and $w'r \notin E$.

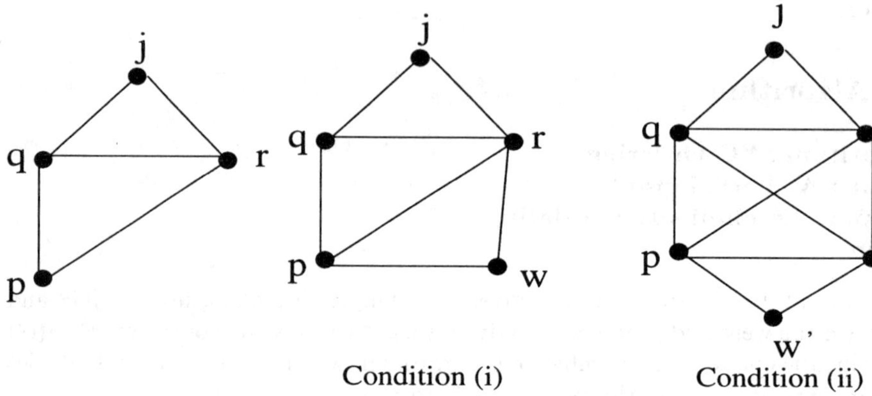

Fig. 1. The cases of Lemma 5

Proof: We are given that $p > q$. Hence when p is chosen either p has lexicographically higher label than q or p and q have the same label and p is chosen in the tie. Let p have lexicographically higher label. This implies that there exists one vertex w which is already numbered and is adjacent to p but not adjacent to q i.e., $pw \in E$ and $qw \notin E$. Since $r, w > p$, by peo property, $rw \in E$. Hence we have a $w > p$ such that it is adjacent to p, r and not adjacent to q. Thus condition(i) of lemma holds.

Let p and q have the same lexicographic labels. Now, p must have at least as much *cur-sep-wt* as that of q. Clearly $\{q, r\}$ is a subset of a separator between j and p. Hence when r is numbered q will get a *cur-sep-wt* of 1. Hence p must have a *cur-sep-wt* of at least 1. Moreover, there must be a separator which contains p but not q, for if every separator that contains p also contains q , then the *cur-sep-wt* of q is more than that of p since there is a separator which contains q but not p (this is nothing but the one that contains $\{q, r\}$ separating j and p). Hence there exists a vertex w which is numbered earlier to p, q and $\{p, w\}$ is a subset of a separator which does not contain q.

The above mentioned w may be r itself. That is $\{p, r\}$ is a separator. If this is so condition (i) of the lemma holds as there is a vertex w' such that $\{p, r\}$ is a separator for w', q. If w is not r then condition (ii) of the lemma holds as there is a vertex w' with q, w' being separated by $\{p, w\}$. Now $qw \in E$ if not $\{p, r\}$ would have been a subset of a separator between q and w, this is not true because we assumed that $\{p, r\}$ is not contained in the separator which contains only p but not q. Hence $qw \in E$. $rw \in E$ since r, w are higher neighbors of p. Also $pw' \in E$ and $ww' \in E$. Notice that $w' > j$ since w' has lexicographically higher label than j. □

Theorem 6. *Numbering the vertices of a graph G using the SEO-algorithm generates a strong elimination ordering if and only if the given graph is a strongly chordal graph.*

Proof: The only if part of the proof is obvious. For the if part, we prove the contrapositive. Let us suppose that when a vertex is numbered with number i, for the first time in the numbering process the strong elimination property is violated. That is there are two vertices with numbers p, q such that $p > q > i$, and p, q are adjacent to i but $N(q) \not\subseteq N(p)$. This implies that there exists a vertex j' such that $j' \in N(q)$ but $j' \notin N(p)$. The following arguments show that if such a situation arises there is an induced *n-sun*. Choose $j = max\{\ j' | j' \in N(q)\ and\ j' \notin N(p)\}$. Since $j > i$ and $jp \notin E$, j has lexicographically higher label than i. Hence there exists a r' which is already numbered and is adjacent to j but not to i. Choose $r = max\ \{\ r' > p\ such\ that\ r'j \in E\ and\ r'i \notin E\}$. See Figure 2(b).

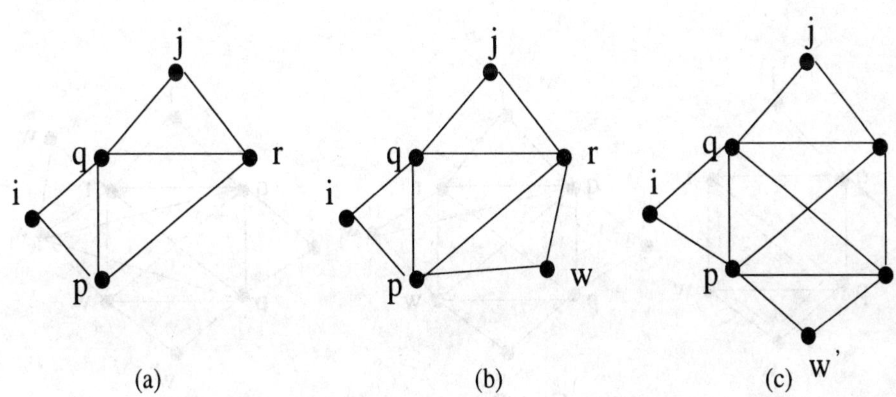

Fig. 2. Strong elimination property failing at i

Considering $r > p > q > j > i$ and existing adjacencies it follows by peo property that $pr \in E$ $qr \in E$. Now apply the Lemma 5 to r, p, q, j. Suppose condition (i) of the Lemma 5 occurs. Then there is a $w > j$ such that $wp \in E$, $wr \in E$ and $wq \notin E$. If $jw \in E$ then by peo property $qw \in E$. Also if $iw \in E$ then $qw \in E$. Hence there is an induced *3-sun*.

Suppose condition (ii) of the Lemma 5 occurs. Then there exists w and w' such that $w > p$ and $q > w' > j$ with $pw \in E$ $w'p \in E, w'w \in E, w'q \notin E\ and\ w'r \notin E$. Here again $iw' \notin E$ and $jw' \notin E$ for if $iw' \in E$, by peo property

$w'q$ would be an edge and if $jw' \in E$, by peo property $w'q$ would be an edge. Hence $i, j,$ *and* w' are independent. Now two cases arise.

Case A: $r > w$

Apply the Lemma 5 to $r > w > q > j$. Two sub cases arise corresponding to the two conditions of the lemma. Refer to Figure 3.

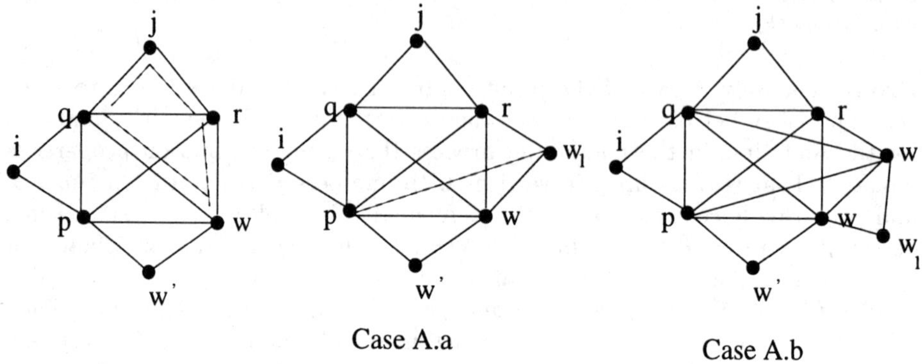

Fig. 3. The case when $r > w$

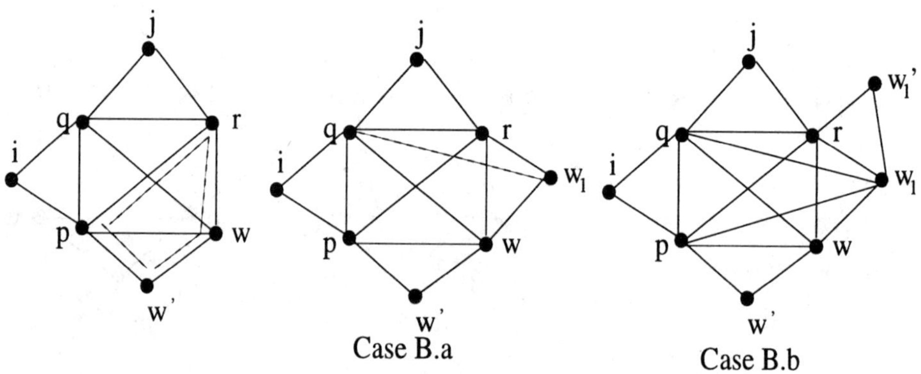

Fig. 4. The case when $w > r$

Case A.a: There is a $w_1 > q$ such that $w_1 w \in E$,$w_1 r \in E$ and $w_1 q \notin E$. Now $w_1 p \in E$ or $w_1 p \notin E$. In the former case, there would be an induced 3-sun and in the latter case there would be an induced 4-sun in the graph.

Case A.b: There exists w_1, w_1', such that $w_1 > w$ $w_1 w \in E, w_1 w_1' \in E$, and $w w_1' \in E$. Here, $p w_1 \in E$, for p and w are greater than q and are neighbors of q. We note that Lemma 5 can again be applied and an additional independent vertex of a sun can be discovered.

Case B: $w > r$
Now apply the Lemma 5 to $w > r > p > w'$. Here again two cases arise. Refer to Figure 4.
Case B.a : There exists a w_1 such that $w_1 r \in E$, $w_1 w \in E$ and $w_1 p \notin E$. Again, either $w_1 q \in E$ or $w_1 q \notin E$. In the former case, we have a 3-sun and in the latter there exists a 4-sun.
Case B.b: There exists w_1 and w_1' such that $rw_1 \in E, w_1 w_1' \in E, rw_1' \in E$ and $pw_1' \in E$.

If $w_1 q \notin E$, then p, q, r, i, j, w_1 would be a 3-sun and we will be through. Otherwise Lemma 5 can again be applied and and an additional independent vertex of a sun can be discovered.

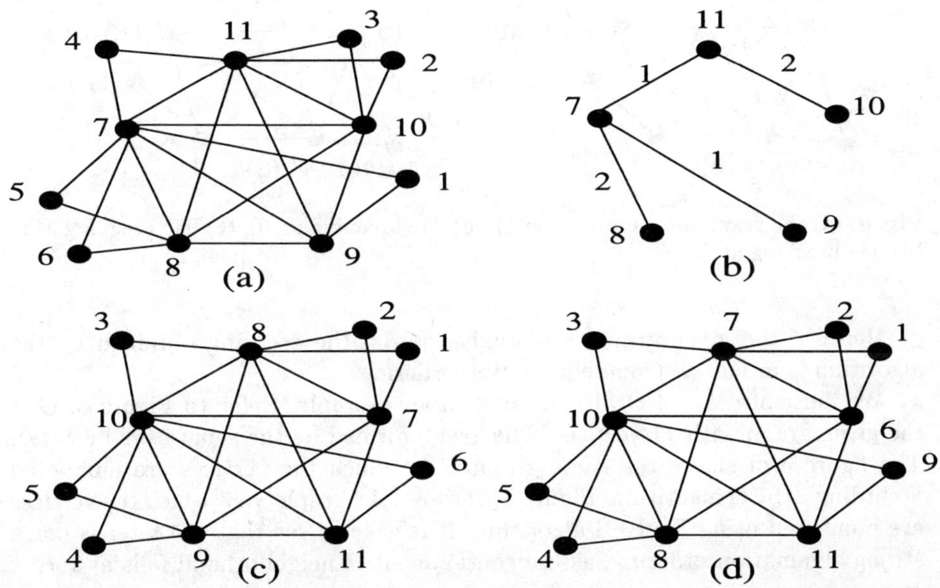

Fig. 5. (a) The given graph G. (b) The graph $S(G)$. (c) An ordering generated by SEO. (d) An ordering generated by LexBFS.

As noted earlier, in the cases A.b and B.b the Lemma 5 can be further applied and in this way the independent vertices of the sun are identified and the size of the sun keeps growing. The process of discovering independent vertices cannot proceed infinitely as there are only finite vertices in the already numbered graph. Eventually, we reach a stage where there is no need to further discover the independent vertices and when this stage is reached the entire induced *n-sun* is discovered. (Note that all the sun vertices are numbered earlier to i). Hence whenever there is a failure of the strong elimination property in the ordering it can be shown that there is an induced *n-sun* among the already numbered vertices.

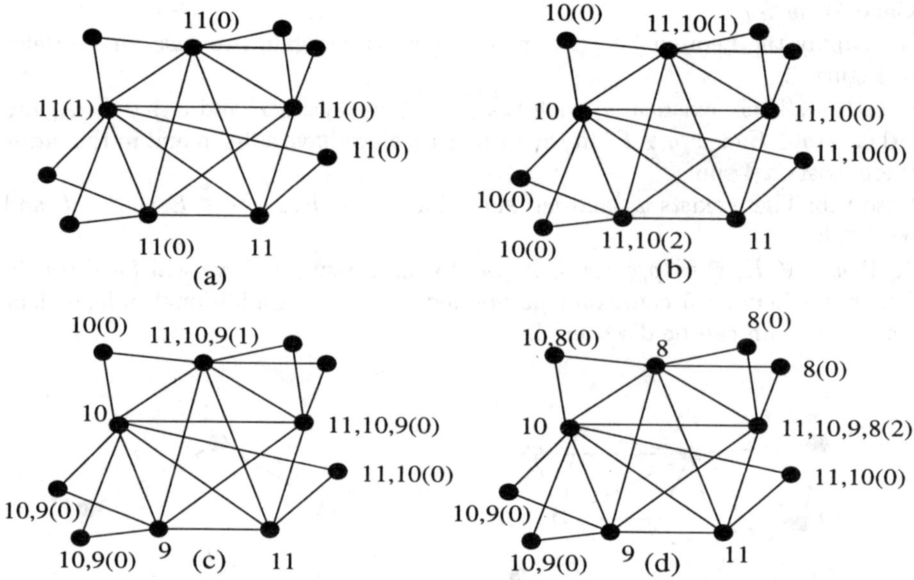

Fig. 6. (a)The graph after numbering 11 (b) Tie breaking at 10. (c) Tie breaking at 9. (d) Tie breaking at 8.

Hence if the given graph is strongly chordal the ordering obtained by the algorithm is in fact a strong elimination ordering. □

We illustrate the SEO algorithm with an example. Refer to Figure 5. G is the given graph with 11 vertices. The graph formed by the separators be $S(G)$. The figure 5(c) shows the same graph G in which the vertices are numbered according to SEO algorithm. Figure 5(d) shows the graph G, in which the vertices are numbered using LexBFS algorithm. It is easy to see that the later is not a strong elimination ordering. as the containment of neighborhood fails at vertex 1.

The first few stages of the algorithm are given in the Figure 6. The lexicographic labels at each vertex are given as a string of integers and are separated by commas. At each vertex the number in the brackets indicates the cur-sep-weight.

6 Complexity

The complexity of the proposed algorithm can be analyzed as follows. Determining the edge weights of $S(G)$ dominates the computation. Except for this the algorithm takes linear time. To construct the weighted graph $S(G)$, one has to traverse all the edges in each of the separators and hence it takes $O(k^2n)$ time where k is the size of the largest minimal vertex separator and n denotes the number of vertices in the graph.

Now to find out whether or not the given graph is strongly chordal, one has to just check for the Γ-freeness of the adjacency matrix ordered according to the ordering generated by the algorithm. Checking Γ-freeness can be done in time proportional to $O(n+m)$ making use of the technique explained in [8]. Hence *strongly chordal graphs* can be recognized in $O(k^2n)$ time.

7 Conclusions

In this paper we have presented an algorithm to generate a strong elimination ordering of a given strongly chordal graph. We use MCS to compute separator sizes and propose a tie-breaking strategy for LexBFS using the separator sizes such that it generates a strong elimination ordering. The complexity of the algorithm is determined by the cost of computing the edge weights for $S(G)$ and is $O(k^2n)$.The algorithm can be used to recognize strongly chordal graphs in the same time complexity. It would be very interesting to get a better bound for constructing edge weights of $S(G)$.

References

1. C Beeri, R Fagin, D Maier and M Yannakakis, *On the desirability of acyclic database schemes*, Jl. of ACM, 30, 1983, pp: 479-513.
2. R Fagin, *Degrees of Acyclicity for hypergraph and relational database schemes*, Jl. of ACM, 30, 1983, pp: 514-550.
3. M Farber, *Characterization of Strongly Chordal Graphs*, Discrete Math.,43, 1983, pp: 173-189.
4. M Farber and R P Anstee *Characterization of Totally Balanced Matrices*, Jl. of Algorithms, 5, 1984, pp: 215-230.
5. M Farber, *Domination, Independent Domination and Duality in Strongly Chordal Graphs*, Discrete Applied Mathematics, 7, 1884, pp: 115-130.
6. M C Golumbic, *Algorithmic Graph Theory and Perfect Graphs*,Academic Press, New York, 1980.
7. Jeno Lehel, *A characterization of totally balanced matrices*, Discrete Mathematics, 57, 1985, pp: 59-65.
8. Anna Lubiw, *Double Lexical Ordering of matrices*, SIAM Jl. of Computing, 16(5), Oct 1987, pp: 854-879.
9. Shen-Lung Peng and Maw-Shang Chang, *A simple linear-time algorithm for the domatic prtition problem on strongly chordal graphs*, Information processing Letters, 43, 1992, pp: 297-300.
10. D J Rose, *A graph-theoretic study of the numerical solution of sparse positive definite systems of linear equations*, in "R C Reed (ed.), Graph Theory and Computing, Academic Press, 1972", pp: 183-217.
11. D J Rose, R E Tarjan and G S Lueker, *Algorithmic Aspects of Vertex Elimination on Graphs*, SIAM Jl. of Computing, 5, 1976, pp: 266-283.
12. J P Spinrad, *Doubly Lexical Ordering of Dense 0-1 Matrices*, Information Processing Letters, 45, 1993, pp: 229-235.
13. P Sreenivasa Kumar and C E Veni Madhavan, *2-Separator Chordal Graphs*, Proceedings of National Seminar on Theoretical Computer Science, Kharagpur, India, 1993, pp: 37-52.
14. R E Tarjan and R Paige,*Three Partition Refinement Algorithm* , SIAM Jl. Computing, 16, 1987, pp: 973-989.

15. M Yannakakis and R E Tarjan , *Simple Linear-time Algorithms to Test Chordality of Graphs, Test acyclicity of Hypergraphs and Selectively Reduce Acyclic Hypergraphs*, SIAM Jl. Computing, 13(3), 1984, pp: 565-579.

A Parallel Approximation Algorithm for Minimum Weight Triangulation

(Extended abstract)

Joachim Gudmundsson Christos Levcopoulos

Department of Computer Science
Lund University, Box 118, S-221 00 Lund, Sweden
{christos,joakim}@dna.lth.se

Abstract. We show a parallel algorithm that produces a triangulation which is within a constant factor longer than the Minimum Weight Triangulation (MWT) in time $O(\log n)$ using $O(n)$ processors and linear space in the CRCW PRAM model. This is done by developing a relaxed version of the quasi-greedy triangulation algorithm. The relaxed version produces edges that are at most $(1+\epsilon)$ longer than the shortest diagonal, where ϵ is some positive constant smaller than 1, still outputs a triangulation which is within a constant factor longer that the minimum weight triangulation. However, if the same method is applied to the straightforward greedy algorithm the approximation behavior may deteriorate dramatically, i.e. $\Omega(n)$ longer than a minimum weight triangulation, if the lengths of the edges are not computed with high precision.

1 Introduction

Planar triangulation is important because of its multitude of practical applications in surface interpolation, for calculations in numerical analysis and graphical display. Also other important computational geometry problems, like geometric searching and polyhedron intersection, use planar triangulations as a preprocessing phase. There are several optimality criteria which are used to measure how good a triangulation is. One criterion which has been studied extensively in the literature is the total length of the edges. Hence, the triangulation of minimum total length is sometimes called the optimal triangulation.

A *planar straight-line graph* or PSLG is a graph G which consists of a finite set of vertices S, and an edge set E. The vertices in S correspond to distinct points in the plane. A diagonal of G is an open straight-line segment with endpoints in S neither intersecting any edges of G nor including any vertex of G. A *triangulation* of G is a maximal set of non-intersecting diagonals of G. The length of a PSLG T, denoted by $|T|$, is the total edge length in T. A *minimum weight triangulation* of S or MWT(S) is a triangulation of S such that $|T|$ is minimized. Gilbert [2] showed that it can be computed for simple polygons in time $O(n^3)$ by dynamic programming. However, for general point sets, it is unknown whether the MWT can be computed in polynomial time, let alone whether it is in NC. Until recently there did not even exist any polynomial approximation algorithm which was known to guarantee a constant approximation factor. Therefore heuristics for approximating MWT have been considered.

There are several well-known heuristics, for example the *Delaunay triangulation*, *greedy triangulation* and the *quasi-greedy triangulation*. The *Delaunay triangulation* is the dual of the Voronoi diagram. Kirkpatrick [4] showed that for each n one can place n points so that the Delaunay triangulation has length $\Omega(n)$ times the optimum. The greedy triangulation of S, abbreviated GT(S), is obtained by repeatedly producing a shortest possible edge that doesn't intersect any of the previously generated edges. The worst-case ratio between the greedy triangulation and the MWT is $\Theta(\sqrt{n})$, for any n, shown in [8, 5]. Although the greedy triangulation and the Delaunay triangulation can yield "bad" approximations, there are some special cases for which they have been proved to perform well. For example, if the points are uniformly distributed, both the Delaunay triangulation and the greedy triangulation are expected to be within a constant factor from the optimum [1, 10]. Also, if the points lie on their convex hull, then the greedy triangulation approximates the optimum [9]. The only known polynomial time heuristic for the MWT which achieves a constant-factor approximation ratio is the so-called quasi-greedy triangulation (QT), presented by Levcopoulos and Krznaric in [8]. They showed that there is only one certain configuration of points for which the greedy doesn't approximate the optimal. So by handling this case as a special case they achieved a constant factor approximation.

Merks [13] proposed a parallel algorithm which triangulates a set of n points in $O(\log n)$ time using a linear number of processors and $O(n)$ space. The algorithm works by reducing the problem of triangulating a set of points in the convex hull of the points to triangulate the points inside triangles. Another parallel algorithm was proposed by Wang and Tsin [14] which achieves the same results in the CREW PRAM model, but with a different decomposition of the problem. They partition the set of points into $\sqrt{n}$ subsets, then triangulate within the convex hulls and funnel polygons which are formed by the partition. These parallel algorithms are optimal both concerning time and number of processors, since a triangulation algorithm can be used to sort and sorting has a parallel time lower bound of $\Omega(\log n)$. But, none of these algorithms are designed to approximate the MWT. We will present a parallel approximation algorithm for the MWT problem. Using $O(n)$ processors and linear space, the algorithm runs in $O(\log n)$ time and achieves a triangulation which is within a constant factor longer than the optimal. Since $\Omega(n \log n)$ is the lower bound on the time complexity for the triangulation problem in sequential computation, the algorithm is optimal with respect to the time-processor product. The computer model we use is the CRCW PRAM which allows concurrent reads and writes.

The paper is divided into two main parts. In Section 3 we present the parallel triangulation algorithm, and show that it runs in logarithmic time and uses linear amount of space. In Section 4 we prove that the length of the produced triangulation is within a constant factor longer than the optimum. The results in section 4 are achieved by generalizing the corresponding results in [8, 9]. The proofs omitted in this extended abstract can be found in [3].

2 Relaxed Greedy or Quasi-Greedy

In 1995 Levcopoulos, Lingas and Wang [12] showed that the problem of producing the greedy triangulation (or even deciding whether an edge belongs to the greedy triangulation) is P-complete (P-complete are the problems in P that are most resistant to parallelization), and since the quasi-greedy algorithm is a slightly modified version of the greedy algorithm it is easy to show that it also is P-complete by following the proof in [12]. This implies that some relaxations of the two algorithms are necessary to obtain an efficient parallel algorithm with good approximation factor. A natural approach would be to relax the requirement of only adding the shortest edge to the triangulation. Is this possible? First we study the relaxed greedy algorithm RGT, that is the RGT adds a shortest or an almost shortest edge to the triangulation. We shall see that the approximation behavior of the greedy algorithm may deteriorate dramatically, if the length of the edges are not computed with high precision.

A relaxed greedy triangulation algorithm RGT is said to be *ϵ-relaxed* (ϵ-RGT) iff it produces all edges that are at most $(1+\epsilon)$, $\epsilon>0$, times longer than the shortest possible edge that doesn't properly intersect any of the previously generated edges. We start with the following important definition.

Definition 1. *(Definition 6.1 in [6]) A concave chain of a PSLG G is a maximal sequence $v_1, \ldots, v_m$ of at least three vertices (v_1 and v_m may be the same vertex but all others are distinct) such that for $k=1,\ldots,m-1$, (v_k, v_{k+1}) are edges of G, and for $k=2,\ldots,m-1$, (v_k, v_{k+1}) is the next edge around v_k in clockwise order from (v_k, v_{k+1}) and with angle $\geq 180°$.*

Observation 1. *There exists a set S of n points such that* $\frac{|\epsilon-RGT(S)|}{|MWT(S)|}=\Omega(n)$.

Proof. Suppose that we have an ϵ-relaxed greedy algorithm ϵ-RGT. Let $C_1 = \{c_1^1, c_1^2, \ldots, c_1^t\}$ be a nearly horizontal concave chain, the points are ordered from left to right, such that c_1^p lies to the left and above c_1^{p+1} where $1\leq p<t$. And, let $C_2=\{c_2^1, c_2^2, \ldots, c_2^r\}$ be a nearly vertical concave chain, the points are ordered from bottom to top, such that c_2^p lies to the left and below c_1^{p+1} where $1\leq p<r$. The chain C_2 lies above and to the left of C_1, Fig. 1. The number of points in C_1 is $t=m$ and the number of points in C_2 is $r=\log m$. We will denote by $|ab|$ the distance between two points a and b. Let $|c_1^1c_2^1|=l$, $|c_1^1c_1^t|=\epsilon'$, $|c_2^ic_2^{i+1}|=(1+\epsilon')^i\cdot l-l$, and the total distance between c_2^1 and c_2^r is approximately 1.

In a $\epsilon-RGT$ of these points the following is a possible scenario: c_1^1 will be connected to every point in C_2, and then c_2^r will be connected to $c_1^2, c_1^3, \ldots, c_1^t$, Fig. 1. The total edge length added to $\epsilon-RGT$ is $\sum_{i=1}^r |c_1^1c_2^i|+\sum_{i=2}^t |c_2^rc_1^i|\geq t=m$

In a MWT the point c_2^1 will be connected to all the points in C_1 and then c_1^t will be connected to all the points in C_2. The total edge length added to MWT is $\sum_{i=1}^t |c_2^1c_1^i|+\sum_{i=2}^r |c_1^tc_2^i|= \epsilon'\cdot l+2=O(1)$. If $m=n-\log n=O(n)$ then we obtain the observation $\frac{\epsilon-RGT}{MWT}=\Omega(n)$.

By this result it is easy to see that we can't relax the standard greedy algorithm, and still get a non-trivial approximation factor. Note that this implies that using the greedy algorithm in the sequential case requires that the length of the edges must be computed with high precision, otherwise the approximation behavior of the algorithm may deteriorate dramatically. Is it possible to use a relaxed version of the quasi-greedy algorithm?

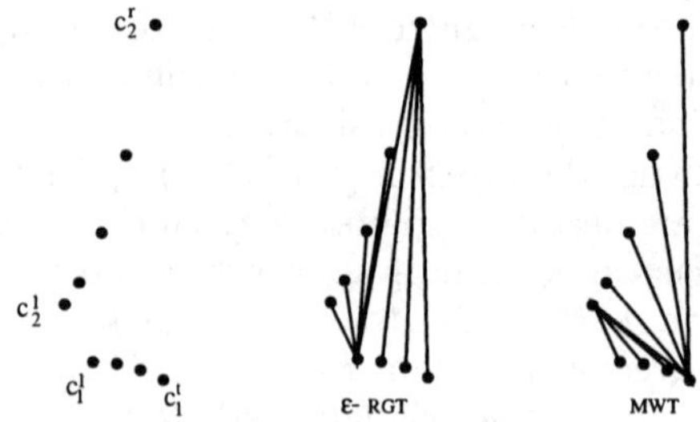

Fig. 1.

3 Parallel Relaxed Quasi-Greedy Triangulation (PRQT)

In this section we present a parallel approximation algorithm that runs in logarithmic time and uses linear space, in the CRCW PRAM model. Next, in Section 4 we prove that the length of the resulting triangulation is within a constant factor longer than the optimum. Let S be a set of n points in the plane. The general idea is to partition the points into subsets and then for each subset produce the locally shortest edges of length at most $(1+\epsilon)\cdot l$, where l is the shortest diagonal of S and ϵ is some constant greater than zero. A special case which we treat separately is when we have l-compvertices, that is a set of vertices that form concave chains, see Definition 2. An l-compvertex will be treated as one single vertex, that is if one vertex in the l-compvertex is to be connected to a vertex not in the l-compvertex, then all other vertices in the l-compvertex are also connected to that vertex.

We need the following definitions from [6].

Definition 2. *An* l-compvertex *(compound vertex) of a PSLG G is a subsequence $v_1, \ldots, v_m$ of a concave chain of G which satisfies the following two properties:*

1. the distance between v_1 and v_m is less than $l \cdot \frac{\epsilon}{8}$, and
2. when we walk on the edges $(v_1, v_2), \ldots, (v_{m-1}, v_m)$, we don't change direction more than 45 degrees in total.

The points in an l-compvertex that aren't endpoints are denoted the *interior points* of the l-compvertex. Let $C=\{v_1, \ldots, v_m\}$ be an l-compvertex in G. C is said to *face* a vertex w not in C iff w can be connected to a vertex v_i, $1 \leq i \leq m$, in C such that $\angle v_{i-1}v_iw$ plus $\angle wv_iv_{i+1}$ is at least 180°.

Definition 3. *We say that a simple polygon P is bipartite iff the vertices of P can be partitioned into two subsets, called poles of P, in such a way that each pole has the following two properties:*

- each vertex of the pole lies on the convex hull of the pole, and
- the convex hull of the pole and the interior of P do not overlap.

A bipartite polygon P is called l-bipartite if, given a partition of its vertices into poles, the distance between any two vertices in the same pole is less than l.

Let v be a vertex of G. If all greedy triangles incident to v have been produced, then v is said to be *hidden*, otherwise we say that v is *manifest*. A manifest vertex v is called an *isolvertex* unless the following two conditions hold simultaneously: (i) there are vertices u and w such that u, v, w is a subsequence of an l-compvertex, and (ii) all greedy triangles incident to v and overlapping with the interior of the convex hull of $\{u, v, w\}$ have been produced.

Now, we are ready to state the following useful fact:

Fact 1. *(Lemma 6.6 in [6]) Let G be any PSLG and let l be the length of the shortest diagonal of G. Assume that all l-bipartite polygons of G are fully triangulated, and that all edges of G that are not inside an l-bipartite polygon have length less than l. Then, given any legal set of l-compvertices of G, and any circle C of radius $O(l)$, C contains $O(1)$ l-compvertices and isolvertices of G.*

To be able to use this result for our algorithm we have to fulfill the condition given in the fact, i.e. all l-bipartite polygons are fully triangulated. This is done by treating the set of vertices in an l-compvertex as a single vertex, that is if a vertex v is to be connected to a vertex c in an l-compvertex C, facing v, then all the vertices in C are also connected to v. If v is a vertex in an l-compvertex C' and C' is facing C then we triangulate the region between C and C'. It is easy to see that the algorithm will fulfill the condition in Fact 1, hence we can use this result when analyzing our algorithm.

The algorithm will be described in pseudo-code, but first we present the algorithm more informally. For convenience we assume that the largest distance between two points in S is 1. Let Q be a square with sides of length 1 that entirely includes S. Every point s in S is assigned its own processor, denoted $P(s)$. These processors are numbered from 1 to n. Start by partitioning the set of points S into subsets. Then the algorithm checks, for each subset, if there are any locally shortest edges of length at most $(1+\epsilon)$ times longer than the globally shortest edge in the subset. If there exists such an edge then this edge is added to the triangulation, provided that the endpoints of the edge don't belong to an l-compvertex. Otherwise, if any of the two endpoints belongs to an l-compvertex then the algorithm triangulates the vertices of the l-compvertex or l-compvertices. The algorithm will add edges in $O(\log n)$ iterations, where each iteration takes $O(1)$ time.

Algorithm PRQT(S)

1. $G \leftarrow \{S, \emptyset\}$
2. $l \leftarrow \frac{1}{10n}$
3. Triangulate all vertices lying closer than $\frac{1}{9n}$ to each other.
4. Find all concave chains, and partition them into l-compvertices.
5. Let Q be a square with sides of length 1 that entirely includes S. Construct a grid within Q, such that the squares have length and height $t=1/n$. The squares in Q are denoted $T_1, T_2, \ldots, T_{O(n^2)}$. Note that according to Fact 1 there are only $O(1)$ l-compvertices and isolvertices in each square.
6. **While** G is not a triangulation of S **do**
   (a) For every possible pair of l-compvertices, denoted C_1 and C_2 in T, lying at distance between l and $(1+\epsilon) \cdot l$ from each other, we check whether there exists a tangent that touches the interior points of C_1 and C_2. If there exists such a tangent, partition C_1 respectively C_2 into two l-compvertices.

(b) **Repeat** (until the entire neighborhood of T is checked)
In the first iteration we check the diagonals with both endpoints in T and in the next eight iterations we check the diagonals with one endpoint in T and one endpoint in any of T's eight adjacent squares (one iteration for each adjacent square). In the first iteration let E be the set of all locally shortest edges, within T, of length between l and $(1+\epsilon')\cdot l$, where $\epsilon'=\epsilon/4$. In the next eight iterations let E be the set of all locally shortest edges of length between l and $(1+\epsilon')\cdot l$, with one endpoint in T and one endpoint in its active neighbor. For each edge e in E with at least one endpoint in an l-compvertex check the six conditions in the quasi-greedy algorithm. When we use the quasi-greedy algorithm we set the multiplicative factor to $1+\frac{\epsilon}{4}$ instead of 1.1 suggested in the standard quasi-greedy algorithm. If the quasi-greedy algorithm suggests a different edge e' then remove e from E and add e'. Now, for all edges $e_1, \ldots, e_b$ in E do the following:
   i. All edges in E that don't have an endpoint in an l-compvertex is added to G.
   ii. If an edge $e \in E$ has exactly one endpoint in $c \in C$, where C is an l-compvertex, one endpoint in $s \in S$ and C is facing s then add to G all possible edges between s and C. Remove the points in C connected to s from the l-compvertex C. The points removed from C are now seen as ordinary isolvertices or hidden vertices. The same is done if s belongs to an l-compvertex C' and C' isn't facing C. Otherwise, if C isn't facing s then just add the edge between s and the interior vertex in c.
   iii. If an edge's both endpoints c_1 and c_2 belong to l-compvertices that face each other then triangulate the region between C and C'. Otherwise, if C doesn't face C' and C' doesn't face C then add the edge between c_1 and c_2 to G.

Until all locally shortest edges of length between l and $(1+\epsilon')\cdot l$ with at least one endpoint in T are checked.

(c) $l \leftarrow (1+\epsilon')\cdot l$
(d) Check if there are any new concave chains.
(e) Merge every incident pair of l-compvertices whose combined total edge length is $\leq l\cdot\frac{\epsilon}{8}$.
(f) If $t \leq 4l$ then merge the squares such that each square in Q has height and length $2t$, hence set $t \leftarrow 2t$

end while
Return G

3.1 The non-trivial steps

Note that the condition in Fact 1 is fulfilled since the algorithm checks in step 6bi-iii if a possible edge has one or both endpoints in an l-compvertex. Before we go into the details we have to note that the number of iterations of the while-loop is $\log_{(1+\epsilon')} n$ since the value of l increases for each iteration, and the number of iterations of the repeat-loop is exactly nine. So to prove that the algorithm works in time $O(\log n)$ we need to prove that each step within the while-loop takes constant time to compute in parallel.

3. *Triangulate all vertices lying closer than* $\frac{1}{9n}$ *to each other.*
Let Q' be a square with sides of length 1 that entirely includes S. Construct a grid within Q', such that the squares have length and height $\frac{1}{9n}$. The

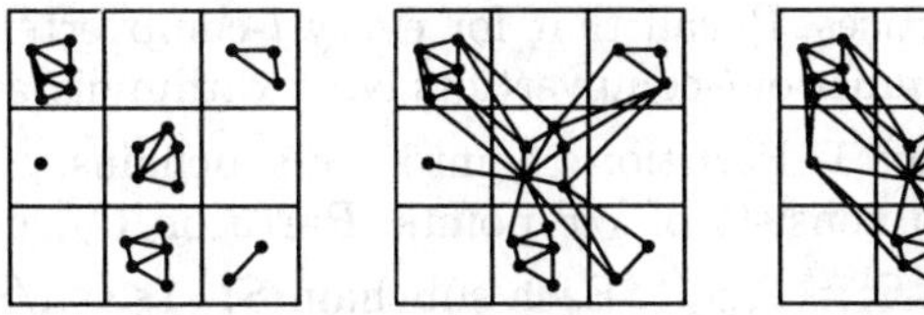

(a) (b) (c)

Fig. 2.

squares in Q' are denoted $T'_{i,j}$, $1{\le}i,j{\le}9n$. For each non-empty square $T'_{i,j}$ triangulate the convex hull of the points within $T'_{i,j}$, Fig. 2a. If there are only two points then produce an edge between these.
Let $T'_{i,j}$ be any square in Q'. For each non-empty neighboring square B of $T'_{i,j}$ we draw two edges between the convex hull in $T'_{i,j}$ and the convex hull in B, such that the region bounded partly by these two segments are maximized. The bounded region is then triangulated, by using some known parallel triangulation algorithm. This is done for each of the, at most eight, non-empty neighbors of $T'_{i,j}$. Finally, we check if there are any bounded regions within $T'_{i,j}$ and its eight neighbors that are not triangulated. If there are such regions (at most eight) then triangulate these regions as well, Fig. 2c. Note that if this step is done in parallel one has to partition the set of squares into disjoint groups, such that a group consists of nine squares that describes a larger square of size $1/3n{\times}1/3n$. Then, the step described above is done in some decided order for the squares in the group such that no two neighboring squares in Q' are processed at the same time. Hence, this step is done, in the parallel case, in nine phases.
By using some known parallel triangulation algorithm with running time $O(\log n)$ this step takes $O(\log n)$ time to compute. Since the total length of these edges is less than 1 (recall that the largest distance between two points in S is 1) the approximation factor will not affect the approximation factor of PRQT by more than a small constant factor.

4. *Find all concave chains, and partition them into l-compvertices.*
Every processor $P(s_i)$, $s_i{\in}S$, checks if s_i belongs to a concave chain. Let $v_1,\ldots,v_m$ be the points in an arbitrary concave chain, where v_i and v_{i-1} are adjacent neighbors in the concave chain. If the distance between two adjacent points is $\le l/10$ then merge these two points into an l-compvertex. If two points want to merge with the same point and all three points can't be merged, then the point with the largest process number decides which points that should be merged. Continue to merge points and l-compvertices until no more merges can be done. Since we have a linear number of processors, this step takes $O(\log n)$ time.

6a. *Check and partition all l-compvertices.*
For every possible pair of l-compvertices, denoted $C_1{=}\{c_1^1,\ldots,c_1^r\}$ and $C_2{=}\{c_2^1,\ldots,c_2^t\}$ in T, lying at distance between l and $(1{+}\epsilon){\cdot}l$ from each other, we check whether there exists a tangent that touches the interior points of c_1 and c_2. If there exists such a tangent, partition c_1, respectively c_2,

into two l-compvertices. Recall that for every l-compvertex C there are at most a constant number of l-compvertices lying within distance $(1+\epsilon)\cdot l$ from C, according to Fact 1. Partition C_1 into $\sqrt{r}$ subchains, $S_1^1,\ldots,S_1^{\sqrt{r}}$, such that each subchain consists of $\sqrt{r}$ points. Partition C_2, in the same way, into $\sqrt{t}$ subchains, $S_2^1,\ldots,S_2^{\sqrt{t}}$. Each subchain S_1^i, $1\leq i\leq\sqrt{r}$, is assigned $\sqrt{t}$ processors, $P_i^1,\ldots,P_i^{\sqrt{t}}$. Note that we will use $\sqrt{t}\cdot\sqrt{r}\leq\max(r,t)$ processors. Every processor P_i^j now checks if there is a possible tangent between C_1 and C_2 that touches S_1^i and S_2^j. If there are several such subchains then we just choose the one farthest away. Each processor has just to check the endpoints of the subchain, so this step is done in constant time. Assume that there exists a tangent between C_1 and C_2 that touches S_1^i and S_2^j. Each point in S_1^i is assigned $\sqrt{t}$ processors. Once again we use $\sqrt{t}\cdot\sqrt{r}\leq\max(r,t)$ processors. For each point $c_{i_s}\in S_1^i$, $1\leq s\leq\sqrt{r}$, check if there is a tangent between C_1 and C_2 that touches c_{i_s} and any of the points in S_2^j.
Hence we can find a tangent between a pair of concave chains in constant time using $O(t)$ processors and, since there are only a constant number, for each l-compvertex we can check all such pairs in parallel in constant time.

6b. Recall that there are only a constant number of l-compvertices and isolvertices in each square T_i, according to Fact 1. Hence we can in constant time check all possible edges of length between l and $(1+\epsilon')\cdot l$.

6biii. If an edge's both endpoints c_1 and c_2 belongs to l-compvertices that face each other then the algorithm triangulates the region between the two l-compvertices. Let C_1 and C_2 be two l-compvertices with shortest distance r between two vertices in C_1 and C_2. A minimal triangulation between the vertices in C_1 and C_2 has length at least $(\#C_1+\#C_2-1)\times r$. A straightforward greedy triangulation has length less than $(\#C_1+\#C_2-1)\times l+l\cdot\frac{\epsilon}{8}$. Hence the approximation factor with regard to an optimal triangulation is at most within a small constant factor. It is easily seen that this also gives a close-to-optimal triangulation for the two concave chains where C_1 and C_2 belong. Otherwise, if C doesn't face C' and C' doesn't face C then add the edge between c_1 and c_2 to G.

6e. For each l-compvertex we know its adjacent l-compvertices, since they belong to the same concave chain. So for each l-compvertex, v, we check its neighbors v_1 and v_2. If the maximal distance between every pair of points in v and v_2 is less than $l\cdot\frac{\epsilon}{8}$ then we merge v and v_2 into one l-compvertex v'. If the maximal distance between every pair of points in v' and v_1 is less than $l\cdot\frac{\epsilon}{8}$ then we merge v' and v_1 into one l-compvertex. Since an l-compvertex is merged at most twice per iteration this step takes constant time.

3.2 The PRQT-algorithm Uses Linear Space

In this section we show how to construct the grid (step 5) in time $O(\log n)$ time such that it uses linear amount of space and allows the algorithm to perform the following two time-critical steps in constant time.

1) Merging four adjacent squares in the grid (step 6f), and
2) finding the neighbors of a square in the grid (step 6b).

We will use a threaded quad-tree [7], where each node represents a square. A quad-tree can be obtained by first enclosing all vertices in S with a square. This square is then partitioned into four squares, which are recursively partitioned into four squares, and so on. A recursion ends (for the PRQT-algorithm) when a square is empty or when the length of the sides of the square is $\leq 1/n$. The induced squares are represented as nodes in a rooted tree, each square having its (at most four) nonempty subsquares as children. This quad-tree may however have much more than a linear number of nodes, because it may contain long paths where each interior node has only one child. A simple refinement that reduces the size to linear is to represent only those squares for which the corresponding nodes have more than one child, that is to compress each of the above mentioned paths into a single edge. Indeed, we do not lose any essential information by such compression. A weakness which remains even in the compressed quad-tree is that for two squares s and q represented in the quad-tree, the nearest common ancestor may be the root even if s and q are adjacent in the grid. Consequently, to find q given only s we may have to follow a long path in the quad-tree. Therefore, we thread (link) nodes that correspond to squares (of equal size) that are adjacent.

In [3] we describe in detail how this structure is built, and then show how the two time-critical steps, stated above, are performed.

4 The ϵ-RQT Achieves a Constant Factor Approximation

In this section we will prove that the approximation algorithm presented in the previous section produces a triangulation of length at most within a constant factor longer than the MWT. The results are achieved by generalizing the corresponding results in [8,9] for the greedy and quasi-greedy algorithm. The proofs of Lemma 1, Lemma 2 and Theorem 1 are given in [3].

For simplicity we will prove the results for the corresponding sequential algorithm. As mentioned above the greedy triangulation is obtained by repeatedly producing a shortest possible edge that doesn't properly intersect any of the previously generated edges. In [8] it was shown that there is only one certain configuration of points for which the greedy algorithm doesn't approximate the optimal, that is when the points form two concave chains facing each other. Hence, in the QT one treats this case as a special case, by checking that every edge added to the triangulation fulfills six conditions. The ϵ-RQT works as the QT but instead of producing a shortest edge it will produce all edges shorter than $1+\epsilon$ times the length of the shortest edge, where ϵ is a positive constant smaller than 1. We need the following results to prove that the ϵ-RQT produces a triangulation which is within a constant factor longer than the MWT.

A convex partition of S is a connected PSLG with vertex set S such that its edges partition the interior of the convex hull of S into bounded convex regions. A *minimum weight convex partition* of S, which we abbreviate by $MWC(S)$, is a convex partition of S such that its total edge length is minimized. Let $\max(v)$ denote the length of a longest edge incident to vertex v in $MWC(S)$. The following fact is straightforward.

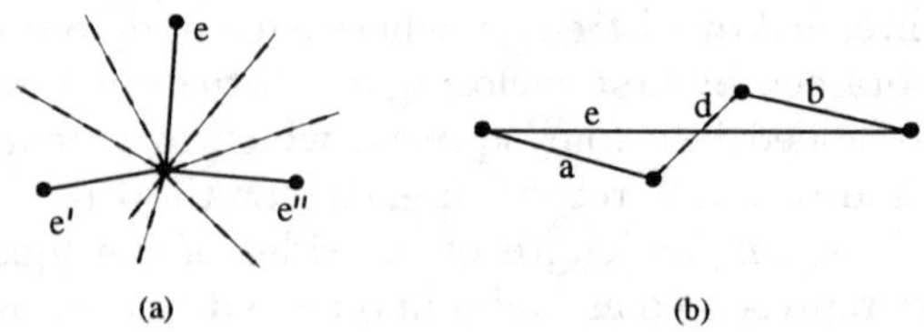

Fig. 3.

Fact 2. *(Observation 2.1 in [8])*
For any set S of vertices it holds that $\sum_{v \in S} \max(v) \leq 2|MWC(S)|$.

Next we define a subgraph of $\epsilon-RQT(S)$ as a convex partition of S. It is obtained by selecting for each vertex $v \in S$ at most three edges of $\epsilon-RQT(S)$, which we call spokes. If v lies on the convex hull of S, then the spokes of v are the two convex hull edges that are incident to v. Otherwise, let e be the shortest edge in $\epsilon-RQT(S)$ incident to v such that there exist greedy edges e' and e'' incident to v with the following three properties.

- e' and e'' are not longer than e,
- e, e' and e'' partition the vicinity of v into three convex regions, and
- within two of these regions bounded by e no edge in $\epsilon-RQT(S)$ incident to v is shorter than e.

Then the spokes of v are the edges e, e' and e'', Fig. 3a. The union of all spokes which we select in this way, by considering all vertices in S, form our *ϵ-relaxed quasi-greedy convex partition*, $\epsilon-RQC(S)$. For a vertex v, let v_M stand for the length of a longest spoke in $\epsilon-RQC(S)$ that was selected for v. We note the following straight-forward observation.

Observation 2. *For any set S of vertices,* $|\epsilon-RQC(S)| \leq 3 \sum_{v \in S} v_M$.

To be able to compare the $\epsilon-RQC$ with the MWC we need Lemma 1.

Lemma 1. *(Modified version of Lemma 5.2 in [8])*
Let S be any set of vertices (in general position) and let v be an arbitrary vertex in S. Then $v_M = O(\max(v))$.

Combining Fact 2, Observation 2 and Lemma 1, we obtain the following result:

Corollary 1. *(Modified version of Corollary 5.3 in [8])*
For any set S of vertices (in general position), $|\epsilon-RQC(S)| = O(|MWC(S)|)$.

Proof. $|\epsilon-RQC(S)| \leq 3 \sum_{v \in S} v_M \leq 3c \sum_{v \in S} \max(v) \leq 6c \cdot |MWC(S)|$, for some constant c.

We now know that the ϵ-relaxed quasi-greedy convex partition is at most within a constant factor longer than a minimum weight convex partition, hence it remains to prove that the convex partition of an ϵ-relaxed quasi-greedy convex partition can be triangulated by edges of at most length $O(MWT(S))$.

Now, let G be a PSLG with vertex set S and let r be a real number greater than zero. An edge e of G is said to be *r-sensitive* [11] if for any diagonal d of S

that properly intersects e, the distance between any endpoint of d to the closest endpoint of e is not greater than r times the length of d. We say that the graph G is *r-sensitive* if all its edges are r-sensitive, Fig. 3b

Given a real number r, we say that a triangulation is r-greedy if it can be produced by repeatedly adding a diagonal, such that its length is not greater than r times the length of the shortest diagonal in the partial triangulation. The standard quasi-greedy is 1.1-greedy, whereas the standard greedy is 1-greedy. Note the following observation.

Observation 3. *The relaxed quasi-greedy triangulation is* $(1+\epsilon)$*-greedy.*

Fact 3. *(Lemma 5.5 in [8])*
Let S be any set of vertices and let c be any real number such that $0<c\leq 1$. *Then any* $(2-c)$*-greedy triangulation T of S is* $(4/c)$*-sensitive.*

Hence from the above fact we have that the relaxed quasi-greedy algorithm is $(4/(1+\epsilon)$-sensitive, and to fulfill the requirements we have to choose ϵ smaller than 1. From Fact 4 we obtain that the $MWC(S)$ can be triangulated such that the length of the triangulation is $O(|MWT(S)|)$, since $|MWC(S)|\leq|MWT(S)|$.

Fact 4. *(Lemma 4.2 in [8])*
For any real number r, $r>0$, let $CP(S)$ be an arbitrary r-sensitive convex partition of S. Then $CP(S)$ can be triangulated by adding diagonals of total length $O(r|CP(S)|+r|MWT(S)|)$.

By using the result in Corollary 1 and Fact 4 it now remains to prove that for a convex polygon P the ϵ-$RQT(P)$ produces a triangulation of length $O(|MWT(P)|)$. This is done in two steps. First we show in Lemma 2 that a convex polygon is partitioned by the ϵ-$RQT(P)$ into triangles and so-called q-bent polygons (to be defined below) by edges of length $\leq c{\cdot}p(P)$, where $p(P)$ is the length of the perimeter of P. Next, we prove in Theorem 1 that for a q-bent polygon P' it holds that $|\epsilon-RQT(P)|\leq \frac{2\cos q-(1+\epsilon)}{2(1+\epsilon)}\times|MWT(S)|$. Hence by combining these two results we obtain the desired result, Theorem 2.

A polygon P is said to be *semi-circular* iff it is convex and it can be drawn within some circle whose diameter is equal to the length of the longest edge of P. The longest edge of a semi-circular polygon is called the *base*. Given a positive real number $q<60$, a polygon P is called q-bent iff P is semi-circular, and the sum of degrees of the two interior angles of P at the endpoints of its base is not greater than $2q$ degrees. Now, let $p(P)$ denote the length of the perimeter of a simple polygon P.

Lemma 2. *(Modified version of Lemma 4.3 in [8])*
For any real number q, $0<q\leq 45$, *there exists some constant c depending on q such that for any convex polygon P there are edges in* $\epsilon-RQT(P)$ *of total length* $\leq c{\cdot}p(P)$ *which partition P into triangles and/or q-bent polygons.*

Theorem 1. *(Modified version of Theorem 3.1 in [9])*
For any q-bent polygon P, $0<q\leq 45$ *and* $0\leq\epsilon<\sqrt{2}-1$, *it holds that*

$$|\epsilon-RQT(P)|\leq\frac{2\cos q-(1+\epsilon)}{2(1+\epsilon)}\times|MWT(S)|.$$

Putting toghether these two results we obtain the following observation.

Observation 4. *(Modified version of Observation 5.4 in [8])*
For any convex polygon P it holds that $|\epsilon{-}RQT(P)|{=}O(|MWT(P)|)$.

Finally we obtain the main result of this section.

Theorem 2. *(Modified version of Theorem 5.10 in [8])*
For any set S of vertices (in general position) it holds that

$$|\epsilon{-}RQT(S)|{=}O(|MWT(S)|).$$

Proof. By combining the results from Corollary 1, Fact 3 and 4, and Observation 4, we obtain the theorem.

References

1. R. C. Chang and R. C. T. Lee. On the average length of delaunay triangulations. *BIT*, 24(3):269–273, 1984.
2. P. D. Gilbert. New results in planar triangulations. Report R-850, Coordinated Sci. Lab., University of Illinois, Urbana, Illinois, USA, 1979.
3. J. Gudmundsson and C. Levcopoulos. A parallel approximation algorithm for minimum weight triangulation. Report LU-CS-TR:97-196, Dept. of Computer Science, Lund University, Lund, Sweden, 1997.
4. D. G. Kirkpatrick. A note on delaunay and optimal triangulations. *Information Processing Letters*, 10(3):127–128, 1987.
5. C. Levcopoulos. An $\omega(\sqrt{n})$ lower bound for the nonoptimality of the greedy triangulation. *Information Processing Letters*, 25(4):247–251, 1987.
6. C. Levcopoulos and D. Krznaric. The greedy triangulation can be computed from the delaunay in linear time. Report LU-CS-TR:94-136, Dept. of Comp. Sci., Lunds University, Lund, Sweden, 1994. Extended abstract published in SWAT'96, LNCS 1097, Springer-Verlag, 1996.
7. C. Levcopoulos and D. Krznaric. Computing a threaded quadtree from the delaunay triangulation in linear time. In *Proc. 7th CCCG*, pages 187–192, 1995.
8. C. Levcopoulos and D. Krznaric. Quasi-greedy triangulations approximating the minimum weight triangulation. In *Proc. 7th ACM-SIAM Sympos. Discrete Algorithms*, pages 392–401, 1996.
9. C. Levcopoulos and A. Lingas. On approximation behavior of the greedy triangulation for convex polygons. *Algorithmica*, 2(2):175–193, 1987.
10. C. Levcopoulos and A. Lingas. Greedy triangulation approximates the optimum and can be implemented in linear time in the average case. In *Proc. 3rd International Conference on Computing and Information*, volume 497 of *LNCS*, 1991.
11. C. Levcopoulos and A. Lingas. C-sensitive triangulations approximate the minmax length triangulation. In *Proc. FST&TCS-12*, volume 652 of *LNCS*, 1992.
12. C. Levcopoulos A. Lingas and C. Wang. On the parallel complexity of planar triangulations. In *FST&TCS-15*, volume 1026 of *LNCS*, 1995.
13. E. Merks. An optimal parallel algorithm for triangulating a set of points in the plane. *International Journal of Parallel Programming*, 15(5), 1986.
14. C. A. Wang and Y. H. Tsin. An $o(\log n)$ time parallel algorithm for triangulating a set of points in the plane. *Information Processing Letters*, 25:55–60, 1987.

The Power of Reachability Testing for Timed Automata

Luca Aceto[1] *, Patricia Bouyer[2], Augusto Burgueño[3] ** and Kim G. Larsen[1]

[1] **BRICS**[†], Department of Computer Science, Aalborg University, Fredrik Bajers Vej 7-E, DK-9220 Aalborg Ø, Denmark.
Email: `{luca,kgl}@cs.auc.dk`, Fax: +45 98 15 98 89

[2] Laboratoire Spécification et Vérification, CNRS URA 2236, Ecole Normale Supérieure de Cachan, 61 av. du Président Wilson, 94235 Cachan Cedex, France.
Email: `bouyer@lsv.ens-cachan.fr`, Fax: +33 1 47 40 24 64

[3] ONERA-CERT, Département d'Informatique, 2 av. E. Belin, BP4025, 31055 Toulouse Cedex 4, France.
Email: `a.burgueno@acm.org`, Fax: +33 5 62 25 25 93

Abstract. In this paper we provide a complete characterization of the class of properties of (networks of) timed automata for which model checking can be reduced to reachability checking in the context of testing automata.

1 Introduction

The main motivation for the work presented in this paper stems from our practical experience with UPPAAL [8], a tool for the verification of behavioural properties of real-time systems specified as networks of timed automata [3]. One of the main design criteria behind UPPAAL has been that of efficiency, and its computational engine has originally been restricted to a collection of efficient algorithms for the analysis of simple *reachability* properties of systems. However, in practice one often wants to examine a model to discover whether it enjoys a number of properties that cannot be directly expressed via reachability. Model checking of properties other than plain reachability ones may currently be carried out in UPPAAL as follows. Given a property ϕ to model check, the user must provide a *test automaton* T_ϕ for it. The test automaton must be such that the original system S has the property expressed by ϕ precisely when

* Partially supported by the Human Capital and Mobility project EXPRESS, a grant from the Italian CNR, Gruppo Nazionale per l'Informatica Matematica (GNIM), and a visiting professorship at the Laboratoire Spécification et Vérification, Ecole Normale Supérieure de Cachan.

** Partially supported by a Research Grant of the Spanish Ministry of Education and Culture and by BRICS. This work was partially carried out while the author was visiting Aalborg University.

† **B**asic **R**esearch **i**n **C**omputer **S**cience, Centre of the Danish National Research Foundation.

none of the distinguished reject states of T_ϕ can be reached by $S\|T_\phi$, i.e., the agent obtained by making the test automaton interact with the system under investigation. This raises the question of which properties may be analyzed by UPPAAL in this manner. In this paper we answer this question by providing a complete characterization of the class of properties of (networks of) timed automata for which model checking can be reduced to reachability testing in the sense outlined above.

In our previous study [2], we have considered SBLL, a property language suitable for expressing safety and bounded liveness properties of real-time systems. In particular, we have shown that SBLL is *testable*, in the sense that suitable test automata may be derived for any property of SBLL. However, as we shall demonstrate in this paper, SBLL is not *expressive complete* with respect to reachability testing because it cannot express all the properties for which test automata can be derived. As the main result of this paper, we present an extension, $L_{\forall S}^-$, of SBLL which is shown to characterize exactly the limit of the testing approach. More precisely we show that:

- every property ψ of $L_{\forall S}^-$ is testable, in the sense that there exists a test automaton T_ψ such that S satisfies ψ if and only if $S\|T_\psi$ cannot reach a reject state, for every system S; and
- every test automaton T is expressible in $L_{\forall S}^-$, in the sense that there exists a formula ψ_T of $L_{\forall S}^-$ such that, for every system S, the agent $S\|T$ cannot reach a reject state if and only if S satisfies ψ_T.

This expressive completeness result will be obtained as a corollary of a stronger result pertaining to the compositionality of the property language $L_{\forall S}^-$. A property language is *compositional* iff every property ϕ of a composite system $S\|T$ can be reduced to a necessary and sufficient property ϕ_T of the component S. As the property ϕ_T is required to be expressible in the property language under consideration, compositionality clearly puts a demand on its expressive power. Let L_{bad} be the property language with only one property ϕ_{nb}, expressing that no reject state can ever be reached (a simple safety property). We prove that $L_{\forall S}^-$ is the least expressive, compositional extension of the language L_{bad} (Thm. 5.4). This yields the desired expressive completeness result because any compositional property language that can express the property ϕ_{nb} is expressive complete with respect to reachability testing (Propn. 5.3).

The paper is organized as follows. After reviewing the variation on the model of timed automata which will be considered in this study (Sect. 2), we introduce test automata and describe how they can be used to test for properties via reachability analysis (Sect. 3). The property language studied in this paper is presented in Sect. 4. We then proceed to argue that the language $L_{\forall S}^-$ is testable (Sect. 4.1). Our main results are presented in Sect. 5. *Ibidem* we show that $L_{\forall S}^-$ is the least expressive, compositional property language that can express the aforementioned safety property ϕ_{nb}, and use this result to derive its expressive completeness with respect to reachability testing.

2 Preliminaries

Timed Labelled Transition Systems Let $\mathcal{A}$ be a finite set of *actions*, and $\mathcal{U}$ be a finite set of *urgent actions* disjoint from $\mathcal{A}$. We use Act to stand for $\mathcal{A} \cup \mathcal{U}$ and let a, b, c range over it. We assume that Act comes equipped with a mapping $\bar{\cdot}$: Act $\to$ Act such that $\bar{\bar{a}} = a$, for every $a \in$ Act. Moreover, we require that $\bar{a} \in \mathcal{A}$ iff $a \in \mathcal{A}$, for every action a. (Note that, since $\mathcal{A}$ and $\mathcal{U}$ are disjoint, it is also the case that $\bar{a} \in \mathcal{U}$ iff $a \in \mathcal{U}$.) We let Act_τ stand for Act $\cup \{\tau\}$, where τ is a symbol not occurring in Act, and use μ to range over it. The symbol τ will stand for an internal action of a system. Let $\mathbb{N}$ and $\mathbb{R}_{\geq 0}$ denote the sets of natural and non-negative real numbers, respectively. We use $\mathcal{D}$ to denote the set of *delay actions* $\{\epsilon(d) \mid d \in \mathbb{R}_{\geq 0}\}$, and $\mathcal{L}$ to stand for the union of Act_τ and $\mathcal{D}$. The meta-variable α will range over $\mathcal{L}$.

A *timed labelled transition system* (TLTS) is a structure $\mathcal{T} = \langle \mathcal{S}, \mathcal{L}, s^0, \longrightarrow \rangle$ where $\mathcal{S}$ is a set of *states*, $s^0 \in \mathcal{S}$ is the initial state, and $\longrightarrow \subseteq \mathcal{S} \times \mathcal{L} \times \mathcal{S}$ is a transition relation satisfying the following properties:

- (Time Determinism) for every $s, s', s'' \in \mathcal{S}$ and $d \in \mathbb{R}_{\geq 0}$, if $s \xrightarrow{\epsilon(d)} s'$ and $s \xrightarrow{\epsilon(d)} s''$, then $s' = s''$;
- (Time Additivity) for every $s, s'' \in \mathcal{S}$ and $d_1, d_2 \in \mathbb{R}_{\geq 0}$, $s \xrightarrow{\epsilon(d_1+d_2)} s''$ iff $s \xrightarrow{\epsilon(d_1)} s' \xrightarrow{\epsilon(d_2)} s''$, for some $s' \in \mathcal{S}$;
- (0-Delay) for every $s, s' \in \mathcal{S}$, $s \xrightarrow{\epsilon(0)} s'$ iff $s = s'$;
- (Forward Persistence of Urgent Actions) for every $s, s', s'' \in \mathcal{S}$, $a \in \mathcal{U}$ and $d \in \mathbb{R}_{\geq 0}$, if $s \xrightarrow{\epsilon(d)} s'$ and $s \xrightarrow{a} s''$, then there exists $\bar{s} \in \mathcal{S}$ such that $s' \xrightarrow{a} \bar{s}$;
- (Backward Persistence of Urgent Actions) for every $s, s', s'' \in \mathcal{S}$, $a \in \mathcal{U}$ and $d \in \mathbb{R}_{\geq 0}$, if $s \xrightarrow{\epsilon(d)} s'$ and $s' \xrightarrow{a} s''$, then there exists $\bar{s} \in \mathcal{S}$ such that $s \xrightarrow{a} \bar{s}$.

As usual, we write $s \xrightarrow{\alpha}$ to mean that there is some state s' such that $s \xrightarrow{\alpha} s'$, and $s \not\xrightarrow{\alpha}$ if there is no state s' such that $s \xrightarrow{\alpha} s'$.

The axioms of time determinism, time additivity and 0-delay are standard in the literature on TCCS (see, e.g., [9]). Those dealing with urgent actions are motivated by the particular kind of timed automaton model considered in verification tools like HyTech [5] and Uppaal [8].

A *delaying computation* is a sequence of transitions $s_0 \xrightarrow{\alpha_1} s_1 \xrightarrow{\alpha_2} \ldots \xrightarrow{\alpha_n} s_n$ $(n \geq 0)$ such that $\alpha_i = \tau$ or $\alpha_i \in \mathcal{D}$, for every $i \in \{1, .., n\}$. Following [9], we now proceed to define versions of the transition relations that abstract from the internal evolution of states as follows:

$$s \stackrel{a}{\Longrightarrow} s' \quad \text{iff} \quad \exists s''.\ \ s \xrightarrow{\tau}^{*} s'' \xrightarrow{a} s'$$

$$s \stackrel{\epsilon(d)}{\Longrightarrow} s' \quad \text{iff} \quad \text{there exists a delaying computation}$$

$$s = s_0 \xrightarrow{\alpha_1} s_1 \xrightarrow{\alpha_2} \ldots \xrightarrow{\alpha_n} s_n = s' \text{ with } d = \sum\{d_i \mid \alpha_i = \epsilon(d_i)\}$$

By convention, if the set $\{d_i \mid \alpha_i = \epsilon(d_i)\}$ is empty, then $\sum\{d_i \mid \alpha_i = \epsilon(d_i)\}$ is 0. We define a collection of transition relations parameterized by a set of urgent actions S as follows:

$$s \xrightarrow{\epsilon(d)}_S s' \quad \text{iff} \quad s \xrightarrow{\epsilon(d)} s' \text{ and } \forall d' \in [0,d[, a \in S, s' \in \mathcal{S}.\ s \xrightarrow{\epsilon(d')} s' \text{ implies } s' \not\xrightarrow{a}$$

$$s \overset{\epsilon(d)}{\Longrightarrow}_S s' \quad \text{iff} \quad \text{there exists a delaying computation} \quad s = s_0 \xrightarrow{\alpha_1}_S s_1 \xrightarrow{\alpha_2}_S \ldots \xrightarrow{\alpha_n}_S s_n = s' \text{ with } d = \sum\{d_i \mid \alpha_i = \epsilon(d_i)\}$$

where the relation $\xrightarrow{\tau}_S$ coincides with $\xrightarrow{\tau}$. Intuitively, $s \xrightarrow{\epsilon(d)}_S s'$ holds if s can delay d units of time, and no action in the set S becomes enabled before time d during this delay activity. Note that, since the set S only contains urgent actions, this amounts to requiring that either $d = 0$ or $s \not\xrightarrow{a}$, for every $a \in S$. Similarly, $s \overset{\epsilon(d)}{\Longrightarrow}_S s'$ holds if there exists a delaying computation of duration d from state s whose delay transitions with positive duration occur only in states in which none of the urgent actions in S are enabled.

Definition 2.1 (Operations on TLTSs).

- Let $\mathcal{T}_i = \langle \mathcal{S}_i, \mathcal{L}, s_i^0, \longrightarrow_i \rangle$ $(i \in \{1,2\})$ be two TLTSs. The parallel composition of $\mathcal{T}_1$ and $\mathcal{T}_2$ is the TLTS $\mathcal{T}_1 \parallel \mathcal{T}_2 = \langle \mathcal{S}_1 \times \mathcal{S}_2, \mathcal{L}, (s_1^0, s_2^0), \longrightarrow \rangle$, where the transition relation $\longrightarrow$ is defined by the rules in below:

(1)	$\dfrac{s_1 \xrightarrow{\mu}_1 s_1'}{s_1 \| s_2 \xrightarrow{\mu} s_1' \| s_2}$	(2)	$\dfrac{s_2 \xrightarrow{\mu}_2 s_2'}{s_1 \| s_2 \xrightarrow{\mu} s_1 \| s_2'}$
(3)	$\dfrac{s_1 \xrightarrow{a}_1 s_1' \qquad s_2 \xrightarrow{\overline{a}}_2 s_2'}{s_1 \| s_2 \xrightarrow{\tau} s_1' \| s_2'}$		
(4)	$\dfrac{s_1 \xrightarrow{\epsilon(d)}_1 s_1' \qquad s_2 \xrightarrow{\epsilon(d)}_2 s_2'}{s_1 \| s_2 \xrightarrow{\epsilon(d)} s_1' \| s_2'}$		$d = 0$ or $\forall a \in \mathcal{U}.\ \neg(s_1 \xrightarrow{a}_1 \wedge s_2 \xrightarrow{\overline{a}}_2)$

  where s_i, s_i' are states of $\mathcal{T}_i$ $(i \in \{1,2\})$, $\mu \in \mathsf{Act}_\tau$, $a, \overline{a} \in \mathsf{Act}$ and $d \in \mathbb{R}_{\geq 0}$. In the above rules, and in the remainder of the paper, we use the more suggestive notation $s \parallel s'$ in lieu of (s, s').
- Let $\mathcal{T} = \langle \mathcal{S}, \mathcal{L}, s^0, \rightarrow \rangle$ be a TLTS and let $L \subseteq \mathsf{Act}$ be a set of actions. The restriction of $\mathcal{T}$ over L is the TLTS $\mathcal{T} \backslash L = \langle \mathcal{S} \backslash L, \mathcal{L}, s^0 \backslash L, \rightsquigarrow \rangle$, where $\mathcal{S} \backslash L = \{s \backslash L \mid s \in \mathcal{S}\}$ and the transition relation $\rightsquigarrow$ is defined by the rules below:

(1)	$\dfrac{s \xrightarrow{\tau} s'}{s \backslash L \overset{\tau}{\rightsquigarrow} s' \backslash L}$	(2)	$\dfrac{s \xrightarrow{\epsilon(d)} s'}{s \backslash L \overset{\epsilon(d)}{\rightsquigarrow} s' \backslash L}$
(3)	$\dfrac{s \xrightarrow{a} s'}{s \backslash L \overset{a}{\rightsquigarrow} s' \backslash L}$		$a, \overline{a} \notin L$

where s, s' are states of $\mathcal{T}$, $L \subseteq \mathsf{Act}$, $a \in \mathsf{Act}$, and $d \in \mathbb{R}_{\geq 0}$.

The reader familiar with TCCS [9] may have noticed that the above definition of parallel composition has strong similarities with that of TCCS parallel composition — the only difference being that in TCCS *all* actions are urgent. This yields precisely the parallel composition operator used in UPPAAL [8].

Timed Automata Let C be a set of clocks. We use $\mathcal{B}(C)$ to denote the set of boolean expressions over atomic formulae of the form $x \sim p$ and $x - y \sim p$, with $x, y \in C$, $p \in \mathbb{N}$, and $\sim \in \{<, >, =\}$. Expressions in $\mathcal{B}(C)$ are interpreted over the collection of time assignments. A *time assignment*, or *valuation*, v for C is a function from C to $\mathbb{R}_{\geq 0}$. Given a condition $g \in \mathcal{B}(C)$ and a time assignment v, the boolean value $g(v)$ describes whether g is satisfied by v or not. (Note that $\mathcal{B}(C)$ is closed under negation.) For every time assignment v and $d \in \mathbb{R}_{\geq 0}$, we use $v + d$ to denote the time assignment which maps each clock $x \in C$ to the value $v(x) + d$. Two assignments u and v are said to agree on the set of clocks C' iff they assign the same real number to every clock in C'. For every subset C' of clocks, $[C' \to 0]v$ denotes the assignment for C which maps each clock in C' to the value 0 and agrees with v over $C \backslash C'$. For an assignment u and a subset C' of C, we write $u \upharpoonright C'$ for the restriction of u to the set of clocks C'. Given two disjoint sets of clocks C_1, C_2, and two valuations v_1, v_2 for the clocks of C_1 and C_2 respectively, $v_1 : v_2$ denotes the valuation for the clocks of $C_1 \cup C_2$ such that $(v_1 : v_2)(x) = v_1(x)$ iff $x \in C_1$ and $(v_1 : v_2)(x) = v_2(x)$ iff $x \in C_2$.

The notion of timed automaton we use in this paper is a variation on the original one introduced by Alur and Dill [3], and underlies that used in, e.g., HyTech [5] and UPPAAL [8].

Definition 2.2. A *timed automaton* is a tuple $A = \langle \mathsf{Act}_\tau, N, n_0, C, E \rangle$ where N is a finite set of *nodes*, n_0 is the *initial node*, C is a finite set of *clocks*, and $E \subseteq N \times N \times \mathsf{Act}_\tau \times 2^C \times \mathcal{B}(C)$ is a set of *edges*. The tuple $e = \langle n, n_e, \mu, r_e, g_e \rangle \in E$ stands for an edge from node n to node n_e (the *target* of e) with action μ, where r_e denotes the set of clocks to be reset to 0 and g_e is the enabling condition (or *guard*) over the clocks of A. All the timed automata we shall consider in this paper will satisfy the following constraint:

- (URGENCY) if $\langle n, n_e, \mu, r_e, g_e \rangle \in E$ and $\mu \in \mathcal{U}$, then g_e is a tautology, i.e., g_e is satisfied by every valuation for the clocks in C.

In what follows, we shall assume that the clocks used in timed automata come from a fixed, countably infinite collection of clocks C_A.

The timed automaton depicted in Figure 1 has five nodes labelled n_0 to n_4, one clock x, actions $a \in \mathcal{U}$ and $b \in \mathcal{A}$, and four edges. The edge from node n_1 to node n_2, for example, is guarded by $x \geq 0$, is labelled with the urgent action a and resets clock x. Note that the guards of edges labelled with the urgent action a are tautologies. A *state* of a timed automaton A is a pair (n, v) where n is a node of A and v is a time assignment for C. The operational semantics of a timed automaton A is given by the TLTS $\mathcal{T}_A = \langle \mathcal{S}, \mathcal{L}, (n_0, [C \to 0]), \longrightarrow \rangle$, where

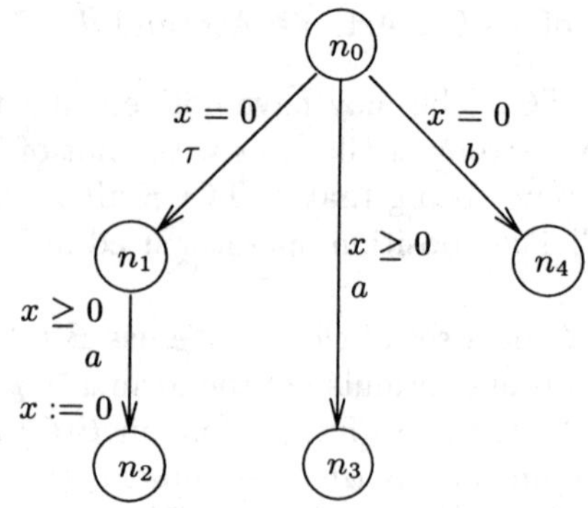

Figure 1: Timed automaton A ($a \in \mathcal{U}$ and $b \in \mathcal{A}$)

$\mathcal{S}$ is the set of states of A, and $\longrightarrow$ is the transition relation defined as follows ($\mu \in \mathsf{Act}_\tau$, $\epsilon(d) \in \mathcal{D}$):

$$(n, v) \xrightarrow{\mu} (n', v') \text{ iff } \exists e = \langle n, n', \mu, r_e, g_e \rangle \in E.\ g_e(v) \wedge v' = [r_e \rightarrow 0]v$$

$$(n, v) \xrightarrow{\epsilon(d)} (n', v') \text{ iff } n = n' \text{ and } v' = v + d$$

3 Testing Automata

As mentioned in Sect. 1, the main aim of this paper is to present a complete characterization of the class of properties of (networks of) timed automata for which model checking can be reduced to reachability analysis. In this section we take the first steps towards the definition of *model checking via (reachability) testing* by defining *testing*. Informally, testing involves the parallel composition of the tested automaton with a *test automaton*. The testing process then consists in performing reachability analysis in the composed system restricted over all non internal actions. We say that the tested automaton fails the test if a special reject state of the test automaton is reachable in the parallel composition (restricted over all non internal actions) from their initial configurations, and passes otherwise. The formal definition of testing then involves the definition of what a test automaton is, how the parallel composition is performed and when the test has failed or succeeded. We now proceed to make these notions precise.

Definition 3.1. A *test automaton* is a tuple $T = \langle \mathsf{Act}_\tau, N, N_T, n_0, C, C_0, E \rangle$ where Act_τ, N, n_0, C, and E are as in Definition 2.2, $N_T \subseteq N$ is the set of *reject nodes*, and $C_0 \subseteq C$ is the set of clocks whose value must be 0 at the beginning of every run of the automaton.

An *initial valuation* for T is any valuation for the set of clocks C that assigns the value 0 to every clock in C_0. An *initial state* of T is any state (n_0, u_0) of T with u_0 an initial valuation.

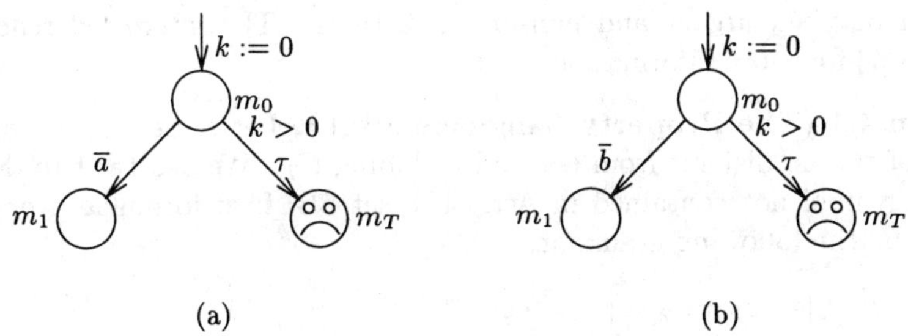

Figure 2: The test automata T_a and T_b

In what follows, we shall assume that the clocks used in test automata come from a fixed, countably infinite collection of clocks C_T disjoint from C_A.

Definition 3.2. Let $\mathcal{T}$ be a TLTS and let T be a test automaton. We say that a node n of T is reachable from a state $(s_1 \parallel s_2)\backslash\mathsf{Act}$ of $(\mathcal{T} \parallel \mathcal{T}_T)\backslash\mathsf{Act}$ iff there is a delaying computation leading from $(s_1 \parallel s_2)\backslash\mathsf{Act}$ to a state whose $\mathcal{T}_T$ component is of the form (n, u).

A state s of $\mathcal{T}$ *fails the test* T from the initial state (n_0, u_0) iff a reject node of T is reachable in $(\mathcal{T} \parallel \mathcal{T}_T)\backslash\mathsf{Act}$ from the state $(s \parallel (n_0, u_0))\backslash\mathsf{Act}$. Otherwise, we say that s *passes the test* T from the initial state (n_0, u_0).

Example 3.3. Consider the timed automaton A of Figure 1 and the test automaton T_b ($b \in \mathcal{U}$) of Figure 2(b), where we label the arrow coming into the initial node m_0 of T_b with the assignment $k := 0$ to denote the fact that clock k is contained in C_0. (This convention will be used throughout the paper.) The reject node m_T of the test automaton is reachable from the initial state of $(A \parallel T_b)\backslash\mathsf{Act}$ as follows. First the automaton A can execute the τ-transition and go to node n_1, thus preempting the possibility of synchronizing on channel b with T_b. Next both automata can let a positive amount of time pass, thus enabling the τ-transition from node m_0 in T_b and making m_T reachable. In this case we say that A fails the test. If we test A using the automaton T_a ($a \in \mathcal{U}$) of Figure 2(a), then, in all cases, A and T_a must synchronize on a and, since a is urgent, no positive initial delay is possible. It follows that the reject node m_T of T_a is unreachable, and A passes the test.

4 Property Languages

In our previous study [2] we considered SBLL, a dense-time property language with clocks suitable for the specification of safety and bounded liveness properties of TLTSs. For the sake of clarity in the subsequent discussion, we now recall the syntax of the language SBLL — modified to take into account the current distinction between urgent and non-urgent actions. The interested reader is referred to [2] for more information.

Definition 4.1 (The Property Language SBLL**).** Let K be a countably infinite set of clocks, disjoint from C_A and including C_T. We use `fail` to denote an action symbol not contained in Act. The set SBLL of formulae over K is generated by the following grammar:

$$\begin{array}{lcl} \varphi & ::= & \mathtt{ff} \mid \varphi_1 \wedge \varphi_2 \mid g \vee \varphi \mid \forall\!\!\forall \varphi \mid \\ & & [a]\varphi \mid \langle a\rangle \mathtt{tt}\ (a \in \mathcal{U}) \mid x\ \underline{\mathtt{in}}\ \varphi \mid X \mid \mathtt{max}(X,\varphi) \\ g & ::= & x \sim p \mid x - y \sim p \end{array}$$

where $a \in \mathsf{Act} \cup \{\mathtt{fail}\}$, $x, y \in K$, $p \in \mathbb{N}$, $\sim \in \{<,>,=\}$, X is a formula variable and $\mathtt{max}(X,\varphi)$ stands for the maximal solution of the recursion equation $X = \varphi$.

Following [7], the formulae in SBLL were interpreted in [2] over extended states of TLTSs, i.e., over pairs of the form $\langle s, v\rangle$, where s is a state of a TLTS and v is a valuation for the clocks in K. For the sake of clarity in the presentation, we recall that the satisfaction relation for SBLL is the largest relation satisfying the relevant implications in Table 1 below and

$$\langle s,u\rangle \models \forall\!\!\forall\varphi \Rightarrow \forall d \in \mathbb{R}_{\geq 0}, \forall s'.\ s \stackrel{\epsilon(d)}{\Longrightarrow} s' \text{ implies } \langle s', u+d\rangle \models \varphi \ .$$

Our main result in *op. cit.* was that the property language SBLL is testable over states of timed automata, in the sense that, for every formula $\varphi \in$ SBLL, we can construct a test automaton T_φ such that every extended state $\langle s,u\rangle$ of a timed automaton satisfies φ iff it passes the test T_φ, in the sense of Defn. 3.2. It is now natural to wonder whether every property φ that is testable in this fashion can be expressed in the property language SBLL. This amounts to asking whether every test automaton T is expressible in the language SBLL, in the sense that there exists a formula ψ_T of SBLL such that every timed automaton A passes the test T if and only if A satisfies ψ_T.

The starting point of our current investigation is the realization that test automata have a greater expressive power than the specification language SBLL. As an example, consider the test automaton T depicted in Fig. 3, where a is an urgent action. It can be shown that the property tested by the automaton in Fig. 3 is *not* expressible in the language SBLL. Intuitively, the property that is tested by the automaton in Fig. 3 requires that, by delaying without enabling an a action in the process, a state can only evolve to one in which it can*not* perform the action b.

The kind of test automaton depicted in Fig. 3 suggests an enrichment of the property language SBLL in which the delay construct $\forall\!\!\forall$ is parameterized by a set of urgent actions, whose elements should not become enabled as a state delays. It is perhaps surprising that, as we shall show in the sequel (cf. Thm. 5.5), this simple extension of SBLL yields a property language that is expressive complete with respect to the collection of reachability properties expressible by means of test automata, in the sense of Defn. 3.2.

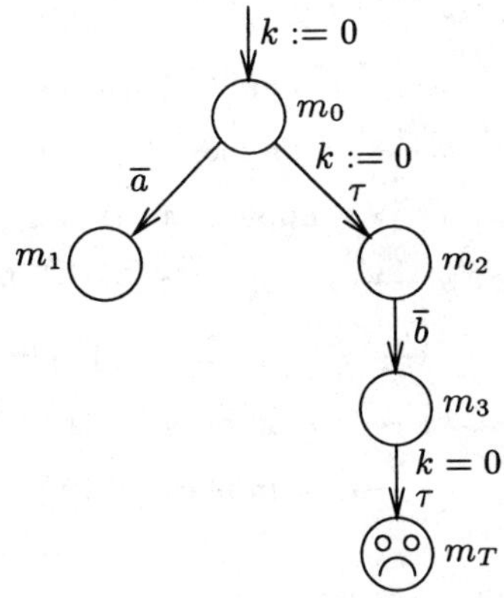

Figure 3: A test automaton that cannot be expressed in SBLL ($a \in \mathcal{U}$)

The property language we study here is an extension of the one considered in [2] (cf. Defn. 4.1), and is closely related to the modal logic L_ν presented in [7], and further investigated in [6].

Definition 4.2. The property language $L_{\forall S}$ consists of the formulae over K generated by the grammar obtained from the one in Defn. 4.1 by replacing constructs of the form $\forall\!\!\forall\varphi$ with $\forall\!\!\forall_S\varphi$, where S is a collection of urgent actions. We use $L_{\forall S}^-$ to stand for the collection of formulae in $L_{\forall S}$ that do not contain occurrences of the basic propositions $\langle a\rangle\mathtt{tt}$.

We write g in lieu of $g \vee \mathtt{ff}$, and clocks(φ) for the collection of clocks occurring in the formula φ. We use the standard definition of closed formulae. In the remainder of this paper, every formula will be closed.

Given a TLTS $\mathcal{T} = \langle S, \mathcal{L}, s^0, \longrightarrow\rangle$, we interpret, as usual, the closed formulae in $L_{\forall S}$ over extended states. We recall that an *extended state* is a pair $\langle s, u\rangle$ where s is a state of $\mathcal{T}$ and u is a time assignment for the formula clocks in K. The satisfaction relation $\models$ is the largest relation included in $\mathcal{S} \times L_{\forall S}$ satisfying the implications in Table 1. We refer the reader to [2] for a discussion of the definition of $\models$. Note that, since `fail` is not contained in Act, every extended state of a TLTS trivially satisfies formulae of the form $[\mathtt{fail}]\phi$. The role played by these formulae in the developments of this paper will become clear in Sect. 5.

4.1 Testing $L_{\forall S}^-$

In Sect. 3 we have seen how we can perform tests on states of TLTSs. We now aim at using test automata to determine whether a given state of a TLTS satisfies a formula in $L_{\forall S}^-$.

$$
\begin{array}{rcl}
\langle s,u\rangle \models \mathtt{ff} & \Rightarrow & \mathit{false} \\
\langle s,u\rangle \models \varphi_1 \wedge \varphi_2 & \Rightarrow & \forall s'.\ s \xrightarrow{\tau}{}^{*} s' \text{ implies } \langle s',u\rangle \models \varphi_1 \text{ and } \langle s',u\rangle \models \varphi_2 \\
\langle s,u\rangle \models g \vee \varphi & \Rightarrow & \forall s'.\ s \xrightarrow{\tau}{}^{*} s' \text{ implies } g(u) \text{ or } \langle s',u\rangle \models \varphi \\
\langle s,u\rangle \models [a]\varphi & \Rightarrow & \forall s'.\ s \overset{a}{\Longrightarrow} s' \text{ implies } \langle s',u\rangle \models \varphi \\
\langle s,u\rangle \models \langle a\rangle \mathtt{tt} & \Rightarrow & \forall s'.\ s \xrightarrow{\tau}{}^{*} s' \text{ implies } s' \xrightarrow{a} s'' \text{ for some } s'' \\
\langle s,u\rangle \models \forall_S \varphi & \Rightarrow & \forall d \in \mathbb{R}_{\geq 0}\ \forall s'.\ \ s \overset{\epsilon(d)}{\Longrightarrow}_S s' \ \text{ implies } \langle s',u+d\rangle \models \varphi \\
\langle s,u\rangle \models x \ \underline{\mathtt{in}}\ \varphi & \Rightarrow & \forall s'.\ \ s \xrightarrow{\tau}{}^{*} s' \text{ implies } \langle s',[x \to 0]u\rangle \models \varphi \\
\langle s,u\rangle \models \mathtt{max}(X,\varphi) & \Rightarrow & \forall s'.\ \ s \xrightarrow{\tau}{}^{*} s' \text{ implies } \langle s',u\rangle \models \varphi\{\mathtt{max}(X,\varphi)/X\}
\end{array}
$$

Table 1: Satisfaction implications

Definition 4.3 (Testing Properties). Let φ be a formula in $L_{\forall S}$, and consider a test automaton $T_\varphi = \langle \mathsf{Act}_\tau, N, N_T, m_0, C, C_0, E\rangle$. For every extended state $\langle s,u\rangle$ of a TLTS $\mathcal{T}$, we say that $\langle s,u\rangle$ passes the test T_φ iff no reject node of T_φ is reachable from the state $(s \parallel (m_0, [C_0 \to 0](u \upharpoonright C)))\backslash\mathsf{Act}$.

The test automaton T_φ *tests* for the formula φ (and we say that φ is *testable*) iff the following holds: for every TLTS $\mathcal{T}$ and every extended state $\langle s,u\rangle$ of $\mathcal{T}$,

$$\langle s,u\rangle \models \varphi \text{ iff } \langle s,u\rangle \text{ passes the test } T_\varphi \ . \tag{1}$$

If (1) holds for arbitrary states of timed automata then we say that the test automaton T_φ *tests* for the formula φ (and that φ is *testable*) over states of timed automata.

Adapting constructions first developed in [2], we can now prove that:

Theorem 4.4. *Every formula in $L^-_{\forall S}$ is testable, and every formula in $L_{\forall S}$ is testable over states of timed automata.*

We remark here that the property languages SBLL and $L_{\forall S}$ are *not* testable because there is no test automaton for the formula $\langle a\rangle\mathtt{tt}$. On the other hand, the languages $L_{\forall S}$ and $L^-_{\forall S}$ are equally expressive over states of timed automata. We refer the interested reader to the full version of this work [1] for more details.

5 Compositionality and Expressive Completeness

We have previously shown that every property φ which can be expressed in the language $L_{\forall S}$ (and, *a fortiori*, in SBLL) is testable over states of timed automata, and that $L^-_{\forall S}$ is testable over states of TLTSs, in the sense of Defn. 4.3. We now address the problem of the expressive completeness of these property languages with respect to test automata and (reachability) testing. More precisely, we study whether all properties that are testable over TLTSs can be expressed in the property languages SBLL and $L^{-}_{\forall S}$—in the sense that, for every test automaton T, there exists a formula ψ_T such that every extended state of a TLTS passes the test T if and only if it satisfies ψ_T. Indeed, we have already enough information to claim that the language SBLL is strictly less expressive than the formalism of test automata. In fact, the automaton depicted in Fig. 3 is nothing but a test automaton for the formula $\forall\!\!\!\forall_{\{a\}}[b]\mathtt{ff}$, which cannot be expressed in SBLL. Our aim in this section is to argue that, unlike SBLL, the language $L^{-}_{\forall S}$ *is* expressive complete, in the sense that every test automaton T may be expressed as a property in the language $L^{-}_{\forall S}$ in the precise technical sense outlined above. In the proof of this expressive completeness result, we shall follow an indirect approach by focusing on the compositionality of a property language $\mathbb{L}$ with respect to test automata and the parallel composition operator $\|$. As we shall see (cf. Propn. 5.3), if a property language $\mathbb{L}$ is compositional with respect to timed automata and $\|$ (cf. Defn. 5.2) then it is complete with respect to test automata and reachability testing (cf. Defn. 5.1). We begin with some preliminary definitions, introducing the key concepts of compositionality and (expressive) completeness.

Definition 5.1 (Expressive completeness). A property language $\mathbb{L}$ over the set of clocks K is *(expressive) complete* (with respect to test automata and testing) if for every test automaton T there exists a formula $\varphi_T \in \mathbb{L}$ such that, for every extended state $\langle s, u\rangle$ of a TLTS, $\langle s, u\rangle \models \varphi_T$ iff $\langle s, u\rangle$ passes the test T.

Compositionality, on the other hand, is formally defined as follows [6]:

Definition 5.2 (Compositionality). A property language $\mathbb{L}$ over the set of clocks K is *compositional* (with respect to test automata and $\|$) if, for every $\varphi \in \mathbb{L}$ and every test automaton $T = \langle \mathsf{Act}_\tau, N, N_T, n_0, C, C_0, E\rangle$ (with C disjoint from clocks(φ)), there exists a formula $\varphi/T \in \mathbb{L}$ over the set of clocks $C \cup \text{clocks}(\varphi)$ such that, for every state s of a TLTS and every valuation u for K,

$$\langle s \,\|\, (n_0, [C_0 \to 0](u \restriction C)), u\rangle \models \varphi \;\Leftrightarrow\; \langle s, [C_0 \to 0]u\rangle \models \varphi/T \ .$$

Our interest in compositionality stems from the following result that links it to the notion of completeness. In the sequel, we use $\mathbb{L}_{bad}$ to denote the property language that only consists of the formula $\forall\!\!\!\forall_{\emptyset}[\mathtt{fail}]\mathtt{ff}$, where $\mathtt{fail}$ is a fresh action not contained in Act.

Proposition 5.3. *Let $\mathbb{L}$ be a property language (over a set of clocks K) that includes $\mathbb{L}_{bad}$. Suppose that $\mathbb{L}$ is compositional with respect to test automata and the parallel composition operator $\|$. Then $\mathbb{L}$ is complete with respect to test automata and testing.*

Since $L^{-}_{\forall S}$ is an extension of $\mathbb{L}_{bad}$, in light of the above proposition an approach to proving that it is expressive complete is to establish that it is compositional with respect to test automata and $\|$. This is the import of the following stronger result:

Theorem 5.4. *The property language $L_{\forall S}^{-}$ is the least expressive extension of $\mathbb{L}_{bad}$ that is compositional with respect to test automata and $\|$.*

In light of Propn. 5.3, we may finally obtain that:

Theorem 5.5. *The property language $L_{\forall S}^{-}$ is complete with respect to test automata and testing.*

For example, the properties tested by the test automata in Figs. 2(a) and 3 may be expressed in $L_{\forall S}^{-}$ as $k \ \underline{\text{in}} \ \forall\!\!\!\forall_{\{a\}}(k = 0)$ and $\forall\!\!\!\forall_{\{a\}}[b]\mathtt{ff}$, respectively.

It is interesting to remark here that the property language $L_{\forall S}^{-}$ is testable also over timed automata with invariants and committed nodes, which are precisely those used in UPPAAL. Moreover, Thm. 5.5 also holds for the model of timed automata with invariants. We refer the interested reader to [4] for details on these results.

References

1. L. ACETO, P. BOUYER, A. BURGUEÑO, AND K. G. LARSEN, *The power of reachability testing for timed automata*, 1998. Forthcoming paper.
2. L. ACETO, A. BURGUEÑO, AND K. G. LARSEN, *Model checking via reachability testing for timed automata*, in Proceedings of TACAS '98, Lisbon, B. Steffen, ed., vol. 1384 of Lecture Notes in Computer Science, Springer-Verlag, 1998, pp. 263–280. Also available as BRICS Report RS–97–29, Aalborg University, November, 1997.
3. R. ALUR AND D. DILL, *A theory of timed automata*, Theoretical Computer Science, 126 (1994), pp. 183–235.
4. A. BURGUEÑO, *Model-checking via Testing and Parametric Analysis of Timed Systems*, PhD thesis, École Nationale Supérieure de l'Aéronautique et de l'Éspace, Toulouse, France, June 1998.
5. T. A. HENZINGER, P.-H. HO, AND H. WONG-TOI, *HyTech: the next generation*, in Proc. of the 16th Real-time Systems Symposium, RTSS'95, IEEE Computer Society press, 1995.
6. F. LAROUSSINIE AND K. G. LARSEN, *Compositional model checking of real time systems*, in Proc. of the 6th. International Conference on Concurrency Theory, CONCUR'95, I. Lee and S. Smolka, eds., vol. 962 of Lecture Notes in Computer Science, Philadelphia, PA, USA, August 21 - 24 1995, Springer-Verlag.
7. F. LAROUSSINIE, K. G. LARSEN, AND C. WEISE, *From timed automata to logic - and back*, in Proc. of the 20th. International Symposium on Mathematical Foundations of Computer Science, MFCS'95, J. Wiedermann and P. Hájek, eds., vol. 969 of Lecture Notes in Computer Science, Prague, Czech Republic, August 28 - September 1 1995, Springer-Verlag, pp. 529–539.
8. K. G. LARSEN, P. PETTERSSON, AND Y. WANG, UPPAAL *in a nutshell*, Software Tools for Technology Transfer, 1 (1997), pp. 134–152.
9. Y. WANG, *Real-time behaviour of asynchronous agents*, in Proc. of the Conference on Theories of Concurrency: Unification and Extension, CONCUR'90, J. Baeten and J. Klop, eds., vol. 458 of Lecture Notes in Computer Science, Amsterdam, The Netherlands, August 27–30 1990, Springer-Verlag, pp. 502–520.

Recursive Mean-Value Calculus

Paritosh K. Pandya* and Y.S. Ramakrishna**

Tata Institute of Fundamental Research
Colaba, Mumbai 400 005, India

Abstract. The Mean-Value Calculus, *MVC*, of Zhou and Li [19] is extended with the least and the greatest fixed point operators. The resulting logic is called μMVC. Timed behaviours with naturally recursive structure can be elegantly specified in this logic. Some examples of such usage are given. The expressive power of the logic is also studied. It is shown that the propositional fragment of the logic, even with discrete time, is powerful enough to encode the computations of nondeterministic turing machines. Hence, the satisfiability of propositional μMVC over both dense and discrete times is undecidedable.

1 Introduction

The Mean-Value Calculus [19] and its antecedent Duration Calculus [18] provide an elegant and powerful logic for the specification of real-time systems. This logic has been used in a number of applications including the requirement capture of real-time systems, giving semantics to real-time and distributed programming notations and capturing circuit behaviour (see the recent survey by Hansen and Zhou [6]).

Mean-Value Calculus, *MVC*, is an interval based logic of time. It uses the notion of *mean-value of a predicate* representing the fraction of the time for which the predicate holds in a bounded closed time interval. This allows real-time properties to be stated. The logical foundations of *MVC* have been studied by Hansen, Zhou, Sestoft and Li (see [6]).

As in most computational systems, repetitive-recursive behaviours occur frequently in real-time systems too. Logics for real-time systems are required to specify such behaviours. It is usually cumbersome to specify recursive behaviours in *MVC*. To overcome this limitation, in this paper we extend *MVC* with the least and the greatest fixed point operators which allow natural recursive descriptions. The resulting logic is called μMVC.

Consider the following specification of a phase of real-time system: "Signal p is sampled at least once every second till its value is found to be true. (Note that the value of p can be arbitrary between sampling points. We exclude the behaviour where p is never detected to be true.)" This can be captured by the following recursive formula.

$$\mu X.\ (EP(\lceil p\rceil^0) \wedge (0 < \ell \leq 1)) \ \vee \ (EP(\lceil \neg p\rceil^0) \wedge (0 < \ell \leq 1)) \frown X$$

* email: pandya@tcs.tifr.res.in

** email: ysr@eng.sun.com

Intuitively, this formula states the following: (A precise meaning of the operators used will be given later in the paper.) Let the formula μX be satisfied by a system behaviour in a time interval $[b, e]$. Then, the first disjunct $(EP(\lceil p \rceil^0) \wedge (0 < \ell \leq 1))$ states that the interval $[b, e]$ is such that p (is sampled and it) holds at the end-point. Moreover the length of the interval is nonzero and at most 1 time unit. The second disjunct, $EP(\lceil \neg p \rceil^0) \wedge (0 < \ell \leq 1))^\frown X$, states that there is an initial subinterval $[b, m]$ of $[b, e]$ with length nonzero but at most 1 and at its endpoint (a sampling of p occurs and) the value of p is false. Moreover, the rest of the interval $[m, e]$ **recursively** satisfies the same formula μX. The least fixed point operator μX ensures that the recursion terminates eventually with the first disjunct being true.

In this paper, we shall formally define the meaning of such recursive formulae. We will also give some proof rules for reasoning about the fixed point operators. Several examples of the use of recursive formulae will be given. The main example that we shall consider is the recursive formulation of the famous car-bee puzzle [5], and a correctness proof of its solution using the laws of μMVC. We will also encode the runs of non-deterministic 2-counter machine within the propositional fragment of the logic μMVC. This shows that even the propositional fragment of μMVC is highly expressive. Unfortunately, this also implies that the propositional fragment is undecidable and unsuitable for automatic verification.

The idea of extending modal logics with fixed point operators is not new. Temporal mu-calculus has been studied by Emerson and Clarke [4] and Banieqbal and Barringer [2]. Modal mu-calculus has been studied by Kozen [7]. Emerson has argued in favour of using recursive formulae for the specification of real-time properties [3]. Stirling [16] provides a recent overview of this topic.

The rest of the paper is organised as follows. A brief overview of the Mean-Value calculus together with its relational semantics is given in Section 2. The fixed point operators are introduced in Section 3. Section 4 gives examples of the use of these fixed point operators. The paper ends with a brief discussion.

2 Mean-Value Calculus: A Relational Semantics

The Mean-Value Calculus is an extension of the first-order real arithmetic and propositional interval temporal logic [9], where the formulae are interpreted over bounded closed intervals.

A state in MVC is a boolean ($\{0, 1\}$ valued) function of time, representing some observable time variant property of a system. Let *Svar* (with typical elements p, q) be the set of *state* variables. States are boolean combinations of such variables. We use constants 0, 1 for states which are everywhere 0 and everywhere 1, respectively. Let P range over states.

For any time interval $[b, e]$, a *term* evaluates to a real value measuring some aspect of the system behaviour in the interval $[b, e]$. The term $\overline{P}$ denotes the *mean-value* of the state P in interval $[b, e]$, whereas symbol ℓ is a term denoting the length of the interval. Let *Gvar* (with typical elements x, y) be the set of *global* (or rigid) variables. Let r range over real constants. A term t has the form

$$\overline{P} \mid \ell \mid x \mid r \mid t_1 \; op \; t_2 \qquad \text{where } op \in \{+, -, *\}$$

For any time interval $[b, e]$, a *formula* of MVC evaluates to *true* or *false* in a given behaviour. Atomic formulae have the form $t_1 = t_2$ and $t_1 < t_2$. Formulae are constructed from these using the usual connectives of first-order logic. The formula $D_1 \frown D_2$, using the modality $\frown$, is satisfied by an interval if it can be chopped into two subintervals such that the first part satisfies D_1 and the second part satisfies D_2. A formula of MVC has the form:

$$t_1 = t_2 \mid t_1 < t_2 \mid D_1 \land D_2 \mid \neg D \mid \exists x.D \mid D_1 \frown D_2$$

Semantics Let T be the set of time points. We will only consider the following two cases. In *dense-time* interpretation, T is taken to be $\Re^0$, the set of non-negative reals. In *discrete-time* interpretation, T is taken to be ω, the set of natural numbers. $MVC(T)$ will denote MVC interpreted over the time domain T.

Let *Intv* be the set of bounded time intervals $\{[b, e] \mid b, e \in T, b \leq e\}$. Notation 2^{Intv} denotes the power set of *Intv*. We shall treat its elements as relations over T. Let $\circ$ denote the relation composition symbol.

A *structure* (or behaviour) θ assigns a *finitely variable* boolean function of time to each state variable p. Such a function changes its value only finitely often in any finite time interval. The structure θ also assigns a real-number to each global variable x. Let Θ denote the space of all structures. A structure θ' is called p-variant of θ if for all $q \in Svar \cup Gvar$, $q \neq p$, we have $\theta'(q) = \theta(q)$. Notation $\theta[r/x]$ denotes x-variant of θ such that $\theta[r/x](x) = r$.

The value of a term t in structure θ and interval $[b, e]$ is denoted by $\hat{\theta}(t)[b, e] \in \Re$. Let $\overline{P}$ denote the mean-value of P in the interval, i.e.

$$\hat{\theta}(\overline{P})[b, e] \stackrel{\text{def}}{=} \begin{cases} \int_b^e \theta(P)(t)dt \;/\; (e - b) & if \quad e - b > 0 \\ \theta(P)(b) & if \quad e - b = 0 \end{cases}$$

In the discrete time domain $\int_b^e \theta(P)(t)dt$ means $\Sigma_{t=b}^{e-1} \theta(P)(t)$. Also,

$$\hat{\theta}(\ell)[b, e] \stackrel{\text{def}}{=} e - b \qquad \hat{\theta}(x) \stackrel{\text{def}}{=} \theta(x)$$

The real constants and operators of arithmetic have their usual meaning. The duration (integral) of P can be defined as $\int P \stackrel{\text{def}}{=} \overline{P} * \ell$.

The semantics of a formula D in a structure θ is denoted by $\mathcal{M}_\theta(D)$ and defined inductively as follows. Note that $\mathcal{M}_\theta(D) \in 2^{Intv}$. Recall that $\circ$ is the relation composition operator.

$$\begin{array}{lll}
\mathcal{M}_\theta(t_1 = t_2) & \stackrel{\text{def}}{=} & \{[b, e] \mid \hat{\theta}(t_1)[b, e] = \hat{\theta}(t_2)[b, e]\} \\
\mathcal{M}_\theta(t_1 < t_2) & \stackrel{\text{def}}{=} & \{[b, e] \mid \hat{\theta}(t_1)[b, e] < \hat{\theta}(t_2)[b, e]\} \\
\mathcal{M}_\theta(D_1 \land D_2) & \stackrel{\text{def}}{=} & \mathcal{M}_\theta(D_1) \cap \mathcal{M}_\theta(D_2) \quad \mathcal{M}_\theta(\neg D) \stackrel{\text{def}}{=} Intv \; - \; \mathcal{M}_\theta(D) \\
\mathcal{M}_\theta(D_1 \frown D_2) & \stackrel{\text{def}}{=} & \mathcal{M}_\theta(D_1) \circ \mathcal{M}_\theta(D_2) \quad \mathcal{M}_\theta(\exists x.D) \stackrel{\text{def}}{=} \cup_{r \in \Re} \mathcal{M}_{\theta[r/x]}(D)
\end{array}$$

Derived Operators We define some useful abbreviations.

- $\lceil P \rceil^0 \stackrel{\text{def}}{=} \ell = 0 \wedge \overline{P} = 1$ holds for all point intervals where P is true.
  $\lceil P \rceil \stackrel{\text{def}}{=} (\ell > 0) \wedge \neg(\ell > 0 ^\frown \lceil \neg P \rceil^0 ^\frown \ell > 0)$ states that P is true *everywhere inside* the extended interval. Formula $\lceil\lceil P \rceil \stackrel{\text{def}}{=} \lceil P \rceil^0 ^\frown \lceil P \rceil$ additionally requires that P holds at the beginning point, and $\lceil\lceil P \rceil\rceil \stackrel{\text{def}}{=} \lceil P \rceil^0 ^\frown \lceil P \rceil ^\frown \lceil P \rceil^0$ requires P to hold at both the end-points.
- Modalities "for some subinterval" D and "for all subintervals" D can be defined respectively by $\Diamond D \stackrel{\text{def}}{=} true ^\frown D ^\frown true$ and $\Box D \stackrel{\text{def}}{=} \neg\Diamond\neg D$.
- $EP(D) \stackrel{\text{def}}{=} true ^\frown (\ell = 0 \wedge D)$ states that D holds at the end-point of the interval.
- $Unit \stackrel{\text{def}}{=} \ell > 0 \wedge \neg(\ell > 0 ^\frown \ell > 0)$ holds for indivisible extended intervals. There are no such intervals in dense-time (due to density property). In discrete time, exactly the intervals of the form $[b, b+1]$ satisfy $Unit$.

We refer the reader to [19, 8] for the proof rules of MVC. The following rules will be used later in the paper.

$$\begin{array}{llcll}
(A0) & (\int P = r) ^\frown (\int P = s) & \Leftrightarrow & (\int P = r + s) & \text{where} r, s \in \Re^0 \\
(A1) & 0 \leq \int P \leq \ell & & & \\
(A2) & \lceil P \rceil \ \ => \ \ \int P = \ell & & & \\
(A3) & \int P \ + \ \int \neg P \ = \ \ell & & &
\end{array}$$

Propositional MVC The following subset of MVC will be called *Propositional MVC*. Note that is fragment does not require the notion of mean-value.

$$\lceil P \rceil^0 \mid D_1 \wedge D_2 \mid \neg D \mid D_1 ^\frown D_2$$

Li [8] has shown that the satisfiability of both $PMVC(\Re^0)$ and $PMVC(\omega)$ formulae is decidable.

3 Open Formulae and Fixed Point Operators

We now consider MVC formulae $F(\overline{X})$ which additionally contain variables in the list $\overline{X}$ as atomic formulae. Such formulae are called *open formulae* and variables $\overline{X}$ are called formula variables. For example, $\lceil P \rceil^0 ^\frown Unit ^\frown X$ is an open formula.

The relational semantics of open formulae can be defined as follows. Let $\sigma : Fvar \to 2^{Intv}$ denote a *valuation* giving the set of intervals $\sigma(X)$ for which X is true. Then, the meaning of $F(\overline{X})$ is inductively given by extension $\mathcal{EM}_\theta^\sigma$ of $\mathcal{M}_\theta$ as follows.

$$\mathcal{EM}_\theta^\sigma(X) \stackrel{\text{def}}{=} \sigma(X)$$

In all other cases, $\mathcal{EM}$ is defined like $\mathcal{M}$. We omit these clauses.

Let $\Sigma = (Fvar \to 2^{Intv})$ be the set of all valuations. For $\chi \in 2^{Intv}$, notation $\sigma[\chi/X]$ denotes a valuation which is like σ except that $\sigma(X) = \chi$. For an open formula, substitution $F[D/X]$ gives the formula obtained by replacing every free occurrence of X by the formula D. As a notational convenience, we emphasize the appearance of X in F by writing $F(X)$. In this case, notation $F(D)$ abbreviates $F[D/X]$

Fixed point operators Consider the recursive equation $X = F(X)$. Then, $\chi \in 2^{Intv}$ is called a solution in X with respect to given θ and σ if

$$\mathcal{EM}_\theta^{\sigma[\chi/X]}(F) \quad = \quad \chi$$

Such a solution is also called a fixed point of $F(X)$ with respect to θ and σ.

A formula $F(X)$ may have zero, one or more fixed points. We are especially interested in the *least* and the *greatest* fixed points (when they exist) and we designate these by the formulae $\mu X.F$ and $\nu X.F$, respectively. In the rest of this section, we investigate the conditions for the existence of these fixed points and give some proof rules governing them.

Let $\sigma \leq_X \sigma'$ iff $\sigma(X) \subseteq \sigma'(X)$ and $\sigma(Y) = \sigma'(Y)$ for all $Y \neq X$. An open formula F is called *monotonic* in X if $(\sigma \leq_X \sigma' \;\Rightarrow\; \mathcal{EM}_\theta^\sigma(F) \subseteq \mathcal{EM}_\theta^{\sigma'}(F))$ for all θ, σ, σ'.

Theorem 1 (Knaster-Tarski). *If $f(x)$ is a monotonic function over a complete lattice $(S, \leq)$ then the set of fixed points (i.e. solutions of $x = f(x)$) form a complete sub-lattice of $(S, \leq)$. The least fixed point, μf, is given by $\sqcap\{\, x \mid f(x) \leq x \,\}$, and the greatest fixed point, νf, is given by $\sqcup\{\, x \mid x \leq f(x) \,\}$.* □

Proposition 1.
- *$(2^{Intv}, \subset)$ is a complete lattice.*
- *$((\Sigma \to 2^{Intv}), \sqsubseteq)$ is a complete lattice where $f \sqsubseteq g$ iff $f(\sigma) \subseteq g(\sigma)$ for all $\sigma \in \Sigma$.*
- *$(\Theta \to \Sigma \to 2^{Intv}, \leq)$ is a complete lattice where $f \leq g$ iff $f(\theta) \sqsubseteq g(\theta)$ for all $\theta \in \Theta$.* □

Theorem 2. *Let F be monotonic in X. Then the semantics of the least and the greatest fixed point formulae $\mu X.F(X)$ and $\nu X.F(X)$ is given respectively by*

$$\mathcal{EM}_\theta^\sigma(\mu X.F) \quad = \quad \cap\{\, \chi \in 2^{Intv} \mid \mathcal{EM}_\theta^{\sigma[\chi/X]}(F) \subseteq \chi \,\}$$

$$\mathcal{EM}_\theta^\sigma(\nu X.F) \quad = \quad \cup\{\chi \in 2^{Intv} \mid \chi \subseteq \mathcal{EM}_\theta^\sigma[\chi/X](F) \,\}$$

□

The following proposition gives sufficient conditions for $F(X)$ to be monotonic.

Proposition 2. *Let F be such that every occurrence of X in F is in the scope of an even number of $\neg$. Such an F will be called* evenly-negated *in X. Then, F is monotonic in X.*

Proof sketch *Note that the operators $\wedge, \vee, \frown$ are all monotonic whereas $\neg$ is anti-monotonic. The result follows from this by structural induction on F.* □

Because of the above theorems, we extend the syntax of MVC to include formulae $\mu X.F(X)$ and $\nu X.F(X)$ where $F(X)$ is *evenly negated.* The resulting logic is called **Recursive Mean-Value Calculus**, or μMVC. The propositional fragment of μMVC (i.e. logic $PMVC$ extended with fixed point operators) will be denoted by $\mu PMVC$. The following proof rules allow reasoning about fixed point operators.

$$(R1)\quad \mu X.F(X) \Leftrightarrow F(\mu X.F(X)) \qquad (R2)\quad \nu X.F(X) \Leftrightarrow F(\nu X.F(X))$$

$$(R3)\quad \frac{F(D) \Rightarrow D}{\mu X.F(X) \Rightarrow D} \qquad (R4)\quad \frac{D \Rightarrow F(D)}{D \Rightarrow \nu X.F(X)}$$

$$(R5)\quad \nu X F(X) \Leftrightarrow \neg \nu X.\, \neg F(\neg X)$$

4 Examples and Expressiveness

In this section, we give some examples of the use of the fixed point operators. One of the main uses of fixed point operators is in giving compositional semantics of the iteration and recursion constructs of real-time programming languages. Several cases of such use are listed in Section 5. Here, we consider some other examples. Many of these point to the expressive power of the logic.

Iteration Let $F(X) \stackrel{\text{def}}{=} (D_1 \vee D_2 {}^\frown X) \wedge D_3$. Then the formula $\mu X.F(X)$ holds for an interval $[b, e]$ provided there is a finite non-decreasing sequence of points $m_0, m_1, \ldots, m_{n+1}$ with $m_0 = b$, $m_{n+1} = e$ such that $[m_i, m_{i+1}]$ satisfy D_2 and $[m_i, e]$ satisfy D_3 for $0 \leq i \leq n-1$, and $[m_n, m_{n+1}]$ satisfies $D_1 \wedge D_3$.

Let $D^* \stackrel{\text{def}}{=} \mu X.(\ell = 0 \vee D {}^\frown X)$. This states that the interval is either a point interval, or it can be partitioned into a finite sequence of subintervals each of which satisfies D. Moskowski [9] has made considerable use of this operator in the context of interval temporal logic.

Palindromes and Context-Free Grammars Palindromes over an alphabet Σ are defined by the grammar $S ::= a_i \mid a_i S a_i$ where $a_i \in \Sigma$. This set of palindromes can be specified by the $\mu PMVC(\omega)$ formula

$$Excl \wedge \mu X.(\lceil a_i \rceil^0 {}^\frown Unit \vee \lceil a_i \rceil^0 {}^\frown Unit {}^\frown X {}^\frown \lceil a_i \rceil^0 {}^\frown Unit)$$

where $Excl \stackrel{\text{def}}{=} (\bigvee_{a \in \Sigma} \lceil\lceil a \rceil\rceil) \wedge (\bigwedge_{a,b \in \Sigma, a \neq b} \lceil\lceil \neg(a \wedge b) \rceil\rceil)$.

A variant of the above encoding also allow us to specify palindromes in $\mu PMVC(\Re^0)$ (see [12]). It is easy to see that the technique used in the above example can be generalised to give a formula $D(G)$ specifying the language of any context-free grammar G (see [12] for details). Equality of two context-free grammars G, G' can be reduced to the validity of the formula $D(G) \Leftrightarrow D(G')$. Since the equality of two context-free grammars is undecidable, we have the following result.

Proposition 3. *The validity (satisfiability) of $\mu PMVC(\omega)$ and $\mu PMVC(\Re^0)$ formulae is undecidable.*

□

4.1 The Car-Bee Problem

The original MVC requires a structure θ to assign a *finitely variable* boolean functions of time to each state variable. MVC can be generalised to allow structures where each state variable is assigned any arbitrary *integrable* boolean function of time (see [5] for details). Note that these functions can be *finitely divergent*, i.e. they may change their values infinitely often within a finite time interval. The following Car-Bee puzzle illustrates such a behaviour.

Car-Bee Problem Car E and Car W move towards each other at uniform and equal speed till they collide after r time units. A bee starts from car E and flies towards car W at twice the speed of a car. On reaching car W the bee instantly reverses its direction and flies towards car E at the same speed till car E is reached. This behaviour is repeated endlessly (thus exhibiting finite divergence) till the cars collide. What is the quantum of time (out of r) spent by the bee in flying towards car W?

We specify the behaviour of the bee using a $\mu MVC(\Re^0)$ formula and prove the correctness of a solution to this problem using the proof rules of the logic. The readers must compare the simplicity of this proof with the previous formulation using MVC without fixed point opeators [5].

Let a state variable B take value 1 when the bee is flying towards the car W, and be 0 at other times. The problem is to compute the value of $\int_0^r B(t)dt$. The specification of B is based on the following analysis. If the velocity of a car is v then the relative speed of a car w.r.t. the other car is 2v whereas that of the bee w.r.t. the other car is 3v. Assuming that the bee is at car E, if the cars take x time units to collide then the bee reaches the car W in $2x/3$ time. From this point the situation is symmetric and the bee reaches the car E again after 2/3 of the remaining time i.e. after $2x/9$ time units. Now the bee is at car E and the above behaviour repeats within the remaining time $x/9$. This gives the following *recursive* formulation of the car-bee problem. Let

$$F(X) \stackrel{\text{def}}{=} \exists x.\ \ell = x \land ((\lceil B \rceil \land \ell = 2x/3) \frown (\lceil \neg B \rceil \land \ell = 2x/9) \frown (\ell = x/9 \land X))$$
$$\mathbf{Bee} \stackrel{\text{def}}{=} \ell = r \land \nu X.F(X).$$

The greatest fixed point captures the fact that there are infinitely many repetitions. Observe that $\mu X.F(X) \Leftrightarrow \mathit{false}$.

Theorem 3. **Bee** $\Rightarrow$ $(\int B = 3r/4)$

Its proof is based on the following lemma.

Lemma 1. *Let* $H(n) \stackrel{\text{def}}{=} \exists y.\ \ell = y \land ((\int B = \frac{3y}{4}(1 - \frac{1}{9^n})) \frown (\ell = \frac{y}{9^n}))$. *Then, for all* $n \in \omega$, *we have* $\nu X.F(X) \Rightarrow H(n)$.

Proof *(by indunction on n)*
Base case

$$
\begin{array}{ll}
 & \nu X.F(X) \\
\Rightarrow & \exists y.\ \ell = y \qquad \{ \textit{ Tautology of MVC } \} \\
\Rightarrow & \exists y.\ \ell = 0 \frown \ell = y \qquad \{ \textit{ Rule A0 } \} \\
\Rightarrow & \exists y. \int B = 0 \frown \ell = y \qquad \{ \textit{ Rule A1 } \} \\
\Leftrightarrow & \exists y.\ (\int B = \frac{3y}{4}(1 - \frac{1}{9^0})) \frown (\ell = \frac{y}{9^0}) \\
\Leftrightarrow & H(0)
\end{array}
$$

Induction Step

$$
\begin{array}{ll}
 & \nu X.F(X) \\
\Leftrightarrow & F(\nu X.F(X)) \qquad \{ \textit{ Rule R2 } \} \\
\Rightarrow & F(H(n)) \\
 & \qquad \{ \textit{ By Ind. Hypothesis and Monotonicity of } F(X) \} \\
\Rightarrow & \exists y.\ \ell = y \wedge (([B] \wedge \ell = \frac{2y}{3}) \frown ([\neg B] \wedge \ell = \frac{2y}{9}) \frown (\ell = \frac{y}{9} \wedge H(n))) \\
 & \qquad \{ \textit{ Definition of } F(X) \} \\
\Rightarrow & \exists y.\ \ell = y \wedge ((\int B = \frac{2y}{3}) \frown (\ell = \frac{y}{9} \wedge H(n))) \\
 & \qquad \{ \textit{ Rules A2, A3 and A0 } \} \\
\Rightarrow & \exists y.\ \ell = y \wedge ((\int B = \frac{2y}{3}) \frown (\int B = \frac{3(y/9)}{4}(1 - \frac{1}{9^n})) \frown (\ell = \frac{y/9}{9^n})) \\
 & \qquad \{ \textit{ Definition of } H(n) \} \\
\Leftrightarrow & \exists y.\ \ell = y \wedge ((\int B = \frac{2y}{3} + \frac{3(y/9)}{4}(1 - \frac{1}{9^n})) \frown (\ell = \frac{y/9}{9^n})) \\
 & \qquad \{ \textit{ Rule A0 } \} \\
\Leftrightarrow & \exists y.\ \ell = y \wedge ((\int B = \frac{3y}{4}(1 - \frac{1}{9^{n+1}})) \frown (\ell = \frac{y}{9^{n+1}})) \\
 & \qquad \{ \textit{ Real arithmetic } \} \\
\Rightarrow & H(n+1) \qquad \{ \textit{ Definition of H(n+1) } \}
\end{array}
$$

□

Proof of Theorem 3 From the above lemma we get that for all $n \in \omega$,

$$(\ell = y \wedge \nu X.F(X)) \Rightarrow \frac{3y}{4}(1 - \frac{1}{9^n}) \le \int B \le \frac{3y}{4}(1 - \frac{1}{9^n}) + \frac{Y}{9^n}$$

By real arithmetic, for all $n \in \omega$,

$$(\ell = y \wedge \nu X.F(X)) \Rightarrow \frac{3y}{4}(1 - \frac{1}{9^n}) \le \int B \le \frac{3y}{4}(1 + \frac{1}{4 * 9^n})$$

Thus, by the completeness of real numbers,

$$(\ell = y \wedge \nu X.F(X)) \Rightarrow \int B = 3y/4$$

□

4.2 Representing Runs of a 2-Counter Machine

A *nondeterministic 2-counter machine* M consists of two counters C and D and a sequence of n instructions with labels $0, \ldots, n-1$. The instructions are of the following form where E ranges over the counters C, D and j, k range over the instruction labels $0, \ldots, n$.

```
increment(E) then jump to j or k
decrement(E) then jump to j or k
if E=0 then jump to j else jump to k
```

After executing an `increment` or `decrement` instruction, the machine non-deterministically jumps to one of the two labels j or k. By convention, the instruction with label n is the halt instruction. Thus, execution may be terminated by jumping to label n. A *configuration* of M is a triple (i, m_1, m_2) where i is the label of the instruction to be executed, and m_1, m_2 are the current values of the counters C, D respectively. The transition relation between the configurations is defined in the obvious way. A run starts with the initial configuration $(0,0,0)$ and is a finite sequence of configurations where successive configurations are related by the transition relation. A halting run is a run which ends with label n.

Theorem 4. *The problem of determining whether a machine M has a halting run is undecidable.*

We shall encode runs of M in $\mu PMVC$. The encoding is sound for both discrete and dense time domains. We use the following state variables $p, s_0, s_1, s_2, s_3, a, c$ and l_i for $0 \leq i \leq n$. All these states are mutually exclusive and at least one of them must be true at each time point; we shall designate this property by $MUTEX$ (we omit the obvious MVC definition).

Let $[b)$ denote a left-closed right open extended time interval in which state b is true. Then, a natural number m is denoted by the behaviour fragment

$$[b)\,\underbrace{[p)[b)\ldots[p)[b)}_{m \;\; times}$$

We shall denote this fragment by abbreviation $COUNT(m)$. A configuration (i, m_1, m_2) is denoted by the following behaviour fragment.

$$[s_0)[l_i)[s_1)COUNT(m_1)[s_2)COUNT(m_2)[s_3)$$

A run is represented by a sequence of such configurations.

The following μMVC formula $CONF$ holds precisely for time intervals representing a configuration (recall the definition of D^* given at the beginning of Section 4).

$$\begin{aligned} COUNTER &\stackrel{\text{def}}{=} \lceil\lceil b\rceil \frown (\lceil\lceil p\rceil \frown \lceil\lceil b\rceil)^* \\ CONF &\stackrel{\text{def}}{=} (\lceil\lceil s_0\rceil \frown (\vee_{i:0\leq i\leq n} \lceil\lceil l_i\rceil) \frown \lceil\lceil s_1\rceil \frown COUNTER \frown \\ &\qquad\qquad \lceil\lceil s_2\rceil \frown COUNTER \frown \lceil\lceil s_3\rceil) \;\wedge\; MUTEX \end{aligned}$$

We define some auxiliary formulae

$$\begin{aligned} label(i) &\stackrel{\text{def}}{=} CONF \wedge (\lceil\lceil s_0\rceil \frown \lceil\lceil l_i\rceil \frown true) \\ iszero(C) &\stackrel{\text{def}}{=} CONF \wedge (true \frown \lceil\lceil s_1\rceil \frown \lceil\lceil b\rceil \frown \lceil\lceil s_2\rceil \frown true) \\ INITCONF &\stackrel{\text{def}}{=} CONF \wedge label(0) \wedge iszero(C) \wedge iszero(D) \end{aligned}$$

where $iszero(D)$ is defined similarly. Formula $label(i)$ holds exactly for configurations with instruction label i. Formula $iszero(C)$ holds for configurations where the value of counter C is 0.

A transition is represented by a pair of configurations occuring consecutively in time; i.e. by intervals satisfying $CONF \frown CONF$. Formula $Inc(C)$ holds for a transition provided the value of counter C has incremented by 1. This formula is central to encoding runs, and should be understood carefully.

$$MATCH(C) \stackrel{\text{def}}{=} \mu X. \left(\begin{array}{l} \lceil\lceil b \rceil \frown \lceil\lceil s_2 \rceil \frown \lceil \neg s_1 \rceil \frown \lceil\lceil s_1 \rceil \frown \lceil\lceil b \rceil \\ \vee \lceil\lceil b \rceil \frown \lceil\lceil p \rceil \frown X \frown \lceil\lceil p \rceil \frown \lceil\lceil b \rceil \end{array} \right)$$

$$Inc(C) \stackrel{\text{def}}{=} \begin{array}{l} (CONF \frown CONF) \ \wedge \\ (\lceil \neg s_1 \rceil \frown \lceil\lceil s_1 \rceil \frown MATCH(C) \frown \lceil\lceil p \rceil \frown \lceil\lceil b \rceil \frown \lceil\lceil s_2 \rceil \frown true) \end{array}$$

Similarly, we can define $Dec(C)$, which encodes the fact that the value of counter has decremented, and $Unchange(C)$ which encodes the fact that counter C has not changed. Similarly, also $Inc(D)$, $Dec(D)$ and $Unchange(D)$. We omit these details.

Execution of an instruction with label i is represented by a formula $D(i)$. Let the instruction with label i be `increment` C `then jump to` j `or` k. Then,

$$D(i) \stackrel{\text{def}}{=} \begin{array}{l} ((CONF \wedge label(i)) \frown (CONF \wedge (label(j) \vee label(k)))) \\ \wedge \ Inc(C) \ \wedge \ Unchange(D) \end{array}$$

Let the instruction with label i be `if C=0 then jump to` j `else jump to` k. Then,

$$D(i) \stackrel{\text{def}}{=} \begin{array}{l} \left(\begin{array}{l} (CONF \wedge label(i) \wedge iszero(C)) \frown (CONF \wedge label(j)) \\ \vee \ (CONF \wedge label(i) \wedge \neg iszero(C)) \frown (CONF \wedge label(k)) \end{array} \right) \\ \wedge \ Unchange(C) \ \wedge \ Unchange(D) \end{array}$$

A finite halting run of M is encoded by the formula

$$HALT(M) \stackrel{\text{def}}{=} \begin{array}{ll} & (INITCONF \frown true) \ \wedge \ CONF^* \\ \wedge & \Box(CONF \frown CONF \Rightarrow (\vee_{i:0 \leq i < n} \ D(i))) \\ \wedge & true \frown (CONF \wedge label(n)) \end{array}$$

Then it is easy to verify that every model $(\theta, [b, e]) \models HALT(M)$ corresponds to a halting run of M.

Proposition 4. *$HALT(M)$ is satisfiable if and only if M has a halting run.* □

Theorem 5. *The satisfiability of $\mu PMVC$ is undecidable.* □

MVC can be extended with an outward looking modality $\vec{\Diamond}\ D$ to get a more powerful logic where liveness properties can be specified (see Pandya [10]).

$$(\theta, [b, e]) \models \vec{\Diamond}\ D \ \text{ iff } \ \text{ for some } m : e \leq m, \quad (\theta, [b, m]) \models D$$

Let $\mu PMVC^{-1}$ denote the Proposition MVC with the fixed point operators and the additional modality $\vec{\Diamond}\ D$.

It is easy to construct a formula $RECUR(M)$ in $\mu PMVC^{-1}$ such that $(\theta,[b,e]) \models RECUR(M)$ if and only if the behaviour θ in interval $[b,\infty]$ corresponds to an infinite run of M in which the label 0 occurs infinitely often (see [12] for details). It is known that the problem of determining whether M has such a run is highly undecidable. Hence we get the following result [12].

Theorem 6. *Satisfiability of $\mu PMVC^{-1}$ formulae is Σ_1^1 hard.* □

5 Discussion

We have extended MVC with the least and the greatest fixed point operators to give a logic μMVC. We have given some examples of the use of fixed point operators in naturally specifying the recursive behaviour of timed systems.

A major motivation for introducing fixed point operators has been to capture the semantics of recursion in timed langauges. Duration Calculus has been extensively used to give logical semantics of many real-time programming notations. This includes Timed CSP [11], the synchronous programming language Esterel [13], Sequential Hybrid Programs [14] and Verilog [17]. In each of these languages, the formalisation of the iteration and recursion constructs can be elegantly achieved using the fixed point operators. For example, the semantics of the loop construct in Esterel has been given [13] by the formula

$$D(\text{loop S end}) \stackrel{\text{def}}{=} \mu X.D(S);\ X$$

The semantics of recursion in Timed CSP has been given [11] by the formula

$$D(recX.F(X)) \stackrel{\text{def}}{=} \nu X.D(F(X))$$

Schneider and Xu [17] have also used the fixed point operators to capture the semantics of iteration constructs of Verilog. A novel semantics of the `while` construct for sequential hybrid pograms using a combination of least and greatest fixed points can be found in [14]. In aid of brevity, we just list these uses here without giving details.

In order to evaluate the expressive power of the fixed point operators in interval logics, we have encoded finite runs of nondeterministic 2-counter machines within Propositional MVC, or $\mu PMVC$. This shows that $\mu PMVC$ is powerful enough to specify all turing computable langauges. Because of this expressive power, it is immediate that the satisfiability of $\mu PMVC$ formulae is undecidable. This makes $\mu PMVC$ quite unsuitable for automatic verification and model checking.

We believe that logics like MVC and μMVC are suitable for requirement capture of real-time systems, where richness rather than decidability is important. They may be used for the verification of real-time systems using the theorem-proving approach [15]. It seems improbable that problems like the carbee problem (Section 4.1) can be handled within simpler decidable logics. At the same time, existence of reasonably rich subsets of μMVC which are decidable remains an open question and a topic of further study. In this context, we conjecture that $\mu PMVC$ formulae with tail recursion are decidable.

Acknowledgements The authors thank K. Narayan Kumar for numerous discussions which helped in shaping this work to its present form.

References

1. R. Alur and T.A. Henzinger. A Really Temporal Logic. *Jour. ACM*, 41(1), 1994.
2. B. Banieqbal and H. Barringer. Temporal Logic with Fixed Points. In *Proc. Temporal Logic in Specification, LNCS 398*, Springer-Verlag, 1989.
3. E. Emerson. Real-time and the Mu Calculus. *In Real-time: Theory in Practice*, REX workshop, Mook, The Netherlands, *LNCS 600*, Springer-Verlag, 1992.
4. E. Emerson and E. Clarke. Characterising Correctness Properties of Parallel Programs using Fixed-points. *LNCS 85*, Springer-Verlag, 1980.
5. M.R. Hansen, P.K. Pandya and Zhou Chaochen. Finite Divergence. *Theoretical Computer Science*, 138:113–139, 1994.
6. M.R. Hansen and Chaochen Zhou. Duration calculus: Logical foundations. *Formal Aspects of Computing*, 9(3):283–330, 1997.
7. D. Kozen. Results on Propositional Mu-calculus. *Thoeretical Computer Science*, 27:333–354, 1983.
8. Xiaoshan Li. *A Mean Value Calculus*. Ph.D. Thesis, Software Institute, Academia Sinica, 1994.
9. B. Moszkowski. A Temporal Logic for Multi-level Reasoning about Hardware. *IEEE Computer*, 18(2):10–19, 1985.
10. P.K. Pandya. Some Extensions to Mean-Value Calculus: Expressiveness and Decidability. In H. Kleine Buning, editor, *Proc. CSL'95, LNCS 1092*, Springer-Verlag, 1995.
11. P.K. Pandya and D.V. Hung. Duration Calculus of Weakly Monotonic Time. To appear in *Proc. FTRTFT'98*, Lyngby, Denmark, *LNCS*, Springer-Verlag, 1998.
12. P.K. Pandya and Y.S. Ramakrishna. A Recursive Mean Value Calculus. *Technical Report TCS-95/3*, Computer Science Group, TIFR, Bombay, 1995.
13. P.K. Pandya, Y.S. Ramakrishna, R.K. Shyamasundar. A Compositional Semantics of Esterel in Duration Calculus. In *Proc. Second AMAST workshop on Real-time Systems: Models and Proofs*, Bordeux, June, 1995.
14. P.K. Pandya, Hanpin Wang and Qiwen Xu. Towards a Theory of Sequential Hybrid Programs. In W.P. de Roever and D. Gries (eds.), *Proc. PROCOMET'98*, Shelter Island, New York, Chapman & Hall, 1998.
15. J.U. Skakkebaek and N. Shankar. Towards a Duration Calculus Proof Assistant in PVS. In *Proc. FTRTFR'94, LNCS 863*, Springer-Verlag, 1994.
16. C. Stirling. Modal and Temporal logics. In *Handbook of Logic in Computer Science, Vol 2.*, Clarendon Press, Oxford, pp. 476–563, 1995.
17. G. Schneider and Qiwen Xu. Towards Formal Semantics of Verilog using Duration Calculus. To appear in *Proc. FTRTFT'98*, Lyngby, Denmark, *LNCS*, Springer-Verlag, 1998.
18. Chaochen Zhou, C.A.R. Hoare and A.P. Ravn. A Calculus of Durations. *Information Processing Letters*, 40(5):269–276, 1991.
19. Chaochen Zhou and Xiaoshan Li. A Mean Value Calculus of Durations. In A.W. Roscoe, editor, *A Classical Mind: Essays in Honour of C.A.R. Hoare*, Prentice Hall International, pp 431–451, 1994.

Efficient Formal Verification of Hierarchical Descriptions

Rajeev Alur

Department of Computer & Information Science
University of Pennsylvania
Philadelphia, PA 19104
Email: alur@cis.upenn.edu
URL: www.cis.upenn.edu/ alur

Model checking is emerging as a practical tool for detecting logical errors in early stages of system design. We investigate the model checking of hierarchical (nested) systems, i.e. finite state machines whose states themselves can be other machines. This nesting ability is common in various software design methodologies and is available in several commercial modeling tools. The straightforward way to analyze a hierarchical machine is to flatten it (thus, incurring an exponential blow up) and apply a model checking tool on the resulting ordinary FSM.

First, we show that this flattening is not necessary in the case of *sequential* hierarchical state machines. We develop algorithms for verifying linear time requirements whose complexity is polynomial in the size of the hierarchical machine. We address also the verification of branching time requirements and provide efficient algorithms and matching lower bounds.

Next, we report on the ongoing research on the analysis of *communicating* hierarchical state machines, and the application of our algorithms to the analysis the ITU standard Z.120 (MSC'96) for message sequence charts.

Reference:

Model checking of hierarchical state machines. R. Alur and M. Yannakakis. In *Proceedings of the Sixth ACM SIGSOFT Symposium on Foundations of Software Engineering*, Nov 1998.

Proof Rules for Model Checking Systems with Data

K. L. McMillan

Cadence Berkeley Labs
2001 Addison St., 3rd floor
Berkeley, CA 94704-1103
mcmillan@cadence.com

Abstract. Model checking is an automated technique for verifying temporal properties of finite-state systems. The technique can be used, for example, to verify the finite control parts of computer hardware designs and communication protocols. However, because it requires exhaustively searching the state space of a system to be verified, it cannot generally be applied directly to systems manipulating data, even if the data types are finite. For unbounded or uninterpreted data types, the model checking problem becomes undecidable.

Nonetheless, reductions akin to "program slicing" can be used to reduce the verification of large systems with unbounded data to model checking problems over tractably small models with finite data types. Such a reduction can be obtained, for example, by enumerating the possible paths of a data item through a system. Symmetry can then be exploited to reduce the cases to a tractable number. Use of model checking in this way can greatly simplify proofs by eliminating the need for global invariants.

This talk will show how a system of three inference rules – circular assume/guarantee, temporal case splitting, and symmetry reduction – can be used in conjunction with model checking to yield quite concise proofs of systems that manipulate data.

Partial Order Reductions for Bisimulation Checking

Michaela Huhn°*, Peter Niebert+, Heike Wehrheim†

°Universität Karlsruhe, Institut für Rechnerentwurf und Fehlertoleranz (Prof. D. Schmid), Postfach 6980, D–76128 Karlsruhe, Germany
huhn@informatik.uni-karlsruhe.de

+Universität Hildesheim, Institut für Informatik (Prof. U.Goltz), Postfach 101363, D–31113 Hildesheim, Germany
niebert@informatik.uni-hildesheim.de

†Universität Oldenburg, Fachbereich Informatik, Abteilung Semantik (Prof. E.-R.Olderog), Postfach 2503, D–26111 Oldenburg, Germany
wehrheim@informatik.uni-oldenburg.de

Abstract. Partial order methods have been introduced to avoid the state explosion problem in verification resulting from the representation of multiple interleavings of concurrent transitions. The basic idea is to build a reduced state space on which certain properties hold if and only if they hold for the full state space. Most often, the considered properties are linear-time properties. In this paper we suggest novel *branching time* reduction techniques which allow checking *bisimulation equivalence* on reduced state spaces. Our reduction takes place on *bisimulation game graphs*, thus jointly treating the systems under consideration. We show that reduction preserves winning strategies of the two players in the bisimulation game.

1 Introduction

Automatic verification of finite state systems is successfully applied in many areas to check that systems satisfy their specifications. However, these techniques all suffer from the so-called state explosion problem which often forbids verification because of complexity. One source of state explosion is the representation of multiple interleavings of concurrent transitions. In the worst case, the state space grows exponentially in the number of components of a parallel system.

The approach to (partially) overcome state explosion we present here belongs to the class of *partial order methods* (PO-methods, for an overview see [Pom96]). The general idea behind PO-methods is the fact that the result of many verification tasks is insensitive to the order in which concurrent transitions are executed by the system. Thus automatic verification can take place on a *reduced* state space which contains just some of a number of different interleavings of

* This work was partially supported with funds of the DFG within the priority program "Design and design methodology of embedded systems".

concurrent transitions. Based on a notion of independence of transitions, PO-techniques incrementally construct this reduced state space by choosing in every explored state only a subset of the enabled transitions for further expansion.

Various conditions on the expansion set guarantee the correctness of the technique, i.e. that the result of verification on the reduced state space is the same as that on the full one. This idea has been successfully applied in many areas, with reductions preserving deadlock-freedom, (Mazurkiewicz) trace equivalence, next-free linear time temporal logic (LTL-X) formulas, failure equivalences or non-emptiness of asynchronous automata These properties are all *linear time* properties. Recently, there has also been some work on extending reductions to *branching time* properties, especially branching time logics, e.g. [GKPP95,WW96].

In the area of process algebras, verification often proceeds by comparing the system and its specification by means of an *equivalence relation.* A whole bunch of equivalence relations has been suggested for this purpose, the most often used one being *bisimulation equivalence* of Park and Milner [Mil89]. Bisimulation is a strong branching time equivalence since it precisely distinguishes the moments of choice. In this paper we develop a new reduction technique for bisimulation checking for systems with an independence relation on *actions* [Maz95].

Preservation of branching time equivalence relations by partial order methods has been studied by De Souza and De Simone [dSdS95] and by Gerth, Kuiper, Peled and Penzcek [GKPP95]. Like us, De Souza and De Simone aim for partial order reductions for the verification task of (strong) bisimilarity checks. They show that bisimilarity of two reduced systems implies bisimilarity of the full systems. For this purpose, they study so-called *partial automata* in which states are attached with information about omitted transitions, which may either already have occurred or will occur later, and define a notion of bisimulation on partial automata. They discuss a number of critical examples and show their result for a restricted class of partial automata. However, the reverse direction (bisimilarity of full automata implying bisimilarity of partial automata) is not shown.

[GKPP95] focus on model-checking of CTL*-X properties. They justify their approach by proving that their partial order reductions preserve *branching bisimulation*, a weak equivalence abstracting from so-called *silent* actions which does not change atomic propositions. Thus with respect to the equivalence check, they prove the full and the reduced system to be branching bisimilar. Technically, Gerth et.al. achieve their goal by adding a further condition to linear-time reduction conditions: The expansion set may either contain *one* or all enabled transitions, and in case of one, the transition must not change atomic propositions.

Starting point for our partial order reductions for bisimilarity are the linear time reduction conditions by Peled and Penzcek [PP95]. We introduce two branching time conditions which ensure a faithful representation of the branching structure in the reduced systems. One of them is in analogy to that from [GKPP95], but for our purposes there are also other cases allowing reductions (see C3 in Section 4). Moreover, since the developed condition is not efficiently computable in general, we develop a strengthening which can be easily determined during the exploration of the state space.

Our goal is to show strong bisimilarity of two reduced systems; hence one must be able to also delay some actions visible with respect to the equivalence check while expanding others. This is in difference to [GKPP95].

An additional difficulty occurs in the comparison of two reduced systems: Either the bisimulation check has to be modified, or it must be guaranteed that in corresponding states, the *same* expansion sets are chosen. Otherwise a bisimulation check on the reduced systems may fail just because accidentally – as in the picture – different expansion sets were chosen. We solve the problem by *jointly* treating both systems. This can quite elegantly be presented by using the characterisation of bisimulation as a *two player game* [Sti93]. Transition systems are bisimilar if and only if a specific player of the bisimulation game has a winning strategy. Instead of reducing transition systems, we reduce *bisimulation game graphs* and show preservation of winning strategies for the two players. For application purposes, the reductions on the game graph can be directly transferred to the joint treatment of both systems in "on-the-fly" algorithms for bisimulation like [FM90]. However, the game characterisation can be used to achieve an asymptotic worst case complexity equal to that of partition refinement algorithms [KS90] for bisimulation, improving the result in [FM90].

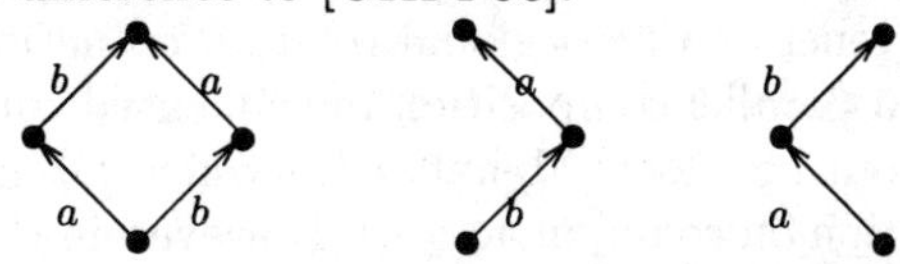

The paper is structured as follows: In Section 2 we introduce the basic notions of bisimulation and global independence relation on actions. Section 3 is concerned with the game characterisation of bisimulation. In Section 4 we give our partial order reductions for bisimulations and the main result.

2 Definitions

In this section, we introduce our models and define bisimulation equivalence.

Partial order reductions require a notion of *independence* on executed actions or transitions of the system. The intuition of independence of actions is that these can be performed in any order with the same effect.

Let *Act* be a finite or infinite set of actions and $I \subseteq Act \times Act$ a symmetric and irreflexive relation called *independency*.

Definition 1. A *labelled transition system* is a tuple $T = \langle S, \rightarrow, s^0 \rangle$, where S is a set of states, $\rightarrow \subseteq S \times Act \times S$ a transition relation and $s^0 \in S$ an initial state. A transition system $\langle S, \rightarrow, s^0 \rangle$ is *I-consistent* if the following holds:

- if $s \xrightarrow{a} s_1, s \xrightarrow{b} s_2, a\ I\ b$, then $\exists s' \,.\, s_1 \xrightarrow{b} s', s_2 \xrightarrow{a} s'$,
- if $s \xrightarrow{a} s_1 \xrightarrow{b} s', a\ I\ b$, then $\exists s_2 \,.\, s \xrightarrow{b} s_2 \xrightarrow{a} s'$ and
- $s \xrightarrow{a} s_1 \bowtie s \xrightarrow{a} s_2 \Rightarrow s_1 = s_2$, where the *event equivalence* $\bowtie \subseteq \rightarrow \times \rightarrow$ is defined as the least equivalence relation including the relation $\rtimes$ with $s \xrightarrow{a} s_1 \rtimes s_2 \xrightarrow{a} s' \Leftrightarrow \exists b \in Act \,.\, s \xrightarrow{b} s_2, s_1 \xrightarrow{b} s' \wedge a\ I\ b$.

The first two properties are known as I-diamond-properties. The third property is in analogy to the event equivalence condition in *transition systems with independence* [SNW93] and has to be added because we extend trace systems by non-determinism. I-consistent transition systems can be seen as a specific type of transition systems with independence in which the independencies are generated by a global relation on actions. They naturally arise as the result of a parallel composition of sequential components, each system executing actions out of a local alphabet (in which all actions are dependent), with synchronisation on common actions. However, in the following we will not refer to a concrete distributed model, but assume I-consistency with respect to a given I.

We aim to check *strong bisimulation equivalence* [Mil89].

Definition 2. Let $T_i = \langle S_i, \rightarrow_i, s_i^0 \rangle$, $i = 1, 2$, be transition systems. A relation $\mathcal{R} \subseteq S_1 \times S_2$ is a *bisimulation relation* if $(s_1, s_2) \in \mathcal{R}$ implies

- if $s_1 \xrightarrow{a}_1 s_1'$, then there exists s_2' with $s_2 \xrightarrow{a}_2 s_2'$ and $(s_1', s_2') \in \mathcal{R}$ and
- vice versa, if $s_2 \xrightarrow{a}_2 s_2'$, then there exists s_1' with $s_1 \xrightarrow{a}_1 s_1'$ and $(s_1', s_2') \in \mathcal{R}$.

States s_1 and s_2 are bisimilar ($s_1 \sim s_2$), if there exists a bisimulation relation relating them, and T_1 and T_2 are bisimilar ($T_1 \sim T_2$) if $s_1^0 \sim s_2^0$.

3 Bisimulation games

As suggested by Stirling [Sti93], an alternative formulation of bisimulation equivalence can be given in terms of *games*, here given in the style of Gale-Stewart games [Tho94]. These are two player games with two different roles, "Control" (player C) and "Disturbance" (player D), who alternately make a move out of a set of possibilities.

We first generally introduce games and strategies as needed. Then we specialise to games characterising bisimulation.

Definition 3 (Game graph, game).
A *game graph* is a bipartite graph $G = (V, V_C, V_D, \longrightarrow)$ with

- $V = V_C \uplus V_D$, sets of vertices reflecting game situations, where V_C is the set of vertices where it is C's turn, and similarly V_D reflects situations where it is D's turn (and it is always unambiguously C's or D's turn).
- $\longrightarrow \subseteq V_C \times V_D \cup V_D \times V_C$, the set of possible moves (arcs).

A *game over G starting at $v_0 \in V$* is a finite or infinite sequence of vertices $(v_0, v_1, ..., v_n)$ or $(v_0, v_1, ...)$, such that $v_i \longrightarrow v_{i+1}$ and in the finite case there exists no $v_{n+1} \in V$ with $v_n \longrightarrow v_{n+1}$. Thus a game ends if the player taking the turn has no possible move.

A finite game $(v_0, ..., v_n)$ is *won* by player D if $v_n \in V_C$, in the converse case it is won by player C. Infinite games are won by player C.

The expressive power of the game formalism relies on strategies. For the sake of this paper we can restrict ourselves to history free winning strategies, where the player takes her decision solely on the ground of the current game situation:

Definition 4 (Strategy, winning strategy).
A *(history free) strategy for player C at $v_0 \in V$* is a function $\sigma_C : V_C \longrightarrow V_D$ defined on situations where it is C's turn. Moreover, σ_C must always choose a legal move, i.e. we require $v \longrightarrow \sigma_C(v_C)$. Similarly, a *(history free) strategy for player D at $v_0 \in V$* is a function $\sigma_D : V_D \longrightarrow V_C$. Since we only consider history free strategies we will simply call them strategies.

A game $(v_0, ...)$ *obeys a strategy σ_C* for player C at v_0, if for every $v_k \in V_C$, such that the game also includes a vertex $v_{k+1} \in V_D$, we have $v_{k+1} = \sigma_C(v_k)$. Games obeying a strategy σ_D for player D are defined accordingly.

A strategy σ_C for player C at v_0 is a *winning strategy* iff C wins every game starting at v_0 obeying this strategy. Similarly, a strategy σ_D for player D at v_0 is a *winning strategy* iff D wins every game obeying this strategy.

We call the set of vertices v_0', where C has a winning strategy at v_0' the *winning set W_C of C*, and also define the winning set W_D of D in the obvious way. Observe that in general $W_C \cap V_D$ ($W_D \cap V_C$ resp.) may be non-empty.

Player D can only have a winning strategy if she can force the game to terminate. A technical tool for the analysis of (history free!) winning strategies for player D are *progress measures* [Kla94].

Definition 5 (Progress measure for a region).
Let $G = (V, V_C, V_D, \longrightarrow)$ be a game graph. $V' \subseteq V$ is called a *region* if $v \in V' \cap V_C$ implies that all $v' \in V$ with $v \longrightarrow v'$ also satisfy $v' \in V'$.

A *progress measure for player D* at V' is a function $\mathfrak{m} : V' \longrightarrow \mathcal{O}$ assigning ordinal numbers to vertices, such that

- for $v \in V' \cap V_D$ there exists $v' \in V'$ with $v \longrightarrow v'$ and $\mathfrak{m}(v') < \mathfrak{m}(v)$;
- for $v \in V' \cap V_C$ and for every v' with $v \longrightarrow v'$ we also have $\mathfrak{m}(v') \leq \mathfrak{m}(v)$.

A region is a part of the game graph which player C – once entered – cannot leave. Progress measures characterise winning strategies. A progress measure for player D on a region V' guarantees that in all games starting at a vertex of V' player D may force the game to end in a winning position for herself. We formalise this idea in the following proposition:

Proposition 6. *1. At all vertices $v_0' \in V'$ of a region V' with a progress measure $\mathfrak{m}$ there exists a winning strategy for D.*

2. W_D is a region that has a progress measure. The games are determined, i.e. $V = W_C \uplus W_D$.

3. If V is finite then (2) holds even when restricted to progress measures assigning only finite ordinals (i.e. natural numbers). Furthermore, W_D can be computed in time $O(|V| + |\longrightarrow|)$, and checking $v_0 \in W_D$ for a single vertex v_0 can be done with the same complexity using an on-the-fly algorithm.

The proof combines ideas from [Tho94] and [Kla94], for details see [HWN98]. A progress measure of particular interest is the *rank*:

Definition 7. Let v be a vertex of a game graph $G = (V, V_C, V_D, \longrightarrow)$, such that D has a winning strategy at v. Then the *rank* $\mathfrak{r}(v)$ *of* v is the least ordinal assigned to v by any progress measure for the region W_D.

Proposition 8. *Let* $G = (V, V_C, V_D, \longrightarrow)$ *be a game graph,* $W_D \subseteq V$ *the winning set for* D*. Then the rank function* $\mathfrak{r}$ *is a progress measure for the region* W_D*. Moreover, for* $\mathfrak{r}(v)$ *we have* $\mathfrak{r}(v) = sup\{\mathfrak{r}(v') \mid v \longrightarrow v'\}$ *if* $v \in V_C$ *and* $\mathfrak{r}(v) = inf\{\mathfrak{r}(v') \mid v \longrightarrow v'\} + 1$ *if* $v \in V_D$*.*

Observe that $\mathfrak{r}(v)$ never is a limit ordinal if $v \in V_D$. In the finite case, the rank of a vertex $v \in V_D$ is the length of the shortest path (of rounds consisting of a D and a C move) in the game graph from v to a winning position for D. Now we will specialise to games characterising strong bisimulation (c.f. [Sti93]).

Definition 9 (Bisimulation game).
Let $T_1 = (S_1, \longrightarrow_1, s_1^0)$ and $T_2 = (S_2, \longrightarrow_2, s_2^0)$, as above. The *bisimulation game graph* $G(T_1, T_2) = (V, V_C, V_D, \longrightarrow)$ *for* T_1 *and* T_2 is given by

- $V = V_D \uplus V_C$ with $V_D = (S_1 \times S_2)$ and $V_C = S_1 \times S_2 \times Act \times \{1, 2\}$.
- $\longrightarrow$ contains exactly the following transitions:
  $(s_1', s_2) \longrightarrow (s_1, s_2, a, 1)$ iff $s_1' \xrightarrow{a}_1 s_1$; $(s_1, s_2') \longrightarrow (s_1, s_2, a, 2)$ iff $s_2' \xrightarrow{a}_2 s_2$;
  $(s_1, s_2', a, 1) \longrightarrow (s_1, s_2)$ iff $s_2' \xrightarrow{a}_2 s_2$; $(s_1', s_2, a, 2) \longrightarrow (s_1, s_2)$ iff $s_1' \xrightarrow{a}_1 s_1$.

A V_C vertex $(s_1, s_2, a, 1)$ "means" that the preceding move of player D was to take an a move in T_1 from some state s_1' to s_1.

Proposition 10. *A pair of states* (s_1, s_2) *is bisimilar iff player* C *has a winning strategy at* (s_1, s_2) *in the bisimulation game for* T_1 *and* T_2*.*

Note that the game characterisation allows to apply the on-the-fly algorithm from Proposition 6 (3) to the bisimulation problem. Moreover, the analysis shows that the resulting algorithm has a better asymptotic complexity than the algorithm given in [FM90], which is quadratic in the size of the game graph, whereas the method described here is linear.

4 Partial order reduction

Partial order reduction methods generate reduced state spaces by exploiting the independencies among transitions in order to avoid generating multiple interleavings of the same partial order. The algorithms usually proceed by a depth-first search of the state space starting with the initial state. For every reached state an *expansion set* is computed (a subset of outgoing transitions) and the transition system is thereby further expanded. A number of conditions on the choice of expansion sets guarantees preservation of certain properties. However, reduction conditions for preserving linear time properties are in general not sufficient for branching time. Additional conditions are needed to ensure that the branching structure of a system is faithfully represented in the reduced system. The following two transition systems serve as our running example (taken from [dSdS95]). We have chosen to give the transition systems here and not the game graph since the former are easier to understand. The full transition systems are given in the picture where $a\ I\ c$ and $b\ I\ c$.

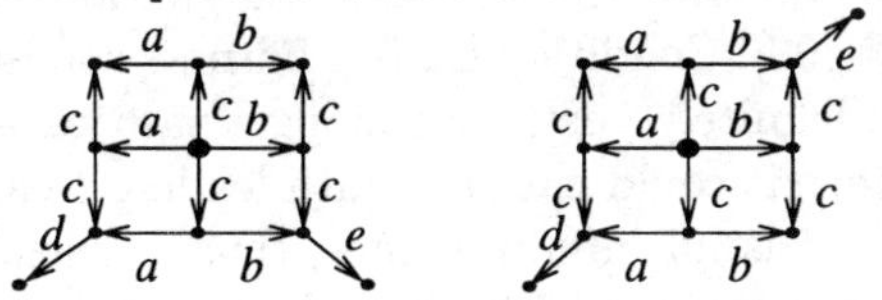

The full systems are obviously not bisimilar. A pair of linear time reductions (e.g. by the ample set method [PP95]) is shown below. The reduction exploits the independency between c and a, b, retaining one representative of every trace. The reduced systems are now bisimilar.

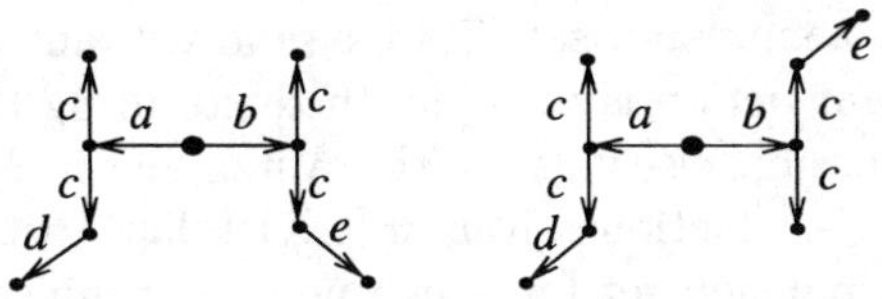

The problem in this example is the delay of a *non-deterministic choice* (two c-transitions) to a point at which some of the possible behaviour after the choice has already been discarded (by the earlier choice between a and b). A reduction selecting both c-transitions for expansion in the initial states (omitting a and b instead) preserves non-bisimilarity of the transition systems. A non-deterministic choice may only be delayed if the expansion set contains a single transition only, not resolving any choices possible now or later.

We will now formulate the reduction conditions on game graphs. The first two conditions are linear time conditions taken from [PP95], the third condition is the new branching time condition.

Reduction algorithm: Let T_1, T_2 be I-diamond-closed transition systems with bisimulation game graph $G(T_1, T_2) = (V, V_C, V_D, \rightarrow)$. Starting at the pair of roots (s_1^0, s_2^0), by a depth-first search (DFS) of the game graph we incrementally construct a reduced game graph $G_{red}(T_1, T_2)$ by choosing only a part of D's possible moves. At the reachable vertices of player C in the reduced game graph all possible moves are kept. For a state s_i in a transition system $(T_i, \rightarrow, s_i^0)$, $i = 1, 2$, let $en_i(s_i) = \{a \mid s_i \xrightarrow{a}\}$ denote the set of labellings of *enabled* actions at s_i. Similarly, we set $en(v) = en_1(s_1) \cup en_2(s_2)$ for $v = (s_1, s_2)$. We say a node $v = (s_1, s_2)$ *allows for a non-deterministic choice on* a in T_i if $|\{s_i \xrightarrow{a} s_i'\}| > 1$. When reaching a vertex $v = (s_1, s_2) \in V_D$, we select a set of actions $E(v) \subseteq en(v)$ for expansion satisfying the following three conditions:

C1 In neither transition systems T_1 and T_2, an action $a \in Act \setminus E(v)$ dependent on $E(v)$ can be executed after s_1, s_2 resp., *before* some action of $E(v)$ is executed.

C2 If $E(v)$ is a proper subset of $en(v)$, then the expansion of v by all moves corresponding to transitions labelled with actions from $E(v)$ does not lead to a vertex on the current search stack (of the DFS algorithm).

C3 Either (**C3a**) $E(v)$ contains a single action a and, moreover, in both transition systems T_1, T_2 at most one a-transition is enabled at s_1, s_2., resp., or (**C3b**) there is no node $v' = (s_1', s_2') \in V_D$ reachable from v without executing actions of $E(v)$ such that v' allows for a non-deterministic choice on some action $a \in Act \setminus E(v)$ in both T_1 *and* T_2.

Moreover, $E(v)$ may only be empty if $en(v)$ is. ■

Condition C1 ensures that we cannot completely cut off a move, may it be one possible now or possible after some successor states which are not yet generated. In the linear time setting, C1 guarantees that the expansion set is an *ample set* [Pel93]. Condition C2 is a fairness condition and ensures that no D-move can be indefinitely postponed along a path generated by a cycle. This must be ruled out since it could cut off a path leading to a winning position for D (remember that C wins all infinite games, thus D must eventually leave all cycles). Condition C3 guarantees that the reduction does not cut off a temporal ordering of choices possible for D on the full graph. In fact, C3 consists of two independent parts: If a singleton satisfies C1 (and C2) and in both transition systems no choice on that action is possible, then executing this action does not influence any choice possible elsewhere in the system in future. C3a is in analogy with branching time PO-reductions given in [GKPP95]. Alternatively, we may keep all actions in the expansion set for which non-deterministic choices in both systems are enabled. In terms of the game, this part of the condition means that such a situation is not under the control of D alone, therefore it may be necessary for D's strategy to enforce the choices at the current node.

At the end of the section we comment on the computation of expansion sets satisfying conditions C1 to C3. These three conditions on the expansion sets guarantee preservation of winning strategies by the reduction.

Theorem 11. *Let T_1, T_2 be finite transition systems. Player C has a winning strategy at v in the reduced game graph $G_{red}(T_1, T_2)$ iff C has a winning strategy at v in the full graph $G(T_1, T_2)$.*

This theorem yields an efficient algorithm for bisimulation checking in two steps: first construct the reduced game graph $G_{red}(T_1, T_2)$, then check for a winning strategy for player C at the root. Note that these two phases can also be executed simultaneously if the algorithm deciding the existence of a winning strategy for C is modified to proceed on-the-fly with the same complexity (see Section 3).

Proof. Let V_{red} denote the set of vertices in the reduced game graph.

Clearly, C has a winning strategy at all vertices $v \in W_C \cap V_{red}$ in the reduced game graph, because the reductions only occur at vertices $v \in V_D$. Consequently, any game obeying the original winning strategy of C in the full graph also leads to a game won by C in the reduced graph.

Player D cannot be guaranteed to inherit a particular winning strategy, because some of her moves might have been eliminated by the reduction. Thus, the difficult part is to show that D has a winning strategy at all vertices $v \in W_D \cap V_{red}$ in the reduced graph. For this we define a progress measure at $W_D \cap V_{red}$.

Let O be the image of the rank function $\mathfrak{r}$ on W_D, so that $(O, \leq)$ is the corresponding well-ordering.

Moreover, let $(V_{red}, \leq_{\text{dfs}})$ be the well-order in which the vertices of V_{red} are *finished* during the depth-first-search (generation) of V_{red}. We define a lexicographical ordering on pairs from $O \times V_{red}$, such that $(\kappa_1, v_1) \leq (\kappa_2, v_2)$ iff $\kappa_1 < \kappa_2$, or $\kappa_1 = \kappa_2$ and $v_1 \leq_{\text{dfs}} v_2$. The order defined in this way is a well-order and thus the elements (κ, v) of $O \times V_{red}$ correspond to ordinals $o(\kappa, v)$. These are the ordinals to define a progress measure by setting $\mathfrak{m}(v) = o(\mathfrak{r}(v), v)$ at vertices $v \in W_D \cap V_{red}$. What remains to be shown is that $\mathfrak{m}$ indeed satisfies the properties of progress measures.

So let $v = (s_1, s_2) \in W_D \cap V_{red}$. Then $\mathfrak{m}$ is defined and we have to show that there exists a move $v \longrightarrow v' \in V_{red}$ such that $\mathfrak{m}(v') < \mathfrak{m}(v)$. There are two cases:

(1) At v no outgoing transitions are removed, i.e., all successors v' of v occur also in the reduced graph. But then there must exist $v \longrightarrow v'$ with $\mathfrak{r}(v') < \mathfrak{r}(v)$, and thus $\mathfrak{m}(v') < \mathfrak{m}(v)$. In particular, this holds for all $v \in W_D \cap V_C \cap V_{red}$.

(2) At v, the set $E(v)$ is a proper subset of $en(v)$, and because of (C2) expanding $E(v)$ at v does not lead to a vertex on the current search stack. This means that $v' <_{\text{dfs}} v$ for all $v \longrightarrow v' \in V_{red}$. As a consequence, it is sufficient to show $\mathfrak{r}(v') \leq \mathfrak{r}(v)$ to obtain $\mathfrak{m}(v') < \mathfrak{m}(v)$ at one of these vertices. This is shown separately in Lemma 12 which gives the technical reason for the correctness of the reduction.

Lemma 12. *Let $v = (s_1, s_2) \in W_D \cap V_D$ be a vertex of the bisimulation game graph, and $E(v)$ be a proper, non-empty subset of $en(v)$ which satisfies the conditions (C1) and (C3). Then there exists a vertex $v_1' = (s_1', s_2', b, k), k \in \{1, 2\}$ with $v \longrightarrow v_1'$ and $b \in E(v)$, such that $v_1' \in W_D$ and $\mathfrak{r}(v_1') \leq \mathfrak{r}(v)$.*

Proof. The proof relies on induction on $\mathfrak{r}(v)$. Since $v = (s_1, s_2) \in W_D$, there exists a vertex v_1 with $v \longrightarrow v_1$ and $\mathfrak{r}(v_1) < \mathfrak{r}(v)$ (due to the properties of progress measures). If $v_1 \in V_{red}$ we are done. The interesting case is that the transitions corresponding to rank decreasing moves $v \longrightarrow v_1$ are labelled with actions $a \notin E(v)$, i.e., the move to a vertex with a properly smaller rank is cut off by the reduction.
In case there is some $b \in E(v)$ such that in just one of the transition systems T_i a b-transition is enabled at s_i, D wins immediately after a b-move (to a vertex with rank zero) and we are done. Thus, if $v = (s_1, s_2)$, one can assume that $E(v) \cap en_1(s_1) = E(v) \cap en_2(s_2)$.
(1) $\mathfrak{r}(v) = 1$. Thus, after the move $v \longrightarrow v_1$, C is blocked. Assume this move corresponds to an a-transition in T_1. From C1 it follows that $a \; I \; b$ for all $b \in E(v)$. Now choose a vertex v_1' such that $v \longrightarrow v_1'$ corresponds to some b-transition, $b \in E(v)$. Then for all vertices $v_2' = (s_1', s_2')$ with $v_1' \longrightarrow v_2'$ (C-move of a b-transition), the a-transition is enabled at the state s_1' in T_1. Hence D can now take the a-transition and wins; thus $\mathfrak{r}(v_2') = 1$ for all such v_2', hence $\mathfrak{r}(v_1') = 1 \leq \mathfrak{r}(v)$.
(2) $\mathfrak{r}(v) > 1$. After the D-move $v \longrightarrow v_1$ corresponding to, say, an a-transition in T_1, C answers with a move $v_1 \longrightarrow v_2$ and $\mathfrak{r}(v_2) \leq \mathfrak{r}(v_1) < \mathfrak{r}(v)$. Now we distinguish whether the selected set $E(v)$ satisfies the first or the second part of C3 - for both parts look at the illustration on page 10.
(2.1) $E(v) = \{b\}$ and in both systems exactly one b-transition is currently enabled. C may have several possibilities for answering the move $v \longrightarrow v_1$ by moves $v_1 \longrightarrow v_2$. At each possible v_2 the set $\{b\}$ can be selected as expansion set satisfying C1 and C3a. This follows from the third condition of I-consistency. By

induction, D may move to a vertex u'_1 via a b-transition and $\mathfrak{r}(u'_1) \leq \mathfrak{r}(v_2)$ and $u'_1 \in W_D$. C has to answer *deterministically* with the only enabled b-transition in the other system by going to some vertex u'_2. Summarising, at all thus reachable vertices u'_2 we have: $\mathfrak{r}(u'_2) \leq \mathfrak{r}(u'_1) \leq \mathfrak{r}(v_2) < \mathfrak{r}(v)$.
Now we show that selecting a b-transition at v does not increase the rank: After D's and C's move via a b-transition we end up at a fixed vertex v'_2 (fixed since in both transition systems just one b-transition is enabled). Now D may again take the a-transition that belongs to the diamond of a and b-transition in T_1 and move to a vertex v'_3. C may answer with all moves corresponding to transitions taken in v_1 leading to some vertex u'_2 again. Next we calculate the rank: By the properties of the rank we get: $\mathfrak{r}(v'_3) = \mathfrak{r}(u'_2)$ for the vertex u'_2 with *maximal* rank and furthermore $\mathfrak{r}(u'_2) = \mathfrak{r}(v'_3) \leq \mathfrak{r}(v'_2) - 1 = \mathfrak{r}(v'_1) - 1$.
Since the rank assigns the minimal progress measure, we have $\mathfrak{r}(v'_1) = \mathfrak{r}(u'_2) + 1$ and with $\mathfrak{r}(u'_2) < \mathfrak{r}(v)$ we get $\mathfrak{r}(v'_1) \leq \mathfrak{r}(v)$.
(2.2) At v_2 we may select $E(v_2) = E(v)$ because $E(v)$ satisfies the conditions C1 and C3b at v_2. By induction, D may move to a vertex u'_1 via a transition labelled with $b \in E(v)$ such that $\mathfrak{r}(u'_1) \leq \mathfrak{r}(v_2)$. Let us assume this b-transition belongs to T_1. Moreover, $u'_1 \in W_D$, i.e. for the vertex u'_2 with maximal rank reachable by a C-move we have $\mathfrak{r}(u'_1) = \mathfrak{r}(u'_2)$.
Now we consider the b-transition at v that belongs to the diamond in T_1. This move is answered by C with a move $v'_1 \longrightarrow v'_2$. Now we remember the a-transition at $v = (s_1, s_2)$ which was used in the full game graph but cut off by selecting $E(v)$. Since $E(v)$ satisfies C3b at v, we know that more than one a-transition can only be enabled in at most *one* of the transition systems. From the third property of I-consistency we deduce that the same holds in all such vertices v'_2. In case there is a non-deterministic choice on a somewhere, say in T_1, D takes the a-transition in T_1 which corresponds to $v \longrightarrow v_1$ or $v_1 \longrightarrow v_2$ leading to a vertex v'_3. In T_2 exactly one a-transition is enabled, i.e. the C-move leads to some vertex u'_2. From $u'_2 \in W_D$ we know $v'_1 \in W_D$. Now again at the vertex u'_2 with maximal rank we get $\mathfrak{r}(u'_2) = \mathfrak{r}(v'_3) \leq \mathfrak{r}(v'_2) - 1 = \mathfrak{r}(v'_1) - 1$.
Thus, we have $\mathfrak{r}(v'_1) = \mathfrak{r}(u'_2) + 1$ and from $\mathfrak{r}(u'_2) < \mathfrak{r}(v)$ we get $\mathfrak{r}(v'_1) \leq \mathfrak{r}(v)$.

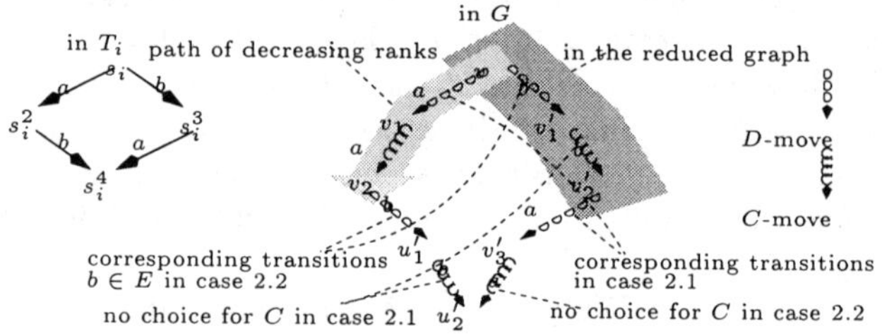

Computing expansion sets. As Peled [Pel93] has shown, computing optimal ample sets is already NP-hard, thus we cannot hope for an efficient algorithm which computes optimal expansion sets satisfying conditions C1 to C3. Instead useful heuristics have to be found. An algorithm for computing expansion sets satisfying condition C1 is developed in [PP95]. In a location-based setting like asynchronous automata or product systems, a strengthening of condition C1 can be locally checked: A chosen set of actions E determines a set of locations $loc(E)$ participating in the execution of these actions. Then it can be checked whether a state[1] exists which coincides with the current state in all locations of $loc(E)$ and which allows for the execution of an action dependent on E. Checking condition C3a is straightforward; for C3b we give an alternative condition C3b′ which is sufficient for ensuring C3b.

C3b′ There is no action $a \in Act \setminus E(v)$ such that in both transition systems T_i, $i = 1, 2$, a state with a non-deterministic choice on a is reachable from s_i before some action of $E(v)$ is executed.

Condition C3b′ is easier to check than C3b because the transition systems are treated separately. In a location-based setting, C3b′ can be checked similarly to C1: Look at states which coincide with the current state in all locations of $loc(E)$ and check for a non-deterministic choice on an action not in E.

Infinite transition systems. Theorem 11 is restricted to finite transition systems and thus to finite game graphs. While this matches the practical needs in the desired application domain, the *theory* does not really depend on it: The finiteness restriction is enforced by the choice of condition C2, a *fairness* condition: Expansion of transitions may not be indefinitely delayed. In the finite case this is guaranteed by condition C2 since eventually we reach a vertex on the search stack and then the complete set of enabled actions has to be expanded. For infinite game graphs different fairness conditions have to be used. However, the proof of Theorem 11 remains valid since a fairness condition can similarly to winning strategies for D be represented by a progress measure $\mathfrak{m}_{\mathsf{fair}}$, which measures the "maximal" distance to the next vertices where all transitions are expanded. Then, in the proof of Theorem 11, this progress measure $\mathfrak{m}_{\mathsf{fair}}$ can be used to replace the order $\leq_{\mathsf{dfs}}$.

5 Conclusions

We have given a partial order reduction scheme for checking strong bisimilarity of two transition systems with the same global dependency relation. The scheme relies on a simultaneous reduction in both systems by applying the reductions to the game graph of the bisimulation game. We believe to have thus provided a more transparent explanation, why the reductions are correct. Furthermore, the approach is compatible with on-the-fly algorithms.

Previous approaches were either limited to weak bisimulation relations (c.f. [GKPP95]), or, as in the case of [dSdS95], on the reduced systems only bisimilarity but not non-bisimilarity can be checked. Furthermore, compared to [GKPP95] we allow for stronger reductions.

The practical experience gathered with other partial order approaches suggests that the reductions resulting from our scheme will often be good. However, only practical experimentation can give an answer here.

[1] This is stronger than condition C1, because reachability of the state is not considered.

The option, to check also preorders and weak relations more efficiently with our method using similar game representations, is an interesting and practically important research topic. Moreover, it should be investigated which of the many partial order reduction approaches different from the on we used can be similarly applied to game graphs as we have done with the ample-set-method.

References

[dSdS95] Monica Lara de Souza and Robert de Simone. Using partial order methods for the verification of behavioural equivalences. In G. von Bochmann, editor, *Formal Description Techniques (FORTE '95)*, 1995.

[FM90] Jean-Claude Fernandez and Laurent Mounier. Verifying bisimulations "on the fly". In *Formal Description Techniques (FORTE)*, pages 91–105, 1990.

[GKPP95] Rob Gerth, Ruurd Kuiper, Doron Peled, and Wojciech Penczek. A partial order approach to branching time model checking. In *Israeli Symp. on Theoretical Computer Science*, 1995.

[HWN98] Michaela Huhn, Heike Wehrheim, and Peter Niebert. Partial order reductions for bisimulation checking. Hildesheimer Informatik-Berichte 8/98, Institut für Informatik, Universität Hildesheim, 1998.

[Kla94] Nils Klarlund. The limit view of infinite computations. BRICS Report Series RS-94-14, Department of Computer Science, University of Århus, Ny Munkegade, building 540, DK-8000 Århus C, Denmark, May 1994.

[KS90] Paris C. Kanellakis and Scott A. Smolka. CCS expressions, finite state processes, and three problems of equivalence. *Information and Computation*, 86:46–68, 1990.

[Maz95] Antoni Mazurkiewicz. Introduction to trace theory. chapter 1, pages 1–42. World Scientific, 1995.

[Mil89] Robin Milner. *Communication and Concurrency*. Prentice-Hall, 1989.

[Pel93] Doron Peled. All from one, one for all: On model checking using representatives. In *International Conference on Computer Aided Verification (CAV)*, volume 697 of *Lecture Notes in Computer Science*, pages 409–423, 1993.

[Pom96] *Workshop on Partial Order Methods in Verification*, volume 29 of *DIMACS Series in Discrete Mathematics and Theoretical Computer Science*. American Mathematical Society, 1996.

[PP95] Doron Peled and Wojciech Penczek. Using asynchronous Büchi automata for efficient model-checking of concurrent systems. In *Protocol Specification, Testing and Verification*, pages 90–100, 1995.

[SNW93] Vladimiro Sassone, Mogens Nielsen, and Glynn Winskel. A classification of models for concurrency. In E. Best, editor, *Concur '93*, volume 715 of *Lecture Notes in Computer Science*, pages 82–96. Springer-Verlag, 1993.

[Sti93] Colin Stirling. Modal and temporal logics for processes. Tutorial handout, Computer Science Dept., Århus University, Århus, Denmark, August 1993. Summerschool in Logical Methods in Concurrency, August 2-13,1993.

[Tho94] W. Thomas. Finite-state strategies in regular infinite games. In P.S.Thiagarajan, editor, *FST&TCS*, number 880 in Lecture Notes in Computer Science, pages 148–158, 1994.

[WW96] Bernard Willems and Pierre Wolper. Partial-order methods for model checking: From linear time to branching time. In *IEEE Symp. Logic in Comp. Sci. (LICS)*, pages 294–303. IEEE Computer Society Press, 1996.

First-Order-CTL Model Checking*

Jürgen Bohn[1] Werner Damm[1] Orna Grumberg[2] Hardi Hungar[1] Karen Laster[2]

[1] {bohn,damm,hungar}@OFFIS.Uni-Oldenburg.DE
[2] {orna,laster}@CS.Technion.AC.IL

Abstract. This work presents a first-order model checking procedure that verifies systems with large or even infinite data spaces with respect to first-order CTL specifications. The procedure relies on a partition of the system variables into *control* and *data*. While control values are expanded into BDD-representations, data values enter in form of their properties relevant to the verification task. The algorithm is completely automatic. If the algorithm terminates, it has generated a first-order verification condition on the data space which characterizes the system's correctness. Termination can be guaranteed for a class that properly includes the data-independent systems, defined in [10].
This work improves [5], where we extended *explicit* model checking algorithms. Here, both the control part and the first-order conditions are represented by BDDs, providing the full power of symbolic model checking for control aspects of the design.

1 Introduction

Symbolic model checking is currently one of the most successful formal methods for hardware verification. It can be applied to verify or debug designs from industrial practice, in particular when it is combined with techniques for abstraction and compositional reasoning. However, the majority of designs will escape even those combined approaches if detailed reasoning about the data path is required. This is because the data part is often too large (or even infinite) and too complicated.

To reduce the data-induced complexity, we combine symbolic model checking for the control part of a design with a generation of first-order verification conditions on data in an algorithm we call *first-order model checking*. Thereby, we achieve a separation of the verification task, where the verification conditions on the data which are computed by our algorithm may be handled afterwards by any appropriate means, for instance by a theorem prover. The algorithm behaves like a symbolic model checker if all system variables are treated as control variables, offering the verification condition generation as an option if the data complexity turns out to be too high.

The algorithm is intended to be applied to a class of applications which permit a clear separation between *control* and *data*. Examples of such systems are embedded control applications, where the control part governs the interaction between the controller and the controlled system, depending in its actions only on some flags derived from the data, and generating data output by finitely many computations. Others are processors with nontrivial data paths.

For such applications, the algorithm will terminate, while in general it will not. The class of systems for which it works properly includes Wolper's data-independent systems [10], where there is neither testing nor computing on data values. Either testing or computing can be permitted, but unrestricted use of both may lead to nontermination

* This research has been funded in part by the MWK under No. 210.3 - 70631/9 - 99 - 14/96.

of our procedure. Due to space limitations, an extensive discussion of the termination issue is not given in this paper.

On a technical level, we take FO-CTL, a first-order version of CTL, as our specification logic. Programs appear in an abstract representation as *first-order Kripke structures*. These extend "ordinary" Kripke structures by transitions with conditional assignments, capturing the effect of taking a transition on an underlying possibly infinite state space induced from a set of typed variables.

Our algorithm incrementally computes for each state of the first-order Kripke structure and each control valuation a first-order predicate over the data variables which characterizes validity of the FO-CTL formula to be proven. The algorithm is developed from a standard CTL symbolic model-checking procedure, not the automata-theoretic approach from [2], as that one does not permit an extension which generates the annotations along the way.

The work presented here extends the previous paper [5] in two respects. First, we now represent and generate first-order annotations symbolically as BDDs. Due to this representation, we can avoid intermediate calls to a theorem prover, as we get, for instance, propositional simplifications "for free". Also, the control valuations are not expanded explicitly, enabling us to cope with much larger control parts. Second, the procedure can now cope with unboundedly many inputs. The addition necessary for that will be pointed out during the description of the algorithm in Sec. 3.

The paper contains a description of our core algorithm, and demonstrates its operation for a simple example problem. There are extensions and optimizations of which we present only one, *control pruning*, which is one of the most important amendments.

Related work: Approaches based on abstraction like the ones in [4, 7] and, to some extent, in [6] try to reduce the state space to a small, resp., finite one, where the proof engineer is required to find suitable abstractions for program variables. In our approach, the verifier's main involvement is in deciding which variables to consider as control.

Using uninterpreted functions in order to model non-finite aspects of the system is more closely related to our work. In such approaches, uninterpreted functions represent terms or quantifier-free first-order formulas, whereas in our work a notion similar to uninterpreted functions represents first-order formulas with quantification.

In [8], systems with infinite memory are verified. States are represented as a combination of an explicit part for data variables and a symbolic part for control variables. Their algorithm, if it terminates, computes the set of reachable states. Thus, they can check only safety properties.

In [9], designs are described by quantifier-free formulas with equality, over uninterpreted functions. A BDD representation of the formulas enables symbolic satisfiability checking. This approach is used for checking design equivalence. No temporal specification logic is considered. There are similar approaches to check the uninterpreted equivalence step functions, e.g. [3].

In [11], data operations on abstract data variables are represented by uninterpreted functions. They check a restricted subset of a first-order linear-time temporal logic with fairness. Their logic allows limited nesting of temporal operators, thus, it is incomparable to our FO-CTL. FO-CTL, on the other hand, allows any nesting of CTL operators, and includes both existential and universal path quantifiers.

In [1], symbolic model checking with uninterpreted functions is used to verify an algorithm for out-of-order execution. They use a reference file (which is similar to our proposition table) to represent system behaviors. Their method is aimed at proving partial and total correctness of out-of-order executions while we verify general FO-CTLproperties.

2 Semantical Foundation

2.1 First-Order Kripke Structures

The basic semantical domain is a Kripke structure, although we will assume that the programming language has its semantics in the more abstract domain of *first-order* Kripke structures.

A *Kripke structure* is a quintuple $(S, R, \mathcal{A}, L, I)$ where S is a not necessarily finite set of *states*, $R \subseteq S \times S$ is the *transition relation*, $\mathcal{A}$ is a set of *atoms*, $L : S \to \mathcal{P}(\mathcal{A})$ is the *labeling function* and $I \subseteq S$ is the set of *initial states*.

We write $s \to s'$ for $(s, s') \in R$. K_s is the structure with the set of initial states set to $\{s\}$. The set $Tr(K)$ of *paths* of a Kripke structure is the set of maximal sequences $\pi = (s_0, s_1, \ldots)$ with $s_0 \in I$ and $s_i \to s_{i+1}$. We use π_i to denote s_i. $|\pi|$ will denote the number of states in the path π, if π is finite. It will be ∞ otherwise.

We now prepare the definition of first-order Kripke structures. A data structure on which a program operates is given by a *signature* $\mathcal{S}$, which introduces typed symbols for constants and functions, and by an interpretation $\mathcal{I}$ which assigns a meaning to symbols, based on an interpretation $\mathcal{I}(\tau)$ of types τ by domains. We assume that the set of types include type `bool` and that there is an equality symbol "$=_\tau$" for each type τ.

For a signature $\mathcal{S}$ and a typed set of variables `V`, we denote by `T(V)` the set of terms and by `B(V)` the set of boolean expressions over `V`. If we enrich the set `T(V)` with a specific constant $?_\tau$ for each type τ, we get the set of *random* terms $\mathtt{T}^+(\mathtt{V})$. For each set `V` of typed variables a set of type-respecting valuations $\mathcal{V}(\mathtt{V})$ is defined. If $\sigma \in \mathcal{V}(\mathtt{V})$ and an interpretation $\mathcal{I}$ are given, we get interpretations $\sigma(\mathtt{t})$ of terms.

To model inputs we consider *random* (or nondeterministic) assignments of the form `v:=?`, and call `v:=t` with $\mathtt{t}\neq ?$ *regular* assignments. Let $\mathcal{I}(\mathtt{v:=t})$ be the semantics of an assignment as a binary relation on $\mathcal{V}(\mathtt{V})$, i.e.,

$$(\sigma, \sigma') \in \mathcal{I}(\mathtt{v:=t}) \Leftrightarrow_{\mathrm{df}} \begin{cases} \sigma'(\mathtt{v}) = \sigma(\mathtt{t}),\ \mathtt{t} \in \mathtt{T(V)} \\ \sigma'(\mathtt{v}) \in \mathcal{I}(\tau),\ \mathtt{t} = ?_\tau \\ \sigma'(\mathtt{w}) = \sigma(\mathtt{w}),\ \mathtt{w} \neq \mathtt{v} \end{cases}$$

A set of assignments is *well-formed*, if the variables on the left-hand sides are pairwise distinct. The semantics of a well-formed set of assignments is the parallel execution of the single assignments. Let `WFA(V)` denote the set of well-formed assignment sets over a set of variables `V`. For a pair `(b,a)` of a condition $\mathtt{b} \in \mathtt{B(V)}$ and a well-formed assignment set $\mathtt{a} \in \mathtt{WFA(V)}$, we set

$$\mathcal{I}(\mathtt{b,a}) =_{\mathrm{df}} (\{\sigma \mid \sigma(\mathtt{b}) = tt\} \times \mathcal{V}(\mathtt{V})) \cap \mathcal{I}(\mathtt{a}).$$

A *first-order Kripke structure* over a signature $\mathcal{S}$ is a tuple $K = (S, \mathtt{V}, R, \mathcal{A}, L, I)$ where S is a finite set of *states*, `V` is a set of typed variables, $R \subseteq S \times \mathtt{B(V)} \times \mathtt{WFA(V)} \times S$ is the *transition relation*, $\mathcal{A}$ is a set of *atoms*, $L : S \to \mathcal{P}(\mathcal{A})$ is the *labeling function*, and $I \subseteq S \times \mathtt{B(V)}$ is the set of *initial states*.

In this paper we use first-order Kripke structures as our programming language. Intuitively, S is used to describe the (rather small set of) program locations, while the valuations $\mathcal{V}(\mathtt{V})$ might become rather big, or even infinite. For example, the following first-order structure K describes a controller that sets an alarm if a frequently read input value grows too fast.

$$S =_{\text{df}} \{s_1, s_2\}$$
$$\mathtt{V} =_{\text{df}} \{\mathtt{alarm{:}bool}, \mathtt{k}, \mathtt{l{:}int}\}$$
$$R =_{\text{df}} \{(s_1, \mathtt{tt}, \{\mathtt{alarm{:=}ff,\ k{:=}1,\ l{:=}?}\}, s_2), (s_2, \mathtt{l\text{-}k{>}80}, \{\mathtt{alarm{:=}tt}\}, s_1), (s_2, \neg\mathtt{l\text{-}k{>}80}, \{\}, s_1)\}$$
$$\mathcal{A} =_{\text{df}} \{\mathtt{in}\}$$
$$L(s) =_{\text{df}} \begin{cases} \{\mathtt{in}\} & \text{if } s = s_1 \\ \{\} & \text{if } s = s_2 \end{cases}$$
$$I =_{\text{df}} \{(s_1, \mathtt{alarm{=}ff})\}$$

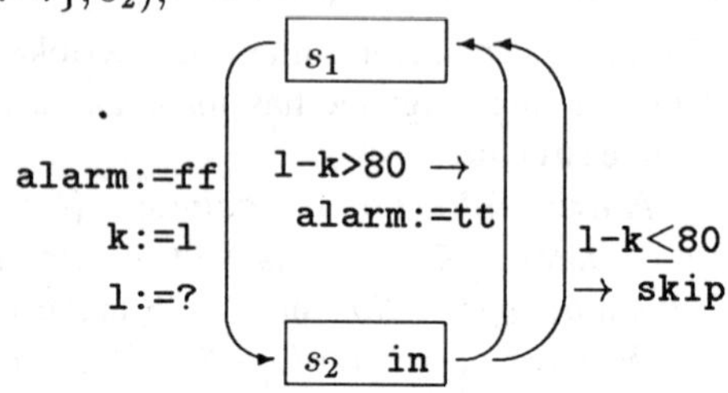

A first-order structure is called *finite* if all its components are finite sets. Finiteness of a first-order structure does not imply that it necessarily represents a finite Kripke structure. Depending on the interpretation, data domains may be infinite, in which case we have a finite description of an infinite-state Kripke structure. We define the semantics of a first-order Kripke structure by means of a regular Kripke structure.

Given an interpretation $\mathcal{I}$ of $\mathcal{S}$, a first-order structure K over $\mathcal{S}$ induces the Kripke structure $K' = \mathcal{I}(K)$ with the components

$$S' =_{\text{df}} S \times \mathcal{V}(\mathtt{V})$$
$$(s_1, \sigma_1) \rightarrow (s_2, \sigma_2) \Leftrightarrow_{\text{df}} s_1 \xrightarrow{\mathtt{b,a}} s_2 \wedge (\sigma_1, \sigma_2) \in \mathcal{I}(\mathtt{b}, \mathtt{a})$$
$$\mathcal{A}' =_{\text{df}} \mathcal{A} \cup \{\, \mathtt{v{=}d} \mid \mathtt{v} \in \mathtt{V}, \mathtt{d} \in \mathcal{I}(\tau(\mathtt{v}))\,\}$$
$$L'(s, \sigma) =_{\text{df}} L(s) \cup \{\, \mathtt{v} = \sigma(\mathtt{v}) \mid \mathtt{v} \in \mathtt{V}\,\}$$
$$I' =_{\text{df}} \mathcal{I}(I) =_{\text{df}} \{\, (s, \sigma) \in S \times \mathcal{V}(\mathtt{V}) \mid (s, \mathtt{b}) \in I \wedge \sigma(\mathtt{b}) = tt\,\}$$

By $K \uparrow \mathtt{x}$ we denote the first-order structure resulting from K if the variable $\mathtt{x}$ is added to the variable set, after renaming a possibly already present $\mathtt{x} \in \mathtt{V}$. Since the added $\mathtt{x}$ does not appear in conditions or assignments, its value is arbitrary in initial states and never gets changed.

2.2 First-Order Temporal Logic

To specify properties of first-order structures, we use first-order computation tree logic, FO-CTL. It has the following negation-free syntax.

$$\phi ::= A \mid \overline{A} \mid \mathtt{b} \mid \phi \wedge \phi \mid \phi \vee \phi \mid \mathbf{q}\,\mathtt{x}.\,\phi \mid \mathbf{Q}\,\psi$$
$$\psi ::= \mathbf{X}\phi \mid \phi\,\mathbf{U}\,\phi \mid \phi\,\mathbf{W}\,\phi$$

where $\mathtt{A} \in \mathcal{A}$, $\mathtt{b} \in \mathtt{B}(\mathtt{V})$, $\mathtt{x} \in \mathtt{V}$, $\mathbf{q} \in \{\forall, \exists\}$ and $\mathbf{Q} \in \{\mathbf{A}, \mathbf{E}\}$.

First-order quantifiers are interpreted *rigidly*, i.e. the value is fixed for the evaluation of the formula in its scope, it does not change over time.

The semantics of a formula ϕ depends on an interpretation $\mathcal{I}$ of $\mathcal{S}$ and a first-order Kripke structure whose variables include all free variables of ϕ. The formula is interpreted over a pair $(s, \sigma) \in \mathcal{I}(K)$. For example, we define

$$(s,\sigma) \models_{\mathcal{I}(K)} A/\overline{A} \Leftrightarrow_{\text{df}} A \in L(s,\sigma)/A \notin L(s,\sigma)$$
$$(s,\sigma) \models_{\mathcal{I}(K)} \mathtt{b} \Leftrightarrow_{\text{df}} \sigma(\mathtt{b}) = tt$$
$$(s,\sigma) \models_{\mathcal{I}(K)} \mathbf{q}\mathtt{x}.\phi \Leftrightarrow_{\text{df}} \mathbf{q}d \in \mathcal{I}(\tau(\mathtt{x})).\ (s,\sigma\{d/\mathtt{x}\}) \models_{\mathcal{I}(K\uparrow\mathtt{x})} \phi \quad \mathbf{q} \in \{\forall,\exists\}$$
$$(s,\sigma) \models_{\mathcal{I}(K)} \mathbf{A}\,\psi \Leftrightarrow_{\text{df}} \forall\pi \in Tr(\mathcal{I}(K)_{(s,\sigma)}).\ \pi \models_{\mathcal{I}(K)} \psi$$
$$\pi \models_{\mathcal{I}(K)} \mathbf{X}\phi \Leftrightarrow_{\text{df}} |\pi| > 1 \wedge \pi_1 \models_{\mathcal{I}(K)} \phi$$
$$\pi \models_{\mathcal{I}(K)} \phi_1\,\mathbf{W}\,\phi_2 \Leftrightarrow_{\text{df}} \text{for all } i < |\pi|, \pi_i \models_{\mathcal{I}(K)} \phi_1, \text{ or there is } j < |\pi|,$$
$$\pi_j \models_{\mathcal{I}(K)} \phi_2, \text{ and for all } i < j,\ \pi_i \models_{\mathcal{I}(K)} \phi_1$$

If $\sigma \in \mathcal{V}(\mathtt{V})$, we denote by $\sigma\{d/\mathtt{x}\}$ the valuation of $\mathtt{V} \cup \{\mathtt{x}\}$ which maps $\mathtt{x}$ to d and agrees further with σ on the valuation of $\mathtt{V}\backslash\{\mathtt{x}\}$. Formally, we lift the standard definition of correctness of a Kripke structure wrt. a CTL formula to the first-order case :

Given an interpretation $\mathcal{I}$ of $\mathcal{S}$, a first-order structure K *satisfies* a FO-CTL formula ϕ, denoted $K \models \phi$, if for every $(s,\sigma) \in \mathcal{I}(I)$, $(s,\sigma) \models_{\mathcal{I}(K)} \phi$.

As in the following example ϕ, we use standard abbreviations in specifications. Expanding logical implication requires moving negation through a formula down to atoms. $\mathbf{AG}\,\phi_1$ is defined by $\mathbf{A}[\phi_1\,\mathbf{W} ff]$ as in CTL.

$$\phi =_{\text{df}} \forall\mathtt{x}\ \mathbf{AG}(\mathtt{in} \wedge \mathtt{l} = \mathtt{x} \rightarrow \mathbf{AXAX}(\mathtt{in} \wedge \mathtt{l\text{-}x} > \mathtt{100} \rightarrow \mathbf{AX}(\mathtt{alarm\text{=}tt})))$$

Note that we use the first-order variable $\mathtt{x}$ to "store" the value of $\mathtt{l}$ through two next-steps such that a comparison between new and old input values becomes possible. In Section 4.3 we check the previously introduced first-order structure against this ϕ.

3 First-Order Model Checking

Model checking of FO-CTL formulas can be described as an iterative computation on the cross product of the first-order Kripke structure with a *tableau* of the formula. After defining this product structure, we will first describe a semantical version of this computation. Afterwards, we will define a syntactic procedure, and finally show how it may be realized by a symbolic, i.e., BDD-based, model checker.

3.1 The Product Structure

The model checking algorithm operates on a product of a first-order Kripke structure with a *tableau* Tab_ϕ of a FO-CTL formula ϕ . Tab_ϕ captures the dependencies between the validity of subformulas of ϕ as known from CTL. In the first-order case here, the subformulas are accompanied by the set of variables which are quantified within the context in ϕ .

Formally, let Tab_ϕ be the smallest set of nodes N which contains $(\phi, \emptyset)$ and is closed with respect to the relations $\rightarrow = \{\, ((\mathbf{QX}\,\phi_1, \mathtt{W}), (\phi_1, \mathtt{W}))\,\}$ and $\mapsto$ defined by

- If $n = (\phi_1 \wedge / \vee \phi_2, \mathtt{W})$, then $n \mapsto (\phi_1, \mathtt{W})$ and $n \mapsto (\phi_2, \mathtt{W})$.
- If $n = (\mathbf{Q}[\phi_1\,\mathbf{U}/\,\mathbf{W}\,\phi_2], \mathtt{W})$, then $n \mapsto (\phi_2, \mathtt{W})$, $n \mapsto (\phi_1, \mathtt{W})$ and $n \mapsto \mathbf{QX}\,\mathbf{Q}[\phi_1\,\mathbf{U}/\,\mathbf{W}\,\phi_2]), \mathtt{W})$.
- If $n = (\mathbf{q}\mathtt{x}.\ \phi_1, \mathtt{W})$, then $n \mapsto (\phi_1, \mathtt{W} \cup \{\mathtt{x}\})$.

Given a finite first-order structure $K = (S, \mathtt{V}, R, \mathcal{A}, L, \underline{I})$ and a FO-CTL formula ϕ with tableau $Tab_\phi = (N, \mapsto, \rightarrow)$, we build the product structure $K \times Tab_\phi = (M, \mapsto', \rightarrow')$ as follows. We are assuming w.l.o.g. that no variable from $\mathtt{V}$ gets quantified within ϕ.

$$M =_{\text{df}} S \times N$$
$$(s,n) \mapsto' (s,n') \Leftrightarrow_{\text{df}} n \mapsto n'$$
$$(s,n) \xrightarrow{\text{b,a}}{}' (s',n') \Leftrightarrow_{\text{df}} n \rightarrow n' \text{ and } s \xrightarrow{\text{b,a}} s'$$

Let ϕ be the example specification from Sec. 2.2, $\phi = \forall \mathbf{x}\, \mathbf{AG}\,(\phi_1)$, with subspecifications

$$\phi_1 =_{\text{df}} \phi_{1,1} \rightarrow \phi_{1,2}$$
$$\phi_{1,1} =_{\text{df}} \texttt{in} \wedge \texttt{l=x}$$
$$\phi_{1,2} =_{\text{df}} \mathbf{AX}\,\mathbf{AX}\,(\phi_{2,1} \rightarrow \phi_{2,2})$$
$$\phi_{2,1} =_{\text{df}} \texttt{in} \wedge \texttt{l-x} > \texttt{100}$$
$$\phi_{2,2} =_{\text{df}} \mathbf{AX}\,(\texttt{alarm=tt})$$

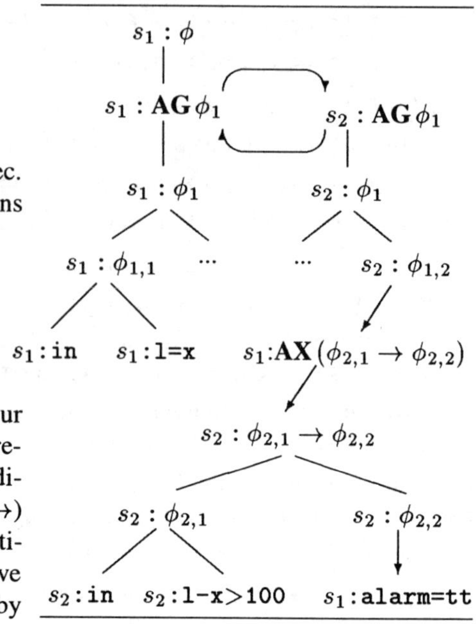

A sketch of the product structure in our example is given on the right. The relation $\mapsto$ is drawn as a line, the conditional assignments labeling the arrows ($\rightarrow$) are missing, as well as the sets of quantified variables. Also, intermediate nodes have been removed from the cycle induced by $\mathbf{AG}\,(\phi_1) = \mathbf{A}[\phi_1\, \mathbf{W} f\!f]$.

Our model-checking procedures will operate on such cross products. The reader will note the similarity between cross products and the information flow in standard CTL model checking, which is opposite to the direction of the arrows.

The nodes labeled by a $\mathbf{W}$ (or $\mathbf{G}$, as in the example) formula are called *maximal* nodes, those labeled by a $\mathbf{U}$ formula are *minimal* nodes. Nodes without successors are called *terminal* nodes. We will say that a node m' in the product structure is *below* some m, if m' is reachable from m via the union of the relations $\mapsto'$ and $\xrightarrow{\text{b,a}}{}'$.

3.2 First-Order Model Checking, Semantically

Let the cross product between a first-order Kripke structure and the tableau of an FO-CTL formula ϕ be given. To each pair $(s, (\phi_1, \texttt{W}))$ in the product structure the set of valuations σ of $\texttt{V} \cup \texttt{W}$ can be assigned s.t. $(s,\sigma) \models_{\mathcal{I}(K)} \phi_1$. Below, we describe a model-checking like procedure which, if it terminates, annotates each node with the correct set of variable valuations. The procedure works iteratively, starting with an initial annotation, and computing the new annotation of a node (s,n) from the annotations of its successor nodes (s',n').

The process starts by initializing all pairs with minimal nodes to $\emptyset$ and all those with maximal nodes $(\phi_1, \texttt{W})$ to $\mathcal{V}(\texttt{V}\cup\texttt{W})$. Pairs with terminal nodes are initialized with the set of valuations satisfying the boolean formula after taking the state labeling into account, i.e.: if $n = (\phi_1, \texttt{W})$ then

$$ann(s,n) =_{\text{df}} \{\sigma \in \mathcal{V}(\texttt{V} \cup \texttt{W}) \mid \sigma(\phi_1') = tt\},$$

where ϕ_1' results from ϕ_1 by replacing atomic formulas A by tt iff $A \in L(s)$ and by $f\!f$ otherwise. In our example this means that $ann(s_1, (\texttt{in},\texttt{x})) = \emptyset$, $ann(s_2, (\texttt{in},\texttt{x})) = \mathcal{V}(\texttt{V} \cup \{\texttt{x}\})$, $ann(s_i, (\texttt{term},\texttt{x})) = \{\sigma \mid \sigma(\texttt{term}) = tt\}$ for $i = 1,2$ and $\texttt{term} =$

alarm=tt, l=x, l-x>100. Nodes which are neither terminal nor maximal or minimal are not initialized.

After each step of the procedure, nodes for which the final annotation has been computed are identified. Initially, this set of nodes consists of the terminal nodes. The criterion for a node to have got its final annotation is that the annotations of all the nodes below it have been stable in the previous step.

It is an invariant of the process of annotation computation, that each annotation computed intermediately, satisfies that for maximal nodes it stays above the semantically correct annotation, and for minimal nodes, it stays below.

A step of the computation consists of updating the annotation of each node which has not yet got its final annotation. No update is done if some direct successor of a node is not yet annotated or if it is of a different mode (maximal/minimal) and not yet finally annotated. Otherwise, the update $ann'(s,n)$ is computed from the current annotations $ann(s',n')$ of the successors as follows ($n = (\mathbf{EX}\,\phi_1, \mathtt{W})$ omitted).

- If $n = (\phi_1 \wedge / \vee \phi_2, \mathtt{W})$, then $ann'(s,n) =_{\mathrm{df}} ann(s, (\phi_1, \mathtt{W})) \cap / \cup\, ann(s, (\phi_2, \mathtt{W}))$.
- If $n = (\mathbf{AX}\,\phi_1, \mathtt{W})$, then
$$ann'(s,n) =_{\mathrm{df}} \bigcap_{(s,n) \xrightarrow{\mathtt{b},\mathtt{a}} (s',n')} \{\sigma \mid \forall \sigma'.(\sigma,\sigma') \in \mathcal{I}(\mathtt{b},\mathtt{a}) \Rightarrow \sigma' \in ann(s',n')\}.$$
- If $n = (\mathbf{Q}[\phi_1\, \mathbf{U} / \mathbf{W}\, \phi_2], \mathtt{W})$, and (s,n') is the successor node of (s,n), then
$$ann'(s,n) =_{\mathrm{df}} ann(s,n').$$
- If $n = (\forall/\exists \mathtt{x}.\, \phi_1, \mathtt{W})$, and (s,n') is the successor node of (s,n), then
$$ann'(s,n) =_{\mathrm{df}} \{\sigma \in \mathcal{V}(\mathtt{V} \cup \mathtt{W}) \mid \forall/\exists d.\, \sigma\{\mathtt{x}/d\} \in ann(s,n')\}.$$

Proposition 1 states that this (semantical) annotation process is semantically sound.

Proposition 1. *If the annotation computation for $K \times Tab_\phi$ terminates, each node is annotated with the correct valuations, i.e., $\sigma \in ann(s, (\phi_1, \mathtt{W}))$ iff $(s,\sigma) \models_{\mathcal{I}(K\uparrow\mathtt{W})} \phi_1$.*

Proof (Sketch). Correctness for nodes which do not lie on cycles, i.e., ones which are neither minimal nor maximal, follows by induction (on the formula size, for instance). Using the invariant that minimal nodes are approximated from below and maximal nodes from above, we see that once a fixed point is reached for one such node, it is the minimal, resp., max., fixed point as required by the characterization of the operator.

Note, however, that while the procedure is sound, it need not terminate if the data domain is infinite. If the data domains are finite, though, it will terminate for the well-known monotonicity reasons.

As a consequence of Proposition 1, we see that a terminating annotation process yields a characterization of the correctness of the system.

Proposition 2. *If the semantical annotation process terminates, then $K \models \phi$ if and only if for every state s, if $(s,\sigma) \in \mathcal{I}(I)$ then $\sigma \in ann(s, (\phi, \emptyset))$ (meaning, by Proposition 1 that $(s,\sigma) \models_{\mathcal{I}(K)} \phi$).*

3.3 First-Order Model Checking, Syntactically

To turn the semantic procedure described above into a syntactic one, we replace the valuation sets $ann(s,n)$ by first-order formulas $\textit{fo-ann}(s,n)$ describing them. We have to check that indeed each step of the computation has a syntactic counterpart.

The initialization of terminal nodes with the formula in the node directly gives us a first-order formula. In analogy to the semantical initialization, minimal nodes are initialized to *ff* and maximal nodes are initialized to *tt*. Disjunction, conjunction and first-order quantification are modeled by the respective formula operators. It remains to define the next-step computations. Starting with a finite first-order Kripke structure, we will have only finitely many successors to each (s,n). Let $n = (\mathbf{QX}\phi, \mathtt{W})$ and $(s,n) \xrightarrow{\mathtt{b},\mathtt{a}}{}' (s',n')$, where $a = \{\mathtt{v}_{i_1}\mathtt{:=?}, \ldots \mathtt{v}_{i_k}\mathtt{:=?}, \mathtt{v}_{j_1}\mathtt{:=t}_{j_1}, \ldots \mathtt{v}_{j_l}\mathtt{:=t}_{j_l}\}$, and let *fo-ann*$(s',n')$ be a first-order description of *ann*(s',n'). Then

$$p' =_{\mathrm{df}} \begin{cases} \neg\mathtt{b} \vee (\forall \mathtt{v}_{i_1}, \ldots, \mathtt{v}_{i_k}.\textit{fo-ann}(s',n'))\,[\mathtt{t}_{j_1}/\mathtt{v}_{j_1}, \ldots, \mathtt{t}_{j_l}/\mathtt{v}_{j_l}] \text{ for } \mathbf{Q} = \mathbf{A} \\ \mathtt{b} \wedge (\exists \mathtt{v}_{i_1}, \ldots, \mathtt{v}_{i_k}.\textit{fo-ann}(s',n'))\,[\mathtt{t}_{j_1}/\mathtt{v}_{j_1}, \ldots, \mathtt{t}_{j_l}/\mathtt{v}_{j_l}] \quad \text{for } \mathbf{Q} = \mathbf{E} \end{cases}$$

describes the contribution of that successor to *fo-ann*$'(s,n)$. Now, if $\mathbf{Q} = \mathbf{A}$ then *fo-ann*$'(s,n)$ is the conjunction of all p' and if $\mathbf{Q} = \mathbf{E}$ then *fo-ann*$'(s,n)$ is the disjunction of all p'. The quantification over the input values stored in the variables $\mathtt{v}_{i_m}$ enables us, differing from [5], to cope with verification tasks where unboundedly many inputs are relevant.

The first-order description provides us with a syntactic procedure for first-order model checking that performs the same steps as the semantical process, except that termination may be harder to detect. To detect stabilization, we permit any kind of formula rewriting. If syntactic equality was the criterion for stabilization, a syntactic procedure would not even terminate for trivial problem instances. On the other hand, capturing propositional reasoning already seems to be sufficient for interesting applications. This is the case in our example.

Proposition 3. *If the syntactic model checking terminates then* $K \models \phi$ *if and only if for every initial state* $(s, \mathtt{b}) \in I$, *the condition* $\mathtt{b}$ *implies fo-ann*$(s, (\phi, \emptyset))$.

Note that, Proposition 3 is independent of any particular interpretation $\mathcal{I}$. We call the generated result of the syntactic model checking for K and ϕ to be the *verification condition*, which is

$$vc(K,\phi) =_{\mathrm{df}} \bigwedge_{(s,\mathtt{b}) \in I} \mathtt{b} \Rightarrow \textit{fo-ann}(s,(\phi,\emptyset)).$$

Thus, $K \models \phi$ iff $\models vc(K,\phi)$. Termination of the syntactic annotation process is difficult to characterize. It depends on properties of the cycles in the product structure. In case of a data-independent system, the procedure can easily be seen to behave well, but there are far more interesting examples. If a cycle does not contain input, [5] provides a sufficient criterion. Even inputs are not harmful if tests do not interfere unrestricted, as for instance our running example shows. A more thorough treatment of this question must be deferred to a full version of this paper.

4 First-Order Model Checking, BDD-Based

First-order explicit model checking is time-consuming and only partly automatic. Thus the syntactic model-checking procedure above would not be terribly efficient if implemented. Our approach is based on the idea of combining BDD procedures for finite (small) data domains with first-order representations for infinite or large data domains. We assume that the variables V of the Kripke structure and quantified variables W from the FO-CTL specification are split accordingly into two classes: *Control* variables C whose valuations will be represented by BDDs, and *data* variables D whose valuations will be represented by first-order predicates.

First-order data predicates enter the BDD representation of an annotation in the form of propositions, which are atomic for the BDD. I.e., the BDD refers via proposition names to first-order formulas. Thus, one part of an annotation BDD B represents sets of control valuations, as an ordinary BDD would do. The rest describes what is left of *fo-ann*(s, n) after partial evaluation w.r.t. control values : first-order formulas, which are viewed as boolean combinations of data propositions. The meaning of the proposition names are kept in a separate *proposition table*. A more detailed description is given in the following subsection.

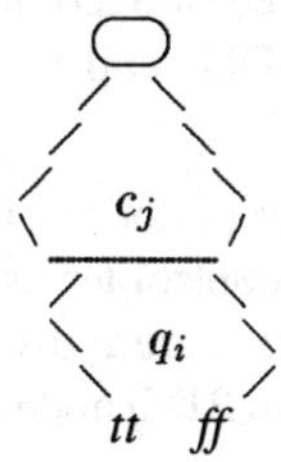

To the left, the general BDD form with control variables and proposition variables is depicted. A specific example BDD is shown to the right. It represents the first-order formula $q_1 \rightarrow (q_3 \vee$ `alarm=tt`$)$ that is the annotation of node s_2 : $\phi_{2,1} \rightarrow \phi_{2,2}$ in our example below.

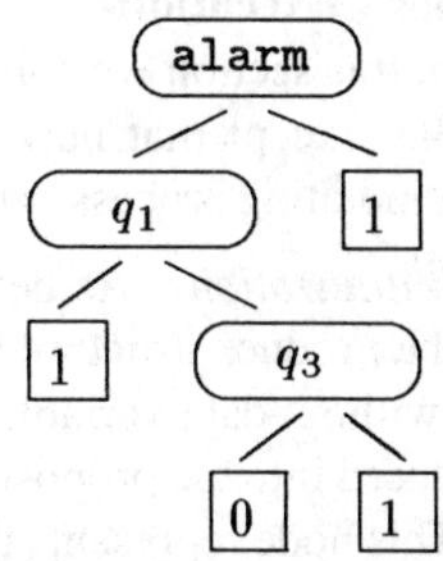

4.1 Representing and Manipulating Data-Dependent Formulas

The proposition table includes, for each proposition variable q_i, the syntactical description of the first-order formula it represents and the set of data variables appearing free in that formula. Note that a proposition does not contain any control variables. The syntax of a proposition may include propositions which are defined earlier in the table. We say that a set of propositions *covers* a first-order formula, if the formula can be written as a boolean combination of these.

Operations : Assignments to be performed along transitions are reflected during model checking by changes to the annotations *fo-ann*(s, n). The effect of taking a transition on control variables is captured canonically using (functional) BDDs.

Assignments of data terms affect the annotations and hence the proposition table. Substitutions can be distributed to single propositions. They may lead to the introduction of new entries in the proposition table, if the result is not already covered by the present set. In our example (see Section 4.3) we apply the data assignment `k:=l` and the random assignment `l:=?` to a proposition q which represents `l-k>80`. Substituting `l'` for `l` and `l` for `k` yields the new proposition $q' \equiv$ `l'-l>80`. Quantifications have to be applied to whole boolean combinations, and they may enforce new propositions, too, e.g. $q'' \equiv \forall$`l'. l'-l>80`. Technically, we maintain a *substitution table* to manage the transformation which is induced on propositions by data assignments. E.g. it would contain q''/q to represent the substitution and quantification effect on q.

Restriction : separate control and data terms We will restrict ourselves to the simple case of a restricted interaction between control and data. This restriction concerns terms in the first-order Kripke structure and specification, but not the dynamically generated formulas *fo-ann*(s, n). We say that control and data are *separated*, if

- right-hand sides of assignments to data variables depend only on data variables,
- right-hand sides of assignments to control variables, conditions and boolean subformulas of the specification are *control terms*, which are generated by the rules :

$$\texttt{ctrl} ::= A \in \mathcal{A} \mid c \in \texttt{C} \mid \texttt{b(D)} \mid \texttt{f(ctrl,...,ctrl)}$$

Intuitively, this means that we may derive a boolean value from data to influence control. Similarly, control can of course influence data via conditions in the first-order structure which enable or disable transitions. The restriction ensures that we are able to represent formulas that are generated during the syntactic annotation process as described above. We conjecture that it is not strictly necessary to impose that restriction. Removing it would complicate our procedure, while its practical merits are debatable.

4.2 Execution

In this section we follow the syntactic model-checking procedure described in Section 3.3, except that now the annotations *fo-ann*(s, n) are represented by BDDs and the annotating process is done partially symbolically.

Initialization: As described in Section 3.3, terminal, minimal and maximal nodes of the product structure are initialized. Node annotations that contain pure control terms (without data variables) are stored as BDDs. In contrast, data dependencies are introduced into the proposition table together with a name q and a link to a single BDD node. This node represents the data proposition in the annotation.

Executing a step: If the annotation *fo-ann*(s, n) that has to be computed for some node (s, n) is a boolean combination of (already represented) subformulas then the representation of *fo-ann*(s, n) is the result of standard operations on BDDs.

Next-step computations of the model checker can be represented as purely boolean operations if no extensions to the proposition table are necessary and no quantifications have to be performed. Otherwise, we can carry out the substitution step symbolically, by enriching the proposition set on demand.

To compute the contribution of a transition $s \xrightarrow{\mathtt{b},\mathtt{a}} s'$ in an **AX** or **EX** evaluation we proceed as follows: we check whether the substitution table is defined for all propositions occurring in the BDD for the successor state. If not, we extend the proposition and substitution table accordingly. Also, there have to be propositions covering the boolean data terms in `b` and in assignments to control variables. The control transformations are captured in a second BDD, which has to be computed only once for the action.

Then, we compute the effect of the assignments as in a conventional symbolic model checker. If random assignments to data do occur in `a`, we have to perform the quantification afterwards. To that end, we extend, if necessary, the proposition table by new propositions with quantified variables and replace the affected parts in the BDDs by the new proposition variables. Finally, we can add the effect of the condition `b`. As a result, we get a BDD which represents the first-order formula *fo-ann*(s, n) from the syntactic model-checking procedure.

4.3 Application to the Example

In the running example, the only control variable is `alarm`, whereas `k`, `l` and `x` are data. The proposition table is initialized by q_1, q_2 and q_3 while the other rows in the table below are filled during a run of the algorithm. Starting the model checking bottom-up with the atomic propositions yields the annotation `ff` for node s_1:`in` and therefore — after some steps — the annotation `tt` for the left subtableau node $s_1{:}\phi_1$. This annotation can be found quickly by performing control pruning as described in Section 5.

The right side of the product structure (on page 6) needs some more attention. We initialize the atoms s_2 : `in` with `tt`, s_2 : `l-x` $>$ `100` with q_1 and s_1 : `alarm=tt` with `alarm=tt`. The annotation of node $s_2 : \phi_{2,2}$ is computed according to the definition in Section 3.3 along both transitions $s_2 \rightarrow s_1$. The first transition yields $\neg q_3 \lor$ `tt=tt` and the second one yields $q_3 \lor$ `alarm=tt`. Their conjunction simplifies to $q_3 \lor$ `alarm=tt`. Quantification is not necessary here, because both assignments are regular. Thus we get for the node $s_2 : \phi_{2,1} \rightarrow \phi_{2,2}$ the annotation $q_1 \rightarrow (q_3 \lor$ `alarm=tt`$)$.

name	proposition	data var	name	proposition	data var
q_1	`l-x>100`	`l`	q_6	`∀ l'.` $(q_4 \rightarrow q_5)$	`l`
q_2	`l=x`	`l`	q_7	q_2`[l''/l'] = l''=x`	`l''`
q_3	`l-k>80`	`l,k`	q_8	q_6`[l''/l]`	`l''`
q_4	q_1`[l'/l] = l'-x>100`	`l'`	q_9	`∀ l''.` $(q_7 \rightarrow q_8)$	
q_5	q_3`[(l',l)/(l,k)] = l'-l>80`	`l',l`	q_{10}	`∀ x.` q_9	

In the next step of the algorithm the transition $s_1 \rightarrow s_2$ is used to manipulate this formula. `alarm` is replaced by `ff`. q_1 and q_3 depend on l that is substituted by the fresh variable l' while k is substituted by l. Afterwards l' is quantified. Note how we omit name clashes when substituting and quantifying l. The generated terms are stored in the proposition table, the substitutions are stored in the substitution table. Finally this step yields q_6 as annotation for node s_1 : $\mathbf{AX}(\phi_{2,1} \rightarrow \phi_{2,2})$. The formula q_6 does not change in the next bottom-up step of the model checking algorithm and also annotates $s_2 : \phi_{1,2}$. This yields $q_2 \rightarrow q_6$ for the node $s_2 : \phi_1$.

When we start the fixed point computation with annotations `tt` and $q_2 \rightarrow q_6$ and then step through both nodes in the loop we reach after some steps the stable description $(q_2 \rightarrow q_6) \land q_9$ for node s_2 : $\mathbf{AG}\,\phi_1$ and q_9 for node s_1 : $\mathbf{AG}\,\phi_1$.

The last step computes $\forall x.\, q_9$ as proof obligation for node $s : \phi$. Slightly simplified, this obligation states $\forall x, l.\, l - x > 100 \rightarrow l - x > 80$. Since this formula is a tautology, the first-order Kripke structure fulfills the specification.

5 Optimization: Control Pruning

Control pruning is an optimization method that allows us to reduce the size of the product structure before the annotation procedure is applied speeding up this procedure. To this end, we will modify the procedure of computing annotations by permitting approximate computations for nodes, whose descendants are not yet stable.

In the simple version discussed here, we introduce a specific proposition "$\perp$" which replaces all data conditions. $\perp$ represents uncertainty. A BDD B depending on it yields a lower approximation of the correct annotation for $\perp = ff$ (i.e., $B[ff/\perp]$ implies the annotation), and an upper approximation for $\perp = tt$. In favorable cases, some annotations can be computed to a value not depending on $\perp$ even if some annotations below still contain it. This permits us to reduce the size of the product structure to be annotated in the accurate procedure, so it also helps to keep the number of propositions small. The process of eliminating all irrelevant nodes after the simple approximation computation where all data propositions are replaced by $\perp$ is called *control pruning*, because it uses only control information to simplify the verification problem.

The approximation of annotations of the left part of the product structure of our example (the part below node s_1 : $\mathbf{AG}\,\phi_1$ in the picture on page 6) is presented on the next page. The approximation proves that the annotations below node $s_1 : \phi_1$ need not be considered again during a detailed model checking process, because the annotation

of this node already yields *tt*.
Applying approximation to the tree below the node $s_2 : \phi_1$ (right side in the product structure on page 6) yields $\bot$ for this node. Thus no optimization is possible there.

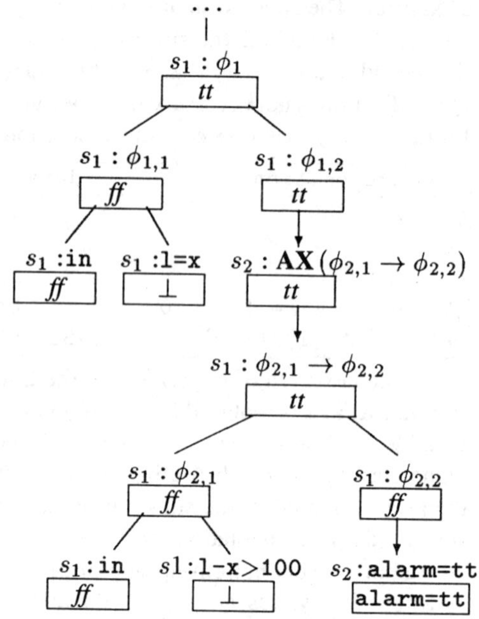

6 Conclusion

The most attractive aspect of our procedure is its closeness to standard symbolic model checking. It is an extension which permits to treat a selected set of variables differently. In fact, the first-order properties can be viewed as abstractions of the data values which are precise wrt. analysed property. In contrast to other frameworks of abstraction, they are computed automatically. Furthermore, they are tailored to the specification to be checked and allow partial evaluation of control to reduce the analysis effort. The method is currently implemented on top of a standard BDD package at OFFIS and will be employed in the context of verification of hybrid ECUs in automotive applications.

References

1. S. Berezin, A. Biere, E. Clarke, and Y. Zhu. Combining symbolic model checking with uninterpreted functions for out-of-order processor verification. submitted for publication.
2. Bernholtz, O., Vardi, M. and Wolper, P. *An automata-theoretic approach to branching-time model checking*, CAV '94, LNCS 818, 142–155.
3. Burch, J.R. and Dill, D.L. *Automatic verification of pipelined microprocessor control*, CAV '94, LNCS 818, 68–80.
4. Clarke, E.M., Grumberg, O. and Long, D.E. *Model checking and abstraction*, ACM TOPLAS, vol. 16,5. 1512–1542. 1994.
5. Damm W., Hungar H., and Grumberg O. *What if model checking must be truly symbolic*. LNCS 987, 1995.
6. Dingel, J. and Filkorn, T. *Model checking for infinite state systems using data abstraction, assumption-commitment style reasoning and theorem proving*, CAV '95, LNCS 939, 1995
7. Graf, S. *Verification of a distributed cache memory by using abstractions*, CAV '94, LNCS 818 (1994), 207–219.
8. A.J. Isles, R. Hojati, and R.K. Brayton. Computing reachability control states of systems modeled with uninterpreted functions and infinite memory. In *Proc. of CAV'98*, LNCS.
9. K. Sajid, A. Goel, H. Zhou, A. Aziz, S. Barber, and V. Singhal. BDD based procedures for the theory of equality with uninterpreted functions. In *Proc. of CAV'98*, LNCS, 1998.
10. Wolper, P. *Expressing interesting properties of programs in propositional temporal logic*, POPL '86, 184–193.
11. Xu Y., Cerny E., Song X., Corella F., and Mohamed O.A.. *Model checking for a first-order temporal logic using multiway decision graphs*. In *Proc. of CAV'98*, LNCS, 1998.

On the Complexity of Counting the Number of Vertices Moved by Graph Automorphisms

Antoni Lozano[1] and Vijay Raghavan[2]

[1] Department LSI, UPC Jordi Girona 1-3, Mòdul C6, Barcelona 08034, Catalonia, E.U.
antoni@lsi.upc.es

[2] Box 1679-B, CS Dept., Vanderbilt University, Nashville, TN 37235, USA
raghavan@vuse.vanderbilt.edu

Abstract. We consider the problem of deciding whether a given graph G has an automorphism which moves at least k vertices (where k is a function of $|V(G)|$), a question originally posed by Lubiw (1981). Here we show that this problem is equivalent to the one of deciding whether a graph has a nontrivial automorphism, for $k \in O(\log n / \log \log n)$. It is commonly believed that deciding isomorphism between two graphs is strictly harder than deciding whether a graph has a nontrivial automorphism. Indeed, we show that an isomorphism oracle would improve the above result slightly—using such an oracle, one can decide whether there is an automorphism which moves at least k' vertices, where $k' \in O(\log n)$. If P $\neq$ NP and Graph Isomorphism is not NP-complete, the above results are fairly tight, since it is known that deciding if there is an automorphism which moves at least n^ϵ vertices, for any fixed $\epsilon \in (0,1)$, is NP-complete. In other words, a substantial improvement of our result would settle some fundamental open problems about Graph Isomorphism.

1 Introduction

The Graph Isomorphism problem (or simply GI) is one of the most famous problems in NP, the reasons being both practical—it is used in such different disciplines as combinatorial designs and organic chemistry—and theoretical. In the latter category, we can point to the fact that GI is still a prime candidate for being an NP-intermediate problem, i.e., one of the kind of problems that Ladner [7] proved must exist in NP which are neither in P nor NP-complete, under the hypothesis that P $\neq$ NP.

One of the most successful approaches for studying GI has been the group theoretical one [5]. The essential starting point here is the observation that many interesting properties of a given graph are revealed by a study of its group of automorphisms, i.e., the set of vertex permutations which preserve adjacency. The consideration of concepts from elementary group theory sheds light on related problems and allows us to gain insight into the complexity and properties of GI itself. A simple question one can ask about the automorphism group of a given graph is what its size (or *order*) is. Perhaps an even simpler question from the group-theoretical point of view is whether the automorphism group is nontrivial, i.e., does the group have any permutation other than the identity? This is precisely one of the best-known open problems related to GI: Graph Automorphism (GA). A many-one reduction is known from GA to GI [8] but not even a Turing reduction is known in the other direction; GA is, therefore, a candidate for an NP-intermediate problem potentially simpler than GI.

Most of the variations of GI considered in the literature turn out to be equivalent to known problems. Some happen to be NP-complete [9] or have polynomial-time algorithms (for example, when the graphs considered have bounded degree [10], which is one of the successes of the group-theoretical approach). Some other variations are equivalent either to GI or to GA. An example of the former kind is the above-mentioned problem of finding the order of the automorphism group of a given graph, which was proved to be GI-equivalent [11]. An example of the latter kind is the following problem posed by Lubiw [9], recently shown to be GA-equivalent by Agrawal and Arvind [1]: given two graphs and k distinct isomorphisms between them, decide if they have yet another isomorphism.

The variations of GI which are not known to be equivalent to known problems are more rare but they are key problems if we wish to understand the relative complexities of GA and GI. For instance, checking, for a fixed constant k, whether the order of the automorphism group of a graph is divisible by k is one such problem, known to be between GA and GI for many-one reductions [2]. The problem we study in this paper, which we call $\mathrm{Mov}_k\mathrm{GA}$, was also posed by Lubiw: given a graph G of n vertices, decide whether G has an automorphism which moves at least $k(n)$ vertices. She observed that $\mathrm{Mov}_k\mathrm{GA}$ is at least as easy as GI and at least as hard as GA when k is any constant function (in fact, it is trivial for $k = 0$ and coincides with GA for $k = 1$). On the other extreme, when k is a linear function of n and even for $k \in \Omega(n^\epsilon)$, where $\epsilon \in (0,1)$, Lubiw shows that $\mathrm{Mov}_k\mathrm{GA}$ is NP-complete. The principal open question in this line of attack is, therefore: what is the complexity of $\mathrm{Mov}_k\mathrm{GA}$ when k is a function which grows more slowly than $k(n) = n^\epsilon$, for example, a function such as $k(n) = \log n$? This range would appear to be rich in NP-intermediate problems, given the behavior at the extremes, and therefore a good area for careful study.

Here we partially answer the above questions We show in Section 3 that when $k \in O(\log n/\log\log n)$, $\mathrm{Mov}_k\mathrm{GA}$ is still Turing equivalent to GA. We also classify more accurately the case when k is a constant function, where $\mathrm{Mov}_k\mathrm{GA}$ is shown to be in fact truth-table equivalent to GA. For $k \in O(\log n)$, we prove in Section 4 that $\mathrm{Mov}_k\mathrm{GA}$ is Turing reducible to GI [1].

The remainder of the paper is organized as follows. Section 2 has definitions of concepts used in the rest of the paper. Section 3 has our results on using a GA

[1] In fact, our result goes in a direction contrary to the intuitive one for Anna Lubiw, who says "The problem [$\mathrm{Mov}_{\log n}\mathrm{GA}$] would seem to be at least as hard as ISOMORPHISM but it is not obviously ISOMORPHISM-complete or NP-complete" [9].

oracle to solve $\mathrm{Mov}_k\mathrm{GA}$, while Section 4 is concerned with the more powerful GI oracle. We conclude with some open problems in Section 5.

2 Preliminaries

The following definitions of group-theoretical concepts may be found in any elementary textbook (for example, [4]).

Let $[n]$ denote the set $\{1, 2, \ldots, n\}$ and S_n the symmetric group of n elements. Let id denote the identity permutation of any permutation group. If $\phi_1, \phi_2 \in S_n$ then the product $\phi = \phi_1\phi_2$ is defined by $\phi(i) = \phi_1(\phi_2(i))$. If G [2] and H are groups then $G \leq H$ denotes that G is a subgroup of H.

Let $G \leq S_n$ and $X \subseteq [n]$. Then the *point-wise stabilizer* of X in G is

$$G_{(X)} = \{\phi \in G \mid \forall x \in X \quad \phi(x) = x\}.$$

Let φ be a permutation and G a subgroup of S_n. We define the *support* of φ and G as follows

$$\mathrm{supp}(\varphi) = \{i \in [n] \mid \varphi(i) \neq i\}$$
$$\mathrm{supp}(G) = \{i \in [n] \mid \exists \varphi \in G \ \varphi(i) \neq i\}$$

If $i \in \mathrm{supp}(\varphi)$ then we say that φ *moves* i and if $i \notin \mathrm{supp}(\varphi)$ then we say that φ *fixes* i (or that i is a *fix-point* of φ). The set of *fix-points* of φ, denoted $\mathrm{fix}(\varphi)$, is the set $[n] - \mathrm{supp}(\varphi)$.

All graphs considered in this paper may be assumed to be labeled and directed. This does not limit the scope of the results so obtained since all the versions of graph isomorphism for graphs are polynomial-time equivalent, irrespective of whether the graphs are undirected or directed, labeled or not [6]. The same comment applies to graph automorphism as well [6].

For any graph G on n vertices, we denote by $Aut(G)$ the group of automorphisms of G. That $Aut(G)$ is a subgroup of S_n easy to see [6]. Moreover, for any $X \subseteq [n]$, the point-wise stabilizer of X in $Aut(G)$, i.e., $Aut(G)_{(X)}$, is a subgroup of $Aut(G)$.

The main problem considered in this paper is that of deciding whether a graph contains an automorphism which moves at least k vertices, where k may be a function of the number of vertices. This problem was called k-FIXED-POINT-FREE AUTOMORPHISM in [9]. It is convenient to cast this as a standard decision problem of deciding membership in a set.

Definition 1. *Let $\mathcal{G}_n$ denote the set of all graphs on n vertices. Let k be any integer function*[3]*. Then,*

$$\mathrm{Mov}_k\mathrm{GA} = \bigcup_{n \geq 1} \{G \in \mathcal{G}_n \mid \exists \varphi \in Aut(G) \quad |\mathrm{supp}(\varphi)| \geq k(n)\}.$$

[2] We use the letter G to denote graphs as well as groups. However, no confusion is likely to arise from this "abuse" since the context always clarifies the issue.

[3] We will implicitly add the modest requirement of polynomial-time computability of k to ensure that $\mathrm{Mov}_k\mathrm{GA}$ is in NP.

An automorphism of a graph G is an automorphism of the complement $\overline{G}$ as well. Moreover, since either G or $\overline{G}$ is (weakly) connected, there is no loss of generality in assuming, as we do henceforth in studying $\mathrm{Mov}_k\mathrm{GA}$, that we deal only with connected graphs.

Given an initially unlabeled graph G on n vertices, and a set $X \subseteq [n] = V(G)$, we denote by $G_{[X]}$ the graph obtained by *labeling* the vertices in X with distinct colors. A labeled vertex is essentially distinguished from the remaining (labeled and unlabeled) vertices of the graph for the purpose of automorphism. In other words, the automorphisms of the graph $G_{[X]}$ are only those automorphisms of $Aut(G)$ which fix X, so that $Aut(G_{[X]})$ is isomorphic to $Aut(G)_{(X)}$, the point-wise stabilizer of X in $Aut(G)$ [11, 6].

A standard "trick of the trade" is the following. Let G be an initially unlabeled graph on n vertices and let $Y = \langle y_1, y_2, \ldots, y_r\rangle$ and $Z = \langle z_1, z_2, \ldots, z_r\rangle$ both be sequences of r distinct vertices of G. Borrowing the notation of [1] with a slight alteration, the graph $G_{[Y]} \uplus G_{[Z]}$ is obtained from G by making copies G_1 and G_2 of G and then labeling vertices y_i in G_1 and z_i in G_2, $1 \leq i \leq r$, with the *same* color. If G is originally weakly connected (as will happen in all our applications) then $G_{[Y]} \uplus G_{[Z]}$ may have the following two kinds of automorphisms only [11, 6]:

- Automorphisms which move vertices in G_1 to vertices in G_1 and vertices in G_2 to vertices in G_2. Such automorphisms fix vertices in Y and Z and may be seen to be in 1-1 correspondence with the cross-product of $Aut(G)_{(Y)}$ and $Aut(G)_{(Z)}$.
- Automorphisms which move *all* the vertices of G_1 to vertices in G_2 in such a way that each vertex y_i in G_1 is mapped to the vertex z_i in G_2, $1 \leq i \leq r$. Such automorphisms are in 1-1 correspondence with the set of automorphisms of $Aut(G)$ which map y_i to z_i, $1 \leq i \leq r$.

3 Using a GA oracle to decide if a few vertices are moved

The main result of this section is that for $k \in O(\frac{\log n}{\log\log n})$, $\mathrm{Mov}_k\mathrm{GA}$ is equivalent to GA. The following overview of the technique we use in this section may help. First, we show (Corollary 1) that the size of the support of any group $G \leq S_n$ in which all automorphisms move at most k elements is at most $2k$. Consequently, we can immediately derive (Corollary 3) that $\mathrm{Mov}_k\mathrm{GA}$ is truth-table reducible to GA, for any *constant* k.

Next, we consider nonconstant functions $k(n)$. Here, the picture is not as clear even if $k(n)$ is a very slowly growing function of n, since one must avoid having to test all possible subsets of $[n]$ of size at most $2k$. To attack this problem, we introduce the notions of a "partial" permutation and consistency of a permutation with a partial specification. Then we show (Lemma 3) that for any permutation group $G \leq S_n$ and any $X \subseteq [n]$, testing whether $G \neq G_{(X)}$ can be done by checking if G contains a permutation ϕ which is distinguishable from all the permutations in $G_{(X)}$ *solely* by its behavior on $\overline{X} \supseteq \mathrm{supp}(G_{(X)})$. The crucial point here is that this enables us to generate the automorphism group of a graph by fixing most of the elements and gradually increasing the support. As long as the current support is not too large, one can check if a partial permutation which is distinguishable from all currently generated automorphisms can be extended to a new automorphism.

We start with the following lemma.

Lemma 1. *Let $G \leq S_n$. If $A_1, \ldots, A_r \subseteq [n]$ are pairwise disjoint and $\phi_1, \ldots, \phi_r \in G$ satisfy*

- $A_i \subseteq \mathrm{supp}(\phi_i)$ *for* $1 \leq i \leq r$ *and*
- $\phi_i \in G_{(\bigcup_{j=1}^{i-1} A_j)}$ *for* $1 < i \leq r$

then there exists a permutation ϕ in G such that

$$|\mathrm{supp}(\phi) \cap \bigcup_{i=1}^{r} A_i| \geq \sum_{i=1}^{r} \left\lceil \frac{|A_i|}{2} \right\rceil .$$

Proof. We proceed by induction on r. For $r = 1$, the statement is trivial. Suppose the lemma holds for $r - 1 \geq 1$ and assume that the antecedent of the lemma holds for r. Let ϕ be the permutation given by the induction hypothesis such that $|\mathrm{supp}(\phi) \cap \bigcup_{i=1}^{r-1} A_i| \geq \sum_{i=1}^{r-1} \left\lceil \frac{|A_i|}{2} \right\rceil$ holds.

Now, either $|A_r \cap \mathrm{supp}(\phi_r \phi)| \geq \left\lceil \frac{|A_r|}{2} \right\rceil$, or not. Since $\mathrm{supp}(\phi_r \phi) \supseteq \mathrm{supp}(\phi) \cap \bigcup_{i=1}^{r-1} A_i$, in the former case the induction hypothesis guarantees that $\phi_r \phi$ provides the permutation which satisfies the lemma. In the latter case, it must be true that $|A_r \cap \mathrm{supp}(\phi)| \geq \left\lceil \frac{|A_r|}{2} \right\rceil$ and consequently ϕ itself satisfies the lemma. ∎

Corollary 1. *Let $G \leq S_n$. Then $|\mathrm{supp}(G)| \leq 2 \cdot \max_{\phi \in G} |\mathrm{supp}(\phi)|$.*

Proof. Let $\phi_1, \phi_2, \ldots, \phi_{|G|}$ be an enumeration of G in any order and define the sets $A_i, 1 \leq i \leq |G|$, by $A_i = \mathrm{supp}(\phi_i) - \bigcup_{j>i} \mathrm{supp}(\phi_j)$. Then the sets A_i are pairwise disjoint and $\bigcup_{i=1}^{|G|} A_i = \mathrm{supp}(G)$. The corollary now follows directly from Lemma 1. ∎

Comment 1 *The constant 2 in Corollary 1 may not be the best possible. However, one can construct examples to show that the best value is not smaller than 3/2.*

Corollary 2. *Let $G \leq S_n$ and let $k = \max_{\phi \in G} |\mathrm{supp}(\phi)|$. Then, $|G| \leq (2k)!$.*

Proof. Follows from Corollary 1. ∎

Now, we can reduce $\mathrm{Mov}_k\mathrm{GA}$ to GA when k is a constant.

Corollary 3. *For any constant $k \geq 1$,* Mov_kGA *is $\leq_{tt}^{p}$-reducible to* GA.

Proof. The following algorithm can be used to decide Mov_kGA using GA for a particular graph G. Generate up to $r = (2k)!$ automorphisms of G in lexicographical order. Using the algorithm in [1], this can be done in time $n^{O(\log(r))}$. If $|Aut(G)| < r$, then we can check all the automorphisms to see if there is one of support at least k. If not, Corollary 2 guarantees us that there will be an automorphism in $Aut(G)$ which moves at least k vertices.

Since the algorithm in [1] makes the queries to GA nonadaptively, we obtain a $\leq_{tt}^{p}$ reduction to GA. ■

In the following, we need the notion of a "partial" permutation. Let $\phi \in S_n$ and $Y \subseteq [n]$. The *partial permutation* ϕ_Y is defined as follows:

$$\phi_Y(i) = \begin{cases} \phi(i), & \text{if } i \in Y \text{ and } \phi(i) \in Y \\ \text{undefined}, & \text{otherwise} \end{cases}$$

We say that a permutation ϕ is a *pseudo-extension* of ρ_Y if either ϕ is an extension of ρ_Y or $\text{Dom}(\rho_Y) \subseteq \text{fix}(\phi)$.

Let $G \leq S_n$. The set of permutations *consistent* with ρ_Y in G is:

$$\mathcal{C}(G, \rho_Y) = \{\phi \in G \mid \phi \text{ is a pseudo-extension of } \rho_Y \text{ or } (\rho^{-1})_Y\}.$$

The set $\mathcal{C}(G, \rho_Y)$ will be used in the main theorem of this section. The following lemma, implicit in [1], motivates this idea in conjunction with a GA oracle.

Lemma 2. *Let G be any graph on n vertices, $\rho \in S_n$, and $X \subseteq [n]$. Let $Y = \langle y_1, y_2, \ldots \rangle$ be any enumeration of* $\text{Dom}(\rho_X)$ *and let $Z = \langle \rho(y_1), \rho(y_2), \ldots \rangle$. Then, $G_{[Y]} \uplus G_{[Z]}$ has a nontrivial automorphism if and only if $\mathcal{C}(Aut(G), \rho_X) \neq \{\text{id}\}$.*

Proof. First, note that $\text{Dom}((\rho^{-1})_X) = \text{Im}(\rho_X)$ and $\text{Im}((\rho^{-1})_X) = \text{Dom}(\rho_X)$. As mentioned at the end of Section 2, any nontrivial automorphism ϕ in a graph consisting of two connected components, such as $G_{[Y]} \uplus G_{[Z]}$ can only be of two forms:

- ϕ is comprised of two automorphisms: ϕ_1, which is an automorphism of $G_{[Y]}$ alone, and ϕ_2, which is an automorphism of $G_{[Z]}$ alone, and at least one of these is nontrivial, say ϕ_1. Now ϕ_1 is an automorphism of G which fixes all the vertices in Y and therefore, $\text{Dom}(\rho_X) \subseteq \text{fix}(\phi_1)$.
- ϕ moves all the vertices of $G_{[Y]}$ to vertices in $G_{[Z]}$ and corresponds to an automorphism ϕ' of $Aut(G)$ which maps vertex $y \in Y$ to vertex $z = \rho(y) \in Z$. That is, ϕ' is an extension of ρ_X.

In either case we get a nontrivial automorphism in $\mathcal{C}(Aut(G), \rho_X)$. Observe, for the converse, that the above proof can be followed backwards if $\mathcal{C}(Aut(G), \rho_X) \neq \{\text{id}\}$. ■

Lemma 3. *Let $G < S_n$ be a group and $X \subseteq [n]$. Then, $G_{(\overline{X})} \neq G$ if and only if there exists a permutation $\phi \in G - G_{(\overline{X})}$ such that $\mathcal{C}(G_{(\overline{X})}, \phi_X) = \{\mathrm{id}\}$.*

Proof. Suppose $G_{(\overline{X})} \neq G$. Let ϕ be a permutation of *minimal* support in $G - G_{(\overline{X})}$. We will show that $\mathcal{C}(G_{(\overline{X})}, \phi_X) = \{\mathrm{id}\}$, proving the lemma.

Suppose, to the contrary, that $\mathcal{C}(G_{(\overline{X})}, \phi_X) \neq \{\mathrm{id}\}$. Assume that ϕ' is a nontrivial pseudo-extension of ϕ_X in $G_{(\overline{X})}$ (the proof for ϕ' being a pseudo-extension of $(\phi^{-1})_X$ is identical since $\mathrm{supp}(\phi^{-1}) = \mathrm{supp}(\phi)$). Consider any element $a \in \mathrm{supp}(\phi')$. Now, $a \in \mathrm{supp}(\phi)$ (otherwise ϕ' cannot be a pseudo-extension of ϕ_X by definition).

- If $\phi_X(a) = b$, then $\phi'(a) = b$ (again by the definition of $\mathcal{C}(G_{(\overline{X})}, \phi_X)$), but then $\phi'^{-1}\phi$ fixes a but no element in $\mathrm{supp}(\phi) \cap \overline{X}$. However, this contradicts the minimality of ϕ.
- If $\phi_X(a)$ is undefined, let $x = \phi(a)$, $y = \phi^{-1}(a)$, and let $b = \phi'(a)$. Observe that:
  1. x belongs to $\overline{X}$ (otherwise, $\phi_X(a)$ would not be undefined).
  2. $\phi'(y) = y$. Otherwise, suppose that $\phi'(y) = z \neq y$. Then, $y \in X$ and $\phi_X(y) = a$ imply that $z = \phi'(y) = a$. However, this in turn implies that $\phi'^{-1}\phi$ is a permutation of smaller support than ϕ in $G - G_{(\overline{X})}$, a contradiction.

  Consider $\phi'' = \phi\phi'\phi^{-1}$. Now,

  $$\phi''(x) = \phi\phi'\phi^{-1}(x) = \phi\phi'(a) = \phi(b) \neq x \tag{1}$$

  because $\phi(a) = x$ and $a \neq b$. Also,

  $$\phi''(a) = \phi\phi'\phi^{-1}(a) = \phi\phi'(y) = \phi(y) = a. \tag{2}$$

  From Equation 1, ϕ'' is a permutation in $G - G_{(\overline{X})}$. But the facts that $\mathrm{supp}(\phi'') \subseteq \mathrm{supp}(\phi)$ and that a is a fix-point of ϕ'' (by Equation 2) contradict the minimality of ϕ.

■

Now we are ready for the main result of this section.

Theorem 2. $\mathrm{Mov}_k\mathrm{GA}$ *can be decided in time $O(k^{O(k)} + kn^2)$, for any function k, with GA as oracle.*

Proof. Consider the algorithm in Figure 1 for deciding $\mathrm{Mov}_k\mathrm{GA}$.

We first discuss the correctness of the approach in the algorithm and then show how all the steps can be implemented within the claimed time bounds by using GA as an oracle.

The correctness of the algorithm is relatively straightforward. The set X maintains the current subset of $\mathrm{supp}(Aut(G))$ that we are considering and the set H maintains the current $Aut(G)_{(\overline{X})}$. Initially, X contains no vertex and H

Input: Graph G, a positive integer k.
Assume that the vertices are numbered $1, 2, \ldots, n = |V(G)|$.
1. $X \leftarrow \emptyset$; $H \leftarrow \{\mathrm{id}\}$
2. **while** $Aut(G) \neq H$ **do**
3. Find an automorphism $\phi \in Aut(G) - H$
4. $X \leftarrow X \cup \mathrm{supp}(\phi)$
5. **if** $|X| \geq 2k$ **then**
6. Halt and answer "Yes"
7. **endif**
8. $H \leftarrow Aut(G)_{(\overline{X})}$
9. **if** $\exists \phi \in H : |\mathrm{supp}(\phi)| \geq k$ **then**
10. Halt and answer "Yes"
11. **endif**
12. **endwhile**
13. Answer "No."

Fig. 1. Algorithm for Deciding $\mathrm{Mov}_k\mathrm{GA}$

contains id only. Each iteration through the **while** loop discovers a new automorphism ϕ in $Aut(G) - Aut(G)_{(\overline{X})}$, causing X to increase. If now $|X| \geq 2k$, then Corollary 1 guarantees us that $Aut(G)$ contains at least one automorphism of support at least k. So we can halt and answer "yes" in this case (line 6). Otherwise, as long as $|X| < 2k$, we simply enumerate all the automorphisms in $Aut(G)_{(\overline{X})}$ and check whether any of them has support at least k. If so, we can again halt and answer "yes" immediately (line 10); if not, we test if there are more automorphisms to be found (i.e., if $Aut(G)_{(\overline{X})} \neq Aut(G)$) and continue through the **while** loop.

The heart of the algorithm lies in testing $Aut(G)_{(\overline{X})} \neq Aut(G)$ of line 2 and if so, finding some automorphism ϕ in $Aut(G) - Aut(G)_{(\overline{X})}$. We now show how these steps can be accomplished using GA. (These are the only steps of the algorithm which use GA.)

To test if $Aut(G)_{(\overline{X})} \neq Aut(G)$, we generate *all* partial permutations $\rho_X : X \longrightarrow X$ and check whether they satisfy the "filtering" condition $\mathcal{C}(Aut(G)_{(\overline{X})}, \rho_X) = \{\mathrm{id}\}$. Note that the filtering condition, for a given ρ_X, can be tested in time linear in $|Aut(G)_{(\overline{X})}| \cdot |X|$. For each partial permutation ρ_X which satisfies the filtering condition, ask GA if $G_{[Y]} \uplus G_{[Z]}$ has a nontrivial automorphism, where $Y = \langle y_1, y_2, \ldots, \rangle$ and each y_i is a distinct element of $\mathrm{Dom}(\rho_X)$ and $Z = \langle \rho(y_1), \rho(y_2), \ldots \rangle$.

From Lemma 2, it follows that if GA answers "yes" in the above procedure then we must have a nontrivial automorphism ϕ in $\mathcal{C}(Aut(G), \rho_X)$. Since the filtering condition ensures that $\mathcal{C}(Aut(G)_{(\overline{X})}, \rho_X)$ does not contain a nontrivial automorphism, it follows that ϕ must be in $Aut(G) - Aut(G)_{(\overline{X})}$, enabling one to decide that $Aut(G)_{(\overline{X})} \neq Aut(G)$ Finally, note that Lemma 3 guarantees that if $Aut(G)_{(\overline{X})} \neq Aut(G)$, then indeed there will be a permutation ϕ such that $C(Aut(G)_{(\overline{X})}, \phi_X) = \{\mathrm{id}\}$. Hence, at least when we consider the partial permutation $\rho_X = \phi_X$, GA is bound to answer "yes." In other words, one can decide that $Aut(G)_{(\overline{X})} = Aut(G)$ if GA answers "no" to all the questions in this procedure. Therefore, the above procedure is also correct whenever it concludes that there is no automorphism in $Aut(G) - Aut(G)_{(\overline{X})}$.

Assuming that we have tested and found that $Aut(G)_{(\overline{X})} \neq Aut(G)$, finding an automorphism in line 3 of the algorithm in Figure 1 can be achieved by using a standard trick. We adaptively add labels to vertices in whichever graph GA answered "yes" until all mappings of an automorphism in $Aut(G) - Aut(G)_{(\overline{X})}$ are found. It is easy to see that a mapping can be found in $O(n^2)$ time, starting from the initial graph.

We now estimate the time complexity of the entire algorithm. The **while** loop is entered at most $2k$ times, since each iteration increases the number of vertices found to be in $\mathrm{supp}(Aut(G))$ and the algorithm stops if at least $2k$ vertices are found in the support. In each iteration, there are two "expensive" steps. The first one is in doing the test in line 2 and then finding an automorphism in line 3, as explained above. The second one is in line 8, when all automorphisms in $Aut(G)_{(\overline{X})}$ are to be assigned to the set H.

The former step is bounded by $O(kn^2 + km)$, where m is the total number of partial permutations. Now m may be bounded by $\sum_{r=0}^{2k} \binom{2k}{r} \frac{(2k)!}{(2k-r)!}$ since the size of the set X is at most $2k$. In turn, this expression is seen to be less than $(2k+1)2^{2k}(2k)^{2k} \in k^{O(k)}$.

The latter step is implemented as follows. In a preprocessing step, the set X is partitioned into equivalence classes of vertices based on the following relation: $u \equiv v$ if and only if u and v have the same neighbors (both in-neighbors and out-neighbors) in $\overline{X}$. These equivalence classes can be found in $O(n^2)$ time. Clearly, an automorphism in $Aut(G)_{(\overline{X})}$ can move a vertex u to a vertex v only if $u \equiv v$. Moreover, a permutation ϕ of vertices in X is an automorphism in $Aut(G)_{(\overline{X})}$ if and only if both the following conditions hold:

- If $\phi(u) = v$ then $u \equiv v$, and
- ϕ is an automorphism of the subgraph of G induced by X.

For a given permutation ϕ, these checks can be carried out in $O(k^2)$ time, given the preprocessed equivalence classes and an $O(1)$ test for equivalence. Therefore, the entire step, which can be repeated at most $O(k)$ times in the loop, can be implemented in $O(n^2 + k^2 \cdot (2k)!) = O(n^2 + k^{O(k)})$ time by checking all possible permutations ϕ of vertices in X by "brute force," i.e., without using the GA oracle. (Indeed, the algorithm in [1] which uses GA to generate automorphisms may be used instead, but this would yield the inferior $O(n^2 + k^{O(k \log k)})$ bound for this step.) Putting these facts together gives the claimed time bounds of the theorem. ∎

This leads to our equivalence result between GA and Mov_kGA when k is a slow-growing function of n.

Corollary 4. $\mathrm{Mov}_k\mathrm{GA}$ *is polynomial-time Turing equivalent to* GA *for* $k \in O(\frac{\log n}{\log\log n})$.

Proof. That $\mathrm{Mov}_k\mathrm{GA} \leq_T^p \mathrm{GA}$ follows from the above theorem by noting that $k^{O(k)}$ is at most a polynomial in n when $k \in O(\frac{\log n}{\log\log n})$.

The proof in the other direction is more straightforward. In order to decide if a given graph G has a nontrivial automorphism using a $\mathrm{Mov}_k\mathrm{GA}$ oracle, use the following procedure. Let C_i be a directed cycle on i vertices. If G is isomorphic to $C_{k(n)-1}$ then clearly G has a nontrivial automorphism. Otherwise, G is in GA if and only if the disjoint union of G and $C_{k(n)-1}$ is in $\mathrm{Mov}_k\mathrm{GA}$. ■

4 Using a GI oracle to deciding if more vertices are moved

The results of the previous section can be improved a little when one has access to the more powerful GI oracle instead of the GA oracle. The key idea here is that instead of generating all the automorphisms of a graph G (as in the previous section) one can decide $\mathrm{Mov}_k\mathrm{GA}$ by simply checking, for every subset X of $\mathrm{supp}(Aut(G))$ of size at least k, whether there is an automorphism which has support precisely X.

Theorem 3. $\mathrm{Mov}_k\mathrm{GA}$ *can be decided in time* $O(2^{O(k)}n^2)$, *for any function* k, *with GI as oracle.*

Proof. The following algorithm can be used to decide $\mathrm{Mov}_k\mathrm{GA}$ using GI as an oracle.

Given a graph G, we can find $S = \mathrm{supp}(G)$ easily using GI as an oracle (see, for example, [11]). If $|S| \geq 2k$, then we are done: by Corollary 1, there must be a permutation with support at least k. Otherwise, suppose that $|S| < 2k$ and define, for each $X \subseteq S$, the following quantities:

1. q_X, the number of permutations in $Aut(G)$ with support exactly X, i.e.,
$$q_X = |\{\phi \in Aut(G) \mid \mathrm{supp}(\phi) = X\}| \quad \text{, and}$$
2. r_X, the number of permutations in $Aut(G)$ with support a subset of X, i.e.,
$$r_X = |\{\phi \in Aut(G) \mid \mathrm{supp}(\phi) \subseteq X\}|.$$

For each set $X \subseteq S$, the quantity r_X can be found by using Mathon's result on counting the number of automorphisms with a GI oracle [11]. This is because r_X is precisely $|Aut(G)_{(\overline{X})}|$, the size of the point-wise stabilizer of $\overline{X}$ in G. Next, the quantities q_X can then be found by a dynamic programming approach using the identities:

$$q_\emptyset = |\{\mathrm{id}\}| = 1 \quad \text{and} \quad \forall X \neq \emptyset, \;\; q_X = r_X - \sum_{Y \subset X} q_Y.$$

Now, there exists a permutation with support at least k if and only if there exists some set X of at least k elements for which q_X is nonzero.

The time complexity of this procedure is dominated by the $2^{|S|} = 2^{O(k)}$ calls to Mathon's procedure for counting automorphisms, which takes $O(n^2)$ time. ∎

Corollary 5. $\mathrm{Mov}_k\mathrm{GA} \leq_T^p \mathrm{GI}$ *for* $k \in O(\log n)$.

5 Conclusions

Deciding whether a graph on n vertices has an automorphism which moves at least $k(n)$ vertices is:

- Equivalent to Graph Automorphism, when $k \in O(\frac{\log n}{\log \log n})$.
- No harder than Graph Isomorphism, when $k \in O(\log n)$.
- NP-complete, when $k \in \Omega(n^\epsilon)$, for any fixed $\epsilon \in (0, 1)$.

(The first two items are shown in this paper. The last item is a result of Lubiw [9].)

This raises a few questions, which we leave as open problems:

1. *Is there some function* $k \in o(n^\epsilon)$*, for every fixed* $\epsilon \in (0, 1)$*, such that* $\mathrm{GI} \leq_T^p \mathrm{Mov}_k\mathrm{GA}$*?*
A positive answer to this question would shed some more light on the relative complexity of GI and GA, by the above results. Specifically, if $\mathrm{GI} \leq_T^p \mathrm{Mov}_k\mathrm{GA}$ for $k \in O(\log n)$ then by Theorem 2, GI has at most a quasi-polynomial factor of n (i.e., $n^{O(\log n)}$) larger time complexity than GA.
2. *Does* $\mathrm{Mov}_k\mathrm{GA}$ *have efficient program checkers? Does it have efficient parallel program checkers?*
It is known that GA has efficient parallel program checkers[4] while the checker known for GI is not parallel. Thus, proving a parallel checker for a problem like $\mathrm{Mov}_{\log n}\mathrm{GA}$ would tell us about its similarity to GA rather than to GI. To start with, it is easy to observe that $\mathrm{Mov}_k\mathrm{GA}$, for $k \in O(\frac{\log n}{\log \log n})$, has indeed efficient program checkers[5] while $\mathrm{Mov}_k\mathrm{GA}$, for any constant function k, has efficient parallel checkers[6].

[4] In the sense of Blum and Kannan [3], who define the concept as an algorithmic alternative to program verification.

[5] By using the so called *Beigel's trick* for program checking [3], which shows that if problem π_1 has efficient program checkers and problem π_2 is Turing-equivalent to π_1 then π_2 has efficient program checkers.

[6] As observed in [1], Beigel's trick can be redeployed for parallel program checkers by requiring truth-table equivalence instead of Turing equivalence.

3. *Is there a GA-oracle based algorithm for enumerating $Aut(G)$ for a graph G on n vertices, in time polynomial in n and $|Aut(G)|$?*
   This question is motivated by the way the GA-equivalence result was obtained in the paper. Agrawal and Arvind [1] give a quasi-polynomial time algorithm for enumerating $Aut(G)$ (their algorithm has complexity $n^{\log(|Aut(G)|)}$ and makes the queries to GA nonadaptively).

A final open question, perhaps of interest mainly to group-theoreticians, is whether the constant 2 in Lemma 1 can be improved.

Acknowledgements

We are grateful to Albert Atserias for suggesting the problem.

Antoni Lozano was supported in part by ESPRIT project (no. LTR 20244, ALCOM-IT), by the DGICYT (Koala project, no. PB95-0787), and CICYT (no. TIC97-1475-CE).

Vijay Raghavan was partially supported by NSF grant CCR-9510392. Thanks also to the LSI department of UPC, where this work was done on a sabbatical visit.

References

1. M. Agrawal and V. Arvind. A note on decision versus search for graph isomorphism. *Information and Computation*, **131** (2):179–189, 1996.
2. V. Arvind, R. Beigel, and A. Lozano. The complexity of modular graph automorphism. *Proceedings of the 15th Annual Symp. on Theoretical Aspects of Comp. Sci.*, LNCS 1373, pp. 172–182, 1997.
3. M. Blum and S. Kannan. Designing programs that check their work. *Journal of the ACM*,**43**:269–291, 1995.
4. J. D. Dixon and B. Mortimer. *Permutation Groups*, Springer-Verlag, New York, 1991.
5. C. Hoffmann. *Group-Theoretic Algorithms and Graph Isomorphism.* Lecture Notes in Computer Science, 136. Springer–Verlag, New York, 1982 (LNCS 136).
6. J. Köbler, U. Schöning, and J. Torán. *The graph isomorphism problem: its structural complexity*, Birkhäuser, Boston, 1993.
7. R. Ladner. On the structure of polynomial-time reducibilities. *Journal of the Assoc. Comput. Mach.*, **22**:155–171, 1975.
8. A. Lozano and J. Torán. On the nonuniform complexity of the graph isomorphism problem. *Proceedings of the 7th Structure in Complexity Theory Conference*, pp. 118–129, 1992.
9. A. Lubiw. Some NP-complete problems similar to graph isomorphism. *SIAM Journal of Computing*, **10** (1): 11–21, 1981.
10. E. Luks. Isomorphism of graphs of bounded valence can be tested in polynomial time. *J. Comput. System Sci.*, **25**: 42–65, 1982.
11. R. Mathon. A note on the graph isomorphism counting problem. *Information Processing Letters*, **8**:131–132, 1979.

Remarks on Graph Complexity

(Extended Abstract)

Satyanarayana V. Lokam [1]
satya@math.luc.edu
Department of Mathematical and Computer Sciences
Loyola University Chicago
Chicago, IL 60626

Abstract. We revisit the notion of graph complexity introduced by Pudlák, Rödl, and Savický [PRS]. Using their framework, we show that sufficiently strong superlinear monotone lower bounds for the very special class of *2-slice functions* would imply superpolynomial lower bounds for some other functions. Given an n-vertex graph G, the corresponding 2-slice function f_G on n variables evaluates to zero on inputs with less than two 1's and evaluates to one on inputs with more than two 1's. On inputs with exactly two 1's, f_G evaluates to 1 exactly when the pair of variables set to 1 corresponds to an edge in G. Combining our observations with those from [PRS], we can show, for instance, that a lower bound of $n^{1+\Omega(1)}$ on the (monotone) formula size of an explicit 2-slice function f on n variables would imply a $2^{\Omega(l)}$ lower bound on the formula size of another explicit function g on l variables, where $l = \Theta(\log n)$.
We consider lower bound questions for depth-3 bipartite graph complexity. We prove some weak lower bounds on this measure using algebraic methods. For instance, our results give a lower bound of $\Omega((\log n/ \log\log n)^2)$ for bipartite graphs arising from Hadamard matrices, such as the Paley-type bipartite graphs. A lower bound of $n^{\Omega(1)}$ on the depth-3 complexity of an explicit bipartite graph would give superlinear size lower bounds on log-depth boolean circuits for an explicit function. Similarly, a lower bound of $2^{(\log n)^{\Omega(1)}}$ would give an explicit language outside the class Σ_2^{cc} of the two-party communication complexity.

1 Introduction and Overview

Proving superlinear (superpolynomial) lower bounds on the circuit size (formula size) of an explicit boolean function is a major challenge in theoretical computer science. On the other hand, remarkable results have been proved in restricted models such as constant depth circuits [Ha,Ra2,Sm], monotone circuits [AB,Ra3], and monotone formulas [RW,KaWi,RM]. In general, techniques from these results on restricted models are considered unlikely to be useful to attack the general question. In fact, there are functions with exponential lower bounds on the monotone complexity, but with polynomial upper bounds on their complexity over a complete basis [Ta]. However, for the special class of *slice functions*, monotone complexity and general complexity differ only by a

[1] Part of the work done while the author was a postdoctoral fellow at University of Toronto.

small polynomial amount [Be]. An n-variable boolean function f is called a *k-slice function* if $f(x) = 1$ whenever $|x| > k$ and $f(x) = 0$ whenever $|x| < k$, where $|x|$ denotes the number of 1's in the input assignment x. When $|x| = k$, $f(x)$ may be nontrivially defined. A function is called a slice function if it is a k-slice function for some $0 \leq k \leq n$. There are NP-complete languages whose characteristic functions are slice functions [Du]. Hence, assuming P $\neq$ NP, it is conceivable that superpolynomial size lower bounds over a complete basis may be provable by proving superpolynomial size *monotone* lower bounds for such slice functions.

For the approach via slice functions described above to yield superpolynomial lower bounds, we must consider a nonconstant k, because a k-slice function has complexity at most $O(n^k)$. But we will show in this paper that for constant k, in fact for $k = 2$, sufficiently strong superlinear lower bounds on k-slice functions would already imply superpolynomial lower bounds for some *other* functions derived from the 2-slice functions. More specifically, a lower bound of $n^{1+\Omega(1)}$ on (even monotone) formula size of an n-variable 2-slice function f implies a lower bound of $2^{\Omega(l)}$ on the formula size of an l-variable function g. We show this using the framework of graph complexity introduced by Pudlák, Rödl, and Savický [PRS].

Note that the nontrivial part (for $|x| = 2$) of a 2-slice function is essentially a (labeled) graph. Conversely, with every n-vertex graph G we can associate an n-variable 2-slice function f_G (see Definition 4).

The model of graph complexity [PRS] is a common generalization of the models of boolean circuits and two-party communication complexity. Measures of graph complexity such as affine dimension and projective dimension of graphs have been proposed and studied in [PR2,Ra1,PR1] as criteria for lower bounds on formula size and branching program size of boolean functions. Separation questions about classes of two-party communication complexity [Yao,BFS] can be reformulated as lower bound questions about bipartite graph complexity as studied in [PRS].

In graph complexity, an n-vertex graph G is constructed or computed as follows. We are given a set of atomic n-vertex graphs (these are analogous to the input variables in a circuit or a formula), called *generators*. In each step of the computation, we can perform a set-operation on the sets of edges of graphs we have constructed so far. Starting with the generators and performing the allowed operations on intermediate graphs, we would like to obtain G as the result of the computation. Complexity of G is the minimum cost of such a computation to construct G. By stipulating the structure of the computation (such as circuits), the set of generators (such as complete bipartite graphs), and the allowed set-operations (such as union and intersection), we get various measures of the cost of the computation and a corresponding definition of the complexity of G.

With a boolean function f on $2l$ variables, we can naturally associate a bipartite graph G_f with color classes $\{0,1\}^l$ such that (x, y) is an edge of G_f iff $f(x, y) = 1$. Let $n = 2^l$, so that G is an $n \times n$ bipartite graph. In [PRS], it is shown that a lower bound of $\psi(\log n)$ on the circuit size (formula size) complexity of

G_f, with complete bipartite graphs as generators and union and intersection as operators, would imply a lower bound of $\psi(l)$ on the boolean circuit size (formula size) of f. Hence superlogarithmic (superpolylogarithmic) lower bounds on the complexity of some explicit bipartite graphs would yield superlinear (superpolynomial) lower bounds on the circuit size (formula size) of explicit boolean functions, resolving long-standing open questions in computational complexity.

In this paper, we make the simple observation that lower bounds on graph complexity are implied by lower bounds on 2-slice functions. We prove that a lower bound of $n \log n \cdot \beta(n)$, for any $\beta(n) = \omega(1)$, on the *monotone* formula size of a 2-slice function implies a lower bound of $\beta(n)$ on the formula complexity of the corresponding graph. Similar results hold for circuit size. Combining this relation with the results from [PRS] we prove that sufficiently strong lower bounds on the monotone complexity of the very special class of 2-slice functions imply lower bounds on the complexity of general boolean functions.

Next, we consider lower bounds on graph complexity. As mentioned above, the model of graph complexity is more general than the models of boolean circuits and two-party communication complexity. Thus, proving lower bounds on graph complexity is even harder. However, studying the graph-theoretic structure of boolean functions may provide insights into their complexity. Understanding the properties of graphs that imply high graph complexity may suggest candidate functions with high boolean complexity. Lower bound arguments for such boolean functions may in turn exploit tools from the well-studied area of graph theory.

Pudlák, Rödl, and Savický [PRS] prove some nontrivial formula size lower bounds in graph complexity. Their lower bounds are on *star-formula* complexity of graphs. A star-formula for a graph is a formula with union and intersection operators and "stars" as the generators, where a *star* is a complete bipartite graph with a single vertex on one side and all other vertices on the other side. In this paper, we focus on the *bipartite-formula* complexity of graphs. Here the generators are complete bipartite graphs, and the operators are union and intersection. Results in this more general model translate more readily into the frameworks of boolean function complexity and two-party communication complexity.

In [PRS], a lower bound of $\Omega(n \log n)$ is proved for the star-formula complexity of some bipartite graphs. This immediately implies a lower bound of $\Omega(\log n)$ on the bipartite-formula complexity. To get any new lower bounds on boolean formula complexity, this needs to be improved to at least $\Omega(\log^3 n)$. The methods used in [PRS] cannot give bounds beyond $\Omega(\log n)$. Furthermore, [PRS] also show that certain Ramsey type properties of graphs (absence of large cliques and independent sets) *do not* imply strong enough lower bounds on graph complexity to give new results in boolean function complexity.

We prove lower bounds on *depth-3* bipartite-formula complexity of some bipartite graphs. Our results give a lower bound of $\Omega((\log n / \log\log n)^2)$ for bipartite graphs arising from Hadamard matrices such as the Paley-type bipartite graphs. In fact, our lower bounds are expressed in terms of the spectrum of the ± 1 incidence matrix associated with the bipartite graph. Our methods are based on approximating polynomials for boolean functions [NS] and rank lower bounds on real matrices under sign-preserving perturbations [KW].

Our lower bounds are still too weak to imply any new results in boolean circuit or communication complexity. We will note that depth-3 bipartite-formula complexity is related to depth-3 boolean formulas and the class Σ_2^{cc} of the two-party communication complexity model [BFS]. Lower bounds on depth-3 boolean circuits have been pursued in much of recent research [HJP,PPZ,PSZ]. One motivation for "strongly" exponential depth-3 lower bounds comes from Valiant's [Va] result that depth-3 lower bounds of $2^{\omega(l/\log\log l)}$ for an l-variable boolean function would imply superlinear size lower bounds on log-depth circuits computing that function. Currently, the best known lower bound on depth-3 circuits is $\Omega(l^{1/4}2^{\sqrt{l}})$ for the parity function [PPZ]. One approach to develop tools for depth-3 lower bounds in boolean complexity is to understand the corresponding (more general) question in graph complexity. Such an approach might lead to graph-theoretic criteria for depth-3 lower bounds in boolean complexity (just as it lead to the notions of affine and projective dimensions as criteria for unrestricted boolean complexity).

A lower bound of $n^{\Omega(1)}$ on the depth-3 bipartite-formula complexity of an explicit bipartite graph would give the "strongly" exponential lower bounds mentioned above and hence would imply superlinear size lower bounds on log-depth circuits for an explicit function. But the current lower bounds on depth-3 bipartite-formulas are too weak even to give (the current best) $2^{\sqrt{l}}$ lower bound on depth-3 boolean formulas. In fact, *generalizing* the best known $2^{\sqrt{l}}$ lower bound (or even the weaker bound of $2^{l^{\Omega(1)}}$) on depth-3 boolean complexity to the framework of graph complexity would resolve a long-standing open question in communication complexity: a lower bound of $2^{\log n^{\Omega(1)}}$ on depth-3 bipartite-formula complexity of an explicit bipartite graph gives an explicit language outside the class Σ_2^{cc} of the two-party communication complexity. Such strong bounds on graph complexity, however, remain as interesting open questions in this area.

2 Models of Graph Complexity

The complexity of a graph measures the difficulty of constructing a target graph using a given collection of primitive graphs, called *generators*, and a given basis of operations on sets of edges. All the graphs involved are assumed to have the same set of vertices, typically $V = \{1, \ldots, n\}$. A set operation on graphs refers to the operation on the corresponding edge sets. For instance, the result of $G_1 \cup G_2$ on graphs $G_1 = (V, E_1)$ and $G_2 = (V, E_2)$ is the graph $G = (V, E_1 \cup E_2)$. Models of graph complexity are defined analogous to the standard models of circuits and formulas where the generator graphs play the role of input variables and the set operations play the role of gates. We now give some formal definitions, most of which are based on [PRS].

Fix a set of generator graphs $\mathcal{G}$ with vertex set V and a basis $\mathcal{O}$ of set operations. A *graph circuit* with generators $\mathcal{G}$ and basis $\mathcal{O}$ is a sequence of equations or *gates* $g_1, \ldots, g_s$ such that each g_i, for $i = 1, \ldots, s$, is of the form

$$G_i = H \text{ for some } H \in \mathcal{G},$$

or

$$G_i = G_j \circ G_k \text{ where } \circ \in \mathcal{O} \text{ and } j, k < i.$$

(Here we are assuming for simplicity that $\circ$ is binary; analogous equations can be written for operations of other arities.) The output graph G_s of the last gate is the graph computed by the circuit. The *circuit complexity* of a graph G, with respect to generators $\mathcal{G}$ and basis $\mathcal{O}$, is the smallest s for which there exists a circuit that computes G.

As usual, we can imagine a circuit to be a directed acyclic graph (DAG) with the input nodes (of in-degree 0) labeled by the generator graphs and the internal nodes (gates) labeled by set operations from the basis. The target graph appears at the root (of out-degree 0) of this DAG. The length of the longest path in the DAG is the *depth of the circuit.* Number of nodes is its size.

A *graph formula* is a graph circuit in which the out-degree of each gate is at most one. Thus a graph formula can be represented as a tree with the leaves labeled by generator graphs and the internal nodes labeled by operations from the basis. The size of a formula is the number of leaves in its tree. The *formula complexity* of a graph is the smallest size of a formula that computes the graph (with respect to a fixed set of generators and a basis).

We can also define the natural restricted models such as *constant depth* graph circuits and formulas. In these models, we allow unbounded fanin and assume that the operations from the basis are naturally extendable to an unbounded number of operands (for example, union, intersection, and symmetric difference of sets have this property).

In what follows, we concentrate on formula complexity. Similar defintions and results can be stated for circuit complexity.

In this paper, we will consider graph complexity with the set operations of UNION and INTERSECTION only. We will naturally want the sets of generators to be *complete* in the sense that every graph should be constructible from these generators and using $\cap$ and $\cup$ operators in a circuit or a formula. Definitions 1 and 2 below give two such sets of generators.

Definition 1 *Fix the vertex set V where $|V| = n$. The set of* stars *is defined to be $\mathcal{S} = \{G \subseteq \binom{V}{2} : G \cong K_{1,n-1}\}$.*

For a graph G on V, the star-formula complexity *of G, denoted $L_{\mathcal{S}}(G)$, is the smallest size of a graph formula computing G using the stars $\mathcal{S}$ as the set of generators and $\cup$ and $\cap$ as the basis.*

A standard counting argument shows that $L_{\mathcal{S}}(G) = \Omega(n^2/\log n)$ for most graphs G. It is also known [Bu,PRS] that for all graphs G, $L_{\mathcal{S}}(G) = O(n^2/\log n)$. Pudlák et al. [PRS] show that the star-formula complexity of the complement of a graph can be substantially larger than the complexity of the graph itself.

We are especially interested in the complexity of bipartite graphs because of their direct relevance to lower bounds on boolean circuits and communication complexity.

Definition 2 *Fix the color classes U and V. Let $\mathcal{B}$ denote the following set of complete bipartite graphs:*

$$\mathcal{B} = \{A \times V : A \subseteq U\} \cup \{U \times B : B \subseteq V\}.$$

For a bipartite graph $G \subseteq U \times V$, the bipartite-formula complexity *of G is the smallest size of a graph formula computing G using $\mathcal{B}$ as the set of generators and $\cup$ and $\cap$ as the basis. Bipartite-formula complexity of G is denoted by $L_{\mathcal{B}}(G)$.*

The following relation holds between bipartite complexity and star complexity.

Proposition 1 (PRS) *Let $G \subseteq U \times V$ be a bipartite graph, $|U| = |V| = n$. Then $L_{\mathcal{S}}(G) \leq L_{\mathcal{B}}(G) \cdot n + 2n$, where the stars are on the vertex set $U \cup V$.*

Another observation of [PRS] is useful to translate a lower bound on star-complexity of general, i.e. not necessarily bipartite, graphs to a lower bound on bipartite graphs:

Proposition 2 (PRS) *Let G be a graph on W, $|W| = 2n$. Then there exists a partition $W = U \cup V$, $|U| = |V| = n$, such that the bipartite graph $G \cap U \times V$ satisfies*

$$L_{\mathcal{S}}(G \cap U \times V) \geq \frac{L_{\mathcal{S}}(G)}{\lceil \log_2 2n \rceil}.$$

Definition 3 *Let f be a boolean function on $2l$ variables, written as $f : \{0,1\}^l \times \{0,1\}^l \longrightarrow \{0,1\}$. Let $n := 2^l$. The $n \times n$ bipartite graph $G_f \subseteq \{0,1\}^l \times \{0,1\}^l$ is defined by including the edge (x,y) in G_f iff $f(x,y) = 1$, where $x, y \in \{0,1\}^l$.*

Note that the AND and OR operations on boolean functions correspond to UNION and INTERSECTION operations on the edge sets of their corresponding graphs. In other words, $G_{f_1 \wedge f_2} = G_{f_1} \cap G_{f_2}$ and $G_{f_1 \vee f_2} = G_{f_1} \cup G_{f_2}$. This suggests a syntactic transformation of a boolean formula (assuming all negations are pushed to the leaves) into a graph formula. But what about the input literals of the boolean formula? The literals are simply the projection functions and the graphs corresponding to projection functions are complete bipartite graphs isomorphic to $K_{n/2,n}$ and $K_{n,n/2}$. For instance, G_{x_i} is the complete bipartite graph $\{x \in \{0,1\}^l : x_i = 1\} \times \{0,1\}^l$. Thus each literal can be translated into a generator in $\mathcal{B}$. With this transformation of a boolean formula for f into a bipartite-formula for G_f, it follows that

$$L_{\mathcal{B}}(G_f) \leq L(f), \tag{1}$$

where $L(f)$ is the minimum size formula (with tight negations) computing f.

Given an $n \times n$ bipartite graph G, where n is a power of 2, we can clearly define a function f such that $G_f = G$. Thus we get the following criterion for lower bounds on boolean formula size:

Proposition 3 (PRS) *An explicit $n \times n$ bipartite graph G, where $n = 2^l$, with lower bound of $L_{\mathcal{B}}(G) \geq \psi(\log n)$ would give an explicit function f on l variables with formula size lower bound $L(f) \geq \psi(l)$.*

Since the proof of this proposition is essentially syntactic, similar relations hold for several restricted models of formulas and circuits as well.

Note, however, that graph complexity of G_f could be much smaller than the boolean complexity of f. This is because in a bipartite-formula we have access to an exponential (in n) number of generators $\mathcal{B}$, whereas the transformation above uses only the $2 \log n$ "canonical" generators corresponding to the projection functions. In fact, the generators in $\mathcal{B}$, in case of graphs $G \subseteq \{0,1\}^l \times \{0,1\}^l$, can be viewed as defining (arbitrary) boolean functions of either the first l or the last l variables. This interpretation captures the connection between two-party communication complexity and graph complexity. In particular, bounded depth bipartite formulas of size $2^{(\log \log n)^c}$ define the complexity classes of the "polynomial hierarchy" of the two-party communication model [BFS].

3 2-Slice Functions

In this section, we relate graph complexity to the boolean complexity of 2-slice functions.

Definition 4 *A boolean function $f : \{0,1\}^n \longrightarrow \{0,1\}$ is a* 2-slice function *if $f(x) = 0$ for all x with $|x| < 2$ and $f(x) = 1$ for all x with $|x| > 2$. On inputs x with $|x| = 2$, f may be nontrivially defined. The inputs x such that $|x| = 2$ and $f(x) = 1$ can be identified with the edges of a graph G with vertex set $\{1, \dots, n\}$ in an obvious way.*

Conversely, every graph G on n vertices gives rise to a 2-slice function f_G on n variables: Given a graph $G = ([n], E)$, we define the function f_G by

$$f_G(x) = \begin{cases} 1 & \text{if } |x| > 2, \\ 0 & \text{if } |x| < 2, \\ 1 & \text{if } |x| = 2 \text{ and } X \in E(G), \\ 0 & \text{if } |x| = 2 \text{ and } X \notin E(G). \end{cases}$$

Here X denotes the set with characteristic vector x, i.e., $X = \{i : x_i = 1, 1 \leq i \leq n\}$ for $x \in \{0,1\}^n$.

Recall that for $1 \leq i \leq n$, the star S_i is defined as the graph with vertex set $V(S_i) = \{1, \dots, n\}$ and edge set $E(S_i) = \{\{i,j\} : j \neq i\}$.

Lemma 1. *Let T_g be a star-formula computing the graph $G = ([n], E)$. Let T_b be the boolean formula obtained from T_g by replacing $\cup$'s by $\vee$'s and $\cap$'s by $\wedge$'s and the star S_i by the variable x_i. Let $f : \{0,1\}^n \longrightarrow \{0,1\}$ be the function computed by T_b. Then, $\forall x$ with $|x| = 2, f(x) = 1$ iff $X \in E$.*

Proof : By induction on the number of operators in T_g that computes G.

In the base case we have zero operators in T_g and this computes a single star S_i for some $i, 1 \le i \le n$. The corresponding T_b is x_i. Clearly the inputs X of size 2 such that $f(x) = 1$ are exactly the edges of S_i.

For the inductive step, first consider the case when the top gate of T_g is $\cup$. Let $T_g = T_{g_1} \cup T_{g_2}$, and let T_{g_i} compute G_i for $i = 1, 2$, so that $G = G_1 \cup G_2$. Correspondingly, we get $T_b = T_{b_1} \vee T_{b_2}$ and $f = f_1 \vee f_2$, where T_{b_i} computes f_i. If $X \in G$, then $X \in G_i$ for $i = 1$ or $i = 2$. By induction hypothesis $f_i(x) = 1$ and therefore $f(x) = 1$. Conversely, suppose $f(x) = 1$ and $|x| = 2$. Then for at least one $i \in \{1, 2\}$, we have $f_i(x) = 1$. By induction hypothesis $f_i(x) = 1$ iff $X \in G_i$ when $|x| = 2$. Thus $X \in G_i$ and therefore $X \in G$.

The proof when the top gate of T_g is $\cap$ is similar. ∎

Theorem 1 *Let G be an n-vertex graph and f_G be the associated 2-slice function on n variables. Let $L_{mon}(f_G)$ be the* {AND, OR} *(monotone) formula complexity of f_G and let $L_S(G)$ be the star-formula complexity of the graph G. Then,*

$$L_{mon}(f_G) \le L_S(G) + O(n \log n).$$

Proof : Let f be the function from Lemma 1 obtained from an optimal star-formula for G. Note that $f_G \equiv f \wedge Th_2^n \vee Th_3^n$, where Th_k^n denotes the k-th threshold function on n variables. Now we use the fact that for constant k there are monotone formulas of size $O(n \log n)$ to compute Th_k^n [Fr]. ∎

Theorem 2 *Let $f : \{0,1\}^n \longrightarrow \{0,1\}$ be a 2-slice function where $n = 2^l$. Suppose that $L_{mon}(f) \ge n \log n \cdot \beta(\log n)$, for some $\beta(\log n) = \omega(1)$. Then there exists a function $g : \{0,1\}^m \longrightarrow \{0,1\}$ such that $L(g) = \Omega(\beta(m))$.*

Proof : Let f be a 2-slice function on n variables where $n = 2^l$, and let G be the associated graph. From Theorem 1, $L_S(G) \ge L_{mon}(f) - O(n \log n)$. Using Proposition 2, there exists an $n/2 \times n/2$ bipartite subgraph H of G such that $L_S(H) \ge L_S(G)/O(\log n)$. From Proposition 1, $L_B(H) \ge L_S(H)/n - 2$. Combining the three inequalities, we have $L_B(H) \ge \Omega\left(L_{mon}(f)/n \log n\right)$.

Since H is a bipartite graph with $n/2 = 2^{l-1}$ vertices on each side, we can identify its color classes with $\{0,1\}^{l-1}$ and define a function g on $m = 2l - 2$ variables such that the $G_g = H$ (as defined in Section 2) and from Inequality 1 in Section 2, we get $L(g) \ge L_B(H) \ge \Omega\left(L_{mon}(f)/n \log n\right)$. It follows that a lower bound of $n \log n \cdot \beta(\log n)$ on $L_{mon}(f)$ would give a lower bound of $\Omega(\beta(m))$ on $L(g)$, since $m = O(\log n)$. ∎

Corollary 1 *An explicit n-variable 2-slice function f with $L_{mon}(f) \ge n^{1+\epsilon}$, for a constant $\epsilon > 0$, would give an explicit m-variable function g such that $L(g) = 2^{\Omega(m)}$.*

4 Depth-3 Lower Bounds

In this section, we consider lower bounds on depth-3 bipartite formulas computing bipartite graphs $G \subseteq U \times V$, $|U| = |V| = n$. Recall that the leaves of the formula are graphs from $\mathcal{B} = \{A \times V : A \subseteq U\} \cup \{U \times B : B \subseteq V\}$.

Let us first observe that the bottom gates of a bipartite formula need not have fan-in more than 2: if the bottom gate is an $\cap$, then it actually computes a complete bipartite graph $A \times B$, where $A \subseteq U$ and $B \subseteq V$, and this can be written as the intersection of at most two graphs from $\mathcal{B}$; if the bottom gate is a $\cup$, then it is easy to see that it computes the complement of a complete bipartite graph $\overline{A \times B}$, and again the complement of a complete bipartite graph can be written as a union of at most two graphs from $\mathcal{B}$.

Without loss of generality, we consider $\cup\cap\cup$ formulas. By the remark above, we can write such a formula as $G = \bigcup_i \bigcap_j G_{ij}$, where G_{ij} is the complement of a complete bipartite graph, i.e., $\overline{A_{ij} \times B_{ij}}$ for some $A_{ij} \subseteq U$ and $B_{ij} \subseteq V$.

Our lower bound proof is based on approximating polynomials for the OR function [NS] and variation ranks under sign-preserving changes [KW].

Nisan and Szegedy [NS] give the following construction of ϵ-approximating polynomials for the OR function. They assume a constant ϵ. The refined analysis to bring out the dependence on ϵ is due to Hayes and Kutin [HK]. Proof is omitted from this extended abstract.

Lemma 2 (NS,HK). *The* OR*-function of n boolean variables can be ϵ-approximated by a real polynomial of degree at most $O(\sqrt{n}\log(2/\epsilon))$. More precisely, for every $0 < \epsilon < 1/2$, there is a real polynomial p of degree at most $O(\sqrt{n}\log(2/\epsilon))$ such that for every $x \in \{0,1\}^n$, $|\text{OR}(x) - p(x)| \leq \epsilon$.*

In the following, we will use the notation $\exp(x)$ to denote c^x for some constant $c > 1$ (c *may* depend on the context). For a bipartite graph $G \subseteq U \times V$, we will let $G(x,y) = 1$ if $(x,y) \in G$ and $G(x,y) = 0$ if $(x,y) \notin G$.

Lemma 3. *Suppose the $n \times n$ bipartite graph $H \subseteq U \times V$ is written as a union of d complete bipartite graphs:*

$$H = \bigcup_{i=1}^{d} (A_i \times B_i), \quad \textit{where } A_i \subseteq U,\ B_i \subseteq V.$$

Then, for every ϵ, where $0 < \epsilon < 1/2$, there is a real matrix M_H such that

- *For all $(x,y) \in U \times V$, $|M_H(x,y) - H(x,y)| \leq \epsilon$,*
- $\text{rank}(M_H) \leq \exp(\sqrt{d}\log(2/\epsilon)\log d)$.

Proof : Let R be the incidence matrix of H, and similarly let R_i be the incidence matrices of the complete bipartite graphs $A_i \times B_i$, $1 \leq i \leq d$, covering H. Note that R is simply the entry-wise OR of the R_i. Furthermore, each R_i is of rank one as a real matrix. We obtain M_H from R using the approximating polynomials for the OR-function given by Lemma 2.

Suppose $p(z_1, \ldots, z_d)$ is an ϵ-approximating polynomial of degree $k := c \cdot \sqrt{d}\log(2/\epsilon)$ for the OR-function of d boolean variables. Syntactically substitute the matrix R_i for z_i in this polynomial, but interpret the product as entry-wise product of matrices, i.e., a monomial $z_i z_j$ is replaced by $R_i \circ R_j$, where for matrices A and B, $(A \circ B)(x, y) := A(x, y)B(x, y)$. Note that if A and B are rank-1 matrices, then $A \circ B$ is also a rank-1 matrix. Thus, a monomial $z_{i_1} \cdots z_{i_t}$ is replaced by the rank-1 0-1 matrix $R_{i_1} \circ \cdots \circ R_{i_t}$. The matrix obtained by computing the polynomial $p(R_1, \ldots, R_d)$ in this way gives us the desired matrix M_H.

It is clear that $M_H(x, y) = p(R_1(x, y), \ldots, R_d(x, y))$. From the properties of p, it is easy to see that for all x, y, $|M_H(x, y) - H(x, y)| \leq \epsilon$. Since M_H is a linear combination of rank-1 matrices, one for each monomial, it follows that rank of M_H is at most the number of monomials in p which is bounded by $\sum_{j=0}^{k} \binom{d}{j} \leq \mathsf{exp}(k \log d)$. ■

Lemma 4. *Let G be an $n \times n$ bipartite graph $G \subseteq U \times V$. If G is realized by a depth-3 bipartite formula $\mathcal{L}$ i.e.,*

$$G = \bigcup_{i=1}^{t} \bigcap_{j=1}^{d_i} \overline{(A_{ij} \times B_{ij})}, \ \text{where } A_{ij} \subseteq U, B_{ij} \subseteq V,$$

then there exists a matrix M such that

i) *If $G(x, y) = 0$, then $|M(x, y)| \leq 1/3$,*
ii) *If $G(x, y) = 1$, then $2/3 \leq M(x, y) \leq t + 1/3$,*
iii) $\mathsf{rank}(M) \leq t\mathsf{exp}(\sqrt{L}\log\sqrt{L})$, *where $L = \sum_{i=1}^{t} d_i$ denotes the length of the formula $\mathcal{L}$.*

Proof : Let $G_1, \ldots, G_t$ be the input graphs to the top gate, i.e., $G = \cup_{i=1}^{t} G_i$. Since each G_i, $i = 1, \ldots, t$, is an intersection of complements of complete bipartite graphs, its complement, $\overline{G_i}$ is computed by a union of complete bipartite graphs. Thus we can apply Lemma 3 to these complements $\overline{G_i}$. Let M_i' be the real matrix given by Lemma 3 that ϵ_i-approximates $\overline{G_i}$, where $\epsilon_i := d_i/3L$.

Let $M_i := J - M_i'$, where J is the $n \times n$ all-ones matrix. It is obvious that M_i ϵ_i-approximates G_i. Furthermore,
$\mathsf{rank}(M_i) \leq 1 + \mathsf{rank}(M_i') \leq \mathsf{exp}(\sqrt{d_i}\log(L/d_i)\log d_i) \leq \mathsf{exp}(\sqrt{L}\log\sqrt{L})$.

Let $M := M_1 + \cdots + M_t$. We want to see the relation between M and G:

If $G(x, y) = 0$, then $\forall i$, $G_i(x, y) = 0$, and hence $\forall i$, $|M_i(x, y)| \leq \epsilon_i$. It follows that $|M(x, y)| \leq \sum_{i=1}^{t} \epsilon_i = 1/3$.

If $G(x, y) = 1$, then $\exists i$, $G_i(x, y) = 1$ and for this i, $1 - \epsilon_i \leq M_i(x, y) \leq 1 + \epsilon_i$. Hence, we have $1 - \epsilon_i - \sum_{j \neq i} \epsilon_j \leq M(x, y) \leq \sum_{j=1}^{t}(1 + \epsilon_j)$. So, in this case, $2/3 \leq M(x, y) \leq t + 1/3$.

Moreover, $\mathsf{rank}(M) \leq \sum_{i=1}^{t} \mathsf{rank}(M_i) \leq t\mathsf{exp}(\sqrt{L}\log\sqrt{L})$. ■

We now show that for some "interesting" graphs G any matrix satisfying (i) and (ii) of Lemma 4 must have a large rank and hence conclude a lower bound on the depth-3 complexity of G using (iii).

Lemma 5 (KW). *Let A be an $n \times n$ ± 1 matrix and let B be a real matrix such that $1 \leq |b_{ij}| \leq \theta$ and $\mathsf{sign}(a_{ij}) = \mathsf{sign}(b_{ij})$ for all i,j. Then $\mathsf{rank}(B) \geq n^2/(\theta \|A\|^2)$, where $\|A\|^2$ is the largest eigenvalue of the matrix AA^* and A^* is the conjugate transpose of A.*

Theorem 3 *Let G be an $n \times n$ bipartite graph and let A_G be its ± 1 incidence matrix, i.e., $A_G(x,y) = -1$ if (x,y) is an edge of G and $A_G(x,y) = +1$ if (x,y) is not an edge of G. Then any depth-3 bipartite formula for G must have size at least a constant times*

$$\frac{\log^2(n/\|A_G\|)}{\log\log^2(n/\|A_G\|)}.$$

Proof : Given a depth-3 formula for G of size L, let M be the matrix given by Lemma 4. Define $B := 3J - 6M$, where J is the $n \times n$ all-ones matrix. Note that if $G(x,y) = 0$, then $B(x,y) \geq 1$, and if $G(x,y) = 1$, then $B(x,y) \leq -1$ and that $|B(x,y)|$ is always at most $6t$. Hence B is a sign-preserving variation of A_G and we can apply Lemma 5: $\mathsf{rank}(B) = \Omega(n^2/(t\|A_G\|^2))$. On the other hand, $\mathsf{rank}(B) \leq \mathsf{rank}(M) + 1$. So, from Lemma 4, part iii), we get that $\mathsf{rank}(B) \leq t \cdot \exp(\sqrt{L}\log\sqrt{L})$. Combining the two estimates on $\mathsf{rank}(B)$ and observing that $t \leq L$, we get

$$\exp(\sqrt{L}\log\sqrt{L}) = \Omega(\frac{n^2}{\|A_G\|^2}).$$

Solving for L proves the theorem. ■

An $n \times n$ Hadamard matrix is a ± 1 matrix such that $HH^\top = nI$. It is obvious that $\|H\| = \sqrt{n}$.

Corollary 2 *For any graph G such that A_G is an Hadamard matrix, the depth-3 bipartite formula complexity of G is at least $\Omega((\log n/\log\log n)^2)$. An example of such a graph is the Paley-type bipartite graph.*

References

[AB] Alon, N., Boppana, R. : The Monotone Circuit Complexity of Boolean Functions, *Combinatorica, 7(1) 1987, pp. 1 – 22.*

[BFS] Babai, L., Frankl, P., Simon, J. : Complexity classes in Communication Complexity Theory, 26th IEEE FOCS, 1986, pp. 337 – 347.

[Be] Berkowitz, S. : On some Relationships Between Monotone and Non-monotone Circuit Complexity, *Technical Report, University of Toronto, 1982.*

[Bu] Bublitz, S. : Decomposition of Graphs and Monotone Formula size of Homogeneous Functions, *Acta Informatika, 23, 1986, pp. 689 – 696.*

[Du] Dunne, P. : The Complexity of Central Slice Functions, *Theoretical Computer Science, 44 (1986), pp. 247 – 257.*

[Fr] Friedman, J. : Constructing $O(n \log n)$ size Monotone Formulae for the k-th Elementary Symmetric Polynomial of n Boolean Variables, *SIAM jl. Comp., 15(3) 1986, pp. 641 – 654.*

[Ha] Håstad, J. : Almost Optimal Lower Bounds for Small Depth Circuits, in S. Micali (ed), *Advances in Computer Research, Vol 5: Randomness and Computation*, JAI Press, 1989.

[HJP] Håstad, J., Jukna, S., Pudlák, P.: Top-Down Lower Bounds for Depth-3 Circuits, *34th IEEE FOCS, pp. 124 - 129.*

[HK] Hayes, T., Kutin, S. : *personal communication.*

[NS] Nisan, N., Szegedy, M. : On the degree of Boolean Functions as Real Polynomials, *24th ACM STOC, 1991, pp. 462 - 467.*

[KW] Krause, M., Waack, S. : Variation Ranks of Communication Matrices and Lower Bounds for Depth-Two Circuits having Symmetric Gates with Unbounded fan-in, *32nd IEEE FOCS, 1991, pp. 777 - 782.*

[KaWi] Karchmer, M., Wigderson, A. : Monotone Circuits for Connectivity require Sper-Logarithmic Depth, *SIAM jl. Disc. Math. 3(2) 1990, pp. 255 - 265.*

[PRS] Pudlák, P., Rödl, V., Savický, P. : Graph Complexity, *Acta Informatica, 25 (1988), pp. 515 - 535.*

[PR1] Pudlák, P., Rödl, V. : A Combinatorial Approach to Complexity,*Combinatorica, 14 (1992), pp. 221 - 226.*

[PR2] Pudlák, P., Rödl, V. : Some Combinatorial-Algebraic Problems from Complexity Theory, *Discrete Mathematics, 136 (1994), pp. 253 - 279.*

[PSZ] Paturi, R., Saks, M., Zane, F. : Exponential Lower Bounds on Depth 3 Boolean Circuits, *29th ACM STOC, 1997, pp.*

[PPZ] Paturi, R., Pudlák, P., Zane, F. : Satisfiability Coding Lemma, *38th IEEE FOCS, 1997, pp. 566 - 574.*

[Ra1] Razborov, A. A. : Applications of Matrix Methods for the theory of Lower Bounds in Computational Complexity, *Combinatorica, 10 (1990), pp. 81 - 93.*

[Ra2] Razborov, A. A. : Lower Bounds on the size of Bounded Depth Networks over a Complete Basis with Logical Addition, *Mat. Zametki 4194) 1987, pp. 598 - 607 (in Russian)*, English translation in: *Math. Notes 41(4)1987, pp. 333 - 338.*

[Ra3] Razborov, A. A. : Lower Bounds on the Monotone Complexity of some Boolean Functions, *Dokl. Akad. Nauk SSSR 281(4) 1985, pp. 798 - 801 (in Russian)*, English translation in: *Soviet Math. Dokl. 31(1985), pp. 354 - 357.*

[Ra4] Razborov, A. A. : A Lower Bound on the Monotone Network Complexity of the Logical Permanent, *Mat. Zametki 37(6) 1985, pp. 887 - 900 (in Russian)*, English translation in: *Math. Notes 37(6) 1985, pp. 485 - 493.*

[RW] Raz, R., Wigderson, A. : Monotone Circuits for Matching require Linear Depth, *JACM, 39(3) 1992, pp. 736 - 744.*

[RM] Raz, R., McKenzie, P. : Separation of the Monotone NC Hierarchy, *38th IEEE FOCS, 1997, pp. 234 - 243.*

[Sm] Smolensky, R. : Algebraic Methods in the theory of Lower Bounds for Boolean Circuit Complexity, *19th STOC, 1987, pp. 77 - 82.*

[Ta] Tardos, É. : The gap between Monotone and Non-monotone Circuit Complexity is Exponential, *Combinatorica, 8(1) 1988, pp. 141 - 142.*

[We] Wegener, I. : *The Complexity of Boolean Functions,* Wiley-Teubner Series in Computer Science, (Teubner, Stuttgart/wiley, Chichester, 1987.)

[Va] Valiant, L. : Graph-Theoretical Methods in Low-level Complexity, *6th MFCS, LNCS vol. 53, Springer-Verlag, 1977, pp. 162 - 176.*

[Yao] Yao, A. : Some Complexity Questions related to Distributive Computing, *11th ACM STOC, 1979, pp. 209 - 213.*

On the Confluence of Trace Rewriting Systems

Markus Lohrey

Universität Stuttgart, Institut für Informatik
Breitwiesenstr. 20–22, 70565 Stuttgart
e–mail: lohreyms@informatik.uni-stuttgart.de

Abstract. In [NO88], a particular trace monoid M is constructed such that for the class of length–reducing trace rewriting systems over M, confluence is undecidable. In this paper, we show that this result holds for every trace monoid, which is neither free nor free commutative. Furthermore we will present a new criterion for trace rewriting systems that implies decidability of confluence.

1 Introduction

The theory of *free partially commutative monoids* generalizes both the theory of free monoids and the theory of free commutative monoids. In computer science, free partially commutative monoids are commonly called *trace monoids* and their elements are called *traces*. Both notions are due to Mazurkiewicz [Maz77], who recognized trace monoids as a model of concurrent processes. [DR95] gives an extensive overview about current research trends in trace theory.

The relevance of trace theory for computer science can be explained as follows. Assume a finite alphabet Σ. An element of the free monoid over Σ, i.e., a finite word over Σ, may be viewed as the sequence of actions of a sequential process. In addition to a finite alphabet Σ, the specification of a trace monoid (over Σ) requires a binary and symmetric independence relation on Σ. If two symbols a and b are independent then they are allowed to commute. Thus, the two words $sabt$ and $sbat$, where s and t are arbitrary words, denote the same trace. This trace may be viewed as the sequence of actions of a concurrent process where the two independent actions a and b may occur concurrently and thus may be observed either in the order ab or in the order ba.

This point of view makes it interesting to consider *trace rewriting systems*, see [Die90]. A trace rewriting system is a finite set of rules, where the left–hand and right–hand side of each rule are traces. Trace rewriting systems generalize both semi–Thue systems and vector replacement systems. Considered in the above framework of concurrent processes, a trace rewriting system may be viewed as a set of transformations that translate sequences of actions of one process into sequences of actions of another process. Thus, trace rewriting systems may for instance serve as a formal model of abstraction.

For all kinds of rewriting systems, the notion of a terminating system and the notion of a confluent system are of central interest. Together, these two properties guarantee the existence of unique normal forms. Unfortunately, both properties are undecidable even for the class of all semi–Thue systems. On the other hand it is a classical result that for the class of terminating semi–Thue systems, confluence is decidable. Unfortunately even this result does not hold in general if trace rewriting systems are considered. More precisely, in [NO88] a concrete trace monoid is presented such that for the class of length–reducing trace rewriting systems over this trace monoid, confluence is undecidable. Therefore it remains the problem to determine those trace monoids for which confluence is decidable for the class of terminating trace rewriting systems. This question will be solved in Section 4, where we prove that confluence of length–reducing systems is decidable only for free or free commutative monoids. This result will be obtained by a reduction to the case of trace monoids with three generators, see Section 3. This undecidability result leads to the question whether there exist (sufficiently large) subclasses of trace rewriting systems for which confluence becomes decidable, see [Die90] for such a subclass. In Section 5 we present a new criterion which implies decidability of confluence. Due to space limitations some proofs are only sketched or completely omitted. They can be found in [Loh98].

2 Preliminaries

In this section we will introduce some notions concerning trace theory. For a more detailed study, see [DR95]. The interval $\{1,\ldots,n\}$ of the natural numbers is denoted by $\overline{n}$. Given an alphabet Σ, the set of all finite words over Σ is denoted by Σ^*. The empty word is denoted by 1. As usual, $\Sigma^+ = \Sigma^* \backslash \{1\}$. The length of $s \in \Sigma^*$ is denoted by $|s|$. For $\Gamma \subseteq \Sigma$ we define a *projection morphism* $\pi_\Gamma : \Sigma^* \longrightarrow \Gamma^*$ by $\pi_\Gamma(a) = a$ if $a \in \Gamma$ and $\pi_\Gamma(a) = 1$ otherwise. Given a word s and factorizations $s = tlu = vmw$, we say that t is *generated* by the occurrences of l and m in s (that are uniquely defined by the two factorizations above) if $t = 1 = u$ or $v = 1 = w$ or $(l \neq 1 \neq m$ and $(t = 1 = w$ or $u = 1 = v))$. A *deterministic finite automaton*, briefly dfa, over Σ is a tuple $\mathcal{A} = (Q, \Sigma, \delta, q_0, F)$, where Q is the finite set of states, $\delta : Q \times \Sigma \to Q$ is the transition function, $q_0 \in Q$ is the initial state, and $F \subseteq Q$ is the set of final states. The language $L(\mathcal{A}) \subseteq \Sigma^*$ that is accepted by $\mathcal{A}$ is defined as usual.

An *independence alphabet* is an undirected graph (Σ, I), where Σ is a finite alphabet and $I \subseteq \Sigma \times \Sigma$ is an irreflexive and symmetric relation, called *independence relation.* The complement $I^c = (\Sigma \times \Sigma) \backslash I$ is called a *dependence relation.* The pair (Σ, I^c) is called a *dependence alphabet.* Given an independence alphabet (Σ, I) we define the *trace monoid* $\mathbb{M}(\Sigma, I)$ as the quotient monoid $\Sigma^*/\!\equiv_I$, where $\equiv_I$ denotes the least equivalence relation that contains all pairs of the form $(sabt, sbat)$ for $(a,b) \in I$ and $s,t \in \Sigma^*$. Elements of $\mathbb{M}(\Sigma, I)$, i.e., equivalence classes of words, are called *traces.* The trace that contains the word s is denoted by $[s]_{\equiv_I}$ or briefly $[s]$. For the rest of this section let (Σ, I) be an arbitrary independence alphabet and let $M = \mathbb{M}(\Sigma, I)$. Since for all words $s, t \in \Sigma^*$, $s \equiv_I t$ implies $|s| = |t|$, we can define $|[s]| = |s|$. If $\Gamma \subseteq \Sigma$ then the trace monoid $N = \mathbb{M}(\Gamma, I \cap \Gamma \times \Gamma)$ is a submonoid of M and we may view $\pi_\Gamma : \Sigma^* \longrightarrow \Gamma^*$ as a morphism $\pi_\Gamma : M \longrightarrow N$ between trace monoids. A *clique covering* of the dependence alphabet (Σ, I^c) is a sequence $(\Sigma_i)_{i\in\overline{n}}$ of alphabets such that $\Sigma = \bigcup_{i=1}^n \Sigma_i$ and $I^c = \bigcup_{i=1}^n \Sigma_i \times \Sigma_i$. Given a clique covering $\Pi = (\Sigma_i)_{i\in\overline{n}}$, we will use the abbreviation $\pi_i = \pi_{\Sigma_i}$. Furthermore let $\pi_\Pi : M \longrightarrow \prod_{i=1}^n \Sigma_i^*$ be the morphism that is defined by $\pi_\Pi(u) = (\pi_i(u))_{i\in\overline{n}}$. It is well–known that π_Π is injective. Thus, M is isomorphic to its image under π_Π which we denote by $\langle\Pi\rangle$. Its elements are also called ***reconstructible*** tuples, see [CM85] pp. 186. A necessary but not sufficient condition for $(s_i)_{i\in\overline{n}} \in \langle\Pi\rangle$ is $\pi_i(s_j) = \pi_j(s_i)$ for all $i, j \in \overline{n}$. If the cliques $\Sigma_1, \ldots, \Sigma_n$ are pairwise disjoint then π_Π is also surjective and $M \simeq \prod_{i=1}^n \Sigma_i^*$. In the rest of this section let $\Pi = (\Sigma_i)_{i\in\overline{n}}$ be an arbitrary clique covering of the dependence alphabet (Σ, I^c) and let $\pi = \pi_\Pi$. Given a factorization $u = vw$ of $u \in M$, we obtain a unique factorization $\pi(u) = \pi(v)\pi(w)$ of the reconstructible tuple $\pi(u)$ (where concatenation of tuples is defined component wise). But the converse is false. A factorization $\pi(u) = (s_i)_{i\in\overline{n}}(t_i)_{i\in\overline{n}}$ corresponds to a factorization of u only if $(s_i)_{i\in\overline{n}} \in \langle\Pi\rangle$ (which implies $(t_i)_{i\in\overline{n}} \in \langle\Pi\rangle$). Since $\pi(u) \in \langle\Pi\rangle$, this already holds if the weaker condition $\pi_i(s_j) = \pi_j(s_i)$ holds for all $i, j \in \overline{n}$. Given a trace $l \in M$ and a factorization $\pi(u) = (s_i)_{i\in\overline{n}}\,\pi(l)(t_i)_{i\in\overline{n}}$, we say that the occurrence of $\pi(l)$ in $\pi(u)$ that is defined by this factorization is reconstructible if $\pi_i(s_j) = \pi_j(s_i)$ for all $i, j \in \overline{n}$. This implies $(s_i)_{i\in\overline{n}}, (t_i)_{i\in\overline{n}} \in \langle\Pi\rangle$ and thus the factorization above defines a unique occurrence of the trace l in u.

In the following we introduce some notions concerning trace rewriting systems. For a more detailed study, see [Die90]. Let $\rightarrow$ be an arbitrary binary relation (for which we use infix notation) on an arbitrary set A. The reflexive and transitive closure of $\rightarrow$ is denoted by $\rightarrow^*$. The inverse relation $\rightarrow^{-1}$ of $\rightarrow$ is also denoted by $\leftarrow$. A *$\rightarrow$–merging* for $a, b \in A$ is a finite sequence of the form $a = a_1 \rightarrow \ldots \rightarrow a_n = b_m \leftarrow \ldots \leftarrow b_1 = b$. We say that the situation $a \leftarrow c \rightarrow b$ is *$\rightarrow$–confluent* if there exists a $\rightarrow$–merging for a and b. The notion of a *terminating* (*confluent, locally confluent*) relation is defined as usual, see e.g. [BO93]. Newman's lemma states that a terminating relation is confluent iff it is locally confluent. A *trace rewriting system*, briefly TRS, over M is a finite subset of $M \times M$. Let $\mathcal{R}$ be a TRS over M. An element $(l, r) \in \mathcal{R}$ is usually denoted by $l \rightarrow r$. Let $c = (l \rightarrow r) \in \mathcal{R}$. For $u, u' \in M$, we write $u \rightarrow_c u'$ if $u = vlw$ and $u' = vrw$ for some $v, w \in M$. We write $u \rightarrow_\mathcal{R} u'$ if $u \rightarrow_d u'$ for some $d \in \mathcal{R}$. We say that the TRS $\mathcal{R}$ is *terminating* (*confluent, locally confluent*) if $\rightarrow_\mathcal{R}$ is terminating (confluent, locally confluent). For $i \in \overline{n}$ we define the rules $\pi_i(c)$ and $\pi(c)$ by $\pi_i(c) = (\pi_i(l) \rightarrow \pi_i(r))$ and $\pi(c) = ((\pi_i(l))_{i\in\overline{n}} \rightarrow (\pi_i(r))_{i\in\overline{n}})$. The TRSs $\pi_i(\mathcal{R})$ and $\pi(\mathcal{R})$ are defined in the obvious way. Note that $\pi(u) \rightarrow_{\pi(c)} \pi(v)$ ($\pi(u) \rightarrow_{\pi(\mathcal{R})} \pi(v)$) need not necessarily imply $u \rightarrow_c v$ ($u \rightarrow_\mathcal{R} v$). The reason is that in the rewrite step $\pi(u) \rightarrow_{\pi(c)} \pi(v)$ a non reconstructible occurrence of $\pi(l)$ may be replaced by $\pi(r)$. We introduce the following notations. Given $(s_i)_{i\in\overline{n}}, (t_i)_{i\in\overline{n}} \in \langle\Pi\rangle$, we write $(s_i)_{i\in\overline{n}} \Rightarrow_{\pi(c)} (t_i)_{i\in\overline{n}}$ if for some $(u_i)_{i\in\overline{n}}, (v_i)_{i\in\overline{n}}$ it holds $s_i = u_i\pi_i(l)v_i$, $t_i = u_i\pi_i(r)v_i$, and $\pi_i(u_j) = \pi_j(u_i)$ for all $i, j \in \overline{n}$. We write $(s_i)_{i\in\overline{n}} \Rightarrow_{\pi(\mathcal{R})} (t_i)_{i\in\overline{n}}$ if $(s_i)_{i\in\overline{n}} \Rightarrow_{\pi(d)} (t_i)_{i\in\overline{n}}$ for some $d \in \mathcal{R}$. With these notations it is obvious that $u \rightarrow_c v$ iff $\pi(u) \Rightarrow_{\pi(c)} \pi(v)$ and $u \rightarrow_\mathcal{R} v$ iff $\pi(u) \Rightarrow_{\pi(\mathcal{R})} \pi(v)$. In particular, $\mathcal{R}$ is confluent iff $\Rightarrow_{\pi(\mathcal{R})}$ is confluent on $\langle\Pi\rangle$. $\mathcal{R}$ is called *length–reducing* if $|l| > |r|$ for every $(l \rightarrow r) \in \mathcal{R}$. Obviously, if $\mathcal{R}$

Rules for the absorbing symbol 0:
(1a) $(1, x0) \rightarrow (1, 0)$ for $x \in \Gamma$
(1b) $(1, 0x) \rightarrow (1, 0)$ for $x \in \Gamma$
(1c) $(c, 0) \rightarrow (1, 0)$

Rules for deleting non well–formed words:
(2a) $(1, \triangleleft y) \rightarrow (1, 0)$ for $y \in \Gamma \backslash \{\$\}$
(2b) $(1, \triangleleft \$ y) \rightarrow (1, 0)$ for $y \in \Gamma \backslash \{\$\}$
(2c) $(1, x \triangleright) \rightarrow (1, 0)$ for $x \in \Gamma$

Main rules:
(3a) $(c, \triangleright A^{|w|+2}) \rightarrow (1, \triangleright q_0 w \triangleleft)$
(3b) $(c, B) \rightarrow (1, 0)$

Rules for shifting \$-symbols to the left:
(4a) $(1, a\beta\$\$) \rightarrow (1, a\$\beta)$ for $\beta \in \Sigma \cup \{\triangleleft\}$
(4b) $(1, a\$\beta\$\$) \rightarrow (1, a\$\$\beta)$ for $\beta \in \Sigma \cup \{\triangleleft\}$

Rules for simulating $\mathcal{M}$: Let $q, q' \in Q$ and $a' \in \Sigma \backslash \{\Box\}$.
(5a) $(1, q \triangleleft \$\$) \rightarrow (1, a'q'\triangleleft)$ if $\delta(q, \Box) = (q', a', R)$
(5b) $(1, bq \triangleleft \$\$) \rightarrow (1, q'ba'\triangleleft)$ if $\delta(q, \Box) = (q', a', L)$
(5c) $(1, qa\$\$) \rightarrow (1, a'q')$ if $\delta(q, a) = (q', a', R)$
(5d) $(1, bqa\$\$) \rightarrow (1, q'ba')$ if $\delta(q, a) = (q', a', L)$
(5e) $(1, \triangleright qa\$\$) \rightarrow (1, \triangleright q'\Box a')$ if $\delta(q, a) = (q', a', L)$

Fig. 1. The system $\mathcal{R}_w$. Let $a, b \in \Sigma$ be arbitrary.

is length–reducing, then $\mathcal{R}$ is also terminating. By the well–known critical pair lemma it is possible to construct a finite set of critical pairs for a terminating semi–Thue system, see [BO93] for more details. Therefore it is decidable whether a terminating semi–Thue system is confluent. In [NO88], a trace monoid M is presented such that even for the class of length–reducing TRSs over M, confluence is not decidable. This problem will be considered in the next section for arbitrary trace monoids. More precisely, let CONFL(M) be the following computational problem:
INPUT: A length–reducing TRS $\mathcal{R}$ over M QUESTION: Is $\mathcal{R}$ confluent ?
For technical reasons we will also consider the problem $CONFL_{\neq 1}(M)$ which is defined in the same way, but where the input is a length–reducing TRS whose right–hand sides are all different from the empty trace 1.

3 Independence alphabets with three vertices

A trace monoid $M = \mathbb{M}(\Sigma, I)$ with $|\Sigma| = 2$ is either the free monoid $\{a, b\}^*$ or the free commutative monoid $\{a\}^* \times \{b\}^*$. In both cases CONFL(M) is decidable. If $|\Sigma| = 3$ then there exist up to isomorphism two cases, where M is neither free nor free commutative. The first case arises from the independence alphabet that is defined by the graph $[a - c - b]$ and will be considered in this section. The corresponding trace monoid is $\{a, b\}^* \times \{c\}^*$. The second case arises from the independence alphabet $[a - b \quad c]$ and is considered in [Loh98].

Lemma 1. $\text{CONFL}_{\neq 1}(\{a, b\}^* \times \{c\}^*)$ is undecidable.

Proof. First we prove the undecidability of $\text{CONFL}_{\neq 1}(\Gamma^* \times \{c\}^*)$ for a finite alphabet $\Gamma = \{a_1, \ldots, a_n\}$ where $n > 2$. This alphabet Γ can be encoded into the alphabet $\{a,b\}$ via the morphism $\phi : a_i \mapsto aba^{i+1}b^{n-i+2}$ for $i \in \overline{n}$. The following proof is a variant of a construction given in [NO88]. Let $\mathcal{M} = (Q, \Sigma, \Box, \delta, q_0, \{q_f\})$ be a deterministic one–tape Turing machine, where Q is the finite set of states, Σ is the tape alphabet, $\Box \in \Sigma$ is the blank symbol, $\delta : Q\backslash\{q_f\} \times \Sigma \to Q \times (\Sigma\backslash\{\Box\}) \times \{L,R\}$ is the transition function, q_0 is the initial state and $q_f \neq q_0$ is the final state. We may assume that δ is a total function. Thus, $\mathcal{M}$ terminates iff it reaches the final state q_f. Assume that the problem whether $\mathcal{M}$ halts on a given input $w \in (\Sigma\backslash\{\Box\})^+$ is undecidable. For instance, $\mathcal{M}$ may be a universal Turing machine. Let Γ be the disjoint union $\Gamma = Q \cup \Sigma \cup \{0, \triangleright, \triangleleft, A, B, \$\}$. For every $w \in (\Sigma\backslash\{\Box\})^+$, we define a TRS $\mathcal{R}_w$ over $\{c\}^* \times \Gamma^*$ by the rules of Figure 1. Note that $\mathcal{R}_w$ is length–reducing and that all right–hand sides are non empty. Since we excluded the case $w = 1$, we do not have to consider the pair $(1, \triangleright q \triangleleft \$\$)$ in the last group of rules. We claim that $\mathcal{R}_w$ is confluent iff $\mathcal{M}$ does not halt on input w. Note that for every rule $(l_1, l_2) \to (r_1, r_2) \in \mathcal{R}_w$ it holds $r_i = 1$ if $l_i = 1$ for $i \in \{1,2\}$. This property assures that $\mathcal{R}_w$ is confluent iff all situations $(t_1, t_2) \; {}_{\mathcal{R}_w}\!\!\leftarrow (s_1, s_2) \to_{\mathcal{R}_w} (t_1, t_2)$ are confluent, where the replaced occurrences of left–hand sides $(l_1, l_2), (m_1, m_2)$ in (s_1, s_2) satisfy the following: For every $i \in \{1,2\}$, s_i is generated by the occurrences of l_i and m_i in s_i and for some $i \in \{1,2\}$ these two occurrences are non disjoint in s_i, i.e., have some letters in common. Most of these situations are easily seen to be confluent. For instance, in the situation $(1, Bv\triangleright q_0 w \triangleleft) \;{}_{(3a)}\!\!\leftarrow (c, Bv\triangleright A^{|w|+2}) \to_{(3b)} (1, 0v\triangleright A^{|w|+2})$ (where $v \in \Gamma^*$ is arbitrary) both traces can be reduced to $(1,0)$ since the left trace contains a factor of the form $x\triangleright$ which may be rewritten to 0 with rule (2c). The only difficult situation is $(1, \triangleright q_0 w \triangleleft vB) \;{}_{(3a)}\!\!\leftarrow (c, \triangleright A^n vB) \to_{(3b)} (1, \triangleright A^n v0)$, where $v \in \Gamma^*$ is arbitrary. Since $(1, \triangleright A^n v0) \to^*_{(1a)} (1,0)$, the truth of the following claim proves the lemma.

Claim: $\mathcal{M}$ does not halt on input w iff $\forall v \in \Gamma^* : (1, \triangleright q_0 w \triangleleft vB) \to^*_{\mathcal{R}_w} (1,0)$.

Let $\mathcal{R}_\mathcal{M}$ be the subsystem that consists of the rules in group (4) and (5). First assume that $\mathcal{M}$ halts on input w. Then there exists an $m \geq 1$ such that $(1, \triangleright q_0 w \triangleleft \$^m B) \to^*_{\mathcal{R}_\mathcal{M}} (1, \triangleright u q_f v_1 \$^2 v_2 \$^2 \ldots v_{l-1} \$^2 v_l \$^2 \triangleleft \$^k B)$, where $u \in \Sigma^*, l \geq 0, v_1, \ldots, v_l \in \Sigma$ and $k \geq 2$. Since $\mathcal{M}$ cannot move from the final state q_f, the last pair is irreducible. Now assume that $\mathcal{M}$ does not halt on input w. First consider the case $v = \$^m$ for $m \geq 0$. We obtain

$$(1, \triangleright q_0 w \triangleleft \$^m B) \to^*_{\mathcal{R}_\mathcal{M}} (1, \triangleright u q v_1 \$^{\alpha_1} v_2 \$^{\alpha_2} \ldots v_{l-1} \$^{\alpha_{l-1}} v_l \$^{\alpha_l} \triangleleft \$^{\alpha_{l+1}} B),$$

where $u \in \Sigma^*, l \geq 0, v_1, \ldots, v_l \in \Sigma$, and $\alpha_1, \ldots, \alpha_{l+1} \in \{0,1\}$. By rule (2a) or rule (2b) the last pair can be rewritten to $(1, \triangleright u q v_1 \$^{\alpha_1} v_2 \$^{\alpha_2} \ldots v_{l-1} \$^{\alpha_{l-1}} v_l \$^{\alpha_l} 0)$ which reduces to $(1,0)$ with the rules of group (1). Now assume $v = \$^m y v'$, where $m \geq 0, y \in \Gamma\backslash\{\$\}$ and $v' \in \Gamma^*$. Similarly to the derivation above, we obtain

$$(1, \triangleright q_0 w \triangleleft \$^m y v' B) \to^*_{\mathcal{R}_\mathcal{M}} (1, \triangleright u q v_1 \$^{\alpha_1} v_2 \$^{\alpha_2} \ldots v_{l-1} \$^{\alpha_{l-1}} v_l \$^{\alpha_l} \triangleleft \$^{\alpha_{l+1}} y v' B),$$

where $u \in \Sigma^*, l \geq 0, v_1, \ldots, v_l \in \Sigma$, and $\alpha_1, \ldots, \alpha_{l+1} \in \{0,1\}$. Since $y \in \Gamma\backslash\{\$\}$ again either by rule (2a) or rule (2b) the last pair can be rewritten to $(1, \triangleright u q v_1 \$^{\alpha_1} v_2 \$^{\alpha_2} \ldots v_{l-1} \$^{\alpha_{l-1}} v_l \$^{\alpha_l} 0 v' B)$ which reduces to $(1,0)$ with the rules of group (1). This concludes the proof.

Note that the system $\mathcal{R}_w$ is not length–increasing in both components, i.e., for all $(l_1, l_2) \to (r_1, r_2) \in \mathcal{R}_w$, $|l_1| \geq |r_1|$ and $|l_2| \geq |r_2|$. Together with Theorem 2 of Section 5 this gives a very sharp borderline between decidability and undecidability for the case of a direct product of free monoids. The following result can be shown using similar techniques.

Lemma 2. $\mathrm{CONFL}_{\neq 1}(\mathbb{M}(\{a,b,c\}, \{(a,b),(b,a)\}))$ is undecidable.

4 The general case

A confluent semi–Thue system remains confluent if we add an additional symbol (that does not appear in the rules) to the alphabet. This trivial fact becomes wrong for TRSs, see [Die90], pp. 125 for an example. Thus, the following lemma is not a triviality.

Lemma 3. Let (Σ, I) be an independence alphabet and let $\Gamma \subseteq \Sigma$. Let $M = \mathbb{M}(\Sigma, I)$ and let $N = \mathbb{M}(\Gamma, I \cap \Gamma \times \Gamma)$. Thus, $N \subseteq M$. If $\mathrm{CONFL}_{\neq 1}(M)$ is decidable then $\mathrm{CONFL}_{\neq 1}(N)$ is also decidable.

Proof. Given a length–reducing TRS $\mathcal{P}$ over N whose right–hand sides are all non empty, we will construct a length–reducing TRS $\mathcal{R}$ over M whose right–hand sides are also all non empty such that $\mathcal{P}$ is confluent iff $\mathcal{R}$ is confluent. The case $\Gamma = \Sigma$ is trivial. Thus, let us assume that there exists a $0 \in \Sigma \backslash \Gamma$. Let $\mathcal{R} = \mathcal{P} \cup \{[ab] \to [0] \mid a \in \Sigma \backslash \Gamma \text{ or } b \in \Sigma \backslash \Gamma\}$. Note that $\mathcal{R}$ is length–reducing. Assume that $\mathcal{P}$ is confluent and consider a situation $u_1 \ {}_{\mathcal{R}}\!\leftarrow u \to_{\mathcal{R}} u_2$. If $u \in N$ then we must have $u_1 \ {}_{\mathcal{P}}\!\leftarrow u \to_{\mathcal{P}} u_2$. Confluence of $\mathcal{P}$ implies that $u_1 \to_{\mathcal{P}}^{*} v \ {}_{\mathcal{P}}^{*}\!\leftarrow u_2$ for some $v \in N$ and thus $u_1 \to_{\mathcal{R}}^{*} v \ {}_{\mathcal{R}}^{*}\!\leftarrow u_2$. If $u \notin N$ then u must contain some letter from $\Sigma \backslash \Gamma$. This must also hold for u_1 and u_2. Furthermore $u_i \notin \Sigma \backslash (\Gamma \cup \{0\})$ for $i \in \{1, 2\}$, which holds since all right–hand sides of $\mathcal{P}$ are non empty. Thus, u_1 and u_2 can both be reduced to $[0]$. Now assume that $\mathcal{R}$ is confluent and consider a situation $u_1 \ {}_{\mathcal{P}}\!\leftarrow u \to_{\mathcal{P}} u_2$. Thus, $u_1 \ {}_{\mathcal{R}}\!\leftarrow u \to_{\mathcal{R}} u_2$ and confluence of $\mathcal{R}$ implies $u_1 \to_{\mathcal{R}}^{*} v \ {}_{\mathcal{R}}^{*}\!\leftarrow u_2$ for some $v \in M$. Since symbols from $\Sigma \backslash \Gamma$ do not appear in u_1 or u_2 it follows $u_1 \to_{\mathcal{P}}^{*} v \ {}_{\mathcal{P}}^{*}\!\leftarrow u_2$.

Now we are able to prove our first main result.

Theorem 1. $\mathrm{CONFL}(M)$ is decidable iff M is a free monoid or a free commutative monoid.

Proof. The decidability of $\mathrm{CONFL}(M)$ in the case of a free or free commutative monoid is well–known. Thus, assume that $M = \mathbb{M}(\Sigma, I)$ is neither free nor free commutative. First note that M is a direct product of free monoids iff the dependence alphabet (Σ, I^c) is a disjoint union of complete graphs iff (Σ, I) does not contain an induced subgraph of the form $[a - b \quad c]$. Thus, by Lemma 2 and Lemma 3, if M is not a direct product of free monoids then $\mathrm{CONFL}_{\neq 1}(M)$ (and thus also $\mathrm{CONFL}(M)$) is undecidable. Thus, assume that $M = \prod_{i=1}^{n} \Sigma_i^*$. Since M is neither free nor free commutative we have $n > 1$ and there exists an $i \in \overline{n}$ such that $|\Sigma_i| > 1$. But then $[a - c - b]$ is an induced subgraph of (Σ, I). Lemma 1 and Lemma 3 imply the undecidability of $\mathrm{CONFL}_{\neq 1}(M)$ and $\mathrm{CONFL}(M)$.

5 A decidability criterion

In this section we present a new and non trivial criterion that implies decidability of confluence for terminating TRSs. For our considerations, we need the concept of a recognizable trace language. For a more detailed introduction into this topic, see for instance chapter 6 of [DR95]. One of the fundamental results about recognizable trace languages states that a trace language is recognizable iff it is recognized by a special kind of automaton, namely a so called asynchronous automaton, see [Zie87]. Since we will need only this type of automata, we use it for the definition of recognizable trace languages.

A (finite) *asynchronous automaton* $\mathcal{A}$ over the trace monoid $M = \mathbb{M}(\Gamma, I)$ is a tuple $\mathcal{A} = (Q, \Gamma, (\delta_a)_{a\in\Gamma}, q_0, F)$, where

- $Q = \prod_{i=1}^{m} Q_i$ is a direct product of finite sets of (local) states,
- for every symbol $a \in \Gamma$, there exists a non empty set $dom(a) \subseteq \overline{m}$ such that for all $(a, b) \in I$ it holds $dom(a) \cap dom(b) = \emptyset$,
- for every symbol $a \in \Gamma$, δ_a is a (partially defined) local transition function $\delta_a : \prod_{i\in dom(a)} Q_i \to \prod_{i\in dom(a)} Q_i$,
- $q_0 \in Q$ is the initial state, and $F \subseteq Q$ is the set of final states.

The (partially defined) global transition function $\delta : Q \times \Gamma \to Q$ of $\mathcal{A}$ is defined as follows. For $(p_i)_{i\in\overline{m}} \in Q$ and $a \in \Gamma$, $\delta((p_i)_{i\in\overline{m}}, a)$ is defined iff $\delta_a((p_i)_{i\in dom(a)})$ is defined. If this is the case it holds $\delta((p_i)_{i\in\overline{m}}, a) = (q_i)_{i\in\overline{m}}$, where (i) $q_i = p_i$ for $i \notin dom(a)$ and (ii) $(q_i)_{i\in dom(a)} = \delta_a((p_i)_{i\in dom(a)})$. For a word $s \in \Gamma^*$, $\delta((p_i)_{i\in\overline{m}}, s)$ is then defined in the usual way. Note that for $(a, b) \in I$ it holds $\delta((p_i)_{i\in\overline{m}}, ab) = \delta((p_i)_{i\in\overline{m}}, ba)$. Thus, it is possible to define $\delta((p_i)_{i\in\overline{m}}, [s])$ for $[s] \in M$. The language accepted by $\mathcal{A}$ is $L(\mathcal{A}) = \{u \in M \mid \delta(q_0, u) \in F\}$. A trace language $L \subseteq M$ is called *recognizable* iff there exists an asynchronous automaton $\mathcal{A}$ over M with $L = L(\mathcal{A})$. Since it holds $L(\mathcal{A}) = M$ iff $\mathcal{A}$, considered as a dfa over Γ, accepts Γ^* the following holds.

Fact 1 The following problem is decidable.
INPUT: An asynchronous automaton $\mathcal{A}$ over M QUESTION: $L(\mathcal{A}) = M$?

Fact 2 If $K \subseteq M$ is recognizable and $L \subseteq N$ is recognizable then $K \times L \subseteq M \times N$ is also recognizable (use the well–known product construction).

The following lemma is crucial for the proof of the next theorem.

Lemma 4. Let $\mathcal{R}$ be a terminating TRS over $\mathbb{M}(\Sigma, I)$ and let $\Pi = (\Gamma_i)_{i\in\overline{n}}$ be a clique covering of (Σ, I^c) such that

- For all $i \in \overline{n}$ and all $(l \to r) \in \mathcal{R}$ it holds $\pi_i(l) \neq 1$.
- For all $i, j \in \overline{n}$ and all $(l \to r) \in \mathcal{R}$, if $\pi_i(\pi_j(l)) = 1$ then also $\pi_i(\pi_j(r)) = 1$.

Then $\Rightarrow_{\pi_\Pi(\mathcal{R})}$ is confluent on $\langle \Pi \rangle$ (and thus $\to_\mathcal{R}$ is confluent) iff all situations

$$(t'_i)_{i\in\overline{n}} = (s_i\pi_i(p)s'_i)_{i\in\overline{n}} \;{}_{\pi_\Pi(\mathcal{R})}\!\Leftarrow\; (s_i\pi_i(l)s'_i)_{i\in\overline{n}} = (t_i)_{i\in\overline{n}} = \\ (u_i\pi_i(m)u'_i)_{i\in\overline{n}} \Rightarrow_{\pi_\Pi(\mathcal{R})} (u_i\pi_i(r)u'_i)_{i\in\overline{n}} = (t''_i)_{i\in\overline{n}} \quad (1)$$

with the following properties are $\Rightarrow_{\pi_\Pi(\mathcal{R})}$–confluent.

- $(l \to p), (m \to r) \in \mathcal{R}$ and $(t_i)_{i \in \overline{n}}, (s_i)_{i \in \overline{n}}, (u_i)_{i \in \overline{n}} \in \langle \Pi \rangle$.
- For all $i \in \overline{n}$, the occurrences of $\pi_i(l) \neq 1$ and $\pi_i(m) \neq 1$ in t_i generate t_i.
- For some $i \in \overline{n}$, the occurrences of $\pi_i(l)$ and $\pi_i(m)$ are non disjoint in t_i.

The fact that the two replaced occurrences of $\pi(l)$ and $\pi(m)$ can be assumed to generate t_i is easy to see. Non-disjointness of the occurrences can be assumed due to the two conditions imposed on $\mathcal{R}$. These conditions assure that if two disjoint and reconstructible occurrences of $\pi(l)$ and $\pi(m)$ exist in $(t_i)_{i \in \overline{n}} \in \langle \Pi \rangle$ and (say) $\pi(l)$ is replaced by $\pi(p)$ then the occurrence of $\pi(m)$ in the resulting tuple is still reconstructible. Let us state now our second main result.

Theorem 2. The following problem is decidable.
INPUT: A TRS $\mathcal{R}$ over a trace monoid $M = \mathbb{M}(\Sigma, I)$ such that there exists a clique covering $(\Sigma_i)_{i \in \overline{n}}$ of the dependence alphabet (Σ, I^c) with the following properties:

> $\pi_i(\mathcal{R})$ is terminating for every $i \in \overline{n}$ and $\pi_i(\pi_j(l)) = 1$ implies $\pi_i(\pi_j(r)) = 1$ for all $i, j \in \overline{n}$ with $i \neq j$ and all $(l \to r) \in \mathcal{R}$.

QUESTION: Is $\mathcal{R}$ confluent?

Note that for instance the second condition on $\mathcal{R}$ trivially holds if $M = \prod_{i=1}^{n} \Sigma_i^*$ with the clique covering $(\Sigma_i)_{i \in \overline{n}}$. Another class to which the theorem may be applied are special TRSs (i.e. every rule has the form $l \to 1$) such that for every left-hand side l and every clique Σ_i it holds $\pi_i(l) \neq 1$. On the other hand, Theorem 2 cannot be applied to the system $\mathcal{R}_w$ from the proof of Lemma 1, since for instance the projection onto the first component is not terminating.

Proof. Let $\Pi = (\Sigma_i)_{i \in \overline{n}}$ be a clique covering of (Σ, I^c) such that $\pi_i(\mathcal{R})$ is terminating for every $i \in \overline{n}$ and let $\pi = \pi_\Pi$. Thus, $\mathcal{R}$ must be terminating. Moreover, there cannot exist a rule $(1 \to \pi_i(r)) \in \pi_i(\mathcal{R})$, i.e., for every $(l \to r) \in \mathcal{R}$ and every $i \in \overline{n}$ it holds $\pi_i(l) \neq 1$ and therefore Lemma 4 applies to $\mathcal{R}$. Fix two rules $(l \to p), (m \to r) \in \mathcal{R}$ and let $l_i = \pi_i(l)$ and similarly for p, m, and r. Consider the situation shown in (1) in Lemma 4. The conditions imposed on (1) imply that for every $i \in \overline{n}$ either (1) $t_i = l_i w_i m_i$ for some $w_i \in \Sigma_i^*$ or (2) $t_i = m_i w_i l_i$ for some $w_i \in \Sigma_i^*$ or (3) l_i and m_i are non disjoint and generate t_i. Furthermore there must exist at least one $i \in \overline{n}$ such that case (3) holds. Thus, for every partition $\overline{n} = I_1 \cup I_2 \cup I_3$ with $I_3 \neq \emptyset$ we have to consider all $(t_i)_{i \in \overline{n}} \in \langle \Pi \rangle$ such that for all $i \in I_k$ case (k) holds. Fix such a partition $\overline{n} = I_1 \cup I_2 \cup I_3$ and let $I_{1,2} = I_1 \cup I_2$, $\Sigma^{(k)} = \bigcup_{i \in I_k} \Sigma_i$ for $k \in \{1, 2, 3\}$. Moreover, since for every $i \in I_3$ there exist only finitely many possibilities for the string t_i we may also fix the tuple $(t_i)_{i \in I_3}$. After these two choices, the only unbounded component in the tuple $(t_i)_{i \in \overline{n}}$ is the reconstructible factor $(w_i)_{i \in I_{1,2}}$. Since the occurrences $(l_i)_{i \in \overline{n}}$ and $(m_i)_{i \in \overline{n}}$ must be reconstructible in $(t_i)_{i \in \overline{n}}$ it is easy to see that $\pi_j(t_i) = \pi_i(t_j) = 1$ for all $i \in I_1, j \in I_2$. Similarly for all $i \in I_3, j \in I_{1,2}$ it must hold $\pi_i(w_j) = 1$. Thus, we have to consider all tuples $(w_i)_{i \in I_{1,2}} \in M_1 \times M_2$, where $M_1 = \langle (\Sigma_i \backslash (\Sigma^{(2)} \cup \Sigma^{(3)}))_{i \in I_1} \rangle \simeq \mathbb{M}(\Sigma^{(1)} \backslash (\Sigma^{(2)} \cup \Sigma^{(3)}), I)$ and $M_2 = \langle (\Sigma_i \backslash (\Sigma^{(1)} \cup \Sigma^{(3)}))_{i \in I_2} \rangle \simeq \mathbb{M}(\Sigma^{(2)} \backslash (\Sigma^{(1)} \cup \Sigma^{(3)}), I)$. We will prove that the set of all tuples $(w_i)_{i\in I_{1,2}} \in M_1 \times M_2$ for which there exists a $\Rightarrow_{\pi(\mathcal{R})}$-merging for the corresponding tuples $(t'_i)_{i\in\overline{n}}$ and $(t''_i)_{i\in\overline{n}}$ (that are uniquely determined by the w_i via the two choices made above) is a recognizable trace language, which proves the theorem by Fact 1.

Let $\mathcal{R}_k = \{(\pi_i(l))_{i\in I_k} \to (\pi_i(r))_{i\in I_k} \mid (l \to r) \in \mathcal{R}\}$ for $k \in \{1,2,3\}$ and let $\mathcal{R}_{1,2} = \{(\pi_i(l))_{i\in I_{1,2}} \to (\pi_i(r))_{i\in I_{1,2}} \mid (l \to r) \in \mathcal{R}\}$. Obviously, there exists a $\Rightarrow_{\pi(\mathcal{R})}$-merging for $(t'_i)_{i\in\overline{n}}$ and $(t''_i)_{i\in\overline{n}}$ iff there exist a $\Rightarrow_{\mathcal{R}_{1,2}}$-merging for $(t'_i)_{i\in I_{1,2}}$ and $(t''_i)_{i\in I_{1,2}}$ as well as a $\Rightarrow_{\mathcal{R}_3}$-merging for $(t'_i)_{i\in I_3}$ and $(t''_i)_{i\in I_3}$ such that both mergings can be combined to a $\Rightarrow_{\pi(\mathcal{R})}$-merging, i.e., both mergings have the same length, in the k-th step for some $(l \to r) \in \mathcal{R}$ the rules $(\pi_i(l))_{i\in I_{1,2}} \to (\pi_i(r))_{i\in I_{1,2}}$ and $(\pi_i(l))_{i\in I_3} \to (\pi_i(r))_{i\in I_3}$, respectively, are applied, and finally the two replaced reconstructible occurrences of $(\pi_i(l))_{i\in I_{1,2}}$ and $(\pi_i(l))_{i\in I_3}$ give a reconstructible occurrence of $\pi(l)$. Since $\mathcal{R}_3$ is terminating it is possible to construct all $\Rightarrow_{\mathcal{R}_3}$-mergings for the fixed tuples $(t'_i)_{i\in I_3}$ and $(t''_i)_{i\in I_3}$. Fix one of these mergings. Since a finite union of recognizable trace languages is again recognizable it suffices to prove that the set of all tuples $(w_i)_{i\in I_{1,2}} \in M_1 \times M_2$ such that there exists a $\Rightarrow_{\mathcal{R}_{1,2}}$-merging for $(t'_i)_{i\in I_{1,2}}$ and $(t''_i)_{i\in I_{1,2}}$ which can be combined with the fixed $\Rightarrow_{\mathcal{R}_3}$-merging to a $\Rightarrow_{\pi(\mathcal{R})}$-merging is recognizable.

Recall that $\pi_j(t_i) = \pi_i(t_j) = 1$ for all $i \in I_1, j \in I_2$. The properties of $\mathcal{R}$ imply that every tuple $(s_i)_{i\in I_{1,2}}$ that appears in a $\Rightarrow_{\mathcal{R}_{1,2}}$-merging for $(t'_i)_{i\in I_{1,2}}$ and $(t''_i)_{i\in I_{1,2}}$ also satisfies $\pi_j(s_i) = \pi_i(s_j) = 1$ for all $i \in I_1, j \in I_2$. But this implies that every $\Rightarrow_{\mathcal{R}_1}$-merging for $(t'_i)_{i\in I_1}$ and $(t''_i)_{i\in I_1}$ can be combined with every $\Rightarrow_{\mathcal{R}_2}$-merging for $(t'_i)_{i\in I_2}$ and $(t''_i)_{i\in I_2}$, assumed that both mergings fit to our chosen $\Rightarrow_{\mathcal{R}_3}$-merging. By Fact 2 it suffices to prove that the set of all tuples $(w_i)_{i\in I_1} \in M_1$ such that there exists a $\Rightarrow_{\mathcal{R}_1}$-merging for $(t'_i)_{i\in I_1} = (p_i w_i m_i)_{i\in I_1}$ and $(t''_i)_{i\in I_1} = (l_i w_i r_i)_{i\in I_1}$ that can be combined with our fixed $\Rightarrow_{\mathcal{R}_3}$-merging is recognizable (the corresponding statement for M_2 can be proven analogously).

In order to allow this combination only rather restricted $\Rightarrow_{\mathcal{R}_1}$-mergings for $(p_i w_i m_i)_{i\in I_1}$ and $(l_i w_i r_i)_{i\in I_1}$ are allowed. More precisely, let the k-th step (in the $\Rightarrow_{\mathcal{R}_3}$-part or the $\Leftarrow_{\mathcal{R}_3}$-part) in our fixed $\Rightarrow_{\mathcal{R}_3}$-merging be of the form $(s_i)_{i\in I_3} \Rightarrow_{\mathcal{R}_3} (s'_i)_{i\in I_3}$, where $s_i = u_i\pi_i(l)u'_i$, $s'_i = u_i\pi_i(r)u'_i$, $(l \to r) \in \mathcal{R}$. Then we have to consider exactly those $\Rightarrow_{\mathcal{R}_1}$-mergings for $(p_i w_i m_i)_{i\in I_1}$ and $(l_i w_i r_i)_{i\in I_1}$ such that the k-th step has the form $(s_i)_{i\in I_1} \Rightarrow_{\mathcal{R}_1} (s'_i)_{i\in I_1}$, where $s_i = v_i\pi_i(l)v'_i$, $s'_i = v_i\pi_i(r)v'_i$, and $\pi_j(v_i) = \pi_i(u_j)$ for all $i \in I_{1,2}$, $j \in I_3$. In particular, the rule from $\mathcal{R}_1$ that must be applied in each step of a $\Rightarrow_{\mathcal{R}_1}$-merging for $(p_i w_i m_i)_{i\in I_1}$ and $(l_i w_i r_i)_{i\in I_1}$ is fixed. For the further consideration we may therefore exchange its left– and right–hand side. Thus, we only have to deal with a fixed sequence of rules over $\langle(\Sigma_i\backslash\Sigma^{(2)})_{i\in I_1}\rangle$. For the following let $\Gamma_i = \Sigma_i\backslash\Sigma^{(2)}$ for $i \in I_1$ and let $\Gamma = \Sigma^{(1)}\backslash\Sigma^{(2)}$.

From the previous discussion it follows that in order to prove the theorem it suffices to prove that for given $\alpha \in \mathbb{N}$ (which is the length of the fixed sequence of rules over $\langle(\Gamma_i)_{i\in I_1}\rangle$), $(l_{i,k})_{i\in I_1}, (r_{i,k})_{i\in I_1} \in \langle(\Gamma_i)_{i\in I_1}\rangle$, $u_{i,j,k} \in \Gamma_i \cap \Sigma_j$ (that are fixed for the rest of this section) where $i \in I_1$, $j \in I_3$, $k \in \overline{\alpha+1}$ the set of all tuples $(w_i)_{i\in I_1} \in M_1$ such that

$$\begin{aligned}\exists (s_{i,1})_{i\in I_1}, \ldots, (s_{i,\alpha+1})_{i\in I_1} \in \langle (\Gamma_i)_{i\in I_1}\rangle \; \forall k \in \overline{\alpha}, i \in I_1, j \in I_3 : \\ s_{i,1} = p_i w_i m_i, \quad s_{i,\alpha+1} = l_i w_i r_i, \quad s_{i,k} = v_{i,k} l_{i,k} v'_{i,k}, \\ s_{i,k+1} = v_{i,k} r_{i,k} v'_{i,k}, \quad (v_{i,k})_{i\in I_1} \in \langle (\Gamma_i)_{i\in I_1}\rangle, \quad \pi_j(v_{i,k}) = u_{i,j,k}\end{aligned} \tag{2}$$

is recognizable in M_1. Since M_1 is recognizable in $\langle (\Gamma_i)_{i\in I_1}\rangle$ and recognizable languages are closed under intersection it suffices to prove that set of all tuples $(w_i)_{i\in I_1} \in \langle (\Gamma_i)_{i\in I_1}\rangle$ such that (2) holds is recognizable. This will be proven in the rest of this section. We need the following notions.

For the rest of the section let X_i for $i \in I_1$ be an infinite enumerable set of variable symbols with $X_i \cap X_j = \emptyset$ for $i \neq j$ and let $\bigcup_{i\in I_1} X_i = X$. We assume $X \cap \Gamma = \emptyset$. For all $i \in I_1$, let $x_i \in X_i$ be a distinguished variable. For $S \in (\Gamma \cup X)^*$ let $\mathrm{Var}(S)$ denote the set of all variables that appear in S. Let Lin_i denote the set of all words $S \in (\Gamma_i \cup X_i \backslash \{x_i\})^*$ such that every variable $x \in \mathrm{Var}(S)$ appears only once in S. We write $S \preceq_i T$ iff $S, T \in \mathrm{Lin}_i$ and the word $\pi_X(S) \in X_i^*$ is a prefix of $\pi_X(T)$. We write $S \simeq_i T$ iff $S \preceq_i T$ and $T \preceq_i S$. A *substitution* is a function $\tau : X \to \Gamma^*$ such that $\tau(x) \in \Gamma_i^*$ for all $x \in X_i$ and $i \in I_1$. The homomorphic extension of τ to the set $(\Gamma \cup X)^*$ that is defined in the obvious way is denoted by τ as well. For every $x \in X$ and $i \in I_1$, we introduce a new symbol $\pi_i(x)$. Let $\pi_i(X) = \{\pi_i(x) \mid x \in X\}$. Every π_i may be viewed as a morphism $\pi_i : (X \cup \Gamma)^* \to (\pi_i(X) \cup \Gamma_i)^*$. For a substitution τ we define $\tau(\pi_i(x)) = \pi_i(\tau(x))$. A *system of word equations with regular constraints*, briefly SWE, is a finite set Δ that consists of *equations* $S = T$ with $S, T \in (\Gamma_i \cup X_i \cup \pi_i(X))^*$ for some $i \in I_1$ and *regular constraints* of the form $x \in L(\mathcal{A})$ where $x \in X_i \backslash \{x_i\}$ and $\mathcal{A}$ is a dfa over Γ_i for some $i \in I_1$. A *solution* τ for Δ is a substitution $\tau : X \to \Gamma^*$ such that $\tau(S) = \tau(T)$ for all $(S = T) \in \Delta$ and $\tau(x) \in L(\mathcal{A})$ for all $(x \in L(\mathcal{A})) \in \Delta$. Let $L(\Delta) = \{(\tau(x_i))_{i\in I_1} \in \langle (\Gamma_i)_{i\in I_1}\rangle \mid \tau \text{ is a solution of } \Delta\}$.

In (2) we ask for the set of all $(w_i)_{i\in I_1} \in \langle (\Gamma_i)_{i\in I_1}\rangle$ such that $(p_i w_i m_i)_{i\in I_1}$ can be transformed into $(l_i w_i r_i)_{i\in I_1}$ by a fixed sequence of rules where furthermore the projections onto the alphabets Σ_j ($j \in I_3$) of the prefixes that precede the replaced occurrences of the left–hand sides are fixed. In the simpler case of a fixed sequence of ordinary string rewrite rules over some Γ_i ($i \in I_1$) it is easy to construct finitely many data of the form $S^{(i)} \simeq_i T^{(i)}$ such that $s \in \Gamma_i^*$ can be transformed into $t \in \Gamma_i^*$ by an application of that sequence iff for some of the constructed data $S^{(i)}, T^{(i)}$ and some substitution τ it holds $s = \tau(S^{(i)})$, $t = \tau(T^{(i)})$. If we further fix the projections onto every alphabet Σ_j ($j \in I_3$) of the prefixes that precede the replaced occurrences of the left–hand sides then we have to add to the above data fixed values for some of the $\pi_{\Sigma_j}(x)$ ($j \in I_3$, $x \in \mathrm{Var}(S^{(i)})$). These additional data may be expressed as regular constraints for the variables in $\mathrm{Var}(S^{(i)})$. If we go one step further and consider the direct product $\prod_{i\in I_1} \Gamma_i^*$, instead of a free monoid, the only thing that changes is that we need for every component $i \in I_1$ data of the above form. Finally if we consider the situation in (2), we have to enrich the above data further since we have to guarantee that reconstructible occurrences of left–hand sides will be replaced. This can be achieved by adding a (synchronization) equation of the form $\pi_i(S_k^{(j)}) = \pi_j(S_k^{(i)})$ (where $i, j \in I_1$, $i \neq j$ and $S_k^{(i)} \preceq S^{(i)}$ for every $i \in I_1$) for the k–th rewrite step, which assures reconstructibility. These consideration lead to the following lemma that can be proven by induction on $\alpha \geq 0$.

Lemma 5. There exists a finite set $\mathcal{S}$ of SWEs (which can be constructed effectively), where every $\Delta \in \mathcal{S}$ has the form

$$p_i x_i m_i = S^{(i)},\ l_i x_i r_i = T^{(i)},\ \pi_i(S_k^{(j)}) = \pi_j(S_k^{(i)})\ (i, j \in I_1, k \in \overline{\alpha}),\ \mathcal{C} \tag{3}$$

(with $S_k^{(i)} \preceq S^{(i)} \simeq T^{(i)}$ for all $i \in I_1$, $k \in \overline{\alpha}$ and $\mathcal{C}$ being regular constraints) such that for $(w_i)_{i \in I_1} \in \langle (\Gamma_i)_{i \in I_1} \rangle$ it holds (2) iff $(w_i)_{i \in I_1} \in L(\Delta)$ for some $\Delta \in \mathcal{S}$.

Thus, in order to prove Theorem 2 it suffices to show that for a SWE Δ of the form (3) the set $L(\Delta)$ is recognizable. The next lemma proves the recognizability of the set of solutions of SWEs of a simpler form.

Lemma 6. Let $S^{(i)} \in \mathrm{Lin}_i$, $Y_i = \mathrm{Var}(S^{(i)})$, $Y = \bigcup_{i=1}^{n} Y_i$ and for all $i, j \in I_1$ with $i \neq j$ let $S^{(i)} = S_{j,1}^{(i)} \ldots S_{j,\alpha_{i,j}}^{(i)}$ be factorizations of $S^{(i)}$, where $\alpha_{i,j} = \alpha_{j,i}$. Let Δ be the SWE

$$x_i = S^{(i)},\ \pi_j(S_{j,k}^{(i)}) = \pi_i(S_{i,k}^{(j)}),\ y \in L(\mathcal{A}_y)\ (i \neq j \in I_1,\ k \in \overline{\alpha_{i,j}},\ y \in Y). \tag{4}$$

Then $L(\Delta) \subseteq \langle (\Gamma_i)_{i \in I_1} \rangle$ is a recognizable trace language.

Proof. Let $\mathcal{A}_x = (Q_x, \Gamma_i, \delta_x, q_x, \{p_x\})$ for $x \in Y_i$, $i \in I_1$. We may assume that for $x \neq y$ it holds $Q_x \cap Q_y = \emptyset$. From these automata we can easily construct a dfa (with 1–transitions) $\mathcal{A}^{(i)} = (Q^{(i)}, \Gamma_i, \delta^{(i)}, q^{(i)}, p^{(i)})$ that recognizes the language $\{\tau(S^{(i)}) \mid \forall x \in Y_i : \tau(x) \in L(\mathcal{A}_x)\}$. The dfa $\mathcal{A}^{(i)}$ reads the word $S^{(i)}$ from left to right but instead of reading a variable $x \in Y_i$ it jumps via a 1–transition into the initial state of the dfa $\mathcal{A}_x$. If it reaches the final state of $\mathcal{A}_x$ the dfa jumps back into the word $S^{(i)}$ at the position after the variable x. The idea is to modify the so called mixed product automaton (see [Dub86]) of the dfas $\mathcal{A}^{(i)}$ (which recognizes the language $\{(w_i)_{i \in I_1} \in \langle (\Gamma_i)_{i \in I_1} \rangle \mid \forall i \in I_1 : w_i \in L(\mathcal{A}^{(i)})\}$) such that it checks whether the additional equations $\pi_j(S_{j,k}^{(i)}) = \pi_i(S_{i,k}^{(j)})$ are satisfied for all $i, j \in I_1$, $k \in \overline{\alpha_{i,j}}$ with $i \neq j$. More formally, let $\mathcal{A} = (\prod_{i \in I_1} Q^{(i)}, \Gamma, (\delta_a)_{a \in \Gamma}, (q^{(i)})_{i \in I_1}, \{(p^{(i)})_{i \in I_1}\})$ be the asynchronous automaton, where $dom(a) = \{i \in I_1 \mid a \in \Gamma_i\}$ for every $a \in \Gamma$. The local transition function is defined as follows. For all $i, j \in I_1$, $k \in \overline{\alpha_{i,j}}$ with $i \neq j$ let $Q_{j,k}^{(i)} \subseteq Q^{(i)}$ be the set of states of $\mathcal{A}^{(i)}$ that corresponds to the subword $S_{j,k}^{(i)}$ of $S^{(i)}$ (which contains all states in Q_x if $x \in \mathrm{Var}(S_{j,k}^{(i)})$). Then the idea is to allow an a–transition only if for all $i, j \in dom(a)$ with $i \neq j$ there exists a $k \in \overline{\alpha_{i,j}}$ such that the i–th component of the asynchronous automata currently is in a state from $Q_{j,k}^{(i)}$ and the j–th component of the asynchronous automaton is in a state from $Q_{i,k}^{(j)}$, i.e., both components are in the same layer. Thus, $\delta_a((q_i)_{i \in dom(a)})$

is defined for $(q_i)_{i \in dom(a)} \in \prod_{i \in dom(a)} Q^{(i)}$ iff for all $i, j \in dom(a)$ with $i \neq j$ there exists a $k \in \overline{\alpha_{i,j}}$ such that $q_i \in Q^{(i)}_{j,k}$ and $q_j \in Q^{(j)}_{i,k}$. If this is the case then $\delta_a((q_i)_{i \in dom(a)}) = (\delta^{(i)}(q_i, a))_{i \in dom(a)}$. It is easy to see that $L(\Delta) = L(\mathcal{A})$.

Now the proof of Theorem 2 can be completed by proving that every SWE Δ of the form (3) can be reduced to a finite set $\mathcal{S}$ of SWEs of the form (4) such that $L(\Delta) = \bigcup\{L(\Theta) \mid \Theta \in \mathcal{S}\}$. The rather technical proof of this fact is carried out in [Loh98].

6 Conclusion

We have shown that for the class of length–reducing trace rewriting systems over a given trace monoid M, confluence is decidable iff M is free or free commutative. Thus, we have located the borderline between decidability and undecidability for this problem in terms of the underlying trace monoid. Furthermore we have presented a new criterion that implies decidability of confluence for terminating systems. Other interesting classes of systems for which it is an open question, whether confluence is decidable are special or monadic trace rewriting systems (which are defined analogously to the semi–Thue case, see [BO93]) as well as one–rule trace rewriting systems, for which confluence can be decided in almost all cases, see [WD95].

Acknowledgments I would like to thank Volker Diekert and the anonymous referees for valuable comments.

References

[BO93] Ronald V. Book and Friedrich Otto. *String–Rewriting Systems*. Springer–Verlag, 1993.

[CM85] Robert Cori and Yves Métivier. Recognizable subsets of some partially abelian monoids. *Theoretical Computer Science*, 35:179–189, 1985.

[Die90] Volker Diekert. *Combinatorics on Traces*. Number 454 in Lecture Notes in Computer Science. Springer, Berlin-Heidelberg-New York, 1990.

[DR95] Volker Diekert and Grzegorz Rozenberg, editors. *The Book of Traces*. World Scientific, Singapore, 1995.

[Dub86] Christine Duboc. Mixed procuct and asynchronous automata. *Theoretical Computer Science*, 48:183–199, 1986.

[Loh98] Markus Lohrey. On the confluence of trace rewriting systems. Available via http://inf.informatik.uni-stuttgart.de/ifi/ti/personen/Lohrey/98a.ps, 1998.

[Maz77] Antoni Mazurkiewicz. Concurrent program schemes and their interpretations. DAIMI Rep. PB 78, Aarhus University, Aarhus, 1977.

[NO88] Paliath Narendran and Friedrich Otto. Preperfectness is undecidable for Thue systems containing only length-reducing rules and a single commutation rule. *Information Processing Letters*, 29:125–130, 1988.

[WD95] Celia Wrathall and Volker Diekert. On confluence of one-rule trace-rewriting systems. *Mathematical Systems Theory*, 28:341–361, 1995.

[Zie87] Wiesław Zielonka. Notes on finite asynchronous automata. *R.A.I.R.O. — Informatique Théorique et Applications*, 21:99–135, 1987.

A String-Rewriting Characterization of Muller and Schupp's Context-Free Graphs

Hugues Calbrix[1] and Teodor Knapik[2]

[1] **College Jean Lecanuet**, BP 1024
76171 ROUEN Cedex, France
HugCalbrix@aol.com

[2] **IREMIA**, Université de la Réunion, BP 7151,
97715 SAINT DENIS Messageries Cedex 9, Réunion
knapik@univ-reunion.fr

Abstract. This paper introduces Thue specifications, an approach for string–rewriting description of infinite graphs. It is shown that *strongly reduction–bounded* and *unitary reduction–bounded* rational Thue specifications have the same expressive power and both characterize the context–free graphs of Muller and Schupp. The problem of strong reduction–boundedness for rational Thue specifications is shown to be undecidable but the class of unitary reduction–bounded rational Thue specifications, that is a proper subclass of strongly reduction–bounded rational Thue specifications, is shown to be recursive.

1 Introduction

Countable graphs or, more precisely, transition systems can model any software or digital hardware system. For this reason at least, the study of infinite graphs is, in authors opinion, an important task. Obviously, dealing with infinite graphs requires a finite description. When viewed as systems of equations, some graph grammars [9] may have infinite graphs as solutions. In this paper another approach is introduced. The idea comes from the categorist's way of expressing equations between words (of the monoid generated by the arrows of a category) by means of commutative diagrams.[1]

By orienting them, equations between words are turned into string–rewrite rules. String–rewriting systems were introduced early in this century by Axel Thue [17] in his investigations about the word problem and are also known as semi–Thue systems. Later, semi–Thue systems became useful in formal languages theory (see [15] for an overview) and, as pointed out in this paper, are also of interest as finite descriptions of infinite graphs. Other approaches relating semi–Thue systems to infinite graphs may be found in [16], [5] and [4]. In the latter paper, the class of Muller and Schupp's context–free graphs [12] is characterized by means of prefix rewriting using labeled rewrite rules.

[1] The idea underlying the definition of the Cayley graph associated to a group presentation leads to a similar result.

The link between infinite graphs and semi–Thue systems introduced in this paper raises the following question. Which classes of graphs may be described by semi–Thue systems ? As a first element of the answer, a string–rewriting characterization of context–free graphs of Muller and Schupp is provided as follows. Sect. 2 is devoted to basic definitions. Thue specifications and their graphs are defined in Sect. 3. Two classes of Thue specifications are described in Sect. 4 and the main result is established in Sect. 5. In Sect. 6 the authors investigate whether these classes are recursive. Short conclusion closes the paper.

2 Preliminaries

Assuming a smattering of string–rewriting and formal languages, several basic definitions and facts are reviewed in this section. An introductory material on above topics may be found in e.g. [2], [11] and [14].

Words. Given a finite set A called *alphabet*, the elements of which are called *letters*, A^* stands for the *free monoid* over A. The elements of A^* are all *words* over A, including the *empty word*, written ε. A subset of A^* is a *language* over A. Each word u is mapped to its *length*, written $|u|$, via the unique monoid homomorphism from A^* onto $(\mathbb{N}, 0, +)$ that maps each letter of A to 1. When $u = xy$ for some words x and y, then x (resp. y) is called a *prefix* (resp. *suffix*) *of* u. If in addition $y \neq \varepsilon$ (resp. $x \neq \varepsilon$), then x (resp. y) is a *proper prefix* (resp. *suffix*) *of* u. The set of suffixes of u is written $\mathrm{suff}(u)$. This notation is extended to sets in the usual way: $\mathrm{suff}(L) = \bigcup_{u \in L} \mathrm{suff}(u)$ for any language L. When $u = xyz$ for some words x, y, z (resp. such that $xz \neq \varepsilon$), then y is called a *factor* (resp. *proper factor*) *of* u. A word u *properly overlaps on left* a word v if $u = xy$ and $v = yz$ for some words x, y, z such that $x \neq \varepsilon$.

Semi–Thue systems. A semi–Thue system $\mathcal{S}$ (an *sts* for short) over A is a subset of $A^* \times A^*$. A pair (l, r) of $\mathcal{S}$ is called *(rewrite) rule*, the word l (resp. r) is its lefthand (resp. righthand) side. As any binary relation, $\mathcal{S}$ has its domain (resp. range), written $\mathcal{D}\mathrm{om}(\mathcal{S})$ (resp. $\mathcal{R}\mathrm{an}(\mathcal{S})$). Throughout this paper, only finite semi–Thue systems are considered.

The *single–step reduction relation* induced by $\mathcal{S}$ on A^*, is the binary relation $\rightarrow_{\mathcal{S}} = \{(xly, xry) \mid x, y \in A^*,\ (l, r) \in \mathcal{S}\}$. A word u *reduces* into a word v, written $u \rightarrow^*_{\mathcal{S}} v$, if there exist words $u_0, \ldots u_k$ such that $u_0 = u$, $u_k = v$ and $u_i \rightarrow_{\mathcal{S}} u_{i+1}$ for each $i = 0, \ldots, k-1$. The integer k is then the *length of the reduction* under consideration. A word v is *irreducible* with respect to (w.r.t. for short) $\mathcal{S}$ when v does not belong to $\mathcal{D}\mathrm{om}(\rightarrow_{\mathcal{S}})$. Otherwise v is *reducible* w.r.t. $\mathcal{S}$. It is easy to see that the set of all irreducible words w.r.t. $\mathcal{S}$, written $\mathcal{I}\mathrm{rr}(\mathcal{S})$, is rational whenever $\mathcal{D}\mathrm{om}(\mathcal{S})$ is so, since $\mathcal{D}\mathrm{om}(\rightarrow_{\mathcal{S}}) = A^* (\mathcal{D}\mathrm{om}(\mathcal{S})) A^*$. A word v is a *normal form* of a word u, when v is irreducible and $u \rightarrow^*_{\mathcal{S}} v$.

An sts $\mathcal{S}$ is *terminating*, if there is no infinite chain $u_0 \rightarrow_{\mathcal{S}} u_1 \rightarrow_{\mathcal{S}} u_2 \rightarrow_{\mathcal{S}} \cdots$. An sts is *left–basic*, if no righthand side of a rule is a proper factor of a lefthand side nor is properly overlapped on left by a lefthand side. An sts $\mathcal{S}$ over A is *special* (resp. *monadic*), if $\mathcal{R}\text{an}(\mathcal{S}) = \{\varepsilon\}$ (resp. $\mathcal{R}\text{an}(\mathcal{S}) \subseteq A \cup \{\varepsilon\}$ and $|l| > |r|$ for each $(l, r) \in \mathcal{S}$).

Graphs. Given an alphabet A, a *simple directed edge–labeled graph G over A* is a set of *edges*, viz a subset of $D \times A \times D$ where D is an arbitrary set. Given $d, d' \in D$, an edge from d to d' labeled by $a \in A$ is written $d \xrightarrow{a} d'$. A (finite) *path* in G from some $d \in D$ to some $d' \in D$ is a sequence of edges of the following form: $d_0 \xrightarrow{a_1} d_1, \ldots, d_{n-1} \xrightarrow{a_n} d_n$, such that $d_0 = d$ and $d_n = d'$.

For the purpose of this paper, the interests lies merely in graphs, the vertices of which are all accessible from some distinguished vertex. Thus, a graph $G \subseteq D \times A \times D$ is said to be *rooted on a vertex* $e \in D$, if there exists a path from e to each vertex of G. The following assumption is made for the sequel. Whenever in a definition of a graph a vertex e is distinguished as root, then the maximal subgraph rooted on e is understood.

Pushdown Machines and Context–free Graphs. An important class of graphs with decidable monadic second–order theory is characterized in [12]. The graphs of this class are called *context–free* by Muller and Schupp and may be defined by means of pushdown machines.

A *pushdown machine*[2] over A (a *pdm* for short) is a triple $\mathcal{P} = (Q, Z, T)$ where Q is the set of *states*, Z is the *stack alphabet* and T is a finite subset of $A \cup \{\varepsilon\} \times Q \times Z \times Z^* \times Q$, called the set of *transition rules*. A is the *input alphabet*. A pdm $\mathcal{P}$ is *realtime* when T is a finite subset of $A \times Q \times Z \times Z^* \times Q$.

An *internal configuration* of a pdm $\mathcal{P}$ is a pair $(q, h) \in Q \times Z^*$. To any pdm $\mathcal{P}$ together with an internal configuration ι, one may associate an edge–labeled oriented graph $\mathcal{G}(\mathcal{P}, \iota)$ defined as follows. The vertices of the graph are all internal configurations accessible from the configuration ι. The latter one is the root of the graph. There is an edge labeled by $c \in A \cup \{\varepsilon\}$ from (q_1, h_1) to (q_2, h_2) whenever there exists a letter $z \in Z$ and two words $g_1, g_2 \in Z^*$ such that $h_1 = g_1 z$, $h_2 = g_1 g_2$ and $(c, q_1, z, g_2, q_2) \in T$.

It may be useful to note that the context–free graphs of Muller and Schupp are exactly (up to isomorphism) all HR–equational (in the sense of [6], also called regular in [4]) as well as VR–equational (in the sense of [1]) graphs of finite degree. Finally, since any pdm over A is a realtime pdm over $A \cup \{\varepsilon\}$, realtime pdm's are as powerful as pdm's for describing graphs. In other words, the graphs of realtime pdm's form a complete set of representatives of Muller and Schupp's context–free graphs.

3 Thue Specifications and Their Graphs

The key ideas of this paper are introduced in the present section.

---

[2] It is a pushdown automaton with no specified accepting configurations.

Definition 3.1. *An (oriented) Thue specification (an ots for short) over an alphabet A is a triple $\langle \mathcal{S}, L, u\rangle$ where $\mathcal{S}$ is a semi–Thue system over A, L is a subset of $\mathfrak{Irr}(\mathcal{S})$ and u is a word of L. An ots is rational if L is so.*

The semantics of a Thue specification may be defined as a category of models similarly to [10] but this topic is not developed in the sequel. In fact, for the purpose of this paper only the initial model, referred to in the following as *the model*, is relevant. Without summoning up the initial semantics, it may be simply defined as follows.

Definition 3.2. *The model of an ots $\langle \mathcal{S}, L, u\rangle$ is the graph, written $\mathcal{G}(\mathcal{S}, L, u)$, defined as follows. The vertices of the graph are all words of L that are accessible via edges from the root u of the graph. The edges of $\mathcal{G}(\mathcal{S}, L, u)$ are labeled by the letters of A. There is an edge $v \xrightarrow{a} w$ whenever w is a normal form of va.*

It should be noted that termination of $\mathcal{S}$ is not required in this definition. Thus a vertex v of $\mathcal{G}(\mathcal{S}, L, u)$ has no outgoing edge labeled by a if and only if no normal form of va belongs to L.

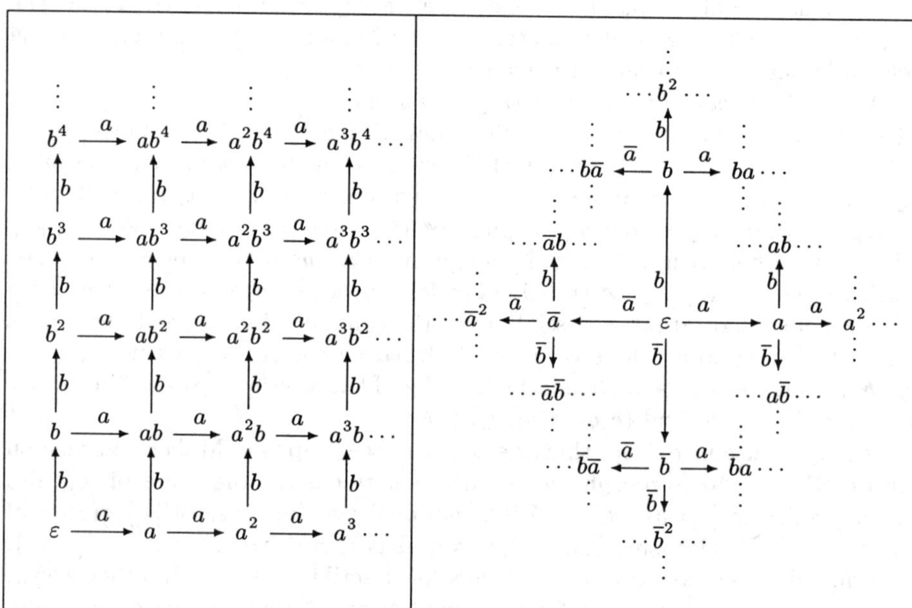

Fig. 1. Graphs $\mathcal{G}(\mathcal{S}_1, \mathfrak{Irr}(\mathcal{S}_1), \varepsilon)$ and $\mathcal{G}(\mathcal{S}_2, \mathfrak{Irr}(\mathcal{S}_2), \varepsilon)$

Example 3.1. Over the alphabet $A_1 = \{a, b\}$, consider a single–rule sts $\mathcal{S}_1 = \{(ba, ab)\}$. The set of irreducible words is a^*b^*. The graph $\mathcal{G}(\mathcal{S}_1, \mathfrak{Irr}(\mathcal{S}_1), \varepsilon)$ (see Fig. 1) is isomorphic to $\omega \times \omega$.

Example 3.2. Over the alphabet $A_2 = \{a, b, \overline{a}, \overline{b}\}$ consider the following sts: $\mathcal{S}_2 = \{(a\overline{a}, \varepsilon), (\overline{a}a, \varepsilon), (b\overline{b}, \varepsilon), (\overline{b}b, \varepsilon)\}$. The set of irreducible words w.r.t. $\mathcal{S}_2$ is the set of all reduced words representing the elements of the free group generated by $\{a, b\}$. The graph[3] $\mathcal{G}(\mathcal{S}_2, \mathfrak{Irr}(\mathcal{S}_2), \varepsilon)$ (see Fig. 1) is isomorphic to the Cayley graph of the two–generator free group.

4 Two equivalent conditions

This section introduces two notions that help characterizing Thue specifications that generate the context–free graphs of Muller and Schupp.

An sts $\mathcal{S}$ over A is *strongly reduction–bounded* on a subset L of $\mathfrak{Irr}(\mathcal{S})$ when there exists a positive integer k such that for each word u of L and each a in A, the length of any reduction of ua is less than k. The integer k is then called a *reduction bound* of $\mathcal{S}$ (on L). An sts $\mathcal{S}$ is *unitary reduction–bounded* on a subset L of $\mathfrak{Irr}(\mathcal{S})$ when it is strongly reduction–bounded on L and 1 is a reduction bound of $\mathcal{S}$.

An ots $\langle \mathcal{S}, L, u \rangle$ is *strongly reduction–bounded* (resp. *unitary reduction–bounded*) if $\mathcal{S}$ is strongly reduction–bounded (resp. unitary reduction–bounded) on L.

The system $\mathcal{S}_1$ from Example 3.1 is not strongly reduction–bounded on $\mathfrak{Irr}(\mathcal{S}_1)$. Indeed, the word b^n is irreducible and n is the length of the reduction of the word $b^n a$ into its normal form ab^n. Since n is an arbitrary positive integer, $\mathcal{S}_1$ has no reduction bound.

On the contrary, the sts $\mathcal{S}_2$ from Example 3.2 is unitary reduction–bounded on $\mathfrak{Irr}(\mathcal{S}_2)$. As a matter of fact, given a nonempty word $w = uc$ of $\mathfrak{Irr}(\mathcal{S}_2)$ with $c \in A_2$, for any $d \in A_2$ the normal form of wd is u if $c = \overline{d}$ or $d = \overline{c}$, and wd otherwise. In both cases the length of the corresponding reduction is not greater than 1. It may be observed that $\mathcal{G}(\mathcal{S}_2, \mathfrak{Irr}(\mathcal{S}_2), \varepsilon)$ is a tree.

The next proposition and the subsequent comment establish inclusions between some familiar classes of semi–Thue systems (see e.g. [2] and [15]) on one hand, and strongly (resp. unitary) reduction–bounded semi–Thue systems on the other hand.

Proposition 4.1. *For all finite semi–Thue systems $\mathcal{S}$ the following holds.*

1. *If $\mathcal{S}$ is special then $\mathcal{S}$ is unitary reduction–bounded.*
2. *If $\mathfrak{Ran}(\mathcal{S}) \subseteq \mathfrak{Irr}(\mathcal{S})$ and no word of $\mathfrak{Ran}(\mathcal{S})$ is properly overlapped on left by a word of $\mathfrak{Dom}(\mathcal{S})$ then $\mathcal{S}$ is unitary reduction–bounded.*
3. *If $\mathcal{S}$ is terminating left–basic then $\mathcal{S}$ is strongly reduction–bounded.*

Proof. Both (1) and (2) are obvious. Let then $\mathcal{S}$ be a finite terminating left–basic semi–Thue system over A. Let $w \in \mathfrak{Irr}(\mathcal{S})$ and $a \in A$. Consider the longest suffix v of w such that $va \in \mathfrak{Dom}(\mathcal{S})$. Observe that, since $\mathcal{S}$ is left–basic, each reduction of wa concerns only va. Let therefore k be the maximum of the lengths of all reductions of the words of $\mathfrak{Dom}(\mathcal{S})$. Obviously, k is a reduction bound of $\mathcal{S}$. □

[3] For each edge, there is the opposite edge (not depicted) corresponding to the formal inverse of the label.

It may be noted that no converse of statements (1), (2) or (3) of the above proposition holds. Indeed, the semi–Thue system $\{aa \to a\}$ over $\{a\}$ is unitary reduction–bounded but is not special; a is properly overlapped on left by aa hence the system is not left–basic. On the other hand, Proposition 4.1 cannot be strengthened to the case of monadic semi–Thue systems. The semi–Thue system $\{ab \to b\}$ over $\{a, b\}$ is monadic without being strongly reduction–bounded.

The following result demonstrates that the strongly reduction–bounded rational ots and unitary reduction–bounded rational ots have the same expressive power for describing graphs.

Proposition 4.2. *Given any strongly reduction–bounded rational ots $\langle \mathcal{S}, R, u\rangle$, one may construct a unitary reduction–bounded rational ots $\langle \mathcal{S}', R', u'\rangle$ such that the graphs $\mathcal{G}(\mathcal{S}, R, u)$ and $\mathcal{G}(\mathcal{S}', R', u')$ are isomorphic.*

Proof. Let k be a reduction bound of $\mathcal{S}$ and $m = \max_{l \in \mathcal{D}om(\mathcal{S})} |l|$ be the maximum length of the lefthand sides of $\mathcal{S}$. Consider any reduction of length n of a word wa such that $w \in R$ and $a \in A$. If $|wa| > mn$, then only a proper suffix of wa is reduced. The length of the reduced suffix cannot exceed mn. Since $n \leq k$, for any reduction, the length of the reduced suffix cannot exceed mk.

Let $\mathcal{S}' = \mathcal{S}'_{\#} \cup \mathcal{S}'_A$ be an sts over $A \cup \{\#\}$, where $\# \notin A$, defined as follows:

$$\mathcal{S}'_{\#} = \{(\#wa, \#v) \mid a \in A,\ w \in R, v \in \mathcal{I}rr(\mathcal{S}),\ wa \xrightarrow[\mathcal{S}]{*} v \text{ and } |wa| < mk\},$$

$$\mathcal{S}'_A = \{(wa, v) \mid a \in A,\ w \in \mathrm{suff}(R), v \in \mathcal{I}rr(\mathcal{S}),\ wa \xrightarrow[\mathcal{S}]{*} v \text{ and } |wa| = mk\}$$

and let $R' = \#R$.

Unit reduction–boundedness of $\mathcal{S}'$ on R' is established as follows. Let $w \in R'$ and $a \in A'$. If $a = \#$ then $wa \notin R'$. Assume then that $a \in A$. Observe first that, if $wa \to_{\mathcal{S}'_{\#}} x$ for some $x \in (A')^*$ then $x \in \mathcal{I}rr(\mathcal{S}')$. Assume therefore by contradiction that there is a reduction $wa \to_{\mathcal{S}'_A} x \to_{\mathcal{S}'} y$ for some $x, y \in (A')^*$. Let w_1 be the longest prefix of w this reduction is not concerned with and let w_2 be the remaining suffix, viz $w = w_1 w_2$. Now, either $w_2 \in \mathrm{suff}(R)$ (when $x \to_{\mathcal{S}'_A} y$) and $|w_2| > mk$ or $w_2 = \#w'_2$ (when $x \to_{\mathcal{S}'_{\#}} y$) for some $w'_2 \in R$ such that $|w'_2| > mk$. Hence, there exists a reduction of $w_2 a$ (resp. $w'_2 a$) w.r.t. $\mathcal{S}$ the length of which exceeds k. This contradicts the assumption that k is a reduction bound of $\mathcal{S}$ on R.

Observe that for all $w \in R$, $v \in \mathcal{I}rr(\mathcal{S})$ and $a \in A$, v is a normal form of wa w.r.t. $\mathcal{S}$ if and only if $\#v$ is a normal form of $\#wa$ w.r.t. $\mathcal{S}'$. Hence, the mapping $w \mapsto \#w$ restricted to the vertices of $\mathcal{G}(\mathcal{S}, R, u)$ extends to a graph isomorphism between $\mathcal{G}(\mathcal{S}, R, u)$ and $\mathcal{G}(\mathcal{S}', R', u')$ where $u' = \#u$. $\square$

5 Main result

Proposition 4.2 together with the statements of this section lead to the main result of this paper.

Proposition 5.1. *Given any realtime pdm $\mathscr{P}$ over A and an internal configuration ι of $\mathscr{P}$, one may construct a unitary reduction–bounded rational ots $\langle \mathcal{S}, R, u\rangle$ such that the graphs $\mathcal{G}(\mathscr{P}, \iota)$ and $\mathcal{G}(\mathcal{S}, R, u)$ are isomorphic.*

Proof. Let $\mathscr{P} = (Q, Z, T)$ be a realtime pdm over A and let $\iota = (q_0, h_0)$ be an internal configuration of $\mathscr{P}$. Without loss of generality A, Q and Z may be assumed pairwise disjoint. Set $A' = A \cup Q \cup Z$. Define an sts $\mathcal{S}$ over A' as follows

$$\mathcal{S} = \{(zqa, hq') \mid (a, q, z, h, q') \in T\}$$

and let $u = h_0 q_0$. It is well known that the pushdown store language of a pdm is rational. The following language is therefore rational:

$$R = \{hq \mid (q, h) \text{ is an internal configuration of } \mathscr{P} \text{ accessible from } \iota\} \ .$$

Moreover $R \subseteq \mathcal{I}\mathrm{rr}(\mathcal{S})$.

Observe that $\mathcal{S}$ is unitary reduction–bounded on R. Indeed, let $v \in R$ and $a \in A'$. For va to be reducible, there must exist $w \in \mathcal{I}\mathrm{rr}(\mathcal{S})$ and a rewrite rule (zqa, hq') such that $v = wzqa$. Consequently, $va \to_{\mathcal{S}} whq'$. But no word of $\mathcal{D}\mathrm{om}(\mathcal{S})$ may overlap hq' on left. Since w is irreducible, so is whq'.

The fact that is $\mathcal{G}(\mathscr{P}, \iota)$ and $\mathcal{G}(\mathcal{S}, R, u)$ are isomorphic is readily established by induction on the distance of vertex from the root, using the following one–to–one mapping of the vertices of $\mathcal{G}(\mathscr{P}, \iota)$ onto the vertices of $\mathcal{G}(\mathcal{S}, R, u)$: $(q, h) \mapsto hq$. □

In order to establish the converse, the following lemma is useful.

Lemma 5.1. *Given a pdm $\mathscr{P} = (Q, Z, T)$ over A, an internal configuration ι of $\mathscr{P}$ and a rational subset R of Z^*Q, one may construct a pdm $\mathscr{P}'$ together with ι' such that the graph $\mathcal{G}(\mathscr{P}', \iota')$ is isomorphic to the restriction of $\mathcal{G}(\mathscr{P}, \iota)$, rooted on ι, to the following set of vertices: $\{(q, h) \in Q \times Z^* \mid hq \in R\}$. Moreover $\mathscr{P}'$ is realtime if $\mathscr{P}$ is so.*

The following proof uses a device similar to a predicting automaton of [11]. More precisely, $\mathscr{P}'$ is constructed so that the contents of its pushdown store encodes a successful run of a finite automaton accepting R.

Proof. Let $\mathscr{A} = (D, d_0, \delta, F)$ be a finite deterministic and complete automaton over A that accepts R. Here D is the set of states of $\mathscr{A}$, $d_0 \in D$ is the initial state, $\delta\colon D \times A \to D$ is the transition function and $F \subseteq D$ is the set of final states of $\mathscr{A}$.

A is the input alphabet of $\mathscr{P}'$ and the stack alphabet is $Z' = D \times Z$. Consider a map $\kappa\colon D \times Z^* \to (D \times Z)^*$ defined as follows

$$\begin{aligned} \kappa(d, \varepsilon) &= \varepsilon, && \text{for all } d \in D,\\ \kappa(d, zg) &= \langle d, z\rangle \kappa(\delta(d, z), g), && \text{for all } \langle d, z\rangle \in D \times Z \text{ and } g \in Z^*. \end{aligned}$$

Let $\iota' = (d_0, \kappa(d_0, h_0))$. On the whole $\mathscr{P}' = (Q, Z', T')$ where

$$T' = \{(a, q, \langle d, z\rangle, \kappa(d, h), q') \mid (a, q, z, h, q') \in T,\ d \in D,\ \delta(d, zq) \in F,\ \delta(d, hq') \in F\} \ .$$

Observe that an edge $(q, gz) \xrightarrow{a} (q', gh)$ is in the restriction of $\mathcal{G}(\mathscr{P}, \iota)$ to $\{(q,h) \mid hq \in R\}$ rooted on ι if and only if the vertex (q, gz) is in this restriction and

$$\kappa(d_0, gz) = H\langle d, z\rangle \quad \text{for some } H \in (Z')^* \text{ and some } d \in D,$$
$$\delta(d, zq) \in F,\ \delta(d, hq') \in F \text{ and}$$
$$(a, q, z, h, q') \in T\ .$$

Hence equivalently, there is an edge $(q, \kappa(d_0, g)\langle d, z\rangle) \xrightarrow{a} (q', \kappa(d_0, g)\kappa(d, h))$ in $\mathcal{G}(\mathscr{P}', \iota')$. Since $\iota' = (d_0, \kappa(d_0, h_0))$, the result follows by induction from the above. □

It may be noted that the size of the resulting pdm $\mathscr{P}'$ is in $O(nk)$, where n is the number of states of the finite automaton $\mathscr{A}$ accepting R used in the construction and k is the size of $\mathscr{P}$. Indeed $|Z'| = n|Z|$ and $|T'| \leq n|T|$.

The converse of Proposition 5.1 is stated in the following.

Proposition 5.2. *Given any unitary reduction–bounded rational ots $\langle \mathcal{S}, R, u\rangle$ over A, one may construct a realtime pdm $\mathscr{P}$ and an internal configuration ι of $\mathscr{P}$ such that the graphs $\mathcal{G}(\mathcal{S}, R, u)$ and $\mathcal{G}(\mathscr{P}, \iota)$ are isomorphic.*

In the following proof a word $w \in \mathfrak{Irr}(\mathcal{S})$ is cut into factors $w = x_1 \ldots x_n y$, so that all words x_i are of equal length m and $|y| < m$, where m is the maximum length of the lefthand sides of $\mathcal{S}$. Then w is encoded by an internal configuration $(q_y, z_1 \ldots z_n)$ where $z_1, \ldots, z_n$ are letters of the stack alphabet that is in one–to–one correspondence with the words over A of length m.

Proof. A pushdown machine $\mathscr{P}' = (Q', Z', T')$ is defined first together with an internal configuration ι' so that $\mathcal{G}(\mathscr{P}', \iota')$ is isomorphic to $\mathcal{G}(\mathcal{S}, \mathfrak{Irr}(\mathcal{S}), u)$. Set $m = \max_{l \in \mathfrak{Dom}(\mathcal{S})} |l|$. Define a pdm $\mathscr{P}'$ as follows. The set Q of the states is indexed by irreducible words, the length of which is strictly less than m viz $Q = \{q_w \mid w \in \mathfrak{Irr}(\mathcal{S}) \text{ and } |w| < m\}$. The stack alphabet $Z' = Z'' \cup \{z_0\}$ has the bottom symbol $z_0 \notin Z''$ and Z'' is an arbitrary set that is in one–to–one correspondence f with the set of irreducible words of length m,

$$f\colon \{w \in \mathfrak{Irr}(\mathcal{S}) \mid |w| = m\} \to Z''\ .$$

The set T' of transition rules of $\mathscr{P}'$ is constructed as follows.

- For any $a \in A$, any $q_w \in Q$ and any $z \in Z''$, one has
  1. $(a, q_w, z, z, q_{wa}) \in T$ when $f^{-1}(z)wa \in \mathfrak{Irr}(\mathcal{S})$ and $|wa| < m$,
  2. $(a, q_w, z, zf(wa), q_\varepsilon) \in T$ when $f^{-1}(z)wa \in \mathfrak{Irr}(\mathcal{S})$ and $|wa| = m$,
  3. $(a, q_w, z, \varepsilon, q_{vr}) \in T$ when $f^{-1}(z)wa = vl$ for some $v \in \mathfrak{Irr}(\mathcal{S})$ and $(l, r) \in \mathcal{S}$ such that $|vr| < m$,
  4. $(a, q_w, z, f(x_1) \ldots f(x_n), q_y) \in T$ when $f^{-1}(z)wa = vl$ for some $v \in \mathfrak{Irr}(\mathcal{S})$ and $(l, r) \in \mathcal{S}$ such that $vr = x_1 \ldots x_n y$, where $x_1, \ldots, x_n, y \in \mathfrak{Irr}(\mathcal{S})$ are such that $|x_1| = \cdots = |x_n| = m$ and $|y| < m$.
- For any $a \in A$ and any $q_w \in Q$, one has
  1. $(a, q_w, z_0, z_0, q_{wa}) \in T$ when $wa \in \mathfrak{Irr}(\mathcal{S})$ and $|wa| < m$,
  2. $(a, q_w, z_0, z_0 f(wa), q_\varepsilon) \in T$ when $wa \in \mathfrak{Irr}(\mathcal{S})$ and $|wa| = m$,

3. $(a, q_w, z_0, z_0, q_{vr}) \in T$ when $wa = vl$ for some $v \in \mathrm{Irr}(\mathcal{S})$ and $(l, r) \in \mathcal{S}$ such that $|vr| < m$,
4. $(a, q_w, z_0, z_0 f(x_1) \dots f(x_n), q_y) \in T$ when $wa = vl$ for some $v \in \mathrm{Irr}(\mathcal{S})$ and $(l, r) \in \mathcal{S}$ such that $vr = x_1 \dots x_n y$, where $x_1, \dots, x_n, y \in \mathrm{Irr}(\mathcal{S})$ are such that $|x_1| = \dots = |x_n| = m$ and $|y| < m$.

Define now the internal configuration ι' of $\mathscr{P}'$ corresponding to the root of the graph $\mathcal{G}(\mathcal{S}, \mathrm{Irr}(\mathcal{S}), u)$ as follows. If $|u| < m$, set $\iota' = (q_u, z_0)$. Otherwise one has $u = x_1 \dots x_n y$ for some $x_1, \dots, x_n, y \in \mathrm{Irr}(\mathcal{S})$ such that $|x_1| = \dots = |x_n| = m$ and $|y| < m$. Set then $\iota' = (q_y, z_0 f(x_1) \dots f(x_n))$.

It is easy to check that the one–to–one mapping $(q_w, z_0 h) \mapsto f^{-1}(h)w$ of the vertices of $\mathcal{G}(\mathscr{P}', \iota')$ onto the vertices of $\mathcal{G}(\mathcal{S}, \mathrm{Irr}(\mathcal{S}), u)$ extends to a graph isomorphism. Moreover $\mathscr{P}'$ is realtime.

Obviously, $\mathcal{G}(\mathcal{S}, R, u)$ is a restriction (on vertices) of $\mathcal{G}(\mathcal{S}, \mathrm{Irr}(\mathcal{S}), u)$ to R rooted on u. Define $\mathcal{C}_{R'} = \{(q_w, z_0 h) \mid h \in (Z'')^*,\ q_w \in Q',\ f(h)w \in R\}$ and $R' = \{z_0 h q_w \mid (q_w, z_0 h) \in \mathcal{C}_{R'}\}$. Observe that R' is rational. Moreover, the restriction of $\mathcal{G}(\mathscr{P}', \iota')$ to $\mathcal{C}_{R'}$ rooted on ι' is isomorphic to $\mathcal{G}(\mathcal{S}, R, u)$. Now, according to Lemma 5.1, one may construct a pdm $\mathscr{P}$ and an internal configuration ι of $\mathscr{P}$ such that the graph $\mathcal{G}(\mathscr{P}, \iota)$ is isomorphic to $\mathcal{G}(\mathcal{S}, R, u)$. □

It is not too difficult to figure out that size resulting from the construction described above is doubly exponential w.r.t. the maximum length of the lefthand sides of $\mathcal{S}$.

In view of the results established so far, it is straightforward to conclude this section as follows. Both strongly reduction–bounded and unitary reduction–bounded rational ots characterize the class of Muller and Schupp's context–free graphs. Moreover, since the transition rules of a pdm may be seen as labeled prefix rewrite rules, the graphs of suffix–bounded rational ots can also be generated by prefix rewriting. This remark is rather obvious insofar as prefix rewriting generate exactly context–free graphs of Muller and Schupp [4].

6 Decision Problems

The criterion of strong reduction–boundedness defines a class of Thue specifications, the graphs of which have decidable monadic second–order theory due to the result of Muller and Schupp [12]. It may be asked whether the class of strongly reduction–bounded rational ots is recursive. The answer is positive for the subclass of unitary reduction–bounded rational ots.

Proposition 6.1. *There is an algorithm to solve the following problem.*
Instance: *A finite semi–Thue system $\mathcal{S}$ and a rational subset R of $\mathrm{Irr}(\mathcal{S})$.*
Question: *Is $\mathcal{S}$ unitary reduction–bounded on R ?*

Proof. Let $\mathcal{S}$ be a finite sts over A. For each rule (r, l) and each $a \in A$ set $R_{(l,r),a} = ((Ra)l^{-1})r$. Observe that

$$\bigcup_{\substack{(l,r)\in\mathcal{S}\\ a\in A}} R_{(l,r),a} = \{v \mid \exists u \in R, \exists a \in A \text{ s.t. } ua \underset{\mathcal{S}}{\to} v\} .$$

Thus, $\mathcal{S}$ is unitary reduction–bounded if and only if $R_{(l,r),a} \subseteq \mathfrak{Irr}(\mathcal{S})$ for each $(l,r) \in \mathcal{S}$ and $a \in A$. Since both $\mathcal{S}$ and A are finite, there is a finite number of inclusions to test, all between rational languages. □

It is not surprising that the above result may be extended as follows.

Proposition 6.2. *There is an algorithm to solve the following problem.*

Instance:	*A finite semi–Thue system $\mathcal{S}$, a rational subset R of $\mathfrak{Irr}(\mathcal{S})$ and a positive integer k.*
Question:	*Is k a reduction bound of $\mathcal{S}$ on R ?*

Proof. The proof is similar to the one of Proposition 6.1. One has to test the inclusion in $\mathfrak{Irr}(\mathcal{S})$ of the languages of the form $((\cdots(((Ra)l_1^{-1})r_1)\ldots l_k^{-1})r_k)$ for each sequence $(l_1,r_1)\ldots(l_k,r_k)$ over $\mathcal{S}$ of length k and each $a \in A$. □

As established above, one may decide whether an integer is a reduction bound of a semi–Thue system. However the decision procedure sketched in the proof does not allow, in general, to establish the existence of a reduction bound. The problem, whether a reduction bound exists, may be addressed in the context of the strong boundedness problem for Turing machines.

As defined in [13], a Turing machine $\mathscr{T}$ is *strongly bounded* if there exists an integer k such that, for each finite configuration uqv, $\mathscr{T}$ halts after at most k steps when starting in configuration uqv. The *strong boundedness problem* for Turing machines is the following decision problem.

Instance:	A single–tape Turing machine $\mathscr{T}$.
Question:	Is $\mathscr{T}$ strongly bounded ?

Now, one may effectively encode an arbitrary deterministic single–tape Turing machine $\mathscr{T}$ into a semi–Thue system $\mathcal{S}$ over an appropriate alphabet A and define an effective encoding χ of the configurations of $\mathscr{T}$ into words of $\mathfrak{Irr}(\mathcal{S})A$ that satisfy the following property.

> Starting from uqv, $\mathscr{T}$ halts after k steps if and only if any reduction of $\chi(uqv)$ into an irreducible word is of length k.

Such an encoding χ may consist in the following. Consider a configuration uqv where a Turing machine is in a state q, uv is a tape inscription such that the tape head is positioned on the first letter of v or on the blank $\Box$, if $v = \varepsilon$. Let $m = \max(|u|,|v|)$ and let u' (resp. v') be the suffix (resp. prefix) of $\blacksquare^m u$ (resp. $v\Box^m$) of length m, where $\blacksquare$ is an additional symbol. Consider now a letterwise shuffle of u' and the reversal $\tilde{v}'$ of v'. Enclose it in a pair of # and append $\overline{q}$ on right. For instance with $u = abc$ and $v = de$ (resp. $u = ab$ and $v = cde$) we get $\#a\Box becd\#\overline{q}$ (resp. $\#\blacksquare eadbc\#\overline{q}$). Formally a configuration uqv is encoded as follows:

$$\chi(uqv) = \#((\blacksquare^{\max(0,|v|-|u|)}u) \sqcup\!\sqcup (\Box^{\max(0,|u|-|v|)}\tilde{v}))\#\overline{q}$$

where $\sqcup\!\sqcup$ denotes the letterwise shuffle of two words (of equal length)

$$a_1\ldots a_n \sqcup\!\sqcup b_1\ldots b_n = a_1b_1\ldots a_nb_n \ .$$

It is not too difficult to simulate in such representation each move of the Turing machine by a single rewrite step w.r.t. an appropriate sts. However, one needs to distinguish whether the tape head is in the part of the tape initially occupied by u or by v. In the former situation the symbols of the states of the Turing machine are used directly whereas in the latter situation, their bared versions (as $\overline{q}$) are used. A complete many–one reduction of the strong boundedness problem for Turing machines into the strong reduction–boundedness problem for semi–Thue systems may be found in a preliminary version of this paper [3].

Now, the strong boundedness problem is undecidable for 2–symbol single–tape Turing machines (cf. Proposition 14 of [13]). This gives the following undecidability result.

Proposition 6.3. *There exists a rational set R for which the following problem is undecidable.*
Instance: *A finite semi–Thue system $\mathcal{S}$.*
Question: *Is $\mathcal{S}$ strongly reduction–bounded on R ?*

7 Conclusion

Thue specifications and their graphs have been introduced and two classes of Thue specifications have been defined: strongly reduction–bounded and unitary reduction–bounded ots. It has been established that both unitary and strongly reduction–bounded rational Thue specifications characterize the context–free graphs of Muller and Schupp. Moreover, the membership problem for the class of strongly reduction–bounded rational ots has been shown to be undecidable whereas, for its proper subclass of unitary reduction–bounded rational ots, this problem has been established as being decidable.

An important property of context–free graphs is the decidability of their monadic second–order theory. However the class of Muller and Schupp's context–free graphs is not the only well–known class of graphs with decidable monadic second–order theory. More general classes of such graphs are described in e.g. [1], [5], [7] or [8]. Beyond, other classes of infinite graphs, the monadic second–order theory of which is not necessarily decidable, are currently under investigation. How Thue specifications are linked via their graphs to all these classes, is considered for further research.

References

[1] K. Barthelmann. On equational simple graphs. Technical Report 9/97, Johannes Gutenberg Universität, Mainz, 1997.

[2] R. V. Book and F. Otto. *String–Rewriting Systems.* Texts and Monographs in Computer Science. Springer–Verlag, 1993.

[3] H. Calbrix and T. Knapik. On a class of graphs of semi–Thue systems having decidable monadic second–order theory. Technical Report INF/1998/01/01/a, IREMIA, Université de la Réunion, 1998.

[4] D. Caucal. On the regular structure of prefix rewriting. *Theoretical Comput. Sci.*, 106:61–86, 1992.

[5] D. Caucal. On infinite transition graphs having a decidable monadic second-order theory. In F. M. auf der Heide and B. Monien, editors, *23th International Colloquium on Automata Languages and Programming*, LNCS 1099, pages 194–205, 1996.

[6] B. Courcelle. The monadic second–order logic of graphs, II: Infinite graphs of bounded width. *Mathematical System Theory*, 21:187–221, 1989.

[7] B. Courcelle. Graph rewriting: An algebraic and logic approach. In J. van Leeuwen, editor, *Formal Models and Semantics*, volume B of *Handbook of Theoretical Computer Science*, pages 193–242. Elsevier, 1990.

[8] B. Courcelle. The monadic second–order theory of graphs IX: Machines and their behaviours. *Theoretical Comput. Sci.*, 151:125–162, 1995.

[9] J. Engelfriet. Contex–free graph grammars. In G. Rozenberg and A. Salomaa, editors, *Beyond Words*, volume 3 of *Handbook of Formal Languages*, pages 125–213. Springer–Verlag, 1997.

[10] J. A. Goguen, J. W. Thatcher, and E. G. Wagner. An initial approach to the specification, correctness and implementation of abstract data types. In R. T. Yeh, editor, *Data Structuring*, volume 4 of *Current Trends in Programming Methodology*, pages 80–149. Prentice Hall, 1978.

[11] J. E. Hopcroft and J. D. Ullman. *Introduction to Automata Theory, Languages, and Computation.* Addison–Wesley, 1979.

[12] D. E. Muller and P. E. Schupp. The theory of ends, pushdown automata and second–order logic. *Theoretical Comput. Sci.*, 37:51–75, 1985.

[13] F. Otto. On the property of preserving regularity for string–rewriting systems. In H. Comon, editor, *Rewriting Techniques and Applications*, LNCS 1232, pages 83–97, 1987.

[14] G. Rozenberg and A. Salomaa, editors. *Handbook of Formal Languages*, volume 1. Springer–Verlag, 1997.

[15] G. Sénizergues. Formal languages and word rewriting. In *Term Rewriting: French Spring School of Theoretical Computer Science*, LNCS 909, pages 75–94, Font-Romeu, May 1993.

[16] C. C. Squier, F. Otto, and Y. Kobayashi. A finiteness condition for rewriting systems. *Theoretical Comput. Sci.*, 131(2):271–294, 1994.

[17] A. Thue. Probleme über veränderungen von zeichenreihen nach gegebenen regeln. *Skr. Vid. Kristiania, I Mat. Natuv. Klasse*, 10:34 pp, 1914.

Different Types of Monotonicity for Restarting Automata*

Petr Jančar[1], František Mráz[2], Martin Plátek[2], and Jörg Vogel[3]

[1] Technical University of Ostrava, Dept. of Computer Science, 17. listopadu 15, 708 33 Ostrava, Czech Republic, e-mail: Petr.Jancar@vsb.cz

[2] Charles University, Department of Computer Science, Malostranské nám. 25, 118 00 Praha 1, Czech Republic, e-mail: mraz@ksvi.mff.cuni.cz, platek@ksi.mff.cuni.cz

[3] Friedrich Schiller University, Computer Science Institute, 07740 Jena, Germany, e-mail: vogel@informatik.uni-jena.de

Abstract. We consider several classes of rewriting automata with a restart operation and the monotonicity property of computations by such automata. It leads to three natural definitions of (right) monotonicity of automata. Besides the former monotonicity, two new types, namely *a*-monotonicity and *g*-monotonicity, for such automata are introduced. We provide a taxonomy of the relevant language classes, and answer the (un)decidability questions concerning these properties.

1 Introduction

The restarting automata (or automata with an operation restart) serve as a formal tool to model analysis by reduction in natural languages. They integrate properties of classical paradigms of algebraical linguistics as e.g. configurations, in a similar way as Marcus grammars (see [11]), to express current syntactic methods of (European) computational linguistics in a formal way. In this paper we stress certain properties of (right) monotonicity, to separate syntactic phenomena transformable in (context-free, almost deterministic) rules from the phenomena not transformable in such rules.

Analysis by reduction consists in stepwise simplification of an extended sentence so that the (in)correctness of the sentence is not affected. Thus after some number of steps a simple sentence is got or an error is found. Let us illustrate the analysis by reduction on the sentence

'Martin, Peter and Jane work very slowly.'

The sentence can be simplified for example in the following way:

'Martin, Peter and Jane work slowly.'
'Martin, Peter and Jane work.'
'Martin and Peter work.' or *'Peter and Jane work.'* or *'Martin and Jane work.'*
'Martin works.' or *'Peter works.'* or *'Jane works.'*

* Supported by the Grant Agency of the Czech Republic, Grant-No. 201/96/0195

The last three sentences are the variants of simple sentences which can be reduced from the original sentence.

'Full' analysis by reduction is used in (European) linguistics as a (purely) syntactic basis for establishing (in)dependencies in any dependency based grammar (see e.g. [10], [4]). From the previously outlined sample of analysis by reduction, it can be e.g. derived that between the words *Martin, Peter, Jane* no *dependencies* can be established (because the order of their deleting is fully free [they are actually coordinated]). On the other hand, we can see that the word *very* must be deleted always before the word *slowly.* That means that *slowly* cannot be considered dependent on *very* but vice versa *very* can be (and actually is) established dependent on *slowly.*

An *RRWW*-automaton can be roughly described as follows. It has a finite control unit, a head with a lookahead window attached to a list, and it works in certain cycles. In a cycle, it moves the head from left to right along the word on the list; according to its instructions, it can at some point once rewrite the contents of its lookahead by a shorter string and (possibly) move to the right-hand side again. At a certain place, according to its instructions it halts or 'restarts' – i.e. resets the control unit to the initial state and places the head on the left end of the shortened word. The computation halts in an accepting or a rejecting state.

Analysis by reduction can be modelled in a straightforward way by *RRW*-automata, which are the *RRWW*-automata using only the input alphabet symbols during their rewriting. *RRW*-automata have the so called 'error preserving property', which means: if a word (sentence) is not correct then after an arbitrary number of cycles the reduced word (sentence) is also not correct. The *RRWW*-automata which can use non-input symbols do not ensure the error preserving property automatically but, on the other hand, they are able to recognize all *CFL*.

Among the types of reducing, *deleting* is significant – it resembles the contextual grammars (see [11], [3]). Contextual grammars work in a dual way – they insert contexts into a string. The reducing by deleting only, which keeps the error preserving property, can be very useful for creating a grammar-checker. It allows to localize the syntactic inconsistencies in a very transparent way. Let us consider an erroneous variant of the sample sentence:

'Martin, Peter and Jane works very slowly.'

We can get the following error core by using stepwise error-preserving reductions by deleting only :

'Peter and Jane works.'

We consider several classes of restarting automata here, the most general is that of *RRWW*-automata. For such automata, the property of *(right) monotonicity of computations* has been introduced in [5]. It leads to (at least) three natural definitions of monotonicity of automata; we call them (strong) monotonicity, *a*-monotonicity and *g*-monotonicity. Only the first type was studied in [5]. Here we consider the other two as well; we provide a taxonomy of the relevant language classes, and answer the (un)decidability questions concerning these properties.

The new types of monotonicity are more suitable for adequate grammar-checking (they allow better separation of syntactic inconsistencies), the g-monotonicity is the most suitable monotonicity to model the 'full' analysis by reduction inside the context-free languages. On the other hand the original 'strong' monotonicity is close to the paradigm of a 'smallest (cheapest) possible' reduction analysis to a given language.

Section 2 defines *RRWW*-automata and its subclasses (*R*-, *RR*-, *RW*-, *RRW*-, *RWW*-automata) as well as the mentioned three types of monotonicity properties. Section 3 summarizes relations to the context-free languages (restarting automata recognize a subclass of context-sensitive languages). Section 4 exhibits the 'decidability border' for the monotonicity properties, providing decidability as well as undecidability results. Section 5 (almost completely) compares the considered models w.r.t. language recognition power. Some additional remarks can be found in Sect. 6.

2 Definitions

An *RRWW-automaton* $M = (Q, \Sigma, \Gamma, k, I, q_0, Q_A, Q_R)$ is a device with a finite state control unit, with the set of states Q, and one head moving on a finite linear (doubly linked) list of items (cells). The first item always contains a special symbol ¢, the last one another special symbol \$, and each other item contains a symbol from the union of two disjoint finite alphabets Σ and Γ (not containing ¢, \$). Σ is called *the input alphabet*, Γ *the working alphabet.* The head has a lookahead 'window' of length k ($k \geq 0$) – besides the current item, M also scans the next k right neighbour items (or simply the end of the word when the distance to \$ is less than k).

In the *restarting configuration* on an *word* $w \in (\Sigma \cup \Gamma)^*$, the word ¢$w$\$ is stored in the items of the list, the control unit is in the fixed, *initial state* $q_0 \in Q$, and the head is attached to that item which contains the left sentinel (scanning ¢, looking also at the first k symbols of the word w). A computation of M starts in an *initial configuration* which is a restarting configuration on *an input word* ($w \in \Sigma^*$). We suppose that the set of states Q is divided into two classes – the set of *nonhalting states* (there is at least one instruction which is applicable when the unit is in such a state) and the set of *halting states* (any computation finishes by entering such a state); the set of halting states is further divided into the set of *accepting states* Q_A and the set of *rejecting states* Q_R.

The *computation* of M is controlled by a finite set of *instructions* I. Instructions are of the following three types ($q, q' \in Q, a \in \Sigma \cup \Gamma \cup \{¢, \$\}$, $u, v \in (\Sigma \cup \Gamma)^* \cup (\Sigma \cup \Gamma)^* \cdot \{\$\}$):

(1) $(q, au) \to (q', MVR)$
(2) $(q, au) \to (q', REWRITE(v))$
(3) $(q, au) \to RESTART$

The left-hand side of an instruction determines when it is applicable – q means the current state (of the control unit), a the symbol being scanned by the head, and u means the contents of the lookahead window (u being a string of length k or less if it ends with \$). The right-hand side describes the activity to be performed.

In case (1), M changes the current state to q' and moves the head to the right neighbour item of the item containing a.

In case (2), the activity consists of deleting (removing) some items (at least one) of the just scanned part of the list (containing au), and of rewriting some (possibly none) of the nondeleted scanned items (in other words au is replaced with v, where v must be shorter than au). After that, the head of M is moved right to the item containing the first symbol after the lookahead and the current state of M is changed to q'. There are two exceptions: if au ends by \$ then v also ends by \$ (the right sentinel cannot be deleted or rewritten) and after the rewriting the head is moved to the item containing \$; similarly the left sentinel ¢ cannot be deleted or rewritten.

In case (3), *RESTART* means entering the initial state and placing the head on the first item of the list (containing ¢).

Any computation of an *RRWW*-automaton M is naturally divided into certain phases. A phase called *cycle* starts in an restarting configuration, the head moves right along the input list (with a bounded lookahead) until is resumed in an new restarting configuration. We demand that the automaton makes exactly one *REWRITE*-instruction in each cycle – i.e. new phase starts on a shortened word. A phase of a computation called *tail* starts in an restarting configuration, the head moves right along the input list (with a bounded lookahead) until one of the halting states is reached. M can also once rewrite during the tail.

It immediately implies that any computation of any *RRWW*-automaton is finite (finishing in a halting state).

In general, an *RRWW*-automaton is *nondeterministic*, i.e. there can be two or more instructions with the same left-hand side (q, au). If it is not the case, the automaton is *deterministic*.

An input *word* w *is accepted by* M if there is a computation which starts in the initial configuration with $w \in \Sigma^*$ (bounded by sentinels ¢,\$) on the list and finishes in an *accepting configuration* where the control unit is in one of the accepting states. $L(M)$ denotes the language consisting of all words accepted by M; we say that M *recognizes the language* $L(M)$.

By *RWW*-automata we mean *RRWW*-automata which do restart immediately after any *REWRITE*-instruction.

By *RRW*-automata we mean *RRWW*-automata with empty working alphabet. *RRW*-automata use only the input symbols in the rewriting, i.e. in all instructions of the form (2) above, the string v contains symbols from the input alphabet Σ only).

By *RR*-automata we mean *RRW*-automata which use deleting without rewriting (i.e. in all instructions of the form (2) above, the string v can always be obtained by deleting some symbols from au).

By *R*-automata we mean *RR*-automata which do restart immediately after any *REWRITE*-instruction.

The notation $u \Rightarrow_M v$ means that there exists a cycle of M starting in the restarting configuration with the word u and finishing in the restarting configuration with the word v; the relation $\Rightarrow_M^*$ is the reflexive and transitive closure of $\Rightarrow_M$.

We often (implicitly) use the next obvious proposition:

Proposition 1 (The error preserving property). *Let $M = (Q, \Sigma, \Gamma, k, I, q_0, Q_A, Q_R)$ be an arbitrary RRWW-automaton, u, v arbitrary input words from Σ^*. If $u \Rightarrow_M^* v$ and $u \notin L(M)$, then $v \notin L(M)$.*

Now we introduce the monotonicity property of computations of *RRWW*-automata. Let $Dist(u \Rightarrow_M v)$, for an arbitrary cycle $u \Rightarrow_M v$, denote the distance of the last item in the lookahead window at the place of rewriting (one rewriting is obligatory in an arbitrary cycle) from the right sentinel ($) in the current list. We say that a computation C of an *RRWW*-automaton M is *monotonic* if for the sequence of its cycles $u_1 \Rightarrow_M u_2 \Rightarrow_M \cdots \Rightarrow_M u_n$ the sequence $Dist(u_1 \Rightarrow_M u_2)$, $Dist(u_2 \Rightarrow_M u_3)$, $\ldots$, $Dist(u_{n-1} \Rightarrow_M u_n)$ is monotonic, i.e. not increasing. Notice, that the tails are not considered for the monotonicity.

We will distinguish between three types of monotonicity:

- By a *monotonic RRWW-automaton* we mean an *RRWW*-automaton where all its computations are monotonic.
- By an *accepting-monotonic (a-monotonic) RRWW-automaton* we mean an *RRWW*-automaton where all the accepting computations are monotonic.
- By a *general-monotonic (g-monotonic) RRWW-automaton* we mean an *RRWW*-automaton where for an arbitrary accepting computation on some word w there is an monotonic accepting computation on w.

For brevity, prefix *det-* denotes the deterministic versions of *RRWW*-automata similarly *mon-* the monotonic, *a-mon-* the *a*-monotonic, and *g-mon-* the *g*-monotonic versions. $\mathcal{L}(\mathcal{A})$, where $\mathcal{A}$ is some class of automata, denotes the class of languages recognizable by automata from $\mathcal{A}$. E.g. the class of languages recognizable by deterministic monotonic *R*-automata is denoted by $\mathcal{L}(det\text{-}mon\text{-}R)$.

For some results concerning *RRW*-automata we need the notion of *nonmonotonicity-resultant word* for an *RRW*-automaton M; such a word w arises as a result of two consecutive cycles by M which violate monotonicity (such word exists iff M is nonmonotonic; it can be accepted by M iff M is not *a*-monotonic).

We will use the following proposition.

Proposition 2. *Given an RRW-automaton M, there exists a (deterministic) finite state automaton A_M recognizing the set of all nonmonotonicity-resultant words for M.*

The respective nondeterministic finite state automaton A'_M, while scanning the input word, guesses two possible places of rewriting in two preceding cycles violating the monotonicity property, and checks that M can restart in both cycles. A_M is a deterministic version of A'_M.

It will be useful to note the following 'pigeonhole' fact.

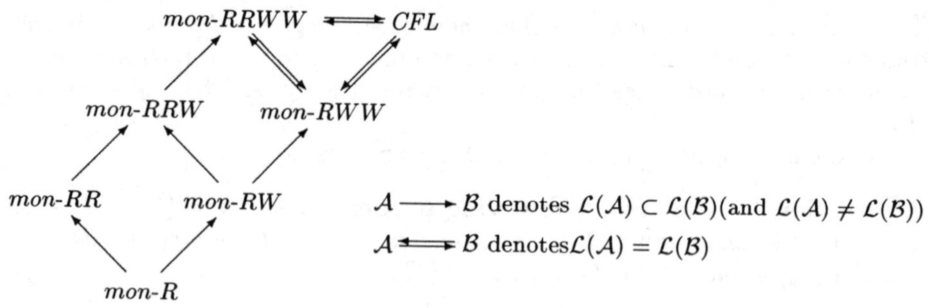

Fig. 1. Relations between classes of languages recognized by monotonic versions of *RRWW*-automata from [6]. If there is no directed path between two classes, then these classes are incomparable.

Lemma 3. *Let* $M = (Q, \Sigma, \Gamma, k, I, q_0, Q_A, Q_R)$ *be an arbitrary RRWW-automaton. There is a constant p such that for an arbitrary cycle or tail starting on a word* $w_1 v w_2$ *(for some words* $w_1, v, w_2 \in (\Sigma \cup \Gamma)^*$*), where* $|v| \geq p$*, the subword* v *can be written* $v_1 auv_2 auv_3$*, (for some words* $v_1, u, v_2, v_3 \in (\Sigma \cup \Gamma)^*$ *and symbol* $a \in \Sigma \cup \Gamma$*),* $|u| = k$ *and* $|auv_2| \leq p$ *where both occurrences of a are entered in the same state by M during the given cycle or tail (including the possibility that both are not entered at all) and in the cycle or tail nothing in* auv_2 *is deleted or rewritten.*

We will use the fact that, for any $i \geq 0$, the given cycle can be naturally extended for the 'pumped' word $w_1 v_1 (auv_2)^i auv_3 w_2$ (including also the case of removing – $i = 0$).

3 Monotonic Restarting Automata and *CFL*

The relations between *CFL* and several classes of *RRWW*-automata were already studied in papers [5, 6]. In [7], there were shown two characterizations of the class of deterministic context-free languages (*DCFL*) by deterministic monotonic *RW*-automata, namely *DCFL* = $\mathcal{L}$(*det-mon-R*) = $\mathcal{L}$(*det-mon-RW*). Figure 1 shows all the relations proved in [6] where *mon-* versions of *RRWW*-automata were studied. Slightly generalizing Theorem 4 from [5], we can get the next lemma, and deduce the next theorem:

Lemma 4. *Let M be an arbitrary RRWW-automaton. Then we can construct a pushdown automaton (PDA) P which accepts exactly the words which can be accepted by M by monotonic computations. Moreover, if M is deterministic then P is deterministic as well.*

Theorem 5. *a) For any* $X \in \{RWW, RRWW\}$*:*

$$\mathcal{L}(mon\text{-}X) = \mathcal{L}(a\text{-}mon\text{-}X) = \mathcal{L}(g\text{-}mon\text{-}X) = CFL.$$

b) For any $X \in \{R, RR, RW, RRW, RWW, RRWW\}$*:*

$$\mathcal{L}(det\text{-}mon\text{-}X) = \mathcal{L}(det\text{-}a\text{-}mon\text{-}X) = \mathcal{L}(det\text{-}g\text{-}mon\text{-}X) = DCFL$$

4 Decidability Questions for Monotonicity Properties

Decidability of the monotonicity property for *RW*-automata was shown in [7]; in fact, the result can be strengthened for *RRWW*-automata:

Theorem 6. *For RRWW-automata, (the property of) monotonicity is decidable.*

A detailed proof appears in [6].

Regarding *a*-monotonicity, the question for *RRW*-automata is still decidable (but by a more complicated construction sketched in the proof below); for *RWW*-automata (and hence also *RRWW*-automata) it becomes undecidable.

Theorem 7. *For RRW-automata, a-monotonicity is decidable.*

Proof. Let M be a given *RRW*-automaton. M is not a-monotonic iff M can accept some word by a nonmonotonic computation; but that means that it can accept some nonmonotonicity-resultant word by a monotonic computation.

Combining *PDAP* from Lemma 4 and A_M from Proposition 2, we can construct a *PDAP'* which accepts just the nonmonotonicity-resultant words accepted by M by monotonic computations. It suffices to check whether P' recognizes the empty language. □

Theorem 8. *For RWW-automata, a-monotonicity is undecidable.*

Proof. We use the well known undecidable problem: given two context-free grammars G_1, G_2, decide whether $L(G_1) \cap L(G_2) = \emptyset$. For technical reasons, we can only consider grammars with the terminal alphabet $\{a, b\}$ and with rules of the type $X \to \alpha$ where $length(\alpha) = 2$ (of course, any generated word has length 2 at least).

Observe that for any such G, an 'obvious' *RWW*-automaton recognizing $L(G)$ can be constructed. $\{a, b\}$ is its input alphabet, $V(G)$ (the set of nonterminals) is its working alphabet, it has just one nonhalting state, the lookahead window of length 1, and it performs (nondeterministically) the bottom-up analysis – it moves right and whenever 'sees' the right-hand side α of a rule $X \to \alpha$, it can replace it by X; it accepts just when the starting nonterminal is left.

Using the described idea, we can, given G_1, G_2, construct an *RWW*-automaton M_1 for the language $\{ucv \mid u \in L(G_1), v \in L(G_2)\}$ (it just performs the 'bottom-up analysis' according to G_1 before c and according to G_2 after c – merging these two analyses arbitrarily. M_1 is obviously *not* a-monotonic whenever there are $u \in L(G_1), v \in L(G_2)$.

By an obvious modification (reversing right-hand sides in G_1) we can get M_2 recognizing $\{ucv \mid u \in (L(G_1))^R, v \in L(G_2)\}$ (^{R} denotes the reversal operation), which is more suitable for our aims.

Now we show how we can, given G_1, G_2, construct an *RRW*-automaton M with the input alphabet $\{\#, c\}$, the working alphabet $\{a, b\} \cup V(G_1) \cup V(G_2)$ s.t. if $L(G_1) \cap L(G_2) = \emptyset$ then $L(M) = \emptyset$ (and hence M is (trivially) a-monotonic) and if $L(G_1) \cap L(G_2) \neq \emptyset$ then M accepts at least one word by a nonmonotonic computation (and hence is not a-monotonic).

M expects the input $\#^i c \#^j$ for some i, j. It is intended to 'generate' a word $u^R cu$ ($u \in \{a,b\}^*$) and then to behave like M_2 (in fact, the phases can be merged arbitrarily). Besides the instructions taken from M_2, its additional instructions enable to replace the string $\#\#c\#\#$ by xcx, where $x \in \{a,b\}$ (a generating step; M will have lookahead window of length 4), and to replace $\#\#x$ ($x\#\#$) by $x\#$ ($\#x$) – a shifting left (right) step.

If there is $u \in L(G_1) \cap L(G_2)$ then there obviously is an appropriate i s.t. M accepts $\#^i c \#^i$ by a nonmonotonic computation; if $L(G_1) \cap L(G_2) = \emptyset$ then M can not accept any word. □

From the described construction we can immediately conclude:

Corollary 9. *Given an RWW-automaton M, it is undecidable whether or not $L(M) = \emptyset$.*

Finally we show that the property of g-monotonicity is undecidable even for R-automata (our simplest model).

Theorem 10. *For R-automata, g-monotonicity is undecidable.*

Proof. We use the well known undecidable Post correspondence problem (PCP) for reduction. Let an instance I of PCP be a sequence of words $u_1, u_2, \ldots, u_n$, $v_1, v_2, \ldots, v_n \in \{0,1\}^*$; the question is whether I has a solution, i.e. whether there are indices $i_1, i_2, \ldots, i_r$ for some $r > 0$ s.t. $u_{i_1} u_{i_2} \ldots u_{i_r} = v_{i_1} v_{i_2} \ldots v_{i_r}$.

We show that, for any instance I, an R-automaton M can be constructed s.t. M is g-monotonic iff I has no solution.

First let us say that the pair (u,v) of words in $\{0,1,a\}^*$ is a *candidate* iff there are $i_1, i_2, \ldots, i_r$ for some $r > 0$ s.t. $u = (u_{i_1} a u_{i_2} a \ldots u_{i_{r-1}} a u_{i_r})^R$ and $v = v_{i_1} a v_{i_2} a \ldots v_{i_{r-1}} a v_{i_r}$. Define a homomorphism $h : \{0,1,a\}^* \to \{0,1\}^*$ by $h(0) = 0$, $h(1) = 1$, $h(a) = \lambda$, where λ denotes the empty word. Observe that I has a solution iff there is a pair (u,v) which is a candidate and $h(u^R) = h(v)$.

Let us define the following languages over the alphabet $\{0,1,a,b,c\}$; in their definitions we automatically assume $u, v \in \{0,1,a\}^*$ and $x \in \{c, \lambda\}$. Let $L_1 = \{ubvx \mid h(u^R) \neq h(v)\} \cup \{ubbvx \mid (u,v) \text{ is not a candidate}\}$. L_1 is obviously recognized by a (deterministic) monotonic R-automaton M_1. It repeatedly 'cuts' around b or bb; when finding the appropriate mismatch, it verifies that there is no b in the rest of the word and at most one c at the end, and accepts.

Now define $L_2 = L_1 \cup \{ubbbvx \mid h(u^R) \neq h(v) \text{ or } (u,v) \text{ is not a candidate}\}$. Note that $L_2 = L_1 \cup \{ubbbvx \mid u,v \text{ arbitrary}\}$ iff I has no solution. L_2 is recognized by an 'obvious' (nondeterministic) monotonic R-automaton M_2 – it behaves like M_1 but when finding three b's 'in the middle', it removes one or two of them (and restarts).

We add a further possibility to M_2, by which the desired M arises: when finding 'the middle' bbb, it can decide to move to the right end, and in case of finding c there, it removes c with one preceding symbol and restarts. In this way, we added nonmonotonic accepting computations. In case that I has no solution,

M still recognizes L_2 and is g-monotonic. On the other hand, if I has a solution then there obviously are words outside L_2 (e.g. words of the form $ubbbvc$, where $h(u^R) = h(v)$ and (u, v) is a candidate) which are accepted by M – but only using nonmonotonic computations (starting by deleting c and the last symbol from v); i.e. M is not g-monotonic in this case. □

The described construction immediately implies:

Corollary 11. *Given two R-automata M_1, M_2, it is undecidable whether or not $L(M_1) \subseteq L(M_2)$ as well as whether or not $L(M_1) = L(M_2)$.*

Since $DCFL = \mathcal{L}(det\text{-}mon\text{-}R) \subseteq \mathcal{L}(R)$ (cf. Theorem 5 b)), the undecidability of the inclusion problem follows already from its undecidability for $DCFL$; on the other hand, the equivalence problem is decidable for $DCFL$ ([9]).

5 A Taxonomy of Monotonic Restarting Automata

Clearly, an arbitrary $RRWW$-automaton can be simulated by some linear bounded automaton. Thus, all the languages recognizable by $RRWW$-automata are context-sensitive. Subclasses of $RRWW$-automata yield a hierarchy of corresponding classes of languages. In this section we will prove all the relations between classes of languages recognized by different types of rewriting automata with a restart operation which are depicted in Fig. 2.

Each inclusion ($\subseteq$) corresponding to an arrow whose starting point is lower than the end point follows trivially from definitions. Therefore the 'real' task is to show that the inclusions are *proper* ($\subset$) – by exhibiting the appropriate sample languages – or that they are equalities, in fact; in addition, we choose the sample languages so that any two classes which are not connected by a directed path in the figure are clearly incomparable. Now we describe the chosen sample languages:

$L_1 = \{f, ee\}.\{c^n d^n \mid n \geq 0\} \cup \{g, ee\}.\{c^n d^m \mid m \geq 2n \geq 0\}$
$L_2 = \{c^n d^n \mid n \geq 0\} \cup \{c^n d^m \mid m > 2n \geq 0\}$
$L_3 = \{(ab)^{2^n - 2m}(abb)^m \mid m, n \geq 0,\ 2m < 2^n\}$
$\quad \cup \{(abb)^{2^n - m}(ab)^m \mid m, n \geq 0,\ m < 2^n\}$
$L_4 = \{a^{n_1+n_2} b a^{n_2+n_3} c a^{n_3} d a^{n_1} \mid n_1, n_2, n_3 \geq 0\}$
$L_5 = \{ww^R \mid w \in (cd + dc)^*\} \cup \{wddw^R \mid w \in (cd + dc)^*\}$
$L_6 = \{a^n b^n c \mid n \geq 0\} \cup \{a^n b^{2n} d \mid n \geq 0\}$

The facts which are needed to be proved for sample languages are summarized in the next table; e.g. the second row denotes that $L_2 \in \mathcal{L}(PDA) - \mathcal{L}(RRW)$, i.e. $L_2 \in CFL - \mathcal{L}(RRW)$, which is proved in [6].

Language	Recognized by	Not recognized by	Proof
L_1	*mon-RW*	*RR*	[6]
L_2	*PDA*	*RRW*	[6]
L_3	*R*	*PDA*	[7]
L_4	*g-mon-R*	*a-mon-RRW*	Lemma 12
L_5	*a-mon-R*	*mon-RW*	Lemma 13
L_6	*mon-RR*	*RW*	[6]

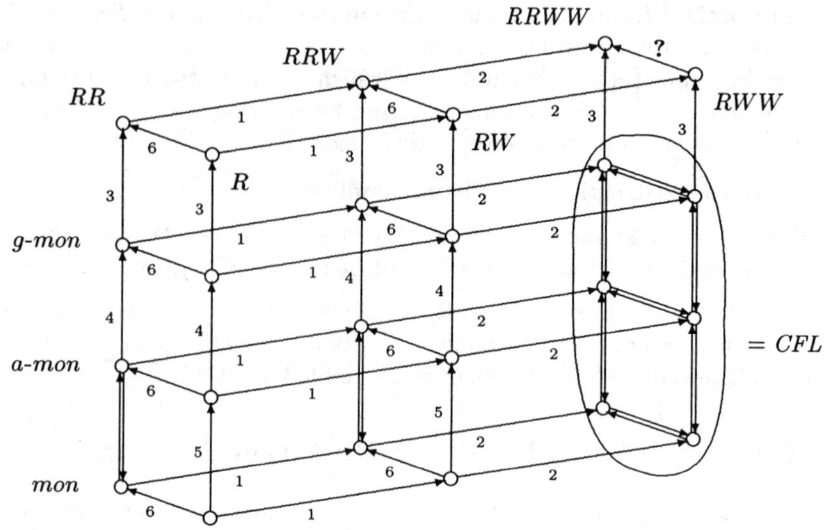

Fig. 2. The relations between classes of languages recognized by rewriting automata with a restart operation with different types of monotonicity. $\mathcal{A} \xrightarrow{x} \mathcal{B}$ denotes that $\mathcal{L}(\mathcal{A}) \subset \mathcal{L}(\mathcal{B})$ and L_x is a sample language from $\mathcal{L}(\mathcal{B}) - \mathcal{L}(\mathcal{A})$, in the case $x = ?$ the relation is an open problem. $\mathcal{A} \Longleftrightarrow \mathcal{B}$ denotes that $\mathcal{L}(\mathcal{A}) = \mathcal{L}(\mathcal{B})$. Lower three layers of the figure correspond to monotonic, a-monotonic and g-monotonic versions of the corresponding classes of automata from the top layer. E.g. the lowest arrow with index 1 means that $\mathcal{L}(mon\text{-}R) \subset \mathcal{L}(mon\text{-}RW)$ and $L_1 \in \mathcal{L}(mon\text{-}RW) - \mathcal{L}(mon\text{-}R)$. If there is no oriented path between any two depicted classes, then these classes are incomparable.

The seven equalities on the right of the figure follow from Theorem 5 a). The remaining two follow from Lemma 14.

As depicted in the figure, one problem remains open.

We end this section by sketchy proofs of the technical lemmas referred above.

Lemma 12. $L_4 \in \mathcal{L}(g\text{-}mon\text{-}R) - \mathcal{L}(a\text{-}mon\text{-}RRW)$

Proof. A *g-mon-R*-automaton recognizing L_4 is almost obvious. (It can 'cut' around b for some time, then around c, and around bcd in the end).

Further we will show that L_4 cannot be recognized by any *a-mon-RRW*-automaton. Let us suppose that L_4 is recognized by an *a-mon-RRW*-automaton M. Because of possible pumping (according Lemma 3), sufficiently long words $w = a^{n_1+n_2}ba^{n_2+n_3}ca^{n_3}da^{n_1}$ from L_4 cannot be accepted by tails. In the case of $n_2 = 0$ and n_1,n_3 sufficiently large, an accepting computation of M on w must start by a cycle with rewriting near c or near the d only (because the word after the first cycle of an accepting computation must be from L_4). Because of possible pumpings (according Lemma 3) in front of b and between b and c in w, it is possible also for large n_2 to rewrite near c or the d and restart in a new restarting configuration. Simultaneously, the given words cannot be recognized neither only by changes in tail (near c or near d) of such word, nor only by changes in front (near the b); the monotonic computation must start by rewriting near the b. It means that there exists an accepting computation by M which starts by rewriting in tail and continues by changes in front of a word – a contradiction. □

Lemma 13. $L_5 \in \mathcal{L}(a\text{-}mon\text{-}R) - \mathcal{L}(mon\text{-}RW)$

Proof. $L_5 = L_{51} \cup L_{52}$, where $L_{51} = \{ww^R \mid w \in (cd+dc)^*\}$ and $L_{52} = \{wddw^R \mid w \in (cd+dc)^*\}$. An *a-mon-R*-automaton M recognizing L_5 can be sketched as follows. On an input word from L_{52} it has the only accepting computation consisting of stepwise deleting around the 'center' dd, which is monotonic. On an input word from L_{51}, M has the only possible accepting computation starting by guessing (and marking by dd) the position of the center of the word and continuing monotonicly on the resulting word from L_{52}.

Now suppose that some *mon-RW*-automaton M with the size of lookahead k recognizes L_5. Sufficiently long words $w = (cd)^n(dc)^n$ cannot be accepted by tails. Otherwise we can get a contradiction by pumping techniques. After the first cycle $w \Rightarrow_M w_1$ of an accepting computation on w, M gets some word $w_1 \neq w, w_1 \in L_{51} \cup L_{52}$ and in the cycle M restarted without scanning the right sentinel. If $w_1 \in L_{51}$ then $wddw_1^R \Rightarrow_M w_1ddw_1^R$ is possible, $wddw_1^R \notin L_5$ and $w_1ddw_1^R \in L_5$ – a contradiction to the error preserving property (Proposition 1). If $w_1 \in L_{52}$ then M has an accepting computation for the word $w(cd)^k dd(dc)^k w^R$ which can start by rewriting near its center only $w(cd)^k dd(dc)^k w^R \Rightarrow_M wudduu^R w^R$, for some $u \in (cd+dc)^*$. But even after such cycle it can make a cycle $wuddu^R w^R \Rightarrow_M w_1uddu^R w^R$ which causes nonmonotonicity – a contradiction.

Hence, an arbitrary *RW*-automaton M recognizing L_5 is nonmonotonic. □

Lemma 14. $\mathcal{L}(a\text{-}mon\text{-}RR) = \mathcal{L}(mon\text{-}RR)$
$\mathcal{L}(a\text{-}mon\text{-}RRW) = \mathcal{L}(mon\text{-}RRW)$

Proof. Apparently, $\mathcal{L}(mon\text{-}X) \subseteq \mathcal{L}(a\text{-}mon\text{-}X)$, for $X \in \{RR, RRW\}$.

To show the opposite inclusions, we sketch a construction of a *mon-RRW*-automaton M' equivalent to a given *a-mon-RRW*-automaton M (i.e. $L(M') = L(M)$). M' simulates cycles by M and simultaneously checks whether the word after the current cycle will be a nonmonotonicity-resultant word for M (using finite state automaton A_M from Proposition 2). If the resulting word would be a nonmonotonicity-resultant word, M' rejects it (this cannot violate monotonicity because tails do not influent monotonicity). Otherwise M' restarts or halts in the same way as M. Actually, M' rejects nonmonotonicity-resultant words even if they arise by a monotonic computation, but as M is *a*-monotonic, such words are rejected by M later.

Moreover if M is an *RR*-automaton then M' is also an *RR*-automaton. □

6 Additional Remarks

Some subclasses of *RRWW*-automata can be considered as strictly length-reducing rewriting systems. G. Sénizergues gave in [8] a characterization of *DCFL* by basic, confluent, strictly length-reducing, finite, controlled rewriting systems. The conditions to be a basic controlled rewriting system in some sense resembles monotonicity.

It would be also worth to compare *RRWW*-automata with shrinking pushdown automata used in [1] for recognition of languages generated by the so called growing context-sensitive grammars. It is easy to see that even *RWW*-automata recognize all languages generated by such grammars.

References

1. Buntrock, G., Otto, F.: Growing Context-Sensitive Languages and Church-Rosser Languages. In: STACS'95, Lecture Notes in Computer Science, Vol. 900. Springer-Verlag, Berlin Heidelberg New York (1995) 313–324
2. Dassow, J., Păun, Gh.: Regulated Rewriting in Formal Language Theory. Springer-Verlag, Berlin Heidelberg New York (1989)
3. Ehrenfeucht, A., Păun, Gh., Rozenberg, G.: Contextual Grammars and Formal Languages. In: Rozenberg, G., Salomaa, A. (eds.): Handbook of Formal Languages, Vol. 2: Linear Modeling: Background and Application. Springer-Verlag, Berlin Heidelberg New York (1997) 237–293
4. Kunze, J.: Abhängigkeitsgrammatik. Studia Grammatica XII. Berlin (1975)
5. Mráz, F., Plátek, M., Jančar, P., Vogel, J.: Restarting Automata with Rewriting. In: Plášil, F., Jeffery, K.J. (eds.): SOFSEM'97: Theory and Practice of Informatics. Lecture Notes in Computer Science, Vol. 1338. Springer-Verlag, Berlin Heidelberg New York (1997) 505–512
6. Jančar, P., Mráz, F., Plátek, M., Vogel, J.: On Monotonicity for Restarting Automata. Accepted to workshop Mathematical Linguistics on MFCS'98, Brno (1998)
7. Jančar, P., Mráz, F., Plátek, M., Vogel, J.: On Restarting Automata with Rewriting. In: Paun, Gh., Salomaa, A. (eds.): New Trends in Formal Languages (Control, Cooperation and Combinatorics). Lecture Notes in Computer Science, Vol. 1218. Springer-Verlag, Berlin Heidelberg New York (1997) 119–136
8. Sénizergues, G.: A Characterisation of Deterministic Context-Free Languages by Means of Right-Congruences. Theoretical Computer Science **70** (1990) 671–681
9. Sénizergues, G.: The Equivalence Problem for Deterministic Pushdown Automata is Decidable. In: Degano, P., Gorrieri, R., Marchetti-Spaccamela, A. (eds.): Proc. ICALP'97. Lecture Notes in Computer Science, Vol. 1256. Springer-Verlag, Berlin Heidelberg New York (1997) 671–681
10. Sgall, P., Panevová, J.: Dependency Syntax – a Challenge. Theoretical Linguistics, Vol.15, No.1/2. Walter de Gruyter, Berlin New York (1988/89) 73–86
11. Marcus, S.: Contextual Grammars and Natural Languages. In: Rozenberg, G., Salomaa, A. (eds.): Handbook of Formal Languages, Vol. 2: Linear Modeling: Background and Application. Springer-Verlag, Berlin Heidelberg New York (1997) 215–235

A Kleene Iteration for Parallelism[1]

Kamal Lodaya
Institute of Mathematical Sciences
CIT Campus
Chennai 600 113 – India.
kamal@imsc.ernet.in

Pascal Weil
LaBRI
Université Bordeaux 1 & CNRS
351 cours de la Libération
33405 Talence Cedex – France.
Pascal.Weil@labri.u-bordeaux.fr

Abstract. This paper extends automata-theoretic techniques to unbounded parallel behaviour, as seen for instance in Petri nets. Languages are defined to be sets of (labelled) series-parallel posets — or, equivalently, sets of terms in an algebra with two product operations: sequential and parallel. In an earlier paper, we restricted ourselves to languages of posets having *bounded width* and introduced a notion of *branching* automaton. In this paper, we drop the restriction to bounded width. We define *rational expressions*, a natural generalization of the usual ones over words, and prove a Kleene theorem connecting them to *regular* languages (accepted by finite branching automata). We also show that *recognizable* languages (inverse images by a morphism into a finite algebra) are strictly weaker.

Introduction

The success of automata as a computational model has led to their being generalized in many different ways. Early on, Thatcher and Wright followed an idea of Büchi (as cited in [16]) and constructed automata operating on terms in free algebras, generalizing from strings, which are terms of the free monoid. This led to the development of tree automata and an alternate approach to context-free languages [8].

More recently, Courcelle applied the notion of recognizability to graphs [4]. He showed that for languages of graphs, definability in monadic second-order (MSO) logic implies recognizability. For special classes of graph languages such as context-free graphs, the two notions coincide [5]. Recognizability is defined algebraically and not via automata.

We go back to a very early generalization of automata, that of Petri nets [13]. Although nets are well-researched, the focus has been on examining causality, conflict and concurrency in their behaviour (see the book [15], for example.) There have been a few attempts to study whether results such as the Kleene or Myhill-Nerode theorems extend to Petri nets. Garg and Ragunath [7] obtained a Kleene theorem using *concurrent* rational expressions for all Petri net languages. Grabowski [10] also has a Kleene theorem using languages of (labelled) posets, which provide more information about concurrency. Boudol described "rational parallel place machines" and provided translations into process algebra [2].

[1] Part of this work was done while the second author was visiting the Institute of Mathematical Sciences, in Chennai.

Our idea is to combine the algebraic notion of recognizability with that of regularity. As in a previous paper [11], we work with *sp-languages* (languages of series-parallel posets). Interaction between rationality, recognizability and regularity was investigated for languages of *traces* (see [6] for a recent survey, especially Ochmański's and Zielonka's theorems.) In [11], we obtained a Myhill-Nerode and a Kleene theorem for those languages which have a uniform bound on the "parallel width" of their terms.

Theorem [11] *A bounded width sp-language is series-rational iff recognizable iff regular.*

The *series-rational* languages over the alphabet A are defined by extending the usual rational expressions to include parallel product: every letter $a \in A$ is a series-rational expression; and if e_1 and e_2 are series-rational expressions, then so are $e_1 + e_2$, $e_1 \circ e_2$, $e_1 \| e_2$ and e_1^+. *Recognizability* means the *sp*-language is described by a morphism into a finite algebra. By *regularity*, we mean acceptance by a finite "branching" automaton, which has fork/join transitions in addition to the usual transitions on a letter of the alphabet. This is a restricted form of Petri net.

Bounded width is the key property in proving these theorems. In terms of nets, this translates to the technical notion of 1-safe behaviour.

Differently expressed, the syntax does not allow a "parallel iteration." For instance, the *sp*-language $\{a||bc, a||b(a||bc)c, a||b(a||b(a||bc)c)c, \dots\}$, which we will denote $(a||bc)\circ_\xi(a||b\xi c)^{*\xi}$, is regular but not bounded width and hence not series-rational. $(a||b\xi c)^{*\xi}$ is an example of a *rational iteration*, while $\circ_\xi$ is a *substitution.* These are borrowed from the "generalized" rational expressions of Thatcher and Wright [16]. In our syntax, the iterated variable is restricted to appear only within a parallel term (see Section 2 for details). A syntax like $\mu\xi.(a||bc + a||b\xi c)$ would be used in process algebra, but that also includes infinite behaviour, which we are not considering.

What happens to recognizability and regularity for unbounded width languages? By using techniques from Büchi [3], we establish one direction of a Myhill-Nerode theorem for the unrestricted languages.

Theorem 1 *Recognizable sp-languages are rational.*

The converse is not true. The *sp*-language $\{a||b, a||a||b||b, \dots\}$ (equal number of a's and b's), denoted $(a||b)\circ_\xi(a||b||\xi)^{*\xi}$, is rational but not recognizable.

We turn our attention to acceptance by branching automata. The results are more pleasing: we get both directions of a Kleene theorem.

Theorem 2 *An sp-language is rational iff it is regular.*

All three proofs (of Theorem 1 and the two directions of Theorem 2) are nontrivial. Together they verify a conjecture made in [11], that recognizable *sp*-languages are regular. We can also nicely round off our earlier theorem.

Theorem 3 *A bounded width sp-language is series-rational iff recognizable iff regular iff rational.*

1 *sp*-posets and *sp*-algebras

***sp*-posets.** Let A be an alphabet (a finite non-empty set). An *A-labelled poset* is a poset $(P, \leq)$ equipped with a labelling function $\lambda: P \to A$. This is a generalization of words, which are finite linearly ordered A-labelled sets. We are in fact considering isomorphism classes of labelled posets (also known as *pomsets* [14]), so unless otherwise specified, the underlying sets of distinct posets are always assumed to be pairwise disjoint. All our posets are finite and non-empty.

Let $\mathcal{P} = (P, \leq_P, \lambda_P)$ and $\mathcal{Q} = (Q, \leq_Q, \lambda_Q)$ be A-labelled posets. The *parallel product* $\mathcal{P}||\mathcal{Q}$ of these posets is $(P \cup Q, \leq_P \cup \leq_Q, \lambda_P \cup \lambda_Q)$, and their *sequential product* $\mathcal{P} \circ \mathcal{Q}$ is $(P \cup Q, \leq_P \cup \leq_Q \cup (P \times Q), \lambda_P \cup \lambda_Q)$. It is easily verified that both products are associative, and that the parallel product is commutative.

We say that an A-labelled poset is *series-parallel*, an *sp-poset* for short, if either it is empty, or it can be obtained from singleton A-labelled posets by using a finite number of times the operations of sequential and parallel product.

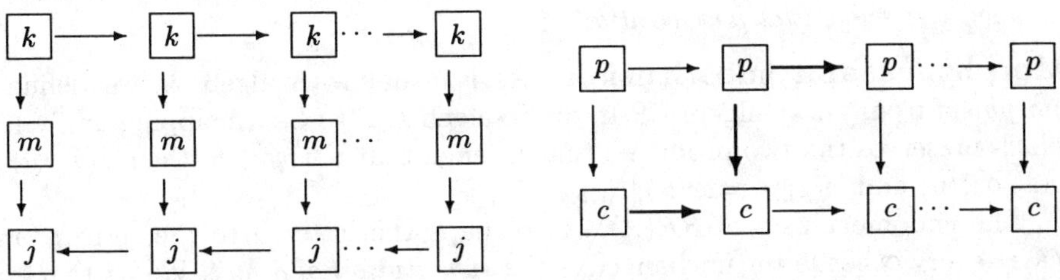

Fig. 1. Posets: series-parallel and not

Example 1.1 Figure 1 shows two posets. Let P_n be the left hand poset having n occurrences of k. Then $P_1 = \{k\}\circ\{m\}\circ\{j\}$ and $P_{n+1} = \{k\}\circ(\{m\}||P_n)\circ\{j\}$.

The right hand poset shows a producer-consumer system, a simple example of message-passing. One can show that this poset is not series-parallel. The trouble can be traced to the N-shaped subposet shown using thick lines. A poset is *N-free* if it does not contain N as a subposet. It is well known that an A-labelled poset $(P, \leq, \lambda)$ is an *sp*-poset if and only if $(P, \leq)$ is N-free [10, 17].

***sp*-algebras.** The notion of *sp*-poset is generalized in the following fashion. An *sp-algebra* is a set S equipped with two binary operations, denoted $\circ$ and $||$ and called respectively *sequential* and *parallel product*, such that $(S, \circ)$ is a semigroup (that is, the sequential product is associative), and such that $(S, ||)$ is a commutative semigroup. Note that no distributivity is assumed. The discussion in the previous section shows that the class of (non-empty) *sp*-posets labelled by the alphabet A, forms an *sp*-algebra.

It is clear from this definition that *sp*-algebras form a variety of algebras (of signature $(2, 2)$), so there exists a free *sp*-algebra over each set A, denoted $SP(A)$. This free algebra was characterized by Bloom and Ésik (see also [9]).

Proposition [1] *$SP(A)$ is isomorphic to the sp-algebra of non-empty A-labelled sp-posets.*

***sp*-terms.** We mildly abuse notation and call the elements of $SP(A)$ *sp-terms*. (We will never have occasion to refer to elements of the free (2, 2)-algebra, which would have been the traditional terms.) Thus $x \circ (y \circ z)$ and $(x \circ y) \circ z$ are the *same sp*-term, conventionally written xyz.

Let $x \in SP(A)$ be an *sp*-term. We say that x is a *sequential term* if it cannot be written as a parallel product $x = y \| z$ $(y, z \in SP(A))$, and that x is a *parallel term* if it cannot be written as a sequential product $x = y \circ z$ $(y, z \in SP(A))$. The only *sp*-terms which are both parallel and sequential are the letters.

More precisely, if $x \in SP(A)$ is an *sp*-term, then x admits a factorization of the form $x = x_1 \| \cdots \| x_n$, where $n \geq 1$ and each x_i is a sequential term, and this factorization is unique up to the order of the factors. It is called the *parallel factorization* of x. The *sp*-term x also admits a unique factorization of the form $x = x_1 \circ \cdots \circ x_n$, where $n \geq 1$ and each x_i is a parallel term. That factorization is called the *sequential factorization* of x.

Morphisms and substitution. As is usual with algebras, we define a *morphism* from an *sp*-algebra S to an *sp*-algebra T to be a mapping $\varphi: S \to T$ which preserves the two products, that is, such that if $x, y \in S$, then $\varphi(x \circ y) = \varphi(x) \circ \varphi(y)$ and $\varphi(x \| y) = \varphi(x) \| \varphi(y)$.

The endomorphism of $SP(A)$ which maps the letter a to the term t, and leaves every other letter unchanged is *the substitution of a by t*. We write $[t/a]x$ for the substitution of a by t in the term x.

Let $\xi \notin A$. We say that t is a *subterm* of x if there exists a $c \in SP(A \cup \{\xi\})$ with exactly one occurrence of ξ such that $x = [t/\xi]c$. c is called a *context* of t in x. t may have several contexts in x.

Example 1.2 In Example 1.1, $P_{n+1} = k(m \| P_n)j$. So P_n is a subterm of P_{n+1}, in the context $c = k(m \| \xi)j$. In other words, $P_{n+1} = [P_n/\xi]c$. The term k is a subterm of P_n in n different contexts. The term $(m \| (kmj))j$ is also a subterm of P_n but the term $(kmj)j$ is not.

We define the *width* of an *sp*-term as the morphism from $(SP(A), \circ, \|)$ into the "tropical" semiring $(\mathbf{N}, \max, +)$ which maps each letter to 1. Alternatively, it is the maximal cardinality of an anti-chain in the corresponding *sp*-poset.

2 Rational *sp*-languages

An *sp-language* is a subset of some free *sp*-algebra $SP(A)$. One of the results of this paper characterizes the "finite state" *sp*-languages in terms of *rational expressions*, as in the case of languages over words.

Let B be an alphabet containing A. (The elements of $B \setminus A$ will be used as *variables*.) We now define rational expressions over B inductively. The treatment follows Thatcher and Wright [16] (see also [8] and [3]).

(1) Every $b \in B$ is a rational expression;

(2) if e_1 and e_2 are rational expressions, then so are $e_1 + e_2$, $e_1 \circ e_2$, $e_1 \| e_2$ and e_1^+;

(3) if e_1 and e_2 are rational expressions, and if $\xi \in B$, then $e_1 \circ_\xi e_2$ is a rational expression;

(4) if e is a rational expression, and if $\xi \in B$, then $e^{*\xi}$ is a rational expression, *provided* every occurrence of ξ or ${}^{*\xi}$ within e is inside a parallel subexpression $e_1 \| \dots \| e_n$.

The last two operations (3) and (4) are called ***substitution*** and ***rational iteration*** (or ***ξ-exponentiation***), respectively. The proviso in (4) is a departure from [16], but a key element in preserving regularity (Section 4).

Now, we associate with each rational expression an *sp*-language in $SP(B)$:

(1) $L(b) = \{b\}$ for $b \in B$;

(2) $L(e_1 + e_2) = L(e_1) \cup L(e_2)$, $L(e_1 \circ e_2) = L(e_1) \circ L(e_2)$, $L(e_1 \| e_2) = L(e_1) \| L(e_2)$ and $L(e_1^+) = L(e_1)^+$ (Kleene iteration);

(3) $L(e_1 \circ_\xi e_2) = [L(e_1)/\xi] L(e_2)$, that is, the set of *sp*-terms obtained from the elements of $L(e_2)$ by replacing each occurrence of ξ by an element of $L(e_1)$ *non-uniformly* (this is an extension of the substitution notation from the previous section);

(4) $L(e^{*\xi}) = L(e)^{*\xi}$, where for any *sp*-language U, we let $U^{*\xi} = \bigcup_{i \geq 0} U_i^\xi$, with $U_0^\xi = \{\xi\}$ and $U_{i+1}^\xi = (U_0^\xi \cup \dots \cup U_i^\xi) \circ_\xi U$. This amounts to taking the least *sp*-language L containing ξ such that $L \supseteq [U/\xi]L$.

Finally, an *sp*-language over A is said to be ***rational*** if it is of the form $L(e)$ for some rational expression e over an alphabet B containing A. For instance, the *sp*-posets of Figure 1 form the rational language $(kmj) \circ_\xi (k(m \| \xi) j)^{*\xi}$.

Substitution and rational iteration play a role similar to concatenation and Kleene star. The operation $\circ_\xi$ is associative, and its iteration yields ${}^{*\xi}$. One can define the ***parallel iteration*** $L^\oplus$ of L as $L^\oplus = L \circ_\xi (\xi \| L)^{*\xi}$ for $\xi \notin A$. Clearly parallel iteration is a form of rational iteration, but the converse is not true: $SP(A) = A^+ \circ_\xi ((A^*(\xi \| \xi))^* A^*)^{*\xi}$ cannot be defined using parallel iteration.

3 Recognizable *sp*-languages

An *sp*-language $L \subseteq SP(A)$ is ***recognized*** by an *sp*-algebra S if there is a morphism $\varphi : SP(A) \to S$ such that $L = \varphi^{-1}\varphi(L)$. An *sp*-language L is ***recognizable*** if it is recognized by a ***finite*** *sp*-algebra.

Example 3.1 Let $a \in A$. Then $a^\oplus$ is recognized by the 2-element *sp*-algebra $\{x, 0\}$ given by $x \| x = x$ and $x \circ x = 0$, mapping letter a to x and every other letter in A to 0. $a^\oplus$ is recognizable but not bounded width.

The rational expressions we have defined serve to describe recognizable languages, which is the content of our next theorem. The proof is a nontrivial extension of the McNaughton-Yamada construction. We follow Büchi's ideas [3, Section 6.6, Exercise 4].

Theorem 1 *Recognizable sp-languages are rational.*

Proof. Let S be a finite *sp*-algebra recognizing L by the morphism $\varphi : SP(A) \to S$, with $L = \bigcup_{f \in \varphi(L)} \varphi^{-1}(f)$. The rational expressions we will construct will be over the alphabet $B = A \cup \{\xi_q \mid q \in S\}$, with extra variables for each element of the algebra. The morphism φ is extended to $SP(B)$ by setting $\varphi(\xi_q) = q$.

Let $L(Z, R, s)$, for Z a set of extra variables, $R \subseteq S$, $s \in S$, be the set of terms t in $SP(A \cup Z)$ such that $\varphi(t) = s$, and for every parallel subterm $t_1||t_2$ of t, $\varphi(t_1||t_2)$ is in R.

Clearly, $\varphi^{-1}(f) = L(\emptyset, S, f)$, so it suffices to construct rational expressions for $L(Z, R, s)$, which is done by induction on $|R|$.

For the base case, when $|R| = 0$, all terms in $L(Z, R, s)$ are sequential and we can use the usual McNaughton-Yamada construction to get a rational expression.

For the induction step, we have to define $L(Z, R \cup \{r\}, s)$, with $r \in S \setminus R$ in terms of expressions involving languages of the form $L(Y, R, q)$. The proof is a bit heavy on notation. We introduce some abbreviations.

We use $\widehat{Z}$ for $Z \cup \{\xi_r\}$ and $\widetilde{R}$ for $R \cup \{r\}$. This notation is extended to languages: $\widehat{L}_q$ stands for $L(\widehat{Z}, R, q)$, $\widetilde{L}_q$ for $L(Z, \widetilde{R}, q)$ and $\widetilde{\widehat{L}}_q$ for $L(\widehat{Z}, \widetilde{R}, q)$. We use L_q for $L(Z, R, q)$.

The following equation allows the construction of a rational expression from the rational expressions for the languages on the right hand side, which exist by the induction hypothesis. (This is just an extension of the expression used in the usual McNaughton-Yamada proof.) It suffices to verify the equation to complete the proof of the theorem.

$$\widetilde{L}_s = L_r \circ_{\xi_r} \Big(\bigcup_{p||q=r} \widehat{L}_p || \widehat{L}_q \Big)^{*\xi_r} \circ_{\xi_r} \widehat{L}_s. \tag{1}$$

Since there is only one variable under consideration, we write $\circ_r$ and ^{*r} instead of $\circ_{\xi_r}$ and $^{*\xi_r}$. We also abbreviate the cumbersome $\bigcup_{p||q=r} \widehat{L}_p || \widehat{L}_q$ by $\widehat{L}_{par}$.

We first show that the right hand side of (1) is included in the left. Let us first look at the language $\widetilde{\widehat{L}}_r = L(\widehat{Z}, \widetilde{R}, r)$. This is the set of terms t using the variable ξ_r such that $\varphi(t) = r$, all whose parallel subterms map to $R \cup \{r\}$. Clearly $\widetilde{\widehat{L}}_r \circ_r \widetilde{\widehat{L}}_r \subseteq \widetilde{\widehat{L}}_r$, and $\xi_r \in \widetilde{\widehat{L}}_r$. Hence $\widetilde{\widehat{L}}_r{}^{*r} = \widetilde{\widehat{L}}_r$.

Now suppose $p||q = r$. Since $r \notin R$, $\widehat{L}_p || \widehat{L}_q \subseteq \widetilde{\widehat{L}}_r$. Since p, q were arbitrary, we get $\widehat{L}_{par} \subseteq \widetilde{\widehat{L}}_r$. Exponentiating both sides, $\widehat{L}_{par}{}^{*r} \subseteq \widetilde{\widehat{L}}_r{}^{*r} = \widetilde{\widehat{L}}_r$.
So $L_r \circ_r \widehat{L}_{par}{}^{*r} \circ_r \widehat{L}_s \subseteq L_r \circ_r \widetilde{\widehat{L}}_r \circ_r \widehat{L}_s \subseteq L_r \circ_r \widetilde{\widehat{L}}_r \circ_r \widetilde{\widehat{L}}_s \subseteq L_r \circ_r \widetilde{\widehat{L}}_s \subseteq \widetilde{L}_s$.

Now we turn to the inclusion from left to right. Consider $t \in \widetilde{L}_s$. By induction on the number n of subterms $t_1||t_2$ in t such that $\varphi(t_1||t_2) = r$, we prove $t \in L_r \circ_r \widehat{L}_{par}{}^{*r} \circ_r \widehat{L}_s$.

If $n = 0$, then t is actually in $L_r \circ_r \widehat{L}_s$. $\widehat{L}_s$ can be written as $\{\xi_r\} \circ_{\xi_r} \widehat{L}_s$, which is a subset of any term of the form $e^{*r} \circ_r \widehat{L}_s$. Using $\widehat{L}_{par}$ as e, we get the *RHS* of (1).

For $n > 0$, consider the outermost parallel subterms $t_1||t_2$ in t with $\varphi(t_1) = p$, $\varphi(t_2) = q$ for some p, q and $p||q = r$. Then $t_1 \in \widetilde{L}_p$ and $t_2 \in \widetilde{L}_q$ have at most $n-1$ parallel subterms mapping to r. By the induction hypothesis, $t_1 \in L_r \circ_r \widehat{L}_{par}{}^{*r} \circ_r \widehat{L}_p$ and $t_2 \in L_r \circ_r \widehat{L}_{par}{}^{*r} \circ_r \widehat{L}_q$.

So $t_1||t_2 \in L_r \circ_r \widehat{L}_{par}{}^{*r} \circ_r (\widehat{L}_p||\widehat{L}_q)$.

Hence each such $t_1||t_2$ is in $L_r \circ_r \widehat{L}_{par}{}^{*r} \circ_r \widehat{L}_{par} \subseteq L_r \circ_r \widehat{L}_{par}{}^{*r}$.

All these parallel subterms can be substituted for variable ξ_r in a subterm $u \in \widehat{L}_s$ to yield t. Hence $t \in L_r \circ_r \widehat{L}_{par}{}^{*r} \circ_r \widehat{L}_s$. □

As stated in the introduction, the converse to Theorem 1 does not hold.

4 Branching automata

To seek a machine characterization of rational *sp*-languages, we now turn to the branching automata defined in our earlier paper [11].

The tuple $\mathcal{A} = (Q, T_{seq}, T_{fork}, T_{join}, I, F)$ is a *branching automaton* over the alphabet A, where Q is the (finite) set of states, I and F are subsets of Q, respectively the set of initial and of final states, $T_{seq} \subseteq Q \times A \times Q$ is the set of sequential transitions, $T_{fork} \subseteq Q \times \mathcal{P}_{ns}(Q)$ and $T_{join} \subseteq \mathcal{P}_{ns}(Q) \times Q$ are respectively the sets of fork and join transitions. Here $\mathcal{P}_{ns}(Q)$ ("nonempty and nonsingleton") stands for subsets of Q of cardinality at least 2.

An element $(q, a, q') \in T_{seq}$ is said to be an a-labelled transition from q to q'. As usual, we write $q \xrightarrow{a} q'$.

An element $(q, \{q_1, \ldots, q_n\})$ of T_{fork} is said to be a *fork transition of arity* n. We denote it by $q \rightarrow \{q_1, \ldots, q_n\}$. Similarly, an element $(\{q_1, \ldots, q_n\}, q)$ of T_{join}, written $\{q_1, \ldots, q_n\} \rightarrow q$, is said to be a *join transition of arity* n.

Let p, q be states of a branching automaton $\mathcal{A}$ and let t be a *sp*-term. The existence of a *run of* $\mathcal{A}$ *on* t *from* p *to* q is inductively defined as follows: There is a run on letter a from p to q if $p \xrightarrow{a} q$. If a term t has sequential factorization $t_1 \ldots t_n$ ($n \geq 2$), there is a run on t from p to q if there exist states $p = p_0, p_1, \ldots p_n = q$ and there exists a run on t_m from p_{m-1} to p_m, for each $1 \leq m \leq n$.

Suppose now that a term t has parallel factorization $t_1|| \ldots ||t_n$ ($n \geq 2$). There is a run on t from p to q if there is a fork at p, sub-runs for the factors and then a matching join ending at q. In order to handle arbitrarily long parallel products with finitely many fixed arity fork transitions, we allow the automaton to do the forking in levels, as follows:

Let $\pi = \{r_1, \ldots, r_s\}$ be a subset of $\{1, \ldots, n\}$. By t_π we mean the parallel term $t_{r_1}|| \ldots ||t_{r_s}$. Now we say there is a run on t from p to q if there exists a partition $\{\pi_1, \ldots, \pi_m\}$ of $\{1, \ldots, n\}$ and there are states p_ℓ, q_ℓ, for $1 \leq \ell \leq m$ such that there is a fork $k = p \to \{p_1, \ldots, p_m\}$, there are runs on t_{π_ℓ} from p_ℓ to q_ℓ, $1 \leq \ell \leq m$, and there is a join $j = \{q_1, \ldots, q_m\} \to q$.

Finally, a branching automaton $\mathcal{A}$ *accepts* the *sp*-term t if there exists a run of $\mathcal{A}$ on t from an initial state to a final state. An *sp*-language L is *regular* if it is the set of *sp*-terms accepted by a finite branching automaton.

Example 4.1 The following automaton has a run on $a||a||b$ from state i to state f. The partition of $\{1,2,3\}$ here is simple: it just has three singletons $\{\{1\},\{2\},\{3\}\}$. The language accepted is $\{a||a||b\}$.

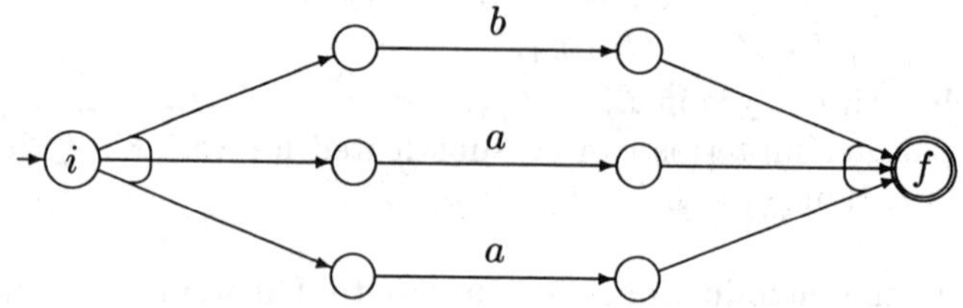

Example 4.2 The following automata accept respectively $SP(A)$ and $(a||b)^{\oplus}$.

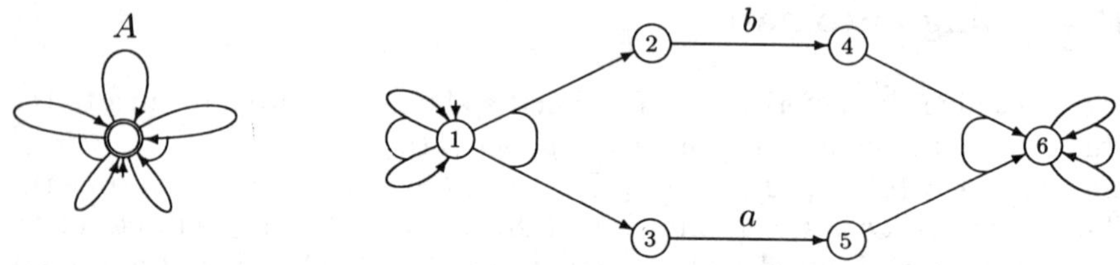

Note the looping forks and looping joins in the two automata. It is these that allow unbounded width terms to be accepted. However, these two automata mix up the states "inside" and "outside" the fork, in the sense defined below. This "misbehaviour" creates technical difficulties in proofs and constructions and must be eliminated, as we argue in [12].

We say that an automaton is *misbehaved* if there exists a fork transition $q \to \{q_1, \ldots, q_n\}$ such that there are runs from each q_i to some final state, or if there is a join transition $\{q_1, \ldots, q_n\} \to q$ such that there are runs from some initial state to each q_i. An automaton is *behaved* if it is not misbehaved.

The two automata in Example 4.2 are misbehaved. In the next proposition, we show that being behaved or misbehaved is a property of the automaton, not of the language. As an example, we give below a behaved automaton for $(a||b)^{\oplus}$.

Proposition 4.3 *Any regular sp-language is accepted by a behaved automaton.*

Proof. Let $\mathcal{A}$ be a branching automaton and let L be the *sp*-language accepted by $\mathcal{A}$. For each fork transition $k = q \to \{q_1, \ldots, q_r\}$, we distinguish (arbitrarily) one of the receiving end states, say, that which is denoted q_r.

We construct a new automaton $\mathcal{B}$ as follows. First we take the disjoint union of $|T_{fork}| + 1$ copies of $\mathcal{A}$, denoted respectively $\mathcal{A}_0$ and $\mathcal{A}_k$ ($k \in T_{fork}$). Next

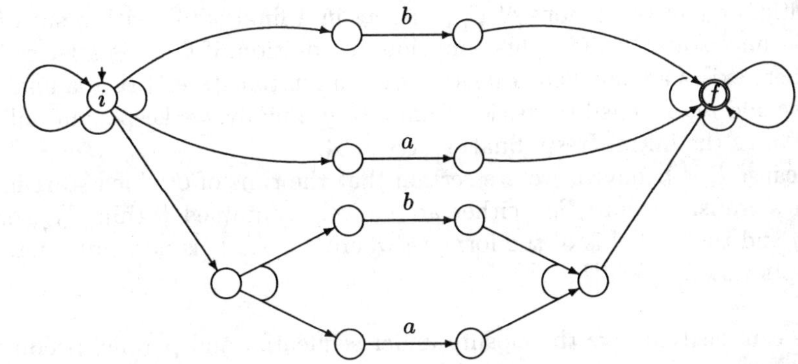

we delete from $\mathcal{A}_0$ all the fork and join transitions. For each fork transition $k = q \to \{q_1, \ldots, q_r\}$ of $\mathcal{A}$, we add to $\mathcal{B}$ a fork transition $q \to \{q_1, \ldots, q_r\}$ where $q, q_1, \ldots, q_{r-1}$ are taken in $\mathcal{A}_0$ and q_r is taken in $\mathcal{A}_k$. Moreover, for each fork transition k of arity r and for each join transition of the same arity, say $j = \{p_1, \ldots, p_r\} \to p$, we add r join transitions $j_{k,m}$ $(1 \leq m \leq r)$ simulating j, with p_m taken in $\mathcal{A}_k$, and with p and the p_h $(h \neq m)$ taken in $\mathcal{A}_0$. Finally, the initial and final states of $\mathcal{B}$ are the same as in $\mathcal{A}$, but taken in $\mathcal{A}_0$. We leave the reader to verify that $\mathcal{A}$ and $\mathcal{B}$ accept the same *sp*-language. □

4.1 Closure properties of regular *sp*-languages

The main theorem of this section is the following.

Theorem 4 *The class of regular sp-languages is closed under union, intersection, inverse and direct image by a morphism, substitution, sequential product and iteration, parallel product and rational iteration.*

For the operations of union, intersection, and inverse and direct image by a morphism, the proof is by simple constructions adapted from the classical theory of automata. It is the behaved automata which enable us to prove closure under substitution.

Lemma 4.4 *Let K and L be regular sp-languages over the alphabet A and let $a \in A$. Then $[K/a]L$ is regular.*

Proof. Let $\mathcal{A}$ be an automaton accepting L and let $\mathcal{B}$ be a behaved automaton accepting K. We construct a new automaton $\mathcal{C}$ as follows. For each a-labelled sequential transition $p \xrightarrow{a} q$ in $\mathcal{A}$, we construct a new copy of $\mathcal{B}$, denoted by $\mathcal{B}_{p,q}$, and we consider the disjoint union of $\mathcal{A}$ and the $\mathcal{B}_{p,q}$. For each transition $p \xrightarrow{a} q$ in $\mathcal{A}$, we delete this transition in $\mathcal{A}$ and we add duplicates of all the sequential and fork transitions of $\mathcal{B}_{p,q}$ originating in an initial state, with p substituted for that initial state on the left-hand side. Dually, we add duplicates of all the sequential or join transitions of $\mathcal{B}_{p,q}$ ending in a final state, with q substituted for that final state on the right-hand side. In addition, if there is a letter b such that there exists a b-labelled transition from an initial state of $\mathcal{B}$ to a final state, then we add a b-labelled transition from p to q. Finally, we keep as initial (resp. final) states the initial (resp. final) states of $\mathcal{A}$.

Because $\mathcal{B}$ is behaved, we are certain that the runs of $\mathcal{C}$ which start in state p with a transition into $\mathcal{B}_{p,q}$ either are entirely contained within $\mathcal{B}_{p,q}$, or visit state q and their label is of the form xy where $x \in K$. It is now immediate that $\mathcal{C}$ accepts exactly $[K/a]L$. □

We can easily derive the closure under sequential and parallel product and iteration, since we can come up with automata for $\{\zeta \circ \xi\}$, $\{\zeta \| \xi\}$, ξ^+ and $\xi^\oplus$. These variables can be substituted to prove closure. We need a final lemma to prove closure under rational iteration.

Lemma 4.5 *Let L be a language over $A \cup \{\xi\}$, such that for each term in L, the letter ξ appears, if at all, only inside a parallel subterm. Then $L^{*\xi}$ is regular.*

Proof. We give a sketch of the proof. Let $\mathcal{B}$ be a behaved automaton accepting L and T_ξ its set of ξ-labelled transitions. We construct a new automaton $\mathcal{C}$ from $|T_\xi| + 1$ disjoint copies of $\mathcal{B}$, denoted $\mathcal{B}_0$ and $\mathcal{B}_{p,q}$, for each $p \xrightarrow{\xi} q$ in T_ξ, with the following modifications:

For each sequential and fork transition out of an initial state of $\mathcal{B}$, we add a transition from the state p in each copy to the same destinations in $\mathcal{B}_{p,q}$. For each sequential and join transition into a final state of $\mathcal{B}$, we add a transition from the same sources in $\mathcal{B}_{p,q}$ to q in each copy.

If there is a sequential transition from an initial to a final state of $\mathcal{B}$, we add a similar transition from p to q in each copy. Hence a run of $\mathcal{B}$ can be simulated by a subrun from p to q in any copy of $\mathcal{C}$. Since this also includes the p and q in $\mathcal{B}_{p,q}$, runs for a term obtained by repeated substitution can also be constructed.

The initial and final states of $\mathcal{C}$ are those of $\mathcal{B}$, taken in $\mathcal{B}_0$, along with a new initial and final state with a ξ transition between them. This makes $\mathcal{C}$ accept ξ.

Hence we can argue that any term $t \in L^{*\xi}$ is accepted by $\mathcal{C}$.

For the converse direction, consider a run of $\mathcal{C}$ accepting t. If t does not make use of any new transitions, it is accepted by $\mathcal{B}_0$, and $t \in L = \{\xi\} \circ_\xi L \subseteq L^{*\xi}$.

Otherwise notice that the condition on occurrence of ξ's and the behavedness of $\mathcal{B}$ make sure that the initial and final states of $\mathcal{C}$ cannot be used inside a subrun for a parallel subterm of t. Hence a run ρ of t on $\mathcal{C}$ using a new transition must begin and end in $\mathcal{B}_0$ and go through the copies $\mathcal{B}_{p,q}$. The automaton construction makes sure that the subrun for each substitution of ξ begins and ends in the same copy. This leads to a proof that t is in $L^{*\xi}$. □

This completes the proof of Theorem 4. In particular, the regular languages are closed under the rational operations, so:

Corollary 5 *Rational sp-languages are regular.*

4.2 Extending McNaughton-Yamada further

Theorem 6 *Every regular sp-language is rational.*

Proof. We use a McNaughton-Yamada construction. Let $\mathcal{A}$ be a branching automaton with state set Q. For each pair of states (p,q), let $L_{p,q}$ be the set of all *sp*-terms which label a run of $\mathcal{A}$ from p to q, and let $\xi_{p,q}$ be a new symbol.

Let x be a *sp*-term and let $x = x_1 \cdots x_k$ be its sequential factorization. Let ρ be a run of $\mathcal{A}$ on x. We say that a fork transition f of $\mathcal{A}$ is used at the upper level by ρ if the sub-run of ρ on some x_i starts with transition f. If $D \subseteq T_{\text{fork}}$ is a set of fork transitions of $\mathcal{A}$ and if $p, q \in Q$, we let $L^D_{p,q}$ be the set of labels of runs of $\mathcal{A}$ which use only fork transitions in D at the upper level. Finally, if f is a fork transition in D, we let $L(D,f,q)$ be the set of labels of runs of $\mathcal{A}$ which start with transition f, end at state q and use f only once at the upper level.

First we consider the case where $D = \emptyset$. Then the elements of $L^{\emptyset}_{p,q}$ are (sequential) words, no fork transitions are used, so the usual McNaughton-Yamada algorithm shows that $L^{\emptyset}_{p,q}$ is rational. Next we assume that $D \neq \emptyset$, and we consider a fork transition $f = r \to \{r_1, \ldots, r_n\} \in D$. Then we have

$$L(D,f,q) = \bigcup_{g=\{s_1,\ldots,s_n\}\to s} \; \bigcup_{\sigma\in S_n} \left(L_{r_1,s_{\sigma(1)}} \| \cdots \| L_{r_n,s_{\sigma(n)}}\right) L^{D-\{f\}}_{s,q}$$

where S_n is the group of permutations of $\{1,\ldots,n\}$, and

$$L^D_{p,q} \;=\; L^{D-\{f\}}_{p,q} \,\cup\, L^{D-\{f\}}_{p,r} L(D,f,r)^* L(D,f,q).$$

Of course, $L_{p,q} = L^{T_{\text{fork}}}_{p,q}$. Thus, using the above formulæ, for each pair of states $p,q \in Q$, we get a rational expression for $L_{p,q}$, where the languages $L_{r,s}$, $r, s \in Q$, only appear within parallel products. In other words, the *sp*-languages $L_{p,q}$ are the solution of a system of equations

$$\xi_{p,q} = \operatorname{expr}_{p,q}(\xi_{r,s};\; r,s \in Q) \qquad p,q \in Q.$$

Solving is done in standard fashion, using the $^{*\xi}$ operation to eliminate each variable. Eventually, we get a simple equation without any argument, that is, a rational expression. Plugging this information back, we iterate these substitutions to find that all the $L_{p,q}$ are rational. □

Corollary 5 and Theorem 6 give us at last our Kleene theorem. We can also quickly dispose of our third theorem by a rather long-winded proof.

Theorem 2 *An sp-language is rational iff it is regular.*

Theorem 3 *A bounded width sp-language is rational iff it is series-rational.*

Proof. The reverse direction is clear. Using Corollary 5, bounded width rational languages are bounded width regular. [11] shows that bounded width regular languages are series-rational. □

Conclusion

In [11], we proved that the three formalisms of algebraic recognizability, rational expressions and automata acceptance coincide in the context of bounded width *sp*-languages. The connection between the latter two formalisms continues to hold in a more liberal setting, where parallelism can be unbounded. But we could not generalize the notion of recognizability to match rational expressions and automata acceptance. This is not surprising. Iteration over a commutative, associative operation is very powerful (recall Parikh's theorem).

We have been unable to define a good analogue of deterministic automata, and to prove (or disprove) that regular *sp*-languages are closed under complement. An obvious lacuna of our approach is the complete absence of communication primitives. That is, our work has more to do with "nets of processes" than with synchronization. Hopefully our theorems are clean enough to provide ideas for extending this approach to a syntax with communication.

References

1. S. Bloom and Z. Ésik. Free shuffle algebras in language varieties, *TCS* **163** (1996) 55–98.
2. G. Boudol. Notes on algebraic calculi of processes, in *Logics and models of concurrent systems* (K.R. Apt, ed.), NATO ASI Series F13 (1985) 261–305.
3. J.R. Büchi. *Finite automata, their algebras and grammars: Towards a theory of formal expressions* (D. Siefkes, ed.), Springer (1989).
4. B. Courcelle. Graph rewriting: an algebraic and logical approach, in *Handbook of Theoretical Computer Science* **B** (J. van Leeuwen, ed.), Elsevier (1990).
5. B. Courcelle. The monadic second-order logic of graphs V: on closing the gap between definability and recognizability, *Theoret. Comp. Sci.* **80** (1991) 153–202.
6. V. Diekert and G. Rozenberg. *The book of traces*, World Scientific (1995).
7. V.K. Garg and M.T. Ragunath. Concurrent regular expressions and their relationship to Petri nets, *Theoret. Comp. Sci.* **96** (1992) 285–304.
8. F. Gécseg and M. Steinby. *Tree automata*, Akadémiai Kiadó, Budapest (1984).
9. J.L. Gischer. The equational theory of pomsets, *TCS* **61** (1988) 199–224.
10. J. Grabowski. On partial languages, *Fund. Inform.* **IV** (1981) 427–498.
11. K. Lodaya and P. Weil. Series-parallel posets: algebra, automata and languages, in *Proc. STACS* (Paris '98), *LNCS* **1373** (M. Morvan, C. Meinel, D. Krob, eds.) (1998) 555–565.
12. K. Lodaya and P. Weil. Series-parallel languages and the bounded width property, *IMSc Tech Rep* **98/07/36** (1998). `http://www.imsc.ernet.in/~kamal/splbwp.ps.gz`.
13. C.A. Petri. Fundamentals of a theory of asynchronous information flow, *Proc. IFIP* (Amsterdam '62), North-Holland (1963) 386-390.
14. V. Pratt. Modelling concurrency with partial orders, *IJPP* **15**(1) (1986) 33–71.
15. W. Reisig. *Petri nets, an introduction*, Springer (1985).
16. J.W. Thatcher and J.B. Wright. Generalized finite automata with an application to a decision problem of second order logic, *Math. Syst. Theory* **2** (1968) 57–82.
17. J. Valdes, R.E. Tarjan and E.L. Lawler. The recognition of series-parallel digraphs, *SIAM J. Comput.* **11** (1981) 298–313.

Quantum Computation and Information

Umesh Vazirani

Computer Science Division,
University of California,
Berkeley, CA 94720.
Email: vazirani@cs.berkeley.edu

Abstract

Quantum computation is a fascinating new area that touches upon the foundations of both quantum physics and computer science. Quantum computers can perform certain tasks, such as factoring, exponentially faster than classical computers. This talk will describe the principles underlying the fundamental quantum algorithms.

The power of quantum computation lies in the exponentially many hidden degrees of freedom in the state of an n quantum bit system — whereas $2^n - 1$ complex numbers are necessary to specify the state, Holevo's theorem states that n quantum bits cannot be used to communicate any more than n classical bits. Nevertheless, there are communication tasks in which these hidden degrees of freedom can be tapped into.

Finally, the state of a quantum system is particularly fragile to noise and decoherence. However, there are beautiful techniques — quantum error-correcting codes — for protecting a given quantum state (with its exponentially many degrees of freedom) against noise and decoherence. These codes can be used to create fault-tolerant quantum circuits — which are immune to a constant rate of decoherence.

Bibliography

1. D. Aharanov, M. Ben-Or, "Fault tolerant quantum computation with constant error," quant-ph/9611025.
2. A. Ambainis, L. Schulman, A. Ta-Shma, U. Vazirani, A. Wigderson, "The Quantum Communication Complexity of Sampling", Proceedings of Symposium on the Foundations of Computer Science, 1998.
3. E. Bernstein, U. Vazirani, "Quantum complexity theory", *Siam Journal of Computing*, **26**, October, 1997 (special issue on quantum computation).
4. A. Calderbank and P. Shor. "Good quantum error-correcting codes exist." *Phys. Rev. A* 54, pp. 1098-1106 (1996).
5. P. Shor, "Algorithms for quantum computation: Discrete logarithms and factoring", *Siam Journal of Computing*, **26**, October, 1997, pp. 1484-1509 (special issue on quantum computatio n).
6. U. Vazirani, "Course Notes on Quantum Computation", http://www.cs.berkeley.edu/ vazirani/qc.html

Author Index